Performance
MANAGEMENT
SYSTEM
a holistic approach

D1586711

-99

Performance
MANAGEMENT
SYSTEM
a holistic approach

PROF. B D SINGH

Sr. Prof. of HRM & Dean (MDP & Consultancy)

IMT, Ghaziabad

EXCEL BOOKS

ISBN: 978-81-7446-861-1

First Edition: New Delhi, 2010

EXCEL BOOKS
A-45, Naraina, Phase I,
New Delhi - 110 028

Published by Anurag Jain for Excel Books, A-45, Naraina, Phase-I, New Delhi -110 028
and printed by him at Excel Printers, C-205, Naraina, Phase-I, New Delhi -110 028

Brief Contents

PART C: PERFORMANCE APPRAISAL FORMATS PRACTISED BY CORPORATES

PART D: LIVE CASES

Detailed Contents

PART D: LIVE CASES

Preface

Veer Bhogya Vasundhara
The World Belongs to the Performer

Performance has been the focal point of an achiever, but in this age of global competitiveness, it has become more critical for the corporates to remain ahead in the race. This has compelled them to visit and revisit their age-old strategies and develop less travelled searching ways and means to enhance their performance. The search is still on.

Performance management system is a sequel to that quest. It is an integrated, holistic and total management system (a 360 degree management system) directed towards endless excellence in performance – giving emphasis on processes and resources on their merit.

HR, which remained neglected in the traditional scheme of management system, received its due share in Performance Management System, because of its inherent, infinite potential for augmenting performance. It was realized that all other resources have limitations and can be easily available, accessible and imitable to the competitors. It is HR which, if made committed, can make the difference and give corporates a distinctive, competitive edge over others.

In traditional management system, Performance Appraisal System was understood as Performance Management System. In fact, they are separate concepts. The Performance Appraisal System was used as control mechanism. It was "judgmental in approach" on the basis of which employees were either rewarded or punished. This was feared by employees and did not evoke positive response and proved dysfunctional, affecting performance adversely.

PMS is "developmental in approach". It focuses on creating, facilitating and enabling performance culture in which individual/team on their own unleash potentials. Its philosophy is enhancing performance by emphasizing on developing "Human Capital".

There are a number of works available on the subject, but they are either sketchy or lopsided. This book attempts to provide a 360 degree view of PMS. In addition, the book contains some latest managerial concepts and practices which are relevant and used in the PMS. It contains some formats used by leading corporates and some live cases on the relevant issues. On the whole, the book would prove to be very useful to the management students.

In essence, the book is an attempt to help the reader to move towards Karmayoga...... Performing Leadership.

PROF. B D SINGH

Acknowledgements

I acknowledge the encouragement and inspiration provided by my esteemed colleagues and dear students at IMT & MDI which gave me confidence to bring out this book.

I am also grateful to different contributors of the articles and case-writers, from whose works I have taken a lot of help.

I acknowledge the support that I drew from the work of T.V. Rao, Prem Chadha, M. Marchigaton, A Wilkinson, Machel Armstrong, Shri A.S. Kohli, T. Deb and many others.

I will be failing in my duty if I do not acknowledge the support that I got from Shri Anurag Jain, the publisher of the Excel Books.

About the Author

Prof. B D Singh has obtained his postgraduate degrees in History and PMIR and LLB from Ranchi University. He did his PGPM (Executive) from IIM, Calcutta. He has worked in various capacities in SAIL, RINL and lastly at NALCO, from where he retired as Director (Personnel and Marketing). Besides having exposure to a number of national and international training programmes, he completed the Advance Management Programme from ASCI, Hyderabad.

Prof. Singh has widely travelled, which includes visits to South-East Asia, the Middle East, Europe, USA, Canada, South Korea, Hong Kong, Japan and Australia. He was the Chairman of Utkal Chapter of NIPM for two consecutive terms and is a life member of NIPM. He is also associated with the HRD Network of India and ISTD, and held the post of Co-Chairman of the Diploma Board of ISTD. He has been associated with many management institutes like ASCI, IIMC, XIMB, FORE, LBS, IGNOU, VVGNLI, as a visiting faculty. He worked as a Professor of HRM at MDI, Gurgaon. He has more than 45 publications on HR, IR and General Management topics. He does consultancy and training extensively, in companies like MUL, Hero-Honda, IPCL, BALCO, SAIL, KPMG, SBI, AAI, PSEB, Moser-Baer, etc. He is on the Editorial Board of *Asia-Pacific Business Review*; *AWARD*, a national journal published by the V.V. Giri National Labour Institute; and *Gyan*, a journal published from CJ-IMT, Mohali. He is on the Governing Board of ACCMAN Institute of Management, Greater Noida and Academic Board of Asia Pacific Institute of Management, Delhi.

Presently, he is working as Sr. Professor (HRM) and Dean (MDP & Consultancy), IMT Ghaziabad.

PART-A

Performance Management

CHAPTER-1

Changing Business Paradigms and Importance of Excellence in - Performance

Business paradigms, platforms and their interaction is very popular and commonly spoken word nowadays. Today one fails to feel most of the very significant events taking place either in economic, business and commerce or the people with their environment in the context of change or progress and to anticipate what lies ahead. People have now begun to understand to their enormous perils those dynamic changes that are related to the evolution of their interactions with one to their business.

What we find, through sweeping areas like globe or to surpass excellence have been changing the fundamental fabric of business and industry. The trade world has witnessed a global village. The technology and also information have revolution that is now appearing the changes and several ways of the done in every moment of all episodes of mankind but never seen in the entire history of the man.

Introduction

Toffler (1971; 1981) observes, "Roaring current of change, a current so powerful that today it overturns institutions, shifts our values and shrivels our roots. The First Wave of change: the agricultural revolution took thousands of years to play itself out. The Second Wave—the rise of industrial civilization—took a mere three hundred years. Today, history is even more accelerative, and it is likely that the Third Wave (information revolution) will sweep across history and complete itself in a few decades".

"We are now living through greatest wave of change on the planet since the enlightenment of the Industrial Revolutions. This is a moment of greater and deeper change than any previous time, because no previous revolution was global in scale or as compressed in time. The acceleration of change and the spatial scope of the change...... mark this moment as different from previous moments....." (Toffler, 1995).

He further adds that the society for the past 300 years has been caught up in a windstorm of change. The storm, far from abating, appears to be gathering more force.

According to Handy (1991), the changes are different this time; they are discontinuous and not part of a general pattern. Handy (1995) further advocates that accepting paradox as a feature of our lives is the first step towards living with it and managing it. He says "More turbulent the times, more complex the world, more the paradoxes". Maynard Jr. and Mehrtens (1993) observe that times are hard and people are consumed by crises. The challenges posed by political, economic and environmental issues persist and intensify. Our society, facing momentous challenges at the beginning of the new millennium, needs visions of the future so attractive, inspiring and compelling that people will shift from their current mindset of focusing on managing crises to anticipating the future. Further, organizations need to understand the changes taking place in every sphere of business, and in the environment that is immediately relevant to their business.

Mind-boggling changes sweeping across the globe at an unprecedented pace have changed the landscape and skyline of business and industry. The wide world has really become a "global village". The technological and Telecommunication revolutions have augmented exponential changes and removed two of the most hitherto insurmountable obstacles in way of human progress – distance and time. Global reach has become easier and business has become possible irrespective of the fact as to which part of the globe one belongs to.

Porter (1980) says that comparative advantage economies of scale in production, logistics, marketing, purchasing, and decreased transportation or storage costs are the prime causes of globalization. Globalization is facilitated by four broad processes: 1) Mobility (key business ingredients such as capital, labour and ideas are increasingly becoming mobile) (Kurtzman, 1993); 2) Simultaneity (goods and services are increasingly available in many places at the same time); 3) Bypass (easier international travel, deregulation and privatization of government monopolies, all of which increase alternatives); and 4) Pluralism (throughout the world, centers are being decentralized).

The growth of globalization is aided by the trade policies of governments, international governmental and non-governmental organizations, including financial institutions such as the World Bank, decline in the costs of communication and transportation, internet, and growth in English-speaking population of the world.

The twentieth century saw dramatic changes within the world of work, and the twenty-first appears to have continued this paradigm of change. Organizations have evolved in terms of purpose, size, structure, management philosophy and relationships with the outside world. Technological advances have revolutionized all work methods, and for many organizations the operational horizon has move from a small geographical area to literally the world; for government, 'being competitive' is now a global (as opposed to a selective international) requirement. Everything has speeded up, including the pace of change itself.

There has been a fierce competition and it has not remained confined within the boundaries of the nations. The world has become boundaryless and therefore competition has also become global. Unlike sports Olympiads which takes place every four years like Olympics. Organizations have to be necessarily the best in order to succeed in global market. The corporations, Nationals and Multinationals, are taking part in business Olympics very frequently.

In fact, it has become a question of survival for the organization to become performing organizations. The Darwin law of survival of the fittest is in operation here also. Organizations have to be necessarily be the fittest in order to survive.

The following two stories depict the present situation:

(a) In the jungle, every morning a phenomenon takes place. The deer tries to run faster and tries to be the fastest. The lion follows her and try to be faster than her. Why do they do that? ....They do that for their survival.

(b) Two friends were traveling in a jungle. After some time, they got tired and stopped for rest, when they heard the roar of a tiger which was menacingly advancing towards them. One of them started putting on his running shoes. "How is this going to help? We can't outrun the tiger" said the other. The first man replied: "I don't have to outrun the tiger; I only have to outrun *you*."

In the present business world, no one is a permanent enemy, and no one is a permanent friend; friendship lasts till the interest is served.

The business paradigms are changing and so are the marketing imperatives. The business houses are under tremendous pressure to visit and revisit, orient and reorient their strategies.

Global Change and Performance: Organizations have to compete for survival. It is survival of the fittest in the true sense of the term.

Performance is the only way to do that. An ordinary performance will not do. Even better performance may not be adequate. It has to be necessarily the best in order to compete and thrive.

Performance is not a chance or a luck, it is result of a series of systematic and integrated activities, conversing to the objectives of the individual, team and the organization.

"Udyogenahi sidhyanti karyani, nahi manorathey nahi suptasya sinhasya pravishanti mukhe mrigah"—Neeti Sloka

"Karmanyevaadhikaraste, ma phalesu kadachana"—The Geeta

"Karma pradhan vishwa kar rakha, ka koi tark badhawahi sakha—Tulsidas

Performance = (Skill to do + Will to do)

Creating skill to do – It means resources and infrastructure required for performance. They are mainly:

- Machine,
- Money,
- Material,
- Men

They determine the capacity of an organization.

Better performance cannot be thought of without state-of-the-art machinery—superior to or equal to the competitors.

Paucity or inferiority of money or material will definitely hamper the performance. Hence, their strategic availability is must.

Men, the most critical and scares of all the resources are not only most important as also most strategic. Sourcing, attracting, developing, retaining and motivating talent are most crucial jobs of a performing organization.

Creating a Will to do

Will to do may also mean will not to do. Will to do is a direct product of organization culture. Such a product is not available in the market. It can not be imported also. It has to be grown and nurtured in the organization itself. This is the precondition for a performing organization.

Corporates of today and tomorrow have to give a re-look and develop a different perspective towards different resources, leading to performance.

In fact, excelling organizations have already re-worked their strategy and started giving maximum emphasis in building "human capital".

HR is a resource which has unlimited potential for performance. All other resources are inanimate resources, have inherent limitations of maximum capacity, easy availability either in the local market or global market. All other resources depreciate while HR is the only resource which appreciates and are capable of development, if given proper organizational climate. They are capable of being doing wonders if given proper and strategic leadership and direction. Properly developed and managed HR builds the performing muscles of the corporation by strategizing, by aligning and by creating a symbiotic working of all the resources, converging on the organizational objective. With thinking facts and self-correcting power, by creative and innovative endowments, they can turn an ordinary performance into an extraordinary one.

Unfortunately, traditional management has put a displaced importance to resources at its command. HR receive the attention that it did not deserved. It was treated as "risk, threat and cost". Naturally the reaction was equal or more than equal in opposite direction, despite best of machines, materials and money, the corporates failed to perform; because there existed a 'will' not to perform or which goes against the requirement of performance.

The real challenge before the corporations and HR profession is to create that will to perform or work culture, where people and groups start thinking and performing themselves in tandem with the organizational goal.

Organizations have to re-look towards their beliefs and assumptions, toward HR, its profession and realize is importance and start giving premium to talent. A ritualistic and pretentious approach will do more harm. Hence, a sincere approach has to dawn upon the organization as a whole and especially the top managers.

Management professionals were compelled to rethink and rework their priorities and approaches towards performing methods and strategies, which gave birth to concepts like 'T.Q.M', 'T.P.M' and a more comprehensive methods "like performance management system". This approach is integrated, holistic, tracing and trekking for improved performance from beginning to the end.

The focal point is performance management system is 'Human Resource', by applying various methods to modify and develop human potential and link the human power with performance. In the centre of the philosophy of performance management system are the assumptions that they are capable of being developed and unfold human potential. The traditional method of simply assessing and evaluating them and using that evaluation for either reward or punishment, had a negative effect. At the end of the performance year, this method was reduced to mostly finding faults and being used as a control mechanism. It created a negative and non-performing culture. It was more of an inquest, after the performance was over. It was judgmental in approach weather an employee is good or bad the element of development was missing.

Performance Management System, on the other hand, starts with the premise that given the clear objective identifying and putting the right competencies on the right job-profiles, giving performance favourable leadership guidance while performing and mentoring, giving employees timely feedback and corrective guidelines and rewarding the performers over non-performance, etc. moves people and teams to work is symbiotic way, generating synergy necessary for excelling team/organizational performance.

Ordinary performance has no place in the global competitive business scenario. It has to be extraordinary and excelling in order to compete.

Before we go to excellence in performance let us see some source of the basic concepts related to performance.

Understanding the Concept of Work

The meaning of work touches upon where we get the concepts that make 'work' meaningful or otherwise. An important and difficult task for any performance manager is to help his/her team members see a powerful personal purpose or a meaning in their jobs. I am reminded of the parable of three stonecutters, eminently narrated by Peter Drucker, who were asked what they were doing. The first one replied, 'I am making a living'. She was working to satisfy her basic physiological needs. The second kept on hammering while she said, 'I am doing the best job of stonecutting in the entire country'. She was possibly fulfilling her achievement motive. The third one looked up with a visionary gleam in her eyes and said, 'I am building a cathedral'. She was surely identifying with the purpose, and responding to her self-actualization need.

Visualizing the ultimate outcome of the total effort. Work is indeed sublime, to do nothing is to be nothing. The dharma of each person to contribute to the larger society in excess of what she consumes out of its resources.

Work means different things to different people and evokes different images and fantasies for them. It bears different connotations in different organizations. Philosophers from Aristotle to Russel, scriptures like the *Bhagavad Gita* and the New Testament, novelists like Gorky have all tried to interpret work. Tandon enlists a number of antecedents that influence us in attributing meanings to work. Concepts of *karma* and *dharma* in the *Bhagwad Gita* have moral and spiritual connotations that influence our motivational perception and performance. Traditional culture, with its distinctive social organization and mindset, like caste roles in the Indian context, influences our work attitudes. The nature of authority relationships in social units like the family can affect authority relationships in formal work units.

"Work-as-life"

- *Economic:* Gainful, productive work performed to meet the economic needs of a person or her family.

- *Cultural:* Functions, such as the rituals of birth, marriage and death, performed as moral duty in the course of one's various life-passages.

- *Psychosocial:* Interpersonal and interfamilial interactions in one's role as member of a social unit.

Work is indeed sublime. Someone said, to do nothing is to be nothing. Work is not just central to our existence—the two are inseparable. When, like the third stonecutter, we perform work for the sheer joy of achieving something worthwhile, we experience true happiness. It is the duty, or dharma of each person to contribute to the larger society in excess of what he/she consumes out of its resources, only by observing this dharma do we qualify as social beings. In doing so, work becomes worship; and dedicated endeavour, the highest form of prayer. As an ideal this provides useful direction.

According to Neff, we can work to destroy ourselves, or to improve a lot. Understanding the intrinsic meaning of work can guide us to better ways of controlling and directing this powerhouse of human energy. The more we know why we work, what we work for, what are its consequences, the more we are able to control our destinies, says Neff.

In the work context, the will to work tends to become antithetical to the will to be free. Unless this incompatibility is managed, and a workable balance achieved, work motivation will remain a constantly challenged commodity that managers have to continually wrestle with.

Given the job security statutes in several countries, and the countervailing power of organized workforce, workers can no longer be coerced to perform. A major function of workplace managers and supervisors is to:

- Kindle and reinforce the will to work implicit in the worker's psyche,

- Innovate ways to build certain psycho-social features into work, the absence of which may weaken or extinguish the will to work

- Help enhance self-esteem of the worker.

Work/Performance described in our ancient scriptures specially in the *Geeta*.

Patanjali—"*Dravya prapti yogah*" (Yogah is creation of wealth).

Karm yogahna yoginam (Yogis are persons who perform actions). "*Yoghasthah kuru karmaan*" (Perform action having become a yogi). According to the *Geeta* or even August Kamte, it is the positive (*adhibantica*) system of constitution of society or *karmyogah*, which is the best and one should determine and perform his *karma* keeping the *dharmah* "code of ethics and morality" in view. The doctrine of *karmyogah* (energism) impresses upon us to be winner like Arjuna by shedding away attachment, excessive greed, ego, selfishness, and inculcating virtues like sacrifice, dedication and greater good of the people as motive of action.

Understanding the Conceptual Aspect of Performance System

'Performance management practice must derive from and be tailored to fit each organization's changing requirements. This will lead to a wide diversity of practices.'

It is, however, helpful to have a general notion of what performance management is about, and so here are some definitions:

An effective performance management system aligns individual performance with the organization's mission, vision and objectives.

American Compensation Association (1996)

Performance management is a process for establishing shared understanding about what is to be achieved, and an approach to managing and developing people in a way which increases the probability that it will be achieved in the short and long-term.

Performance management is a means of getting better results from the organization, teams and individuals within an agreed framework of planned goals, objective and standards.

Armstrong and Murlis (1994)

The performance management process is the process by which the company manages its performance in line with its corporate and functional strategies and objectives. The objective of this process is to provide a proactive closed loop system, where the corporate and functional strategies are deployed to all business processes, activities, tasks and personnel, and feedback is obtained through the performance measurement system to enable appropriate management decisions.

Bitici, Carrie and McDevitt (1997)

The essence of performance management is the development of individuals with competence and commitment, working towards the achievement of shared meaningful objectives within an organization which supports and encourages their achievement.

Lockett (1992)

A systematic approach to improving individual and team performance in order to achieve organizational goals.

Hendry, Bradley and Perkins (1997)

A clear focus on how each employee can contribute to the overall success of the organization lies at the heart of performance management systems.

IDS (1997)

Performance management is a way of translating corporate goals into achievable objectives that cascade down throughout the organization to produce optimum results.

IRS Management Review (1996)

Performance management aims to improve strategic focus and organizational effectiveness through continuously securing improvements in the performance of individuals and teams.

Philpott and Shepard (1992)

Performance management is about 'directing and supporting employees to work as effectively and efficiently as possible in line with the needs of the organization'.

Walters (1995)

These definitions frequently refer to performance management as a process of aligning or integrating organizational and individual objectives to achieve organizational effectiveness. It is interesting to note that only one definition mentions development and only two refer to teams. Yet, in our view, development is the prime purpose of performance management – a view which is shared by Chris Bones (1996), who says that 'performance does not need managing. It needs encouraging, developing supporting and sustaining'.

Performance management is a strategic and integrated approach for delivering sustained success to organizations by improving the performance of those who work in them and by developing the capabilities of teams and individual contributors. Development is perhaps the most important function of performance management. Performance management is concerned with outputs—the achievement of results; and with outcomes—the impact made on performance. But it is also concerned with the processes required to achieve these results and the inputs in term of capabilities (knowledge, skill and competence) expected from the teams and the individuals involved.

The Oxford English Dictionary defines 'performance' as behaviour—the way in which organizations, teams and individuals get work done. Campbell (1990) believes that 'Performance is behaviour and should be distinguished from the outcomes because they can be contaminated by systems factors'.

A more comprehensive view of performance is achieved if it is defined as embracing both behaviour and outcomes. This is well put by Brumbrach (1988): "Performance means both behaviors and results. Behaviors emanate from the performer and transform performance from abstraction to action. Not just the instruments for results, behaviors are also outcomes in their own right—the product or mental and physical effort applied to tasks—and can be judged apart from results."

What does Performance Management set out to do?

❈ The Basic Aims ❈

Two simple propositions provide the foundation upon which performance management is built:

When people (individuals and teams) know and understand what is expected of them, and have taken part in forming these expectations, they will use their best endeavours to meet them.

The capacity to meet expectations depends on the levels of capability that can be achieved by individuals and teams, the level of support them is given by management, and the processes, systems and resources made available to them by the organization.

⌘ Detailed Aims

In more detail, the aims of performance management are to:

- Help to achieve sustainable improvements in organization performance

- Act as a lever for change in developing a more performance-oriented culture

- Increase the motivation and commitment of employees

- Enable individuals to develop their abilities, increase their job satisfaction and achieve their full potential to their own benefit and that of the organization as a whole

- Enhance the development of team cohesion and performance

- Develop constructive and open relationships between individuals and their managers in a process of continuing dialogue which is linked to the work actually being done throughout the year

- Provide opportunities for individuals to express their aspirations and expectations about their work.

⌘ Performance Management Aims – Suggested by other Commentators

The American Compensation Association (1996) states that organizations rely on performance management to:

- Document job responsibilities

- Help define performance expectations

- Provide a framework for supervisors and employees to communicate with each other

- Provide ongoing opportunities for supervisors to coach and encourage personal development

- Align individual performance expectations with organization goals.

⌘ Why is Performance Management Necessary?

The reasons given by the organization listed above appear to be powerful ones for introducing performance management, and the aims listed earlier in this chapter seem to be equally worthy. But it can be argued, especially by line managers, that if it is a normal process of management, why bother to introduce formal and possibly bureaucratic procedures for doing it? Indeed, in any organization there will be some good managers for whom adopting the performance management process is just 'doing what comes naturally'. They can be invaluable as champions, developers and coaches.

Performance management is concerned with creating a culture in which organizational and individual learning and development are a continuous process. It provides means for the integration of learning and work so that everyone learns from the successes and challenges inherent in their day-to-day activities.

What is actually a competency? It is just functional knowledge or something more than that. Is the competency required for a technical consultant different from that of a senior manager in business? Knowledge alone does not predict job performance or success in business. Various other components are required. Generally speaking, competency is any measurable characteristic that differentiates performance in a given job or role in an organization in a given environment. It is the sum total of physical competencies, job knowledge, conceptual and strategic skills, skill in applications and emotional strength or intelligence, which is basically the capacity to act, motivate ourselves, which is basically the capacity to act, motivates ourselves, manage our emotions in ourselves and in our relationships, using this to direct and work with others, and risk-taking to achieve goals. Hence competency mapping has become an important factor in performance development and management.

❃ How does Performance Management work? ❃

We must emphasize again that there is no one right way of 'doing' performance management. It must be tailored to the circumstances and needs of the organization, and it must be operated flexible in accordance with the needs of the individuals affected by it. Having said that, it is possible to set out a typical sequence of processes that in one form or another are found in most performance-management arrangements, certainly in all the organizations we visited during the course of our research. This can be regarded in a sense, as a model of performance management that illustrates its various components. But it should not be regarded as an ideal upon which all approaches to performance management should be modelled in every respect.

The Performance Management Cycle

Performance management is a process, not an event. It operates as a continuous cycle, as shown in Figure 1.1.

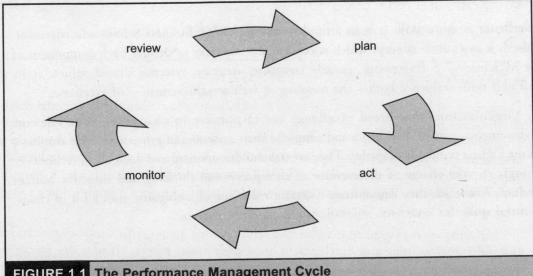

review

plan

monitor

act

FIGURE 1.1 **The Performance Management Cycle**

The above figure is broadly in line with Deming's model for continuous quality management. A variation on this model has been produced by Torrington and Hall (1995), as shown below.

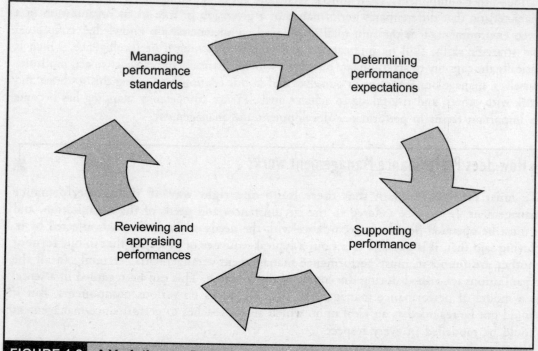

Managing performance standards

Determining performance expectations

Supporting performance

Reviewing and appraising performances

FIGURE 1.2 A Variation on Deming's Model for Continuous Quality Management

Excellence in Performance

"Yogah Karmasu Koushlam". – The Geeta

'Excellence is not a skill. It is an attitude', says an Amity Business School advertisement. Indeed, it is a subtle concept which is relative and not easy to define. Each component of the McKinsey 7-S framework, namely structure, strategy, systems, shared values, style, staff and skills influence both – the meaning as well as achievement – of excellence.

Organisations that breed excellence are responsive to change in their relevant environments, sure of their basics and simple in their systems and procedures with emphasis on the highest standards of quality. They are stakeholder-oriented and don't allow technology or logic to take charge of the exercise of entrepreneurial thinking and intuitive human wisdom. Above all, they demonstrate a certain tolerance of ambiguity, even a bit of chaos, to make space for creativity, innovation and experimentation.

Eight Attributes of Excellence

Peters & Waterman Jr. identify eight attributes – relearning the basics of management, the organizational and managerial behaviour which elicit the best response from stakeholders and which distinguish excellent companies from those are less than excellent:

1. *A Bias for Action:* Given two options, being seen as tuned to action. A preference for doing something – anything – rather than sending an idea through endless cycles of analyses and committee reports. Speed, quickness of action, cutting across bureaucracy, experimenting and providing field for thinking creatively and putting these ideas into action.

2. *Staying Close to the Customer:* Learning about and from the customer. Learning and understanding the needs and preferences of the people whom they serve and responding or catering to those. Exceptional service – prompt with a personal touch and exceptional quality. Operationalizing the belief that the customer is a person, so effort needs to be made to know her and work as close to her as possible.

3. *Autonomy and Entrepreneurship:* Organizing the enterprise into small units and encouraging them to think and act independently and competitively. Allowing for creativity, appropriate risk – taking and imaginative approach in the face of bonafide mistakes and errors of judgment. Bridging the gap between creativity and innovation by achieving a high rate to innovation. Fostering many innovators – champions. Promoting autonomy, initiative, innovation and learning from failure as basic components of the work culture.

4. *Productivity through People:* Primacy and respect for individual members as human beings, their desire to grow and develop – and to stand out. Manifesting their firm belief that the human capital is the fundamental resources – the primary source for achieving performance effectiveness for productive gain. Creating in all members the awareness that their best efforts are crucial and that they will appropriately share rewards of the organization's success. It is easy to borrow money from financial institutions, to buy good technology – but people make all difference.

5. *Hands-on, Value-driven:* Clarifying and articulating the organisation's core values – its basic philosophy, what will one look back on with greatest satisfaction, how will the organization invoke the enormous energies and talents of its people – and breathe life into these values – de-emphasizing the mechanistic side of managing. Manifesting a strong belief in the various attributes of excellence. Insisting that the managers remain in touch with the organisation's core business and promote a strong work culture. Thinking globally and, as they say, acting locally, to uphold the organisation's mission and its basic philosophy while functioning hands on at all levels.

6. *Stick to the Knitting:* Doing what they do well as an organisation. Working through their core competence, and saying in businesses they are thoroughly familiar with. Base diversification strategies on some central skills or strengths of the organization. Willingness to get out of this if it doesn't work.

7. *Simple Form:* Lean Staff – Flexibility and maneuverability in responding to the permanent white waters kind of volatile environment. Maintaining lean staff, especially at the corporate levels – fewer hierarchical layers, and few people at the higher levels, more operatives. Not creating complexity either through structure or through staffing, where avoidable. One dimension – product, or geographical area, or function – has clear primacy. Pursuing delegation for down the line.

8. *Simultaneous Loose-Tight Properties:* Balance between centralization and decentralization. Fostering a climate wherein there is high commitment to the core organizational values combined with tolerance for all those who sincerely subscribe to those values – loose informality, fluidity and flexibility in procedures. Being tight on core values and principles, but liberal on well-designed delegation and autonomous functioning at all levels down to the shop floor. Space for examination.

For Subramanya, 'excellence is not a destination…it is an endless road. The achievement is to have the pleasure of walking on and on…end-lessly'. Excellence-seekers follow Winston Churchill: 'Never, never quit.' They walk on with optimism as their hope helps them visualize the invisible, touch the intangible and materialize the impossible.

To Chanda, one reason for decay of the culture of excellence is that excellence is no longer seen as being rewarded. By inference, a primal feature of a culture of excellence is that it encourages individuals to achieve excellence conversely, that at least it does not inhibit excellence. It is not that those who aspire to excel in their chosen field always have a smooth passage, without sacrificing elsewhere, but that they have greater chances of surviving as achievers. A second reason is that the direction in which 'excellence' lies is rather unclear – somewhat obscure or uncertain. What constitutes excellence, what the society values, is not widely understood – there is ambiguity about the manifest values that encourage or reward excellence-seeking behaviour.

Mediocrity vs. Excellence: Mediocrity and compliance are naturally less painful or risky than a course of excellence and initiative. Logically, then mediocrity and compliance should be the preferred modes of behaviour in an environment of constant change and uncertainty. Excellence and initiative can be extremely threatening not only to those who venture these but also to those others in an organization who choose to play safe. These others are, often moulded in the conventional organization milieu, which spells mediocrity.

Mediocrity, after all, is not quite unnecessary – in fact, all organizations survive because they have a large number of such people, at all levels, which hold the organization together and lend it a stable continuity. Excellence seekers do not follow the laid down path. Instead, they yearn to break new paths, and leave their trail. To use General Patton's dictum, they accept the challenges, so that they may feel the exhilaration of victory. Unbridled, they can rock the organizational boat.

Three questions, therefore, arise:

●   How can the criteria that qualify achievement as excellence be made more explicit?

●   How should excellence be rewarded?

●   Who should be responsible for fostering and perpetuating a culture of excellence?

Criteria for Excellence: Successful seekers of excellence are usually quite clear about the direction of their pursuits. Occasionally, however, they may get distracted or confused by dissonant messages from their environment, and get hijacked into directions in which they neither wish, nor have the capability to achieve with excellence. Lack of opportunities is rarely an issue with those for whom excellence is a genuine value. There are inevitable limits to available opportunities and, it is this scarcity which gives rise to the phenomenon of competitive achievement. Sometimes, this competition eggs individuals on to the achievement of excellence. For earnest individuals, therefore, such constraints offer no alibi. If anything, too many opportunities alluring high achievers to multiple goals may diffuse unidirectional concentrated effort. Other things being equal, there may well be a low ratio of high achievers to opportunities demanding their contribution. Achievement ceases to be excellence if it is attained without challenges. It takes courage to venture into new, hither-to-fore unexplored manors….to test one's limits and break through.

Excellence does not lie only in the domain of the individual. Six sigma is an example of how organizations pursue excellence. Raman reports on this phenomenon in quality improvement – One Sigma = 690,000 defects per million, Two Sigma = 308,000 defects, Three = 66,800 defects, Four Sigma = 6,210 defects, five Sigma = 230 defects, and Six Sigma = 3.4 defects per million …..He suggests that no one will ever achieve this 20-year old technique because by the time anyone even gets close, the customer's requirements will change – and you'll have to start over again with both your design and your processes.

- *Rewarding Excellence:* In the words of St. Francis De Sales, excellence seekers do not wish to be anything but what they are, and try to be that perfectly. Inadequate satisfaction of the lower order material needs – and these have increased exponentially – takes toll, and many people decide to compromise on the urge to satisfy their higher order needs for achievement and self-actualization. But, would those in who burns the genuine desire for high achievement be really dissuaded by compulsions of their material and economic needs? If they do, to what extent shall we acknowledge them as seekers of excellence? Was there any period in history when those who self-actualised really went by Abraham Maslow's hierarchy of needs? One wonders.

- Several organizations emphasize monetary benefits as strong motivators. Granted that money is a strong motivator, a question arises: What does money motivate a person for? It is often assumed that money motivates people to work and excel. This unfortunately, is not borne out by behavioural research. Money is important, but an achiever basically looks for achievement and satisfaction in the area of work for its own sake – money she needs to satisfy some other important needs. In times of human relation crises, organizations look for a solution which money can buy – the easy way out. Rarely do they ask: Are people fully occupied in work? Are they given work that they are most suited for? Are people fully utilized? Do they experience a sense of achievement and success in their tasks and positions? These are questions to which there are no easy answers. Interfirm comparisons or interpersonal comparisons in these areas are hard to make. These require far greater skills and a deeper insight into the human processes than just comparing figures. Many organizations, therefore, don't venture in this area. Often, as defence mechanisms, they deny the relevance of these questions to their problems or to human motivation.

- A question that we need to ask ourselves is – if money-based motivation is the spearhead approach that organizations adopt to deal with human issues, can a culture of excellence – getting recognized and rewarded.

- *Responsibility:* In the organizational context, the excellence seekers' work must not only bear close relevance to the organizational purpose, but also promise to enhance it. Where it is so, organizational management must share the responsibility for nurturing excellence with high potential performers. Sparks of brilliance and excellence are not all that accidental. Organisations that excel do so because they consciously protect, nurture, encourage, and help a few people with the potential for excellence and initiative. However, protagonists of mediocrity and compliance, for a different set of reasons, make persistent efforts to beat down people initiating excellence. They imprison these high-potentials within the organization, which is not able to provide adequate canvas for self- expression, experimenting, discovery, or growth. The dark suffocating environment of mechanistic and routine jobs is, to them, intellectually no better than the prison cells are in a physical sense. Organisations judge their performance against routine standards, totally inappropriate to their genius, while they monitor and evaluate their own performance, which however high, doesn't satisfy them. Denied time and opportunity to work on areas, in which they can excel, they experience continual spells of failure. Nothing can be more damaging to the development of a culture of excellence and innovation than providing such sensitive individuals so many experiences of failure so often.

- People who seek excellence also seek challenges. They are not afraid of meeting these challenges or even failing to meet them if the odds are somewhat equal in between failure and success. Empathy and supportiveness in their work environment certainly helps more than disaffection and hostility. One way of promoting excellence and innovation is to provide excellence seekers with as many experiences of success, however small, as possible, and provide emotional support in the event of failure, so that they stay stimulated. In this way, an organization can raise the level of human aspirations, and allow both routine mediocrity and creative excellence to coexist and complement each other.

- When seekers of excellence find the organizational environmental hostile, and it appears necessary in the interest of their core role responsibilities to toe the line, even the most tenacious of them may be beaten down and made to take recourse to the establishment culture. This may happen right in the beginning of the struggle for certain individuals or, perhaps, at later stages of the conflict between the culture of mediocrity and the culture of excellence. Some fortunate ones may, by exceptions, come across a set of coincidental circumstances that give them requisite support to pursue their chosen goal, but these accidents cannot be equated with a culture of excellence.

- *Seekers of Excellence vs. Seekers of Excellence:* A word to the seekers of excellence themselves. Through unintended, they may sometimes cross each other's paths, thereby creating obstructions. This is certainly possible when there is no coordinating mechanism in place. This can also happen when they believe that the concept of excellence is limited to what they have individually set out to pursue. In fact, this is not so. Excellence revels in diversity: it means different things to different people. Protagonists of mediocrity and compliance may well believe that the only approach that can bring about excellence is their own breed. They may thus work to promote mediocrity and compliance with the same zest, enthusiasm and self righteousness that a so-called protagonist of excellence does to promote excellence. Interestingly, Conan Doyle had this to say, "Mediocrity knows nothing higher than itself, but talent instantly recognizes genius." A culture of excellence must characterize greater detachment and discrimination to identify what excellence is and what it is not. Since both must co-exist, tremendous tolerance for the viewpoints and aspirations of others seems important.

● *To conclude, let me quote John D. Rockfeller:* 'I do not think there is any other quality so essential to success of any kind as the quality of perseverance. It overcomes almost everything, every nature.'

CHAPTER-2

Conceptual Aspects and their Linkages with Performance Management

LEARNING OBJECTIVES

- To give conceptual aspects of performance to students

- To link performance with human resource development

- To impress students that sustainable performance can be achieved only through continuous human resource development

HRM and Performance Management System Linkages

The power of organization is increasingly linked to its intellectual capital rather than its physical assets. People are now the drivers of corporate performance and competitiveness. Therefore, performance management deals with improving organizational performance by improving employee performance, Essentially, the cost of competitiveness involves efficiency and productivity. Dr Mritunjay Arthreya (2004) observed that workforce productivity constitutes around 60 percent of the total cost. Therefore, the growing significance of performance management needs no further emphasis.

The concept of performance management may be categorized into two separate types of management. The first one deals with the performance of an organization as a whole and evaluates the effectiveness of its managers. The second one deals with the system of evaluating employees in order to enable them to achieve reasonable goals and thus ensure that the organization performs better. It is pertinent here to understand what performance is. Brumbrach (1988) defines 'performance' both as behaviour and results. Behaviour emanates from the performer and transforms performance from abstraction to action. Not just the instruments for results, behaviours are also outcomes in their own right—the products of mental and physical effort applied to task and can be judged apart from the results. In the organizational content, performance means successful formulation and implementation of a value creating strategy which either generates or sustains its competitiveness.

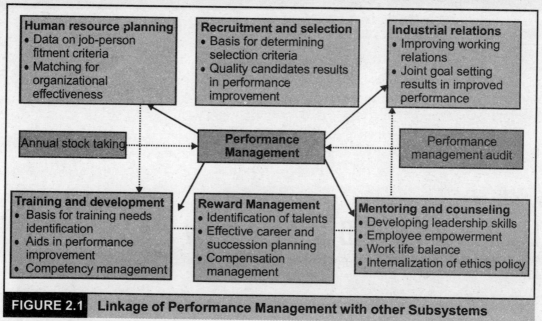

FIGURE 2.1   Linkage of Performance Management with other Subsystems

Performance management is an important organizational tool to clarify performance objectives, standards, critical dimensions, and competencies to enhance individual performance. Performance management works best when an employee's work is planned and goals for achievement are communicated, so that every employee is aware of the work and performance expected of him. Planning and setting performance criteria provides employees with a path of predictable rewards for good performance and the consequences of non-performance. In this way, employees reasonably assume the responsibility for consequences of their performance, whether excellent or marginal. It also provides a rationale basis for various HR decisions such as compensation, promotions, transfers, training, counselling, mentoring, termination, etc.

Performance management provides an opportunity to the employees and their managers to jointly create a plan for achieving shared goals and professional development needs at the same time. It emphasizes the development of capability and capacity of employees to perform consistently, coupled with the agility to respond to a changing dynamic business and work environment. The focus is more on decision-making and accountability at all levels of the organization for integration of operations.

An employee's motivation to perform, to develop personal capabilities, and to improve future performance is influenced by feedback of performance on an ongoing basis. It provides organizations with an opportunity to communicate to employees the mission, strategy, vision, and core values of the organization and personalizes organizational strategy into individual performance objectives seamlessly. It accords an opportunity to employees to use performance management to clarify their expectations, objectives, and values with respect to the organization. This helps in forging a partnership with the organization on the basis of self-awareness, ownership and authenticity, leading to an apt balance between operational objectives and performance and personal/ team development. Armstrong and Baron (2004) observe that performance management establishes a shared understanding about what is to be achieved and an approach to leading and developing people which will ensure that it is achieved.

Performance management is a 'systematic' and 'holistic' approach to identify critical dimensions of performance and to carry out activities necessary to ensure that the mission, objectives, goals, vision, and values of the organization are being met in an effective and efficient manner. It is systematic because it follows a sequence of steps from planning, managing, appraising, and monitoring, with the objective of meeting individual and organizational needs in the possible manner. Being a systematic approach, performance management seeks to connect all the strategic imperatives of the organization to build synergy. It helps in integrating performance management process with other critical organizational systems including leadership development, succession planning, and talent management efforts. Performance management is a 'holistic approach' bringing together many of the elements which go to make up the successful practice of HR management, in particular, learning and development.

Performance management is a multi-dimensional concept and includes inputs, processes, outputs, and outcomes. It is seen as crucial process that helps the organization focus on what each employee and team needs to contribute, so the organization as a whole is successful. Therefore, it is in essence a capability-building tool of organizations to stay adaptive in future.

It integrates various aspects of the business:

1. *Vertical integration*

2. *Functional integration*

3. *Human resource integration:* This ensures effective integration of different subsystems of HR management to achieve the organizational goals with optimum performance. These subsystems include people management, task monitoring, job design motivation, appraisal and reward systems, and training and empowerment.

4. *Goal integration:* It focuses on arriving at a congruence between the needs, aspirations, and goals of the managers with that of the goals and objectives of the organization.

Performance management transforms organizational objectives and strategy into a measurable action plan by getting the right information to and from the right people at the right time and in the right format. It enables employees to better understand their roles and responsibilities. Conversely, this rapid exchange and assimilation of information form all levels of the organization gives managers data to justify changes to their organization's strategy as well. As a strategy of HR management, it also assigns ownership to key metrics and increases accountability to ensure that employees are focuses on their work essential to the objectives and strategy, and that the results achieved by employees are consistently met in an effective and efficient manner.

EXHIBIT 2.1	Key Ingredients of Successful Performance Management	
• Committed leadership	• Transparent performance information
• Build competency-based development plans	• Effective multi-source feedback mechanisms to discuss and address performance issue
• Strong links between performance measures and programme results	• Useful performance measures

Source: Adapted from: J. M. Kamensky (2006).

Hence, performance management helps organizations in management consistent performance in a manner which holds employees and managers accountable for supporting its objectives and strategy, successfully fulfilling assigned job responsibilities, and accomplishing individual performance goals. This would require the following prerequisites:

• Business processes are as simple as possible.

• Lines of leadership and management are clear.

• Employees are empowered, which is an important driver of innovation.

• A distinct organizational culture.

• Workplace interactions are based on honesty, integrity, and trust.

• Openness to change.

EXHIBIT 2.2	Five Keys to Performance Excellence
1.	Results that enable a company to remain competitive
2.	Systems and processes that connect work efforts to desired results
3.	Measurable change in operational procedures
4.	Methods for analyzing and decreasing gaps between current and desired performance
5.	Employees with appropriate skills, knowledge, and behaviors to perform as required

Source: ASTD (1997) as quoted from Ram K. Navaratna, March 2007, HRD Newsletter of National HRD Network.

Purposes of Performance Management

Performance management is a key organizational strategy for improving competitiveness of the organization in a marketplace characterized by Olympian competition. It seeks to attain the following objectives in the organizational context.

1. Formulate strategy determining what the objectives of the organization are and how the organization plans to achieve them.

2. Manage the strategy implementation process, by examining whether an intended strategy is being put into practice as planned.

3. Challenge assumptions by focusing not only on the implementation of an intended strategy, but also on making sure that its content is still valid.

4. Sustain excellence in performance by motivating employees to setting goals that align with organizational strategies.

5. Check position by monitoring whether the expected performance results are being achieved.

6. Comply with the non-negotiable parameters, by making sure that the organization is achieving the minimum standards needed, if it is to survive (e.g., legal requirements, environmental parameters, etc.).

7. Communicate direction to the rest of the employees, by passing on information about what are the strategic goals individuals are expected to achieve.

8. Communicate with external stakeholders.

9. Provide feedback by reporting to employees how they are, their group, and the organization as a whole is performing against the expected goals.

10. Evaluate and reward behaviour in order to focus the employee's attention on strategic priorities, and to motivate them to take actions and make decisions, which are consistent with organizational objectives and strategy.

11. Benchmark the performance of different organizations, plants, departments, teams, and individuals.

12. Develop a dynamic work culture by assimilating people's thoughts, actions and consequences.

13. Inform managerial decision-making process with performance data.

14. Encourage improvements and learning at all levels and across the organization by nurturing natural talents of employees for building their capabilities to demonstrate success in a fair and objective manner.

15. Assess current management potential and assign rating to individual employees for the purpose of succession planning and management.

16. Empower employees to set their own performance criteria so that achieving these objectives becomes their mission.

Therefore, the purposes of performance management can be broadly classified as:

- Strategy comprises the role of managing strategy implementation and challenging assumptions.

- Communication comprises the role of checking position, complying with the non-negotiable parameters, communicating direction, providing feedback, and benchmarking.

- Motivation comprises the role of evaluating and rewarding behaviour, and encouraging improvement and learning.

Elements of Performance Management

Some of the major principles of performance management are enlisted below:

1. It translates organizational objectives into work units, departmental team, and individual goals.

2. It provides clarity of goals and objectives of the organization to all the employees and managers.

3. It is a continuous and integrated process for developing organizational, team, and individual performance.

4. It seeks to build commitment towards organization, team, and individual performance expectations.

5. It empowers individual employees to find avenues for improving performance.

6. It requires an organizational culture that fosters corporate values of openness, mutuality, trust, fairness, and respect, paving the way for two-way communications.

7. It creates a system of regular feedback with positive reinforcement of employee's behavior and action.

8. It provides for evaluation of employees performance against jointly agreed performance criteria in a congenial work environment.

9. It provides for an effective and contextual management of external environment for overcoming obstacles and impediments in the way of effective managerial performance.

10. It is more of a developmental tool rather than administration of financial rewards.

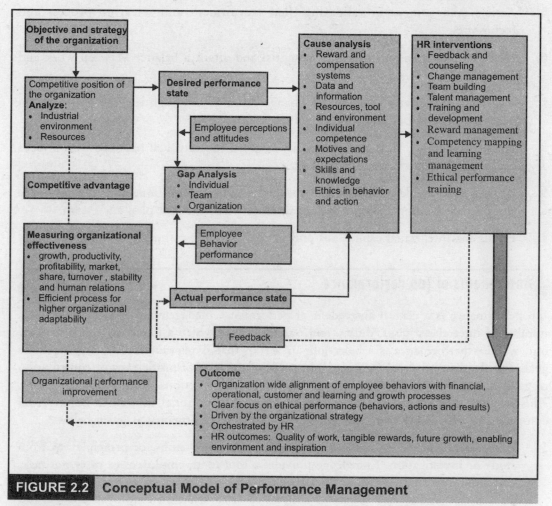

FIGURE 2.2 **Conceptual Model of Performance Management**

Why Performance Management?

Some of the major functions of performance management are enlisted below. Performance Management:

1. Helps in clarifying the mission, vision, strategy, and values of the organization to the employees in order to enable them achieve the same.

2.   Helps in improving various business processes as the deficiencies are highlighted.

3.   Helps in attracting and retaining talents in the organization and helps in establishing a robust talent review system.

4.   Facilitates competency mapping, training and development needs identification, and implementation as part of the performance development tool (employees have the competencies to met both the present and emerging requirements of the organization).

5.   Assists management in validating their recruitment and selection process and techniques.

6.   Helps employees attain their full potential and attain a balance between work and personal life.

7.   Improves organization's ability to change faster by highlighting the gap between potential capabilities and present ability.

8.   Helps in making a shift from industrial relations to individual relations with a focus for employee growth an development

9.   Enables sustainable organizational competitiveness, innovation, and low employee turnover by helping in reviewing organization structure and plan succession.

10. Builds the intellectual capital not only at managerial level but at frontline level too.

⌘ Antecedents of Job Performance ⌘

Job performance is a critical antecedent of performance management. A job consists of a number of interrelated tasks, duties, and responsibilities which a jobholder needs to carry out, whereas performance is a behaviour or action that is relevant for the organization's goals and that can be scaled (measured) in terms of the level of proficiency or contribution to goals that is represented by a particular action or set of actions (John Campbell 1988). This implies that job performance involves certain functional as well as behavioural competencies. A number of factors tend to impact job performance as given below:

1.   *Knowledge:* Knowledge is the acquaintance with facts, truths, or principles, as from study or investigation. Knowledge provides a tool to an employees to carry out tasks and activities in the organizational context. However, knowledge can be in two forms—'declarative knowledge' which is concerned with what an employee knows, and 'procedural knowledge' that refers to what an employee can do. Therefore, it is the ability of an individual employee coupled with his training, education, and experience which makes job performance feasible. An employee with sound functional knowledge will be successful on the job as he knows what he needs to do. A job description provides the list of work areas or the priority of an employee is likely to fail. Hence, a match between job and specific task proficiency is important of successful performance on the job performance in job description, together with ability of the employee to perform the tasks, duties, and responsibilities according to these descriptions.

2. *Motivation:* Mere possession of knowledge or the ability to perform a given job does not guarantee adequate job performance, if the employee lacks the motivation to perform. Only a motivated employee will make a concerted effort to perform. An employee may be motivated by individual as well as organizational factors. Individual factors could be self-efficacy, an urge to excel, reward tied to performance, craving for recognition, etc. While organizational factors could be an enabling culture, feedback environment, existence of performance management system, leadership's support and encouragement, employer branding programmes, etc. Therefore, the second determinant of job performance pertains to motivation of the employees.

3. *Feedback:* Employees tend to perform well at their job if they are provided with feedback that is meaningful and constructive. Such feedback helps employees identify areas of improvement and they tend to work harder to overcome the performance gaps. Existence of a feedback-oriented workplace environment is crucial to improve the performance of employees on an ongoing basis. Therefore, the third determinant of job performance relates to the presence of an effective feedback mechanism in the organization.

4. *Leadership:* Leadership has a profound influence on the employee's morale and motivation and organizational culture. Many time, top leaders had to leave their organizations not because they did not have the job knowledge or the requisite skills, but because of failure set right the organizational culture. Effective leaders tend to solicit employee's involvement in steering their organization forward. They encourage suggestions, trust them, encourage taking risk, and elicit full mental participation of their employees in improving organizations performance and competence. Performance management depends heavily on the motivation and commitment of employees, mediated by leadership. Therefore, the fourth determinant of job performance pertains to effective leadership.

5. *Personality:* Personality is a key dimension of behaviour, and behaviour is a foundation of performance of employees. Personality is shaped by various endogenous and exogenous factors. Personality influences the behaviour and action of the employees and ultimately impacts their job performance. It also impacts felicitation of peer and team performance of an individual employee. Therefore, the fifth determinant of job performance connects to personality of employees.

Hence, we may conclude that knowledge, motivation, feedback, leadership, and personality are the key dimensions of effective job performance. Their presence or absence will leave significant impact on performance management.

Dimensions of Effective Performance Management

Processes are the means by which individual performance is directed, assessed, and rewarded. Performance management should be a continuous process and should be carried out regularly.

People management capability: The knowledge, skills, attitude, and behaviors that the managers need in order to raise the performance standards of their employees. The managers and employees should act together in the same spirit within the overall framework of performance management.

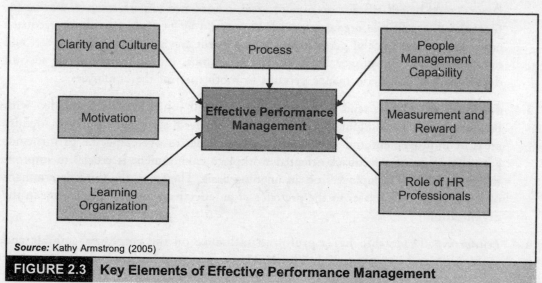

Source: Kathy Armstrong (2005)

FIGURE 2.3   **Key Elements of Effective Performance Management**

EXHIBIT 2.3 **Ten Top Performance Management Tips**	
1. Talk to your people often in order to head-start	6. Keep formal discussions friendly and simple performance management of your people
2. Build feedback in as a natural activity.	7. Be very positive and do not spend extended time on the weaknesses of employees.
3. Be honest in a working relationship for everyone's benefit.	8. Help employees achieve their needs.
4. Notice great performance and celebrate successes.	9. Remember that performance management is not an instrument to manage indiscipline
5. Have an uncomplicated and time-bound system of performance management.	10. Learn from mistakes.

Motivation: The extent to which the organizations communicate performance management and seek commitment of employees towards it. Performance management should be participatory in nature so as to facilitate exchange of performance and development needs.

Measurement and rewards: The performance criteria or indicators that are used to evaluate (a) individual performance and (b) the organizational effectiveness of the whole system, and how these are used to allocate rewards.

Role of HR professionals: The extent to which HR professionals (a) demonstrate subject matter expertise; (b) draw upon relevant theory an research evidence and (c) influence through leaders within organizations to focus energy on the aspects of performance management that make a significant difference to performance. Human resource professionals should follow a win-win approach in order to help managers and their employees succeed.

Learning organization: The extent to which organizations are able to objectively reflect and learn from their own performance management experience, builds on what works, and refining where necessary.

Culture and clarity of purpose: The extent to which an approach to performance management resonates and is congruent with the broader culture of the organization in which it is being applied.

In a nutshell, performance management seeks to balance business alignment with learning and development and performance reward.

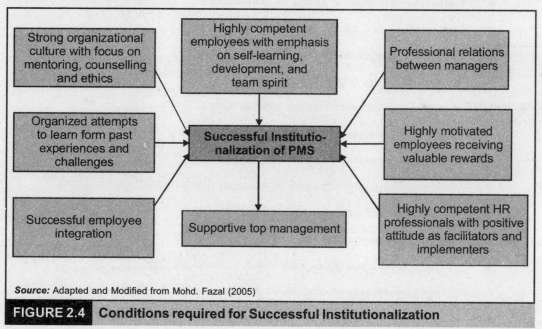

Source: Adapted and Modified from Mohd. Fazal (2005)

FIGURE 2.4 **Conditions required for Successful Institutionalization**

Organization's Ultimate Goal

An organization's ultimate goals determine its strategy. For example, an organization intending to become the world's largest textile company in the shortest possible time (ultimate goal) will increase its production capacities either through organic route such as setting up new manufacturing facilities, or by acquiring other textile organizations. Since acquisition helps increasing production capacities quickly, the organization will pursue acquisition as a strategy for faster growth. But acquisition strategy also involves turning around the performance of the older acquired production units which essentially calls for improving human performance for corporate success.

1. *Organizational objectives and strategy*

   ❖ Achieving organization's ultimate goal

   ❖ Achieving organization's competitive position

   ❖ Comparing organization's strength with changing environment

   ❖ Examining organization's critical issues

   ❖ Analysing organization's opportunities

   ❖ Exploring the best approaches in view of organizational resources and competencies.

2. *Assessment of organizational performance needs*

   ❖ Identifying competencies necessary for achieving organizational objectives and strategy

   ❖ Gathering information about critical issues

   ❖ Determining new and future performance needs

   ❖ Prioritizing organizational improvement measures

   ❖ Recognizing core organizational values.

3. *Setting organizational performance expectations*

   ❖ Determining required vs desired performance

   ❖ Determining current performance status

   ❖ Understanding, aligning, and agreeing on performance expectations

   ❖ Formulating key performance indicators

   ❖ Evolving job objectives

   ❖ Aligning individual goals with organizational strategy.

4. *Establishing performance management process*

   ❖ Designing a framework of performance management encompassing

   ❖ Performance planning

   ❖ Performance managing

   ❖ Performance appraisal

   ❖ Performance monitoring.

5. *Measuring effective of performance management*

   ❖ Identifying opportunities for performance development

   ❖ Providing performance counseling including 360 degree feedback

- ❖ Devising reward strategy and administering reward system
- ❖ Instituting performance management audit
- ❖ Improvement in competitive position of the organization.

Instituting Performance Management Audit

Performance management audit is a diagnostic toll used to assess the PMS of an organization. It is a participative tool that examines various performance-related issues and seeks to identify the strengths and areas of improvement needed in an organization's PMS.

Performance audit helps an organization in the following ways:

- A clear picture of how employees view PMS right now
- A clear picture of how employees think the PMS should be improved
- A clear picture of how PMS can be benchmarked
- A clear picture of what values and integrity in terms of managerial and employees behavior and action is emphasized
- Creating consensus of all stakeholders—shareholders, customers and employees for finding future direction to address new global business challenges.

EXHIBIT 2.4 Performance Management System Checklist for Managers	
Do you have written performance standards for the employees?	Yes/No
Have you communicated the performance standards to the employees?	Yes/No
Are the standards clear and reasonable?	Yes/No
Has HR representative reviewed the standards for any possible problems?	Yes/No
Have you told the employee what critical element he is failing in?	Yes/No
Have you counselled the employee on how to improve to an acceptable Level?	Yes/No
Have you fully assessed and utilized all available resources to help the employee improve? Have you explained and offered them to the employee?	Yes/No
Have you sought employee input regarding what is needed to improve?	Yes/No
Have interim review periods been established to measure the employee's improvement?	Yes/No
Have you advised the employee what he has to do to improve performance and retain the job?	Yes/No
Have you provided all the agreed assistance including training to the employee?	Yes/No
Did you consider any requests for accommodation?	Yes/No

Contd...

Have you taken into account annual, sick, or to her leave taken during the review period?	Yes/No
Did you document the employee's performance, your efforts to assist, the employee's actions and contributions to the improvement plan, etc.?	Yes/No
Do you have copies of any notes of counselling and /or assistance to The employee?	Yes/No
Do you have copies of memoranda of counselling provided to the employee?	Yes/No
Has there been due process prior to the administration of any discipline?	Yes/No
Do you have a just cause to administer progressive discipline and/or use the alternate discipline process, and the document to demonstrate the just cause.	Yes/No

E-performance Management

Organizations recognize that maximizing performance of employees is critical to its success. Changing market conditions, changes in technology, and changes in regulatory requirements all combine to create a dynamic market for human resources. With a talent war on the horizon, increasingly, the cost of employee compensation makes performance management a key component in any strategic human resource plan. As the cost of attracting, retaining, and training competent employee rises, organizations increasingly focus on identifying both the top and bottom performers within the organization. Marginal performers may be counseled out or provided with training/retraining in an effort to return their performance to an acceptable level, while excellent performers are identified and rewarded appropriately. Moreover, since the promotion and development of internal sources has been shown to be significantly less expensive than external recruitment, organizations seek to identify their excellent employees as candidates for advancement within the organization.

With the IT revolution, the paradigm of organizational system has changed drastically. Given stiff competition, cost containment is a major paradigm of organizations intending to stay competitive. The IT-enabled performance management comes as an effective tool to leverage the full benefits of the system at a comparatively much lesser cost of administration. Moreover, the focus of organizations today is on paperless office, flexible systems, and integration across the organization. Electronic performance management (or e-performance management) offers great value for money to the organizations and addresses its needs aptly. E-performance management is essentially a PMS in the form of an online software package with multiplication modules that is fully integrated with the organizational metrics. It provides greater flexibility, tracking, and access of performance management to large number of employees and managers across the organization, across the world at the press of a button. Bititci et al. (2000) point out that the main benefit of using an IT platform for managing the performance management within an organization is that the maintenance of the information contained within the systems becomes much simpler. They also set up some requirements for an IT platform, which is suitable in such a situation. This e-performance management software is readily available in the market as standard product, or can be customized to meet a specific need of the organization.

Nevertheless, the key to successful performance management list in a top-down approach that identifies critical success factors for an organization and filters them through each level of the organization into measurable objective and goals. The result of this breakdown is grouping of competencies and skills for each unique job, which facilitates in setting a robust performance criteria.

Once these competencies and skills are established, the organization requires a tool to capture employee performance relative to both organizational standards and the performance of that employee. E-performance management product provides this capability in the form a web-based, real-time, software tool that is fully integrated with the organizational objectives and strategy.

The e-performance management product allows organizations to maintain a record of core skills and competencies into the employee's performance management process. E-performance management provides templates for a wide application that could be used across organizations spread in different parts of the world through one software module. E-performance management template provide the following features:

- Job or individual-centered performance contracts

- Uploading of performance criteria

- Secure online appraisal with password

- Automatic e-mail notification of completed appraisal to employee and manager

- Workflow system to monitor appraisal progress

- Archive retrieval possible for retrieval of previous period appraisals

- Assigning different weighting protocols

- Viewing competency ratings

- Viewing compensation details

- Career advancement and opportunities available.

As organizations make the transition from the hierarchical structures of the past into learner and flatter structures, the responsibility for evaluating an employee's performance can no longer be restricted to a single manager/appraiser. Changes in organizational design such as cross-functional teams and project-driven organizations require that the performance evaluation task be shared by multiple managers, often from different areas in the organization.

E-performance management provides a flexible tool to manage employee performance in organizations with dynamic structures. It allows employees to collaborate with one or many performance appraisers to identify appropriate performance criteria on a document by document basis. In addition, both employees and appraisers may nominate others on the organization to participate in the review process via the delivered multi-rater process. When an employee performance management process identifies an area of opportunity, or an entirely new area of organizational skill is identified, e-performance management can be used to address these issues by generating employee development plans and employee learning programmes. These development tips and functions allow the organization to provide standardized content for these scenarios, and ensures that a consistent message is communicated to all members of the organization.

E-performance management also helps in screening employees being appraised against the skills and competencies that have been identified for keyed positions.

Moreover, as an employee's performance, skills, or competencies change, their ranking in the succession plan can be updated according to both their individual performance and their performance relative to other succession candidates.

Implementing performance management across and organization creates the potential for a large amount of administrative overhead. Performance management process must be completed and approved, feedback and counseling must be provided fro multiple reviewers, documents rated, deadlines monitored, and many of these activities must be performed multiple times during each performance cycle for each and every employee. E-performance management (e.g., Oracle's PeopleSoft Applications) helps organizations automate many of the administrative processes surrounding performance management. E-performance management enables rule-based routing of performance documents for editing and approval, the delivered language editor and results writer tools enable standardized content to be suggested at the time of appraisal, and the status dashboard enables all parties to track their documents as they move the performance management process, that is, from planning to monitoring and beyond.

E-performance management offers numerous benefits, some of which are listed below:

For managers

- Focused and aligned performance goals have a direct influence on organizational performance

- Employee performance and focus areas are accessible in an instant

- Performance management is a key part of an organization's integrated human resource strategy

- Easy to drill down through performance data for initiating root cause analysis for marginal performers

- Getting instant feedback on performance with drill down to individual employee performance

- No need to write performance contracts each year, simply upload and edit from a previous period

- Development needs emanating from performance discussions are automatically fed into the individual development plan.

For HR professionals

- Organization-wide quality assurance of goals and key performance indicators (KPIs).

⌘ E-performance Management Practices in Indian Organizations ⌘

Technology has changed the face of business. Many HR transactions have been automated especially performance management. We now look at IT-enabled performance management practices of some leading companies in India.

At **Nokia India**, there are no performance appraisal forms. Performance criteria are set by employee in concurrence with his manager in the appraisal tool. Reviewing officer reviews the same. This tool helps to update the goal setting and achievements periodically.

At **PepsiCo**, employees unload their performance targets on MDN, a global portal which is available to PepsiCo employees across the world. Mid-term review and final appraisals facilities by MDN which also guides employees in tracking their career plans by preparing Career Development Action Plan. The data is subsequently used by HR.

At **TCS**, managers use an online system for carrying out performance management system, merit pay, and succession planning activities with ease.

- Progress of goal/KPI setting and appraisal is monitored and managed

- Monitor appraisal bias within the organization

- Paper-based forms are eliminated, making process management more efficient and secure

- Managers are more likely to conduct effective goal/KPI setting and appraisal, given ease of use

- Performance management more likely to become entrenched in the organization.

We conclude in the words of Agha Husan Abedi:

"The conventional definition of management is getting work done through people, but real management is developing people through work."

CHAPTER-3

From HRM to Building Human Capital for Excelling Performance

LEARNING OBJECTIVES

- To make students aware of the linkages between performance management system and human resource management

- To make students aware that performance is the result of committed human recourses

- To give a detailed account of building human capital for excellence in performance

- To make students aware that "human capital" alone can give sustaining capabilities to corporates

Introduction

"Human capital is increasingly being recognized as the important determinant of organizational performance and enhancing the individual has never been so important. Today, it is far more important to empower an individual in such a way that they can be placed anywhere on the globe."

N.S. Rajan, Partner, Human capital, Ernst & Young

Source: *Business Manager*, December 2006.

Senior Management Decisions on Stakeholder Saliency

EXHIBIT 3.1	Stakeholder Systems Model of HRM				
Line Managers	**HR specialist**	**Employees**	**Labors union representatives**	**'Fiduciary' stakeholders: Shareholders and Customers**	**'Silent' stake holders: Community and Environment**
Stake holders perspectives and agendas					
Stakeholder synthesis—Agreement on HR policy					
Perceived fairness/ agreement on aims and objective of HR policy					
System procedural justice					
HR practice					
Perceived fairness of HR system: Fair hearing, access to information, opportunity to challenge, etc.					
System procedural justice					
HR system outcomes					
Perceived fairness of HR decisions on access to training, placement, promotion, salary revision, etc.					
Impact on motivation and performance					
System distribution justice					
HR evaluation measures					
Organization and wider stakeholder satiscation? Efficacy---do HR systems work? Efficiency—Do HR systems operate cost effectively? Effectiveness—Do HR systems contribute to organization goals?					
Equity—Do HR systems embody fairness and integrity?					
System evaluation					

Source: John Simmons (2002).

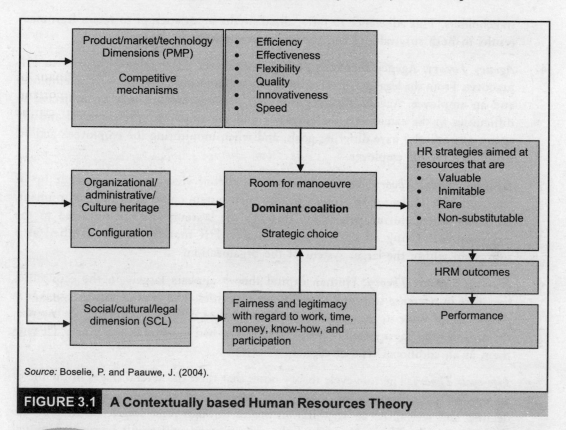

Source: Boselie, P. and Paauwe, J. (2004).

FIGURE 3.1 | **A Contextually based Human Resources Theory**

Theoretical Frameworks of Human Resource Management

The area of HR management today is being supported, developed, and understood using a variety of theoretical frameworks. Jackson and Schuler (1995) provide the following frameworks:

1. *Resource Dependence Theory:* Resource dependence theory stems from the relationship between an organization and its constituencies. This theory emphasizes the need for resources as being primary in the determination of policies and procedures. Organizations are viewed as being able to succeed by gaining and retaining control over scarce valuable resources, such as human resources.

2. *Competitive Advantage Theory:* Competitive advantage theory dictates that a competitive advantage exists if the resource is rare, inimitable, non-substitutable, and valuable. Competitive advantage can be sustained through continued training, support of organizational culture, selection processes, performance management, and other traditional HR practices.

3. *Institutionalist Theory:* Institutionalism suggests that organizations operate in a manner consistent with the rationalized myths that will garner them legitimacy in their external environment. This external environment is made up of a broad variety of

stakeholders. This adherence to rationalized myths in an attempt to retain legitimacy results in both survival and constraints on organizational actions.

4. *Agency Theory:* Agency theory is perhaps one of the most related theories to HR practices. From the legal perspective, an agency relationship exists between an employer and an employee. Agency theory posits that this relationship may be subjected to difficulties to the extent that the employer and the employee (the principal and the agent, respectively) have differing goals, and when monitoring the employee's actions is difficult for the employer.

5. *General System Theory:* The general systems theory views systems as made up of complex, independent parts. Inputs to this open system come from the environment, are transformed during processing through the system, and are returned to the environment. Using an open-systems model, HR management is studied as a subsystem within the larger system of the organization.

6. *Human Capital Theory:* Human capital theory appears largely in the economics literature in reference to people's productive capacities. The crux of this theory is that people are of value to the organization because they make it productive. In essence, the organization has invested in people just as they had invested in machinery, viewing them as an additional type of capital.

7. *Life-cycle Theory:* The Life-cycle theory notes that there are several stages in the life of an organization. These stages have been described as start-up, growth, maturity, decline, and revival. As an organization moves through these stages, HRM practices that fit with the life-cycle stage of the organization will result in organizational effectiveness.

8. *Role Behavior Theory:* Role behaviour focuses on the interdependent role behaviours as building blocs for the organizational system. According to Katz and Kahn (1978), role behaviors are defined as 'the recurring actions of an individual, appropriately interrelated with the repetitive activities of others so as to yield a predictable outcome'. The primary means by which the organization sends role information through the organization, supports desired behaviours, and evaluates role performances in HR management.

9. *Organizational Change Theory:* Organizational change theory focuses on the difference in form, quality or state over time in an organizational entity. Organizational change theory adds two pieces to the understanding of HR management. First, in management in organizational change, organizations need to ensure congruence between the stated goals and stated changes and the enacted changes. Second, people need to change in order to affect organizational changes, which requires an active role being played by HR management.

10. *Transactions Cost Theory:* Transactions cost theory takes an economic viewpoint of the creation of governance structures which establish, monitor, evaluate, and enforce exchanges agreed upon earlier. Central to this theory are two assumptions—'bounded rationality' and 'opportunism'. On the part of employees, the potential for

opportunism exists when the employee is specially trained or possesses specialized knowledge or skills, which have a market value to other organizations. Bounded rationality dictates that there are a limited number of options that can be assessed by any given organization prior to making a decision. Human resource activities seek to take advantage of bounded rationality while attempting to prevent the exercise of opportunism through the execution of contracts, the creation of monitoring and compliance assurance system, and through the revision of the contracts as and when necessary.

11. *Strategic Contingency Theory:* Strategic contingency theory recognizes that there are several strategic typologies. The choice made by an organization of which strategy to pursue requires systematic management of human resources in order to ensure appropriate and successful implementation. Strategic contingency theory posits that the choice between various typologies is dependent upon the environment within which the organization operates.

12. *Organizational Learning Theory:* According to organizational learning theory, perspective prior learning facilities should exist in order to make the learning and application on new, related knowledge feasible. This idea can be extended to include the case in which the knowledge in question is itself a set of learning skills constituting an organization's absorptive capacity.

13. *Information Processing Perspective:* This perspective is based on the premise that organizations are created to facilitate the flow of information for effective individual and organizational decision-making. The focus is on the capacity and facilitation characteristics of organizational structure and practices and practices such as human resources ones that support, encourage, and reward transfer of information within the organization, across its boundaries to international joint venture partners and the international joint venture itself, and that enables the organization to acquire knowledge to transform the data and information.

All these theories are being used today to help develop the area of HR management. Many are also being used to help develop and understand international HR management.

A number of HRM theorists will have reservations in accepting the culturally indigenous HR management practices argument because they might believe that management practice evolved through the period of feudalism till socio-technology. Hence, HR management practices have to be innovative at every evolutionary stage to make them work effectively for the organization. This is because culturally, indigenous HR management practices are evolved along with a country's national culture, and are time-tested. Therefore, adequate consideration has to given to develop synergies between the culturally indigenous HR management practices of the country of focus and an organization's HR management practices that are evolved from 'alien' cultures (Bartlett et al. 2002). Hence, national culture is an essential component of HR management of any multinational corporation.

Components of 'Best Practice'/High Commitment HRM

(Source: adapted from Pfeffer J. *The Human Equation: Building profits by putting people first.* Boston, Harvard Business School Press. 1998)

⌘ Employment Security and Internal Labour Markets ⌘

Pfeffer (1998) regards employment security as fundamentally underpinning the other six HR practices, principally because it is regarded as unrealistic to ask employees to offer their ideas, hard work and commitment without some expectation of employment security and concern for their future careers. The contribution a positive psychological contract makes to open and trusting employment relationships (Holman et al 2003), and the notion of mutuality that is seen as a key component in partnership agreements both relate to this. For example, whilst the partnership agreement at Borg Warner does not contain an explicit statement about employment security, both managers and shop stewards from the company recognize that the plan could not have stayed open without employee support (Suff and Williams 2003, p39).

Pfeffer (1998, p183) reckons that compulsory lay-offs and downsizing undermine employment security, and sees the following as alternatives: (1) proportionately reducing working hours to 'spread the pain' of reduced employment costs across the entire workforce; (2) reducing wages to reduce the labour costs; (3) freezing recruit to prevent overstaffing; and (4) putting production workers into sales to build up demand.

This is some way short of full-blown employment security, and it is clear that employment security is not expected to reduce corporate profits. The employer's financial flexibility is maintained by increasing employee workloads and by ensuring that salaries are related to organizational performance in the event of a downturn in demand.

⌘ Selective Hiring and Sophisticated Selection ⌘

Recruiting and retaining outstanding people and 'capturing a stock of exceptional human talent' (Boxall 1996, p.66-67) is seen as an effective way to achieve sustained competitive advantage. Even though employers have always wanted to recruit the best people available, this is nowadays more likely to be systematized through the use of sophisticated selection techniques and taking greater care when hiring. Increasingly, employers are looking for applicants who possess a range of social, interpersonal and team working skills in addition to technical ability.

For example, Wood and de Menezes (1998) asked about the importance of social and teamworking skills as selection criteria, and Wood and Albanese (1995) found that two of the major facets sought by employers were trainability and commitment. Hoque's (1999) study of large hotels also identified trainability as a major selection criterion. Indeed, in a growing number of situations, it would appear that employers feel that they can provide technical training for people so long as they have the 'right' social skills, attitudes and commitment (Stury et al 2001; Callaghan and Thompson, 2002; Marchington et al 2003b).

The proxies used to measure 'selective hiring' vary widely. They include the following:

- The number of applicants per position (Delaney and Huselid 1996) or as many good applicants as the organization needs (Guest et al 2003).

- The proportion administered an employment test prior to hiring (Huselid 1995; Guest et al 2003)

- The sophistication of (selection) processes, such as the use of psychometric tests (Patterson et al 1997) and realistic job previews (Hoque 1999; Guest et al 2000b, 2003).

These measures capture quite different components of the selection process and on whether the focus is on the overall approach taken by employers or the precise techniques they use. Moreover, some of them emphasize inputs rather than outputs in terms of the quality of those eventually recruited. For example, attracting a large number of applicants for a position may indicate poor HR procedures due to failures to define the job and the field adequately prior to advertising. It is also possible that selective hiring, especially when it focuses on how well new recruits might fit with the prevailing organizational culture, can lead to under-represented groups being excluded from employment. Moreover, an excessive 'cloning' of employees could be problematic if the organization is keen to promote initiative and diversity, and counterproductive if business needs and markets change. On the other hand, there may be situations where it is impossible to attract sufficient applicants due to skills, there may be situations where it is impossible to attract sufficient applicants due to skills shortages—as with some professional jobs in the health and education sectors—where the emphasis shifts to generating a pool of potential recruits rather than finding more sophisticated ways to choose between them.

Recruiting high quality, committed staff is seen as central to 'best practice' HRM, and the use of psychometric tests, structured interviews and work sampling is likely to increase the validity of selection decisions. Competencies to be sought at the selection stage include trainability, flexibility, commitment, drive and persistence, and initiative. The key point about 'best practice' selection is that it should be integrated and systematic, making use of the techniques which are appropriate for the position and the organization, and administered by individuals who have themselves been trained.

⌘ Extensive Training, Learning and Development ⌘

Having recruited 'outstanding human talent', employers need to ensure that these people remain at the forefront of their field, not only in terms of professional expertise and product knowledge but also through working in teams or in interpersonal relations. Boxall (1996, p.67) view this as one element in 'organizational process advantage', the idea that employers aim to synergies the contribution of talented and exceptional employees. There is little doubt that there has been a growing recognition of the importance of individual and organizational learning as a source of sustained competitive advantage as employers introduce more skills-specific forms of training an experience continuing skills shortages in some areas.

Wright and Gardner (2003, p.312) note that this is one of the most widely quotes and important elements of high commitment HRM. The use of the word 'learning' is crucial as it demonstrates employer willingness to encourage and facilitate employee development rather than just providing specific training to cover short-term crises. Different types of measure have been used here: full-fledged 'learning companies' (Hoque 1999), employee development and assessment programmes or task-based and interpersonal skills training. The time and effort devoted to learning opportunities is also important. A range of proxies have been used here such as the number of days' raining received by all workers, the proportion of workers who have been trained, the budget set aside for training, or the establishment of agreed training targets over a two year period. The WERS survey used a simple absence/presence distinction is relation to induction training and formal job training, finding that well over half of all workplaces engaged in this. Training was provided at fewer workplaces in the private sector than the public sector. The CIPD survey (Guest et al 2000a, p.15) reports quite surprisingly, that almost one-quarter of respondents claimed to offer at least one month's training per annum to their staff, although 13 percent admitted that they provided none at all. West et al (2002) used several measures for assessing training in their study of NHS hospitals, each of which related to the amount of money spent, whilst Guest et al (2003) focused instead on the amount of training received by workers.

Of course, there are problems in trying to measure and evaluate the concentration of training and learning. While it is clearly important to establish how much time and resources employers invest in formal training, and whether or not this covers the entire workforce, it is also crucial to identify the type of training which is provided and who has responsibility for managing this. Quite a number of the studies have looked solely at the financial or quantitative aspects—in terms of money or time invested in training—and ignored the quality or relevance of training and learning that is provided. It is now widely acknowledged that most workers are overqualified for the jobs they do (Grugulis 2003), and as such extra training may add little to organizational performance or worker skills. Even where training opportunities are provided, there is often 'no explicit aim within the training of increasing the individuals' skill base or broadening their experience' (truss et al 1997, p.61). Similarly, questions need to be asked about whether or not longer term budget safeguards are established so as to protect training provision (Wood and Albanese 1995) or if training is tied in to 'increased promotability within the organization' (Delery and Doty 1996). The quality of training, both in terms of its focus and its delivery, is clearly more important than a simple count of the amount provided.

✳ Employee Involvement (EI), Information Sharing and Worker Voice ✳

There are a number of reasons why EI is an essential component of the high commitment paradigm (Marchington and Wilkinson 2005). First, open communications about financial performance, strategy and operational matters not only ensures that workers are informed about organizational issues, it also conveys a symbolic and substantive message that they are to be trusted and treated in an open and positive manner. Second, teams working to be successful workers require information in order to provide a basis from which to offer their suggestions and contribute to improvements in organizational performance. Third, participation can provide management with some legitimacy for it actions on the grounds that ideas have been put forward by workers and/or at least considered by them before decisions are ultimately made. As we argue throughout this book, even if management has more power at its disposal than do workers, the employment relationship is not complete and legally defined in detail but open to interpretation and disagreement over how it is enforced on a daily basis.

Information involvement or EI appears in just about every description of, or prescription for, 'best practice' or high commitment HRM. EI can include downward communications, upward problem-solving groups and project teams, all of which are designed to increase the involvement of individual employees in their workplace. The precise mix of EI techniques depends upon the circumstances, but the range of measures used and the 'flexible' definition of involvement of involvement are potentially confusing. Many of the studies restrict this to downward communications from management to employees which measure the frequency of information disclosure (Patterson et al 1997), the regularity of team briefing or quality circles (Wood and Albanese 1995) or the extent to which workers are informed or consulted about business operations or performance (Guest et al 2003). The regularity of attitude surveys also features strongly in many of the studied (e.g. Huselid 1995; Hoque 1999; Guest et al 2000a). Some go further and enquire about the percentage of employees who receive training in group problem-solving (Arthur 1994) or the level at which a range of decisions is made (Delaney and Huselid 1996). The WERS survey analysis only included briefing in its estimates if at least 25 percent of the time at the meeting was devoted to employee questions and discussion (Guest et al 2000a, p16), something that happens at about half the workplaces.

Again, the range of proxies used is so wide that it is difficult to compare results across these studies and arrive at any firm conclusions about the importance of information sharing and EI to high commitment HRM. The fact that EI is often, little more than a cascade of information from management means that any meaningful workers contribution is unlikely. Indeed, one of the objectives of schemes such as team briefing is to reinforce the supervisor as an information disseminator who adapts messages to suit specific operational requirements. This one-way version of information sharing—rather than being seen as educative, empowering and liberating as the terminology might imply—could more easily be interpreted instead as indoctrinating, emasculating and controlling (Marchington and Wilkinson 2005).

Although only a relatively small number of authors (e.g., Huselid 1995; Roche 1999; Batt et al 2002; Dundon et al 2004) specifically include voice as an aspect of high commitment, it seems essential that workers should have the opportunity to express their grievance openly and independently, in addition to being able to contribute to management decision-making on task-related issues. Employee voice may be achieved through trade union representation and collective bargaining as well as through formally established grievance and disputes procedures, but in addition, it could be through speak-up schemes, which offer employees protection if their complaints are taken badly by managers (Marchington et al 2001). In their study of telecommunications, Batt et al (2002, p589) regarded direct participation and union representation as 'complementary vehicles for employee voice at work'.

⌘ Self-managed Teams/Teamworking

This practice has become more prevalent over the last decade for a variety of reasons, not least as a way of pooling ideas and improving work processes in response to Japanese competition. It has been identified by many employers as a fundamental component of organizational success (Marchington 1999). It is also one of the key attributes that employers look for in new recruits, something asked for in references, and it even plays a part in courses organized for school students. Teamwork is typically seen as leading to better decision-making and the achievement of more creative solutions (Pfeffer 1998, p76). Evidence suggests that employees who work in teams generally report higher levels of satisfaction than their counterparts working under more "traditional" regimes, although they also report working hard as well (Wilkinson et al 1997; Edwards and Wright 1998; Geary and Dobbins 2001; Batt and Doellgast 2003).

⌘ High Compensation Contingent on Performance

Pfeffer (1998) reckons that there are two elements to this practice—higher than average compensation and performance—related reward—although both send a signal to employee that they deserve to be rewarded for superior contributions. To be effective, this needs to be at a level in excess of that for comparable workers in other organizations so as to attract and retain high-quality labor. In addition, according to this scenario, rewards should reflect different levels of worker contribution, perhaps being paid as a regular bonus or through profit sharing schemes. Despite the extensive criticism of performance-related pay, it is included in most lists of 'best practice', particularly those conducted in the US. Given that research in the UK is much more critical about the value of incentive pay, it might be better to include the entire reward package in this HR practice so that it is not restricted to pay alone, and it can then relate to employee contributions to organizational performance—whether this is on an individual, team, department or establishment-wide basis.

Huselid (1995) includes two measures for this factor; the proportion of the workforce who have access to company incentive schemes and the proportion whose performance appraisal are used to determine their compensation. MacDuffie (1995) refers to contingent compensation. The UK studies also focus on merit or performance pay. Wood and de Menezes (1998) enquired about merit pay and profit sharing, Guest et al (2000a) included performance related pay for non-managerial staff, whereas Hoque (1999) asked about merit pay and appraisal schemes for all staff and West et al (2002) and Guest et al (2003) focused on appraisal as the key factor. Indeed, in West et al's study, appraisal had an extremely significant impact on performance. Not surprisingly, the proportion of workplaces covered by performance-related reward was rather less widespread in the public sector than in the private (Guest et al 2000a, p16). However, equally surprisingly, given the degree of practitioner interest in inventive pay schemes, about two-thirds of the respondents to the CIPD survey (Guest et al 2000b, p16) said that their organizations did not make use of individual performance related pay for their non-managerial employees.

⌘ Reduction of Status Differences/Harmonization ⌘

Symbolic manifestations of egalitarianism seen in the HR practices of some Japanese companies are meant to convey messages to manual workers and lower grade office staff that they are valuable assets who deserve to be treated in a similar way to their more senior colleagues. It is also seen as a way to encourage employees to offer ideas within an 'open' management culture. This can be seen through egalitarian symbols, such as staff uniforms, shared canteen and car-parking facilities, but it is also underpinned by the harmonization of many terms and conditions of employment—such as holidays, sick-pay schemes, pensions, and hours of work (*IRS Employment Review* 784a 2003). The principal point behind moves to single status and harmonization, is that it seeks to break down artificial barriers between different groups of staff, thus encouraging and supporting teamworking and flexibility. Extending employees share ownership to the workforce as a whole is a further way in which status differences can be reduced, typically through schemes whereby staff are allocated shares according to some predetermined formula. Pfeffer (1998, p38) argues that 'employee ownership, effectively implemented, can align the interests of employees with those of shareholders by making employees shareholders too'. Firms with high shareholders return also often have some form of employee ownership.

The proxies used for harmonization and the reduction of status differentials are also wide and variable. For example, Wood and de Menezes (1998) ask about whether or not any employees have to 'clock in' to work, and about the existence of employee share schemes and welfare facilities/fringe benefits. Hoque's (1999) questions relate very broadly to harmonization and single status. Guest et al's (2000a, 2000b, 2003) questions vary between the highly specific (harmonized holiday entitlements for all staff) through to whether or not the organization has a formal commitment to achieving single status. Over 80 percent of the organizations in the CIPD survey (Guest et al 2000b) claimed to have harmonized holidays and just under half reckoned to have a formal commitment to single status.

Bundles of Human Resource Practices

It should be clear from the previous section that there are often links between these high commitment HR practices. For example, workers are more likely to welcome EI and information sharing if they have employment security and their workplace is relatively status-free. Equally, they are more likely to show an interest in team working if their efforts are rewarded with performance-related incentives, share ownership, and access to training opportunities. Similarly, if sufficient care has been taken at the recruitment and selection stage, new recruits are more likely to adopt flexible working practices and welcome team working, as well as be striving for internal promotion in the future. In isolation, or without the support of a strong organizational culture each of these practices can easily be dismissed as noting more than a short-term fad or fashion. Conversely, the more that HR practices form a coherent and synergistic bundle of related practices, it is argued, the more organizations are likely to enjoy success due to the fact that the high commitment paradigm is more deeply embedded into the culture of the workplace. Benson and Lawler (2003,-157) note that 'research at the work unit level confirms the importance of viewing practices as complementary' and that the high commitment model (in general) outperformed more traditional control-oriented work systems despite the fact that the exact combination of practices is uncertain and may be industry-specific.

By contrast, bundles are 'additive'. Generally speaking, the more practices that are in place the better, so long as some distinctive core exists. In other words, it may be possible to adopt a large number of high commitment HR practices and ignore others, but still gain from the interactive effects of those that are in place. Questions then arise as to how many practices are needed to make a difference, from what areas of HRM these are to be drawn and whether certain practices are fundamental to make the synergies work. Much of Guest et al's recent work has differentiated between organizations on the basis of how many HR practices they use. Their analysis of the WERS data led them to conclude that 'despite trying a variety of approaches and combinations, we could not find any coherent pattern of bundles of practices in the private or the public sectors. The only combination that made any sense was a straightforward count of all the practices' (Guest et al 2000a, p15). Provided a certain minimum number of practices are in place, it is likely (though not automatic) that high commitment HRM will be found in a range of different areas of practice—such as selection, training, EI and harmonization.

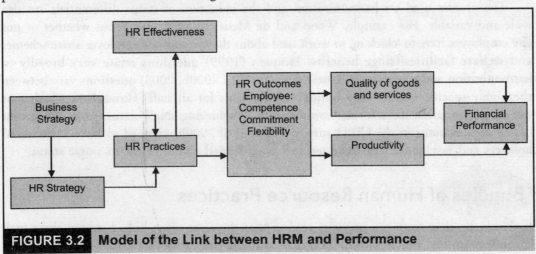

FIGURE 3.2 Model of the Link between HRM and Performance

There are a number of significant findings that confirm, overturn or extend previous work investigating the links between high commitment HRM and performance. First, the researches and the AMO model used, which argue that in order for people to performance better, they must:

- Have the ability and necessary knowledge and skills, including how to work with other people (A)

- Be motivated to work and want to do it well (M)

- Be given the opportunity to deploy their skills both in the job and more broadly contributing to work group and organizational success (O).

⌘ Raising Questions about HRM-Performance Link ⌘

Persuasive as they might appear, and attractive as they might be to HR professionals, studies argue high commitment HRM leads to improved levels of performance have not escaped criticism , including – as we have seen—some by the authors themselves. Drawing on a number of sources (e.g. Holman et al 2003: Wright and Gardner, 2003; Godard, 2004), some of the major concerns are outlined below:

Questions about the Direction of Causality and the 'Black Box'

It will be apparent from the earlier discussion that this is a major issue, and much depends on the theoretical framework adopted by the researcher. Conceptually, it is equally likely that the use of a strong bundle of high commitment HR practices could lead to improved performance, at least at workplace level, as it is that high commitment HRM is made possible and paid for by high levels of organizational performance.

Little Consistency in the HR Practices Included in the Bundle

The number of HR practices in each of the lists varies substantially (from as few as six or seven to twenty more) as does the inclusion or exclusion of specific techniques. For example, despite the importance attached to employment security by Pfeffer, this is not included in several of the lists (e.g. Delaney and Huselid 1996; Patterson et al 1997; Wood and de Menezes 1998). Similarly, while some authors include measures of employee voice other than that achieved through self-managed teams and employee involvement, Pfeffer does not. Perhaps this does not matter if we are clear as to why certain HR practices should be included, but that does not seem to be the case. As Wood (2003, p280) argues, it is much more important to focus on an underlying orientation for integrated management or high commitment HRM that may be reflected in slightly different types of practice rather than spending time trying to identify a set of practices that might be appropriate across all workplaces. However, far too often, the lists seem to be developed on the basis of individual preference, by looking at what other researchers have used or by constructing groupings of practices on the basis of factor analysis, and then attempting to impose some theoretical justification for this ex-post facto. Of those that do have a theoretical model to underpin their approach, even then it is not always clear why certain practices are included and others are not. For example, Huselid (1995, pp.645-647) uses two groups of practices, entitled 'employee skills and organizational structures' – which includes job design, enhanced selectivity, formal training, various forms of participation, and profit sharing-and 'employee motivation' – which comprises performance appraisal linked to compensation and a focus on merit in promotion decision. It seems strange that participation and profit-sharing should be in the first grouping rather than the second given the supposed importance of these as techniques that enhance employee motivation. Patterson et al (1997) also emerge with two groups of practices, subtitled 'acquisition and development of employee skills' and 'job design' and on this occasion, participation and team working find way into the second grouping rather than the first. In short, a simple count of how many HR practices are used tells us little of any theoretical value.

Variations in the Proxies used to Measure High Commitment HRM

The studies use a range of different proxies for he same HR practice. For example, some are straight yes/no or absence/present type measures whereas others ask for the percentage of the workforce covered by a particular aspect of HRM-such as performance related pay. In some cases, the proportions vary between within a particular study between studies with, say 25 percent in one and 90 percent in another. Worse still, they can vary within a particular study between different items. Differences in the way in which practices are counted as present or absent have a major effect on the construction of the overall bundle, and it is rare for there to be an explicit discussion as to why certain levels have been set. Notability, Guest et al (2000b) do openly explain why they went for a figure of 90 percent is some of their questions. More seriously, the mere absence or presence of a practice is irrelevant because what matters is how this is used and what impact it has on the people employed and on organizational performance. Take the example of grievance procedures; these are almost universally employed in organizations, so a proxy based around absence or presence tells us nothing about how people take up grievances, how many they take up, and whether they regard the processes as open and reasonable—arguably more important as a differentiator. A similar point arises in relation to days spend on training. Knowing that the typical employee is trained for about five days per annum is hardly evidence of high commitment HRM if they are trained merely in how to conform to strict rules and procedures—as sometimes happens in call centres (Sturdy et al 2001). Moreover, potential problems also arise when compiling scores of high commitment HRM in deciding whether or not each practice should be weighted equally. This is clearly a problem where there are more measures of a particular item than others; for example, as often occurs with EI. It is possible in this situation that the overall measure gives too much weight to one factor compared with others. Moreover, what happens when, as in the WERS analysis, one practice is widely used—such as a formal statement on equal opportunities—and another, such as job security, is rarely provided? Do these deserve to be equally weighted or is the use of a relatively are practice something that differentiates organizations from their competitors.

Variations in the Proxies used to Measure Performance

One of the major problems is the different types of performance measure that are used, in particular whether they are based on objective or subjective assessments. Many of the studies have focused on the former, using measures of organizational performance such as profitability that have very little obvious linkage with the efforts of individual workers, even though ultimately this is what matters to organizations. This is clearly problematic in multiple organizations within the same industry, and even more complicated in conglomerates that operate across a range of sectors and countries, as well as in public-private partnership and inter organizational networks where it is hard to establish identifiable boundaries between them.

Dangers in Relying on Self-report Scores from HR Managers

Differences can arise depending on the expertise of the person who completes the questionnaire for an organization. For obvious reasons, questions used in telephone surveys tend to be those that are capable of an immediate answer that can be coded easily. As Purcell (1999) notes, this may not get us very far in establishing what factors really make a difference to employee commitment or organizational performance. Further, problems arise because personnel specialists, who are often the respondents in these surveys, often lack detailed knowledge about the competitive strategies utilized by their organizations and the proportion of sales derived form these strategies. At least the Guest et al study did overcome a number of these shortcomings by including managing directors and HR professionals in their sample, but they were unable to get opinions from employees themselves. This is particularly problematic if workers perceptions are not even included in studies when the focus is on' objective' measures of performance. Anxieties such as these mean that considerable caution is needed when interpreting conclusions from these quantitative studies, and one suggestion (Wall et al 2004) is that a team of independent experts could assess how schemes were working rather than relying on internal evaluations alone. For example, someone with a deep knowledge of EI could compare and contrast how these schemes were working across a range of different organizations.

Doubts about how much Autonomy Organizations have in Decision-making

It is implicitly assumed that organizations are free agents that are able to choose precisely which HR practices they wish to employ, considering any forces beyond their own organizational boundaries. Any organization is subject to forces that shape its HR policies, in terms of legal and institutional arrangements or through the pressure exerted by clients or industry bodies. This is most apparent in how the high commitment HRM package might be applied in different countries, and we should not assume the Anglo-Saxon model (based principally on North American and UK research) is early applicable to other countries.

The Universal Application of Best Practice HRM

One key aspect of the celebratory literature is that 'best practice' HRM is capable of being used in any organization, irrespective of product market situation, industry, or workforce,. Pfeffer (1998, pp.33-34) produces evidence from many industries and studies which he claims demonstrates the case for 'putting people first'. These include 'relatively low technology setting such as apparel manufacture to very high technology manufacturing processes. The results seem to hold for manufacturing and for service firms. Nothing in the available evidence suggests that the results are country-specific. The effects of high performance management practices are real, economically significant, and general—and thus should be adopted by your organization'. Support for this argument comes from several other studies. For example, Huselif (1995, p644) states that "all else being equal, the use of high performance or practices and good internal fit should lead to positive outcomes for all types of firms". Delery and Doty (1996, p828) find 'relatively strong support' for the universalistic argument and some support for other perspectives, and suggest that 'some human resource practices always {our emphasis) have a positive effect on performance'. These were: profit sharing, results-oriented appraisals and employment security. There is support form a non-US study as well, with Wood and Albanese (1995, p242) agreeing that certain HR practices have a universal effect.

"Innovative human resource practices are likely to contribute to improved economic performance *only when* {our emphasis} three conditions are met: when employees possess knowledge and skills that managers lack; when employees are motivated to apply this skill and knowledge through discretionary effort; and when the firms' business or production strategy can only be achieved when employees contribute such discretionary effort".

HR as a Strategic Business Partner

The competencies, which exist at different levels of personality are:

1. *Observable (easily assessable) level:*

   ❖ *Knowledge:* Information that an individual has in a particular area.

   ❖ *Skill:* Individual's ability to perform a certain physical or mental task (analyzes and gives decision)

   ❖ *Behaviour:* Action of a person in a given situation

2. *Non-observable (difficult to assess):*

   Personal characteristics:

   ❖ *Traits:* Psychological characteristics and consistent responses shown towards a situation or information

   ❖ *Motives:* The things a person consistently thinks about or wants and, which causes action. Motives drive or direct behaviour towards a select or certain actions or goals.

   ❖ *Self-concept:* Person's attitudes values or self-image.

Decision Tool for Training

The tool used to decide, whether training is to be given or not, after identifying the competency gaps, is given below.

'Can do' refers to the employee ability (competence) to do the job. 'Will do' refers to the employee willingness (motivation) to perform the job.

This results in four alternatives –

Can do/will do: This is the ideal situation; the employee is fully qualified and is doing the job as designed.

Cannot do/Will do: Here the employee is putting out the effort, but is not getting the result (skill problem).

Can do/Won't do: Here the employee possesses the competencies to do the work but does not complete work process as designed (motivational problem).

Cannot do/Won't do: This employee has deficiencies in both skills and motivation. The "will do-can't do" dimension of this model is within the purview of a competency effort. But the 'Can do-Won't do' dimension is not competency-based. It is a matter of attitude.

Human Capital

Human capital is the fountainhead of vast economic benefits that flow from human creativity and commitment, innovation and discovery, imagination and passion. It has been manifested in the development of electric lights, photography, telegraph, telephone, photocopying, automobiles, aircrafts, facsimile, microprocessors, personal computers and e-commerce.

Human capital is based on igniting the entrepreneurial passions of an organization's people. It involves setting up, supporting, and sustaining dynamic internal webs of the flow of ideas, talent, motivation, and resources toward new high growth opportunities. It involves leveraging a company's competitiveness and resources in novel ways towards new concepts of, and approaches to business; and translating them into credible ventures. It involves and denotes a linking up of entrepreneurial spirit, imagination, ideas, skills, knowledge, and capabilities with resources in the service of wealth creation in any business enterprises.

The Pillars of Human Performance

Work performance of an individual may be observed and appraised along three dimensions as follows:

1. An understanding of the context of work, or work situation, in terms of its purpose, nature, conditions, requirements, metrics of appraisals, and so on;

2.   The ability to carry out the work effectively in terms of the requisite knowledge, skills and capabilities required for performance excellence; and

3.   Motivation to carry out the work in terms of one's commitment and best efforts towards excelling in performance.

These three dimensions may be viewed as three pillars of human performance, viz., understanding the context, the ability to be effective, and motivational to excel. These three axes of human performance may be logically applied and instantiated to explicate the nature, norms, and attributes of the human capital as follows:

The first pillar, i.e., understanding the context, implies employees' reflective and critical understanding of the dynamic business environment of their enterprise. It also implies employees' comprehension of their company's vision and strategy, business system design and profit model, competitive logic and core value proposition. More importantly, it implies employees' clarity of understanding regarding their company's processes and mechanisms for the creation, capture, and delivery of value; and the nature and rationale of their own individual and collective efforts toward realizing their company's vision and strategy. The employees' awareness and understanding of their company's business context also orients them towards a better appreciation of the present and potential challenges facing their company; and the requirements of knowledge, skills, and capabilities for coping with them.

The second pillar, i.e., the ability to be effective, in the context of human capital, implies employees' abiding dedication to work excellence in their broadly defined and non-rigid work roles. More importantly, it implies employees' sustained orientation towards learning, upgradation of skills, cultivation of new and needed capabilities, expertise, creative thinking and use of knowledge; for both problem-solving and innovation; streamlining of process, procedures, and routines for eliminating non-value-adding activities; and experimentation and initiatives in search of opportunities. This is so, for the concept of performance excellence, or effectiveness, is neither static nor fixed.

The second pillar is meaningfully shaped by the first (i.e., 'understanding the business context') in terms of the adaptability of human capital to changes in a firm's business environment. The requirements of learning, knowledge, skills and capabilities of, and by employees, and the life cycles of its organization and industry. The requirements of employees' effectively performance would be radically different across disparate organizations like high-technology growth firms, firms in mature or declining industries, or firms caught in industrial shake-outs and consolidation. Even for the same firm, requirements would differ from time-to-time depending upon changes in its competitive situation. The focus of human capital along the second axis of performance is on proactive learning, development, and used of knowledge for customer-valued work excellence.

The third pillar i.e., 'motivation to excel' implies an organization-wide shared ethos of a high degree of commitment to enterprise goals, and a high level of cooperation among employees toward working together to achieve those goals, These, in turn imply a high level of trust and goodwill among employees in pursuit of shared objectives. Both commitment and cooperation are vital for individuals with complementary and specialized knowledge and skills to collaborate creatively for solving difficult problems, developing new products and/or services, achieving performance breakthroughs, creating new competencies, and generating value through relentless improvement an innovation.

Employees in an enterprise, both individually and collectively, must score high on each of the three axes, and consistently across all the three axes and in an expanding manner over time; in order to constitute the firm's human capital. The ability to meet the foregoing requirements of performance in a continuing manner, raises a basic question. What type of person would be capable of scaling the heights of performance, and sustaining the same in a steady-state fashion over time?

Performance excellence and effectiveness in organizations, apart from an individual's ability and motivation, depend primarily on the individual's ability to effectively collaborate with others. Collaboration is a purposive relationship based on trust, mutual regard, and sharing of ideas, information, knowledge, resources and responsibilities. It involves working together to learn, solve problems, innovate, meet tight time schedules, cope with obstacles, deal with unforeseen difficulties, and strive to achieve and exceed organizational goals every day. The nature and range of collaborative activities may vary, the collaborating persons, or team members, may be different from time to time, and job rotation assignments may engender new forms and modes of interpersonal and group interactions across organization levels, space and time. But the imperatives of doing one's best in cooperation with others, helping others when needed, and pursuing stretch goals of the enterprise, remain unchanged.

The Dynamic Nexus of Human Capital at the Enterprise Level

Human capital as an appreciating resource of an enterprise does not exist and develop as an isolated entity. Its growth, development, and evolution are inextricably bound up with its multilateral interactions with certain other salient factors in an enterprise, The state of human capital in an organization is simultaneously the cause and consequence of its interactive relationships with a dynamic nexus of a set of determinate factors. The nature, interrelationships, and dynamics of these factors may very briefly be outlined as follows:

The business environment of a firm as its dominant driver influences the firm's vision and values, shapes the firm's business model and logic of competition; and directs its organizational learning. The firm's business environment, and vision and values, together help shape its social capital i.e., the nature and strength of its internal collaborative structures.

Organizational learning and social capital of the firm together help determine the quality of its human capital. Organizational learning and human capital, in turn, shape the firms's knowledge management system. They also determine and facilitate the knowledge management system's outputs in terms of fostering innovation, developing the firm's competencies/capabilities, streamlining of its processes, and cultivation of relevant expertise in domains of competitive importance. These outputs of the firm's knowledge management system, in turn, serve to enhance and enrich the quality of the firm's human capital. The latter enables and engenders a flexible orchestration of the firm's innovative prowess, competencies/capabilities, streamlined process, and expertise; and leverages them for addressing the challenges and opportunities facing the firm. Such a flexible orchestration of the firm's total stock and flow of knowledge constitutes its intellectual capital (Rastogi, 2000).

The human capital of an enterprise is embedded in a dynamic nexus of its organizational learning, social capital and knowledge management. Its thrust and focus emanate from the firm's business model and strategic of competitiveness in the context of its business environment and vision. As the core of this nexus, human capital engenders the firm's intellectual capital i.e., its overall macro-level capacity and meta-capability for sustaining its competitiveness and business performance. Intellectual capital represents a firm's holistic capacity and capability for mastering the challenge of constant change. Without human capital, however, there is no intellectual capital.

Human capital relentlessly propels an organization toward becoming and being a storehouse of business expertise; a growing pool of cutting-edge competencies, skills, best practices, techniques and tools; a collaborative collectivity of autonomous and peak performing employees; an exemplar of speed and brain-power in all domains of its activity; an agile player responding rapidly to market shifts; and a bearer of a culture of consonant innovation. The organization thence tends to become and remain an effective instrument for continuous creation of wealth in the service of man and society. In this sense, the core of wealth creation process lies in the human capital of organizations in a society.

Six Attributes for HRD Managers

1. *Give voice to the voiceless:* Create forums where forgotten workers, customers, vendors, and citizens can make themselves heard. What they say, if heard by management with care, may keep the organization ticking in feast as well as famine.

2. *Light up dark areas:* An organization is full of overlooked, neglected activities. Hold up a lamp to them and see whether they are healthy or not. Invigorate them through focused training of those in charge. At one Indian research lab in Hyderabad, the management, in its drive for international class, identified forty areas where it needed to excel, including such 'unimportant' activities like gardening, interior décor, estate maintenance, and reception. Invite those servicing 'fringe' activities into the corporate limelight.

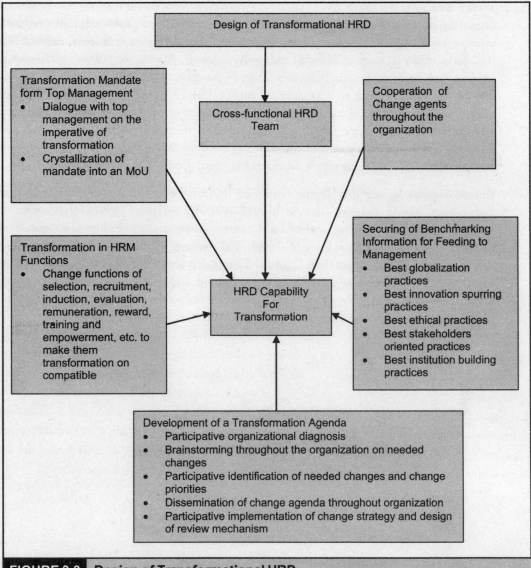

FIGURE 3.3 **Design of Transformational HRD**

3. *Make the meaningless meaningful:* Too many employees see the point of their effort as merely earning a living. They need to be explained the importance of what they are contributing, and can contribute, to the organization's prosperity and the contribution the organization is making to society. Once employees are fired up in this fashion, the can lift up the organization on their shoulders and carry it to a peak.

4. *Get brooms for the dirt:* Organizations commonly operate in a miasma of outdated rules, regulations, procedures, checks, routines, practices and policies. Periodic spring cleaning is essential remaining vital and responsive. Often, yesterday's innovation turns today into an albatross. Peter Drucker's sage question need to be answered periodically: if the corporation were to start all over again, which of its current policies, practices, and activities would it retain?

5. *Drive out past answers by proactive questions:* Some researchers have linked organizations to garbage cans in which past solutions, current problems, and preferred choices are dumped, and past solutions attached themselves to problems, rather than problems eliciting custom tailored solutions (Cohen, March, & Olsen, 1972). Past success, not competition, is frequently Enemy Number 1 in a dynamic industry, for it tends to restrict search to what worked earlier. The 21st century will be a century of queries and challenges, many of the best from knowledge workers, knowledge vendors, and knowledge customers. Those who seek to meet them by rummaging in their old files will court failure. Promote questioning so that the right answers emerge, and seek the answers from the whole world rather than from one's familiar files.

6. *Create beacons for the lost:* If our corporate leaders are to build a vibrant industrial India, they would have to be role models—of the spirit of entrepreneurship, of professionalism, of integrity, and of solid contributions to society. The Gita speaks of dharma. Dharma is not just a set of duties; it is a way of life. It permits the pursuit of the mundane, but in an exalted fashion. The trusteeship that Gandhiji enjoined up businessmen captures the dharma of businessmen well. Our spiritual heritage can make coherent the turbulence of this century. Identify those with the potential to be beacons and make them more luminous through training and exposure.

CHAPTER-4

Historical Perspective of Performance Management System

(WW-I) and the First-even pattern who has saved himself of the abilities of workers for industry prior to World War I. We are now richly influenced by Taylor and inspired that this in management style which was designed to come it as possible to hope that many of the developments in the long this followed, even at that day have been industrial by Taylor. The U.S. Screen with had systemized and used to have the efficiency of U.S. Army offers. It is also have supplanted the scientific systemof performance in that story and amount to see a prominent on the base of merit. The personnel history of this prominence in chapter in he...

LEARNING OBJECTIVES

- To give students a historical perspective of employees evaluation

- To make students aware of the different stages of employees performance measurement

- To make students aware of confidential report-writing

- To trace the history of modern performance management system from mere performance appraisal system

Historical Background

From the very evolution of civilization, people have been developing methods and systems of performance and evaluating the performance in their own ways. But there was no scientific approach for either performance or its evaluation.

According to Koontz (1971), the emperors of the Wei dynasty (AD 221-265) in China had an 'Imperial Rater' whose task was to evaluate the performance of the official family. Centuries later, Ignatius Loyola (1491-1556) established a system for formal rating of the members of the Society of Jesus (the Jesuits).

The first formal monitoring systems, however, evolved out of the work of Frederick Taylor and his followers before World War I. Rating for officers in the US armed services was introduced in the 1920s, and this spread to the UK in the 1950s and 1960s, when it was sometimes rechristened performance appraisal. Management by objectives then came and went in the 1960s and 1970s and, simultaneously, experiments were made with the critical incident technique and behaviourally anchored rating scales. A revised form of results-oriented performance appraisal emerged in the 1970s, which still exists today. The term 'performance management' was first used in the 1970s, but it did not become a recognized process until the latter half of the 1980s.

Merit-rating and Performance Appraisal (Earlier Versions)

W D Scott was the American pioneer who introduced rating of the abilities of workers in industry prior to World War I. He was very much influenced by Taylor and invented the 'man to man comparison' scale, which was Taylorism in action (it is possible to argue that many of the developments in this area that followed, even to this day, have been influenced by Taylor). The W D Scott scale was modified and used to rate the efficiency of US Army officers. It is said to have supplanted the seniority system of promotion in the army and initiated an era of promotion on the basis of merit. The perceived success of this system led to its adoption by the British army.

The pioneering efforts of Scott were developed in the 1920s and 1930s into what was termed the graphic rating scale, used for reports on workers and for rating managers and supervisors.

A typical manager's or supervisor's scale included assessments of various qualities, for example,

Consider his success in winning confidence and respect through his personality inspiring favourable indifferent unfavourable repellent.

Times have changed. The justification made for the use of this sort of rating scale was that they were 'educational'. They ensured, it was said, that shoes making the reports analyzed subordinates in terms of the traits essential for success in their work. The educational impact on employees was described as imparting knowledge that they were being judged periodically on essential traits considered vital and important. The original scale was said to have been based on thorough research by W D Scott and his colleagues into what were the key criteria for rating people at work. But the principle of the scale and the factors used were seized on with enthusiasm by organizations on both sides of the Atlantic as merit-rating or, in the 1950s, performance appraisal, flourished. This was without any research into or analysis of the extent to which the factors were relevant (or even whether dubbing someone 'repellent' was a food idea). Our survey revealed that some organizations are today using lists of competencies that include items suspiciously like some of the traits identified 70 years or more ago. They seemed to have been lifted down from some shelf (or extracted from a 'dictionary of competencies') without any research into the extent to which they were appropriate in the context of the organization. Merit-rating still exists in some quarters, even if it is now called performance management.

Merit-rating often involved (and still involves under the guise of performance appraisal) the quantification of judgments against each factor, presumably in the belief that the quantification of subjective judgments makes them more objective. Some companies use the total merit score as the basis for ranking employees, and this is translated into a forced distribution of performance-pay purposes; for example, the top 10 per cent in the ranking get a 5 per cent increase, the next 20 per cent a 4 per cent increase, and so on. We heard of one manufacturing company that, to iron out rating inconsistencies, used a diabolical device they called 'factorizing'. An average score was calculated for the whole company and the allocation of points in each department was equated to the company average. Inevitably, line managers objected strongly to the implied assumption that there were no differences between departmental performances.

⌘ Criticism of Merit-rating and Performance Appraisal ⌘

Although merit-rating in different guises persists, a strong attack on the practice was mounted by McGregor in his highly influential *Harvard Business Review* article, 'An uneasy look at performance appraisal' to analysis.

This implies a more positive approach. No longer is the subordinate being examined by his superior so that his weaknesses may be determined; rather he is examining himself, in order to define not only his weaknesses but also his strengths and potentials. He is no longer a pawn in a chess game called management development.

McGregor went on to propose that the focus should be on the future rather than the past in order to establish realistic targets and to seek the most effective ways of reaching them. The accent of the review is, therefore, on performance, on actions relative to goals.

There is less of a tendency for the personality of the subordinate to become an issue. The superior, instead of finding himself in the position of a psychologist or a therapist, can become a coach helping a subordinate to reach his own decisions on the specific steps that will enable him to reach his targets.

In short, the main factor in the management of performance should be the analysis of the behaviour required to achieve agreed results, not the assessment of personality. This is partly management by objectives, which is concerned with planning and measuring results in relation to agreed targets and standards, but retains the concept that performance is about behaviour as well as results (a notion that management by objectives ignored).

In short, the main factor in; the management of performance should be the analysis of the behaviour required to achieve agreed results, not the assessment of personality. This is partly management by objectives, which is concerned with planning and measuring results in relation to agreed targets and standards, but retains the concept that performance is about behaviour as well as results (a notion that management by objectives ignored).

A mainly forgotten, but still relevant, research project conducted by Rowe (1964) in the UK came to broadly the same conclusion as McGregor – that managers do not like 'playing at being God' in rating the personalities of their subordinates.

Managers admitted they were hesitant [to appraise] because what they wrote might be misunderstood, because they might unduly affect a subordinate's future career, because they could only write what they were prepared to say and so on.

One comment made to Rowe was that, 'You feel rather like a schoolmaster writing an end-of-term report'. Rowe concluded:

- Appraisers were reluctant to appraise

- The follow-up was inadequate

- No attempt should be made to clarify or categories performance in terms of grades. The difficulty of achieving common standards and the reluctance of appraiser to use the whole scale make them of little use.

These comments, especially the last one, are as relevant today as they were more than 30 years ago and commentators are still producing these precepts as original truths. It is remarkable how much reinventing of the wheel goes on in the field of performance management. Another example is the replacement of the discredited 'management by objectives' by performance management, at least in its earlier versions.

The attack on merit-rating, or on the earlier versions of performance appraisal (as it came to be known in the 1950s), was often made on the grounds that it was mainly concerned with the assessment of traits. These could refer to the extent to which individuals were conscientious, imaginative, self-sufficient, co-operative, or possessed qualities of judgment, initiative, vigour or original thinking. Traits represent 'predispositions to behave in certain ways in a variety of different situations'. Trait theorists typically advance the following definition of personality: 'More or less stable internal factors that make one person's behaviour consistent from one time to another and different from the behaviour other people would manifest in comparable situations' (Hampson 1982). But the belief that trait behaviour is independent of situations and the people with whom an individual is interacting is questionable. Trait measures cannot predict how a person will respond in a particular situation (Epstein and O 'Brien 1985). And there is the problem of how anyone can be certain that someone has such-and-such a trait. Assessments of traits are only too likely to be prompted by subjective judgments and prejudices.

Management by Objectives

The term was first coined by Peter Drucker (1955), when he wrote:

"What the business enterprise needs is a principle of management that will give full scope to individual strength and responsibility and at the same time give common direction of vision and effort, establish teamwork and harmonize the goals of the individual with the common weal. The only principle that can do this is management by objectives and self-control".

Drucker emphasized that 'an effective management must direct the vision and efforts of all managers towards a common goal'. This would ensure that individual and corporate objectives were integrated and would also make it possible for managers to control their own performance: 'Self-control means stronger motivation – a desire to do the best rather than just enough to get by. It means higher performance goals and broader vision'.

McGregor's (1960) contribution arose from his Theory Y concept. He wrote that:

"The central principal which derives from Theory Y is that of integration: the creation of conditions such that the members of the organization can achieve their own goals best by directing their efforts towards the success of the organization."

This is McGregor's principle of 'management by integration and self control', which of managing people. McGregor developed the concept in a way more in line with current thinking on performance management than the bureaucratic focus of management by objectives prevailing in the late 1960s. He wrote that:

"The tactics are worked out in the light of the circumstances. Forms and procedures are of little value... 'Selling' management a programme of target setting and providing standardized forms and procedures is the surest way to prevent the development of management by integration and control."

This principle may not have entered the vocabulary of performance management, but is fully absorbed into current thinking about it. Many writers and management consultants recycle McGregor's philosophy without ever acknowledging its source.

⌘ Definition ⌘

MBO was defined by John Humble (1972) as:

"A dynamic system which seeks to integrate the company's need to clarify and achieve its profit and growth goals with the manager's need to contribute and develop himself. It is a demanding and rewarding style of managing a business."

He described management by objectives as a continuous process of:

- Reviewing critically and restating the company's strategic and tactical plans.

- Clarifying with each manager the key results and performance standards he must achieve, and gaining his contribution and commitment to these, individually and as a team member.

- Agreeing with each manager a job improvement plan which makes a measurable and realistic contribution to the unit and company plans for better performance.

- Providing conditions (an organization structure and management information) in which it is possible to achieve the key results and improvement plan.

- Developing management training plans to build on strengths, to help managers to overcome their weaknesses and to get them to accept responsibility for self-development.

- Strengthening the motivation of managers by effective selection, salary and succession plans.

- Humble emphasized that these techniques are interdependent and illustrated the dynamic nature of the system as shown in Figure 4.1.

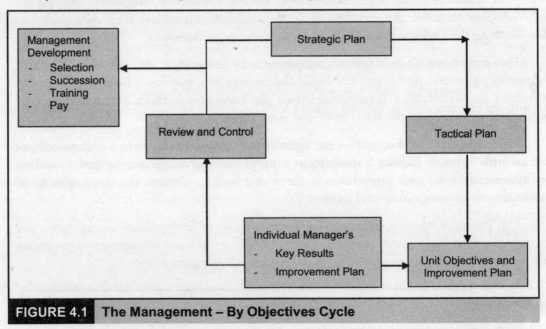

FIGURE 4.1   The Management – By Objectives Cycle

Except for the insistence that this system is exclusively for managers, much of what Humble wrote would be acceptable today as good, if not necessarily best, performance-management practice.

But management by objectives had become thoroughly discredited by the end of the 1970. Why?

⌘ Criticisms of Management by Objectives ⌘

One of the first, and most formidable, attacks on management by objectives was made in the *Harvard Business Review* by Levinson 1970. His criticisms were as follows:

- Every organization is a social system, a network of interpersonal relationships. A person doing an excellent job by objective standards of measurement may fail miserably as a partner, superior, subordinate or colleague.

- The greater the emphasis on measurement and quantification, the more likely the subtle, non-measurable elements of the task will be sacrificed. Quality of performance frequently loses out to quantification.

- It (management by objectives) leaves out the individual's personal needs and objectives, bearing in mind that the most powerful driving force for individuals comprises their needs, wishes and personal objectives.

Another critic writing in the *Harvard Business Review* (a favourite medium for attacks on performance appraisal) was Schaffer (1991), who wrote:

Ironically, management by objectives programmes often create heavy paper snowstorms in which managers can escape from demand making. In many MBO programmes, as lists of goods get longer and thicker, the focus is diffused, bulk is confused with quality, and energy is spent on the mechanics rather than the results. A manager challenged on the performance of her group can safely point to the packet of papers and assert: 'My managers have spent many hours developing their goals for the year.'

The cause of the demise of management by objectives was no doubt the fact that the process became oversystematised (often under the influence of package-oriented management consultants) and that too much emphasis was placed on the quantification of objectives. The originators of the concept may not have advocated lots of forms, and they recognized, as John Humble had, that qualitative performance standards could be included in the system, by which was meant 'a statement of conditions which exist when the result is being satisfactorily achieved'. But these principles were often ignored in practice. In addition, management by objectives often became a top-down affair with little dialogue, and it tended to focus narrowly on the objectives of individual managers without relating them to corporate goals (although that is what was supposed to happen, and it was certainly a major part of Drucker's original concept). The system also tended to concentrate on managers, leaving the rest of the staff to be dealt with by an old-fashioned merit-rating scheme, presumably because it was thought that they did not deserve anything better.

A later comparison of management by objectives and performance management by Fowler 1990 criticized the former because:

- It was not right for all organizations – it required a highly structured, orderly and logical approach which did not fit the opportunistic world of the entrepreneur.

- Only limited recognition was given to the importance of defining the organization's corporate goals and values – the emphasis was on the role of the individual manager.

- Line managers perceived it as a centrally imposed administrative task.

- It became a formal once-a-year exercise bearing little relationship to managers' day-to-day activities.

- There was overemphasis on quantifiable objectives to the detriment of important qualitative factors.

- The system was administratively top-heavy-form-filling became an end in itself.

Critical Incident Technique

The critical incident technique was developed by Flanagan (1954). On the basis of his research, he came to the conclusion that, to avoid trait assessment (merit-rating) and over concentration on output (management by objectives), appraisers should focus on critical-behaviour incidents which were real, unambiguous and illustrated quite clearly how well individuals were performing their tasks. Flanagan advocated that managers should keep a record of these incidents and use them as evidence of actual behaviour during review meetings, thus increasing objectivity. He defended this proposal against the suggestion that he was asking managers to keep 'black books' on the grounds that it was positive as well as negative examples that should be recorded, and that it would be better to make a note at the time rather than rely on memory, which is selective and may recall only recent events.

The critical incident technique did not gain much acceptance, perhaps because the 'black book' accusations stuck, but also because it seemed to be time-consuming. In addition, the problem was raised of converting the incident reports into an overall rating.

But the concept of critical incidents has had considerable influence on methods of developing competence frameworks, where it is used to elicit data about effective or less effective behaviour. The technique is used to assess what constitute good or poor performance by analyzing events observed to have a noticeably successful or unsuccessful outcome, thus providing more factual, 'real' information than by simply listing tasks and guessing performance requirements. Used in this way the critical-incident technique produces schedules of 'differentiating competencies' that define the behavioural characteristics that high-performance display, as distinct from those characterizing less effective people – i.e. the performance dimensions of roles.)

Even if the Flanagan concept of critical incidents has not survived as a specific assessment technique, it does survive as the basis for review processes that rely on factual evidence rather than opinion. The critical incident method can also be used to develop behaviourally anchored rating scales, as described below.

Behaviourally Anchored Rating Scales

Behaviourally anchored ratings scales are designed to reduce the rating errors that it was assumed are typical of conventional scales. They include a number of performance dimensions such as teamwork, and managers rate each dimension on a scale, as in the following example:

1. Continually contributes new ideas and suggestions. Takes a leading role in group meetings but is tolerant and supportive of colleagues and respect other people's points of view. Keeps everyone informed about own activities and is well aware of what other team members are doing in support of team objectives.

2. Takes a full part in group meetings and contributes useful ideas frequently. Listens to colleagues and keeps them reasonably well-informed about own activities, while keeping abreast of what they are doing.

3. Delivers opinions and suggestions at group meetings from time to time, but is not a major contributor to new thinking or planning activities. Generally receptive to other people's ideas and willing to change own plans to fit in. Does not always keep others properly informed or take sufficient pains to know what they are doing.

4. Tendency to comply passively with other people's suggestions. May be withdrawn at group meetings, but sometimes shows personal antagonism to others. Not very interested in what others are doing or in keeping them informed.

5. Tendency to go own way without taking much account of the need to make a contribution to team activities. Sometimes uncooperative and unwilling to share information.

6. Generally uncooperative. Goes own way, completely ignoring the wishes of other team member and taking no interest in the achievement of team objectives.

It is believed that the behavioural descriptions in such scales discourage the tendency to rate on the basis of generalized assumptions about personality traits (which were probably highly subjective) by focusing attention on specific work behaviors. But there is still room for making subjective judgments based on different interpretations of the definition levels of behaviour.

Behaviourally anchored rating scales take time and trouble to develop and are not in common use, except in a modified form as the dimensions in a differentiating competency framework. It is this application that has spread into some performance management processes.

Performance Appraisal (1970s Version)

In the 1970s, a revised approach to performance appraisal was under the influence of the management-by-objectives movement. It was sometimes called 'results-oriented appraisal' because it incorporated the agreement of objectives and an assessment of the results obtained against these objectives. Ratings were usually retained of overall performance and in relation to individual objectives. Trait ratings were also used but, more recently, these have been replaced in some schemes with competence ratings. This form of performance appraisal received a boost during the late 1980s because of the use of performance-related pay based on performance ratings.

Appraisals, as defined by ACAS (1988):

"Regularly record an assessment of an employee's performance, potential and development needs. The appraisal is an opportunity to take an overall view of work content, loads and volume, to look back at what has been achieved during the reporting period and agree objectives for the next."

Appraisal schemes often included ratings of performance factors such as volume of work, quality of work, knowledge of job, dependability innovation, staff development and communication and an overall rating. Some schemes simply reviewed the achievement of objectives but still included the overall rating. Scope might be allowed for self-assessment, and the forms frequently included spaces for work improvement plans, training requirements and the assessment of potential. There was usually an arrangement for 'countersigning' managers to make comments, generally the appraiser's manager – the appraiser's grandparent.

In principle, many organization and personnel specialists believed that formal appraisals were desirable. The ACAS 1988 booklet stated that:

Appraisals can help to improve employees' job performance by identifying strengths and weaknesses and determining how their strengths may be best utilized within the organization and weaknesses overcome.

But many criticisms were made of the ways in which appraisal schemes operated in practice. Levinson 1976 wrote that "it is widely recognized that there are many things wrong with most of the performance appraisal systems in use." He thought that the most obvious drawbacks were that:

- Judgments on performance are usually subjective, impressionistic and arbitrary

- Ratings by different managers are not comparable

- Delays in feedback occur, which create frustration when good performance is not quickly recognized and anger when judgment is rendered for inadequacies long past

- Managers generally have a sense of inadequacy about appraising subordinates, and paralysis and procrastination result from their feelings of guilt about playing God.

Levinson stated that "Performance appraisal needs to be viewed not as a technique but as a process involving both people and data, and as such the whole process is inadequate." He also pointed out that appraisal was not usually recognized as a normal process of management and that individual objectives were seldom related to the objectives of the business.

A slightly more balanced comment was made by Long 1986 on the basis of the (then) Institute of Personnel Management's research into performance appraisal:

"There is no such thing as the perfect performance review system. None are infallible, although some are more fallible than others. Some systems, despite flaws, will be managed fairly conscientiously, others, despite elegant design, will receive perfunctory attention and be ultimately fair. The relative success or failure or performance review, as with any other organizational system, depends very much on the attitudinal response it arouses".

The requirements for success were indeed demanding. These were stated by Lazer and Wikstrom 1977 as follows:

"A 'good' performance appraisal scheme must be job-related, reliable, and valid for the purposes for which it is being used, standardized in its procedures, practical in its administration and suited to the organization's culture".

The problem was that performance appraisal was too often perceived as the property of the personnel department. This was where the forms were kept and where decisions were made about performance-related pay. Line managers frequently criticized the system as being irrelevant. They felt they had better things to do; at worst, they ignored it and, at best, paid lip-service to completing the forms, knowing that they had to make ratings to generate performance pay. Indeed, managers have been known to rate first in accordance with what pay increase individuals should have and then write their comments to justify their marks. In other words, human beings behaved as human beings. Individuals were said to be wary of appraisals and to be as likely to be de-motivated by an appraisal meeting as the opposite.

Perhaps the worst feature of performance appraisal schemes in the 1970s and 1980s (and some still surviving through the 1990s) was that appraisal was not regarded as a normal and necessary process of management. If ratings were based on a review of the extent to which individual objectives were attained, those objectives were not linked to the objectives of the business or department. Appraisal was isolated and therefore, irrelevant.

The concept of "Appraisal: An idea whose time has gone?" was advanced by Fletcher (1993a). He stated that:

"What we are seeing is the demise of the traditional, monolithic appraisal system. In its place are evolving a number of separate but linked processes applied in different ways according to the needs of local circumstances and staff levels. The various elements in this may go by different names, and perhaps the term appraisal has in some ways outlived its usefulness".

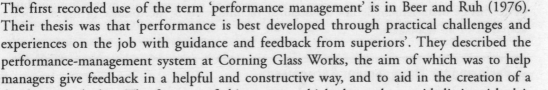

⌘ Beginning of Performance Management System   ⌘

The first recorded use of the term 'performance management' is in Beer and Ruh (1976). Their thesis was that 'performance is best developed through practical challenges and experiences on the job with guidance and feedback from superiors'. They described the performance-management system at Corning Glass Works, the aim of which was to help managers give feedback in a helpful and constructive way, and to aid in the creation of a developmental plan. The features of this system, which the authors said distinguished it from other appraisal schemes, were as follows:

- Emphasis on both development and evaluation

- Use of a profile defining the individual's strengths and development needs

- Integration of the results achieved with the means by which they have been achieved

- Separation of development review from salary review.

Although this was not necessarily a model performance management process, it did contain a number of characteristics still regarded as good practice.

The concept of performance management then lay fallow for some years, but began to emerge in the US in the mid-1980s as a new approach to managing performance. However, one of the first books exclusively devoted to performance management was not published until 1987. It described what had become the accepted approach to performance management as follows:

"Performance management is communication – a manager and an employee arrive together at an understanding of what work is to be accomplished, how it will be accomplished, how work is progressing toward desired results, and finally, after effort is expended to accomplish the work, whether the performance has achieved the agreed-upon plan. The process recycles when the manager and employee begin planning what work is to be accomplished for the next performance period. Performance management is an umbrella term that includes performance planning, performance review, and performance appraisal. Major work plans and appraisals are generally made annually. Performance review occurs whenever a manager and an employee confirm, adjust, or correct their understanding of work performance during routine work contacts."

In the UK, the first published reference to performance management was made at a meeting of the Institute of Personnel Management (IPM) Compensation Forum in 1987 by Don Beattie, then personnel director, ICL, who described how it was used as 'an essential contribution to a massive and urgent change programme in the organization' and had become a part of the fabric of the business.

By 1990, performance management had entered the vocabulary of HRM in the UK as well as in the US. Fowler (1990) defines what has become the accepted concept of performance management:

"Management has always been about getting things done, and good managers are concerned to get the right things done well. That, in essence, is performance management – the organization of work to achieve the best possible results. From this simple viewpoint, performance management is not a system or technique; it is the totality of the day-to-day activities of all managers."

⌘ Performance Management Recognised ⌘

Full recognition of the existence of performance management was provided by the research project conducted by the (then) Institute of Personnel Management 1992. The following definition of performance management was produced as a result:

"A strategy which relates to every activity of the organization set in the context of its human resources policies, culture, style and communications systems. The nature of the strategy depends on the organizational context and can vary from organization to organization."

It was suggested that what was described as a 'performance management system' complied with the textbook definition when the following characteristics were met by the organization:

● It communicates a vision of its objectives to all its employees.

● It sets departmental and individual performance targets that are related to wider objectives.

● It conducts a formal review of progress towards these targets.

● It uses the review process to identify training, development and reward outcomes.

● It evaluates the whole process in order to improve effectiveness.

In addition, 'performance management organization':

● Express performance targets in terms of measurable out puts, accountabilities and training/learning targets

● Use formal appraisal procedures as ways of communicating performance requirements that are set on a regular basis

● Link performance requirements to pay, especially for senior managers.

In the organization with performance management systems, 85 per cent had performance pay and 76 per cent rated performance. The emphasis was on objective-setting and review, which as the authors of the report noted, "leaves something of a void when it comes to identify development needs on a longer-term basis. There is a danger with results-orientated schemes in focusing excessively on what is to be achieved and ignoring the how." It was noted that some organizations were moving in the direction of competency analysis, but not very systematically.

Two of the IPM researchers (Bevan and Thompson, 1991) commented on the emergence of performance-management systems as integrating processes that mesh various HRM activities with the business objectives of the organization. They identified two broad thrusts towards integration:

1. Reward-driven integration, which emphasizes the role of performance pay in changing organizational behaviour and tends to undervalue the part, played by other human resource development (HRD) activities. This appeared to be the dominant mode integration.

2. Development-driven integration, which stresses the importance of HRD. Although performance pay may operate in these organizations, it is perceived to be complementary to HRD activities rather than dominating them.

Some of the interesting conclusions emerging from this research were that:

- 'No evidence was found that improved performance in the private sector is associated with the presence of formal performance management programmes.'

- 'An overwhelming body of psychological research exists which makes clear that, as a way of enhancing individual performance, the setting of performance targets is inevitably a successful strategy.'

- The process of forming judgments and evaluations of individual performance is an almost continuous one. Most often, it is a sub-conscious process, relying on subjective judgments, based on incomplete evidence and spiced with an element of bias.

- There was little consistency of viewpoint on the motivating power of money. The majority (of organizations) felt that the real motivators at management levels were professional and personal pride in the standards achieved, or loyalty to the organization and its aims, or peer pressure. One line manager commented that he was self-motivated: The money comes as a result of that, not as the cause of it. While the principle of pay for performance was generally accepted, the reservations were about putting it into practice – it was often viewed as a good idea – especially for other people – but not something that, when implemented, seemed to breed either satisfaction or motivation.

- The focus has been on the splendid-sounding notion of the performance-orientated culture and of improving the bottom line, and /or the delivery of services. Whilst this is well and good, the achievement of such ends has to be in concert with the aims and the development needs of individuals.

Rationale behind Performance Management

Performance management arrived in the late 1980s partly as a reaction to the negative aspects of merit-rating and management by objectives referred to earlier. Of course, it at first incorporated many of the elements of earlier approaches; for example, rating, objective-setting and review, performance pay and a tendency towards trait assessment. Some of these features have changed. Conceptually, however, performance management is significantly different from previous approaches, although in practice, the term has often simply replaced performance appraisal, just as human resource management has frequently been substituted for personnel management without any discernible change in approach lots of distinctions, not many differences.

Performance management may often be no more than new wine in old bottles or to mix metaphors, a 'flavours of the month'. But it exists, and our research demonstrates that interest is growing why?

The market economy and entrepreneurial culture of the 1980s focused attention on gaining competitive advantage and getting added value from the better use of resources. Performance orientation became important, especially in the face of global competition and recession. The rise of HRM also contributed to the emergence of performance management. The aims of HRM are to:

- Adopt a strategic approach – one in which HR strategies are integrated with business strategies.

- Treat people as assets to be invested in to further the interests of the organization.

- Obtain higher levels of contribution from people by HRD and reward management

- Gain the commitment of employees to the objectives and values of the organization.

- Develop a strong corporate culture expressed in mission and value statements and reinforced by communication.

Advocates of performance management believe that it is a practical approach to the achievement of each of these aims.

The use of performance management in the best-practice companies is not because it is a better technique than performance appraisal, but because it can form one of a number of integrated approaches to the management of performance. The appeal of performance management in its fully realized form is that it is holistic: it pervades every aspect of running the business and helps to give purpose and meaning to those involved in achieving organizational success.

We conclude this chapter by providing a summary of the most recent developments in the history of performance management.

EXHIBIT 4.1	Management by Objectives, Performance Appraisal and Performance Management Compared	
Management by objectives	**Performance appraisal**	**Performance management**
Packaged system	Usually tailor-made	Tailor-made
Applied to managers	Applied to all staff	Applied to all staff
Emphasis on individual objectives	Individual objectives may be included	Emphasis on integrating corporate, team and individual objectives
Emphasis on quantified performance measures	Some qualitative performance indicators may also be included	Competence requirements often included as well as quantified measures
Annual appraisal	Annual appraisal	Continuous review with one or more formal reviews
Top-down system, with ratings	Top-down system, with ratings	Joint process, ratings less common
May not be a direct link to pay	Often linked to pay	May not be a direct link to pay
Monolithic system	Monolithic system	Flexible process
Complex paper work	Complex paper work	Documentation often minimized
Owned by line managers and personnel department	Owned by personnel department	Owned by line management

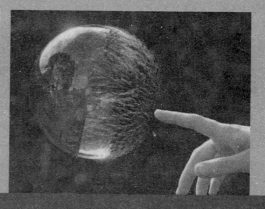

CHAPTER-5

Performance
Management System:
The Past and the Future

LEARNING OBJECTIVES

- To remove the wrong perception of students that performance appraisal and performance management system are one and the same

- To make students aware that while performance appraisal is judgmental, the performance management system is developmental

- To trace the performance management system is a shift to total management system than merely appraisal in the end of the year

Performance Management—A Shift in Approach

PMS is another way of envisioning the totality of a manager's function. It views the managerial function holistically – not a random collection of activities that most managers recognize and undertake as their core function. It provides a systemic dimension to the managerial activities – highlighting their mutual interrelatedness and interdependence. It emphasizes the dynamic, sequential and cyclical nature of these activities, essential to actualize their potential synergistic impact, which is the source of high performance and excellence. By implication, it also explains why focusing on only one or a few of these activities doesn't deliver the results wished-for.

Any system needs certain prerequisites to function smoothly. So does PMS. PMS becomes easier to do and more productive to the extent that:

- It is used holistically, as a system

- The relevant subsystems are in place and accepted

- The organization's philosophy and human environment is conducive to high morale

- The manager is oriented to, and equipped with, high performing attitudes and leadership skills.

PMS represents a concrete form of participatory dyadic relationship between each managee's aspirations and roles, and the organization's objectives and activities. As such, an effective PMS system can set into motion a tremendous ripple effect, releasing productive managee enthusiasm, high retention, and improved client satisfaction.

How is PMS different from appraisal systems?

PMS operationalizes the supervisory role of a manager to maximize performance. It is not something that a line manager has to do in addition to her normal chores. Properly implemented, it saves the manager's time. Like any other change intervention, there can however, be a hump in activity during its initial implementation phase.

Several organizations use the term, PMS, to cover performance appraisal plus some related activities. Some others use parts of what is considered an integrated PMS system. Most organizations see PMS as a troubleshooting tool for the fallouts of performance appraisal. Frequently, PMS is offered as a remedy for problems that arise when traditional performance appraisal is practiced as a stand-alone system. PMS is systematization of normal managerial and supervisory tasks and is believed that such problems are due to a lack of supporting systemic infrastructure, and many of these should disappear, or become insignificant, when appraisal is used as part of a comprehensive PMS system.

Performance appraisal is a part of the PMS system – no more or less important than its other parts. PMS emphasizes the supervisor's essential role to help and support the supervisees in putting extraordinary performance to achieve their goals. Traditional performance appraisal emphasizes the supervisor's role as a judge.

PMS emphasizes that performance is the joint responsibility of the supervisee and the supervisor, whereas performance appraisal substantially sees it as the supervisee's sole responsibility. In organizations, there are any numbers of examples where a supervisor is rated as a high performer even though her supervisees do not perform well. In PMS, this should normally not happen.

For this, a deep understanding of the nature of work and performance is needed.

How are Performance Management Systems Different from Appraisal Systems?

First, it is important to distinguish between performance appraisal systems and performance management systems.

Thus, the main difference between the performance management and appraisal systems is their respective emphasis and spirit. Good organizations in the past have used essentially their performance appraisal systems as performance management systems. They may have used the traditional title. The title seems to mean a lot in communicating the appropriateness of the systems and its emphasis.

- Performance appraisal systems

  - ❖ Focus is on performance appraisal and generation of ratings

  - ❖ Emphasis is on relative evaluation of individuals.

  - ❖ Annual exercise – normally through periodic evaluations are made.

  - ❖ Emphasis is on ratings and evaluation.

  - ❖ Rewards and recognition of good performance is an important component.

  - ❖ Designed and monitored by the HR Department.

  - ❖ Ownership is mostly with the HR department.

  - ❖ KPAs and KRAs are used for bringing in objectivity.

  - ❖ Developmental needs are identified at the end of the year on the basis of the appraisal of competency gaps.

  - ❖ There are review mechanisms to ensure objectivity in ratings

  - ❖ It is a system with deadlines, meetings, input and output and a format.

  - ❖ Format driven with emphasis on the process.

  - ❖ Linked to promotions, rewards, training and development interventions and placements.

- Performance management systems

  ❖ Focus is on performance management.

  ❖ Emphasis is on performance improvements of individuals, teams and the organization.

  ❖ Continuous process with quarterly performance review discussions.

  ❖ Emphasis is on performance planning, analysis, review, development and improvements.

  ❖ Performance rewarding may or may not be an integral part.

  ❖ Designed by HR department but could be monitored by the respective departments themselves.

  ❖ Ownership is with line managers, HR facilitates its implementation. KPAs or KRAs are used as planning mechanisms.

  ❖ Developmental needs are identified on the basis of the competency requirements for the coming year.

  ❖ There are review mechanisms essentially to bring performance improvements

  ❖ It is a system with deadlines, meetings, input, output and a format.

  ❖ Process driven with emphasis on the format as an aid.

  ❖ Linked to performance improvements and through them to other HR decisions as and when necessary.

  ❖ PMS is change in managerial style of doing work.

  ❖ It creates and nurtures performing culture.

  ❖ Framework of Performance Management.

⌘ When can we say that the system is working well? ⌘

The following are the criteria for the system to work well:

1. Line managers take it seriously and the performance plans are completed on time for 80 per cent of the cases in any given year. Completing on time means within two weeks of the stipulated time by the organization.

2. Line managers spend adequate time in performance planning and review discussions. Adequate time may mean about one day or 8 to 10 hours per employee per year, of which, four hours should be individual time. This includes group performance planning, individual planning, attending any performance briefing sessions, identification of developmental needs, etc. This excludes any seminars and workshops used for introducing the performance management system.

3. The performance plans achieve the objectives of clarifying goals, roles, and time frame, and performance standards for each department and individual. They differentiate the work to be done by each employee from that of his/her boss and subordinates.

4. The performance review discussions conducted are of quality and 80 per cent of the employees look forward to these with enthusiasm and treat them as learning opportunities.

5. Organizational support is planned in the form of removing bottlenecks, arranging training programmes, job-rotation and the like after performance planning sessions. Performance improvements are taken seriously and all the employees try their best to assist each other in this.

6. A performance culture is generated in the organization and the performance management system is a part of it and may even be one of the reasons for its generation.

Managing Performance

"Whether you think you can or you think you can't – you are right", says Ford. Performance Management concerns everyone who manages performance – in short .....everyone. Some of us manage teams; some of us may only have one managee; but all of us manage our own performance. Systematic Performance Management can help each one of us.

The leader, some say, is the one who knows the way, shows the way, and goes the way. Managers are called upon to deliver in demanding and changing times, prevent work-orders from piling up, and escape getting swamped by outstanding demands. For this they need people: bright people who have relevant experience; people who learn quickly, use mature judgment; are well organized, steady and disciplined – in short, instant winners, high achievers. Managers value people who are sensitive and can share the manager's sense of urgency and perhaps that of distress. Unfortunately, such instant winners, high achievers are not easy to get. Most managers have, in reality, to make do with average, ordinary people. And with these ordinary people they must deliver extraordinary performance. How can managers get extraordinary performance from their ordinary people? In his "How to get Extraordinary Performance from Ordinary People", Rollin Glaser says, by effectively and systematically managing performance.

Extraordinary performance has to be planned, monitored and reinforced. The manager must relentlessly design it with each managee. It is hard, time-consuming, requires rigorous analysis, involvement, follow-up and motivation. But, which alternatives are as satisfying without sweat?

Managers are hired and rewarded to effectively manage performance – of organizations, of managees, and above all, their own – towards achieving specific goals. Most managers cherish high performance expectations from their managees, monitor their performance, communicate deviance to them and evaluate managee performance based on which they try and secure rewards and punishments for the managees. They consider rewards and punishments a legitimate source of their own power and influence with their managees.

Several managers recognize and accept main components of a PfM programme as their usual core functions. Several organizations use the following managerial initiatives to optimize people's task performance:

- Goal setting, or establishing objectives and expectations through formal or informal means.

- Delegating or assigning work at higher levels of responsibility.

- Developing managees to learn job skills and to better perform their present as well as future roles and responsibilities.

- Appraising – appraisal interviewing, praising good performance, coaching and counseling to help people cope more effectively with work or non-work problems that retard their performance.

Successful managers already use some, if not all, of these. What is not always recognized, however, is the interrelatedness and interdependence of these processes and their potential for synergistic impact on performance. PfM as a system attempts just that. 'Luck is what happens when preparation meets opportunity,' says Elmer Letterman. PfM encourages individuals to anticipate opportunity and prepare consciously.

In conclusion, performance appraisal system has been used as a "judgmental tool" to reward or punish the employee. It is an annual affair, having hardly any feedback system. It has evoked negative reaction and as hardly helped to improve the performance. On the other hand, performance management system is a "360 degree approach" towards continuous performance improvement through human resource development. It is "developmental" in approach and focuses on building a wholesome and robust performance management culture through term-committed human capital.

CHAPTER-6

Performance Management Basic Theories – Systems and Processes

LEARNING OBJECTIVES

- To make students aware of the different processes and concepts associated with performance management.

- To give students a behavioural and theoretical base for understanding the different processes and systems

- To make students aware of the different steps involved in performance management system—from vision, mission, and objective, to goal setting, performance agreement stipulating group targets and individual targets and other different elements required in performance management system

- To provide leadership while getting enhanced performance from the followers it also makes provisions for feedback for improved performance, it makes the chapter indicate for reward for better performance and developmental packages for deficiencies in performance.

Introduction

A performing organization is the based on sound systems and should take into account all the forces and factors impinging on performance. It is generally known as:

$$Input \longrightarrow Throughput \longrightarrow Output.$$

Input denotes all resources that are required including facilitating systems.

The throughput denotes processes required.

Output denotes performance.

An organization develops vision, mission and objectives.

It develops strategic approaches towards all resources required for performance but focus goes on to Human Resources, which has the potentials to generate excelling capabilities. This is entirely different from the traditional approaches towards performance. Performance Management System is one such approach.

Performance is achievement of organizational objectives or goals. The Performance Management System is a "360° approach" to achieve the organizational goal, through robust systems and flowing procedures. These systems and procedures emphasize the HR aspects involved in the system an procedures. Previous chapters have explained the concepts of performance management system—this chapter deals with systems and processes of Performance Management Systems.

Theoretical Base of Performance Management System

The following theories are important. Hence, before proceeding further, it is necessary to discuss them here.

✠ Goal-setting Theory ✠

Goal-setting theory was established by Locke (1981). The theory postulates that the goals pursued by employees can play an important role in motivating superior performance. People examine whether their current behavior is sufficient to achieve the goals or not. If they find that their goals will not be achieved by their current behavior, they will either modify their behavior, or choose more realizable goals. People's feeling of satisfaction is determined by a comparison between what they receive and what they feel they should receive. Accordingly, if managers translate organizational goals for employees as being worthwhile for employees to accept and pursue, they can harness a source of motivation to perform, and direct it for securing strategic outcomes. When setting goals, objective measures, as employees assign them higher credibility and typically accept their validity (Lawler 1995).

Peter Drucker's M.B.O puts this principle into practices. In fact, the very inception of Performance Management System starts with goal-setting which provides destination and direction which induce employees to move in the right direction.

⌘ Expectancy Theory (Vroom's) ⌘

Victor Vroom made an important contribution to the understanding of the concept of motivation and the decision processes that people use to determine how much effort they will expend on their jobs. Criticizing Herzberg's Two Factors theory, he said that a person's motivation towards an action at any time would be determined by an individual's perception that a certain type of action would led to a specific outcome and his personal preference for this outcome. This model is based on the belief that motivation is determined by the nature of the reward people expect to get as a result of their job performance. Because man is a rational human being, he will try to maximize the perceived value of such rewards. People will be highly motivated if they are made to believe that if they behave in a particular way, they will receive a certain type of outcome according to their personal preference. There are three variables in Vroom's model given in the form of an equation. Since the model is a multiplier, all the three variables must have high positive value to imply motivated performance choices. If any of the variable is zero, the probability of motivated performance tends to be zero.

Motivation = Valence × Expectancy × Instrumentality

All these three variables are explained as follows:

1. *Valence:* Valence means the attraction (or repulsion) or an outcome to the individual. Whenever an individual has preference for a reward, valence is the strength of that preference. The valence is something subjective and varies from person to person. Valence is deemed to be positive for an individual if he prefers attaining the outcome to not attaining it. Valence is zero, if the individual prefers attaining the outcome to not attaining it. Valence is zero, if the individual is indifferent towards the outcome and the valence will be negative if the individual prefers not attaining the outcome to attaining it. In simple words, we can say that the worker must value the reward as desired and satisfactory. It is not the actual value of the reward, but the perceived value of the reward in the mind of the worker which is important. For example, a person who is more interested in getting recognition for the hard work, will not have any valence for cash reward.

2. *Expectancy:* Expectancy is also referred to as the Effort-Performance Probability. It refers to the extent to which the person believes his efforts will lead to the first level outcome i.e., completion of the task. Expectancy is the probability that a particular action will lead to the outcome, it is the perception in the mind of the individual of the likelihood hat a particular action or behavior will lead to a certain outcome. Since it is an association between effort and performance, its value an range between 0 and 1. If the individual feels that the probability is higher, he will put more efforts to achieve the desired outcome.

3. *Instrumentality (Performance-Reward Probability):* Instrumentality refers to the probabilities attached by the individual to each possible performance outcome alternative just as the individual previously assigned probabilities to various levels of effort leading to different levels of performance (expectancy). In simple words, instrumentality refers to the belief and expectation of a person that his performance will lead to a particular desired reward. For example, if an individual wants a promotion and feels that superior performance is very important in reviewing the promotion. Superior performance is the first level outcome and the promotion is the second level outcome. Superior performance (First level outcome) will be instrumental in obtaining the desired promotion (Second level outcome). The value of instrumentality also varies between 0 to 1 as it is also the probability of achieving the desired outcome.

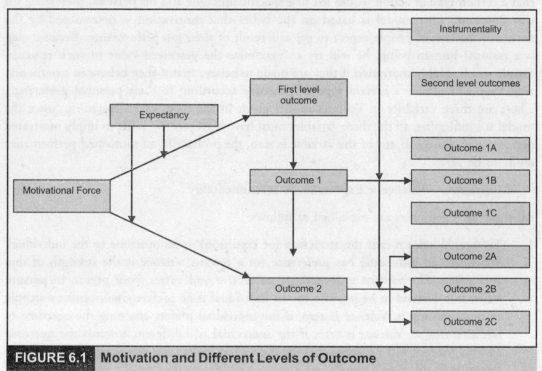

FIGURE 6.1 **Motivation and Different Levels of Outcome**

As the relationship suggests, (Motivation = V × E × I) motivational force will be highest when all the three factors are high and the force will be reduced when any one or more of valence, expectancy or instrumentality approaches zero.

The management must recognize and determine the situation as it exists and take steps to improve up on these factors for modification of behaviour, so that highest value can be achieved individually. Management for example, can deal with the different situations in the following ways:

EXHIBIT 6.1	Dealing with Low Performance, Effort and Reward

(i) Low Effort-Performance Expectancy

Reasons	Steps to be taken
Lack of necessary skills and training, so that the workers do not know that their extra efforts will lead to better performance.	Management should provide opportunities for training to improve skills in order to improve effort-performance relationship.

(ii) Low Performance-Reward Instrumentality Relationship

Reasons	Steps to be taken
Reward policy may be inconsistent and may depend upon factors other than performance which the worker may not be aware of or may not consider fair.	Management should re-evaluate the appraisal techniques and formulate policies that strengthen this relationship as just and equitable.

(iii) Low Reward-Valence

Reasons	Steps to be taken
The rewards may not be desirable for the workers. Some workers may find monetary rewards desirable while some others may value recognition more.	Management must investigate the desirability of the rewards which are given on the basis of performance.

Porter and Lawler Model of Motivation

Lyman Porter and Edward Lawler came up with a comprehensive theory of motivation, combining the various aspects that we have so far been discussing and using two additional variables in their model. Though built in large part on Vroom's expectancy model, Porter and Lawler's model is a more complete model of motivation. This model has also been practically applied in their study of managers. This is a multi variate model which explains the relationship that exists between job attitudes and job performance. This model is based on four basic assumptions about human behaviour:

1. As mentioned above, it is a multivariate model. According to this model, individual behavior is determined by a combination of factors in the individual and in the environment.

2. Individuals are assumed to be rational human beings who make conscious decisions about their behaviour in the organizations.

3. Individuals have different needs, desires and goals.

4. On the basis of their expectations, individuals decide between alternate behaviours and such decided behavior will lead to a desired outcome.

The various elements of this model are explained in the following figure:

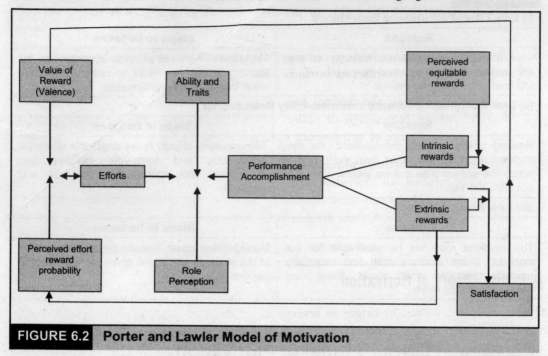

Porter and Lawler Model of Motivation

The various elements of this model are as follows:

1. *Effort:* Effort refers to the amount of energy which a person exerts on a job.

2. *Value of Reward:* First of all people try to figure out whether rewards that are likely be received from doing a job will be attractive to them. This is referred to as valence in Vroom's theory.

    A person who is looking for more money, for example, extra vacation time may not be an attractive reward. If the reward to be obtained is attractive or valent, then the individual will put extra efforts to perform the job, otherwise he will lower his effort.

3. *Perceived Effort Reward Probability:* In addition, before people put forth any effort, they will also try to assess the probability of a certain level of effort leading to a desired level of performance and the possibility of that performance leading to certain kinds of rewards. Based on the valence of the reward and the effort reward probability, people can decide to put in a certain level of work effort.

4. *Performance:* Effort leads to performance. The expected level of performance will depend upon the amount of effort, the abilities and traits of the individual and his role perceptions. Abilities include knowledge, skills and intellectual capacity to perform the job. Traits which are important for many jobs are endurance, perseverance, and goal directedness. Thus, abilities and traits will moderate the effort-performance relationship. In addition, people performing the jobs should have accurate role perception which refers to the way in which people define their jobs. People may

perceive their role differently. Only those, who perceive their roles as is defined by the organization, will be able to perform well when they put forth the requisite effort.

5. *Rewards:* Performance leads to certain outcomes in the shapes of two types of rewards namely extrinsic rewards and intrinsic rewards.

    Extrinsic rewards are the external rewards given by others in the organization in the form of money, recognition or praise. Intrinsic rewards are internal feelings of job, self esteem and sense of competence that individuals feel when they do a good job.

6. *Satisfaction:* Satisfaction will result from both extrinsic and intrinsic rewards. However, for being satisfied, an individual will compare his actual rewards with the perceived rewards if actual rewards meet or exceed perceived equitable rewards, the individual will feel satisfied and if these are less than the equitable rewards, the individual will feel dissatisfied.

✂ Equity Theory of Motivation

The equity theory owes its origin to several prominent theorists. However, it is J. Stacey Adam's formulation of the theory which is most highly developed and researched statement on the topic. According to Adams, equity theory is based on the simple assumption that people want to be treated fairly. Many employees are concerned not only with satisfying their own needs but also compare what others receive. The theory defines equity as the belief that we are being treated fairly in relation to others and inequity as the belief that we are treated unfairly in relation to others. Employees feel satisfied or dissatisfied with comparative observations of their friends, neighbours and colleagues. Whenever the employee feels that he is lacking in some way in comparison to others, he tends to work hard to reach the level of others. People are motivated by the inequity they note with others. The equity theory helps in understanding both the causes and likely consequences of feelings of inequitable treatment among organization members.

Adams has defined two specific words viz. person and other. Person is any individual for whom equity or inequity exists. Other is defined as any individual with whom a person is in relevant exchange relationship or with whom a person compares himself. Adams describes the equity comparison process in terms of input/output rations. Inputs are an individual's contribution to the organization. Such as the person's training, education, skills, experience, ethic background, effort and loyalty. Outputs are what he receives in return. An individual can receive many positive and negative outcomes from the organization. The outcomes which an individual receive are in the form of pay, working conditions, recognition, social relationships, level of supervision, etc. The individual alone decides whether an outcome is positive or negative.

People assess the ratio between their outcomes and their relevant inputs. Each person compares this ratio with the ratio of another person or group of people. Let us call the person making the comparison one person and the object of comparison the other. The following figure shows the results of comparisons:

1. $\dfrac{\text{Person's Outcomes}}{\text{Person's Inputs}} = \dfrac{\text{Other's Outcomes Equity}}{\text{Other's Inputs}} \rightarrow \text{Equity}$

2. $\dfrac{\text{Person's Outcomes}}{\text{Person's Inputs}} < \dfrac{\text{Other's Outcomes}}{\text{Other's Inputs}} \rightarrow \dfrac{\text{Negative}}{\text{Inequity}}$

3. $\dfrac{\text{Person's Outcomes}}{\text{Person's Inputs}} > \dfrac{\text{Other's Outcomes}}{\text{Other's Inputs}} \rightarrow \dfrac{\text{Positive}}{\text{Inequity}}$

A feeling of equity results when an individual perceives the ratios as equal. The situation happens in a work environment where a person feels that he and his co-worker are paid the same amount and their relevant inputs are also the same. A feeling of equity can also occur when other's outcomes are higher (or lower) than the person's and when other's inputs are also higher (or lower). This form of equity is common in organizations. A person does not feel inequitably treated if his superior is getting a higher salary than him.

In case, there is inequality in the ratios of outcomes and inputs, people can experience two types of inequity—positive and negative. In negative inequity, people feel that they are underpaid for what they give the organization and in positive inequity they feel that they are paid more than their work is worth. The amount of inequity is proportional to the size of the perceived discrepancy in the two ratios. The basic equity theory assumes that upon feelings inequity, the person is motivated to reduce it. Further, the greater the inequity the greater the motivation to reduce it. Thus, inequity as a motivation force will act as follows:

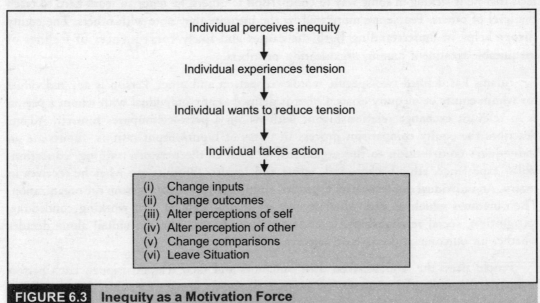

Individual perceives inequity

Individual experiences tension

Individual wants to reduce tension

Individual takes action

    (i)   Change inputs
    (ii) Change outcomes
    (iii) Alter perceptions of self
    (iv) Alter perception of other
    (v) Change comparisons
    (vi) Leave Situation

FIGURE 6.3   **Inequity as a Motivation Force**

Responses to Inequity

It is not that the person feeling inequity alone gets motivated to restore equity. The person with a feeling of equity also gets motivated but to maintain the current situation. The person with a feeling of inequity can try a number of alternatives viz.:

1. *Change Inputs:* A person can change his inputs depending upon whether the perceived inequity is positive or negative. Under a condition of negative inequity, he may reduce his efforts, productivity or quality of work. Under a condition of positive inequity he may increase those inputs.

2. *Change Outcomes:* A person may attempt to change his outcomes by requesting a salary increase or asking for a bigger office. Anything perceived to be an outcome important to the individual can shift his ratio of inputs to outcomes.

3. *Alter Perceptions of Self:* Rather than actually changing the inputs and outcomes, people may change their perceptions of their inputs or outcomes. If they feel overpaid, they may begin to 'see' more responsibility and duty in their job. If they feel underpaid they may reduce the perceived importance of the job by suggesting to themselves that 'it is just another job'.

4. *Alter Perception of Other:* People may change their perceptions of the inputs and outcomes by comparison with other. A person who feels overpaid may impute more importance to the task of the other party than in the past.

5. *Change Comparisons:* If comparing oneself with Specific Person creates feelings of inequity, choosing someone else for comparison purposes may result in less uncomfortable feelings.

6. *Leave Situation:* A person may withdraw from the situation that produced the feeling of inequity. The withdrawal can be permanent such as leaving the organization for some other organization, or it can be temporary, such as increased absences or tardiness.

TABLE 6.1 Developing Performance Management System	
Determining the organization's mission statement and objectives	Defining and measuring individual performance—what is meant by performance in a particular organization, and how do performance management processes enhance performance
Enhancing communications within the organization so that employees are not only aware of the objectives and the business plan, but also in a position to contribute to their formulation	Implementing appropriate reward strategies
	Developing employees to improve performance and career progression in the future

A Model of Performance Management System

1. Organizational objectives and strategy

   ❖ Organization's ultimate goal

   ❖ Organization's competitive position

   ❖ Comparing organization's strength with changing environment

   ❖ Examining organization's critical issues

   ❖ Analyzing organization's opportunities

   ❖ Exploring best approaches in view of organizational resources and competencies

2. Assessment of organizational performance needs

   ❖ Identifying competencies necessary for achieving organizational objectives and strategy

   ❖ Gathering information about critical issues

   ❖ Determining new and future performance needs

   ❖ Prioritizing organizational improvement measures

   ❖ Recognizing core organizational values

3. Setting organizational performance expectations

   ❖ Determining required vs desired performance

   ❖ Determining current performance status

   ❖ Understanding, aligning, and agreeing on performance expectations

   ❖ Formulating key performance indicators

   ❖ Evolving job objectives

   ❖ Aligning individual goals with organizational strategy

4. Establishing performance management process

   ❖ Designing a framework of performance management encompassing

   ❖ Performance planning

❖ Performance managing

❖ Performance appraisal

❖ Performance monitoring

5. Measuring for performance management

    ❖ Identifying opportunities' for perfor

    ❖ Providing performance counselling in

    ❖ Devising reward strategy and adminis

    ❖ Instituting performance management a

    ❖ Improvement in competitive position of

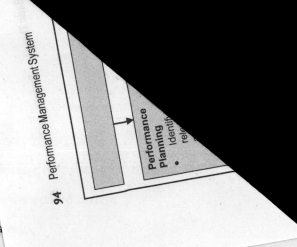

⌘ Processes have to be Organizationally Journal ⌘

A good performance management process must fit the strategic direction and culture of the organization. Following are guiding principles that are consistently found in effective performance management process and that can be adapted by the organization:

● Performance management links the goals of the individual employee to goals of the organization.

● The employee and manager collaborate to set goals and review performance.

● Performance management process is forward-looking; past performance is summarized and future goals are set.

● The process is based on a two-way communication between the employee and the manager.

● The process monitors and measures results (what) and behavior (how).

● The process does not evaluate personal traits, such as initiative–these are too subjective.

● The manager provides both positive feedback for a job well done and constructive feedback when improvement is needed.

● Training and development opportunities are provided for improving performance.

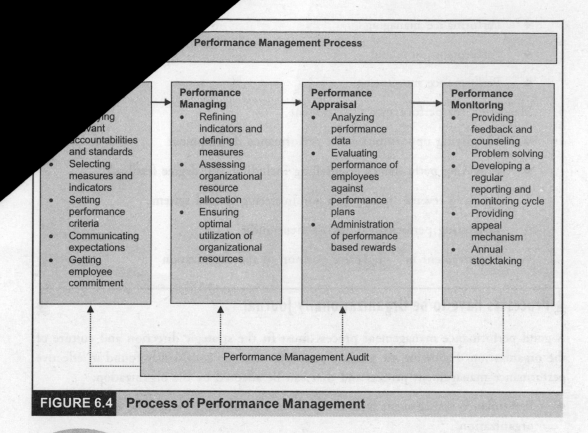

FIGURE 6.4 **Process of Performance Management**

The figure contains the following text:

Performance Management Process

[Performance Planning]
- ...ving
  ...vant
  ...accountabilities
  and standards
- Selecting
  measures and
  indicators
- Setting
  performance
  criteria
- Communicating
  expectations
- Getting
  employee
  commitment

Performance
Managing
- Refining
  indicators and
  defining
  measures
- Assessing
  organizational
  resource
  allocation
- Ensuring
  optimal
  utilization of
  organizational
  resources

Performance
Appraisal
- Analyzing
  performance
  data
- Evaluating
  performance of
  employees
  against
  performance
  plans
- Administration
  of performance
  based rewards

Performance
Monitoring
- Providing
  feedback and
  counseling
- Problem solving
- Developing a
  regular
  reporting and
  monitoring cycle
- Providing
  appeal
  mechanism
- Annual
  stocktaking

Performance Management Audit

Corporate Mission and Strategic Goals

Vision and mission objectives have to be based on the best in the line of business—the benchmarked business organization. Higher the competition, it is better because we do all that is required to raise our systems and procedures to meet the challenge.

Benchmarking

"If you know yourself and your enemy well, you can win thousands of wars". (For further details, see Part B)

Corporates have to ensure world-class quality and follow the norms of Six Sigma.

Six Sigma is an example of how organizations pursue excellence. Raman (power 24) reports on this phenomenon in quality improvement—

One Sigma   = 690,000 defects per million,

Two Sigma   = 308,000 defects,

Three Sigma = 66,000 defects,

Four Sigma   = 6,210 defects,

Five Sigma   = 230 defects, and

Six Sigma = 3.4 defects per million. He suggests that no one will ever achieve this 20-year old technique because by the time anyone even gets close, the customer's requirements will change and you'll have to start over again with both your design and your processes. (For further details, see Part B)

These provide the starting-point of the performance-management process. The aim is to ensure that each of the activities in the sequence is aligned to those goals and contributes to their achievement.

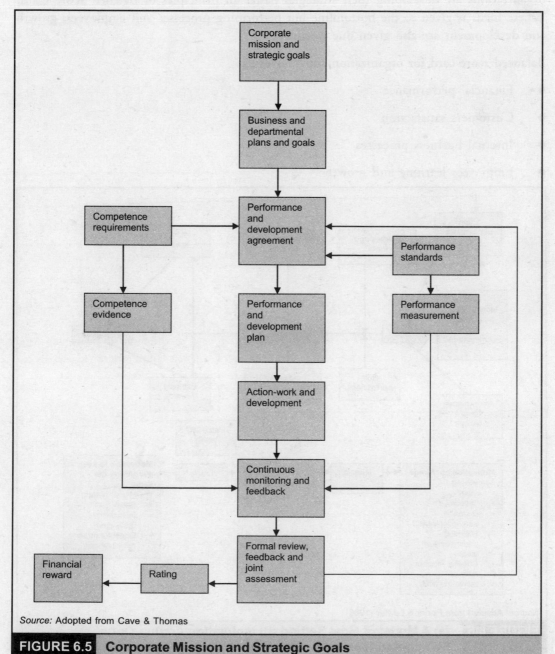

Source: Adopted from Cave & Thomas

FIGURE 6.5 **Corporate Mission and Strategic Goals**

Corporate and Departmental Plans and Goals

These flows directly from the corporate goals but some alterations may take place so that departmental views about what can be achieved are taken into account before the business goals are finalized. In fact, a performing organization develops its objectives and strategies keeping in mind the sustainable excellence in performance. For that, the performing organizations are developing their strategies based on principles of Balance Score Card. Where focus is given to the bottomline but performing processes and employees; growth and development are also given due weightage.

Balanced score card for organization and individual

- Financial performance
- Customers satisfaction
- Internal business processes
- Employees learning and growth

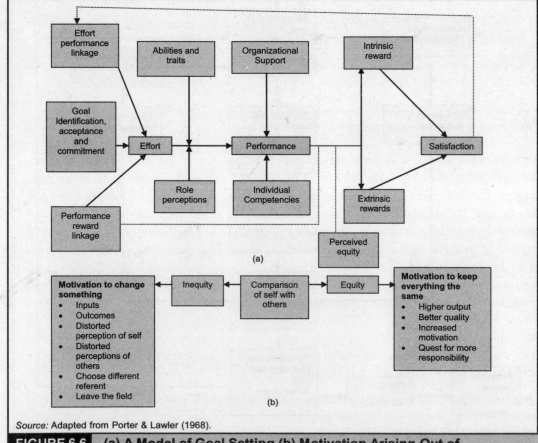

Source: Adapted from Porter & Lawler (1968).

FIGURE 6.6 **(a) A Model of Goal Setting (b) Motivation Arising Out of Self-comparison with others**

Organization are vision and mission driven. All activity in the organizations, therefore, have to be integrated for achievement of those corporate objectives. Performance Management Systems is a top-down approach – the activities of various departments, teams and individuals travels down in terms of concrete, and tangible sub-objectives which are to be shared with the employees, their competencies matched and linked with the schemes for rewarding high performance and developing deficient ones.

⌘ Instituting Performance Management Audit

Performance management audit is a diagnostic tool used to assess the PMS of an organization. It is a participative tool that examines various performance-related issues and seeks to identify the strengths and areas of improvement needed in an organization's PMS.

Performance audit helps an organization in the following ways:

● A clear picture of how employees view PMS right now

● A clear picture of how employees think the PMS should be improved

A clear picture of how PMS can be benchmarked (for further details, see Part B)

● A clear picture of what values and integrity in terms of managerial and employee behaviour and action is emphasized.

● Creating consensus of all stakeholders – shareholders, customers and employees for finding future direction to address new global business challenges.

⌘ Performance and Development Agreement

The performance and development agreement, sometimes called the performance contract, is the agreement on objectives and accountabilities reached by individuals with their managers. The agreement is usually reached at a formal review meeting and recorded during or after the meeting on a performance review form. The processes of discussion and agreement are easier if both parties (the manager and the individual) prepare for the meeting by reviewing progress against agreed work or learning objectives, considering what plans need to be made to improve performance or develop competences and skills, thinking about future objectives, and examining any areas where the manager could provide more support through help, guidance, coaching or the provision of additional resources or facilities. Many organizations ask both managers and individuals to complete a pre-review meeting questionnaire which will provide an agenda for the review. A performance agreement defines the work to be done, the results to be attained, the performance standards to be achieved and the competence levels required.

For individuals, the work to be done is agreed in terms of key result areas or principal accountabilities or, sometimes, in the case of relatively routine jobs, by reference to main tasks or duties. In more dynamic roles, existing accountabilities may have to be reassessed and new ones agreed as part of a revised agreement. In some cases, it may simply be necessary to confirm existing arrangements. The individual agreement should be based on an open, two-way and unambiguous discussion. This covers the areas listed below:

- What the person is doing now

- What the person might have to do in the future because of changing requirements

- How the work should be done (competence or process requirements)

- What the expected outputs and outcomes of the work (performance requirements and standards) are

- What knowledge, skills and ability are required to do the work (input requirements)

- Any core values the individual would be expected to uphold—these may refer to such areas as quality, teamwork, customer service, responsibility to the community and care for environmental issues. The purpose of the discussion would be to define expectations on how the person's behaviour should support these values. The core values may be expressed in a list of competencies.

- What support the person requires—from the manager, from co-workers, from resources or information.

As Antonioni (1994) emphasizes, it is essential that agreement is concluded on process goals (how the work is done) as well as output goals (what has to be achieved). And looking at it from a total quality management (TQM) view, he also stressed that the most important need 'centres on information regarding key external and internal customers' needs and expectations. Each internal customer has performance requirements that must be made explicit.' It is here that KPA (Key Performance Area), KRA (Key Results Area), & KPI (Key Performance Indicators are worked out).

Identifying KRAs helps individuals employees in a number of ways as enumerated here:

- Clarify their roles

- Align their roles to the organization's business or strategic plan

- Focus on results rather than activities

- Communicate their role's purposes to others

- Set goals and objectives

- Priorities their activities, and therefore improve their time/work management

- Make value-added decision.

Key results areas capture about 80 percent of a work role. The remainder of the role is usually devoted to areas of shared responsibility. For example, 'image of the organization is usually a very senior official's key result area, but hopefully, all employees contribute to this outcome.

Key results area are worded using as few terms as possible, with no verbs, that is, about results, not actions, and no direction/measurement. They simply describe the areas for which one is responsible for results.

Individuals undertake the following steps to determine the KRAs for their roles:

- Enlist main day-to-day responsibilities/activities.

- For each activity, ask 'Why do I do this?'

- Review the answers to 'why' questions, looking for common themes or areas.

- Identify KRAs from these themes.

- Share KRAs, preferably with those they report to, those they work along with, and with those who report to them.

The KRA approach has three main advantages:

- Areas such as innovation, customer response time, and employee development are included rather than being overlooked.

- It is the first stage of objective setting.

- It makes it easier to assess current performance.

The discussion on individual or team goals in the light of how they fit in with these internal customer expectations may lead to a reconsideration of departmental goals, and even of corporate goals—especially if people are being asked to do more than they can reasonably be expected to accomplish.

Basically the same process can be followed for teams, i.e., agreeing what work should be done, how it should be done, what should be achieved, and what team skills are required.

Further consideration is given to the objective and competence agreement and definition aspects of the performance and development agreement.

⌘ The Performance and Development Plan ⌘

The performance and development-planning part of the performance-management sequence is primarily a joint exploration of what individuals need to do and know to improve their performance and develop their skills and competences, and how their managers can provide the support and guidance they need. This requires Competence Mapping and Machine and potential development.

Competency is underlying characteristics required to perform a given task, activity, or role. Competency has the following forms – knowledge, skills and attitude.

Thus, competency relates to the cluster of related knowledge, attributes, skills, training, and other personal characteristics that –

- Affects a major part of one's job
- Correlates with performance on the job
- Can be measured against well-established standards
- Can be improved via training and development.

The performances aspect of the plan obtained agreement on what has to be done to achieve objectives, raise standards and improve performance. It also establishes priorities—the key aspects of the job to which attention has to be given. Agreement is also reached at this stage on the basis upon which performance will be measured and the evidence that will be used to establish levels of competence. It is important that these measures and evidence requirements should be identified and fully agreed upon now, because they will be used jointly by managers and individuals and collectively by teams to monitor progress and demonstrate achievements.

Methods of measuring performance and analyzing evidence of levels of competence are considered.

For individuals, this stage includes the preparation and agreement of a personal development plan (PDP). This provides an action plan for individuals with the support of their managers and the organization. It may include formal training but, more importantly, it will incorporate a wider set of development activities such as self-managed learning, coaching, project work, job enlargement and enrichment, an element of self-assessment by the individual. If multisource assessment (360-degree feedback) is practiced in the organization, this will be used to discuss development needs.

Personal development planning is s key part of the performance and development management process, and is considered fully.

Performance Development and Support

Performance management helps people to get into action so that they achieve planned and agreed results. It is a work—and people—related activity, and focuses on what has to be done, how it is done and what is achieved. But it is equally concerned with developing people, helping them to learn, and providing them with the support they need to do well, now and in the future.

The emphasis should be on managing performance throughout the year. This will involve continuous monitoring and feedback and formal reviews, as described below:

It is also necessary to enhance what Alan Mumford (1989) calls, 'deliberate learning from experience'. Which means learning from the problems, challenges and successes inherent in people's day-to-day activity. The premise is that every task individuals undertake presents them with a learning opportunity. This will be the case as long as they are encouraged to reflect on what they have done and how they have done it, and draw conclusions on what they need to do when they are next presented with a similar task or have to undertake a different task requiring the use of the newly acquired skills.

Support should also be provided on a continuing basis through coaching and counseling, and by providing the facilities and resources necessary to meet expectations. As Marchington and Wilkinson (1996) state, 'performance management requires ongoing and unsolicited support in order to be effective; that is, the telephone call or the "change" conversation just to check that all is going well, which many busy managers tend to overlook in their efforts to satisfy formal organizational requirements.'

⌘ Continuous Monitoring and Feedback ⌘

Perhaps one of the most important concepts of performance management, and it bears frequent repetition, that it is a continuous process of managing and developing performance standards which reflects normal good practices of direction setting, monitoring and measuring performance, providing feedback and taking action accordingly. Performance management should not be imposed on managers as something 'special' that they have to do. Neither should it be imposed on individuals and teams as something 'special' that is done to them. Performance management does no more than provide a framework within which managers, individuals and teams work together to gain a better understanding of what is to be done, how it is to be done, what has been achieved, and what has to be done to do even better in the future.

These sentiments could be dismissed as no more than managerialist rhetoric. And indeed they are managerialist, in the sense that they promote the notion of continuous improvement to support the achievement of the purpose of the organization, and therefore of its management. But organizations are there to achieve a purpose, and it can be argued that if performance management helps them to do so, then to describe it pejoratively as managerialist is to miss the point. Of course, this argument is valid only if management appreciates that performance management should respect the needs of all stakeholders. Individual needs for job satisfaction, growth, security, recognition and reward have to be understood and reconciled with the needs of the organization. And the continuous process of managing performance throughout the year can be carried out in a way that respects different needs as well as recognizing mutual interests.

As stated by the American Compensation Association (1996), it is important to develop performance management on the basis of 'open, honest, positive, two-way communication between supervisors and employees throughout the period'. From the viewpoint of performance, this means instant feedback to individuals and teams on the things they have done well or not so well. If people can be provided with the information they need to monitor their own performance, so much the better. It is not available readily, they can be encouraged to seek it. The aim is to provide intrinsic motivation by giving people autonomy and the means to control their work.

Interim informal reviews can be held as required—monthly, quarterly, etc. They can be used to provide more structured feedback and, importantly, to revise objectives and plans in response to changing circumstances.

Progress in implementing the personal development plan can also be monitored during the year.

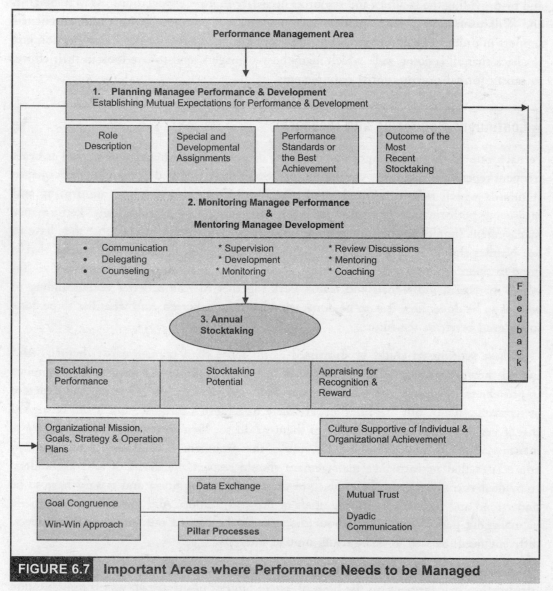

FIGURE 6.7 Important Areas where Performance Needs to be Managed

Why Set Objectives?

An organization is essentially a well-integrated combine of person who produce results necessary to fulfill specific common goals, using certain resources. Organizational performance therefore is, to a very great extent, the performance of its people.

For Drucker, objectives are needed in every area where performance and results directly and vitally affect the survival and prosperity of the business.

Objectives help establish a shared framework for measuring performance, with a manager and managee having common understanding help achieve clarity.

Work-Standards and Goal-setting Approach

This is a modification of Management by Objectives (MBO) approach. Many organizations preset quantitative, measurable work standards and goals.

Organizational and Individual Performance Plans

Job descriptions——————— Competency Management————(See details in part-B)

- Detailed job description for a Director
- Individual objectives
- Individual performance plans

Performance Standards

- The quantity of outcome
- Its quality
- The time taken to produce the outcome
- The resources used or the cost incurred to produce it.

Two Challenging Problems

1. Impact of environment in making achievement of targeted performance easy or difficult.

   ❖ Building performance indicators in a performance plan.

   ❖ Monitoring progress in the light of these indicators.

   ❖ Taking Stock of performance against planned goals and achievements.

2. Sustainability of performance standards in a dynamic, fast-changing context.

Parameters

It is sometimes easier to develop standards, which combine two or three of the parameters of quality, quantity, time, and cost, e.g. twenty (quantity) corrected news columns (quality) to be composed by a composer (cost) in a newspaper press, in a shift of eight hours (time).

Prioritizing Goals

Goals or objectives must cover all the important aspects of a managee's role. Lopsided objectives that emphasize a few areas, neglecting others, may be a sure recipe for failure. Yet, all goals are not equal as regards their contribution to role responsibilities—some are more critical than others to the managee's role performance. Differing priorities in performance plans would reflect such differences. One method of prioritizing that Maslanek proposes is allocating percentage weights to rank-order goals. While allocating weightage can be hard and disputable in many cases, rank ordering through discussion is certainly feasible.

Smart Goals

To elaborate this acronym:

S   Specific, with Standards. The goal specifies what and how much is to be done and describes the level of performance and outcome that will meet expectations. It tends to stretch the managee and is clear, unambiguous, easy to understand and challenging.

M   Measurable and Mutual. The goal provides shared measurable indices for meeting standard in terms of quantity, quality, time, cost, etc.

A   Adjustable and Achievable. The goal states how flexible it is to meet unforeseen contingencies. While being challenging, it remains within the reach of the managee—effectively using her competencies and demonstrating high commitment—and is thus achievable in the normal course.

R   Relevant and Realistic. The goal is within the managee's control, involves some important accountability and addresses results that concern her role responsibility. It is relevant and aligned to organizational objectives.

T   Trackable and Timely. The goal can be tracked and reviewed periodically, and indicates the time-frame for completion.

Steps involved in Developing SMART Goals

Step 1: Develops appropriate training plans based on identified training needs: conducts training courses and/or coordinates their delivery/implementation with outside consultants, ensuring a curriculum that best meets staff needs (accountabilities).

Step 2: Develop and deliver five management-training workshops (action) by a specified date (time frame).

Step 3: Performance meets expectations when 75 percent of the participants' evaluations indicate the workshops are above-average (measurable standard).

Mentoring Managee Performance and Mentoring Managee Development

(MMP and MMD) is the heart and soul of PfM. It is the performing phase.

⌘ Drivers of Organizational Performance ⌘

In today's complex and diverse context, managees – largely knowledge workers – are the key drivers of organizational performance.

1. Motivation

2. Behaviour

3. Positive work motivation

⌘ Planning on the Left Side and Managing on the Right ⌘

About a quarter of a century age, Mintzberg spoke something of what we know today as emotional intelligence and spiritual intelligence.

● Objectivity

● Subjective self

● Emotional Intelligence and Spiritual Intelligence,

● Logical analysis – linear, sequential, etc. while discounting the intuitive –simultaneous, relational, holistic, etc.

⌘ Managerial Leadership ⌘

For Field Marshal Bernard Montgomery, 'Leadership is the capacity and will to rally men and women to a common purpose and the character which inspires confidence'.

Attributes

● Communicating Organizational Vision and Strategy

● Knowing Customer Needs

● Championing Organization-initiated Change

● Anticipating Impact of Competition

● Creating an Environment that Fosters Risk-taking

● An Understanding of Other Cultures and Languages.

Mistakes

- Deviating from the Organization's Strategy
- Inadequate Focus on Customer Needs
- Failure to Anticipate Impact of Competition
- Lack of Openness to Learning and New Ideas
- Failure to Invest Enough to Hire the Right People
- Not Communicating Organizational Vision with Clarity
- Inadequate Development of Managees' Trust
- Failure to Foster Risk-taking
- Failure to Leverage New Technology
- Lack of Understanding of Other Cultures

⌘ Situational Leadership   ⌘

In their book *Leadership and the One-Minute Manager*, Blanchard, Zigarmi elaborate a model of Situational Leadership. According to them, 'A whole manager is flexible and is able to use four different leadership style.

Style 1

Directing: The leader provides specific instructions and loosely supervises task-performance.

Style 2

Coaching: The leader continues to direct and closely supervise task accomplishment, but also explains decisions, solicits suggestions and supports progress.

Style 3

Supporting: The leader facilitates and supports subordinates' efforts towards task accomplishment and shares responsibility for decision-making with them.

Style 4

Delegating: The leader turns over responsibility for specific task-accomplishment, including decision-making and problem-solving, to subordinates.

Directive Behaviour involves telling people clearly what to do, how to do it, where to do it and when to do it, and then closely supervising their performance.

Supportive Behaviour involves listening to people, providing support and encouragement for their efforts, and then facilitating their involvement in problem-solving and decision-making.

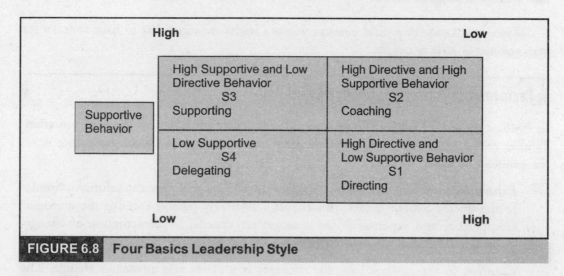

FIGURE 6.8   Four Basics Leadership Style

Development Levels

● **Competence** involves relevant knowledge and skills, which can be learnt and gained from formal education, on-the-job or off-the-job training, and/or experience.

● **Commitment** involves 'confidence' and motivation' where confidence means a managee's self-assuredness in her ability to duly accomplish a task without intensive supervision, and motivation means her achievement orientation and enthusiasm for the task.

Using Situational Leadership Style

The authors portray a linkage between the four development levels and the four leadership style.

TABLE 6.2   Development Level and Leadership Styles

Development Level	Appropriate Leadership Style
D1 Low Competence + High Commitment	**S1** **Directing** Structure, Control and Supervisor
D2 Some Competence + Low Commitment	**S2** **Coaching** Direct and Support
D3 High Competence + Variable Commitment	**S3** **Supporting** Praise, Listen and Facilitate
D4 High Competence + High Commitment	**S4** **Delegating** Turn Over Responsibility for day-to-day Decision-making

Managerial/Leadership Grid concept where a leader-managers has to have concern for performance as well as people.

⌘ Performance Manager's Change Agent Role ⌘

In PMS, a significant role of the manager is as an agent of change in her work situation. Tandon enlists three roles that a change agent can take—actual choice depending upon the problem at hand:

(i) *Expert:* As an expert, the manger diagnoses problems and provides solutions. Similar to the doctor-patient model, this entails a relatively passive role for the managee. Competence and expertise of the manager are crucial. Implementation of change, using this role, is largely dependent upon the expert power of the manager.

(ii) *Catalyst:* In the catalyst role, the manager stimulates and advocates change. The managee is actively involved along with the manager in diagnosing problem and developing solutions. Here the manager's ability to re-educate and persuade the managee is crucial to effective change.

(iii) *Process Consultant:* In this role, the manager assists the managee in finding her own solutions. The process is one of changing, but not providing answers. Facilitative and persuasive strategies characterize the manager's behaviour in this role.

Organizational Human Relations

Sometime ago, Chris Argyris futuristically hypothesized certain changes forthcoming in organizational human relations' policies and practices in *Human Relations: A Look into the Future*. These are of interest in the context of PfM – especially MMP and MMD. These predicted changes are briefly listed below:

● From an approach that expects *people always to be friendly to the one where people feel free to dislike others as well as to be friendly.* Argyris argues that it is unrealistic to expect people to like one another all the time. He believes that freedom to express honest hostilities, if done effectively, can enhance cooperative effort, and release a lot of energy used up in withholding feelings.

● From a view that *human beings are the most important part of an organization* to the more realistic one that importance of human beings as part of an organization varies under different conditions. According to Argyris, most 'self-responsible' managees consider 'the tensions and frustrations inherent in production bogies, budgets, etc.' as legitimate and understand the logic of organizational demands made on them. The managees may even consider an under expression of human resource primacy 'as conscious manipulations that betray the management's basic lack of confidence in the individual'.

● From the belief that *managers should become 'inseparable and indistinguishable' from the organization* to the one that *'people should give of themselves without giving up themselves'*

Argyris predicts this because, in his view, inseparable and indistinguishable managers can breed organizational sickness in a fast-relevance and the best fit warrant managerial mobility. A concept of commitment that looks for the managers to become inseparable and indistinguishable from the organization can compromise authenticity and, according to Argyris, cause a manager to distort reality in order not to see the real impact of his leadership upon the organization.

- From an assumption that *maximum communication among individuals is necessary* to the one that *optimum communication is most effective*. According to Argyris, too much communication can 'clog up the channels with much noise'. Over-communicating managements often 'forget to listen' or 'communicate information that either baffles the employees or makes them defensive'. Argyris asserts that 'One sign of trust in a human relationship is appropriate silence'.

- From a concept that *'an effective organization is one with high production, low turnover, low absenteeism and low grievance rates', to the one that the total health of an organization spells effectiveness.* Argyris alludes to research to suggest that low turnover, low absenteeism and low grievance rates are not requisite conditions for achieving the traditional objectives of profit, which can be achieved even by managers who are 'apathetic, indifferent to the company and alienated from their management and from each other'. Besides, such emphasis on 'low turnover, low absenteeism, and low grievance rates' can make an organization so 'rigid and defensive' that it overlooks the need for change to maintain organizational growth.

- From the belief that *'superiors can develop subordinates to be more skillful in interpersonal competence and diagnosing accurately administrative situations' to the one that 'no one can develop anyone else except himself. The door to development is locked from the inside'.* Argyris points out that onus for development on the manager means developing managees in the image of the currently effective executive, which can be dicey, since in a fast-changing world, 'today's managerial skills of success may pave the way for tomorrow's failure'. Argyris suggests that the responsibility of the organization is not to develop people, but to 'develop the climate and the opportunities for self-development'.

- From the objective of executive development programmes *'to change the executive behaviour'*, to the one of helping *the executive become more aware of herself and become more tolerant or accepting or herself, and therefore of others*. Objective of change in behaviour conveys that the existing behaviour is faulty. Besides the fact that it is hard to pinpoint what the correct behavior is, such a message invariably creates defensiveness and resistance. In the situational concept of leadership, for instance, managerial effectiveness requires proficiency in 'a number of different kinds of leadership patterns' to respond to a concept of 'reality-centered' leadership. Besides, to Argyris, it is wild to assume that short duration events can influence people 'to change their basic values and behaviour that have taken a lifetime to develop'. He recommends that if people can be enabled to truly take care of their own emotions, they will begin to care more for others. As they develop 'a high sense of inner worth', experience lesser defensiveness, increased internal freedom and creativity, they will begin to permit others to achieve the same.

- From the objective of executive development programs which *teach an executive how to behave or to think* to the one of *helping the executive learn how to learn*. According to Argyris, development and change are the main future characteristics of management. Teaching the executive what one ought to read, how one ought to behave and think emphasizes end results, which may not remain constantly relevant. He considers, 'Emphasizing the processes of how to learn, how to diagnose administrative situations, how to learn from experience' as timeless wisdom. He describes the change from developing 'learned men' to developing 'learning men'.

- From the assumption that *human relationship problems are caused primarily by poor organizational planning, poor budgets, incentive systems, etc.* to the one that *effective organizational planning, budgets, incentive system, etc. also can cause human problems.* Argyris names research to support that 'organization and managerial controls, if used correctly, can cause employees to feel dependent, subordinate, submissive and to use relatively few of their adult abilities'. Managees can adapt to poor organizational plans by 'absenteeism, turnover, apathy, indifference', etc. He also refers to the possibility of managees 'wages as compensation for dissatisfaction and not necessarily as a reward for past performance, or as a motivation for future performance'. He believes that the economic man may exist; and 'this may be one of the deepest human problems our society will face'.

⌘ Equity Theory ⌘

The ratio of their own outcomes to their inputs, to the ratio of comparable another's outcomes to inputs,

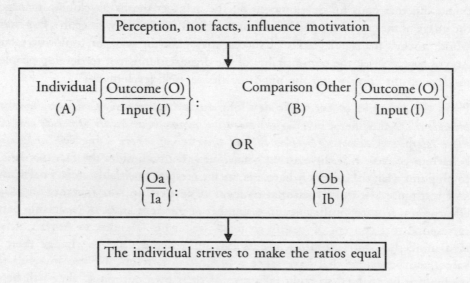

⌘ Movers of Human Behavior

According to Hackman, et al., there are three psychological states that are critical in determining a person's motivation and satisfaction on the job:

- *Experienced Meaningfulness:* The individual must perceive his/her work as worthwhile or important by some system of values.

- *Experienced Responsibility:* She must believe that she personally is accountable for the outcomes of her efforts.

- *Knowledge of Results:* She must be able to determine, on some fairly regular basis, whether or not the outcomes of her work are satisfactory.

Achievement, Affiliation and Power Motives

McClelland and his colleagues did considerable research on what motives contribute to the success of a manager, and in what way. They considered three motives significant to this context. These are:

- **Need for Achievement;** meaning the desire to do something better or more efficiently than before.

- **Need for Affiliation;** meaning the desire to establish or maintain friendly relations with others.

- **Need for Power;** meaning the desire to have impact on others (not dictatorial power but the need to be strong and influential).

⌘ Enriching Performance through Diversity

Organizations function in an increasingly democratic multipolar world. According to Kouzes & Posner, it is no longer possible for them—whether in business, government, or nonprofit sectors—to thrive by being responsive only to the world as defined by the elite. To be successful in a multipolar world, leaders in all roles, at all levels and in all walks of life, must learn to appreciate and value diversity, not merely tolerate it, or manage it, as they say. They see diversity as a significant consequence of urbanization following the industrial revolution of the early 1900s. They believe that organizations—being radically designed around processes, not functions, with greater freedom of movement across boundaries within and outside the organization—are themselves becoming more diverse.

⌘ Some Monitoring and Mentoring Behaviours of the Manager

- Praising good performance.

- Faulting a behaviour without rejecting the person.

- Sharing feelings rather than pronouncing value judgments.

- Demonstrating and demanding integrity in behaviour and intent.

- Being easily accessible to fulfill legitimate needs of her managees.

- Nurturing effective managees through continual reaffirmation of their worth to the organization.

A supportive workplace, where members engage in mutual help, is however, more likely to produce effective performers—and effective performance—than a sterile group managed by the book——any book.

Effective performance managers set challenging goals, which are nevertheless within the managee's reach to achieve. Unachievable goals do not stretch the managee capacities or motivate. They frustrate. A good mean sure of developmental goal-setting is that at least three out of four managees regularly meet their targets.

The Pygmalion effect demonstrates that high expectations produce high performance from managees. Research on self-fulfilling prophecies has shown that managers who genuinely have a positive prognosis about their managees' success in meeting goals or targets are usually rewarded by their managees proving them right. Similarly, managers with negative expectations from their managees are presented with failures. (For further details, see Part B)

Monitoring Employee's Performance and Development Supervision

Monitoring managee performance is an essential part of supervisory leadership, and naturally follows planning managee performance. This is a phase in which the cycle of PfM: Planning → Monitoring → Stocking occurs several times.

Monitoring and its Objectives

PfM explicitly promotes the value that a manager and her managee accept joint responsibility for monitoring progress on the tasks and goals agreed upon during the initial performance planning or expectation setting meeting and subsequent review meetings. Managers use instruments like written reports, review discussions and on-the-spot inspections to track:

- Timely and quality fulfillment of managee tasks and goals.

- Help and support legitimately needed by the managee's tasks, including those agreed upon during planning and review meetings.

Process of Monitoring

The manager observes managee performance through:

1. Periodic written reports

2. Scheduled meetings

3.   On-the-spot inspections, or field or site visits in case of managees whose location is different from that of the manager.

4.   Relevant and reliable information from other available sources.

In the course of monitoring, the manager provides feedback to the managee(s) and asks for feedback from the managee(s) during

1.   Group or team meetings to discuss common issues, problems, etc.

2.   One-on-one meetings to discuss specific issues and problems encountered by individual managee(s).

The manager and the managee, thereafter, discuss corrective measures needed, actions to be taken by either or both of them and other help or support needed to accomplish the requisite tasks and goals.

⌘ Communication

1.   **Factual levels** where the manager and the managee discuss data and information, observed behaviours or events, organizational policies, guidelines, procedures and precedents, known or anticipated constraints.

2.   **Reflective levels** where the more subtle views, feelings, values, beliefs and assumptions which influence a situation are shared and clarified.

3.   **Intuitive or interpretive levels** where manager and the managee attempt to understand the factual and the reflective data, what these mean, and what their implications or ramifications are for the managee's performance.

4.   **Decisional levels** where the manager and the managee reach conclusions or agreements in the nature of decisions action plans or procedures for implementation or follow-up.

Reflecting on Interpersonal Communication

Degree and patterns of communication effectiveness in interpersonal relationships can often be understood by reflecting privately how one presents and uses oneself in communicating with others in one's daily contacts and activities. Undertaking such a reflection is often both interesting and helpful.

Listening: 'A good leader encourages followers to tell him what he needs to know, not what he wants to hear'.

Review Discussion

Promoting Constructive Controversy: "A successful man is one who can lay a firm foundation with the bricks others have thrown at him", says David Brinkley. "If there are two people who think alike, one is redundant", say some others.

'When thoughtful dissent and diversity stimulates innovative thinking, arouses curiosity, encourages active search, 'repeated exposure to diversity and controversy'.

How do Periodic Reviews Work Better and Help?

Periodic reviews help the performance manager:

- Correct planning assumptions and errors mid-course before it is too late.

- Monitor and encourage progress, and keep the work on track.

- Strengthen dyadic relationship between the manager and her employee.

⌘ Monitoring Employee Performance & Mentoring Employee Development ⌘

For further details, see Part B

'The future belongs to those who see possibilities before they become obvious', says John Sculley former CEO of Pepsi and Apple Computers. All development must ultimately lead also to the ability of a person to so envision her future. Some broad purposes of employee development in this context are:

1. Improving performance-effectiveness of employees.

2. Developing employee with requisite knowledge, problem-solving and social skills to meet the needs of their current and future roles and tasks.

3. Creating conditions that allow and encourage individual employees to grow into what they are capable of becoming.

There are several legitimate development options for each employee that could interest the employee, and/or organization. These may be immediate—role-related aimed at improving the employee's current role-performance; or futuristic—career-related that address the needs to capture opportunities palpable in the near future, or those for her potential development towards improved long-term prospects. All these various kinds of employee development goals are relevant and important. Employees with their unique attributes will need different, customized development packages that the managers must envision and develop. Four of these merit are mentioned in the context of PfM:

(a) Those in response to planned self-development initiatives from the managee.

(b) Those necessitated by determination or review of performance standards.

(c) Those indicated by the ongoing monitoring (observation and feedback) process.

(d) Those called for as outcomes of the appraisal process.

On-site efforts involve intensive interaction between managee and her supervisor, supportive problem-solving feedback from the supervisor, opportunity to exercise greater responsibility, job rotation and special assignments, etc.

Off-site efforts may consists of formal training through courses, programmes, or workshops either within the organization or outside, aimed primarily at imparting knowledge in specific areas, relating to the organization and its processes, the managee's role or its tasks, development of skills in solving problems and in interacting with people.

Organization development interventions are essential, because training can merely impart knowledge, develop skills as well as create awareness about different attitudes and their implications. Application of what is learnt in the classroom would, however, require simultaneous developments within the organization that help and encourage such application.

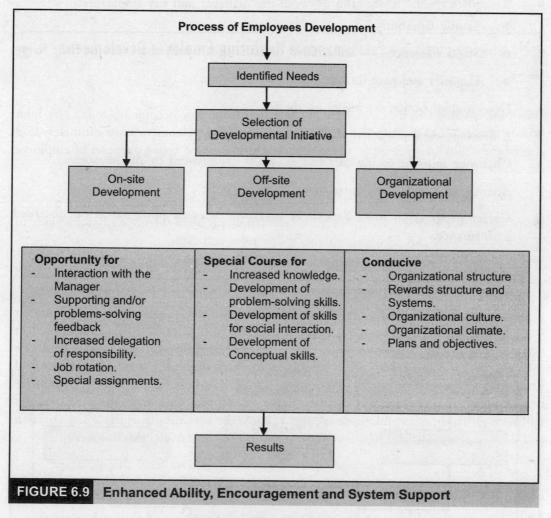

FIGURE 6.9 **Enhanced Ability, Encouragement and System Support**

In this 'The 10 Commandments of Development', Dennis R. Briscoe suggests the following principles that successful development initiatives usually respond to:

1. *All development is essentially self-development:* The door to learning, they say, is locked from inside. No development can take place unless the managee has an inner urge to develop. The organization must provide a favorable—even seductive—learning

environment, but the primary responsibility for her personal and professional growth must vest in the managee.

2. Managee development is an essential part of a manager's job.

3. Organizations must recognize the totality of an individual:

 ❖ Aspiration

 ❖ Work and lifestyle values

 ❖ Personal as well as work needs and interests

 ❖ Family situations

 ❖ Stress tolerances——self-defined limits within which they manage their lives

 ❖ Capacity and pace for learning.

4. Development occurs essentially on the job.

5. A developmental job offers challenge or stretches.

6. Challenge must be continually and gradually experienced by the managee.

7. Alternating stretch and let-up consolidates learning.

8. Career progression must depend as much on assessed potential as on observed performance.

9. Successful development programmes require imaginative monitoring.

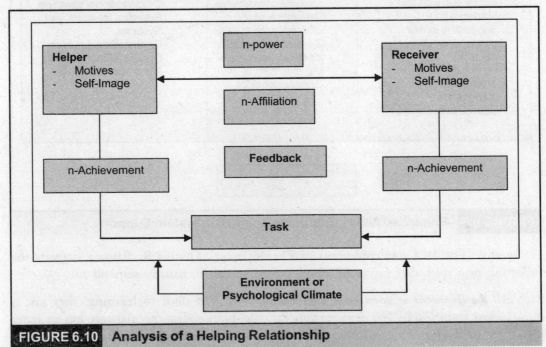

FIGURE 6.10 Analysis of a Helping Relationship

Mentoring

Engendering Trust: The magic of trust can't be explained better than through what is called the Placebo Effect——by which the period of recovery of a patient is significantly related to the level of confidence she has in the medicine and/or the doctor. The higher the level of confidence, the lower the period of recovery. (For further details, see Part B)

Role Efficacy

Dimensions of Role Efficacy

1. *Centrality Vs. Peripherality:* The dimension of centrality measures the role occupant's perception of the significance of the role. The more central that a managee feels his her role is in the organization, the higher will be his her role efficacy.

2. *Integration Vs. Distance:* Integration between the self and the role contributes to role efficacy and self-role distance diminishes efficacy.

3. *Proactivity Vs. Reactivity:* When a role occupants takes some initiative and does something independently, that person is exhibiting proactive behaviour. On the other hand, if she merely responds to what others expect, the behaviour is reactive.

4. *Creativity Vs. Routinism:* When a role occupants perceive that they do something new or unique in their roles, their efficacy is high. The perception that they do only routine tasks lowers role efficacy.

5. *Linkage Vs. Isolation:* Inter-role linkage contributes to role efficacy. If role occupants perceive interdependence with others, their efficacy will be high. Isolation of roles reduces efficacy.

6. *Helping Vs. Hostility:* One important aspect of efficacy is the individual's perception of how he/she gives or receives help. A perception of hostility decreases efficacy.

7. *Superordination Vs. Deprivation:* One dimension of role efficacy is the perception that the role occupants contributes to some larger entity.

8. *Influence Vs. Powerlessness:* The role occupants' feeling that they are able to exercise influence in their roles increases their efficacy. The influence may be in terms of decision-making, implementation, advice or problem-solving.

9. *Growth Vs. Stagnation:* When a role occupants has opportunities——and perceives them as such—to develop in his/her role through learning new things, role efficacy is likely to be high. Similarly, if the individual perceives his/her role as lacking in opportunities for growth, the role efficacy will be low.

10. *Conformation Vs. Avoidance:* When problems arise, they can either be confronted to find solutions or they can be avoided. Confronting problems to find solutions contributes to efficacy and avoidance reduces efficacy.

Pygmalion Effect or self-fulfilling prophecy has to be displayed by the Leader/Manager. (See detail in part B)

"Treat a man as he is, he will remain as he is, Treat a man as he can and should be, he will become as he can and should be."

Change employees' thinking about themselves. Let them know the potential in them. Transform their negativity into positivity.

In a speech at Harvard University in 1943 Winston Churchill observed that the empires of the future will be empires of the mind. He might have added that the battles of the future will be battle for talent. If we are able to create people who are committed to the welfare of the organization and trained and tuned to the requirements of organization then they will steer the organization towards its ultimate business goals and will help achieving excellence.

Somebody has rightly said, "A company is only as great as the people who work for it. "People or people policies can make or break any business. When employees are encouraged to express their creativity, the result is a more fulfilled and sustained workforce. Happy people work harder and are more likely to stay at their jobs. Workplace stress stifles creativity of employees while it is the most required thing in today's time. According to James M. Kouses and Barry Z. Posner, "We have minds and hearts both are to be used at work!"

"The individual is the fountainhead of creativity and innovation only by releasing the energy and fire of our employees we can win in any business anywhere in the globe".

Annual Stocktaking

✢ Foci of Stocktaking Discussions

Stocktaking discussions are most productive when work-focused and development-oriented; and therefore concentrating on:

1. Extent to which the appraisee has achieved or failed to achieve, requisite results.

2. Ways to deal with unanticipated obstacles and difficulties encountered by the managee during the year.

3. Action plans for better performance by the managee, including plans for her personal and professional development.

These give best results and most comfort to both managee as well as the manager, when they are futuristic—how can things be done differently, and better, in future—rather than being past-oriented or fault-finding. This is not to say that lessons from the experience under review are to be ignored in the futuristic treatment of issues. It is the tenor of discussion that needs to be helping in order to generate constructive motivation.

Stocktaking discussions need not be a one-time event. These can be seen as occurring periodically during the entire year. Its first phase is at the start of the year when the manager and the managee identify key performance areas, set performance standards and expectations for performance during the year.

The second phase is a series of interactions throughout the year to review outcomes of the first phase, and also to monitor, guide, motivate, and develop the manage while she performs or struggles to meet performance expectations.

The last phase concerns the stocktaking progress when measurement, analysis and evaluation of actual achievements are made in relation to the set performance standards.

⌘ Content of Stocktaking Discussions ⌘

A comprehensive discussion looks at:

1. Achievement or non-achievement of performance goals and extent of shortfall, if any.

2. Causes for such achievement or non-achievement. Can the reasons for non-achievement be mitigated, and how—through training, by modifying organizational systems, revising performance standards or by influencing environmental forces, or by other means. Can the reasons for achievement be captured as learning and sustained as future assets?

3. Determining what, in the content or context of performance tasks, is positive and helpful and therefore, needs to be retained and reinforced.

4. Determining what, in the content or context of performance tasks, is negative and hindering and therefore, needs to be remedied or changed.

5. Drawing lessons to be used for planning the next performance cycle.

A purposeful stocktaking discussion limits itself primarily to those attributes of the managee – her skills, knowledge or attitudes, which are amenable to learning or changing. Discussions that bring up value judgments or other issues which can not be easily learnt like intelligence, imaginativeness, etc., do not really help in identifying proactive measures to help improve future performance. These are more likely to be perceived as the manager's justification – in advance – for a negative appraisal to follow, than as a helping intervention.

Advantages of Stocktaking Discussion

Some advantages of an ongoing interaction during the various phases of a PMS cycle are:

● There can be opportunities to try remedial measures during the current year, rather than the next one.

● There are fewer surprises for the managee, and the ultimate appraisal may come along predictable lines.

- Chances are that the appraisal exercise becomes less feared.

- Dyadic discussions begin to appear routine and less traumatic events.

Common Characteristics of Stocktaking Discussions

In the course of such a discussion, the process of interaction may vary depending upon the styles and stances adopted variously by the manager and the managee, and also the overall organizational climate in which the interaction takes place. The three types of appraisal discussions described by Maier represent three most-frequently seen situations. Some common characteristics of these situations are:

1. These require a one-on-one communication between manager and the managee.

2. Usually, the situation has high emotional overtones.

    These situations call for a high level of communication skills on the part of both manager and the managee.

3. These situations call for a high level of communication skills on the part of both manager and the managee.

The manager is called upon to simultaneously play somewhat conflicting roles of a judge and a coach, which he/she must be able to effectively balance in order to give the managee a satisfying level of opportunity to influence the process by presenting relevant data. To illustrate a useful role of the manager, the analogy of interaction between a doctor and her patient is often used, with a three-fold role of the doctor:

1. Electing symptoms by skillful questioning.

2. Active listening to probe and arrive at likely causes.

3. Drawing on her professional knowledge and experience to suggest corrective measures.

While using this analogy, it is important to understand that stocking discussions don't necessary respond to pathological situations. While steps in the analogy are useful, these may need to be adapted appropriately, recognizing that the managee is not a patient and that the discussion is not held necessarily at the initiative of the managee, which is essentially the case in a doctor-patient interaction. And, that is exactly where the difficulties for stocking discussions arise. If a managee has as much confidence in the manager's ability – requisite knowledge and skills—to deal with her problems as a patient has in a doctor, and if he/she as much trusts the manager's intent to help her, stocktaking discussion may not, in a sense, be such a pain.

Conditions for Effective Discussions

Norman Maier stresses on some prerequisites for an effective discussion:

- Clear definition of the managee's role and responsibilities in the organization.

- Identification of key indicators for defining the managee's performance more pointedly.

- Organizational standards of performance which are realistic and achievable, given available resources.

Some other conditions that help these discussions become effective are:

- Effective communication skills, including active listening skills.

- Positive and supportive psychological climate to reduce anxiety levels of the managee and the manager.

- Mutuality of purpose and genuine participation of both—managee and the manager— to make discussions a joint exploration towards improving managee performance.

Manager's image as:

- **Authentic**, bona fide and honest-to-purpose. Tough-minded—able to squarely confront the reality of the situation without the need to push unpleasant facts under the carpet.

- **Supportive**, having genuine concern for the managee – his/her well being and personal development.

- *Positive and empathic:* Able to see outcomes and willing to engage proactively with the managee to identify ways of obviating similar problems and difficulties in future.

- **Open** and keen to seek the managee's views and suggestions, and engage with her to examine these in the overall organizational context.

Where managers or the managees fail to respond adequately to the issues arising during the discussions, the causes may be seen in either of the following.

- Ambiguity in initial performance planning tools.

- Inadequate skills of the participants

- Participants' inability to understand their respective roles in this developmental process.

Facts/Data Collection Regarding Performance

Information on performance is collected by using forms, which can be filled out on paper or electronically.

- *Basic employee information:* This section of the form includes basic employee information such as job title, division, department and other work group information, employee number, and pay grade or salary classification. In addition, forms usually include the dates of the evaluation period, the number of months and years the rater has supervised or worked with the employee, an employee's starting date with the company and starting date in the current job, the reason for appraisal, current salary and position in range, and the date of the next scheduled evaluation.

- *Accountabilities, objectives, and standards:* If the organization adopts a results approach, this section of the form would include the name and description of each accountability, objectives agreed upon by manager and employee, and the extent to which the objectives have been achieved. In many instances, the objectives are weighted in terms of importance, which facilitates the calculation of an overall performance score. Finally, this section can also include a subsection describing conditions under which performance was achieved, which may help explain why performance achieved the (high or low) level described. For example, supervisor may have the opportunity to describe specific circumstances surrounding performance during the review period, including a tough economy, the introduction of a new line of products, and so forth.

- *Competencies and indicators:* If the organization adopts a behavior approach, this section of the form includes a definition of the various competencies to be assessed, together with their behavioral indicators.

- *Major achievements and contributions:* Some forms include a section in which a rater is asked to list the two or three major accomplishments of the individual being rated during the review period. These could refer to results, behaviours, or both.

- *Developmental achievements:* This section of the form includes information about the extent to which the developmental goals set for the review period have been achieved. This can include a summary of activities, such as workshops attended and courses taken, as well as results, such as new skills learned. Evidence of having learned new skills can be documented, for example, by obtaining a professional certification.

- *Developmental needs, plans, and goals:* This section of the form is future-oriented and includes information about specific goals and timetables in terms of employee development. As noted before, some organizations choose to create a separate development form and do not include this information as part of the performance appraisal form.

- *Stakeholder input:* Some forms include sections to be filled out by other stakeholders, such as customers with whom the employee interacts. Overall, stakeholders are defined as people who have firsthand knowledge of and are affected by the employee's performance.

- *Employee comments:* This section includes reactions and comments provided by the employee being rated. In addition to allowing formal employee input, which improves the perceived fairness of the system, the inclusion of this section helps with legal issues because it documents that the employee has had an opportunity to participate in the evaluation process.

- *Signatures:* The final section of most forms includes a section in which the employee being rated, the rater, and the rater's supervisor provide their signatures to show they have seen and discussed the content of the form. The HR department may also provide approval of the content of the form.

CHAPTER-7

Annual Performance Appraisal System

LEARNING OBJECTIVES

- To understand the conceptual aspects of performance appraisal system

- To make students aware of the formats that are used for measuring the performance in different companies

- To make students aware of multi-rating systems of feedback

- To make students aware of assessing the potential of any plan

- To give them some feel about appraisals of expatriate employee

Introduction

Performance appraisal or evaluation is the process of identifying, measuring and developing human performance in organizations. An effective appraisal system must not only accurately measure current performance levels, but also contain mechanisms for reinforcing strengths, identifying deficiencies and feeding such information back to ratees in order that they may improve future performance. This record, developmental aspect of appraisal is as important as the measurement aspect.

The term performance itself denotes judgment behavior which has been evaluated. Performance appraisal is thus the process of observing and identifying, measuring and developing human behavior in the organization. These activities are described as follows:

- Observation and identification refers to the process of viewing or scrutinizing job behaviors. It consists of choosing what job behaviors to look at among all that are emitted by a ratees, as well as how often to observe them. The choices inherent in this process add subjectivity to appraisal.

- Measurement refers ascertaining the extent, degree, level, etc., of a behavior. After rater choose what information to examine, they compare this information about rate behavior against a set of organizational or personal expectations for each job. The degree to which observed behavior meets or exceeds the expectations determines its desirability, or the level of performance it reflects, such as excellent or satisfactory.

- Development refers to performance improvement over time. An appraisal system must contain mechanisms to communicate the expectations and measurement process to persons being appraised, motivate them to remove any deficiencies uncovered and reinforce them to build on strengths in order to improve future performance.

When PA is considered in terms of its utility to an organization, several operational PA objectives seem critical. These include, (1) the ability to provide adequate feedback to employees to improve subsequent performance, 2) the identification of employee training needs, 3) the identification of criteria used to allocate organizational rewards, 4) the validation of selection techniques to meet Equal Employment Opportunity (EEO) requirements and 5) the identification of promotable employees from internal labor supplies. In order to accomplish these objectives, the PA system must, of course, be an accurate measure of performance.

A PAs adequacy to provide feedback and improve performance requires that it possess the following characteristics: be unambiguous and clearly specify the job related performance expected, use behavioral terminology, set behavioral target for ratees to work toward and use a problem solving focus which culminates in a specific plan for performance improvement. If PAs are to identify training needs, the format must specify rate deficiencies in behavioral terms, include all relevant job dimensions, and identify environmental deterrents to desired performance levels.

PAs are also used in the allocation of organizational rewards such as merit pay and punishments, such as disciplinary actions. Effective reward allocation may require a valid

PAs which ranks employees according to a quantifiable scoring system. Sufficient variance in scores is essential to differentiate across performers. In allocating rewards, PAs must also be used for disciplinary action, which may range from warnings to termination. Thus, the documentation required for such decisions must also be facilitated by the PA format. With the recent passage of Civil Service Reform Act and its provision typing performance to merit pay and bonuses, the importance of PAs in the public sector has been greatly heightened.

PAs must be designed to facilitate the validation of selection techniques. The process requires, in general terms and at a minimum, measures of employee output or job-related dimensions that tap the behavioral domain of the job analysis, the facilitation of inter-rater reliability measures, professional and objective administration of the PA and continual rater observation of rate performance.

The identification of promotion potential requires that job related PAs have several dimensions in the incumbent's is the same, or similar to, the job to which the incumbent be promoted. This indicates the incumbent's ability assume increasingly difficult assignments. The PA must rank ratees comparatively, measure the contribution to departmental objectives and perhaps capture a ratee's career progression and long-term goals.

The final but perhaps most important PA objective is accuracy in measuring performance. In some ways, it would be conceived as essential for meeting the PA objectives mentioned above. The issues of concern here would include PA formats which minimize raters response set errors (i.e. easy leniency, restriction of range, halo) those which ratees with other measures of performance using alternative formats (e.g., direct indices such as salary), those which obtain reliability across raters, those which have the flexibility to reflect changes in the job environment and those possessing credibility with raters, that they complete the format seriously.

Thus, there are several criteria which PAs should meet to be fully operational. But which types of formats-those which measure worker behavior, or which measures the outcomes of that behaviour—are more effective? No simple answer is available, but the utility of various types of behavior-based formats can best be ascertained by comparing them against the PA objectives identified above.

Comparison of Formats

Global ratings: The first PA format alternative is unidimensional, global rating which uses a rater's overall estimate of performance without distinguishing between critical job elements or dimensions. There are numerous problems in the use of unidimensional formats and when compared to the six PA objectives described above, they generally, fall far short. Unidimensional PA formats are also questionable as measures of performance criteria) from a legal standpoint because they are not used on job analysis and thus are not job-related.

Trait-based scales: There are numerous multidimensional (or graphic) approaches to measuring performance. They are more useful than global scales because they recognize that job performance consists of separate dimensions, or job elements. The first of these is the familiar trait-based scale using dimensions such as loyalty, dependability, etc. Other dimensions traditionally found on these formats are cooperation, initiative and self-confidence. There are problems in the use of trait-based scales centering found potential ambiguity and subjectivity. That is specifically what is meant by "lack of cooperation?" Thus, many trait-based scales are generally evaluated as only poor to fair relative to PA objectives. Further, and perhaps most important, trait-based scales are typically not sufficiently job-related or based on a thorough job analysis. Thus an organization's vulnerability to Equal Employment Opportunity (EEO) litigation is not alleviated.

Behavior-based scales: A significant step beyond global and trait-based scales. These are based upon a job analysis and attempt to determine what an employee actually does at work. A behavior-based scale provides specific feedback to employees because it is based on the activities required of the job. It captures specific information across emloyees for reward allocation and about each employee specifically in the assessment of training needs because it identifies the activities (dimensions) in which an employee may be deficient. For promotion potential, a dimension-based scale can certainly be useful because it may specify the kinds of behaviors incumbents are to demonstrate in their present jobs. Performance on these dimensions can then be compared to the dimensions required in the next job level (for which the employee is a promotion candidate).

Behavior-based scales are often seen as more accurate than the previous two PA formats because of their job-relatedness and specificity. Thus we can expect less error and higher inter rater agreement (and/or reliability). Finally, because dimension-based scales can meet the legal requirements for criterion measure, these certainly can be an improvement for the validation of selection procedures.

The major drawback with dimension-based scales is that although they provide specification of the particular activities of an employee, the scale points are of limited use if they are only numerically and/or adjective-anchored. They provide little specific feedback on what behavior led to the particular rating given, even though the area of performance deficiency has been identified. Thus, a dimension-based PA may be deficient in assessing an employee's specific behaviors within the job dimensions since only adjective or numerical anchors are used.

Behavioral expectation scales or behaviorally anchored rating scales (BARS) are also dimensional scales. The scale points are behavioral statements illustrating various degrees of performance, not merely adjectives or numbers. Thus, BARS are far more specific in terms of identifying employee behavior relative to performance on a specific job dimension. These are also more sophisticated than dimension based formats and require more time to develop.

Behavior-based scales seem to provide excellence feedback to employees in specifying not only what activities employees are to engage in, but also the behaviors a rater perceives that a ratee has demonstrated during the performance period. In fact, performance improvement has been demonstrated through the used of behavior-based systems.

TABLE 7.1	Objectives of Performance Appraisal Systems	
1. Feedback/ development requires:	**2. Assessing training needs/requires:**	**3. Identifying promotion potential requires:**
• Specifying behavioral terminology on the format. • Setting behavioral targets for ratees to work toward. • Job-related, problem-solving performance review which ends with a plan for performance improvement.	• Specify deficiencies in behavioral terms. • Rating on all relevant job dimensions. • Identifying motivation/attitude and environmental conditions as causes of inadequate performance.	• Job-related criteria. • Job dimensions dealing with ability to assume increasingly difficult assignments built into the form. • Ability to rank ratees comparatively. • Measuring of contribution to organization/department objectives. • Assessing of ratee's career aspirations and long-range goals.
4. Rewards allocation requires:	**5. Validation of selection techniques requires:**	**6. Measurement accuracy requires:**
• Ability to rank order ratees or results in quantifiable, performance scores. • Facilitating a variance or spread of scores to discriminate between good, bad, fair, etc., ratees. • Measuring contributions to organization/department objectives. • Accuracy and credibility with employees.	• Job relatedness and a comprehensive list of dimensions tapping the behavioral domain of the job. • Systematic job analysis to derive criteria. • Assessing interrater reliability. • Professional, objective administration of format. • Continual observation of rate performance by raters.	• Reducing rater response set errors(e.g., leniency, restriction of range, halo). • Agreeing iwht other performance measures not on the format (e.g., direct indices such as salary, number of promotions.) • Reliability across multiple raters. • Flexibility to reflect changes in job or environment. • Job-related criteria. • Commitment of raters to observe rate performance frequently and complete format seriously.

Effectiveness-based systems: Another multidimensional system is results, or effectiveness, based scaling. Effectiveness-based scales attempt to provide "objective" indicators for levels of performance and are, of course, typically called Management by Objectives (MBO) systems. Although it is a multidimensional approach in that there are often many objectives which are to be accomplished, effectiveness-based scaling is unique in that what it provides is a measure of an employee's contribution, not an employee's activities or behaviors.

Ratees evaluated with effectiveness-based scaling are being evaluated not on what they do but what they produce; not on how they spend their time, but what they produce; not on how they spend their time, but what they contribute. This is an important difference and a major shortcoming of the previously discussed PA approaches. Obviously, it is difficult to develop specific indicators of employee contribution, but it can be done for many jobs. It is accomplished with more ease in lower level jobs and entry-level jobs within an organization than higher level jobs.

Thus, effectiveness-based scales offer something that is critical and often overlooked in the assessment of performance appraisal. MBO systems are often used to measure unit productivity to which a manager presumably makes a contribution.

What are the Causes of Problems?

Regardless of what format is used, problems can deter PA system effectiveness. The cause of the ineffectiveness of any particular PA system is a function of many variables, acting singly or in groups, which characterize the job, organizational setting and users. However, most often specific causes are located within the following broad problem categories: human judgment, raters, criteria and formats, organization policy, legal requirements and Equal employment Opportunity (EEO) legislation and inflexibility. Each of these six broad categories contains several possible sources of PA problems, discussed briefly below.

Problems in a PA system ultimately can only be judged as to their degree of severity and dysfunctional consequences in light of the original objectives developed for each system. For example, a PA system may sacrifice some degree of applicability across job-type (and would, possibly, have higher developmental costs) in order to have a greater amount and specificity of information about performance available to a certain group of ratees. Hence, it may have greater ability to pinpoint performance deficiencies and thus reduce costs of unnecessary training programs. If the objectives of a PA system are predetermined and prioritized, the system can be designed to make such trade-offs rationally and at minimal cost. Further, after PA design and implementation, problems diagnosed can be judged as to seriousness and corrective action planed in light of objectives. This relationship between PA objectives and both the design and revision of PA systems, while considering various PA problems, is emphasized in the discussion to follow.

Problem No. 1 – Human Judgment: A fundamental source of problems in PA is the subjectivity and individuality which accompanies the human judgment process. Individual differences among people influence their attitudes, values, perceptions, behavior and judgment, a fact as true the PA setting as it is in all others. Intelligence, cognitive style, amount of education, age, sex and self-esteem are few of the individual level characteristics which have been found to influence the making of judgments of others. The expectation raters' supervisors hold for them as well as a rater's own level of job performance and competence, have also been found to effect ratings.

All these factors, however, act in an implicit manner. They reflect "honest" or legitimate differences in personality, background or ability between participants in PA which influence their perception—their view of reality and thus perceptions of the behavior of ratees. While these individual differences typically do not result in deliberate attempts to bias or prejudice ratings, their result on PA (e.g., inaccuracies) is similar.

Besides these unintentional PA errors resulting from individual differences, are those overt, deliberate attempts to distort Pas based upon personal prejudices and biases against others of a certain religion, national origin, race, sex, age, political ideology etc. The result can be the setting of different performance standards for two people performing the same job or the distorting of PA results upward or downward to correspond to one's prejudices.

TABLE 7.2	Generalized Evaluation of PA Formats Compared to PA Objectives					
Objective/ Format	Feedback/ development	Assessing Training needs	Identification of promotion potential	Reward allocation	Selection system validation	Measurement accuracy
Global	Poor	Poor	Poor to Fair	Poor	Poor	Poor
Trait-based	Poor	Poor	Poor to Fair	Poor to Fair	Poor to Fair	Poor to Fair
Behavior-based (if behaviorally-anchored)	Very good to Excellent	Very Good	Very Good	Very Good	Very good to Excellent	Good
Effectiveness Based	Fair to Good	Fair to Good	Fair to Good	Very Good to Excellent	Fair to Good	Very Good to Excellent

TABLE 7.3	Source of Problems in Appraisal Systems				
Human Judgment	Raters	Criteria and Formats	Organizational Policy	Legal Requirement and Equal Employment Opportunity Legislation	Inflexibility
Subjectivity and/or individual nature of decision making; international bias and prejudice	Lack of information on rate performance, lack of knowledge of ratees' job, possession of erroneous information, differing expectations due to level in hierarchy and role.	Ambiguity, lack of specificity and behaviorally-based language, not communicated explicitly to rates	No commitment to appraisal, failure to use results in reward allocation, no standard policy regarding raters' tasks in appraisal or frequency of appraisal, no allowance for user participation in system development.	Failure to develop appraisal criteria from job analysis; rating systems administered subjectively, use of results to discriminate on basis of race, sex, etc.	Inability of system to reflect dynamic nature of jobs and organizational context; credibility loss from outdated systems.

Credibility and Effectiveness of Appraisal Systems

Even when performance criteria are quantifiable and visible, figure can be distorted or interpreted erroneously by such judgmental factors as perceived amount of effort or initiative and hence intentional bias still enter the process.

Problem No 2 – Raters: PA problems stem from conscientious raters who possess inadequate and/or erroneous information about rate performance. Many supervisors, due to their own job duties which may physically separate them from their subordinate ratees, are able to observe rate performance too infrequently to accurately judge typically performance over a long period. But non-representative sampling or allowing a typical positive or negative performance occurring during their infrequent observation periods to bias their judgments of performance over the entire period can lead to inaccurate appraisals.

In addition, members of each hierarchical level within an organization may view a ratee's performance from a different vantage point or hold differing expectations for desired performance based upon their roles, Thus a ratee's supervisor may be in an excellent position to judge the ratee's technical competence, but not his or her ability to effectively interact with others. Peer raters may possess the best information regarding a ratee's interpersonal effectiveness. Supervisors of ratees, as critics and evaluators of their subordinates, typically judge performance are harshly than do job incumbents themselves.

Problem No. 3: Criteria and PA Formats: The identification of specific, consistent, performance criteria is the first objective of a PA system, as discussed earlier. The easiest way to assure that a ratee's performance can be evaluated based upon only the whim of a rater is of course to keep the criteria ambiguous and/or secret, to change them capriciously, or never to develop them at all as discussed above, each type of appraisal format has advantages and disadvantages relative to this issue of defining the criteria against which to base evaluations. The overall objective, of course, is to develop a format which identifies and defines the criteria in explicit, concrete terms.

For example, if a supervisor (rater) is given the authority to set merit raises for a group of subordinates (rates) and the PA format which is used to measure performance is of the global type involving overall ranking, the supervisor can easily feel trapped. Of course, the supervisor might have a definite and accurate overall impression as to the relative performance of his or her ratees and can easily discriminate between the excellent and average performers. But if the top performers are given merit raises and the others are not, the supervisor needs a rationale for this action to give to those who were denied the merit raise. The global PA format provides little help since it does not specify and define the exact criteria used in PA or the different levels of performance within each criterion. To develop a formal, written rational for each rating may not only be seen as too bothersome for many raters but they may find it difficult to articulate the exact criteria to ratees. The result is often that either extreme leniency is used on many ratings or that all ratees are rated about the same and hence each receives a smaller merit raise. Thus, expediency rather than discrimination between good and poor performers characterizes the PA system and its credibility is destroyed.

Problem No. 5 – Legal requirements and Equal Employment Opportunity (EEO) Legislation: The risk of precipitating charges of discrimination as a result of policy decisions based upon a PA results is now itself a serious cause of problems in PA Systems. The ramification of subjective, unsustained PAS can be devastating to an organization. Recently, through several pieces of legislation, court decisions and guidelines of various federal agencies, the issue of discrimination in employment as a result of PAs has become more visible and spelled out in more detail than ever before.

Organizations must present PA forms and any instructions given to raters as part of the evidence for the validity of such selection techniques as employment tests. Thus, the use, of for example, an application blank, would be judged acceptable in certain situations only if answers to particular items on the blank were found to correlate highly with the probability of future job "success" of workers in the job. Job "success" is demonstrated typically by results of a PA system. The PA system is thus open to scrutiny by the courts and must therefore be thorough and as bias-free as possible.

Violation of civil rights legislation can also come from the use of Pas directly in promotion decisions. The following excerpts from discussions of recent court cases involving PAs illustrate the potential consequences of an inadequate system.

The court found the following as a basis for discrimination: "Recommendations by foremen were based on standards which were vague and subjective and were made without written instructions concerning qualifications necessary for promotion...one company was required to offer training programs to upgrade personnel, to provide foremen with written instructions delineating objective criteria....The other company was ordered to post announcements of pre-foremen training classes, to post notices of qualifications required for salaried positions.

Using performance ratings for determining personnel layoffs was found to be in violation of Title VII of the Civil Rights Act when an employer failed to validate the appraise methods according to EEOC guidelines. The evaluations were judged invalid because they were based on subjective observations (two of three evaluators did not observe the employee on a daily basis, evaluations were not admixture and scored under controlled and standardized conditions. The courts ordered the company to reinstate the employees with nominal back pay and required the company not to use performance ratings until they have been validated.

Problem No 5 – Inflexibility: The final cause of problems in PA systems is the dynamic nature of jobs and job performance and the static nature of any written PA document typically developed several months before it is to be used. As job responsibilities, duties, requirements and job environments change over time, a PA format may become obsolete before it is even used! Further, as workers' performance levels change over time, perhaps due to training and experience, the standards set in PA formats may be too low, geared only for newer worker. Even the same jobs within classes are not identical.

One solution is, of course, to continually develop new PA formats as all of the above factors change and to develop separate PA formats for each and every position. But this solution is an economic impossibility. A solution often used by organizations is to develop a few categories of formats—perhaps one format for operating level workers, one for clerical workers, one for technical workers, and one for managers. A reasonable solution? Yes, provided raters are knowledgeable, competent, use identical standards, observe performance equally, are generally bias-free and are provided with specific, detailed criteria. But in the all too often instances when the "ideal" rater is unavailable, PA formats applicable across job types may lead to subjectivity and possibly to litigation for discrimination.

The view of PA systems presented above is, admittedly problematic. Yet it is a realistic one as many organizations find their appraisal system to be the source of continual problems.

As discussed, no system is capable of alleviating all appraisal problems completely. Yet there are a few things which can be done to enhance a system's effectiveness.

The first way to improve appraisal systems is to recognize that the appraisal process entails far more than measurement and the use of a form. It also includes observation and identification of performance, as well as development of performance. As discussed, PA systems have several objectives. They must be developed in light of both the trade-off between these objectives and the potential problem sources in appraisal.

The second mechanism for improved appraisal is to integrated the best aspects of the various formats. Behavior based system, such as Behaviorally-Anchored Rating Scales (BARS), specify criteria in very concrete terms to improve accuracy, provide detailed feedback to ratees and help comply with legal requirements due to the job-relatedness of criteria. Effectiveness-based systems, such as Management by objectives (MBO) are very popular due to their ability to measure and quantify results, redirect effort to important tasks and allow for rate participation in goal-setting.

Performance Appraisal

Performance appraisal is a systematic evaluation of present potential capabilities of personnel and employees by their superiors, or a professional form outside. It is a process of estimating or judging the value, excellent qualities or status of a person or thing. It is a process of collecting, analyzing, and evaluating data relative to job behavior and results of individuals. The appraisal system is organized on the principle of goals and management by objectives. Management decisions on performance utilize several integrated inputs: goals and plans, job evaluation, performance evaluation, and individual history. It connotes a two-dimensional concept-at one end of the continuum lies the goals set by the authority, and at the other end, the performance achieved by the individual or any given group.

Performance appraisal can be either formal or informal. Usage of formal systems schedule regular sessions in which to discuss an employee's performance. Informal appraisals are unplanned, often just chance statements made in passing about an employee's performance. Most organizations use a formal appraisal system. Some organizations use more than one appraisal system for different types of employees or for different appraisal purposes. Organizations need to measure employee performance to determine whether acceptable standards of performance are being maintained. The five primary criteria on which the value of performance may be assessed are — quality, timeliness, cost effectiveness, need for supervision, and interpersonal impact. If appraisals indicate that employees are not performing at acceptable levels, steps can be taken to simplify jobs, train, and motivate workers, or dismiss them, depending upon the reasons for poor performance.

The results of appraisal are normally used to:

1. Estimate the overall effectiveness of employees in performing their jobs,

2. Identify strengths and weaknesses in job knowledge and skills,

3.   Determine whether a subordinate's responsibilities can be expanded,

4.   Identify future training and development needs,

5.   Review progress towards goals and objectives,

6.   Determine readiness for promotion, and

7.   Motivate and guide growth and development.

⌘ Objectives of Performance Appraisal ⌘

Performance appraisal plans are designed to meet the needs of the organization and the individual. It is increasingly viewed as central to good human resource management. This is highlighted in Cumming's classification of performance appraisal objectives. According to Cummings and Schwab (1973), the objectives of performance appraisal schemes can be categorized as either evaluation or developmental. The evaluative purpose have a historical dimension and are concerned primarily with looking back at how employees have actually performed over a given time period, compared with required standards of performance. The developmental performance appraisal is concerned, for example, with the identification of employees' training and development needs, and the setting of new targets.

The broad objectives of performance appraisal are:

1.   To help the employee to overcome his weaknesses and improve his strengths so as to enable him to achieve the desired performance.

2.   To generate adequate feedback and guidance from the immediate superior to an employee working under him.

3.   To contribute to the growth and development of an employee through helping him in realistic goal setting.

4.   To provide input to system of rewards (comprising salary increments, transfers, promotions, demotions or terminations) and salary administration.

5.   To help in creating a desirable culture and tradition in the organization.

6.   To help the organization to identify employees for the purpose of motivating, training and developing them.

7.   To generate significant, relevant, free, and valid information about employees.

In short, the performance appraisal of an organization provides systematic judgments to backup wage and salary administration; suggests needed changes in one's behavior, attitudes, skills, or job knowledge; and uses it as a base for coaching and counseling the individual by his superior. Appraising employee performance is, thus, useful for compensation, placement, and training and development purposes.

⌘ Uses of Performance Appraisal ⌘

The appraisal systems do not operate in isolation; they generate data that can contribute to other HRM systems—for example to succession planning and manpower planning.

Some of the common uses of appraisals include:

- Determining appropriate salary increases and bonuses for workers based on performance measure.

- Determining promotions or transfer depending on the demonstration of employee strengths and weaknesses.

- Promoting effect communication within organizations through the interchange of dialogue between supervisors and subordinates.

- Motivating employees by showing them where they stand, and establishing a data bank on appraisal for rendering assistance in personnel decisions.

Organizations use performance appraisals for three purposes – administrative, employee development, and programme assessment, Programme appraisal commonly serve an administrative purpose by providing employers with a rational for making many personnel decisions, such as decisions relating to pay increases, promotions, demotions, terminations and transfers. Valid performance appraisal data are essential to demonstrate that decisions are based on job related performance criteria. An employee's performance is often evaluated relative to other employees for administrative purposes, but may be assessed in relation to an absolute standard of performance. Performance appraisal for employee development purposes provide feedback on an employee's performance. The intent of such appraisals is to guide and motivate employee's to improve their performance and potential for advancement in the organization. Appraisal data can also be used for employee development purposes in helping to identify specific training needs of individuals. Programme assessment requires the collection and storage of performance appraisal data for a number of uses. The records can show how effective recruiting, selection, and placement have been in supplying a qualified workfare. Performance measures can be used to validate selection procedures and can also be used as "before" and "after" measures to determine the success of training and development programmes.

In brief, the various used of performance appraisal can be classified into two broad categories. One category concerns the obtaining of evaluation data on employees for decision-making for various personnel actions such as pay increasing, promotions, transfer, discharge, and for selection test validation. The other main use is or employee development including performance improvement training, coaching, and counseling.

⌘ Planning the Appraisal ⌘

A meaningful performance appraisal is a two-way process that benefits both the employee and the manager. For employees, appraisal is the time to find out how the manager thinks they are performing in the job. For a manager, a formal appraisal interview is a good time to find out how employees think they are performing on the job. The planning appraisal strategy has to be done:

Before the Appraisal

1. Establish key task areas and performance goals.

2. Set performance goals for each key task area.

3. Get the facts.

4. Schedule each appraisal interview well in advance.

During the Appraisal

1. Encourage two-way communication.

2. Discuss and agree on performance goals for the future.

3. Think about how you can help the employee to achieve more at work.

4. Record notes of the interview.

5. End the interview on an upbeat note.

After the Appraisal

1. Prepare a formal record of the interview.

2. Monitor performance.

3. Feedback session— tell and sale, tell and listen, problem solving

4. Developing need based training programme

5. Working out reward based incentives

⌘ Approaches to Performance Appraisal ⌘

George Odiorne has identified four basic approaches to performance appraisal.

Personality-based systems: In such systems the appraisal form consists of a list of personality traits that presumably are significant in the jobs of the individuals being appraised. Such traits as initiative, drive, intelligence, ingenuity, creativity, loyalty and trustworthiness appear on most such lists.

Generalised descriptive systems: Similar to personality-based systems, they differ in the type of descriptive term used. Often they include qualities or actions of presumably good managers: "organizes, plans, controls, motivates others, delegates, communicates, makes things happen," and so on. Such a system, like the personality-based system, might be useful if meticulous care were take to define the meaning of each term in respect to actual results.

Behavioural descriptive systems: Such systems feature detailed job analysis and job descriptions, including specific statements of the actual behavior required from successfully employees.

Result-centered systems: These appraisal systems (sometime called work-centered or job-centered systems) are directly job related.

They require that manager and subordinate sit down at the start of each work evaluation period and determine the work to be done in all areas of responsibility and functions, and the specific standards of performance to be used in each area.

When introducing performance appraisal a job description in the form of a questionnaire has to be preferred. A typical questionnaire addressed to an individual would cover the following points:

- What is your job title?

- To whom are you responsible?

- Who is responsible to you?

- What is the main purpose and what are your main areas of responsibility?

- What is the size of your job in such terms of output or sales targets, number of items processed, number of people managed, number of customers? What targets or standards of performance have been assigned for your job? Are there any other ways in which it would be possible to measure the effectiveness with which you carry out your job?

- Is there any other information you can provide about your job?

⌘ Components of Performance Appraisal ⌘

The components that should be used in a performance appraisal system flow directly from the specific objectives of appraisal. The following components are being used in a number of Indian organizations.

1. Key Performance Areas (KPAs)/Key Result Areas (KRAs)

2. Tasks/targets/objectives; attributes/qualities/traits

3. Self appraisal

4. Performance analysis

5. Performance ratings

6. Performance review, discussion or counseling

7. Identification of training/development needs

8. Ratings/assessment by appraiser

9. Assessment/review by reviewing authority

10. Potential appraisal.

⌘ General Contents of a Performance Appraisal

- Traits—Attitude, accountability, initiative, drives etc.

- Behaviour—Motivated or otherwise

- Result or output

⌘ Types of Performance Appraisal

There are two types of performance appraisal systems which are normally used in organizations : (i) close-ended appraisal system and, (ii) open-ended appraisal system.

In the close ended appraisal system, commonly used in government organizations and public enterprises, a confidential report is submitted on the performance of the employee. Only where an adverse assessment is made against an individual, the concerned individual is informed about the same. The main shortcoming of this system is that an individual is not informed about his/her inherent strengths and weaknesses and, therefore, is not given an opportunity to respond to the assessment made on him/her. The employees are, therefore, in a constant dilemma as to how their performance is viewed by the management.

In the open-ended appraisal system, unlike in the close ended system, the performance of the individual is discussed with him, and he is ranked in a five or ten point rating scale. The company uses this tool primarily for rewarding a good performer or for other considerations like promotions. The main weakness of this system is that all the employees are ranked in a particular scale, and whereas the good performers are rewarded, there is no concerted effort to motivate the average performers are rewarded, there is no concerted effort to motivate the average performers in performing better. Another weakness of the grading system is that the appraisal may turn out to be more subjective in nature due to insufficient data maintained on the individual. This system also leads to unnecessary comparisons made on different individuals performing similar jobs.

Performance appraisal can be a closed affair, where the appraisees do not get any chance to know or see how they have been evaluated; or it can be completely open, where the appraisees have the opportunity of discussing with their superiors during the evaluation exercise.

⌘ Concerns and Issues in Appraisal

1. Identifying job responsibilities and duties and performance dimensions, standards and goals.

2. Prioritizing and weighing performance dimensions and performance goals.

3. Determining appropriate methods for appraising performance.
4. Developing suitable appraisal instruments and scoring devices.
5. Establishing procedures that enhance fair and just appraisals of all employees.
6. Providing performance feedback to all employees.
7. Rating observed and identified performance to the rewards provided by organization.
8. Designing, monitoring and auditing processes to ensure proper operation of the system and to identify areas of weakness.
9. Granting employees opportunities for appeal whenever and wherever such action is appropriate.
10. Training of employees in all phases of the appraisal system.

The basic issues addressed by performance appraisal are:

- What to appraise?
- How to appraise fairly and objectively?
- How to communicate the appraisal and turn the total process into a motivator?
- How the performance appraisal results can be put to good use?
- How to implement the performance appraisal system smoothly?

Steps in the Appraisal Programme

As in other personnel programmes, performance appraisal forms a line responsibility to be accomplished with advice and help of the personnel department. Indeed, the appraisal programme is likely to be an utter failure if it lacks the support of top management; if superiors are not adequately trained, or have no trust in its value; if the results of appraisal are not discussed with the subordinates; and if the appraisal is not used to serve the purposes it is meant.

Pigors and Myers suggest several steps to develop and administer the programme effectively.

1. The personnel department may attempt to obtain as much as possible the agreement of line management in respect to the needs and objective of the programme. A choice has to be made among different kinds of appraisal methods judiciously.
2. The personnel department has to examine the plans of other organizations as well as the relevant literature in the field to formulate the most suitable plan for the appraisal programme.
3. Attempts should be made to obtain the co-operation of supervisors in devising the appraisal form and discuss with them the different factors to be incorporated, weights

and points to be given to each factor, and description or instructions to be indicated on the form.

4. The personnel or industrial relations manager tends to explain the purpose and nature of the programme to all the superiors and subordinates to be involved and affected by it. Care should be taken to take into confidence the representatives of the union, if it exists in the company.

5. Attempt is to be made to provide intensive training to all the supervisors with a view to obtaining unbiased and uniform appraisal of their subordinates.

6. Care may be taken to acquire line and staff co-ordination and mutual checking of appraisals with a view to achieving intra and inter-departmental consistency and uniformity.

7. There should be an arrangement for periodic discussion of he appraisal by the superior with each of the subordinates to express himself, If he feels that the appraisal has been biased and that. It should be otherwise.

8. As soon as the appraisal has been duly discussed, attempts may be made to recommend for salary increases or promotion, if these decisions seem plausible in the light of appraisals.

9. There should be provision for challenge and review of appraisals, If the employees or their union representatives are dissatisfied with the personnel decisions which the management has taken on the basis of these appraisals. These steps, if followed carefully, are likely to help the superiors to evaluate their subordinates effectively.

Performance appraisals are of different types:

1. Job-Focused
2. Person-focused
3. Role-focused
4. Hybrid

Methods of Performance Appraisal

Structure and Sayles have classified performance appraisal into three groups: traditional performance rating, newer-rating method, and result-oriented appraisal. A brief description of each is as follows:

⌘ Traditional Performance Rating

Traditional rating involves completion of a form by the immediate supervisor of the individual who is being evaluated. In some cases, attempts are made to accomplish the rating by a committee consisting of the immediate supervisor, the supervisor's superior and one or two more officers of the company who are familiar with the ratees. Although ratings by the committee bring several viewpoints together and overcome the superior's bias, if any, they are highly time-consuming. The conventional rating scale form incorporates several factors, such as, job knowledge, judgment, organizing ability, dependability, creativity, dealing with people, delegation, and leadership. The rating is assigned by putting a tick mark horizontally. Frequently, descriptive phrases are given in the form to guide the rater while evaluating the ratees. This method is very simple to understand and easy to apply. On the basis of ratings on specific factors, it is possible to identify areas in which the individual requires further development. The ratings on specific factors can be summated to obtain a composite performance score.

The merit-rating scales are frequently criticized from the standpoints of clarity in standards, differing perceptions, excessive leniency or strictness, the central tendency, the halo effect, and the impact of an individual's job. The basic criticism of the traditional performance rating is concerned with its emphasis on personality traits instead of job performance. Such rating is highly subjective in the absence of objective standards.

Other criticisms of traditional performance rating relates to – First, there is a divergence of opinion among raters so to what is meant by such standards as "unsatisfactory", "good" and so on. Second, there may be divergent perceptions and accordingly, different standards of judgments among the raters. Third, the raters may be susceptible to excessive leniency or strictness error. Fourth, there is an error of central tendency involving a cluster of ratings near the middle of the scale. Fifth, there is a chance of the occurrence of a halo effect. Sixth, there is a tendency on the part of the raters to assign high ratings to individuals holding high-paid jobs.

⌘ Newer Rating Methods ⌘

Because of several inadequacies in the traditional rating scale, attempts have been made to devise new procedures which are less susceptible to the above weaknesses. Among these included rank order, paired comparison, forced distribution forced choice, critical incident and field review. These methods are discussed below:

(i) *The Rank-order Procedure:* It is effective where ten or lesser number of individuals are to be evaluated. According to this procedure, each individual is assigned such ranks as first, second, third and so on. If the evaluation process involves several traits, the ranking is made separately for each trait. Although this method is simple to understand and easy to apply, this technique becomes cumbersome and difficult when a large number of employees are to be evaluated in the organization.

(ii) *Paired-comparison System:* Under this, each individual is compared with every other individual. The appraiser is required to put a tick-mark against the name of the individual whom he consider better on the trait in question. The final ranking is determined by the number of times he is judged better than the other. This method becomes complicated when the number of individuals for evaluation is large.

(iii) *The Forced Distribution Procedure:* It is form of comparative evaluation in which an evaluator rates subordinates according to a specified distribution. Here judgments are made on a relative basis, i.e., a person is assessed relative to his performance in the group he works. This procedure can be used for numerous traits if required by evaluating the individuals separately on each trait. The forced distribution method is primarily used to eliminate rating errors such as leniency and central tendency.

(iv) *The Forced Choice Technique:* It forces the rather to select form a series of several statements or traits, the one which best fits the individual and one which least fits, and each of these statements is assigned a score. Since the appraiser does not know the score value of statements, this method prevents the rater from deliberately checking only the most favorable trait. Moreover, the appraiser is unable to introduce personal bias into the evaluation process because he does not know which of the statements is indicative of effective performance. This enhances the overall objectivity of this procedure.

(v) *The Critical Incident Method:* This technique of performance appraisal was developed by Flanagan and Burns. Under this procedure, attempts are made to devise for each job a list of critical job requirements. Superiors are trained to be on the lookout for critical incidents on the part of the subordinates in accomplishing the job requirements. The superiors enlist the incidents as they happen and in the process, tend to build up a record of each subordinate with debit on the minus side and credit on the plus side. The merit of this procedure is that all evaluations are based on objective evidence instead of subjective rating.

(vi) *The Field Review:* It is an appraisal by someone outside the employee's own department, usually someone form the corporate office or form the employee's own human resources department. The field review process involves review of employee records, an interviews with the employee, and sometimes with the employee's superior. Field review as an appraisal method is used primary in making promotion decisions at the managerial level. Field reviews are also useful when comparable information is needed from employees in the different units or locations.

Results-Oriented Appraisal

The results—oriented appraisals are based on the concrete performance targets which are usually established by superior and subordinates jointly. This procedure has been known as Management by Objectives (MBO).

MBO

The definition of MBO, as expressed by its foremost proponent, Dr. George S. Odiorne, is: "Management by objectives is a process whereby the superior and subordinate managers of an organization jointly identify its common goals, define each individual's major areas of responsibility in terms of the results expected of him, and use these measures as guides for operating the unit and assessing the contribution of each of its members."

Much of the initial impetus for MBO was provided by Peter Drucker (1954) and by Douglas McGregor (1960). Drucker first described management by objectives in 1954 in the Practice of Management. Drucker pointed the importance of managers having clear objectives that support the purposes of those in higher positions in the organization.

McGregor argues that by establishing performance goals for employees after reaching agreement with superiors, the problems of appraisal of performance are minimized. MBO in essence involves the setting out clearly define goals of an employee in agreement with his superior. Carroll and Tosi (1973), in an extensive account of MBO, note its following characteristics:

1. The establishment of organizational goals.

2. The setting of individual objectives in relation to organizational goals.

3. A periodic review of performance as it relates to organizational goals.

4. Effective goal-setting and planning by top management.

5. Organizational commitment.

6. Mutual goal-setting.

7. Frequent individual performance reviews.

8. Some freedom in developing means of achieving objectives.

MBO is, thus, a method of mutual goal-setting, measuring progress towards the goals, taking action to assure goal attainment, feedback, and participation. It is a result-oriented philosophy, enabling an employee to measure progress toward a goal which the employee often has helped to set In the goals-setting phase of MBO, a superior and subordinate discuss job performance problems and a goal is agreed upon. Along with mutual goal-setting, a major component of MBO is the performance review session between the superior and subordinate, which takes place regularly to evaluate progress towards specified goals.

The key features of management by objectives are as under:

1. Superior and subordinate get together and jointly agree the list the principal duties and areas of responsibility of the individual's job.

2. The subordinate sets his own short-term performance goals or targets in cooperation with his superior.

3. They agree upon criteria for measuring and evaluating performance.

4. From time to time, as decided upon, the superior and subordinate get together to evaluate progress towards the agreed-upon goals. At those meetings, new or modified goals are set for the ensuing period.

5. The superior plays a supportive role. He tries, on a day-to-day basis, to help the subordinate achieve the agreed upon goals. He counsels and coaches.

6. In the appraisal process, the superior plays the role of a judge and more of the role of one who helps the subordinate attain the organization goals or targets.

7. The process focuses upon results accomplished and not upon personal traits.

There are four main steps in MBO:

1. *Define the job:* Review, with the subordinates, his or her key responsibilities and duties.

2. *Define expected results (set objectives):* Here specify in measurable terms what the person is expected to achieve.

3. *Measure the results:* Compare actual goals achieved with expected results.

4. *Provide feedback, appraise:* Hold periodic performance review meetings with subordinates to discuss and evaluate the latter's progress in achieving expected results.

MBO as a mutual goal setting exercise is most appropriate for technical, professional, supervisory, and executive personnel. In these position, there is generally enough latitude and room for discretion to make it possible for the person to participate in setting his work goals, tackle new projects, and discover new ways to solve problems. This method is generally not applied for lower categories of workers because their jobs are usually too restricted in scope. The is little discretionary opportunity for them to shape their jobs.

MBO may be viewed as a system of management rather than an appraisal method. A successful installation of MBO requires written mission statements that are prepared at the highest levels of top management. Mission statements provide the coherence in which top-down and bottom-up goal setting appear sensible and compatible. MBO can be applied successfully to an organization that has sufficient autonomy, personnel, budget allocation, and policy integrity. Managers are expected to perform so that goals are attained by the organization. Too often MBO is installed top-down in a dictatorial manner with a little or no accompanying training. If properly implemented, it serves as a powerful and useful tool for the success of managerial performance.

MBO is a tool that is inextricably connected with team building so that the work commitment of team members can be increased and their desire to excel in performance can be inspired. It is important to have effective team work among a group of managers or a group of subordinates.

The group of employees or subordinates must be looked upon as a team that needs to be brought together. Goals should be set by manager-subordinate pairs, and also by teams. The basic superior-subordinate relationship in an organization is in no way undermined in this concept of team goal setting. Lines of responsibility, authority, and accountability remain clear.

MBO has many benefits, some of which are enlisted below:

1. Providing a way for measuring objectively the performance of subordinates.

2. Co-ordinates individual performance with company goals.

3. Clarifies the job to be done and defines expectations of job accomplishment.

4. Improves superior-subordinate relationship through a dialogue that takes place regularly.

5. Foster increased competence, personal growth, and opportunity for career development

6. Aids in an effective overall planning system.

7. Supplies a basis for more equitable salary determination, especially incentive bonuses.

8. Develops factual data for promotion criteria.

9. Stimulates self-motivation, self-discipline and self-control.

10. Serves as a device for integration of many management functions.

MBO has certain potential problems such as:

1. It often lacks the support and commitment of top management.

2. Its objectives are often difficult to establish.

3. Its implementation creates excessive paperwork if it is not closely monitored.

4. It concentrates too much on the short run at the expense of long-range planning.

5. It may lead to be excessive time consuming.

Traditionally, in most performance evaluations a supervisor evaluates the performance of subordinate. Recently, a new approach has been enunciated by the western management gurus, which is known as 360 degree appraisal—a performance management in which people receive performance feedback from those on all sides of them in the organization—their boss, their colleagues and peers, and their own subordinates, and internal and external customers. The list can grow to include vendors and consultants, human resource professionals, suppliers and business associates, even friends and spouses. The 360 degree feedback refers to the practice of using multiple raters often including self-ratings in the assessment of individuals. Thus, the feedback comes from all around. It is also a move towards participation and openness. Many American companies are now using this 360 degree feedback. Companies that practice 360 degree appraisals include Motorola, Semco Brazil, British Petroleum, British Airways, Central Televisions, and so on. Barring a few multinational companies, in India this system of appraisal is uncommon.

This form of performance evaluation can be very beneficial to managers because it typically gives them a much wider range of performance-related feedback than a traditional evaluation. That is, rather than focusing narrowly on objective performance, such as sales increase or productivity gains, 360 degree often focuses on such things as interpersonal relations and style. Of course, to benefit from 360 degree feedback, a manager must have thick skin. The manager is likely to hear some personal comments on sensitive topics, which may be threatening. Thus, a 360 degree feedback system must be carefully managed so that its focus remains on constructive rather than destructive criticism.

⌘ Balance Score Card ⌘

The Balance Score Card (BSC) creates a template of measurement of organizational performance as well as individual performance. It is a measurement-based management system, which enables organizations to clarify vision and strategy before initiating action. It is also a monitoring system that integrates strategy into performance measures and targets, thus making it operational and highly effective. It helps cascade corporate level measures to lower level so that the employees can see what they must do well to improve organizational effectiveness and helps focus the entire organization on what must be done to create breakthrough performance. BSC was introduced in 1992 by Dr. Robert Kaplan and David Norton and has been successfully adopted by numerous companies worldwide.

Experts from various departments are brought together to evaluate individuals groups specially their potentials for promotions.

Errors in Performance Appraisal

Differences in perception and value systems influence evaluations. For instance, two raters observe an employee disagreeing with a supervisor. One perceives this as insubordination, but the other sees it as a willingness to stand up to for what he believes in. Individual rather bias can seriously compromise the credibility of an appraisal. Some of the common syndromes are:

Halo Effect: This is a tendency let the assessment of a single trait influence the evaluation of the individual on other traits too.

Horns Effect: This is a tendency to allow one negative trait of the employee to color the entire appraisal. This results in an overall lower rating than may be warranted.

Leniency or Constant Error: Depending upon the appraiser's own value system which acts as a standard, employees may be rated leniently or strictly. Such as ratings do not carry any reference to actual performance of the employees. Some appraisers consistently assign high values to all employees, regardless of merit. This is a leniency error. The strictness tendency is a reverse situation, where all individuals are rated too severely and performance is understated.

Central Tendency: This is the most common error that occurs when a rather assigns most middle range scores or values to all individuals under appraisal. Extremely high or extremely low evaluations are avoided by assigning 'average ratings' to all.

Spill-over Effect: This refers to allowing past performance to influence the evaluation of present performance.

Personal Bias: Perhaps the most important error of all arises form the fact that are very few people are capable of objective judgments entirely independent of their values and prejudices.

The above errors have evoked concerns about performance appraisal. McGregor (1960), with his concern for the human side of enterprise, appraisal represented a judgment and demotivating process. Similar concerns were voiced by Deming (1982) who suggested that appraisal was 'a deadly disease which blamed individuals for problems systematic to organizations. Margerison (1976) went as far as to predict that appraisal would 'fall apart at the seams' due to a combination of managerial indifference, employee ambivalence and union opposition. This theme was reiterated by Fletcher (1993), who suggested that the days of standardized appraisal were numbered. But, despite these gloomy predictions, the use of performance appraisal has flourished.

⌘ Problems in Performance Appraisal

1. Design defect

2. Implementation defect

3. Raters' bias

Competency-based Performance Assessment

Performance management is a strategic and integrated approach for delivering sustained success to organizations by improving the performance of those who work in them and by developing the capabilities of teams and individual contributors. Development is perhaps the most important function of performance management. Performance management is concerned with outputs—the achievement of results; and with outcomes—the impact made on performance. But it is also concerned with the processes required to achieve these results and the inputs in term of capabilities (knowledge, skill and competence) expected from the teams and the individuals involved).

According to one survey, 31 percent of the organizations surveyed included some form of competency assistance in the performance management process. On the basis of the 1991 survey, Fletcher and Williams suggested that, "The interest in competencies perhaps signifies a much more explicit concern with means and not just ends", but they also remarked that if competencies are not defined on the basis of empirical research to determine which of them are associated with effective performance, then there is a danger that the competencies in themselves will lack validity and the assessments made by managers may lack reliability and validity.

Performance management is regarded as a number of inter-linked processes rather than a single system. It was, therefore, common to find performance management carefully aligned with communications strategies, competency development, job design and evaluation, payment systems and motivation practices.

⌘ Performance Defined

The Oxford English Dictionary defines 'performance' as behaviour—the way in which organizations, teams and individuals get work done. Campbell (1990) believes that

'Performance is behaviour and should be distinguished from the outcomes because they can be contaminated by systems factors'.

A more comprehensive view of performance is achieved if it is defined as embracing both behavior and outcomes. This is well put by Brumbrach (1988): "Performance means both behaviors and results. Behaviors emanate from the performer and transform performance from abstraction to action. Not just the instruments for results, behaviors are also outcomes in their own right—the product or mental and physical effort applied to tasks—and can be judged apart from results."

Performance could, therefore, be regarded as behaviour—the way in which organizations, teams and individuals get work done. Campbell believes that 'Performance is behaviour and should be distinguished from the outcomes because they can be contaminated by systems factors.'

What is Competency?

Competencies are defined as "Skills and abilities, described in behavioral terms that are coach able, observable, measurable and critical to successful individual or organization's performance". While goals are the "What" of performance, competencies are the "How" of performance.

Companies are the knowledge, skills and personal attributes required for excellent performance in a job, role or specific business. Competency development is a carefully crafted process of research and data-gathering about firm's managers and employees as they perform their daily work, with the goal of determining the specific knowledge, skills and personal attributes required for excellent performance in these actual jobs, roles or businesses.

The competencies and the need to develop them translate into a personal development plan and the whole links into what is being tried to be achieved within the organization. Severn Trent Water has developed an interesting definition of competency as 'grouping of knowledge, skills and behaviors which may well be required in whole or in part within a variety of managerial situations'. Competency analysis is concerned with the behavioral dimensions of the roles.

Indicator of behaviours for achieving higher levels of performance can be categorized as given below:

- Personal drive
- Impact on results
- Analytical power
- Strategic thinking
- Creative thinking

- Decisiveness
- Commercial judgments
- Team management and leadership
- Interpersonal skills
- Ability to communicate
- Ability to adapt and cope with change and pressures
- Ability to plan and control projects

According to Lockett 1992, "The essence of performance management is the development of individuals with competence and commitment, working towards the achievement of shared meaningful objectives within an organization which supports and encourages their achievement."

Performance management is concerned with creating a culture in which organizational and individual learning and development are a continuous process. It provides means for the integration of learning and work so that everyone learns from the successes and challenges inherent in their day-to-day activities. The drive to enhance performance is making ever-greater demands on the knowledge and skills of the workforce and on people, who carry a much greater responsibility for their own performance.

The performance management for teams deserves more attention. War makes an effective team, the competencies required for teamwork and a definition o what can be regarded as a team for performance management purpose? Peer pressure in teamwork is an important factor. Performance management processes are important in tightly knit and long standing project teams.

Some of the key competencies for team work according to Hay/McBer (Gross 1995) are:

- Interpersonal Understanding
- Influence
- Customer Service Orientation
- Adaptability
- Team Work
- Oral Communication
- Achievement Orientation
- Organizational Commitment

Performance measurement for teams will be related to the purpose of the team and its particular objectives and standards of performance.

⌘ Underlying Characteristics ⌘

Competencies are underlying characteristics of people and indicate "ways of behaving or thinking, generalizing across situations, and enduring for a reasonably long period of time."

Five types of Competency Characteristics

1. *Motives:* The things a person consistently thinks about or wants that cause action. Motives "drive, direct, and select" behavior toward certain actions or goals and away from others.

    Example: Achievement-motivated people consistently set challenging goals for themselves, take personal responsibility for accomplishing them, and use feedback to do better.

2. *Traits:* Physical characteristics and consistent responses to situations or information.

    Example: Reaction time and good eyesight are physical trait competencies of combat pilots.

    Emotional self-control and initiative are more complex "consistent responses to situations." Some people don't "blow up" at others and do act "above and beyond the call of duty" to solve problems under stress. These trait competencies are characteristic of successful managers.

    Motives and competencies are intrinsic operant or self-starting "master traits" that predict what people will do on their jobs long term, without close supervision.

3. *Self-concept:* A person's attitudes, values, or self-image.

    Example: Self-confidence, a person's belief that he or she can be effective in almost any situation is part of that person's concept of self.

    A person's values are respondent or reactive motives that predict what he or she will do in the short-term and in situations where others are in charge. For example, someone who values being a leader is more likely to exhibit leadership behavior if he or she is told a task or job will be "a test of leadership ability." People who value being "in management" but do not intrinsically like or spontaneously think about influencing others at the motive level often attain management positions but then fail.

4. *Knowledge:* Information a person has in specific content areas.

    Example: A surgeon's knowledge of nerves and muscles in the human body.

    Knowledge is a complex competency. Scores on knowledge tests often fail to predict work performance because they fail to measure knowledge and skills in the ways they are actually used on the job. First, many knowledge tests measure rote memory, when what is really important is the ability to find information. Memory of specific facts is less important than knowing which facts exist that are relevant to a specific problem, and where to find them when needed. Second, knowledge tests are "respondent." They measure test takers' ability to choose which of several options is the right response, but not whether a person can act on the basis of knowledge. For example, the ability to choose which of five items is an effective argument is very different from the ability to stand up in a conflict situation and argue persuasively. Finally, knowledge best predicts what someone can do, not what he or she will do.

5. *Skill:* The ability to perform a certain physical or mental task.

    Example: A dentist's physical skill to fill a tooth without damaging the nerve; a computer programmer's ability to organize 50,000 lines of code in logical sequential order.

Mental or cognitive skill competencies include analytic thinking (processing knowledge and data, determining cause and effect, organizing data and plans) and conceptual thinking (recognizing patterns in complex data).

The type or level of a competency of has practical implications for human resource planning. As illustrated in fig. Knowledge and skill competencies tend to be visible, and relatively surface, characteristics of people. Self-concept, trait and motive competencies are more hidden, "deeper," and central to personality.

Surface knowledge and skill competencies are relatively easy to develop; training is the most cost-effective way to secure these employee abilities.

Core motive and trait competencies at the base of the personality iceberg are more difficult to assess and develop; it is most cost-effective to select for these characteristics.

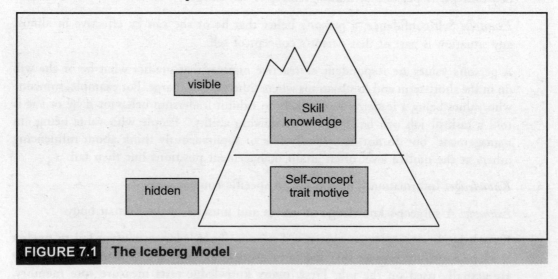

FIGURE 7.1 **The Iceberg Model**

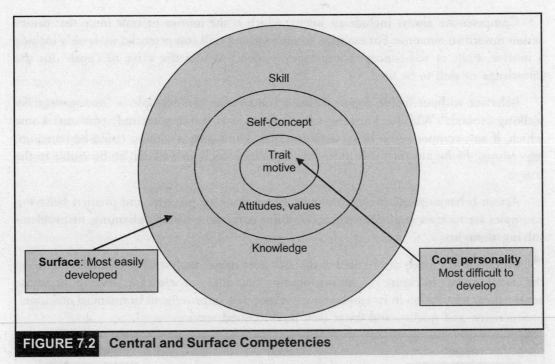

FIGURE 7.2   Central and Surface Competencies

Self-contempt competencies lie somewhere in between. Attitudes and values such as self-confidence (seeing one's self as a "manager" instead of a "technical/professional") can be changed by training, psychotherapy, and/or positive development experiences, albeit with more time and difficulty.

Many organizations select on the basis of surface knowledge and skill competencies ("we hire MBAs from good schools") and either assume that recruits have the underlying motive and trait competencies or that these can be instilled by good management. The converse is probably more cost-effective: organizations should select for core motive and trait competencies and teach the knowledge and skills required to do specific jobs. Or as one personnel director put it, "You can teach a turkey to climb a tree, but it is easier to hire a squirrel."

In complex jobs, competencies are relatively more important in predicting superior performance than are task-related skills, intelligence, or credentials. This is due to a "restricted range effective." In higher level technical, marketing professional, and managerial jobs, almost everyone has an I.Q. of 20 or above and an advanced degree from a good university. What distinguishes superior performers in these jobs is motivation, interpersonal skills, and political skills, all of which are competencies. It follows that competency studies are the most cost-effective way to staff these positions.

⌘ Causal Relationships ⌘

Motive, trait, and self-concept competencies predict skill behavior actions, which in turn predict job performance outcomes, as in the motive/trait – behavior – outcome causal flow model shown in figure.

Competencies always include an intent, which is the motive or trait force that causes action toward an outcome. For example, knowledge and skill competencies invariably include a motive, trait, or self-concept competency, which provides the drive or "push" for the knowledge or skill to be used.

Behavior without intent doesn't define a competency. An example is "management by walking around." Without knowing why a manager is walking around, you can't know which, if any, competency is being demonstrated. The manager's intent could be boredom, leg cramps, the monitoring of work to see if quality is high, or a desire "to be visible to the troops."

Action behaviours can include thought, where thinking precedes and predicts behavior. Examples are motives (e.g., thinking about doing something better), planning, or problem-solving thoughts.

Casuals fowl models can be used to do "risk assessment" analyses. For example, following the casuals arrows in Figure 7.3, an organization that does not select for, develop, or arouse achievement motivation in its employees can expect less improvement in financial outcomes, productivity, and quality, and fewer new products and services.

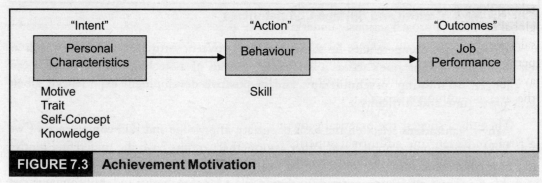

FIGURE 7.3 Achievement Motivation

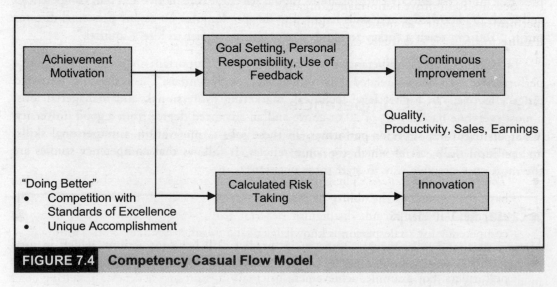

FIGURE 7.4 Competency Casual Flow Model

Criterion Reference is critical to our definition of competence. A characteristic is not a competency unles. it predicts something meaningful in the real world. Psychologist William James said the first rule for scientists should be that "A difference which makes no difference is no difference." A characteristic or credential that makes no difference in performance is not a competency and should not be used to evaluate people.

- *Superior Performance:* This is defined statistically as one standard deviation above average performance, roughly the level achieved by the top 1 person out of 10 in a given working situation.

- *Effective Performance:* This usually really means a "minimally acceptable" level of work, the lower cutoff point below which an employee would not be considered competent to do the job.

"One standard deviation" is used to define superior performance for two reasons. First, many research studies have documented the economic value of this level of performance to organizations. Depending on the complexity of the job, the value of one standard deviation above the mean is 19 to 48 percent of output for non-sales jobs, and 48 to 120 percent for sales. A minimum estimate of economic value of superior performance can be calculated by taking these percentages multiplied by the average salary per year for the job. In fact, this global estimate approach seriously undervalues jobs that Southeast firms found that superior salespeople (earning an average of $41,777), sold on average $6.7 million and average performers sold on average $3 million. The superior group sold 123 percent more than the average salespeople, a difference worth not 120 percent but 8,857 percent (or 89 times) the average employee salary.

These data suggest the practical economic value of a competency model that can help a firm find even one additional superior salesperson: $3.7 million—a benefit that can justify considerable investment in competency research.

Second, to improve performance, organizations should use the characteristics of superior performers as their "template," or "blueprint," for employee selection and development. Failure to do so is essentially to select and train to mediocrity—an organization's current average level of performance.

Categorizing Competencies

Competencies can be divided into two categories, "threshold" and "differentiating" according to the performance criterion they predict.

- *Threshold Competencies:* These are the essential characteristics (usually knowledge or basic skills, such as the ability to read) that everyone in a job needs to be minimally effective but that do not distinguish superior from average performers. A threshold competency for a salesperson is knowledge of the product or ability to fill out invoices.

- *Differentiating Competencies:* These factors distinguish superior form average performers. For example, achievement orientation expressed in a person's setting goals higher than those required by the organization, is a competency that differentiates superior from average salespeople.

Mapping Competencies

Competency Mapping beings with identifying key competencies for an organization and/or a job and incorporating those competencies throughout the various processes (i.e. job evaluation, training, recruitment) of the organization. With a competency based job description, the second step involves mapping those competencies throughout the organization's human resources processes. The competencies of the respective job description also become factors for assessment on performance evaluation. Using competencies helps in more objective evaluations based on displayed or not displayed behaviours. Taking competency mapping one step further, the results of performance evaluation can be used to identify in what competencies individuals need additional development or training.

Building Competency Models

There are three ways in which competencies models may be developed:

1. *Behavioral Indicators:* Behavioural indicators describe the behaviours, thought patterns, abilities and traits that contribute to superior performance.

2. *Evaluative Competency Levels:* Exceptional competencies of high performers are set as standards for evaluating competency levels of employees.

3. *Competencies Describing Job Requirements:* This approach is useful for organizations having multiple competency models. Competencies required in a particular job are described. Job specific competency models help in structuring focused appraisal and compensation decisions.

Profiling Competency Framework for a Particular Role

To identify role-specific competencies required industry specific, functional and behavioral competencies, which need to be developed for enhanced performance. The approach for developing a competency framework for a particular role is as proposed below:

1. Understand strategic business context of the organizations in term of its structure and environmental variables.

2. Detail role description for positions. Defining and scaling (relative importance and mastery level) of specific behaviours for each identified competency as a measure of performance.

3. Develop competency framework taking into consideration the core values and the culture of the organizations in addition to specific functional and level requirements. This should jell with the vision and mission of the company.

4. Validate the competency framework through a workshop, which should include functional experts and top management personnel in order to define critical and desirable competencies. And also to substantiate the extent to which the competencies differentiate between high and average performers by validating the content and criteria.

The competency framework includes technical competencies, behavioural competencies and the proficiency levels required for each competency. Each competency should be detailed in terms of behavioral indicators that enable observation and assessment.

Potential Assessment Centre for Competency Mapping

The linkage between competencies and roles is achieved through a competency mapping exercise, through which the most critical, success driving behaviors for specific roles are established. Against the validated competency framework, an individual's potential is identified through an Assessment Centre process as outlined below:

- Design Assessment Centre
- Conduct Assessment Centre
- Map individual competencies and gaps
- Finally assess organizational capability and gaps.

A link between people and competencies is established through an effective system of measuring the proficiency of an individual on the desired competencies for the role. The link between people and roles is established through effective measuring tools that evaluate the performance of the person in the role. On-the-job performance of the individual is evaluated on the basis of a performance management system.

The Assessment Centre is a powerful tool in the hands of the management for selection and development. As a selection tool it can be used for management promotions, fast tracks schemes, high potential list and change of functional role. As a development tool, it is helpful in succession planning, identifying training needs and career development.

Designing and conducting a potential Assessment Centre should follow basic principles in term of accuracy, fairness, reliability, legality, efficiency, multiple assessors, multiple tests and optimal stress to increase performance. It would involve two types of exercises, i.e., group exercises and individual exercises.

⌘ Group Exercises ⌘

For potential assessment, the following group exercises are conducted:

- *Assigned Role Exercises:* Used to assess negotiating skills, decision-making skills, and risk-taking skills;

- *Unassigned Role Exercises:* Used to assess ability to handle uncertainty, change orientation, ethical behaviour and global orientation; and

- *Team Exercises:* Used to assess ability to work in a team and solve problems efficiently.

⌘ Individual Exercises ⌘

For potential assessment, the following individual exercises are conducted:

- *In-Basket Exercises:* Used to assess ability to plan, organize, decide, manage and delegate;

- *Learning skill Inventory/Psychometric Inventories:* Used to assess ability to learn, leverage knowledge and indicate behavioral patterns; and

- *Interpersonal Effectiveness Module:* Used to assess interpersonal effectiveness, excommunication skills, patience and interpersonal skills.

Inputs for analysis of an individual's potential and behavioral patterns are also collected through multilateral feedback (self, peer, subordinate, customer and superior assessment), behavioral event interviews, career aspiration interview, career history, etc. In order to minimize assessors' bias and ensure objectivity and uniformity multiple trained assessors for each competencies assessment are used.

The competencies gaps can be find out by comparing the desired competency (proficiency) levels and displayed competency levels as indicated in the figure given below:

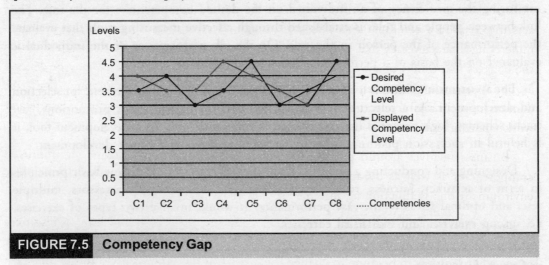

FIGURE 7.5 Competency Gap

Based on the above exercises, feedback details for individuals on their strengths and developmental areas are prepared. Positive gaps between desired and displayed competencies indicate areas of improvement; negative gaps indicate strengths. Each gap area needs to be analyzed and prioritized into major and minor gaps. These gaps are to addressed at the individual, departmental and organizational levels by agreeing on milestones for each individual in terms of projects, job rotations, transfer, training and job enrichment. Setting up a Development Monitoring Cell in HR would help in creating a project plan with deadlines and escalation possibilities with a feedback system for feedback from bosses and individuals. Average assessment results are used to identify strengths and gaps in an organization's capabilities.

Competency Mapping and Performance Management

Traditionally, a number of factors that gave the measure of performance were technical skills, number of years of experience, education, personality traits, IQ, etc. Organizations have been relying on scholastic achievements, standardized tests and other pedagogical measures to recruit, keep and assess their workforce. However, researchers were forced to rethink this strategy due to the fact that people fitting in these criteria were not always successful in their jobs. This issue was first publicly addressed in 1973 by Harvard University Psychologist, in his paper titled, "Testing for Competency rather than for Intelligence" wherein he observed that the most academic overachievers are not always the most successful people in their profession. According to him, job selection and performance should be based on desired, observable behaviour instead of traditional standardized tests. Although there was no empirical basis for McClelland's conclusions, the approach gained popularity and acceptance within the human resource community and continues to do so.

Competencies are a broader term referring to an individual's demonstrated knowledge, skills, behaviours, experience, life view and values and constitute observable, behavioral acts that require a combination of all these attributes to execute. Competencies are those underlying characteristics that are indicative of one's performance in terms of how he or she behaves and thinks in a work situation and over a period of time. This may be defined as behaviors that determine and demonstrate exceptional performance. They are demonstrated in a job context and, as such, are influenced by an organization's culture and work environment.

Business revolves around people. Breakthroughs in performance come via improved competencies as well as by acquiring new competencies depending upon the business environment one is functioning in.

So we have on the one hand competencies for any given post and human resources of the organization on the other hand. The two require to be matched. Besides we have to see what requires to be done to change the quality of human resources in the direction of required competencies. An ideal match is perhaps never reached but one can strive towards it.

Various human resource systems in an organization can be integrated with competencies as the focal point as described in Table 7.4.

TABLE 7.4	Human Resources Systems in an Organization	
S.No.	**HR System**	**Competencies as Focal Point**
1.	Workforce Planning	• Organization competency gap analysis
2.	Selection	• Position profiling
		• Interview questions to match positional requirement
3.	Performance management	• Competencies linked to goals
4.	Compensation	• Pay increase based on competency development
		• Recognition based on demonstrating competencies
		• Career bands based on competencies
5.	Career Development	• Competencies as road map for career development
6.	Training	• Competency assessment tools
		• Development activities linked to competencies
7.	Leadership Development	• Leadership competency profiles
8.	Succession Planning	• Planning for future leadership needs

There are four elements in the performance management process against which managers are assessed. These are:

- *Strategic Contribution:* What managers need to do in terms of the achievement of targets;

- *Role Performance:* What managers need to do in terms of maintaining and continually improving their core role;

- *Common Responsibilities and Behaviours:* A measure of behavior in accordance with company values; and

- *Competency Assessment:* What managers need to do in terms of developing their underlying skills and knowledge.

This process has been specifically designed to provide an integrated approach to managing performance by giving direction, targets and feedback and ensuring appropriate individual and team development.

Competency Model

It is the 'road map' that defines the behaviour imperative to achieve desired results. It helps employees understand how and what to deliver. It is a flexible tool and supports specific needs like employee orientation, employee development, performance management, coaching, developing career strategies, assessments and succession planning.

The initial step is to get every employee to benchmark himself. Considering that employees have different competencies, the setting up of standards should vary. When the benchmarks set are inefficient, the organization loses some of its good performers, as they believe they have accomplished the highest in the company. Similar damage is done when the standards are very high the average performers get disillusioned at the targets achieved. Benchmarks should enable the full realization of employee potential.

The main reason for the growing use of competency mapping in business lies in their strategic value as performance improvement vehicles for both organizations and individuals. Competency mapping has several performance-related benefits. These highlight the clusters of knowledge, skills and personal attributes that lead to high performance. These can be understood and learned by all organization members through use of effective training, development, performance management and compensation systems.

Competency mapping serve as behavior-based standards of performance against which people and organizations can be measured over time. As such, they provide both a behavioural and conceptual vision for the kinds of performance necessary to fulfill business strategies.

Indian Oil has recently carried out this exercise for its senior executives. Based on the gap identified with respect to benchmark roles and competencies, fresh training inputs have been planned for a select group of executives. Job rotations and career successions planning would be linked to this process in due course of time.

Companies like Amoco, DuPont, Federal Express, Proctor and Gamble and Sony have been developing competency models not only to improve employee performance in the workplace but also to improve the quality of the employees hired. Initiative has been taken by Indian companies including Indian Oil Corporation for competency mapping and they plan to integrate this with their Performance Management System.

Competency Mapping – A Tool for Optimizing the Human Capital

Competency mapping forms an excellent tool for optimizing the human capital. By identifying the key competencies for an organization or a particular position in an organization, and using it for job evaluation, recruitment, training and development, performance management, succession planning, etc. the organization effectively communicates what it actually expects from them. The competency framework serves as the bedrock for all HR applications. As a result of competency mapping, all the HR processes like talent induction, management development, appraisals and training yield much better results.

Competency mapping involves identifying the competencies that will be needed by people working in an organization. The level of competency needed by employees at each level must also be specified. This depends on the type of job they do and the environment in which the organization functions. Once this is identified, the remaining process becomes easier. The next step will be to match the existing level of competencies with what is actually required, and take measures to bridge the gap.

"Can a round peg fit a square hole? So can't a wrong employee in a right organization."

The future of an organization lies with the people working there. The organization will have to find a correct person who will fulfill its expectations or will have to chisel and shape up the existing employee to fit its expectations. The more efficient they become in facing the demands of the environment, the more effective will be the organization.

✼ Core Competencies, Behaviour Pattern and Elemental Build up ✼

Communication Skills

This does not necessarily refer to the English speaking skill. There are various factors leading to effective communication.

Competency	Behavioural aspects	Elements
Communication Skills	• Ability to express ones thoughts clearly • Ability to make others understand you • Ability to listen to others • Ability to write your thoughts clearly • Ability to summarize ones ideas in a precise way	Group skill Initiative Empathy Patience

Interpersonal Relationship Building Ability

This deals with how well a person is able to socialize and make a close bond with others around him.

Competency	Behavioural aspects	Elements
Interpersonal Relationship Building Ability	• Ability to work in groups or wok as a team • Ability to initiate talks • Ability to understand other's problems • Ability to empathize with others • Courage to apologize on committing mistakes	• Group skill • Initiative • Empathy • Patience

Negotiating Ability

The need for this skill arises when two or more parties argue on a common issue and each party wants a conclusion on it prefers.

Competency	Behavioural aspects	Elements
Negotiating Ability	• Ability to reason • Ability to be ethical during the process • Ability to predict the next argument of opponents • Ability to survive till the end and not to surrender • Ability to associate various arguments and think logically	• Stress management • Risk taking • Reasoning • Responsibility taking

Critical Thinking Ability

The business environment is full of uncertainties and surprises. One must have the ability to think and act under unforeseen and critical situations.

Competency	Behavioural aspects	Elements
Critical Thinking Ability	• Ability to think logically under stress • Ability to remain confident under critical situations • Ability to take risk • Ability to take up responsibility when something goes wrong	• Stress management • Risk taking • Reasoning • Responsibility taking

Data Management Ability

The documents and files possessed by a company are of great importance. The information has to be managed effectively.

Competency	Behavioural aspects	Elements
Forecasting Ability	• Ability to receive correct data • Ability to transmit accurate data • Ability to store data in order and safely • Ability to understand how much of data is to be revealed to a person	• Data reception ability • Data transmission ability • Data storing ability

Forecasting Ability

As already said, the business environment is highly uncertain. One has to possess the ability to foresee future changes and competitions.

Competency	Behavioural aspects	Elements
Forecasting Ability	• Constant review of business environment • Updating oneself with global business happenings • Adequate logic and reasoning	• Prediction • Environment scanning • Reasoning

Creativity

It is not only the quality of the product that plays a role in the market. It is also how different our products are compared to that of our competitors, which attracts our customers. This requires creativity. This will also bring about a huge difference in the way regular day-to-day activities are carried out.

Competency	Behavioural aspect	Elements
Creativity	• Ability to think differently • A keen sense of colors • Ability to present differently • Courage to accept and present the ideas	• Accepting creativity • Practicing creativity • Encouraging creativity

Business Environment Understanding

Success is possible in business only if proper understanding and analyses of the happenings of the business environment is made.

Competency	Behavioural aspects	Elements
Business Environment Understanding	• Regular scanning of the business environment • Updating the happenings in the global business environment • Proper understanding of the happenings within the organization • Ability to relate the happenings in the outer world to the business	• Updating skill • Environmental scanning ability • Organizational understanding

Coordination/Partnership Skill

Any business cannot survive if people were to work as individuals. It requires people of one department to coordinate and work with people of other department. Also people of the same department must be able to coordinate among themselves and also with external environment.

Competency	Behavioural aspects	Elements
Coordination/Partnership Skill	• Ability to work in teams • Knowledge about the activities of other departments • Ability to receive and transfer information	• Job skill • Information handling • Team working

Instruction Following Ability

However flat today's organizations have become; there still exists a certain amount of hierarchy. Employees must be able to receive orders from their superior and execute the instructions correctly.

Competency	Behavioural aspects	Elements
Instruction Following Ability	• Ability to listen keenly to the instructions given • Ability to accept instructions • Ability to be oriented towards the target • Ability to retain interest in the work being done. • Ability to build trust in the minds of superior about the quality of work one does	• Trust building • Target orientation • Interest retention • Instruction accepting

Knowledge Updating

Any employee must be in a position to update his/her knowledge with regard to the happenings of the outside world. This is absolutely necessary for servicing in today's business environment.

Competency	Behavioural aspects	Elements
Knowledge Updating	• Ability to scan external environment • Ability to search for information • Ability to logically relate the information obtained	• Business environment understanding • Information searching • Information relating

Presentation Skill

Employees in any organization will have to present their reports or analyses to people within the organization and also the others outside.

Competency	Behavioural aspects	Elements
Presentation Skill	• Proper body language • Ability to simplify the presentation • Ability to have a control over the audience • Ability to answer the questions asked	• Body language • Simplifying the facts • Convincingly answering • Audience controlling

Analyzing/Problem Solving Ability

When faced with unexpected situations, the employee must be able to tackle it. In case any problem arises; the employee must be able to solve it.

Competency	Behavioural aspects	Elements
Analyzing/ Problem solving ability	• Ability to identify the actual problem • Ability to think under stress • Ability to reason out or think logically • Ability to give long term solutions • Ability to take up responsibility when something goes wrong	• Problem identification • Long-term solution giving • Initiative • Reasoning • Responsibility accepting

Counseling Ability

When employees have some problem, naturally their performance in the organization goes done. The problem could be in their personal life or in the organization. Whatever be the case, the employees require a good counselor who can lend their support to the employees with problems.

Competency	Behavioural Aspects	Elements
Counseling Ability	• Ability to lend a listening ear to the people with problem • Ability to listen without interrupting or advising • Ability to empathize with the other person • Ability to accept the person the way he/she is • Ability to have a proper body language	• Understanding skill • Empathy • Body language • Listening skill

Other Competencies

Apart from these competencies, there are others that are specific to the job done. The requirements of those competencies vary depending upon the time and situation. Those skills are:

• Financial forecasting ability

• Customs handling ability

- Computer knowledge
- Customer handling ability, etc.

Potential Appraisal

In consonance with the philosophy of human resource development that has replaced the erstwhile personnel management in many organizations, more emphasis has been laid on the appraisal of the employees potential in addition to their performance. Performance is a thing of the past, while potential includes the possible knowledge, skills, and attitudes the employee may possess for better performance.

The purposes of a potential review are:

1. To inform employees of heir future prospectus.

2. To enable the organization to draft a management succession program.

3. To update training and recruitment activities.

4. To advice employees about the work to be done to enhance their career opportunities.

The following are some of the requirements and steps to be followed when introducing a potential appraisal systems.

1. *Role Description:* A good potential appraisal system would be based on clarity of roles and functions associated with the different roles in an organization. This requires extensive job description to be made available for each job. These job descriptions should spell out the various functions involved in performing the job.

2. *Qualities Required:* Besides job descriptions, it is necessary to have a detailed list of qualities required to perform each of these functions. These qualities may be broadly divided into four categories-(1) technical knowledge and skills, (2) managerial capabilities and qualities, (3) behavioral capabilities, and (4) conceptual capabilities.

3. *Indicators of Qualities:* A good potential appraisal system besides listing down the functions and qualities would also are various mechanisms for judging these qualities in a given individual. Some of the mechanisms of r judging these qualities are- (2) rating by others, (b) psychological tests, (c) simulation games and exercises, (d) performance appraisal records.

4. *Organizing the System:* Once the functions, the qualities required to perform these functions, indicators of these qualities, and mechanisms for generating these indicators are clear, the organization is in a sound position to establish and operate the potential appraisal system. Such establishment requires clarity in organizational policies and systematization of its efforts.

5. *Feedback:* If the organization believes in the development of human resources it should attempt to generate a climate of openness. Such a climate is required for helping the employees to understand the strengths and weaknesses and to create opportunities

for every employee to know the results of assessment. He should be helped to understand the qualities actually required for performing the role for which he thinks he has the potential, the mechanisms used by the organization to appraise his potential, and the results of such an appraisal.

A good potential appraisal system provides opportunities continuously for the employee to know his strengths and weaknesses. These are done through periodic counseling and guidance sessions by either the personnel department or the managers concerned. This should enable the employee to develop realistic self-perceptions and plan his own career and development.

Self-appraisal

Development or change takes place only if the appraise is interested in development or change. Such a desire is normally an outcome of self-review or reflection. It is an opportunity for the appraisee to recapitulate and list down his accomplishments and failures. The most important part of self-appraisal is the process of review and reflection through performance analysis.

A thorough performance analysis done prior to the review discussion helps in making the review discussion fruitful. Review discussion aims at making the appraiser and the appraise understand each other better by communicating the performance analysis of the appraisee's performance. It is in this discussion that the appraiser should:

1. Complement that appraisee for his accomplishment s and good qualities;

2. Understand and appreciate his difficulties and make action plans to help him in the future;

3. Understand the appraisee's perception of the situation and correct the perceptions if necessary;

4. Help him to recognize his strong points and weak points;

5. Communicate the expectations of the appraiser form the appraisee; and

6. Identify developmental needs of the appraisee and chalk out a course of action for meeting these needs.

Team working is the trend therefore, Team Appraisal for –

1. Common purpose/goal

2. Agreed norms

3. Independent function

4. Each member has specific role

5. Complimentary skill

6. Common leadership

7. Mutual accountability

   Example: Indian cricket team

Performance Appraisal Assessment

The quality of an appraiser is much more crucial than the appraisal methods, It is desirable to make the immediate superior a party to the appraisal program. The assessment can be accomplished by an individual or by a combination of the immediate superior, other managers acquainted with the assessee's work, a higher level manager, a personal officer, the assessee himself, and the assessee's subordinates. Training of appraisers has been largely stressed as a measure to improve performance appraisals. Appraisers can be trained with a view to improving their ability to evaluate subordinates and discuss evaluations with them effectively.

The following questions can provide an assessment of performance appraisal system:

1. What purposes does the organization want its performance appraisal system to serve?

2. Do the appraisal forms really get the information to serve the purposes?

3. Are the appraisal forms designed to minimum errors and ensure consistency?

4. Do the processes for the appraisal serve the purpose of effective communication between the appraiser and the appraisee?

5. Are superiors rewarded for correctly evaluating and developing their employees?

6. Are the evaluation and developmental components separated?

7. Are superiors relatively free from task interference in doing performance appraisal?

8. Are the appraisals being implemented correctly?

The following questions serve as guidelines for assessing the end-product of performance appraisal:

1. Did the appraisal session motivate the subordinate?

2. Did the appraisal build a better relationship between the supervisor and the subordinate?

3. Did the subordinate come out with a clear idea of where he or she stands?

4. Did the superior arrive at a fairer assessment of the subordinate?

5. Did the superior learn something new about the subordinate?

6. Did the subordinate learn something new about the superior and pressures he or she faces?

7. Does the subordinate have a clear idea of what corrective actions to be taken to improve his/her own performance?

Executive Performance Contents and Criteria

1. Job Knowledge
2. Quality of Work
3. Leadership
4. Problem Solving and Decision Making
5. Planning and Organizing
6. Responsibility and Accountability
7. Customer Service
8. Business Judgment
9. Ability to Work with Others
10. Motivating Others
11. Creativity
12. Initiative and Enthusiasm
13. Interpersonal Competence
14. Communication Skills
15. Integrity and Courage
16. Honesty and Sincerity

BOX 7.1	Sample Format of Criteria used in Performance Assessment

Periodicity of Appraisal (tick any one):

Quarterly _____ Half-yearly _____ Yearly

Performance Criteria (tick any one):

Exceeds Performance _____ Meets Performance

Below Performance _____ Standards _____ Standards

Performance Appraisal Guidelines

- Keep the system simple, and keep the paperwork burden down.
- It is a managerial tool to be used for improving results under the manager's province. But it should not be punitively and unjustly.

- Establish and maintain two entirely different performance appraisal systems: One geared to making pay decisions and the other designed to yield information about employee development.

- Once a system has been decided upon, apply it for several years; in other words don't tinker with the system annually.

- Do not rely on formal performance appraisals to do the entire job in communicating on performance; day-to-day informal contacts must do the bulk of the job.

- Review performance formally at least once in a year and also whenever there has been a repetition of negative employee behaviour.

Performance Appraisal in Practice

Traditionally appraisals are carried out by the supervisors of the employees. Some companies do follows self appraisal and compare the same with the traditional appraisal of the supervisors. A new approach has been recently enunciated by the western management gurus, which is known as 360 degree appraisal whereby appraisals are required to be carried out not only by the supervisors, but also by those supervised (subordinates) and peers. This approach also needs a re-look in the context of leadership concepts being practiced universally. If one requires to be appraised on how well he performs the leadership role, the appraisal should originate form the followers (bottom to top approach) and not form their supervisors alone.

While the supervisors can appraise, on the performance standards, goals, targets, achievements, the leadership attributes need to be appraised only by those being supervised. This argument is quite valid for higher level executives including CEOs. Therefore, all the three approaches top-bottom, bottom-top and peer level appraisal – will be very relevant. Perhaps, appropriate weightage is required to be assigned for appraisals being carried out in the 360 degree system, which is yet to take off seriously in many organizations.

It is quite disappointed to not that appraisals are not being carried out with the due importance and seriousness they deserve, though the systems provide scope for periodic and timely appraisals. Normally appraisals are being carried out once a year or at the most twice a year as per the existing practice. Many organizations do follow monthly and quarterly appraisals for managers (trainees) till they are confirmed, and follow the by-annual or annual appraisal system thereafter. Appraisal is a continue process, to e scientifically carried out day in day out, If one has to seriously carry out appraisals.

Performance Review and Feedback

Performance review or evaluation interview is necessary with a view to communicate effectively with each employee on his performance. The main thrust of the system is to effectively develop the communication process between the appraiser and the appraisee so that individual strengths and weaknesses are identified and necessary corrective actions taken. If the performance of the employee falls short of the standards set in the process of goal setting, the employee is encouraged to improve his performance. Similarly, if the employee has exceeded the standard, he is encouraged to accept a higher goal.

Evaluation interviews are not easy to conduct, and if they are poorly handled they may lead to hostility and greater misunderstanding. Performance review can be quite beneficial to the organization and to the individual involvement if done properly. Consequently, many companies have spent a great deal of time and effort on training their supervisors to handle evaluation interviews more effectively. To ensure that no essential part of the interview is left out, supervisors are often encouraged to follow a standardized outline. For example:

1. The supervisor tells the subordinate the purpose of the interview, and that it is designed to help him do a better job.

2. The supervisor then presents the evaluation, giving the strong points first and then the weak points.

3. Next the supervisor asks for general comments on the evaluation.

4. The supervisor then tries to encourage the subordinate to give his own picture of his progress, the problems he is meeting, what he can do to solve them, and how his supervisor can help him.

The interviews ends with a discussion of what the subordinate can do by himself to overcome his weak points and what the supervisor can do to help. The supervisor tries to accept any criticism or aggression on the part of the subordinate without argument or contradiction.

Feedback is important in letting your employees know how they are doing. Without feedback, employee tend to assume that their performance is acceptable. If they make the wrong assumption for an extended period of time, a serious performance problem can develop-one that may be hard to correct. There are two types of feedback—positive and corrective. Providing regular feedback is important if you want to demonstrate to your employees that your employees that you care about them. It is also another way to make the human-touch appraisal process an ongoing activity.

Feedback in Performance Review— Mirroring the Strength and Weaknesses

Mirror, Mirror on the wall-

Who is fairest of all—Snow-white

"A successful man is one who can lay a firm foundation with the bricks others have thrown at him" says David Brinkley.

If there are two people who think alike, one is redundant, say some other.

Feedback communication is most critical activity in performance management system.

A dyadic process between the employee and his boss.

1. Assumption that the reviewer has superior competence and knowledge, has absorbed performance closely for longer period.

2. Another set of assumption are how we see our self and how others see us. This increases our self-awareness.

Enhanced self-awareness is key to high performance as leader.

Feedback is transmitting information from one part of the system to another part to do corrective action or initiate new action. Built in the system itself. Feedback is considered positive because it is with view to further development and improvement. It is helping people to help themselves. It is to assist appraise to make change in his work life or to accept or adjust to change. It helps –

1. To voice concern to problems

2. To come to term with his own feelings.

3. Understand his own motives and aspirations more clearly.

4. To sharpen his saw.

"In given 8 hours to cut a tree, I will spend 6 hours to sharpen my axe." – Abraham Lincoln

"Sharpening our skills from time to time is the key to success".

Performance feedback provides information that helps employee to alter, change and maintain/develop their, skills, behaviors and/or attitudes so that the organization continues to operate effectively. Self feedback is highly desirable feature of PMS but there is always a need for managers, colleagues and customers (internal + external) to provide holistic feedback based on their suggestion.

A customized version of Johari Window as a way of evaluating awareness effectiveness of manager-managee roles in the context of career planning. (Potential identification) 360° feedback involves collective awareness perception about persons behaviour and impact that behavior is likely to have on performance.

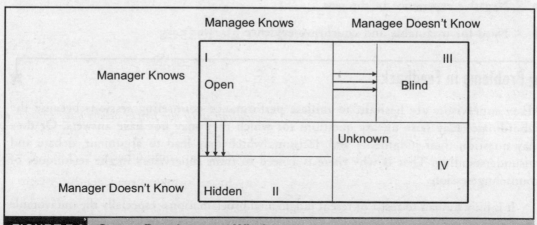

FIGURE 7.6 *Career Development Windows*

⌘ Two Types of Feedback

Positive/Praise: Good feedback includes information on both good and poor performance. Although most people are a lot more comfortable giving feedback on good performance than they are on poor performance, some guidelines must be followed when giving praise so that the feedback is useful in terms of future performance. First, praise should be sincere and given only when it is deserved. If praise is given repeatedly and when it is not deserved, employees are not able to see when a change in direction may be needed. Second, praise should be about specific behaviors or results and be given within context so that employees know what they need to attempt to repeat in the future. For example, a manager can say the following: "John, thanks for providing such excellent service to our client. Your efforts helped us renew our contract with them for another two years. It's these types of behaviors and results that our group needs to achieve our goal for this year. And, this is exactly what our company is all about – providing outstanding customer service." Third, in giving praise, managers should take their Time rather than rushing through the information and looking embarrassed. Finally, avoid giving praise by referring to the absence of the negative, for example, "not bad" or "better than last time." Instead, praise should emphasize the positives and be phrased in terms of "I like the way you did that….." or "I admire how you did that…."

Negative Feedback: Negative feedback includes information that performance has fallen short of accepted standards the goal of providing negative feedback is to help employees improve their performance in the future; it is not to punish, embarrass, or chastise them. However, it is important to give negative feedback when this is warranted because the consequences of not doing so can be detrimental for the organisation as a whole.

In spite of the need to address poor performance, managers are usually not very comfortable providing negative feedback. Why is this so? Consider the following reasons:

- Negative reactions and consequences

- Negative experience in the past

- Need for irrefutable and conclusive evidence

⌘ Problems in Feedback

Many supervisors are hesitant to initiate performance counseling sessions because the subordinates may raise uneasy questions for which they may not have answers. Or they may question their judgments and decisions which may lead to argument, debate and misunderstanding. That is why there is a need to train supervisors in the techniques of counseling session.

It is only human to resist or resent judgmental proclamations- especially the unfavorable ones-even where these are accompanied by rational explanation; and it is natural that such resistance or resentment substantially blocks positive response.

Where the process is analytical, with a view to exploring ways of improving the managee's role performance or identifying her developmental and growth needs, the response can be more open and receptive.

Judgemental process can be unilateral, but analytical processes are best when inclusive and participatory.

Letting an employee know where he stands' is a fairly comprehensive process, while for recognizing a managee's good work the discussion can be much more selective in content. It is clear, however that each type of discussion requires somewhat different skills to handle.

Delivering feedback is an art that requires the manager to put on a host of hats and play a range of roles like that: of (1) a counselor, (2) a parent. (3) a psychiatrist, (4) a friend and (5) sometimes, but only some times, a boss'. Acquiring feedback skills, both in giving and receiving feedback requires years of experience, genuine interest in the managee's well-being, an innate sense of fair play, maturity that enables managers to process managee reactions online ad shift roles as appropriate.

⌘ Need for Feedback after Performance ⌘

General Perceptions

Most theories of work motivation point out that before employees can improve their performance, they must know how well they are currently doing.

Enquiries help employees to analyze and understand –

1.   His job performance and job behaviors

2.   His strength & weakness

3.   His potential

4.   His environment

In order to improve performance employees need feedback & also guidelines in reaching the next levels of performance. Feedback has to be positive & corrective in nature.

Two important principles to be kept in view are shown below:

1.   Feedback should be given as close as possible in time to when the relevant performance occurs.

2.   The performance should be documented

   (i)   Managee's performance as planned a start of the year.

   (ii)   Managee's performance plan as modified during the year.

   (iii) Managee's actual performance recorded during the year.

   (iv) Actual overall performance of the managee's workgroup during the year etc.

Feedback sessions can be uncomfortable & anxiety provoking experience for both the parties, the appraiser can be apprehensive about discussing a negative evaluation with the appraise. The same way it becomes difficult for the appraise to accept & digest negative feedback.

1.   Most of the time it creates ugly situation.

2.   Therefore conducting feedback in reviews requires a great deal of skill and expertise.

Objective/Importance of Feedback Discussion

Feedback session aims at development of appraise as well as appraiser. However, it focuses more on appraisee in:

1.   Helping him to realize his potential as a manager or a leader etc.

2.   Helping him to understand himself – his strengths and his weakness.

3.   Providing him an opportunity to acquire more insight into his behavior and analyze the dynamics of such behavior.

4.   Helping him to have better understanding of environment.

5.   Increasing his personal and interpersonal effectiveness by giving him feedback about his behavior and assisting him in analyzing his interpersonal competence. Encouraging him to set goals for further improvements

6.   Encouraging him to generate alternatives for dealing with various problems.

7.   Creating an empathic atmosphere to share and discuss his tensions, conflicts, concerns and problems.

8.   Helping him to develop various action plans for further improvement.

9.   Helping him to review in a non-threatening way his progress in achieving various objectives.

The main objective of performance counseling is to help the employee to overcome his weaknesses and to reinforce his strength. In this sense it is a developmental process where the supervisor and the subordinate discuss the past performance with a view to help the subordinate to improve and become more effective in future.

Appraisal reports serve as spring board for discussion. One of the fallout effects of this dyadic interaction is the identification of training needs. Counseling provides an opportunity to the supervisor to give feedback to the subordinate on the performance and performance related behavior. Feedback can be an effective tool provided that:

1.   Both negative and positive feedback are communicated.

2.   It is not just an opinion but is backed by data. In other words it should be descriptive and not evaluative.

3. It focuses on behaviour rather than on the individual.

4. It is timely. Delayed feedback is neither helpful nor effective. On the other hand, it might be seen as criticism which may further deteriorate the distortions.

For appraiser, it helps –

1. To know more about appraise

2. To know conditions at work (task clarity, ability, motivation, organizational support)

3. To enable appraiser to influence appraise in terms of opportunity to make an impact & prove himself.

4. To know/develop leadership style.

Suggestions to Enhance Feedback Effectiveness

1. *Timeliness:* Feedback should be delivered as close to the performance event as possible. For feedback to be most meaningful, it must be given immediately after the event.

2. *Frequency:* Feedback should be provided on an ongoing basis, daily if possible. If performance improvement is an ongoing activity, then feedback about performance should also be provided on an ongoing basis.

3. *Specificity:* Feedback should include specific work behaviors, results and the situation where these behaviors and results were observed. Feedback is not about the employee and how the employee "is," but about behaviors and results and situations in which these behaviors and results took place.

4. *Verifiability:* Feedback should include information that is verifiable and accurate. It should not be based on inferences or rumors. Using information that is verifiable leads to more accurate feedback and subsequent acceptance.

5. *Consistency:* Feedback should be consistent. In other words, information on specific of performance should not vary unpredictably between overwhelming praise and harsh criticism.

6. *Privacy:* Feedback should be given at a place and time that avoids any potential embarrassment. This applies to both criticism and praise, because some employees, due to personality or cultural background, may not wish to be rewarded in public.

7. *Consequences:* Feedback should include contextual information that allows the employee to understand the importance and consequences of the behaviors and results in question. For example, if an employee has become frustrated and behaved inappropriately with an angry customer and the customer's complaint has not been addressed satisfactorily, feedback should explain the impact of these behaviors (i.e., the customer's problem was not resolved, the customer was upset, and likely to not give repeat business to the organization).

8. *Description first, evaluation second:* Feedback should first focus on describing behaviors and results rather than on evaluating and judging behaviors and results. It's better first to report what has been observed and, once there is agreement on what happened, to evaluate what has been observed. If evaluation takes place first, employees may become defensive and feedback may be rejected.

9. *Performance continuum:* Feedback should describe performance as a continuum, going from less to more in the case of good performance and from more to less in the case of poor performance. In other words, feedback should include information on how to display good performance behaviors more often and poor performance behaviors less often. Thus, performance is a matter of degree, and even the worst performer is likely to show nuggets of good performance that can be described as a starting point for a discussion on how to improve performance.

10. *Pattern identification:* Feedback is most useful if it is about a pattern of poor performance rather than isolated events or mistakes.

    Identifying a pattern of poor performance also allows for a better understanding of the causes leading to poor performance.

    (i) *Confidence in the employee:* Good feedback includes a statement that the manager has confidence that the employee will be able to improve her performance. It is important for the employee to hear this from the manager. This reinforces the idea the feedback is about performance and not the performer. Note, however, that this should be done only if the manager indeed believes the employee can improve her performance. In the case of a chronic poor performance, this type of information could be used out of context later if the employee is fired.

    (ii) *Advice and idea generation:* Feedback can include advice given by the supervisor on how to improve performance. In addition, however, the employee should play an active role in generating ideas on how to improve performance in the future.

Conditions for Effective Feedback Discussions

1. *General climate of openness & mutuality:* A climate of minimum trust and openness is essential for effective Feedback discussion and for building a psychological safe environment.

2. *General helpful & empathic attitude of management:* Feedback discussion involves effective helping which is not possible unless the appraiser has a helping attitude and has empathy for the appraise.

3. *Sense of uninhibited participation by the subordinates in the performance review process:* It is a process of developing dialogue which eventually contributes to better understanding on the part of appraise.

4. *Dialogic relationship in goal setting & performance review:* Joint participation by the employee and his reporting officer is necessary both in goal setting as well as in the

performance review. Without such a collaborative effort, Feedback discussion does not achieve its purpose.

5. *Focus on work-oriented behaviour:* The main purpose of feedback discussion is to help the employee in improving his performance.

6. *Focus on work-related problems & difficulties:* Analysis of performance, therefore, becomes the basis of feedback discussion.

7. *Avoidance of discussion of salary & other rewards:* The main purpose of Feedback discussion is to use performance appraisal in planning and improvement of the employee, rather than understanding relationship between performance and reward. Bringing such a discussion into the feedback discussion may vitiate its main purpose.

   (i)   Feedback discussion is a means and not the end in itself.

   (ii) Performance improvement and development requires congenial culture and involvement of employees.

   (iii) While giving feedback, facilitating climate is require to be created.

✤ Different Types of Feedback Interviews ✤

- "Tell & Sell"
- "Tell & Listen"
- "Problem-solving".

Tell & Sell

In a tell and sell feedback interview, the supervisor tells the employee how good or bad the employee's performance has been and then attempts to persuade the employee to accept this judgment. The employee has no input into the evaluation. Because it is very directive and one-sided, the tell and sell feedback can lead to defensiveness, resentment, and frustration on the part of the subordinate. The employee may accept the results of the interview and may not be committed to achieving the goals that are set. This may lead to poor performance in the future.

Skill requires –

Directive leadership

1. To persuade and secure workable acceptance

2. To show restrain caution, control

3. To use influence and power effectively

4. To motivate employee to accept

5. To deal with and soften resistance

6. To show patience, retain control

7. To manage unexpressed conflicts

8. To motivate managees through authoritarian leadership.

This type is used for young, new, in experienced employee – who are in search of a father figure in position of authority, a mediocre willing to follow authority.

In terms of time and effort, this type of discussion is efficient and economical; and can produce positive results under the right conditions.

Tell & Listen

In the tell and listen approach to the feedback interview, the supervisor tells the employee what has been right and wrong with the employee's past performance but then gives the employee a chance to react. The extent of the subordinate's participation in the interview can vary widely. The subordinate may simply be given an opportunity to react to the supervisor's statements or may be permitted to offer a full self-assessment, challenging the supervisor's assessment.

This type provides for in-depth exploration. The manager communicates his conclusions or feedback to the managee, and then provides an opportunity for his to respond. The manager patiently listens to the managee's facts and arguments without interrupting or refuting him. In the active-listening mode, he, in fact, prompts and encourages the managee to bring out any frustration and negative feelings.

Manager assumes the role of a counsellor through:

1. *Active listing:* To understand the managee's point of view, feelings and attitudes.

2. *Patience:* To provide space and opportunity to the managee for fully expressing himself/herself without inhibition or embarrassment.

3. *Empathy:* Understanding managee feelings, and communicating understanding.

4. *Summarizing feelings and content:* To indicate progress, and to emphasize certain benchmark points during the discussions and in conclusion.

5. *The ability to stay open:* Not to become defensive

6. The ability of not to dwell on face-savers that can frustrate the value of feedback.

7. The ability to keep an open mind, such that managee's legitimate facts and logic can duly influence the manager's conclusions.

Managees can be effectively motivated if the discussion leads for:

1. Solving some job and role-task problems.

2. Improving dyadic understanding and chemistry between manager and the managee.

3.   Creating a better understanding of, or solving, some personal issues of either the manager or the managee.

4.   Bringing about improvements in the work climate and context.

Some other positive outcomes for the managee can be:

1.   Changes in job assignments and performance standards or expectations,

2.   Modifications in assessment of various factors impacting managee performance, based on facts and logic presented by the managee,

3.   Greater interest towards initiatives for managee development.

This type also has potential for the manager receiving feedback from the managee in the form of facts and logic that the managee presents along with other verbal or non-verbal communication. This can result in efforts to improve performance through:

1.   Supervision that is more managee-centered.

2.   Work methods that are more efficient.

3.   Job assignments that are more suited to the managee's talent.

4.   Performance expectations for the future that are more realistic to fulfill.

5.   Stronger faith in upward communication.

Tell and Listen discussion provides an opportunity for the manager to get an insight into the managee's needs –

- Social/personal

- Psychological

- Work-related

- Interest-related

Problem-solving Type

Recent trends show a shift favouring a problem solving approach to performance discussions, with emphasis on managee development. Unlike *Tell and Sell* and *Tell and Listen* types, in Problem-solving discussion feedback is not directly communicated to the managee. The manager stimulates the managee to review performance and to discuss opportunities and enabling factors as well as problems and hindering forces in his work context. He is encouraged to share his satisfactions and frustrations, personal and professional strengths and weaknesses, high and low points during the performance period, achievements and innovations, additional support needed for future performance, etc.

In this type, manager doesn't play the judge at all; rather he assumes the role of what Maier calls the "helper". This is so, because this type holds managee development as its primary objective, rather than communicating feedback.

Given a degree of initial rapport the goal of managee development establishes an almost instant mutual agenda for both manager and the managee, with the managee implicitly relating with the helping role of the manager. This facilitates the managee accepting reality and sharing his performance problems and difficulties with the manager. The manager can fortify this rapport into a more enduring helping relationship by showing his eagerness to discover managee interests and also to examine the various ideas and suggestions for improvement that the managee comes up with and prompting him to examine and reality-test these ideas and suggestions.

Where the managee comes up with half-baked ideas or makes naive suggestions, problem-solving discussion is the best-perhaps the only way to help him explore more deeply, by stimulating the rational and the analytical in his frame. The manager's knowledge and experience can help a managee see and overcome his/her shortcomings only if the manager is able to share these positively and constructively with the managee.

As the title suggests, this type extensively involves generating alternate solutions, and then exploring and evaluating these alternatives to arrive at the most suitable and feasible alternative. It is a creative process.

Problem-solving discussion uses most skill applicable to the Tell and Listen type. When the managee comes up with several ideas and suggestions, it is helpful if the manager jots them down. This can aid in summarizing, and also manifest the manager's seriousness and interest.

Skillful questioning- intended to help the managee examine his idea, suggestions, or plans- usually conveys that the manager wants to get the complete picture.

Problem-solving discussion, like the Tell and Listen type promotes upward communication; thereby pooling the contribution of people with two different perspectives on the same situation. This sets the stage for decisions, which have both high quality, and high acceptance.

Problem-solving approach can work only if the managee actively participates in it. It cannot work where he remains passive; and the manager may have no option but to call upon one of the other two types.

Content of Stocktaking Discussions

A comprehensive discussion looks at:

1. Achievement or non-achievement of performance goals and extent of shortfall, if any.

2. Causes for such achievement or non-achievement. Can the reasons for non-achievement be mitigated, and how- through training, by modifying organizational systems, revising performance standards or by influencing environmental forces, or by other means. Can the reasons for achievement be captured as learning and sustained as future assets?

3. Determining what, in the content or context of performance tasks, is positive and helpful and therefore needs to be retained and reinforced.

4. Determining what, in the content or context of performance tasks, is negative and hindering and therefore needs to be remedied or changed.

5. Drawing lessons to be used for planning the next performance cycle.

A purposeful feedback discussion limits itself primarily to those attributes of the managee — his skills, knowledge or attitudes, which are amenable to learning or changing – (SKA) – Competencies development activities to be planned.

List of Managerial Competencies

- Planning ability
- Organizing ability
- Co-ordination
- Supervision
- Leadership and dynamism
- Initiative
- Resourcefulness
- Creativity and Imaginativeness
- Development of subordinates
- Contribution to team spirit
- Analytical abilities
- Delegation
- Public relations
- Sociability
- Self-confidence

What constitute feedback discussion?

1. Communication
2. Influencing
3. Helping

Communication

The appraiser essentially communicates with the Appraisee. Communication involves— 1 receiving messages (listening), 2 giving messages (responding), 3 and giving feedback.

Listening

- Listening an effective Communication skill.

- An open ear is the only believable sign of an open heart.

- Listening is a caring attitude.

- Hearing is done through the ears while listening is through an intellectual and emotional process that integrates physical and emotional inputs in search of meaning and understanding.

- An effective listener listens not only to the words but to the hidden meaning behind the words. Effective listening is not a passive process. It plays an active role in the process of communication.

- Listener should have reason or purpose of listening.

- It is important for the listener to suspend judgement.

- The listener should resist distractions.

- The listener should wait before responding to the speaker.

- The listener should repeat verbatim what the speaker says.

- The listener should rephrase in his own words the contents and feelings of what the speaker says, to the speaker's satisfaction.

- The listener should use the time differential between the rate of speed (speak 100-150 wpm) and rate of speed (Listen 400-500 wpm) to reflect upon the content and research for meaning.

- The listener should be ready to respond to the speaker's comment.

Responses

Appraiser Responses

- Unhelpful
- Alienating
- Not encouraging creative acts
- Passive listening
- Lack of verbal response
- Critical
- Pointing inconsistencies
- Repeated mention of weaknesses

- Effective & Helpful
- Empathic Levelling
- Rapport building
- Identifying feelings
- Supportive
- Recognizing Criticizing availability
- Trusting

- Belittling
- Reprimanding
- Directive
- Prescribing
- Ordering
- Threatening
- Giving no options
- Pointing out only one acceptable way
- Quoting rules and Regulations

- Exploring
- Questions
- Reflecting
- Sharing
- Probing
- Closing
- Summarizing
- Concluding
- Contracting for follow-up and help

Giving Feedback

Interpersonal feedback is an important input for increasing self-awareness. It helps in reducing the blind area of a person, helping him to become more aware about his strengths and weaknesses.

Sharing interpersonal perceptions through the feedback and the self-disclosure processes, thus, becomes instrumental in creating a more open, positive, win-win relationship between the managee and her supervisor. One outgrowth of this concept is the greater awareness of interdependency underlying the managee- manager relationship, which is a tremendous force in enhancing their mutual value to each other, and to the organization.

Influencing

PRD (Performance Review and Development) also involves influencing the appraise in several ways. The manager cannot escape the fact that he is influencing his employee in such a way that the latter is able to move in some direction, Providing positive reinforcement so that desirable behaviour is further strengthened,

Helping

Helping also functions in a similar way. It involves three different elements. Helping behaviour is based on mutuality of relationship. The appraise responds as much to the appraiser's needs as the former does to the latter's. And finally, helping primarily involves identification of developmental needs of the appraise so that he may be able to develop and increase his effectiveness. Also, help appraise to have access to developmental facilities.

Sequential Process of PRD

The typical sequence of events for such a meeting is the following:

1. *Explain the purpose of the meeting:* The first step includes a description of the purpose of the meeting and the topics to be discussed.

2. *Self-appraisal:* The second step includes asking the employee to summarize her accomplishments during the review period. This is more easily accomplished when the employee is given the appraisal form to be used by the supervisor before the meeting. This portion of the meeting allow the employee to provide her perspective regarding performance. The role of the supervisor is to listen to what the employee has to say and to Summarize what he hears. This is not an appropriate time for the supervisor to disagree with what the employee says.

3. *Share ratings and explain rationale:* Next, the supervisor explains the rating he provided for each performance dimension and explains the reasons that led to each score. It is more effective to start with a discussion of the performance dimensions for which there is agreement between the employee's self appraisal and the supervisor's appraisal. This is likely to reduce tension and to demonstrate to the employee that there is common ground and that the meeting is not confrontational.

4. *Developmental discussion:* Once the supervisor and employee agree on the scores given to each performance dimension, there should be a discussion of the developmental plan. At this point, the supervisor and the employee should discuss and agree on the developmental steps that will be taken to improve performance in the future.

5. *Employee summary:* Next the employee should summarize in her own words, the main conclusions of the meeting: what performance dimensions are satisfactory, which need improvement, and how improvement will be achieved. This is an important component of the meeting because it gives the supervisor an opportunity to learn if he and the employee are in accord.

6. *Reward discussion:* The next step during the meeting includes discussing the relationship between performance and any reward allocation. The supervisor should explain the rules used to allocate rewards and how the employee would be able to reach higher reward levels as a consequence of future performance improvement.

7. *Follow-up meeting:* Before the meeting is over, it is important to schedule the next performance-related formal meeting. It is important that the employee sees that there will be a formal follow-up and that performance management is not just about meeting with the supervisor once a year. Usually, the next meeting will take place just a few weeks later to review whether the developmental plan is being implemented effectively.

8. *Approval and appeals process discussion:* Finally, the supervisor asks the employee to sign the form to attest that the evaluation has been discussed with him. This is also an opportunity for the employee to add any comments or additional information she would like to see included on the form. In addition, if disagreements about ratings have not been resolved, the supervisor should remind the employee of the appeals process.

9. *Final recap:* Finally, the supervisor should use the "past-present-future model." In other words, the supervisor summarizes what happened during the review period in

terms of performance levels in the various dimensions, reviews how rewards will change based on this level of performance, and sums up what the employee will need to do in the next year to maintain and enhance performance.

Be empathetic	open – up.
Attending	Attaching seriousness & importances
Listening	Active one
Acceptance	By paraphrasing, mirroring or reflecting
Encourage participation Exploration	
Problem Identification/ Diagnosis	Strength and weakness and plan for improvement Generating several alternative causes for problems
Action Planning	Training need, job-rotation, more responsibilities, role-clarity etc.
Searching	Alternatives.
Decision-making	About the final alternative(s)
Supporting	Action plan.

BOX 7.2 **Eleven Golden Rules for Conducting Performance Review Meeting**

1. Be prepared – Not casual – fully equipped with relevant information.

2. Create the right atmosphere

3. Work out

4. A clear structure of the meeting- enough time to employee to talk

5. Use praise – Praise keeps people to relax and comfortable

6. Let Individual do most of the talking

7. Invite self-assessment –

   Ask questions like

   (i)   How do you feel you have done?

   (ii) What do you feel are your strength?

   (iii) What do you like most/ least about your job?

   (iv) Why do you think you did not meet target?

8. Discuss performance and not personality

9. Encourage analysis of performance

10. Do not deliver unexpected criticisms

11. Agree for Plan of actions – realistic, measurable, progressive etc.

⌘ Six Suggestions ⌘

1. *Coaching approach on result:* If I attack you, what will you do? Defend yourself. Same thing happens, when you attack employee during interview "Attack the variance and not the person." Coaching approach on result reduces the likelihood of reactions

2. *Get down to the cases:* Be specific about the result. Identify the variance you are concerned about. Cite data. Provide example.

3. *Determine causes:* When exploring causes, tell employee to identify three or four causes. Do not reject his suggestion, jointly identify these which are more complicated and Important. Use your expertise to keep him.

4. Make it a two way process give enough space.

5. Set up Action-plan

   (i) Considering several possible actions to correct a given cause of failure.

   (ii) Concentrate on one or two actions.

   (iii) Be specific about who, what, when

   (iv) Follow – up and report back.

   (v) Reduce plan in writing.

6. *Provide Motivation:* Stress the benefits to the employees in achieving the necessary results. Benefit has to be of consequence to the employee – it could be advancement, increase in compensation, additional responsibility and status or it could be a sense of accomplishment etc.

   Jointly map out the competences chart, help him to acquire/enhance them. That help employee to unleash his potentials which is beneficial to the individual and the organization to achieve competitive edge.

Live Examples

1. US telecom company Hughes, uses 'a competency based performance enhancement model' wherein 'each position in the organization is defined in terms of 23 key competencies, categorized into four groups: attitude-based, knowledge-driven, skill-centered, and value-based'. These competency formulations help measure adequacies and shortfalls. Relevant training and development input can be considered for areas where the competencies fall short of requirements, provided the managee shows interest and the inputs are likely to help reduce the gap. These inputs, where successful, are expected to maximize productivity as well as make managees aware of their professional standing.

2. Engineering major Larsen & Toubro uses what it calls 'a competency matrix'. It lists 73 competencies that vary across managerial levels to measure performance, and gauge

developmental needs of managees. Each listed competency has associated knowledge, skills, and attributes. The company appraises individual employees on the listed competencies and zeroes on the functional, managerial, and behavioural skill gaps. Subsequently customized reinforcement is provided. Further, as the matrix is linked to business strategy on the one hand and training needs on the other, strategic needs drive the company's development policies, making the process of re-learning and re-skilling easier and more focused.

Dr. Reddy's Laboratories

It is essential that Appraiser and Reviewing Authority hold a meeting to help the appraise integrate his/her personal performance with the feedback being provided by appraise and reviewing authority. At this meeting, review the enablers and constraints that helped/hindered the performance of the employee. Also during this meeting, focus on assessing the strengths and areas of improvement of the appraise in relation to his/her performance.

This feedback session should also clarify the extent to which the employee has achieved his/her objectives so that employee has a deeper understanding of what has been achieved and how the performance can be improved next year. At the end of the session, the employees should feel a Sense of pride in their accomplishments and a desire to improve in their development areas. Treating employee with respect and helping them plan for performance improvements is a far better way of motivating them than criticizing or attaching blame.

Case Study

Preventing Defensiveness

Spencer is Jeff's manager and needs to talk to him about his poor performance over the previous quarter. Jeff enters the room and sits across the desk from Spencer.

Jeff: Spencer, you wanted to talk to me?

Spencer: Yes Jeff, thanks for coming by. I wanted to talk about your performance last quarter. (Spencer's phone rings and he answers it. Five minutes later Jeff is still waiting for Spencer. Jeff finally gets frustrated and Spencer notices Jeff looks at his watch several times.)

Sorry for the interruption Jeff, I know it is frustrating to be kept waiting.

Jeff: I am very busy. Can we get on with this?

Spencer: Yes absolutely. As you know you had some problems meeting all of your goals last quarter.

Jeff: Now wait a second, I met the most important goal.

Spencer: Yes, you did, but you missed the other four.

Jeff: Just by a little and it wasn't my fault.

Spencer: Jeff, you need to accept responsibility for your own performance and not push blame onto others. You need to meet your goals this coming quarter or I will have to take more serious action.

Jeff: One bad quarter and you threaten to fire me? I can't believe this.

Spencer: Just meet all of your goals and I won't have to take that action.

Given this background, what could Spencer have done to combat Jeff's defensiveness more effectively?

Potential Appraisal Management

In a competitive world, past achievements do not always guarantee future success. The risks of failure are high, especially for those who have been operating in a protected environment. Economic reforms are constantly exposing organizations to higher levels of competition. To face competition, firms need to advance at high speed in all areas – technology, processes, management, finances, quality, cost, new market creation, new product inventories and, above all, increased efficiency, motivation and productivity on the part of the employees. Competing organizations from other countries have easy access to the best technologies, easy and unlimited finance, well-established management systems and practices, high quality orientation, brand equity and simple flat and cost-effective structures with fewer but very competent people to handle all these. In such circumstances, firms have no options but to become more technology driven, market sensitive and customer focused, quality centered, cost effective, systems driven and managerially effective. To achieve these, it is necessary to have competent managers in strategic advantages; without them, they cannot serving long.

Rationalizing Organizational Structures

Too many hierarchical levels have been created in the past for a variety of reasons. The levels of differentiation was unnecessary. Differentiation of roles and the increased number of layers add to delays, reduce speed, give a false idea of easy profitability and frustrate more employees than motivating them. They increase inefficiency, frustration and also create unrealistic aspirations.

The managerial structures need to be rationalized to include a maximum of there to four levels. At best these could be junior, middle, senior and top management cadres. The culture should be that of a peer culture and performance culture.

Aligning Compensation Plans

To keep the motivation levels high, there could be running scales and appropriate compensation mechanisms so that people do not get frustrated if they do not get promoted. Increased years of service and consistent high performance should be recognized and should be valued more than promotion. It is possible to design compensation systems that keep the motivation levels of people high and aspiration for promotion low and limited.

Promotion policies should be rationalized and they should be based on competence. Mere changes in salary grades and compensation without changes in tasks (responsibilities, accountabilities and nature of jobs performed) should be treated as upgradations and not as promotions. They should be considered as valuable and should be given to more employees. Promotions, however, should be limited to those who are required to perform new roles or tasks and carry higher levels of responsibilities, or meet different kinds of challenges. Anything that is a promotion should be accompanied by:

- Grade changes;

- Designation changes;

- Changes in compensation structure and emoluments;

- Changes in responsibilities with a reasonably significant number or quality of tasks to be performed in the new role.

✿ Potential Appraisal is a Necessity ✿

Competent people should handle strategic and critical roles. Hence, there is a need to constantly identify competent people. This need is what makes potential appraisal very significant.

To have competent people, we must know competency requirements. To know the competency requirements, we must know the job profile or the list of tasks to be performed. There should then be a reliable and valid method of assessing the extent to which a given employee has the competence to perform the new tasks, Potential appraisal is nothing but an assessment of the extent to which a given individual has the potential to perform the new task or new job. Such potential assessment can either be a simple or a complicated matter depending on a number of things.

It is simple if the employee is already performing most or all the tasks in his/her current job. In such cases, appraisal of current performance is a good indicator of future potential and the performance appraisal period is an appropriate time to assess potential. For example, if a deputy manager (production) has to be promoted to manager (production) most of the tasks will remain the same. Normally, such promotions are more a case of re-designation.

However, potential appraisal is complicated if the employee is to be considered for a new job or task. Here one has to gather evidence of the person's potential to perform the new job and past performance is not adequate as an indicator. The best way to judge a person's potential and therefore ability to succeed in the new role is to actually put the person on the job and then assess him. However, there are a lot of practical constraints to this. For one, the organization cannot afford to take such risks and, second, there would be many aspirants for a particular post. The next best alternative available in such situations is to simulate the job and observe the person's performance.

This is where the assessment centre as a methodology gains significance. Assessment centers are specially established centers to create such simulated job conditions and observe a person's performance, thereby assessing his potential to occupy that position. Again, it is not necessary to simulate the entire job. In any case, in a promotion, 60-70 per cent of the work can be handled well as a result of past experiences. It is the remaining part which is critical and requires a different set of competencies. Therefore, this critical part of the job can be studied, competencies identified and methods designed to evaluate these competencies.

Promotions should be preceded by a thorough testing of competencies or potential for holding the position to which the employee is being promoted. It is here that the assessment centre becomes relevant. Such an assessment centre should communicate to employees that the firm is focusing on performance culture and competency culture.

Most organizations include potential appraisal as a part of the performance appraisal. This has advantages but also several disadvantages.

1. Potential is about the future while performance deals with the past. Good performance in the past in a given job need not be a good indicator of the likely performance in future in a role that the individual has not performed.

2. Biases of the boss who is just one level above may creep into potential appraisal.

3. Potential should relate to competencies while performance related to KPAs and other tasks assigned to the individual. Potential is about assessing people against competencies required for higher level roles.

4. Performance on a given job is partly dependent on the support provided by the organization including his reporting officer and reviewing officer and their judgement may be more reflective of the situation in which the performer has performed rather than his actual capabilities.

5. It is only fair to create the conditions under which the individual is likely to perform the new job and test him out in relation with the situation as well as his competencies. That is how assessment centers become relevant tools for promotion decisions.

Combining the potential appraisal with performance appraisal may be appropriate under the following conditions:

1. There is no significant difference in the current job of the individual and the future job for which his potential is being tested.

2. The competencies required by the new job are the same as those needed by the current.

3. The current job offers adequate opportunity for the individual to demonstrate the competencies needed for the future job.

4. The reporting officer or the reviewing officer is experienced enough and unbiased so as to judge accurately the potential of the individual.

5. It is useful to supplement the data with 360 degree feedback and assessment centres.

Assessment Centre

An assessment centre is a comprehensive, standardized procedure in which multiple assessment techniques such as situational exercises and job simulation Business games, discussions, reports and presentations) are used to evaluate individual employees' for a variety of decisions. Most frequently the approach has been applied to individuals being considered for selection, promotion, placement or special training and development in management.

Promotion

A decision to promote is essentially a decision to select from within the organization those most likely to succeed at higher level jobs. Any method used by the organization to take promotion decisions such as performance appraisal data, interviews, etc. should be supplemented by data from the assessment centre. Since, the assessment centre method is used to study the likely performance and behavior of a person in a role not previously performed by him/her; it can be used to supplement promotion decisions. Using additional inputs not only results in a more appropriate decision, it also helps eliminate individual biases and imparts more transparency and fairness to the promotion system. High validity has been reported in use of assessment centre data for promotions to first level supervisory and middle management levels; while no validity studies have been reported for higher levels of management.

Tools Used in Assessment Centres

As mentioned above, the main characteristics of assessment centres are multiple methods of assessment using multiple assessors. The main assessment tools that are used are:

Psychometric Tests

In general three types of tests or questionnaires can be used in assessment centres: aptitude tests, ability tests and personality tests. Aptitude tests are those which attempt to evaluate verbal and numerical reasoning ability. Ability tests attempt to measure awareness. Knowledge and other such aspects. They also measure simple skills like problem solving ability, etc. For e.g., a chapter pencil test could be administered to find out the familiarity or level of skill of the individual in relation to computer literacy, financial management skills, etc. Personality tests are those tests which are aimed at studying various dimensions of personality rather than the ability. MBTI and 16 PF are tests used in many organizations. While ability and aptitude tests have right or wrong answers, personality tests do not have the same.

The tests are selected for assessment taking the following points into consideration:

- Objective—what needs to be measured;
- Reliability and validity;

- Length of time required to administer the test;

- Availability of qualified experts to administer, scope and interpret the tests;

- Cost involved

Interviews—Background Interviews, Critical Incident/ Situational Interviews, Behavior Event Interviews

Generally structured interviews are used in assessment centers to increase inter-assessor reliability. Questions are decided; sample responses are formed and classified as good, bad or average. This, in turn, is used to rate the participant's response.

Background interviews are generally used if the participant's performance on his current and previous jobs would be an indicator of his success for the role for which he is being assessed. The participant is required to give specific examples of how he has performed job duties or handled job problems in the past.

In a nutshell, potential appraisal has following elements unleashing latent but unrealized abilities:

1. Ability to take risk

2. Analytical ability

3. Innovative, creative ability

4. Initiativeness & Proactiveness

5. Leadership skills

6. Level headedness

7. IQ, EQ, SQ (value)

The purpose of Potential Appraisal is to convert workhorses and problem children kinds of employees transformed into "Star Performers".

Design of 360 Degree Feedback Instruments for Leadership Development: An Experience at Infosys

360 Degree feedback instruments have been in use for more than 15 years now. One study states that by 1996, 90% of the Fortune 1000 companies had already used the 360 Degree Feedback instruments in some way or the other [FHLPS 1996]. A 360 Degree Feedback instrument is a multi-rater appraisal and feedback system that helps an individual get feedback from his manager, peers, direct reports and clients. This instrument has been used to assess managerial effectiveness as well as in leadership development [AW 2003, CTC 1998]. The effectiveness of the instrument depends on a number of factors including

– openness in the organization, a balanced use of the feedback, relevance and quality of the statements, openness of the member in interpreting the feedback in the right spirit, and selecting the right set of respondents. The effectiveness in essence depends on the readiness of the organization as well as readiness of the individual [TVR 2003].

In the context of using 360 Degree Feedback instruments for leadership development, organizations may either use a standard off-the-shelf 360 Degree Feedback instrument or design a completely customized instrument. Yet another approach is to customize a standard off-the-shelf instrument. The argument offered for using an off-the-shelf instrument is the context in variant nature of leadership, so if a research organization has already done the necessary research on the different dimensions of leadership, it makes immense sense to use the instrument in an "As-Is" form. At the other end, there are organizations that feel that leadership is context dependent, so the instrument needs to be customised to the needs of the organization [CTC 1998]. At Infosys, we have taken the latter approach because we feel that manifestation of leadership is different in different circumstances and so the instrument has to be customized to ensure that the feedback is relevant and appropriate to the needs.

The second dimension in designing a 360 Degree Feedback instrument is the input for the instrument. There are instances where the instrument has been derived from a set of traits [AW 2003] and in other cases from a set of well-defined competencies [CM 2003]. We at Infosys have adopted a competency-based leadership development model and hence our 360 Degree Feedback instrument is also based on leadership competencies.

Design a competency-based 360 Degree Feedback instrument is dependent on a good understanding of the competencies and their manifested behaviour across multiple roles within an organization. In order for these instruments to be focused and highly relevant to all roles, the ideal state is to design such an instrument for every role in an organization. Since this is an expensive proposition, most organizations have a generic instrument addressing the needs of a set of roles. The effectiveness of the instrument as a development tool is to a large extent dependent on how well the competencies are defined for the set of roles for which it is administered.

The definition of the competencies is the first step. This is followed with the process of translating the definitions into statements that effectively measure the competencies. This is an iterative process involving proper wording of the statements, validation for understand ability of these statements, relevance of the statements to the competencies, and simplicity. These characteristics of the statements are ensured through a set of validation steps that are explained in section 4.

In this paper we use the Infosys Leadership Development processes as the context to explain the challenges and complexities of designing 360 Degree Feedback instruments for Tier-1 and Tier-2 leaders within the Leadership Development Framework of the company. The lessons learnt in this exercise are likely to be generic enough to be applied to the design of 360 Degree Feedback instruments in similar situations.

Section 2 of this paper sets the context for definition of tier wise leadership competencies. Section 3 describes the methodology for designing a 360 Degree Feedback instrument.

Section 4 describes further work necessary to refine the instrument, while section 5 concludes with the lessons learnt in this exercise.

⌘ The Infosys Context ⌘

Infosys uses a stratified three-tiered approach to leadership development. Tier-1 consists of Independent Business Units Heads (IBU HEADS), Practice Heads, Vice President-Sales and Function Heads. Tier-2 comprises of members who have the potential to occupy Tier-1 position in 3 years and Tier-3 has members who can serve as the pipeline for Tier-2 in 3-5 years. The pool for each tier accordingly is from different levels in the organization. The rationale for adopting a stratified leadership development process is because we believe that the leadership needs of the three tiers are different and it is essential to make this distinction to ensure that the leadership development services are focused and well delivered.

Leadership Competencies

In order to ensure that leadership development is effective, the first step was to identify the leadership competencies that are relevant to Infosys. A team of professionals studied various leadership competencies and worked with the senior management of Infosys to arrive at a set of 8 competencies that were seen to be relevant and essential for all leaders at Infosys. The team also defined each competency by a set of attributes specified as phrases. The Figure gives the details of the competency framework of leadership at Infosys. The team had to also understand how these leadership competencies manifest for each of the three tiers. The aim of this understanding was to ensure that the 360 Degree Feedback instrument was customized for each tier. In this chapter, we focus on their challenges of creating a customized 360 Degree Feedback instrument for each tier.

Challenges in Understanding the Manifestation of Competency for Multiple Tiers of Leadership

This subsection deals with the challenges faced in understanding the meaning and/or implication of the manifested behaviours of leadership across multiple tiers. The challenges are exemplified by using two roles viz., Vice President-Sales (Tier-1) and Delivery Manager (Tier-2). To facilitate a better understanding of the context, we have outlined the key components of these roles in the following paragraphs.

Vice President-Sales (Tier-1)

The Vice President-Sales (VP-Sales) is responsible for the revenue growth and client acquisition of a particular geographic region where Infosys operates. He is supported in his efforts by a frontline sales force and interfaces with multiple groups: marketing, software delivery teams, technology and industry specialists. The relevant Leadership Competency Framework is illustrated in Figure.

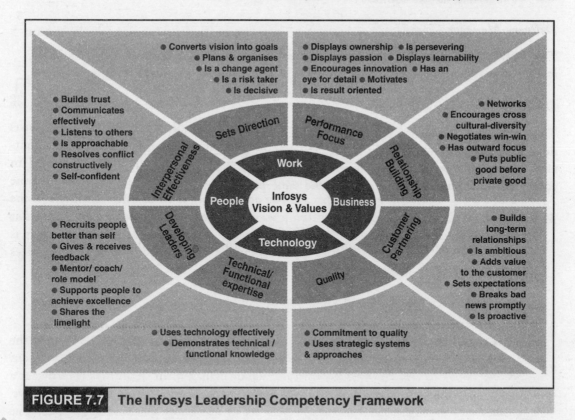

FIGURE 7.7 The Infosys Leadership Competency Framework

Contribution to the Sales Strategy

This involves giving inputs about the region, client expectations, and helping the Senior Management and Sales and Marketing teams to evolve the sales strategy.

Planning and Execution for Sales Targets

This involves creating and executing the operational plan for the region in accordance with the sales strategy.

Planning and Execution for Client Acquisition

This involves looking ahead beyond the current year and planning for client based on the long-term strategy. This is important in order to ensure that some time and effort is budgeted for the long term.

Ensuring Good Client Relationship

This involves maintaining relationships with all clients in the region, and specifically with key executives of the client organizations.

Delivery Manager (Tier-2)

The Delivery Manager (DM) manages 200 to 250 software professionals across multiple levels and is responsible for client deliveries. The key components of this role are as follows:

Delivery of Software Solutions

This includes ensuring that the various projects in his delivery unit are planned, designed, developed and delivered to meet client expectations on quality, schedule, productivity and effectiveness of the software solution. In addition, he has to ensure that these solutions adhere to the organizational norms on the same parameters.

Management of the Teams in the Unit

The DM is responsible for people management which include the following:

1. Optimal people utilization.

2. Performance Management and employee motivation.

3. Development of his employees- ensure sufficient opportunities to learn and enable this process.

4. Resolution of day-to-day people issues.

5. Resolution of critical issues.

These issues typically relate to specific client requirements that are escalated by his project team, decisions related to scope and re-negotiation with the client, and decisions related to exceptions in resource requirement due to any unforeseen circumstances.

For the two roles discussed above, the manifestation of the competencies listed in Table 7.5 Are materially different. In the next few paragraphs, we have attempted to illustrate the distinctive components of leadership competencies and their respective manifestation in the context of the roles of VP-Sales and Delivery Manager.

In this illustration, we explore one attribute for the Setting Direction competency:

TABLE 7.5	Competency and Attributes required for VP-sales and DM		
Competency	**Attribute**	**VP-Sales**	**DM**
Setting Direction	Converts vision into goals	Understanding the organization vision and ensures that his client retention and acquisition strategy is in line with the same and legal, the organization's vision is to generate a larger proportion of its revenues from higher value add services. In this context, the VP-Sales is able to conceptualize hot to "go-to-market" with industry or horizontal solutions which lead to higher margin business for the company.	Understands the organization's and client's expectations of quality and timeliness in software delivery and is able to meet and exceed these expectations at his unit level, e.g., ensures that the quality goals of the practice are implemented well in his unit.

Explanatory Note: Infosys is an organization whose primary source of revenue is from software application development and maintenance services. The company of late is moving up the value chain by providing higher-end services such as technology infrastructure management, system integration, customized industry vertical solutions, etc. However, since the primary revenue source is still from software application development and maintenance, there is tremendous competition form both offshore vendors providing similar services from India and global services, Accenture, and CSC. There is pressure on the company to mot to value-added (higher margin) services to protect the current levels of profitability.

The VP Sales is expected to be a key person in implementing this dimension of the organization's vision. The role holder is exacted to be able to reposition the company, leverage its existing brand equity (as a cost-efficient services provider) and get the Chief Information Officer's (CIO's) mind share in the client organization. These elements help translation of the larger organization vision into ground reality.

The Delivery Manager in this context needs to understand their repositioning of Infosys services or solutions (as against being involved in the repositioning himself like the VP-Sales), manage quality expectations of the client, ensure his team is well trained, set clear project goals, and ensure his team delivers as per promise.

While both the activities are critical for the implementation of the vision of the company, the role of the VP-Sales is more complex as compared to the DM for this statement. Hence this difference needs to be appropriately reflected in the 360 Degree Feedback instrument.

The statements in the respective 360 Degree Feedback instruments for this attributes are as follows:

Tier-1: Converts organization vision into unit specific goals Creates innovative action plans that drive the business.

Tier-2: Translates the department/unit vision into team specific goals

It is evident that the VP-Sales clearly has a higher degree of organizational impact and this is reflected in the statements in the respective 360 Degree Feedback instruments above.

⌘ Methodology

The key challenge was to create a 360 Degree Feedback instrument for each tier that reflects the complexity of multiple roles in that tier. In order to do this effectively, we evolved the following methodology:

Competency Definition and Designing the Draft Instrument

Select a set of roles in a tier for the competency definition of the Tier-ideally all roles in a tier.

For each role in the tier:

1. Get an understanding of the role using the job description for the role

2. Describe each leadership attributes in operational terms

3. Verify with the role holder(s) and the concerned manager(s)

4. Abstract an operational definition for each attribute based on description of that attribute for various roles in each tier Design a draft 360 Degree Feedback instrument

5. Validate the draft instrument with relevant sample Tier-1 and Tier-2 members.

The main challenge of this activity is to be able to define and abstract the nuances of each role in a particular tier. We have tried to illustrate the same with the help of two roles in Tier-1 – VP-Sales and IBU-Head. The VP-Sales job has been described in section 2. The broad areas of focus of the IBU-Head are – top-line and bottomline management, brand management, sustainable business model evolution, people development, capability building to support the business needs, and relationship building with clients.

The task now is to illustrate the leadership competencies and attributes in the context of these roles. Let us exemplify an attribute: "Has outward focus" which is part of the "Relationship Building" competency. The operational definition of this attribute for VP-Sales is: "Understands the client's needs and sells solutions appropriate to the needs, using Infosys' capabilities and go-to-market solutions appropriate to the needs, using Infosys's capabilities and services". The operational definition for the same for an IBU-Head is "Understands the client's needs, and builds generic capabilities and go-to-market solutions appropriate to the needs". Similarly, we followed the same process for 10 Tier-1 roles and then arrived at a multidimensional definition for each attribute of the competency. For the "Has outward focus" attribute, the Tier-1 operational definition is as follows:

- Able to generate solutions from the business perspective of the external/internal client.

- Continually seeks diverse perspectives when carrying out his job responsibilities.

- Continuously scans the external environment for new paradigms, changes in business model and is able to align the solutions of his unit to the immediate and future needs of his client.

For each of the attributes across the 8 competencies, we listed these operational definitions. The final list included more than 150 statements for Tier-1. To keep the 360 Degree Feedback instrument compact, we then decided to look at only those key statements which best measure the competencies. After multiple iterative steps, we chose a set of 60 key statements that constituted the draft Tier-1 360 Degree Feedback instrument.

In the Tier-1 draft instrument, for the "Has outward focus" attribute we chose " able to generate solutions from the business perspective of the external/ internal client". This was chosen since in spirit it subsumes all the three components of the definition listed above.

Validating the Instruments

After the draft instruments were ready, we went through a series of steps to validate the robustness of the statements included. The stage wise validation process is as follows:

Content Validation

We administered the draft instruments to a selected sample of Tier-1 and Tier-2 members. We included a couple of columns in the draft instrument(s), in one of which the respondents were expected to common on the clarity of the statement (ambiguity test). In the second column, the respondents were expected (ambiguity test). In the second column, the respondents were expected to indicate the leadership competency, which was closely linked to the particular statement (test of association).

After administering the draft instruments, we analysed the results, which revealed the following:

1. The respondents by and large understood the statements there were very few statements that did not pass the ambiguity test.

2. There were issues in the test of association primarily between the Setting Direction and Performance Focus competencies. Respondents seemed to have interchangeably used these competencies. One of the reasons for this was possible multiple overlapping zones between these two competencies. In order to validate this, we felt we needed a larger sample set and so chose to postpone addressing this issue to the next version of the instrument.

Statistical Tests

We performed a simple statistical test of correlation, the objective of which was to reduce the number of statements in the final instruments. We wanted to see how closely each statement was related to the overall competency groups scores. Figure 7.8 shows the format used in this exercise.

After plotting the data in the above format, we did a correlation analysis of the competency average score with the individual statement scores (for each statement in the competency). To illustrate, we did a correlation analysis of the competency average score with the individual statement scores (for each statement in the competency). To illustrate, we did a correlation between $(X_1, X_2, X_3,....,X_{30})$ and $(Y^1_1, Y^1_2, Y^1_3,...., Y^1_{30})$, $(X_1, X_2, X_3,.....,X_{30})$ and $(Y^2_1, Y^2_2, Y^2_3,......, Y^2_{30})$ and so on. Since there are 60 statements in all, 60 such correlation coefficients were computed.

Respondent Data

Statements	1	2	3	4		27	28	29	30
Setting direction	X_1	X_2	X_3	X_4		X_{27}	X_{28}	X_{29}	X_{30}
1.	Y^1_1	Y^1_2	Y^1_3	Y^1_4		Y^1_{27}	Y^1_{28}	Y^1_{29}	Y^1_{30}
2	Y^2_1	Y^2_2	Y^2_3	Y^2_4		Y^2_{27}	Y^2_{28}	Y^2_{29}	Y^2_{30}
3									
....									
....									
....									
......									
Performance Focus (Average)									
.....									
......									
57									
58									
59									
60									

Statements   Correlation Matrix

FIGURE 7.8   **Format used for Statistical Test**

Given the small sample size, it was essential to select statements that had a high correlation coefficient with the competency. We therefore looked at a cut-off of 0.7. However, it was essential to validate if the statements with correlation coefficient lower than 0.7 were unique or were subsumed-as judged by an expert panel-b, a set of other statements in the same competency.

Those that were subsumed were dropped. There were 8 such statements that were dropped in the process. We finally had 52 statements in the Tier-1 instrument.

Refining the Instrument

The first cycle of Tier-1 and Tier-2, instruments were rolled out in March-April 2003. These instruments have been used by the members to create their Personal Development Plans (PDPs). Going forward, we want to further refine the instrument by adopting the following process:

- List all the data sets of all the participants in the format prescribed in Figure.

- Do the correlation exercised across all responses

Look at statements with correlation coefficients in the following ranges:

- >0.7
- 0.6-0.7
- 0.4-0.6
- <0.4

Statements having a correlation coefficient greater than 0.7 will be automatically selected for the next roll-out.

For statements with correlation coefficient in the range 0.6-0.7, we propose to do an expert panel discussion with the supervisors of the members and see if these statements are relevant for measuring the respective competencies and then either include or reject, based on the response.

Statements with correlation coefficient in the range 0.4-0.6 also have the expert panel review as above. In addition to that, we propose to do content validation and association test with a much larger sample size than in the pilot. If both these validation tests are passed, the statements will be included in the next iteration of the instrument.

Statements with correlation coefficient less than 0.4 will be dropped from the next iteration of the instrument.

Lessons Learnt

In this section, we list the key learning of this exercise that could be useful for professional designing competency based 360 Degree Feedback instruments. It is important to understand the nuances of a competency/attribute and its manifestation in different roles to ensure that the instrument is appropriate.

It is important to be exhaustive while defining a competency, whereas while designing the instrument is should be as compact as possible. Given these two conflicting requirements it is essential for the professional not only to be rigorous in the analysis but also use judgment in the wording and selection of the statements.

The process of validation is extremely important but should not be restricted to statistical tests alone. In our experience, we have noticed that statistical tests are only indicative and we must also rely on our judgment before a statement is eliminated from the final instrument. The judgement call is always tricky since a statement could add unique value to the competency in spite of having a low correlation. We strongly recommend that professionals designing the instrument go through a process of debate, expert panel reviews, and other validation steps, before dropping a statement merely on the basis of low correlation scores.

Expatriate Performance Appraisal: Problems and Solutions

For more and more companies, gaining a competitive edge increasingly means making decisions that reflect an acute understanding of the global marketplace—how other countries utilize and view marketing strategies, accounting and financial systems, labor laws, leadership, communication, negotiation and decision-making styles. Gaining a knowledge of these components is most directly accomplished by sending managers to work in an overseas subsidiary and utilizing them on reentry.

Research show clearly that expatriates develop valuable managerial skills abroad that can be extremely useful to their development as effective senior managers. Based on current research on expatriates, including our own surveying and interviewing of more than 150 of them., probably the most significant skills expatriates develop as a result of their overseas assignments include the following:

- Being able to manage a workforce with cultural and sub cultural differences

- Being able to plan for, and conceptualize, the dynamics of a complex, multinational environment

- Being more open-minded about alternative methods for solving problems

- Being more flexible in dealing with people and systems

- Understanding the interdependencies among the firm's domestic and foreign operations.

These skills are the natural outgrowth of the increased autonomy and ʻpotential impact expatriates experience in their international assignment, In fact, in our study, 67 percent reported having more independence, and they Also indicated they had more potential impact on the operation's performance than in their domestic position. With increased decision-making responsibilities in a foreign environment, expatriates are subjected to a fairly intense working environment in which they must learn the ropes quickly.

The skills expatriate managers gain are obviously crucial to effectively managing any business operation, particularly at the international and multinational level. Nightmares abound in the business press of the inept decisions sometimes made by top management due to ignorance of cross-cultural differences in business practices. The ability to plan and conceptualize based on the complex interdependencies of a global market environment with significant cultural differences is required of top management in MNCs.

In short, expatriates can become a very valuable human resource for firms with international or multinational operations. However, one of the most serious stumbling blocks to expatriates' career paths is the lack of recognition of the value of expatriation and the informality with which firms accurately evaluate their expatriates' overseas performance. Although the attributes expatriates gain overseas can and do translate into concrete advantages. For their firms, a quick glance at the skills previously listed indicates intangibles that are often difficult to measure and usually are not measured—or are measured inaccurately—by present performance evaluation methods. Hence, it is critical to more closely examine this potential stumbling block to expatriates' careers and to make specific recommendations to improve the process and accuracy of such reviews.

⌘ Appraising the Expatriate's Performance   ⌘

Several problems are inherent to appraising an expatriate's performance. First, an examination of those who evaluate an expatriate's job performance is relevant. Those evaluators include the host national management and often the home office management.

Host National Management's Perceptions of Actual Job Performance

That local management evaluates the expatriate is probably necessary; however, such a process sometimes is problematic. Local management, typically evaluates the expatriate's performance from its own cultural frame of reference and set of expectations. For example, one American expatriate manager, we talked to, used participative decision making in India but was thought of by local workers as rather incompetent because of the Indian notion that managers, partly owing to their social class level, are seen as the experts. Therefore, a manager should not have to ask subordinates for ideas. Being seen as incompetent negatively affected local management's review of this expatriate's performance, and he was denied a promotion on return to the United States. Local management's appraisal is not the only potential problem. However, in fact, based on our research with expatriates, local management's evaluation is usually perceived as being more accurate than that of the home office.

Home Office Management's Perceptions of Actual Job Performance

Because the home office management is geographically distanced from the expatriate, it is often not fully aware of what is happening overseas. As a result, for middle and upper management, home office management will often use a different set of variables than those used by local management. Typically, more visible performance criteria are used to measure the expatriate's success (for example, profits, market share, productivity levels). Such measures ignore other, less visible variables That in reality drastically affect the company's performance. Local events such as strikes, evaluation of the currency, political instability, and runaway inflation are examples of phenomena that are beyond the control of the expatriate and are sometimes "invisible" to the home office.

One expatriate executive told us that in Chile he had almost single-handedly stopped a strike that would have shut down their factory completely for months and worsened relations between the Chileans and the parent company in the United States. In a land where strikes are commonplace, such an accomplishment was quite a coup, especially for an American. The numerous meetings and talks with labor representatives, government officials, and local management required an acute understanding of their culture and a sensitivity beyond the ability of most people. However, because of exchange rate fluctuations with its primary trading partners in South America, the demand for their ore temporarily decreased by 30 percent during the expatriate's tenure. Rather than applauding the efforts this expatriate executive made to avert a strike and recognizing the superb negotiation skills he demonstrated the home office saw the expatriate as being only somewhat better than a mediocre performer. In other words, because for home office management the most visible criterion of the expatriate's performance was somewhat negative (sales figures), it was assumed that he had not performed adequately. And though the expatriate's boss knew a strike had been averted, the bottomline concern for sales dollars overshadowed any other significant accomplishments.

The expatriate manager must walk a tightrope. He must deal with a new cultural work group, learn the ins and outs of the new business environment, possibly determine how to work with a foreign boss, find out what foreign management expects of him,' and so on. He must also understand "the-rules of the game" on the home front. It is difficult, and sometimes impossible, to please both. Attempting to please both can result in a temporarily, or permanently, railroaded career. So it was with an individual who was considered a high potential in a semiconductor firm. He was sent to an overseas operation without the proper product knowledge preparation and barely kept his head above water because of the difficulties of cracking a nearly impossible market. On returning to the United States, he was physically and mentally exhausted from the battle. He sought a much less challenging position and got it because top management then believed they had overestimated his potential. In fact, top management never did understand what the expatriate was up against in the foreign market.

In fact, expatriates frequently indicate that headquarters does not really understanding their experience—neither the difficulty of it nor the value of it. One study found that one-third of the expatriates felt that corporate headquarters did not understand the expatriate's experience at all. In a 1981 Korn/Ferry survey, 69 percent of the managers reported they felt isolated from domestic operations and their U.S. managers. It is clear from others' and our own research that most U.S. senior management does not understand the value of an international assignment or try to utilize the expatriate's skills gained abroad when they return to the home office. The underlying problem seems to be top management's ethnocentricity.

Management Ethnocentricity

Two of the most significant aspects of management's inability to under-stand the expatriate's experience, value it and thereby more accurately measure his or her performance are (1) the communication gap between the expatriate and their home office and (2) the lack of domestic management's international experience.

The Communication Gap: Being physically separated by thousands of miles and in different time zones poses distinct problems of communication. Not only does the expatriate have difficulty talking directly with his manager, but usually both the U.S. manager and the expatriate executive have plenty of other responsibilities to attend to. Fixing the day-to-day problems tends to take precedence over other concerns, such as maintaining contact with one's boss (or subordinate) in order to be kept up to date on organizational changes or simply to inform him or her of what one is doing. Most of the expatriates in our research indicated they had very irregular contact with their home office and that often it was not with their immediate superior. Rarely did the boss initiate direct contact with the expatriate more than once or twice a year.

The Lack of International Experience: The old Indian expression "To walk a mile in another man's moccasins" has direct meaning here. How can one understand what another person's overseas managerial experience is like its difficulties, challenges, stresses, and the like without having lived and worked overseas oneself? According to one study, more than two-thirds of upper management in corporations today have never had an international assignment. If they have not lived or worked overseas, and if the expatriate and U.S. manager are not communicating regularly about the assignment, the U.S. manager cannot evaluate the expatriate's performance appropriately.

Of course, how the U.S. manager and foreign manager perceive the expatriate's performance will depend partly on the expatriate's actual performance and partly on the 'managers' perceptions of the expatriate's performance. Up to now, we have discussed the 'managers' *perceptions of the* expatriate's performance. Let's now turn our attention to what usually corn-poses the expatriate's *actual* performance to better understand why evaluating it is problematic.

Actual Job Performance

As repeatedly mentioned by the expatriates in our study and in other research, the primary factors relating to the expatriate's actual job performance include his or her technical job know-how, personal adjustment to the culture, and various environmental factors.

Technical Job Know-How: As with all jobs, one's success overseas partly depends on one's expertise in the technical area of the job. Our research indicates that approximately 95 percent of the expatriates believe that technical competency is crucial to successful job performance. Although common sense supports this notion, research shows that technical competence is not sufficient in itself for successful job performance. For example, an engineer who is an expert in his or her field and who tends to ignore cultural variables that are important to job performance will likely be ineffective. He or she might be less flexible with local personnel, policies, and practices because of his or her reliance on technical know-how or because of differences in cultural views. As a result, the host nationals might become alienated by the expatriate's style and become quite resistant to his or her objectives and strategies. A less experienced engineer, with less technical competence, might be more willing to defer to the host country's employees and their procedures and customs. A shade of humility is always more likely to breed flexibility, and in the long run, the less experienced engineer might develop the trust of the foreign employees and might well be more effective than the experienced engineer.

We have been given numerous examples by expatriates, in fact, where this has been the case. One expatriate who represented a large construction firm was sent to a worksite in India. The expatriate was an expert in his field and operated in the same fashion as he did in the United States. He unintentionally ignored local work customs and became an object of hatred and distrust. The project was delayed for more than six months because of his behavior.

Adjustment to a New Culture: Just as important as the expatriate's technical expertise is his or her ability to adapt to the foreign environment, enabling him or her to deal with the indigenous people. Nearly every expatriate in our survey felt understanding the foreign culture, having an ability to communicate with the foreign nationals, and being able to reduce stress were as—if not more—important to successful job performance than was technical competence. Regardless of how much an expatriate knows, if he or she is unable to communicate with and understand the host nationals, the work will not get done. An expatriate's adjustment overseas is also related to at least two personal variables (1) one's marital and family status (that is, whether accompanied by a spouse and children) and (2) the executive's own personal and the family's predisposition to acculturation. Research clearly indicates that expatriates who have their family abroad are often less successful because of the stress on the family of being in a foreign environment. The stress on the spouse negatively affects the employee's concentration and job performance. With an increasing number of dual-career couples being affected by expatriation, the problems are even keener. A number of expatriates reported that their formerly career-positioned spouse suffered from depression most of the time they were overseas. Moving from experiencing the dynamics of a challenging career to having no business-world activity and being unable to communicate the most basic needs is a grueling transition for many career-oriented spouses.

Company variables affecting cultural and work adjustment also come into play. The thoroughness of the company's expatriate selection method and the type and degree of cross-cultural training will affect expatriate adjustment and performance. In other words, if the firm is not selective about the personality of the expatriate or does not appropriately prepare the employee and dependents, the firm may be building in failure before the manager ever leaves the United States.

All these factors influence the expatriate's learning curve in a foreign business environment. More time is thus required to learn the ins and outs of the job than for the expatriate's domestic counterpart who might have just taken a comparable position stateside. In fact, most expatriates say it takes three to six months to even begin to perform at the same level as in the domestic operation. Hence, performance evaluations at the company's normal time interval may be too early to accurately and fairly reflect the expatriate's performance.

⌘ A Summary of Factors Affecting Expatriation/Performance ⌘

In summary, an expatriate's performance is based on overseas adjustment, his or her technical know-how, and various relevant environmental factors. Actual performance, however, is evaluated in terms of perceived performance, which is based on a set of fairly complex variables usually below the evaluator's level of awareness. Much of the perceived performance concerns perceptions of the expatriate and his or her situation. Depending on whether the manager assessing the expatriate's performance has had personal overseas experience or is otherwise sensitive to problems associated with overseas work, the performance appraisal will be more or less valid. *The bottom line for the expatriate is that the performance appraisal will influence the promotion potential and type of position the expatriate receives on returning to the United States.* Because expatriates generally return from their experience with valuable managerial skills, especially for firms pursuing an international or global market path, it behooves organizations to carefully review their process of appraising expatriates and the evaluation criteria themselves.

Guidelines on How to Appraise an Expatriate's Performance

⌘ Human Resource Personnel: Giving Guidelines for Performance Evaluation ⌘

Human resources departments can do a couple of things to help guide the evaluator's perspective on the evaluation.

A basic breakdown of the difficulty level of the assignment should be done to properly evaluate the expatriate's performance. For example, working in Japan is generally considered more difficult than working in England or English-speaking Canada. The learning curve in japan will take longer because of the very different ways business is conducted, the language barrier that exists, and the isolation that most Americans feel within the Japanese culture. Major variables such as following should be considered when determining the difficulty level of the assignment:

1. Operational language used in the firm

2. Cultural "distance," based often on the region of the world (for example, Western Europe, Middle East, Asia)

3. Stability of the factors affecting the expatriate's performance (for example, labour force, exchange rate).

Many foreigners speak English, but their proficiency does not always allow them to speak effectively or comfortably, so they rely on their native language when possible. In addition, they usually do not speak English among themselves because it is not natural. In Germany, for example, one expatriate said that while relying on English allowed a minimum level of work to be performed, the fact that he did not speak German limited his effectiveness. Secretaries, for example, had very limited English-speaking skills. German worker spoke English together and therefore unknowingly excluded the expatriate from casual and often work-related conversations. And outside work, he had to spend three to four times the amount of time to accomplish the same things that he did easily in the United States. Most of the problem was because he could not speak good enough German, and many of the Germans could not speak good enough English.

Although sharing the same language facilitates effective communication, it is only the surface level of communication. More deep-rooted cultural-based phenomena can more seriously affect an expatriate's performance. Countries or regions where the company sends expatriates can be fairly easily divided into categories such as these: (1) somewhat more difficult than the United States, (2) more difficult than the United States. Plenty of information is available to help evaluate the difficulty level of assignments. The U.S. State Department and military branches have these types of ratings. In addition, feedback from a firm's own expatriates can help build the picture of the varying level of assignment difficulty.

Rather than having the manager try to subjectively build the difficulty level of the assignment into his or her performance appraisal, human resources could have a built-in, numerical difficulty factor that is multiplied times the quantity obtained by the normal evaluation process (for example, somewhat more difficult = X 1.2; more difficult = X 1.4; much more difficult = X 1.6).

⌘ Evaluator: Trying to Objectify the Evaluation ⌘

Several things can be done to try to make the evaluator's estimation more objective.

1. Most expatriates agree that it makes more sense to weight the evaluation based more on the on-site manager's appraisal than the home-site manager's notions of the employee's performance This is the individual who has been actually working with the expatriate and who has more information to use in the evaluation. Having the on-site manager evaluate the expatriate is especially valid when the on-site manager is of the same nationality as the expatriate. This helps avoid culturally biased interpretations of the expatriate s performance.

2. In reality, however, currently the home-site manager usually per-forms the actual written performance evaluation after the on-site manager has given some Input. When this is the case, a former expatriate from the same location should be involved in the appraisal process. This should occur particularly with evaluation dimensions where the manager is trying to evaluate the individual against criteria with which he or she is unfamiliar relative to the overseas site. For example, in South America the dynamics of the workplace can be considerably different from those of the United States. Where stability characterizes the United States, instability often characterizes much of Latin America. Labor unrest, political upheavals, different labor laws, and other elements all serve to modify the actual effects a supervisor can have on the productivity of the labor force in a company in Latin America. A manager who has not personally experienced these frustrations will not be able to evaluate an expatriate's productivity accurately. In short, if production is down while the expatriate is the supervisor, the American boss tends to believe it.

3. On the other hand, when it is a foreign, on-site manager who is making the written, formal evaluation, expatriates agree that the home-site manager should be consulted before the on-site manager completes a formal terminal evaluation. This makes sense because consulting the home-site\manager can balance an otherwise hostile evaluation caused by an intercultural misunderstanding.

One expatriate we interviewed related this experience. In France, women are legally allowed to take six months off for having a baby. They are paid during that time but are not supposed to do any work related to their job. This expatriate had two of the three secretaries take maternity leave. Because they were going to be coming back, they were not replaced with temporary help. The same amount of work, however, still existed. The American expatriate asked them to do some work at home, not really understanding the legalities of such a request. The French women could be fired from their job for doing work at home. One of the women agreed to do it because she felt sorry for him. When the American's French boss found out one of these two secretaries was helping, he became very angry and intolerant of the American's actions. As a result, the American felt he was given a lower performance evaluation than he deserved. When the American asked his former boss to intercede and help the French boss understand his reasoning, the French boss modified the performance evaluation to something more reasonable to the American expatriate. The French manager had assumed the American should have been aware of French laws governing maternity leave.

⌘ Performance Criteria ⌘

Here again, special consideration needs to be given to the expatriate's experience. Expatriates are not only performing a specific function, as they would in their domestic operation, they are also broadening their under standing of their firm's total operations and the inherent interdependencies thereof. As a result, two recommendations are suggested.

1. Modify the normal performance criteria of the evaluation sheet for that particular position to fit the overseas position and site's characteristics.

   Using the. Latin American example referred to before might serve to illustrate this point. In most U.S. firms, maintaining positive management-labor relations is not a primary performance evaluation criterion. Stabilizing the workforce is not highly valued because the workforce is already usually a stable entity. Instead, productivity in terms of number of units produced is a highly valued outcome. As such, motivating the workforce to work faster and harder is important. In Chile, however, the workforce is not so stable as it is in the United States. Stability is related to constant production—not necessarily to increasing production—and a stable production amount can be crucial to maintaining marketshare. In this case, if an expatriate is able to maintain positive management-labor relations such that the workforce goes on strike only two times instead of twenty-five times, the expatriate should be rewarded commensurately. In other words, while the expatriate's U.S. counterpart might be rated primarily on increases in production, the expatriate in Chile should be rated on stability of production.

   How can such modifications in the normal performance criteria be determined? Ideally, returned expatriates who worked at the same site or in the same country should be involved in developing the appropriate criteria or ranking of the performance criteria or both. Only they have first-hand experience of what the possibilities and constraints are like at that site. This developmental cycle should occur approximately every five years, depending on the stability of the site—its culture, personnel, and business cycles. Reevaluating the criteria and their prioritization periodically will make sure the performance evaluation criteria remain current with the reality of the overseas situation. If expatriate availability is a problem, outside consultants who specialize in international human resource management issues can be hired to help create country-specific performance evaluation forms and criteria.

2.   Include an expatriate's insights as part of the evaluation.

"Soft" criteria are difficult to measure and therefore legally difficult to support. Nevertheless, every attempt should be made to give the expatriate credit for relevant insights into the interdependencies of the domestic and foreign operations. For example, if an expatriate learns that the reason the firm's plant in India needs supplies by certain dates is to accommodate cultural norms—or even local laws—such information can be invaluable. Previously, no one at the domestic site understood why the plant in India always seemed to have such odd or erratic demands about delivery dates. And no one in India bothered to think that their U.S. supplier didn't operate the same way. If delivering supplies by specific dates asked for by their India colleagues ensures smoother production or increased sales and profits for the Indian operation, and if the expatriate is a critical link in the communication gap between the United States and India, the expatriate should be given credit for such insights. This should be reflected in his or her performance review.

To obtain this kind of information, either human resource or operational personnel should formally have a debriefing session with the expatriate on Jus or her return. It should be in an informal interview format so that specific and open-ended questions can be asked. Questions specific to the technical nature of the expatriate's work that relate to the firm's interdependencies should be asked. General questions concerning observations about the relationship between the two operations should also be included.

There is another, even more effective way this aspect of performance review can be handled. At regular intervals, say, every three to six months, the expatriate could be questioned by human resource or operational personnel domestic site about how the two operations might better work together. Doing it this way helps maximize the possibility of noting all relevant insights.

❈ Conclusion ❈

With the marketplace becoming increasingly global, the firms that carefully select and manage their internationally assigned personnel will reap the benefits. Today, there is about 20 percent turnover rate for expatriates when they return. Such a turnover rate is mostly due to firms not managing their expatriates' careers well. Firms are not prepared to appropriately reassign expatriates on their reentry. This obviously indicates that firms do not value the expatriate's experience. This further carries over into the lack of emphasis on appropriately evaluating an expatriate's performance. Appropriately evaluating an expatriate's performance is an issue of both fairness to the expatriate and competitive advantage to the firm. With the valuable experience and insights that expatriates gain, retaining them and effectively positioning them in a firm will mean the firm's business strategy will be increasingly guided by those who understand the companies' worldwide operations and markets.

CHAPTER-8

Performance and HRD

HR Developmental Dimensions

Human resource development in the organization context is a process by which the employees of an organization are helped, in a continuous and planned way to:

1. Acquire or sharpen capabilities required to perform various functions associated with their present or expected future roles;

2. Develop their general capabilities as individuals and discover and exploit their own inner potentials for their own and/or organizational development purposes; and

3. Develop an organizational culture in which supervisor-subordinate relationships, teamwork and collaboration culture in which supervisor-subordinate relationships, teamwork and collaboration among subunits are strong and contribute to the professional well-being, motivation and pride of employees.

This definition of HRD is limited to the organizational context. In this context of a state or nation, it would differ.

HRD is a process, not merely a set of mechanisms and techniques. The mechanisms and techniques such as performance appraisal, counseling, training, and organization development interventions are used to initiate, facilitate, and promote this process in a continuous way. Because the process has no limit, the mechanisms may need to be examined periodically to see whether they are promoting or hindering the process.

Organizations can facilitate this process of development by planning for it, by allocating organizational resources for the purpose, and by exemplifying an HRD philosophy that values human beings and promotes their development.

Hence, the goals of the HRD systems are to develop:

- The capabilities of each employee as an individual.

- The capabilities of each individual in relation to his or her present role.

- The capabilities of each employee in relation to his or her expected future role(s).

- The dyadic relationship between each employee and his or her supervisor.

- The team spirit and functioning in every organizational unit (department, group, etc.)

- Collaboration among different units of the organization.

- The organization's overall health and self-renewing capabilities which, in turn, increase the enabling capabilities of individuals, dyads, teams, and the entire organization.

Such a concept of development will focus on the different units available in the organization for different purposes. The individual and his role are important units of for some purposes. For others, groups, departments and the entire organization are more relevant units.

Development in this sense becomes a massive effort. While training may play the major role in designing and monitoring development efforts in the organization, other parts of the organization have to share in such an effort. In fact, the person, or the groups for whom the efforts of development are made, is also a partner in this process of development. The four partners or agents of development can be identified as: (a) the person or role, (b) the immediate boss of the person, (c) the human resource management department, and (d) the organization. The various foci and the four agents of development are shown in Exhibit 8.1.

EXHIBIT 8.1	The Development Dimensions of the Personnel Function

1. Analysing the Role

    (a) Task analysis

    (b) Key performance areas

    (c) Critical attributes

    (d) Job evaluation

2. Matching the Role and the Person

    (a) Selection/recruitment

    (b) Placement

    (c) Potential appraisal

    (d) Promotion

    (e) Career development, career and succession planning

3. Developing the Persons in the Role

    (a) Performance appraisal

    (b) Feedback and counseling

    (c) Mentoring

    (d) Career development

    (e) Training

4. Developing the Role for the Person

    (a) Job rotation

    (b) Job enrichment/redesigning

    (c) Role effectiveness and efficacy

5. Developing Equitability

    (a) Management of salary and amenities

    (b) Management of incentives and rewards

    (c) Standardizing and administering procedures

Contd...

6. Developing Self-renewing Capability

    (a) Communication

    (b) Organization development

    (c) Organizational learning

    (d) Developing culture and climate

7. Coping with Collective Power

⌘ Development Dimensions of the Personnel Function ⌘

1. *Analysing the Role:* One of the main aspects of HRM is to analyse the role in terms of responsibilities or key functions/performance areas of the role, and the competencies required to perform the effectively.

2. *Matching the Role and the Person:* Once the organization is clear about the dimensions of the roles or the jobs, it tries to get the best people for these jobs. After people are recruited they are put in different places. Recruitment and placement are important aspects of HRM. Placement is useful for giving varied experiences to people recruited. Another aspect of matching role and person is reflected in potential appraisal, finding out who has potential to match the requirement of the job. Obviously, the next step is promotion of people by placing them in appropriate roles for which the organization is searching people. Promotion is only one part of long term and succession planning.

3. *Developing the Persons in the Role:* Individuals develop not only through training, but, and in fact more through effective supervision, by helping them to understand their strengths so that they can leverage them for better performance. Similarly, they are helped to find out in what they have to be more effective in their jobs. Performance appraisal is not complete unless the performance is properly reviewed and feedback is given, and people are helped to understand their strengths and weaknesses. We are discussing this aspect ahead, along with performance coaching or counseling. It is also important to give opportunity to young and bright persons to deal with their problems; such help is provided generally by senior persons who are not necessarily related in job with the person seeking help. This process of mentoring is also discussed ahead. One important aspect relating to employee development, but unfortunately not adequately dealt with, is training.

4. *Developing the Role for the Person:* Very little attention has been given to role, although job rotation is being practiced in most of the organizations, and some organizations have also tried out job enrichment based on Herzberg's concept of motivators. The chapter on this discusses development of roles, including role effectiveness and role efficacy. Traditionally, HR function has given attention to individual employees and teams have been generally neglected. It is important for all organizations. We have devoted sufficient attention to this aspect.

5. *Developing Equitability:* Satisfaction level of employees depends to a great extent on their perceived justice being done to them without any discretion, as reflected in practices like management of compensation, rewards, and various amenities. People have high performance and develop competencies only if these are rewarded by the organization. Reward does not mean financial reward only, many rewards may be non-financial too. Equitability can also be developed by standardizing administrative procedures, so that people do not have any feelings that decisions are subjective.

6. *Developing Self-renewing Capability:* An organization should be concerned not only with its growth, but also with its health. It needs to diagnose its problems from time-to-time and take steps to develop new competencies to cope with the various problems and challenges it would be facing. This can be done through action research that is concerned with development of competencies through effective teams to diagnose the problems and initiate the process of collaborative work to deal developing with such problems. In Organization Development (OD), the focus is on developing process competency to increase organization effectiveness. OD aims at maintaining profiles of organizational health, monitoring organizational health, assisting sick departments helping interested units and departments in self-renewal, conflict management, creation of strong teams and so on and establishing processes that built a climate to promote enabling capabilities in the organization. OD in the earlier years, mainly in the 1960s (and party in the 1970s) was team/group-based. Most of the OD interventions in organizations started with deep process work beginning at the top level. OD has now widened considerably, it is no more confined to managers, it has been attempted with workers also. Attention has also been given to organizational learning, to develop the competence of an organization to analyse its experience and learn from it. The third aspect of self-renewal is research orientation in HRD, which means consciously and continually collecting data in order to understand the various issues, and designing ongoing interventions based on such data. For example, data were collected, and used effectively in L&T on the working of the appraisal system including counseling. Such data can help to improve implementation of the appraisal system. HRD related research is important, it helps in analysing data and information generated by the HRD in L&T has already established the orientation and several other organizations are in the process of introducing such "Research-orientation". For example, data related to HRD are being systematically analysed.

❈ Communication and Development of Culture ❈

The two often neglected aspects are discussed in some details below:

Communication

Many organizations have paid attention to communication. Over the years, some innovative and successful practices have been evolved in a number of Indian organizations. For example, in BHEL (Bhopal Unit), Management Employees Communication Meetings (MECOMs) have been effectively used. A MECOM is an open forum, in which more than 700 persons participate. It has contributed to mutual sharing of information and concerns and better understanding between management and employees. It has helped in effective implementation of decisions. Establishing this system was not easy: great deal of OD work had to be done prior to and during the evolution of MECOM.

In Tata Iron and Steel Company (TISCO), the Chairman keeps communication with his employees by answering every letter that is addressed to him (some 80,000 in a year) and has an open house at his residence between 7 and 9 every morning where anyone can walk in and discuss personal or work-related problems. He also holds dialogues with large groups, sometimes consisting of as many as 2500 persons. A very systematic attention has been paid to communication in VSAT Industries (including regular business-related communication with the union) with great benefits.

Communication ensures the flow of goal-oriented information and messages between different individuals and groups. In all directions, it helps them perform their roles more effectively. Communication minimizes distortion of information (studies have shown that in downward communication the information loss in terms of original messages is about 40 percent by the time it reaches the worker). Communication also minimizes hierarchical and psychological distance and maximizes collaboration amongst individuals and teams in an organization. More specifically, the following are the objectives of communication in an organization: information sharing, feedback, control, influence, problem-solving, decision-making, facilitating change, and facilitating group development. There are mainly four directions of organizational communication:

1. *Downwards communication:* The following types of communications are suggested along with some mechanisms:

    (a) *Diffusion of routine information:* This can be better done through circulars, bulletin boards and so on.

    (b) *Diffusion of procedural information:* This can be done by circulars, especially prepared notebooks and manuals.

    (c) *Socialization:* As already suggested, socialization individuals in the value system of the company should be done through induction booklets, special programmes, and meetings. Sharing of information from higher levels with the employees may also help employees to feel they are a part of the organization.

    (d) *Job-related information:* This needs to be done by interpersonal communication between the job holder and his reporting officer.

    (e) *Feedback on individual performance:* The most effective way of this communication is the appraisal review and coaching meetings held on the basis of performance appraisal results.

    (f) *Employee development:* Employee development is done through dyadic communication, based on trust between a manager and his employee, training programmes, and group meetings. A more effective communication for development is by the model set by senior managers.

2. *Upward communication:* Upward communication is as necessary as downward communication. There are several purposes for such communication. These are suggested below, along with possible mechanisms of developing them.

    (a) *Management control:* Use of management information ensuring regular flow of information helps in achieving effective management control.

    (b) *Feedback:* Feedback from lower levels to higher levels is very useful. Such feedback can be provided by use of special questionnaires and interviews. Exit interviews conducted when people are leaving the organization are used for feedback on important aspects which the people at higher level must know.

    (c) *Problem-solving involvement:* The effective mechanisms for solving person-related problems of lower levels management by the higher levels are grievance procedures and periodical meetings called by the higher level management. Another good method which may help the people at lower levels in the organization to participate in problem-solving is a suggestion scheme, which may help the people at lower levels in the organization to participate in problem-solving is a suggestion scheme which, however, needs to be well designed, properly executed, and periodically reviewed to save becoming ritualistic. A small task force may be constituted to prepare a scheme, and monitor it for sometime. Periodical meetings allowing all employees to express their feelings and give feedback to the management, to help them to take follow-up action on problems has been found to be useful in some organizations. VST Industries have introduced the scheme in a planned way (Vidyasagar, in NHN, 1989: 150).

3. *Horizontal communication:* Communication across business groups, regions and units is very important to develop collaboration and reduce bureaucratization. The following tasks can be achieved with different mechanisms as suggested below:

    (a) *Experience sharing:* Functional group meetings (like those of Finance, HRD, R&D, EDP people and others) from different business groups, along with other relevant people from the corporate departments may be helpful.

    (b) *Problem-solving:* Participation of people from different business groups in solving common problems can be achieved by setting up a special task force (group to work out details and, in many cases, to implement action plans) and a problem clinic (group to diagnose problems and suggest alternative solution, using special techniques of diagnosis).

    (c) *Coordination:* Standing committees are meant to make coordination more effective.

4. *External communication:* Communication with external agencies, like current and potential customers, government agencies, competitors and potential collaborators

resource providers (banks and financial institutions) is very important, but often gets little attention. The following purposes can be served by the suggested mechanisms:

(a) *Image building:* Annual reports, balance sheets, brochures, advertisements and the like are important mechanisms, deserving detailed planning in terms of form and content. Participation of company executives in professional bodies like management associations, chambers of commerce sub-committees also help significantly.

(b) *Credibility building:* Balance sheet and correspondence (prompt, purposive, and precise) contribute to the credibility of the company.

(c) *Influencing:* An organization should not shy away from its role of influencing policies and decisions in the concerned industries and other forums. Well-prepared dialogue by the top management and participation in conference and forums must receive the attention they deserve. One general weakness of Indian companies is the lack of expertise and seriousness in influencing external agencies. One of the most important roles of corporate management is to develop an aggressive (in the positive sense) posture and competence to deal with critical issues. This ability has been amply demonstrated by many organizations.

Principles in Designing HRD System

Of course, HRD systems must be designed differently for various organizations. Although the basic principles may remain the same, the specific components, their relationships, the processes involved in each, the phasing, and so on, may differ from organization to organization.

Designing in integrated HRD systems requires a thorough understanding of the principles and models of human resource development and a diagnosis of the organization culture, existing HRD practices in the organization, employee perceptions of these practices, and the developmental climate within the organization. The following principles related to focus, structure, and functioning should be considered when designing integrated HRD systems.

⌘ Focus of HRD System ⌘

1. *Focus on enabling capabilities:* The primary purpose of HRD is to help the organization to increase its "enabling" capabilities. These include development of human resources, development of organizational health, improvement of problem-solving capabilities, development of diagnostic ability (so that problems can be located quickly and effectively), and increased employee productivity and commitment.

2. *Balancing adaptation and change in the organizational culture:* Although HRD systems are designed to suit the organizational culture, the role of HRD may be to modify that culture to increase the effectiveness of the organization. There always has been a

controversy between those who believe that HRD should be designed to suit the culture and those who believe that HRD should be able to change the culture. Both positions seem to be extreme. HRD should take the organization forward, and this can be done only if its design anticipates change and evolution in the future.

3. *Attention to contextual factors:* What is to be included in the HRD systems, how is it to be subdivided, what designations and titles will be used, and similar issues should be settled after consideration of the various contextual factors of the organization—its culture and tradition, size, technology, levels of existing skills, available support for the function, availability of outside help and so on.

4. *Building linkages with other functions:* Human resource development systems should be designed to strengthen other functions in the company such as long-range corporate planning, budgeting and finance, marketing, production, and other similar functions. These linkages are extremely important.

5. *Balancing specialization and diffusion of the function:* Although HRD involves specialized functions, line people should be involved in various aspects of HRD. Action is the sole responsibility of the line people, and HRD should strengthen their roles.

⌘ Structure of HRD System ⌘

1. *Establishing the identity of HRD:* It is important that the distinct identity of HRD be recognized. The person in charge of HRD should have responsibility for this function exclusively and should not be expected to do it in addition to any other function. Multiple responsibilities produce several kinds of conflict. This person should report directly to the chief executive of the organization.

2. *Ensuring respectability for the function:* In many companies, the personnel function does not have much credibility because it is not perceived as a major function within the organization. It is necessary that HRD be instituted at a very high level in the organization and that the head of the HRD department be classified as a senior manager. Both the credibility and usefulness of HRD depend on this.

3. *Balancing differentiation and integration:* The human resource development function often includes personnel administration, human resource improvement and training, and industrial relations. These three functions have distinct identities and requirements and should be differentiated within the HRD department. One person may be responsible for OD, another for training, another for potential appraisal and assessments, etc. At the same time, these roles should be integrated through a variety of mechanisms. For example, inputs from manpower planning should be available to line managers for career planning and HRD units for potential appraisal and development. Data from recruitment should be fed into the human resources information system. If salary administration and placement are handled separately, they should be linked to performance appraisals. Differentiation as well as integration mechanisms are essential if the HRD system is to function well.

4. *Establishing linkage mechanisms:* HRD has linkages with outside systems as well as with internal subsystems. It is wise to establish specific linkages to be used to manage the system. Standing committees for various purposes (with membership from various parts and levels of the organization), task groups, and ad hoc committees for specific tasks are useful mechanisms.

5. *Developing monitoring mechanisms:* The HRD function is always evolving. It, therefore, requires systematic monitoring to review the progress and level of effectiveness of the system and to plan for its next step. A thorough annual review reappraisal every three years will be invaluable in reviewing and planning the system. It may be helpful to include persons from other functions in the organization in the HRD assessment effort.

⌘ Functioning of HRD System

1. *Building feedback and reinforcing mechanisms:* The various subsystems within HRD should provide feedback to one another. Systematic feedback loops should be designed of this purpose. For example, performance and potential appraisals provide necessary information for training and OD, and OD programmes provide information for work redesign.

2. *Balancing quantitative and qualitative decisions:* Many aspects of HRD, such as performance and potential appraisals, are difficult to quantity. Of course attempts should be made to quantify many variables and to design computer storage of various types of information, but qualitative and insightful decisions are also necessary and desirable. For example, in considering people for promotions, quantitative data are necessary inputs, but other factors must also be taken into consideration. Thus, a balance between the mechanical and the human factors is necessary.

3. *Balancing internal and external expertise:* A human resource development system requires the development of internal expertise and resources, specifically in content areas that are used frequently within the organization. For expertise that is required only occasionally, the use of external resources or consultants may be the most feasible. It is necessary to plan for an economical and workable balance between the two. It is preferable to use internal personnel to conduct training; however, an organization that uses only in-house expertise may not benefit from new thinking in the field. On the other hand, a company that relies solely on external HRD helps does not develop the internal resources that are necessary for effective functioning.

4. *Planning or the evolution of HRD:* Various aspects of HRD can be introduced into the organization in stages, depending on its needs, size and level of sophistication. Some aspects may require a great deal of preparation. Rushing the introduction of an aspect of HRD may limit its effectiveness. Each stage should be planned carefully, with sequenced phases built one over the other. This may include:

    (a) **Geographical phasing** introducing the system In a few parts of the organization and slowly spreading it to other parts. This may be necessary in a large or widely located organization.

(b) **Vertical phasing** introducing the system at one or a few levels in the organization and expanding up or down gradually.

(c) **Functional phasing** introducing one function or subsystem, followed by other functions. For example, introducing job specifications (identification of critical attributes of jobs) before introducing a complete potential-appraisal system.

(d) **Sophistication phasing** introducing simple forms of subsystems, followed after some time by more sophisticated forms.

Making HR a Business Partner

1. Train HR people in business to get a holistic business perspective

2. Get involved in larger organizational issues and handle coordination at that level

3. Align HR strategies with business strategies

4. Keep in mind business strategies forums, hold strategic discussions meetings, and prepare discussion paper

5. Convene business strategies forums hold strategic discuss meetings, and prepare discussion paper

6. Initiate process of discussion on strategy formulation form the frontline upward

7. Help in searching state of the art practices to discuss with the business team.

Training

Training is required at every stage of work and for every person at work. To keep oneself update with the rapidly changing technologies, concepts, values and environment, training plays a vital role. Training programmes are also necessary in any organization for improving the quality of work of the employees, at all levels. It is also required when a person is moved from one assignment to another of a different nature. Taking into account this context, this unit aims at providing insight into the concept, need and methods of training, also areas of evaluation of training, retraining and dimensions of organizational learning.

Need and Benefits of Training

There are some other reasons also for which this training becomes necessary. Explained below are various factors, giving rise to the need for training.

- Employment of inexperienced and new labour requires detailed instructions for effective performance on the job.

- People have not to simply work, but work effectively with the minimum of supervision, minimum of cost, waste and spoilage, and to produce quality goods and services.

- Increasing use of fast-changing techniques in production and other operations requires training into newer methods for the operatives.

- Old employees need refresher training to enable them to keep abreast of changing techniques and the use of sophisticated tools and equipment.

- Training is necessary when a person has to move from one job to another because of transfer, promotion or demotion.

Hence, a well-planned and well-executed training programme should result in:

- Reduction in waste and spoilage;

- Improvement in methods of work;

- Reduction in learning time, supervisory burden, machine breakage, maintenance cost and accident rate;

- Improvement in quality of products, production rate;

- Improvement of morale and reduction in grievances;

- Improvement of efficiency and productivity;

- Reduction in manpower obsolescence;

- Enabling the organization to provide increased financial incentives, opportunity for internal promotion and raising of pay rates;

- Wider awareness among participants, enlarged skill; and

- Personal growth.

✼ Organizing Training Programmes ✼

A good system training starts with the identification of training needs. The following sources can be used for identifying training needs.

Performance Review Reports: Performance review reports help in identifying directions in which the individuals should be trained and developed. On the basis of the annual appraisal reports, various dimensions of training can be identified. Training needs identified on the basis of performance appraisal, provide good information for organizing in-company training, and on-the-job training for a select group of employees.

Potential Appraisal: Training needs identified on the basis of potential appraisal, would become inputs for designing training programmes or work-out training strategies for developing the potential of a selected group of employees who are identified for performing future roles in the organization.

Job rotation: Working in the same job continuously for several years without much change may have demotivating effects. Some organizations plan job rotation as a mechanism of maintaining the motivation of people. Training is critical in preparing the employees before placing them in a new job.

Continuing Education: Besides these, most of the training programmes that are organized today, aim at equipping the managers with new technology. These training programmes attempt to help the managers raise their present level of effectiveness.

✤ Methods of Training

The methods of training are as follows:

Analysis of an Activity: List in a logical sequence, the activities in producing product or service or part thereof, and determine what new knowledge or skill is called for or which aspects of present knowledge or skills need to be modified.

Analysis of Problems: To analyse 'problems' and determine what additional skills, knowledge or insight are required to handle it.

Analysis of Behaviour: To analyse typical behaviour by individuals or groups and determine the corrective action involving training.

Analysis of an organization: To analyse organizational weaknesses to produce clues to both individual and group training needs.

Appraisal of Performance: To analyse performance and determine if someone should get something, be it additional knowledge, skill or understanding.

Brainstorming: To bring together a homogenous group and to ask individuals in the group to call out any ideas they have for answering a 'how to' question and identify items which call for additional knowledge, skill or attitude.

Buzzing: To ask an audience of supervisors, managers, professional, personnel or others (as long as it is homogenous) as to what the desirable next steps are in the organization's training programme or 'what additional areas of knowledge (or skill or understanding), do we need to handle our work better'.

Card Sort: To write statements or potential training needs on cards, hand them over to the persons whose ideas are sought, to arrange these cards in what they feel is their order of importance for various training needs.

Checklist: To break down a job, process, programme, activity, or area of responsibility into a list of detailed parts or steps arranged in logical sequence. Then to have checked off by each employee the items about which he feels he would like to have more skill or knowledge.

Committee: To constitute an advisory committee composed of persons responsible for or with a direct interest in an activity to identify training needs.

Comparison: To compare what an individual is doing (or contemplates doing) with what others are doing or have done to learn about new ways to handle old problems, keep up-to-date on new techniques and procedures and fight his own obsolesce.

Conference: To identify training needs and make decisions on ways these needs shall be met.

Consultants: To employ outside consultants to determine training needs and develop ways to meet them.

Counselling: To discuss between training practitioner and a person seeking guidance regarding the way he can improve his on-the-job performance or prepare for advancement.

In-basket: To measure or test a manager's ability to handle some of the day to day challenges which come to him in writing in his 'in-box' from various sources.

Incident Pattern: To note in terms of success or failure, the responses to special situations and to study the pattern of deviation.

Informal Talks: To meet and talk informally with people for finding clues to training needs.

Interviews: To arrange a formal meeting with the person or group concerned employing the interview techniques.

Observation: To observe such things as may have value as indicators of training needs, especially needs which are just under-the-surface or emerging.

Problem Clinic: To arrange meetings of a homogenous group to discuss a common problem and develop a solution.

Research: To identify implications for training and development as a result of research.

Role Playing: To get clues to his training needs in a skill, an area of knowledge, or in understanding or attitude by observing how each role player acts in a role playing situation.

Self-analysis: To self-evaluate and know what is needed in theory, additional knowledge, skill or insight.

Simulation: To analyse performance in simulated exercise to reveal individual and/or group training needs.

Skill Inventory: To establish and annually update an inventory of the skills of their employees and to identify gaps or blind spots in reserve or stand-by-skills.

Slip Writing: To write on a slip, the type of training needed and analyse the information on these slips.

Studies: To undertake studies which can turn up training needs which will have to be met if the plans were adopted.

Surveys: To undertake surveys that can be used to take inventory of operations, employee attitudes, implications of advanced planning, etc.

Tests: To perform tests to measure skill, knowledge or attitude and to identify gaps.

Task Force: To constitute a task force which, in analyzing the problem, may in earth training needs which must be met before their recommended solution to the problem can be implemented.

Questionnaire: To develop a questionnaire to elicit information which can be used to determine training needs, delimit the scope of the training, identify course contents, etc.

Workshop: To identify in a workshop, the need for further understanding or insight about organization goals or operations.

⌘ Principles of Training ⌘

Certain principles are followed for developing effective training programmes. Some of these are described below:

1. Every human being is capable of learning.

2. An adequate interest and motive for learning is essential because people are goal-oriented.

3. Learning is active, and not passive.

4. People learn more and faster when they are information of their achievements.

5. People learn more by doing than by learning alone.

6. Time must be provided to practice what has been learnt.

7. A knowledge of the standards of performance makes learning effective.

8. Learning is a cumulative process. An individual's reaction to any lesson is conditioned and modified by what has been learned by him in earlier lessons and by previous experience.

9. Early success increases an individual's chances for effective learning.

10. Effective learning results when initial learning is followed immediately by application.

11. The rate of learning decreases when complex skills are involved.

12. Learning is closely related to attention and concentration.

13. Learning is more effective when one sheds one's half-knowledge, prejudices, biases, likes and dislikes.

14. Learning to be successful should be related to a learner's experiences in life.

15. Trainees learn better when they learn at their own pace.

Training Methods

Various methods of training have been evolved and any one method, or a combination of any tow or more of these can be used, depending upon the training requirements and the level of people to be trained.

⌘ Training for Different Employees ⌘

The employees who are to be trained can be different types and each type would require a different type of training.

Unskilled workers are given training in improved methods of handling machines and materials. The objective here is to secure reduction in cost of production and waste. Training is given on the job itself, by immediate superior officers.

Semi-skilled workers require training to cope with requirements arising out of adoption of mechanization, rationalization and technical processes. Training is given by more proficient workers, bosses or inspectors. It may be given either in the section or department of the worker or in segregated training shops.

Skilled workers are given training through apprenticeship in training centres or in the industry itself.

Salesmen are trained in the art of salesmanship in handling customers, planning their work, and facing challenges of the marketplace. Supervisory staff constitute a very important link in the chain administration. They have to cope with the increasing demands of the enterprise in which they are employed and to develop team spirit among people under their a charge. A training programme for them should aim at helping the supervisors to improve their performance, and to prepare them for assuming greater responsibilities at higher levels of management.

All training methods can be broadly classified as (a) on-the-job-methods, and (b) off-the-job methods.

⌘ On-the-job Methods ⌘

Under these methods, the principle of learning by doing is used. These methods are briefly summarised below:

1. *On-the-job Training:* An employee is placed in a new job is told how it is to be performed. It aims at developing skills and habits consistent with the existing practices of an organization and by orienting him to his immediate problems. Coaching and instructing is done by skilled workers, by supervisors, or by special training instructors. A variety of training aids and techniques are used such as procedure charts, lecture manuals, sample problems, demonstrations, oral and written explanations, tape recorders, etc.

2. *Vestibule Training or Training-Centre:* It involves classroom training imparted with the help of equipment and machines identical to those in use at the place of work. Theoretical training is given in the classroom, while practical work is conducted on the production line. It is often used to train clerks, bank tellers, inspectors, machine operators, typists, etc.

3. *Simulation:* It is an extension of vestibule training. The trainee works in closely duplicated real job conditions. This is essential in cases in which actual onset-job practice is expensive, might result in serious injury, a costly error or the destruction of valuable material or resources, e.g., in aeronautical industry.

4. *Demonstration and Examples:* Here the trainer describes and demonstrates how to do a certain work. He performs the activity himself, going through a step-by-step explanation of the 'why', 'how' and 'what' of what he is doing. Demonstrations are often used in combination with lectures, pictures, text material, discussion, etc. The emphasis under this method is on know-how. The principles and theory of a job must be taught by some other methods.

5. *Apprenticeship:* A major part of training time is spent on the job productive work. Each apprentice is given a programme of assignments according to predetermined schedule which provides for efficient training in trade skills. This method is appropriate for training in crafts, trades and technical areas, specially when proficiency in a job is the result of a relatively long training or apprenticeship period, e.g., job of a craftsman, a machinist, a printer, a tool maker, a pattern designer, a mechanic, etc.

⌘ Off-the-job or Classroom Methods ⌘

Training on the job is not a part of every day activity under these methods. Location of this training may be a company classroom, an outside place owned by the organization, an education institution or association, which is not a part of the company.

These methods are:

1. *Lectures:* These are formally organized talks by an instructor on specific topics. This method is useful when philosophy, concepts, attitudes, theories and problem-solving have to be discussed. The lectures can be used for a very large group to be trained in a short time. These are essential when technical or special information of a complex nature is to be imparted. The lectures are supplemented with discussions, film shows, case studies, role-playing, etc.

2. *The Conference Method:* Under this method, a conference is held in accordance with an organized plan. Mutual problems are discussed and participants pool their ideas and experience in attempting to arrive at better methods of dealing with these problems. The members of the group come to teach each other and to learn together. Conferences may include buzz sessions which divide the conference into small groups of four or five for intensive discussions. These small groups report back to the whole group with their conclusions or questions. This method is ideally suited for analyzing problems and issues, and examining them from different viewpoints. It helps in developing conceptual knowledge, reducing dogmatism and modifying attitudes.

However, it is suitable only for a small group of, say 20-30 persons, because larger group often discourages active participation of all the conferees. Under this method, the conferees should have some knowledge of the subject to be discussed. They should be good stimulating leaders who can adopt a flexible attitudes and encourage members to express themselves with fear. They should also control the more verbose members while brining out the more reserved. They can develop sensitivity to the thoughts and feelings of individuals, summarise material at appropriate times during a discussion, and ensure a general consensus on points without forcing agreement or side-stepping disagreements.

3. *Seminar of Team Discussion:* The group learns through discussion of a paper on a selected subject. The paper is written by one or more trainees. Discussion may be on a statement made by the person in charge of the seminar or on a document prepared by an expert. The material to be analysed is distributed in advance in the form of required reading.

4. *Case Discussion:* Under this method, a real (or hypothetical) business problem or situation demanding solution, is presented to the group and members are trained to identify the problems present, they must suggest various alternatives for tackling them, analyse each one of these, find out their comparative suitability, and decide for themselves the best solution. The trainer only guides the discussion and in the process ensures that no relevant aspect is left out of discussion, and adequate time is spent on each aspect. This method promotes analytical thinking and problem-solving ability. It encourages open-mindeness, patient-listening, respecting others' views and integrating the knowledge obtained from different basic disciplines. Incidentally, it enables trainees to become increasingly aware of obscurities, contradictions and uncertainties encountered in a business. This method is extensively used in professional schools of law and management, and in supervisory and executive training programmes in industry.

5. *Role-Playing:* This method is also called 'role-reversal', 'socio-drama' or 'psychodrama'. Here, trainees act out a given role as they would in a stage play. Two or more trainees are assigned roles in a given role as they would in a given situation, which is explained to the group. Therefore, there are no written lines to be said and, naturally, no rehearsals. The role players have to quickly respond to the situation that is ever changing and to react to it as they would in the real one. It is a method of human interaction which involves realistic behaviour in an imaginary or hypothetical situation.

Role playing primarily involves employee-employer relationships, hiring, firing, discussing a grievance problem, conducting a post appraisal interview, disciplining subordinate, or a salesman making presentation to a customer.

6. *Programme Instruction:* This involves two essential elements: (a) a step-by-step series of bits of knowledge, each building upon what has gone before, and (b) a mechanism for presenting the series and on the trainee's knowledge. Questions are asked in proper sequence and indication given promptly whether the answer are correct.

This programme may be carried out with a book, a manual or teaching machine. It is primarily used for teaching factual knowledge such as Mathematics, physics, etc.

Evaluation of Training

Many organizations, especially industries, have been concerned with the difficult but critical question of evaluation. Training managers or organizers are also concerned with this question. All books on training have dealt with this issues, but no satisfactory and comprehensive accounts of evaluation are available.

Two additional questions are – How should evaluation be done? What specific ways should be adopted for it? These questions relate to the design and techniques of evaluation, respectively.

⌘ Main Clients   ⌘

There are several partners in the training act and process, and all of them are the client of evaluation. Their needs for feedback and use of feedback for improvement (control) will naturally be different with some overlapping. There are four main partners in training (and clients for evaluation):

1.   The participants or learners (P)

2.   The training organization or institute (I) include

     (a)   Curriculum planners (CP)

     (b)   Programme designers (PD)

     (c)   Programme manager (PM)

3.   The faculty or facilitators or trainers (F)

4.   The client organization, the ultimate user and financier of training (O)

     Literature on training evaluation has not paid due attention to this respect.

⌘ Dimensions of Evaluation   ⌘

Attention has been given to the main dimensions of training and most of the suggested models are based on these. Four main dimensions have usually been suggested: contexts, inputs, outputs, and reaction. The last dimension is not in the same category as the other three. Reaction evaluation can be of contextual factors, training inputs, and outcomes of training.

In all discussions of training evaluation, the most neglected aspect has been the training process which cannot be covered by training inputs. The climate of the training organization, the relationship between participants and trainers, the general attitudes and approaches of the trainers, training methods, etc., are very important aspects determining the effectiveness of training. Evaluation of the training process, therefore, should constitute an important element. We may, thus, have four main dimensions of evolution: evaluation of contextual factors (F), evaluation of training inputs (I), evaluation of training process (P), and evaluation of training outcomes (O).

Areas of Evaluation

The various areas of training evaluation need more attention and elaboration. Seven main areas, with some sub-areas under each, are suggested for consideration. These are shown in the exhibit below in sequential order; the exhibit also shows the conceptual model of training, by relating the areas to the dimensions. This model is based on the following assumptions.

EXHIBIT 8.2 Coverage of Evaluation	
Area of Evaluation	**Dimension**

1. Pre-training Factors
   (a) Preparation
   (b) Learning Motivation
   (c) Expectations
	Context

2. Training
   (a) Curriculum including
   (b) Specific Events
   (c) Specific Sessions
	Events

3. Training Management
   (a) Areas of Satisfactory/ Dissatisfaction
   (b) Training Facilities
   (c) other Facilities
	Context

4. Training
   (a) Learning Climate
   (b) Training Methods (Pedagogy)
   (c) Trainer Team Effectiveness
	Process

5. Participant Development
   (a) Conceptual Development
   (b) Learning of skills
   (c) Change in Values/Attitudes
   (d) Change of Behaviour
   (e) Application
	Outcome

6. Organizational Development
   (a) Job Effectiveness
   (b) Team Effectiveness
   (c) Organizational Effectiveness
	Outcome

7. Post-training Factors
   (a) Cost
   (b) Organizational Support
   (c) Organizational Factors Hindering or
      facilitating use of Training
	Context

1. Effectiveness of training depends on the synergic relationship and collaborative working amongst the major partners of training (participants: training organization, trainers and client organization). Hence evaluation should provide the necessary feedback to these for contributing to training effectiveness.

2. Training effectiveness depends not only on what happens during training, but also on what happens before the actual training (pre-training factors). Evaluation cannot neglect these important contextual factors.

3. Various aspects of the training process that are not direct training inputs for example, also contribute to its effectiveness. Evaluation should, therefore, also focus on these factors.

4. The focus or the main task of evaluation should not only be in the nature of auditing (measuring training outcomes in terms of what has been achieved and how much), but should also be diagnostic (why the effectiveness has been low or high), and remedial (how effectiveness can be raised).

Retraining

Retraining programmes are designed as a means of avoiding personal obsolescence. It is the tendency of the individual worker to become outdated in terms of job requirements. This is true of employees at every level in the organization.

However, retaining is focused on rank-and-file workers. This is so because their number is large and technological change makes its immediate impact on those who work closer to technological resources. Besides, they are less equipped to foresee their personal needs and because they require more assistance in advance planning than to others.

Workers require refresher courses to help them recall what they have forgotten and to overcome some practices they have come to accept as satisfactory. They also need to bring them with respect to relevant new knowledge and skill. The need for retraining also arises as a result of technological changes resulting in changes in equipment, tools, and work methods.

The Present Status of Training

Training is not fulfilling its proper role in various organizations. There are, at least, the following five reasons for the plight in which training is at present.

⌘ Call-girl Role

The training unit organizes training events on the initiation or suggestion of the persons who matter in the organization. Training plays a reactive rather than a proactive role. Instead of being a partner in the process of development of the organization, it merely responds to requests made to it. This essentially reduces its effectiveness. This plight is largely shared by the outside consultants and trainers who are invited to do a particular training programme, or even to give one or more talks on specific topics. But this is also true of the in-company training function. While talking to persons in charge of training in various organizations, one gets the impression that they do not have enough opportunity in the organization to innovate and suggest ways of developing it.

So far training has been treated either as a feudal wife or as a call-girl rather than a modern housewife. The role of the wife in the feudal society was to decorate the home and bear children, but not necessarily be a life partner in enjoying life, or sharing problems. A call-girl is invited when she is needed and she also does not participate in the vital decisions of a man's life. Similarly, taking either analogy, training is not able to fulfill the obligation of being really effective in an organization. Training has to become comparably to a real housewife, by not only responding to the needs of the organization, but by determining these needs and being a partner in the process of development. Unless training is treated as a partner in decision-making, it cannot play the role of contributing to organizational effectiveness.

Expectancy of Peripherality

By and large there seems to be a general feeling in the organization that training is a peripheral activity rather than a central one. In many organizations, training is more decorative than functional. In some organizations, training performs the role of the family priest. This role is enjoyed by the training subsystem too. The family priest mainly helps in the performance of religious rituals appropriate to the caste of the family. He also gives pious advice, often to be merely heard and not necessarily acted upon. He however, is not involved in any vital decisions taken by the family. Training, therefore, is often regarded as a useful but not a very essential activity in the organization. Other functions such as production marketing, personnel, and finance are very central and important, and compared to these functions, training is only of secondary importance. This concept of training as a non-essential or a peripheral activity produces several effects in the organization. The personnel connected with the training activity have a low self-image and cannot operate with confidence.

Low Status

Since training is regarded as peripheral, and since it is treated as a service department, only responding to the various demands of the organization, it is unfortunately given rather a low status. This is a vicious circle. No activity can become central in an organization unless the organization expects that activity to be important and gives it high enough status. On the other hand, the status is also a function of the activity being central. The low status of training is reflected in the level at which the TM is being recruited in the organization. In most organizations, he is at such a low level that it becomes difficult of to him assert himself and to be heard with respect. Unfortunately, in Indian organizations, status and grade play an important part in deciding how much say a person would have in the organization. Low status of training, therefore, limits its effectiveness considerably.

⌘ Non-professional Image

Training is becoming a profession. Although it has not been completely professionalized, it has developed its own techniques, and is fast emerging as a profession. However, organizations in India still do not treat training as a profession; in fact, they do not take it seriously. Training is seen as a function which can be managed by anymore who is good in the main activity of the organization. As a result, people appointed to manage training may not have the necessary professional skills which TMs would be required to have. In some cases, those who are found to be less efficient and effective in other functions are transferred to the training function. Such practices reflect the attitude of the management towards training. The example is cited of one organization in which the training system is fairly large. Discussions with persons in various parts of the organization revealed that they were recommending or nominating those persons for appointment as trainers whom they did not find very useful. In some cases, the transfer of people to the training units and back to operations were very frequent. Those who were not trainers were not given any orientation or training before being made to take up their new role as trainers.

⌘ Slow Professionalisation

One factor for which we, who are in the field of training, are responsible is the slow speed with which we are professionalizing training in India. Each profession has its own system of preparation of those persons who want to join it. It develops its own skills of working, its own techniques, and its own standards of ethics. It develops a strong pressure group to ensure that the minimum standards of pre-professional and in-professional training are maintained. The establishment of the Indian Institute of Management and the Indian Society for Training and Development has helped in developing training as a profession. However, the aspirations of training personnel are so low, and their behaviour so different, that they project a weak image of training. They only respond to the need of the organization, rather thinking of ways of transforming their role into a more central one. We need to do a great deal in developing training as a profession.

Making Training a Strategic Function

Turnaround in thinking on training is already evident that it must move from the periphery to the centre, from being a service function to partnership in the main task of the organization. In a recent study of HR re-engineering in 34 large US companies 69% respondents mentioned "repositioning of HR as a strategic business partner with the management" as a re-engineering goal. The same is true.

Training is concerned with increasing organizational effectiveness. So far, the approach of training has been to offer/organize training for specific competencies. The movement is in the direction of training becoming more proactive, and contribute, to strategic thinking of the organization. This swing is sometime seen as abandoning the previous position and taking a new one. Repositioning does not mean taking an "either or" position. Repositioning involves expanding the role and emphasizing the strategic role, of training. While the strategic role is important, the other roles are not to be neglected.

Training should attend both to the current as well as the future needs. The current perspective is more operational, while the futuristic perspective is strategic. The other dimension relevant for the role of training is that of content vs process. While the former emphasizes the development of specific competencies, the latter is concerned with developing learning and empowering capability. If we combine these two dimensions, we get four training modes as shown in the Figure below.

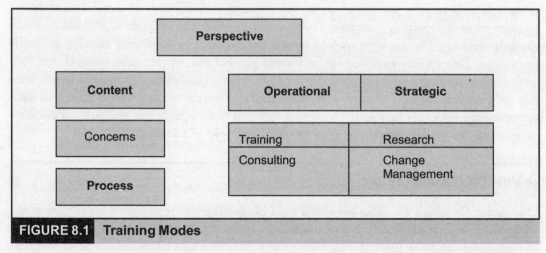

FIGURE 8.1 **Training Modes**

All the four modes of training are important. However, increasingly, training must move towards transformational and strategic roles. Figure shows the foci, objectives and postures, for these four training modes. We shall briefly discuss these, taking the four main roles of training.

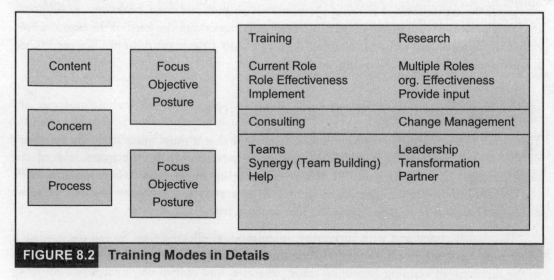

FIGURE 8.2 **Training Modes in Details**

Training Role

Training system should develop needed competencies for various role occupant. The emphasis is on making the current roles in the organization more effective by equipping people occupying these roles with the needed competencies. Training takes current strategy and implements it in terms of development of needed competencies. The trainers should deliver good training. And to do this, they themselves must have the relevant technical competencies.

Research Role: In order to move in the strategic direction, trainers need to search what competencies are needed and will be needed in the organization. Training then assumes two more functions: searching future competencies, and developing them. Since the narrow boundaries of roles are breaking down, a person should develop flexibility to perform various roles. Multi-skilled workers are a good example of such effort. This becomes the first essential step for developing autonomous work groups and self-managed teams. The trainers, who function as researchers, need to develop their deep insight into organizational needs and process. Trainers should develop research competencies, especially those of action research.

Consulting Role: Greater emphasis on organizational effectiveness, rather than only on individual role effectiveness, will require more group process-orientation of trainers. Development of effective teams influence both the effectiveness of the individual team members as well as organizational effectiveness. The emphasis is synergy building, thereby enhancing effectiveness of each member. This can be done if the trainers advance with their research competencies into a consulting role analyse problems, develop and use interventions involving concerned line people to deal with the problems, help in implementing the agreed action plan, and support it to stabilize the decisions. This is one step further in contributing to the strategic process. Training is then seen as a useful function for developing organizational strategy. Trainers should develop both sharper understanding of the organizational strategy, and consulting competencies to play this role effectively. Training function should be used more frequently for international consulting. Trainers then will also develop more hands-on experience, which will make training more realistic and relevant.

Change Management Role: This is the real strategic partnership role. The focus of training is to develop leadership at all levels in the organization—the ability of strategic thinking, taking responsibility, creativity to find alternative solutions, and empowering others. The objective is to transform the organization, to make paradigm shift if needed. Training then becomes a true strategic partner. This is not possible without involvement of the trainers in the main business of the organization, and gaining relevant business knowledge.

Translating Business Strategy into Training Terms

Successful implementation of the business strategy of an organization will require some competencies. Business strategy indicates the broad direction for the future movement of an organization, and preferred ways of doing so. For successful implementation, the organizational tasks must be translated into various functional terms: marketing, financial, technology, human resources, training etc. This helps to make strategy formulation and implementation participative.

The overall organizational or "business" strategy should provide the framework for developing the training strategy to facilitate effective implementation of the strategy. It will include detailed approach to be adopted, competencies to be developed (in what thrust, evaluation etc.). Training strategy, thus, prepared may be reviewed by all the functional leaders preparing the strategies which must be integrated into the main strategy for better synergy.

Another way to translate business strategy into training terms may be to develop strategies for key decisions taken by the organization. For example, if cost reductions of one of the elements in the business strategy, training may develop ways of advancing this concern and achieving concrete results. In a study of 34 large US companies, for example, 78% HR professionals listed "cost reduction" as a top goal.

Training goals get closely linked with business goals. By maintaining an independent strategy, training may send a signal that is not connected with the other functions. Regarding HR. One participant in the study said "If I had to do it again, I'd build HR strategies directly into business strategies and make them seamless".

⌘ Working More Closely with Line Managers ⌘

People dealing with training should work more closely with line people. They are already working with line people in the areas of coaching, counselling, training, strategy planning for the departments etc. When cross-functional task forces and implementation teams are set up, training people should join these. Similarly, when teams are set up to discuss training issues etc., line people should be invited as members. Such close working together may help in integrating training with the various business groups and making training a strategic partner.

Rosow and Zager have made some recommendations to forge stronger links between training and business strategy.

The partnership in training should be based on value-added partnership of the trainers and training system. As strategic partners, training people should raise serious discussion on how organizational strategy should be developed, and how it can implemented faster. Effective partnership comes out of professional competence and credibility.

⌘ Making Training a Strategic Partner ⌘

1. The vice-president responsible for the training function should be actively involved in formulating corporate strategy, to ensure that:

    ❖ Strategic goals are realistically ambitious with respect to the reservoir of skills that will be available to meet them.

❖ The training function will be able to help the top management communicate corporate strategy throughout the organization and to help managers translate the strategy into training needs.

2. The vice-president for the training function should ensure that all training programs (1) are necessary to the corporate strategy; (2) are recommended by (and, if possible, budgeted to) the managers whose employees are to be trained; and (3) help the trainees progress along the career paths jointly set by them and their managers.

3. The effectiveness of a programme should be measured by how fully and how durably the trainees have mastered the subject matter.

4. The most controversial and potentially the largest factor in measuring the cost of a programme is whether the trainee's time spent in training should be considered and added cost. On the other hand, management should count as a cost any additional expense incurred to cover the trainee's work while training is in progress.

5. When an employer invites an employee to be retrained, it should ensure that the employee becomes fully acquainted, as early as possible, with the new position, work unit, and supervisor, whether the position is within or outside the firm. Such acquaintance maximizes the trainee's ability to learn and to apply the new skills.

⌘ Aligning Training Strategy with Corporate Strategy ⌘

1. The chief executive officer (CEO) and senior associates should include a training plan as a critical component of the corporate strategic plan, to ensure that all levels of the organization will have the knowledge and skills to carry out the strategic plan. The training plan should distinguish clearly between (1) tactical programmes designed to keep up with-and even anticipate-changes in technology, competition, and work-force standards, as well as with the rapid obsolescence of occupations.

2. The CEO should regularly monitor the training function to ascertain that (1) program priorities match those of the corporate strategy, (2) programme cost and skill objectives are valid, and (3) programme cost and skill objectives are met.

3. Employers should think of their organizations as in a sense, institutions for continuous learning, and should make them function as such. They should, therefore, aim to involve all employees in all stages of training, from needs analysis through evaluation.

4. Where employees are presented by unions, employers should invite the unions to share in the design and administration of training for their members. Unions should press for and accept such joint programmes, but they should be careful to take on responsibility no faster than they acquire the skills and experience to discharge it.

5. To institutionalize continuous learning throughout the organization, the employer should encourage employees to make special efforts to learn-and/or to help other

employees learn-skills valuable to the employer. Encouragement should take such forms as:

❖ A clear declaration that continuous learning and helping other employees to learn are integral parts of every job and every employee's responsibility.

❖ Favourable structures and mechanisms, for example, learning by objectives, train-the trainer programmes, continuous learning centers, semi-autonomous work teams.

❖ Appropriate rewards, for example, pay raises, eligibility for promotion, recognition by peers.

❖ Where a union is present, a jointly administered training programme and fund.

❖ Training, with focus of competency building amongst various organizational units, requires collaboration amongst several players in the organization. Partnering by different key persons in the organization is important for the success of training.

Towards Learning Organization

Organization-wide learning, widespread and as a clear concept, dates only from the 1970s, and that learning had to be continuous only from the 1980s. Continuous learning that also embraces the environment—the organization in its environment—has been the top agenda since the 1990s.

The organization-wide learning view is already a long way from viewing training as something for individuals, or a class, or a team at work or play. The next step however, and each step after, does not follow at all smoothly. Each calls for reconceiving the change effort and so also the training for it. The very next step makes occasional into permanent effort, and this can usually cannot be done by merely stretching what is already there but often calls for programming, resources, and integration of a different order, and reorganization. The next step again then broadens the perspective beyond the organization to include people outside, and not just as clients, suppliers, or more or less distant regulators or other officials as before and one-by-one, but as essential partners and together.

Turbulence, newly and reluctantly recognized as the now normal state of the environment and fed by instantaneous global information and tremors of all kinds, causes the shift to a continuously learning organization. It is a basic shift, to a different disposition for the organization as a whole. It orients and prepares the organization differently, different even from the recent past when its people expected and then also buckled down to making a learning effort from time-to-time and here and there in the organization, and even when lately that exigency occurred ever more frequently. So the shift is not just for more economy of effort and smoothing out interruptions of normal living and working.

Urgent as it is, understanding this move, from spasmodic organization-wide learning to a continuously learning organization is essential, and can be achieved by collaborative efforts. Exhibits and extracts from major works may serve best for an overview and also for connecting readers with the works themselves for fuller exposition of views of special interest to them.

Exhibit contrasts organizational learning with a continuously learning organization on the six dimensions highlighted in organizational studies since the 1970s. What Chris Argyris calls 'double-loop learning' sets the stage for the rest: not only is something learnt that improves task performance (single-loop learning), but the organization too takes note and modifies its policies, structure, ways of operating, and whatever else is necessary to support that change and to promote further changes. In both cases, learning only registers when it shows in improved performance.

The key difference lies in the scope of that performance in singly-loop learning, even if it be organization-wide, the organizational framework remains unchanged; in double-loop learning, the organization uses the learning, for changing its framework as well. Indeed, when that becomes its culture, it expects and is continuously prepared for using innovative inputs for improving performance directly and also improving itself. Basic to this shift is what Harold Bridger, a founder member of the Tavistock Institute in London, calls the 'double-task': learning for improved performance plus learning how the improvement is effected, for use next time and also to guide adjusting the framework so it can support further learning.

EXHIBIT 8.3	Organization-wide Learning and Learning Organizations	
Organization-Wide learning	**The Learning Organization**	
1. Single-loop learning	Double-loop learning	(Argyris, 1977)
2. Incremental	Transformational	(Argyris and Schon, 1978)
3. Lower-level	Higher-level	(Fiol and Lyles, 1985)
4. Adaptive	Generative	(Senge, 1990)
5. Tactical	Strategic	(Dodgson, 1991)
6. Occasional	Continuous	

Training needs to be reoriented so that it becomes a strategic function, and contributes not only to the development of individuals and teams, but is able to help the organization become a learning organization. Training, therefore, deserves rethinking and replanning.

Mentoring and Performance Coaching

✂ Conditions for Employee Development ✂

For helping and employee to grow and develop in any Organization; it is necessary to understand the conditions associated with development. The following are some such conditions.

1. *The individual should be interested in developing himself:* Development cannot take place if the person himself is not interested in it. The first condition for human

resources development is to ensure the interest of the individual in developing himself. Quite often, higher level officers in the organizations write off some of their employees as not growing or not willing to grow. Such perceptions only show bias. No individual wants to stagnate. Only others, because of their expectations difference between the observer's interest in the employee's development in one direction, being different from the employee's own desire to learn something best. It is an understanding and mutual discussion, it may be possible to create interest in individuals for new areas of development that are congruent with organizational goals and plans.

2. *The individual should know the areas of his potential development:* Although the recent researches in behavior suggest that individuals can learn any skills, there is also ample evidence to show that some individuals can grow faster on some dimensions that on others. These are called aptitudes. While in the developed countries there are enough opportunities for an individual to know about his potential through psychological tests, school coaching services, family guidance services, etc. We do not have such services easily available in India. An individual himself may discover, quite often too late, that he is good at certain things and he is not as good at on his introspective capability and the opportunities he gets to test himself. In organizations where fresh graduates are exposed to a variety of jobs through job rotation procedures, the young men get opportunities to test themselves and their aptitudes in relation to various functions. In organizations which do not have such a job rotation policy at the early stages of employee's career, the chances of round pegs being put in square holes increase. While every individual should attempt to discover his own potential, the organization also has an obligation to create conditions for such a discovery.

3. *The individual should make a clear choice about the direction in which he would like to grow and develop:* Besides discovering his aptitude, the individual should be in a position to make a clear choice about his career. He might discover that he has more than one strength. A combination of his strengths may indicate that he is good at a number of things. Some careers may be more paying than others. Sometimes the individual may have the strengths required for a particular career. Which according to him is rewarding only in a limited way. In such a case, he should be able to take the risk and create opportunities for himself to develop strengths required for new careers. Through a good career planning and training system, the organization should attempt to help him to develop himself. The organization should also help in setting such career goals realistically.

4. *He should be able to identify opportunities for development within and outside the organization:* Identification of potential, strengths, weaknesses, etc., may have a demoralizing effect on the employees if no system exists for developing or overcoming them. Opportunities for the development of individual employees within and outside the organization should be created.

5. *He should identify mechanisms of using these opportunities and get the support he needs from his superiors and the organization:* While the organization should plan for the growth of the employees according to their career plan, it is unrealistic to expect

it to support the career goal of each individual employee. However, it should help the individual to understand the limitations and work out alternative strategies.

6. *He should make efforts to develop:* Mere interest in development does not serve any purpose if the individual is not prepared to invest himself and his energies in his development. Such an investment would depend upon how much he is prepared to act. Development can take place only through concentrated efforts to acquire knowledge and the ability to experiment with that knowledge. High-activity level and risk-taking orientation 'accelerate learning.

7. *He would take outside help to periodically review his progress:* Persons cannot develop in isolation. Most of the development at higher levels is facilitated through human interaction. A person should have either a reference group or a few selected helpers in the environment for periodical reviews. The reference group or selected helpers act as mirrors so that the individual can continuously look at himself in the direction in which he is growing.

8. *A positive emotional and professional climate should be created in the workplace for the employee to progress and review himself:* The responsibilities for creating such a climate lie at every level with higher level officers and the top management of the organization. Such a climate facilitates free expression of feelings, emotions, free exchange of views, opinions and, at the same time fostering of mutual trust.

The identification of potential and development of the employee is a joint responsibility of the employee himself and the organization. While the latter should provide opportunities for the individual to grow, the former should get interested in identifying opportunities, strengths and weaknesses, set himself realistic career goals, and continuously review his growth. The individual has the responsibility to make use of such opportunities and act with drive and determination. One of the most effective instruments in the hands of an employee for development is performance review (feedback and coaching).

Performance review can be done at several stages. While it is the responsibility of the supervisors to guide and counsel their employees in relation to their past, present and future, a formal system of performance review can be employed by organizations. Performance review can be done both for the individual and the group.

❈ Objectives of Performance Coaching   ❈

Coaching aims at developing employees in an organization, by the following.

1. Helping them to realize their potential as managers.

2. Helping them to understand themselves—their strengths and weaknesses.

3. Provide them opportunity to acquire more insight into their behaviour and analyze the dynamics of such behaviour.

4. Helping them to have a better understanding of the environment.

5. Increasing their personal and interpersonal effectiveness by giving them feedback about their behaviour and assisting them in analyzing their interpersonal competence.

6. Encouraging them to set goals for further improvement.

7. Encouraging them to generate alternative for dealing with various problems.

8. Providing them empathic atmosphere for sharing and discussing tensions, conflicts, concerns and problems.

9. Helping them to develop various action plans for further improvement.

10. Helping them to review in a non-threatening way their progress in achieving various objectives.

11. Strengthening the dyadic relationship between the employee and his boss.

⌘ Individual-level Review ⌘

The purpose of performance review is to help the employee grow and develop. Others can help him as quite often he may not aware of his own strengths, just as he may be blind to his weaknesses. Those who continuously interact with the person can act as mirrors. However, such a feedback should be specific and purposeful. It serves three main purposes: (1) general improvement of the person, (2) improvement of his performance in specific tasks, and (3) identification and development of his potential for higher level responsibilities.

1. *General Improvement:* Feedback for the general improvement of an employee is a continuous process. It occurs either inside or outside the organization through colleagues, friends, subordinates, family members, etc. Within the organization, people who work closely can be instrumental in helping the employee continuously assess the impact he is making on people and the environment. Such an assessment would help him to understand his own characteristics and develop as a mature person. No formal system can help in such a continuous interpersonal feedback. However, it can be facilitated through an open climate, a climate of psychological security, and positive attitudes towards one another in the organization.

2. *Improved Performance:* While the senior officer helps their subordinates to perform gains. Usually, managers guide their subordinates more in relation to specific, immediate task-related problems rather than on other aspects of behavior. For example, whenever a subordinate faces a problem, his officer may give a solution for that particular problem. Merely providing the solution to a problem dos not amount to giving feedback. This will not necessarily help the employee to develop the ability to solve future problems by himself this ability to solve problems by himself can be developed through continuous education.

The formal appraisal system is another mechanism of giving feedback discussion. In such a formal system, the tasks are set much in advance. At the end of a specified period of time, both the individual and his senior officer sit together for performance review. Feedback is a critical factor in such a review. In the performance review, the individual points out his own accomplishments in relation to the objectives decided upon. He may also identify the factors that have helped him in achieving whatever he could achieve, and the factors that prevented him from doing better. The individual may also highlight the qualities he has shown in that particular period. After he presents his own assessment, his senior officer tries to help him analyze his own performance in greater depth. He might add a number of other factors which have helped him to achieve whatever he has achieved, and a number of other factors that prevented him from doing better. The senior officer may also focus on the strengths and weaknesses of the appraises. He might also point out the consistencies or inconsistencies of behaviour he observed in the employee. Both the manager and his employee jointly identify the developmental needs and ways of meetings the needs.

3. *Potential Development of the Employee:* Employees develop their potential if they are aware of the opportunities in the organization and also of the mechanisms for developing this potential. Some organizations use mechanism to appraise the potential of an employee. Usually, data are collected about all the employees whose potential is being assessed. It may be useful to give feedback to the employee on such data. Feedback on potential assessment would help the employee to understand his strengths and weaknesses, and help him to modify his career plans accordingly. If the employee has no opportunity to explore the feedback further, it is likely to demoralize him. Since emotions are involved here, it should be handled delicately. Such review should better be done either by one whom the employee trusts, or by an outside expert who has used objective measures of assessing the potential, or by a group of people from the top management who have a border perspective and who can coach the employee. The officers one or two levels above the employee can give such feedback, either formally or informally, after a system of potential appraisal has been introduce to the organization. In such a review with the employee, they would have with them the employee's ratings and other data on his potential. The following points may be kept in mind in the potential appraisal review of the employees.

   (a)   The employee should be given the source of feedback;

   (b)   The employee should be told the limits of the feedback;

   (c)   The employee should be helped to view alternative career opportunities;

   (d)   Before giving such feedback, it should be ensured that the employee believes that there are opportunities to develop his potential and that human behaviour is dynamic and changeable; and

   (e)   While giving the feedback, the relationship of the employee with others who work with him should also be kept in mind.

Feedback to Groups or Teams

Feedback needs to be given to a group of people who constitute a small unit or a department within a large organization. It may help the group to grow and develop as such. Feedback to groups is generally useful in terms of the process mechanisms operating in the group, like decision-making styles, collaborative orientation of the group with other groups, delegation, supervisory styles, morale, etc. Feedbacks can be given either by the organizational leader or through an external agent using the research and surveys. Mechanisms of giving group feedback using survey research are described in the section on research and organization development.

⌘ Conditions for Effective Coaching ⌘

Coaching is a means and not an end in itself. Development does not occur just because there is coaching. Coaching could be an effective instrument in helping people integrate with their organizations and have a sense of involvement and satisfaction. The following conditions are necessary for coaching to be effective:

1. *General Climate of Openness and Mutuality:* If the organization or department in which the employee is working is full of tension, and people do not trust each other, coaching cannot be effective. A climate of minimum trust and openness is essential for effective coaching.

2. *General Helpful and Empathic Attitude of Management:* Coaching involves effective helping, which is not possible unless the coach has a general helping attitude and has empathy for the counselled.

3. *Uninhibited Participation by the Subordinates in the Review Process:* Unless the subordinates in a department or organization feel free enough to participate without inhibition in the process of review and feedback, coaching cannot be effective. Coaching is not a one-way process of communicating to the employee what he should or should not do. It is a process of developing a dialogue which eventually contributes to a better understanding on the part of the counselee.

4. *Dialogic Relationship in Goal Setting and Performance Review:* Performance coaching focuses on the counselee's achievement of the performance goals set in consultation with his manager. Joint participation by the employee and his reporting officer is necessary both in goal-setting and performance review. Without such collaborative effort, coaching cannot achieve its purpose.

5. *Focus on Work-oriented Behaviour:* The main purpose of performance coaching is to help the employee to improve his performance. Coaching can be effective if the focus

is kept on the work-related goals rather than on diffusing attention into various other areas. While doing so, discussion may involve the related and personal issues, but thee are used to refocus on improvement on organization roles rather than on personal or general personality problems.

6. *Focus on Work-related Problems and Difficulties:* Performance coaching is not only related to the achievement of goals, but also to the contextual problems in achieving or not achieving the goals. Analysis of performance, therefore, becomes the basis of coaching.

7. *Avoidance of Discussion of Salary and other Rewards:* Performance coaching may not serve its purpose if it includes discussion about salary raise, rewards, etc. The main purpose of performance coaching is to use performance appraisal in planning and improvement of the employee, rather than in understanding the relationship between performance and rewards like salary, etc. Bringing such discussion in the performance coaching may vitiate the main purpose of coaching.

⌘ The Process of Coaching ⌘

Coaching is given by one who is senior to the person, receiving the help in competence, knowledge, psychological expertise, or in the hierarchical position in an organization. There are three main processes involved in coaching – communication, influencing and helping. The coach essentially communicates with the employee. Communication involves receiving messages (listening), giving messages (responding), and giving feedback. The person who provides coaching does all the three things. Coaching also involves influencing the counselee in several ways. The manager cannot deny the fact that he is influencing his employee in such a way that the latter is able to move in some direction. However, this influence is of a special, that is, enabling the other person to exercise more autonomy, providing positive reinforcement so that desirable behavior is further strengthened, and creating conditions in which the persons able to learn from the behaviour of the coach through the process of identification. The third element in the process, i.e., helping, also functions in a similar way. It involves three different elements. First, helping behaviour is based on the concern and empathy the coach has for his counselee. Secondly, it is also based on the mutuality of relationship; the counselee responds as much to the coach's needs as the latter does to the former's. Finally, helping primarily involves identification of developmental needs of the counselee so that he may be able to develop and increase his effectiveness. This dynamic process of coaching is shown in figure 8.3.

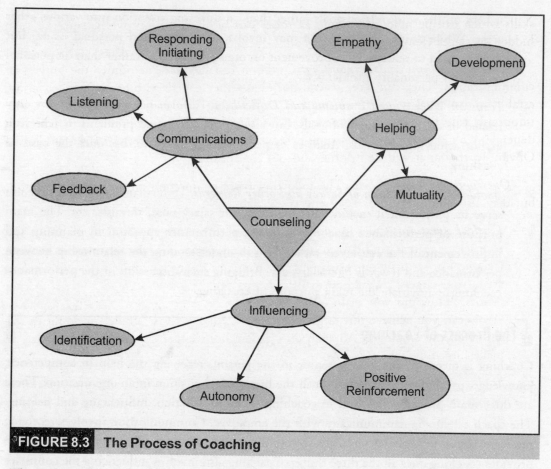

FIGURE 8.3 **The Process of Coaching**

The various elements of the coaching process is explained in more detail below:

Communication

Interpersonal communication is the basis of performance review in which both the employee and his reporting officer are involved. Such a conversation in performance review should be congenial, which may help the employee to be in a receptive mood. It is important to keep in mind that communication is greatly influenced by how problems and issues are perceived by the two persons involved in the conversation. It may get distorted if people are not empathic to each other and do not try to understand each others' point of view. Non-verbal communication is as important as verbal communication. People speak much more through their gestures and postures than through words. The tone and manner of speaking is also important. There are three main elements in communication.

Listening: Listening is the first effective step in communication. Listening involves paying attention to the various messages being sent by the other person. The obvious message is the ideas being communicated (cognitive message). But there may be hidden feelings and concerns which the other person may not be able to put clearly in words. Listening to feelings and concerns is very important for effective coaching. This involves skills which can be practiced. Some exercises can be used to improve listening of such hidden messages (Rao and Pareek, 1978)

Asking Questions and Responding: Question can facilitate or hinder the process of communication. They can serve several purposes—they can in getting more information, establishing mutuality, clarifying matters, stimulating thinking. Questions play a very important role in coaching. Some questions can shut off the employee, or make him dependent on the coach, while some others can build the autonomy of the employee. Obviously, the latter will be helpful, and not the former.

Questions that do not help: The following types of question are not only unhelpful, but they also hinder the process of effective coaching:

1. *Critical questions:* Questions which are used to criticize, reprimand or doubt the counselee, create a gap between him and the counselor. The way the question is asked (skeptical or sarcastic tone) may indicate nature of the question. "Why could you not attain your targets?" Would normally communicate an invitation to examine hindering factors. "How did you again fall short of your target?" is a reprimanding question. "How can you achieve this target since you failed last time?" indicates doubt in the ability of the employee. All such critical questions either shut off the counselee or make him different.

2. *Testing questions:* Questions that are asked to find out whether a person is right or wrong, or how much he knows, are evaluating or testing questions. Such questions may tend to put the other person on the defensive. In a testing question, the person asking the question takes a superior attitude, while the other person is put in a kind of witness box. Such questions may also take the form of a cross-examination. A reporting officer who proposes to find out why his employee was not able to meet his target can easily slip into a cross-examination, testing or evaluating posture. Again, the tone of the interviewer may determine whether the question is a testing question. Such questions are sometimes similar to critical questions.

3. *Resenting questions:* A person may ask questions to indicate his resentment of the behavior of the other person. When an employee in a coaching situation asks: "How should I attain a higher target?", it may indicate his resentment depending on the tone in which such a question is asked.

4. *Leading questions:* Quite often unknowingly, the questions asked indicate what kind of answers are wanted and such answers are actually received. Such a question may be asked after making a statement. For example, a reporting officer may say to his employee: "You could not attain the target because maintenance department did not cooperate. Is that true?" or it may be put in the question form: "Were you not able to attain the target because the maintenance department did not cooperate?" Both are leading questions. A leading question almost seduces the other person to go along the line of thinking of the one who asks the question. This tends to stop further exploration and is not helpful.

Questions that are helpful: The following types of questions may be of help in developing a more healthy relationship in increasing the effectiveness of the other person.

1. *Trusting questions:* Questions which are asked to that the questioner is seeking help or suggestions may indicate the trust he has in the other person. The question "How do you think I can deal with the problem I am facing?" is seeking help from the other person. Such questions may be asked both by the employee and the supervisor.

2. *Clarifying questions:* Questions may be asked to collect information, more facts and figures. Such questions are very helpful. If a coach asks his employee several questions to help him to get more information about various aspects, the employee, in turn, would provide him with relevant information to understand his problems. After listening to a person for some time the coach may paraphrase the counsellee's statement (also called mirroring), and then he may ask a question to confirm whether his understanding is correct. For example, the question, "Are you worried about your lack of knowledge of the new system?" is a clarifying question. A clarifying question helps the manager and the employee to remain at the same level throughout the conversation.

3. *Empathic questions:* Questions about the feelings of a person, his concern, his problem, not so much for finding solutions as to indicate and express concern, may be classified as emphatic questions. When a manager asks an employee: "How is your son feelings now?", he is not merely seeking information, but in fact indicating his personal concern about the health of the employee's son and thereby expressing empathy with the employee. Such questions help to generate more trust, and the necessary rapport with the employee. Empathic questions create a climate of mutual trust and human understanding.

4. *Open questions:* The most useful questions are those which stimulate reflection and thinking in the employee. "Why do you think we have not achieved the targets this year while the other company has?" is an open question inviting the other person to explore the various possible dimensions, and to share them with the person who is asking such a question. Open questions encourage creativity, and a tendency to explore several directions which might have been neglected so far. Such questions are very useful.

5. *Responding to questions:* Coaches sometimes use certain responses, some of which are useful and some dysfunctional. Some coaches may be using certain types of responses more often than others. It is necessary to be aware of this. Responses that alienate the employee, criticize him or order him, are more likely to be dysfunctional. Empathic, supportive, and exploring responses are more functional. Various verbal behaviors in a coaching situation that characterize these responses are shown in Exhibit 8.4.

EXHIBIT 8.4	Coach Responses
Unhelpful	**Effective and Helpful**
Alienating	Empathic
Continuous stress on conformity	Leveling
Not encouraging creative acts	Rapport building
Passive listening	Identifying feelings
Lack of verbal response	Supportive
Critical	Recognizing
Criticizing	Communicating availability
Pointing inconsistencies	Committing support
Repeated mention of weaknesses	Trusting
Belittling	Exploring Questions
Reprimanding	Questions
Directive	Reflecting
Prescribing	Sharing
Ordering	Probing
Threatening	Closing
Giving no potions	Summarizing
Pointing out only one acceptable way	Concluding
Quoting rules and regulations	Contracting for follow up and help

Feedback: Interpersonal feedback is an important input for increasing self awareness. It helps in reducing the blind area of a person, helping him to become more aware about his strengths and weaknesses. If properly used, it results in a higher mutuality between two persons. The process of interpersonal feedback, and conditions which make it effective, have been discussed in detail (Pareek, 1976). The following hints are reproduced from that source:

Feedback will be effective if the person giving feedback (coach) makes sure that it is:

1. Descriptive and not evaluative;

2. Focused on the behaviour of the person and not on the person himself;

3. Data-based and specific and not impressionistic;

4. Reinforces positive new behaviour;

5. Suggestive and not prescriptive;

6. Continuous;

7. Mostly personal, giving data from one's own experience;

8. Need-based and solicited;

9. Intended to help;

10. Focused on modifiable behaviour;

11. Satisfying the needs of both (giver and receiver of feedback)

12. Checked and verified;

13. Well-timed; and

14. Contributes to mutuality and building up of relationship.

From the point of view of the one who receives the feedback, it is necessary that the reaction to feedback is more in terms of exploring ways of improving behaviour rather than of defensive behaviour. The following defensive behavior might not help in using feedback properly; the behaviour which are opposite of these may be helpful.

1. Denying feedback as opposed to owning up responsibility for behavior.

2. Rationalization (explaining away feedback by giving reasons) as opposed to self-analysis to find why such behaviour was shown.

3. Projection (contributing negative feelings to the other persons) as opposed to empathy (trying to understanding the point of view of the other persons).

4. Displacement (expressing negative feelings to one who may not fight) as opposed to exploration (taking help of the other person in knowing more about the feedback given).

5. Quick acceptance without exploration as opposed to collecting more information and data to understand the behaviour.

6. Aggression towards the person giving feedback as opposed to seek his help in understanding the feedback.

7. Humour and wit as opposed to concern for improvement.

8. Counter-dependence (rejecting the authority) as opposed to listening carefully to the person giving feedback.

9. Cynicism (generally strong skepticism that things cannot improve) as opposed to a positive, critical attitude to accept some feedback and to question some other.

10. Generalization (explaining things in a general way) as opposed to experimenting.

Influencing

Influencing would mean making an impact on the person in relationship. Such impact need not necessarily be of a restrictive type. Influencing in coaching would involve the following three aspects:

1. *Increasing Autonomy of the Person:* Usually, influencing is understood only in the sense of restricting the autonomy of the person exerting influence. Positive influencing

is the opposite of this; the autonomy of the other person is increased, and he has larger scope of making his own choice. Even this is influencing, but of a different kind. Flanders makes a distinction between the two modes of influence, viz., the direct mode of influence (which restricts the freedom of the other person), and the indirect mode of influence (which increases the freedom of the other person). Flanders has developed some categories, and encouraging a person in the second category of influence. The reason is obvious. When a person is criticized or punished, some actions for which he is criticized or punished are inhibited and the person avoids doing those in future. This restricts his freedom. On the other hand, if a person is praised or recognized, he feels encouraged to take more initiative in exploring new directions. This results in an increase in the field of his autonomy. In coaching, much more use is made of the indirect mode of influence, by recognizing and expressing feelings, acknowledging and praising good ideas given by the counselee, and raising question which promote thinking and exploration.

2. *Positive Reinforcement:* It has been established by Skinner that change in behaviour cannot be brought about in human beings through punishment or negative reinforcement, but only through positive reinforcement. Influencing would involve providing encouragement and reinforcing success so that the person takes more initiative and is able to experiment with new ideas. Change cannot take place without experiment and risk-taking. And these are encouraged through positive reinforcement.

3. *Identification:* One major influence which helps an employee to develop is the opportunity for him to identify himself with individuals having more experience, skill and influence. This is the first stage in the development of psycho-social maturity, or power motivation. This legitimate need should be fulfilled. Levinson states several barriers which may come in the way of such a legitimate process of identification; lack of time, intolerance for mistakes, complete rejection of dependency needs, repression of rivalry, and unexamined relationship. Levinson suggests that, to help the development of the process of identification it is necessary that the manager also examines his own process, and needs of interacting with the subordinates.

Helping

Coaching is essentially helping. Helping involves several processes but the following three are mainly important.

1. *Concern and Empathy:* Without the manager's concern for his employee, effective helping cannot be provided in a coaching session. Such concern is shown when the coach is able to feel for his subordinate and is able to empathies with him. This would be reflected in the kinds of questions asked and the tone in which the conversation takes place. Managers may constantly ask themselves how much concern and genuine empathy they have for the employees they are coaching. Without such genuine concern, coaching may only degenerate into a ritual and cannot achieve its goals.

2. *Mutuality of Relationship:* Coaching should not be regarded as merely giving help. It is also receiving help on various aspects. Unless such a relationship is established—i.e., both persons involved in the relationship feelings free to ask for and provide help to each other—coaching cannot be effective. Mutuality is based on trust and the genuine perception that each person has enough to contribute. Although the coach is in a superior position, he continues to learn and to receive help from the counsellee.

3. *Identifying Developmental Needs:* The main purpose of performance coaching is to identify the development needs of the employee which can be met through various ways. It is necessary that coaching results in clear and systematic identification of such needs and in subsequent plan as to how these needs will be fulfilled.

Sperry and Hess (1974) have advocated the use of contact coaching, which they defined as "the process by which the manager aids the employee in effective problem-solving, and develop using the techniques or keying, responding and guiding." Contact coaching is based on a transactional analysis approach and makes use of several skills already discussed. Keying refers to reading people. The supervisor uses an appropriate frame of reference to perceive what the employee means by his verbal and non-verbal responses. Responding concerns what the supervisor communicates back to the employee. What is learnt from keying is replayed in a manner which adds to, on subtracts from, the interchanges with the meaning the employee communicates. Guiding is the techniques the supervisor as motivator can increase the employee's drive and direct it so that he accomplishes his objective better.

Morrisey (1972) has suggested a few other techniques, such as a you-we technique, second-hand compliment, advice-request and summary. In the you-we technique, one uses you to complement and we to criticize (you are doing a great job, we have a problem). The second-hand compliment is communicating to the subordinate a compliment for him received from a third party (Mr Raman says that you have done an excellent job for him). The advice-request is asking the employee for suggestions and advice. Summarizing at the end helps in clarifying the decision stake and fixing the responsibilities and integrating the whole discussions.

Values in the Helping Process

The central issue in a helping process relates to the values of the helper. The helping behaviour and strategies flow out of the basic stand he takes in relation to the client. Figure 8 gives in summary the dynamics of the helping process in value terms. The helper should ask himself/herself what values he/she holds, and with what consequences.

Okun (1976) has suggested that the following set of images of people is essential for an effective helping process:

1. People are responsible, and capable of making their own choices and decisions.

2. People are controlled to a certain extent by their environment, but they are able to direct their lives more than they realize. They always have choices and freedom, along

with responsibility, even if they have restricted options due to environmental variables biological or personality predispositions.

3. People want to feel good about themselves and continuously need positive confirmation of their own needs, ranging from basic physiological needs to abstract self-actualization ones (fulfilling physiological, psychological and aesthetic needs).

4. People want to feel good about themselves and continuously need positive confirmation of their own self-worth from significant persons. They want to feel and behave congruently, to reduce dissonance between internal and external realities.

5. People are capable of learning new behaviors and unlearning existing ones and they are subject to environmental consequences of their behaviors which in turn, serve as reinforcements. They strive for reinforcements that are meaningful and congruent with their personal values and belief systems.

6. People's personal problems may arise from unfinished business (unresolved conflicts) stemming from the past (concerning events and relationships) and, although some exploration of causation may be beneficial in some cases, most problems can be worked through by focusing on the here and now, on what choices the personal has now. Problems are also caused by incongruence between internal (how you see things inside) and external (how you see things outside) perceptions in the present.

7. Many problems experienced by people today are societal or systemic rather than personal or interpersonal. People are capable of learning to effect choices and changes within the system as well as from without.

❋ Phases of Performance Coaching ❋

Coaching is helping the employee to grow and develop in the organization. Every manager is coaching his employee, knowingly or unknowingly, in his day-to-day work-life. An effective manager coach is one who helps his employees to become more aware of their strengths and weaknesses and helps them to improve further on the strong points and overcome weaknesses. By the process of mutuality and support, he helps the employee to develop, by providing the proper emotional climate. Mutuality involves working together with the employee and developing future plans of action for the employee's growth and contribution to the organization. Support involves acceptance of the employee as a total person, with his strengths and weaknesses, and encouraging him with warmth.

Coaching requires certain interpersonal skills which can be acquired easily if a manager is genuinely interested in developing his subordinates. Coaching skills are important for a manager, particularly at the time of performance review.

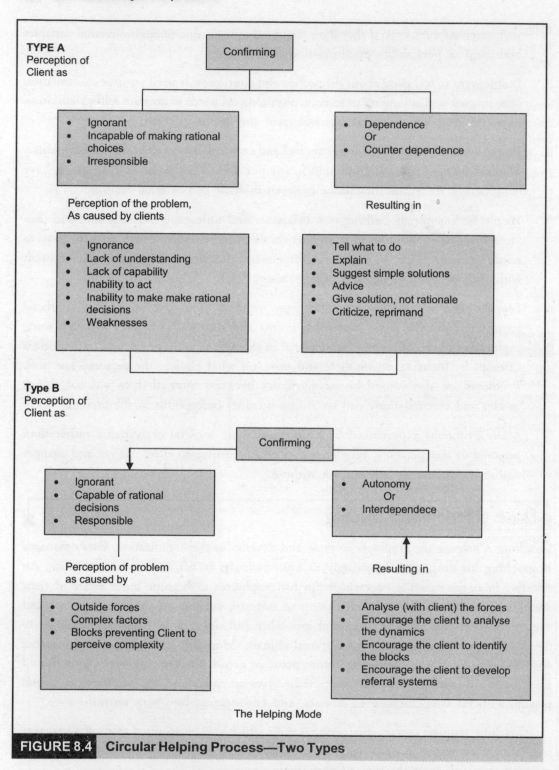

TYPE A
Perception of
Client as

Confirming

- Ignorant
- Incapable of making rational choices
- Irresponsible

- Dependence
  Or
- Counter dependence

Perception of the problem,
As caused by clients

Resulting in

- Ignorance
- Lack of understanding
- Lack of capability
- Inability to act
- Inability to make make rational decisions
- Weaknesses

- Tell what to do
- Explain
- Suggest simple solutions
- Advice
- Give solution, not rationale
- Criticize, reprimand

Type B
Perception of
Client as

Confirming

- Ignorant
- Capable of rational decisions
- Responsible

- Autonomy
  Or
- Interdependece

Perception of problem
as caused by

Resulting in

- Outside forces
- Complex factors
- Blocks preventing Client to perceive complexity

- Analyse (with client) the forces
- Encourage the client to analyse the dynamics
- Encourage the client to identify the blocks
- Encourage the client to develop referral systems

The Helping Mode

FIGURE 8.4 Circular Helping Process—Two Types

Good managers, whenever the necessity arises, coach their employee in their jobs. Annual performance reviews provide formal opportunities for formal coaching. Such a formal coaching process passes through certain stages, which are important for the managers to note. The coaching process has the following three phases: rapport building, exploration, and action planning.

In the rapport-building phase, a good coach attempts to establish a climate of acceptance, warmth, support, openness and mutuality. He does this by empathizing with the employee and his orientations, by listening to his problems and feelings, by communicating his understanding to the employee, and by expressing empathy with and genuineness of interest in him. In the exploration phase, the coach attempts to help the employee to understand himself and his problem better. He may do this by raising questions to help the employee explore his problems and diagnose the problem properly.

In the action planning phase, the coach and the employee jointly work out or plan specific action steps for the development of the latter. The manager makes commitments to provide the specific support to employee for development.

Exhibit 8.5 gives the three phases (and the sub-phases) of the coaching process. Against each sub-phase there are mentioned types of coach behavior which either help or hinder the coaching process.

EXHIBIT 8.5	Sequential Process of Performance Coaching	
Phases	**Helpful Behaviour**	**Hindering Behaviour**
Report Building Attending Listening (to) telephones Feelings Concerns Problems Acceptance (empathy)	Rituals, smile Conversation on personal matters Physical attention (posture) Eye contact Response (verbal and non-verbal) Keeping out telephones, noise Communication of feelings and During conversation Concerns paraphrasing feeling Sharing own experience	Discussion from start Distraction (attending to other things, etc.) Signing letters, talking to others, disturbance, etc. Lack of response, passive listening for a long period
Exploration Exploring Problem Identification Diagnosis	Mirroring or paraphrasing Open questions Encouragement to explore Questions to explore possible problems Encouragement to generate information Identification of a probable problem Exploratory questions Generating several possible causes	Criticizing Avoiding or hedging Suggestion of a problem Suggesting the cause
Action Planning Searching Decision making Supporting	Questions on possible solution Generating alternative solutions Questions on feasibility, priority Pros and cons Discussion of one solution Discussion of an action plan Contingency plan Identification of needed help Monitoring Contract on help	Advising Directing Making a fixed plan Promise of general help

Rapport Building

Rapport building is essential for any effective coaching outcome. This phase involves generating confidence in the employee to open up an frankly share his perceptions, problems, concerns, feelings, etc. The coach-manager should level himself with his employee and tune himself to his orientations. This can be done by adopting the employee's frame of reference.

Attending: The opening phase of coaching is very important in rapport building. General opening rituals may communicate messages of attending to the employee and given importance to the coaching transaction. Inviting rituals like offering the chair, closing the door to indicate privacy, asking the secretary not to disturb or not to connect telephonic calls during the cooperation, may indicate that the coach is attending to the employee. However, all such rituals should come out of the genuine concern for and full attention to the employee during the coaching session.

Listening: It has already been discussed that listening is important for effective coaching. As already stated it is important to listen to what the employee says, as well as to his feelings and concerns. Physical posture (e.g., leaning forward) and keeping eye contact with the employee are indicators of listening.

Acceptance: Establishing a climate of acceptance is a necessary part of establishing rapport. The employee must feel that he is wanted and that his coach is interested in understanding him as a person rather than as a role or a positioning an organization. The coach communicating back to the employee by listening to all the problems of the employee and communicating back to the employee that he is listening. The coach can communicate back to the employee by paraphrasing or mirroring or reflecting what the employee says. For example, when an employee says, "I am really mad. I have tried to do my best in the past year. I have worked twice as hard as anymore else in the office. But I never get promotion," he is expressing his anger. The coach may reflect back and say, "You feel that your superiors have not shown proper recognition for your hard work." Such a reflection or mirroring would help the employee feel that he is being understood ad that his coach s interested in him. This builds a climate of acceptance and facilitates the process.

Exploration: Besides accepting the employee, listening to him, and establishing a climate of openness, the coach should attempt to understand as well as help the employee understand his own situation strengths, weaknesses, problems and needs. Nobody would like to be directly told his weaknesses. Coaching skill lies in making the employee discover his own weaknesses, and identify his problem. At the most, the coach may use open and exploring questions.

Exploring helps an employee to search various dimensions of the problems, or discover unidentified problems and bring to the surface unnoticed issues. Exploring can be done by using questions and suggesting to the employee to talk more on a problem he mentions. As already discussed, a variety of questions may be used.

Problem Identification: After general exploring, questions may be asked to help the employee focus on the problem. It is necessary for the coach to use questions, both to generate information on some concerns and problems and to narrow down focus to identify a more probable problem. For example, if an employee feels that his problem is that others do not cooperate with him, the coach may ask questions to narrow down the problem to the employee's relationship with a few colleagues, and then questions to narrow down the problem to the employee's relationship with a few colleagues, and then questions may be asked to help the employee see what he does that prevents possible cooperation. Eventually, the problem may turn out as to how the employee may deal with competitive relationship, and yet collaborate. Identification of a problem is the necessary step in planning for improvement.

Diagnosis: Diagnosis of the problem is the next step in exploration. Explorations should lead to the diagnosis. Without diagnosis there is little scope for solving any problem. Open questions like "Why do you think people are put off when you talk with them?" "What personal limitations mainly bother you?" may help the employee more towards a better diagnosis. The main attempt should be to generate several alternative causes of a problem.

Action Planning: Managers are expected to guide their employees and contribute to their development. Coaching interviews should end with specific plans of action for the development of the employee. Identifying a training need, job rotation, sponsoring for further training, increased responsibility, role clarity, etc., are some of the likely for further training, increased responsibility, role clarity, etc., are some of the likely outcomes in such action plans. Three sub-phases can be identified in action planning.

Searching: The main contribution of the coach to action planning is the help he provides to the employee in thinking of alternative ways of dealing with a problem. In addition to encouraging the employee in brainstorming such alternatives, the coach at a later stage can also add to this list of alternatives for further exploration. This should, however, be regarded as a contingency plan, to be altered in the light of further experience.

Supporting

The final and crucial stage of coaching is to communicate support and plan for such support in implementing the agreed action plan. Psychological contract of providing help should emerge after considerable exploration and discussion. Support and help should facilitate in further increasing the autonomy of the employee, and not his dependence on the coach. A system for monitoring and follow up of the action plan may be prepared. This closes the coaching interaction.

⌘ Making Coaching Effective ⌘

In performance coaching formally organized by the organization, the employee may not ask for coaching but his superior may organize coaching interviews as an organizational requirement. On such occasions, the employee may be forced into a coaching situation. If coaching is given without having been sought, it is likely to be of limited value. It may prove frustrating both to the coach and to the employee. In such situations, the coach would do well by forgetting about performance coaching and talk to the employee about performance coaching and talk to the employee about his lack of interest in growth. The employee is likely to open up if the coach establishes an open climate. If the employee has serious emotional block in dealing with his superior, there is no use organizing a coaching interview. They need a problem-solving session before that. Hence, before coaching, it must be ensured that the employee is willing to learn from this interview.

Some employees are loyal and some superiors so protective, that there is a danger of employee becoming totally dependent on the coach. The coach should check from time to time through reflection, if he is making the employee too dependent on him. The coach must allow the employee to make his own decisions and perhaps help him in making decisions, but must not take decisions for him.

The employee must understand the purpose of coaching. If he does not understand, or has wrong expectations, he may not receive whatever is said to him in the proper perspective. If it is felt that he has some misunderstandings, it is better to use the first session to clarify him and then schedule another session.

Arguments should be minimized. One argument is sufficient to make both parties defensive. The coach should accept everything the employees says and try to build on it. Acceptance is the best way of bringing about self-realization in the person.

Good coaching sessions fail to produce effective results due to lack of follow-up. Follow-ups through informal exchanges go a along way in communicating interest in the employee. Otherwise, he may feel that the coaching is only artificial and may lose interest in it eventually.

The Process of Mentoring

The word "mentor" comes from the Greek epic story about Odysseus who wandered the world seeking adventure and – you could say – personal development. Before going on his ten-years voyage (none of this weekend workshop stuff for Odysseus!), he left his son Telemachus in the care of an older and trusted friend whose name was Mentor. In Odysseus' absence, Mentor not only helped the boy become a competent young man but also saved his life. This relationship, and the name of the older man who assisted the younger man in developing himself, become a model for what is now known as mentoring.

Mentoring is the process where a person (the mentor) provides support, training, and guidance to a less-experienced, usually younger person (the mentee, mentoree, or protégé). Some benefits of mentoring are that it enhances productivity and teamwork, it encourages continued learning, it improves the self-esteem of the protégé, and it improves the chances of success in the protégé's endeavours.

Levinson et al., (1978) have contributed the most to the understanding of the mentoring process. Levinson's concept of a mentor includes being a teacher, sponsor, counsellor, developer of skills an intellect, host, guide, exemplar, and most importantly supporter and facilitator in the realization of the vision the young person has about the kind of life he wants as an adult. Mentoring integrates characteristics of the parent-child relationship and peer support without being either. According to Levinson, not having a mentor in the formative years of a young person could be a great handicap to one's psychological and career development.

Although young person during their professional journey, knowingly research and discover appropriate mentors, organizations are increasingly paying attention to this phenomenon. Generally, more promising young managers are given mentoring experience. A young manager assigned to a mentor, who is senior in position and age sometimes several levels senior to the protégé; not necessarily from the protégé's department. Mentors are selected on the basis of their interest, availability, and "mentoring competence" (image of competence, empathy, and ability to provide emotional support). One mentor may have not more than five protégés. Tata Iron successfully used this arrangement.

There are two main phases in mentoring process – dependence and interdependence, although counter-dependence may, in some cases, be an intermediary phase between the two. During the dependence phase, admiration for the mentor is followed by identification with him, followed by approval (getting guidance and checking alternative action ideas). The interdependence phase is characterized by trust-building and mutuality when the mentor and the protégé may begin to collaborate and provide emotional support to each other. If the mentor is experienced as overwhelming and overpowering, counter-dependence may develop before interdependence. The protégé may reject the mentor and may develop his own independence. Search of one's own identify may later lead to appreciation of the mentor's role and relationship, leading to interdependence. Several well-known persons in the West having famous mentors passed through the counter-dependence phase and some could not make much progress to interdependence.

Mentoring process is quite similar to the counselling process. The dynamics of the phase discussed with counseling are also applicable to mentoring. The ultimate goal of both counseling and mentoring is to help an employee attain psychological maturity and effectiveness.

Counselling for Better Performance

Counselling is quite often misunderstood. It is wrongly interpreted as a process of correcting or controlling the employee behaviour by giving him negative feedback in an assertive manner by his boss. When employees make mistakes or become unmanageable or non-cooperative, executives often state that they need counselling. Some managers also are known to make statements like "I called him for counselling and gave him a bit of my mind" or "I called him for counselling and told him clearly that I am not going to tolerate his behaviour any more" or "I called him for counselling and finished him off", etc. Unfortunately, due to such misuse of the term "counselling" it has acquired some negative connotations in the minds of some managers. They confuse "verbal threats", "criticism" and "negative feedback" to be counselling. Actually such behaviours prevent counselling.

A second reason why counselling has acquired a negative image in the minds of some executives is because of equating it with clinical counselling and psychotherapy, which are more often associated with problem cases. In fact, a major difference between clinical counselling and performance counselling is precisely this. Performance counselling is normally done in regular course of performance when there are no problems. When there are problems, executives should resort to appropriate methods of solving them rather than to counselling. Because exclusive focus on a particular problem or issue may prevent performance counselling. Performance counselling focuses on the entire performance (tasks and behaviours) during a particular period rather than on a specific problem. However, specific problems may be discussed during counselling as a part of analysing and understanding performance patterns.

In clinical counselling the client goes to a therapist for help on his own initiative and therefore has a high motivation to solve his problems and improve his capabilities to deal with his environment. In performance counseling, the counselor, initiates the discussion as a part of an appraisal system or as a part of some processes that take place in the organization. The onus of making the counselling successful is jointly with the counsellor and the counselee, although the counsellor has a major responsibility by virtue of his position in the organizational hierarchy. It is this, that makes performance counselling complex. The counsellor who is at a higher status level has to carry on the task of helping his subordinate by creating an atmosphere of acceptance. Thus, unlike clinical counselling, in performance counselling the counsellor has an additional task of motivating the counselee to participate effectively in the counselling process. In addition, while continuing to exercise his authority as a boss outside the counselling session, he should generate a climate of acceptance, mutuality, trust and openness during counselling. Recognition of this complexity is essential for the successful implementation of counselling. Failure to recognise this often leads managers to point out inconsistencies in their bosses by statements like – "He was nice during counselling and out of it he is very hard on me." Counselling is a separate event and certainly should lead to more understanding but need not result in "lenience" or "softness" in dealing with people.

While performance counselling should take place at least once in a year as an integral part of the appraisal system outlined in this book, it could be carried out more frequently by managers. It is advisable to have performance counselling discussions quite frequently depending upon the needs of each appraise and the time availability of the counsellor. In fact, the more attention a manager pays to counselling his subordinates, the more time he is likely to gain in the long run as a result of improved capabilities of his subordinates.

Any organization interested in using a good performance appraisal and review system that aims at developing employees has to practice and pay enough attention to performance counselling. Performance appraisal does not serve the purpose of developing employees unless an effective system of performance counselling is introduced and practised in the organization. Performance counselling can be defined as the help provided by a manager to his subordinates in analysing their performance and other job behaviours in order to increase their job effectiveness. Performance counselling essentially focuses on the analysis of performance on the job, and identification of training needs for further improvement.

Counselling is a dyadic process. It is based on the relation between two persons, a manager who is providing help and an employee to whom such help is given or who is a counsellee. It differs from training mainly in its intensity of dyadic relationship and its focus on establishing mutuality and confidentiality. Managers provide such help or counselling at various stages. For example, employee may be provided such personal help soon after his selection or when he is facing difficulties or problems. The focus of performance counselling is the employee's performance on the task assigned to him.

Performance counselling sometimes is also called "coaching" mainly because the purpose, the word "counselling" is a much wider and appropriate term for such a process.

✻ Objectives of Counselling

Counselling aims at development of the counsellee. It involves the following:

1. Helping him to realise his potential as a manager

2. Helping him to understand himself-his strengths and his weaknesses

3. Providing him an opportunity to acquire more insight into his behaviour and analyse the dynamics of such behaviour

4. Helping him to have better understanding of the environment

5. Increasing his personal and interpersonal effectiveness by giving him feedback about his behaviour and assisting him in analysing his interpersonal competence

6. Encouraging him to set goals for further improvement

7. Encouraging him to generate alternatives for dealing with various problems

8. Providing him empathic atmosphere for his sharing and discussing his tensions, conflicts, concerns and problems

9. Helping him to develop various action plans for further improvement

10. Helping him to review in a non-threatening way his progress in achieving various objectives.

✻ Conditions for Effective Counselling

Counselling is a means and not an end in itself. Development does not occur just because there is counselling. Counselling could be an effective instrument in helping people integrate with their organization and have a sense of involvement and satisfaction. The following conditions are necessary for counselling to be effective:

1. *General Climate of Openness and Mutuality:* If the organization or department in which the employee is working is full of tension, and people do not trust each other,

counselling cannot be effective. A climate of minimum trust and openness is essential for effective counselling.

2. *General Helpful and Empathic Attitude of Management:* Counselling involves effective helping which is not possible unless the counsellor has general helping attitude and has empathy for the counsellee.

3. *Sense of Uninhibited Participation by the Subordinates in the Performance Review Process:* Unless the subordinates in a department or organization feel free enough to participate without inhibition in the process of review and feedback, counselling cannot be effective. Counselling is not a one-way process of communicating to the employee what he should or should not do. It is a process of developing dialogue which eventually contributes to better understanding on the part of counsellee.

4. *Dialogic Relationship in Goal Setting and Performance Review:* Performance counselling focuses on the counselee's achievement of the performance goals he had set in consultation with his manager. Joint participation by the employee and his reporting officer are necessary both in goal setting as well as in the performance review. Without such collaboration effort, counselling does not achieve its purpose.

5. *Focus on Work-oriented Behaviour:* The main purpose of performance counselling is to help the employee in improving his performance. Counselling can be effective if the focus is kept on the work-related goals rather than diffusing attention into various other areas. While doing so, discussion may involve other related and personal issues, but these are used to refocus on improvement of organizational roles rather than on personal or general personality problems.

6. *Focus on Work-related Problems and Difficulties:* Performance counselling is not related only to the achievement of goals, but also to the contextual problems in achieving or not achieving the goals. Analysis of performance, therefore, becomes the basis of counselling. Details of performance review and analysis are discussed in Rao Pareek (1978).

7. *Avoidance of Discussion of Salary and Other Rewards:* Performance counselling may not serve its purpose if it includes discussion about salary raise, rewards, etc. The main purpose of performance counselling is to use performance appraisal in planning and improvement of the employee, rather than understanding relationship between performance and reward like salary, etc. Bringing such discussion in the performance counselling may vitiate the main purpose of counselling.

CHAPTER-9

Performance Recognition and Performance-based Reward System

LEARNING OBJECTIVES

- To apprise students of the importance of performance & compensation linked with it

- To give them an idea about the concept & practices of variable pay

- To make students familiar with different emerging practices like gain sharing, profit sharing, stock options etc.

Introduction

The shift towards market economy, and lowering of trade barriers, is perhaps the most important new source of pressure on organisations to raise their performance level. Therefore, never before have organisations been subjected to as much performance and change pressure as they are today, and there is every reason to believe that pressure will continue to increase. Therefore, organisations today are busy evolving performance enhancement management.

What is Performance?

The Oxford English dictionary defines "performance as behaviour – the way in which organisations, teams, and individuals get work done." Campbell (1990) believes that behaviour should be distinguished from outcome because they cannot be contaminated by system factors. A more comprehensive view of performance is achieved, if it is defined as embracing both behaviour and outcome. This is well put by Brumbrach (1998) – "Performance means both behaviour and results. Behaviour emanates the performer and transforms performance from abstraction to action. Not just the instrument from the results, behaviour are also outcome in their own rights – the product of mental and physical efforts apply to task – that can be judged apart from results."

Performance does not mean a mere performance. Performance has to be better than the best – exceeding the benchmark. Excellence denotes outstanding achievement over a long period of time. In other words, an excellent organisation should have sustained competitive advantage over a considerable length of time. In order to do so, it has to constantly improve and change depending upon the way environment moves (Peters 1989). Calingo (2002) highlights that excellent organisations have achieved excellence not only individually over improved values to their customers but also in anticipating changes and discovering the ways of creating products and services as learning organisation. Excellent organisations are world-class organisations that are ready to compete with anybody, anyplace, anytime.

Performance Management

According to Lockett (1992) "the essence of performance management is the development of the individuals with competence and commitment working towards the achievement of shared and meaningful objectives within the organisation, which supports and encourages the achievement." Performance Management is a process which is designed to improve organisation team and individual performance – it is shared/participative process, an integrating process – based on agreements, on accountability, measurement and Review, feedbacks, development and improvements on continuous basis.

Performance management is concerned with creating a culture in which organisational and individual learning and development are continuous process. It provides means for integration of learning and work so that everyone learns from successes and challenges inherent in day-to-day activities. The desire to enhance performance is making ever-greater demand on the knowledge and skills of the workforce and on the people, who carry a much greater responsibility for their own performance. Performance and results are important but concern for people, their well-being and fairness of treatment is equally important.

If organisations want to attract high performers and retain and motivate the high performer, they have to be willing to reward excellent performer highly. This requires abandoning traditional pay structures and practices in which the best performers are only paid a little more than average and below average performer. In today's new economy, companies have to invest money in human capital in order to make them.

Some Safeguards before introducing Performance Pay should be:

- Criteria for measuring performance of work and contribution to company needs to be developed, communicated, understood and accepted

- Clarity in setting target/results for measuring performance

- Regular/Periodic Feedback on Performance

- Reward System/Performance Pay on line with desired target/result to be achieved

- Appropriate ratio in pay which is subject to performance

- Need for a periodic evaluation of the scheme

- Need to recognise that performance when influenced by factors outside control how will they be evaluated (Exchange rates, recession, sudden spurt/fall in demand).

The challenges before compensational reward system are to attract the right kind of human capital and to motivate it to develop and perform in the way that increases shareholders value. Unless their reward and compensation system accomplishes these two objectives, most organisations cannot be affected in a highly competitive business environment. Simply spending large amount of money is not enough; the money must be spent in ways that attract, retain and motivate the right people.

Creating reward systems that focus on excellence and treat employees as human capital investors requires a major change in the way most systems operate. Reward system generally treats employees as jobholders and how well they perform their jobs. Viewing them as human capital investors suggest a different approach to rewards in two respects.

1. It suggests basic reward on the value of human capital that people bring to organisation. What their job is at a particular moment is much less important than the value of their knowledge and skills.

2. It suggests rewarding people according to how effectively they use their human capital – their knowledge, skills, and competencies – to help the organisation improve its business performance.

Creating reward system that recognises the value of human capital and reward performance excellence is not easy. It requires a total departure from traditional compensation system and a careful articulation of existing reward system, business strategy, organisational design, information systems, etc.

Designing performance linked reward system is conditioned by a variety of factors; such as, nature of business, type of technology, the attitude of unions, and human resource strategy of organisation. Therefore, no standard model can be recommended. It has to be customized.

Performance linked reward systems reduce labour cost, result in increase in real wages and motivate performance. They provide a method of observing cost escalation on account of pay increase and thus, help in sustaining the competitiveness of the organisation.

It has been increasingly realised that performance related pay if used in isolation, may have little impact on motivation for performance. Appropriate conditions have to be created in the organisation for performance linked reward system to be motivationally effective. These conditions will involve, for instance, proper information, proper consultation, proper communication, proper training and development of the employees, developing a proactive attitude and performance-oriented culture, providing non-monetary incentives and evolving an efficient management performance.

Employees performance depends on mainly three factors – skill, knowledge & motivation:

Employees performance = f (SKM)

Where;

S = skill & ability to perform task

K = knowledge of facts, rules, principles, & procedures

M = motivation to perform

⌘ Performance Measures ⌘

"If you can not measure you cannot improve" – What is not measured is not worth doing (Production, Quality, Cost, Delivery, Safety etc.) Profitability gets measured on:

- Return on investment
- Return on sale
- Return on total capital
- Return on book quality
- Net income by total assets

Performance is essentially what an employee does or does not do. Employee performance common to most jobs includes the following elements:

- Quantity of output

- Quality of output

- Timeliness of output

- Presence at work

- Cooperativeness

Performance measures provide evidence of whether or not the intended result has been achieved and extend to which the job – holder has produced the result.

Performance measure becomes the basis of generating feedback information.

Performance appraisal is the process of evaluating how well employees perform their jobs when compared to a set of standards, and then communicating that information to those employees. Performance appraisal is also called employee rating, employee evaluation, performance review, performance evaluation, and results appraisal.

The non-compensation system contains many of the reward components that behavioral scientists have been describing for the past 50 years as critical for improving workplace performance. An in-depth analysis of the seven non-compensation dimensions identified in a close interrelation between compensation and non-compensation rewards. The line between these two major reward categories might at first glance appear to be sharply defined, but it soon blurs as they interact and blend together.

1. *Enhance Dignity and Satisfaction from Work Performed:* Possibly the least costly and one of the most powerful rewards an organization can offer to an employee is to recognize the person as a useful and valuable contributor. This kind of recognition leads to employee feelings of self-worth and pride in making a contribution. Few people want simply to be given something. They would much prefer to know that through their own efforts, they have earned and deserved rewards. Every compensation and noncompensation reward component should carry with it the message, "we need you and appreciate your efforts."

2. *Enhance Physiological Health, Intellectual Growth, and Emotional Maturity:* Considering the number of hours a person spends on the job, on travel to and form the work site, and off the job in attempting to resolve job-related problems frequently receive minimal attention until a serious problem occurs. Once this happens, however, it overrides all other employee concerns and activities. Modern health practices recognize the direct relationship between the physiological health and intellectual and emotional well-being of each individual.

3. *Promote Constructive Social Relationships with Co-workers:* An old adage states that "One man is no man." Although there are constant reminders of what one dedicated person can achieve, there are even more reminders that one human alone is weak.

However, with concerted action, people can accomplish almost anything. In this world of extreme specialization, people need and rely on other people more than ever. One of the most valued rewards gained from working is the opportunity to interact in a socially constructive manner with other people to enjoy the comradeship of workplace associates.

4. *Design jobs that Require Adequate Attention and Effort:* Over the past 40 years, organizational scientists have discussed at length the problems arising boredom related to work assignments that were developed in the last quarter of the nineteenth century. Jobs were designed so that workers could be taught quickly how to perform a few highly repetitive tasks. Workers then were required to perform these few tasks for as long as they remained on the job. What first appeared to be an efficient way of melding human resources with machine technology proved to have serious drawbacks.

5. *Allocate Sufficient Resources to Perform Work Assignments:* Requiring employees to perform assignments for which they have neither the knowledge nor the skills opens the door for problems. Not only is the organization likely to suffer because of outcome failures, but employee job-related interest and satisfaction are apt to break down because of the likelihood or inevitability of failure. Most employees seek a sense of accomplishment from their work. They want some degree of challenge, but they also want to feel reasonably, sure that they can succeed.

6. *Grant Sufficient Control over the Jobs to Meet Personal Demands:* From the 1950s to the present time, behavioral scientists have discussed the need to grant employees greater opportunity to participate in organizational decision-making processes. One problem with this participation concept is that organizations are composed of all kinds of people with all kinds of decision-making desires. Some people simply want to be told what to do, to be shown what is an acceptable level of performance, and then to be left alone to do their jobs. A few people in every organization want to tell top management how to run the organization. Between these two extremes is a wide variety of demands for a greater voice in determining how to perform assignments.

7. *Offer Supportive Leadership and Management:* This dimension is difficult to separate from all other noncompensation rewards, but it is so important that it must be recognized as a unique dimension of the non-compensation rewards and not just a component of the other factors.

Designing Reward System

Four main questions in relation to reward system are: who should be rewarded? What rewards should be given? How should assessment be done for deciding the rewards? And how rewards should be given. We shall discuss each issue, with examples of practices in the Indian organizations.

⌘ Whom to Reward? ⌘

Rewards are symbols of appreciation and recognition. Rewards reinforce what the organization values and want to be strengthened. So, almost every one related to the organization can be covered by the reward system.

Individual Employees: Individuals showing exceptional behaviour and high performance should be rewarded. Individuals are being rewarded by all organizations that follow a reward system. Variable pay is one type of reward. We shall discuss below individual rewards under other aspects of reward system. Probably about 20% managers are likely to get rewards. Performance at Polaris is categorized into four levels – Premium, Outstanding, Competent and Learning. These are indexed to the 90th, 75th, 50th and 25th percentile. "The Premium Performers are at the top end of the industry, and that is consistent with our policy of institutionalizing meritocracy at all levels of the company." Among the rewards schemes at Polaris are Konark, aimed at identifying potential leaders and encouraging the "cream to float to the top," At Cognizant "statistically speaking, the top performers have progressed about 70 percent quicker, and have received cash award up to three times higher than the others in the organization. That pretty much sums up our performance ethic."

Teams: As already stated, individuals work in teams, and the organizations need strong, cohesive, competent and self managed teams. Therefore, in future more and more rewards should be given to teams. Teams need to be empowered by giving high performing teams more autonomy and resources. In Tata Cummins, which runs operations through self managed teams of workers, each team is given money every month to use for raising the level of performance. Teams also include departments. High performing department should also be recognized and rewarded.

One of the four ACE awards given by Ericsson-India is Ericsson Champions Trophy, awarded to the Best Unit, to recognize highest achievement of Unit's Balance scorecard: Performance audit through year: Process performance + improvements; Balanced score card perspectives; Customer satisfaction; Follow up of action plans; Accomplishing PD talks; Competence development scores.

The Organization: Exceptional performance by the organization needs to be celebrated. Every one belonging to the organization then has a sense of pride.

Outsiders: Customers, suppliers vendors, etc., can also be covered in the reward system. In Associated Capsules and Universal Capsules, outstanding employees chosen are asked to name any outsider, who in their opinion, has contributed to the business of the company in the last quarter. They may invite that person to the company's dinner and the Chairman writes the invitation letter to such persons. This is a very innovative way to recognizing external persons through internal people. At ICICI recognition extends to the employees' family as well: employees' children who excel in academics or extracurricular activities are recognized through scholarships and sponsorships.

⌘ What to Reward?

As already stated rewards are meant to reinforce desirable behaviour, high performance, values etc., whatever the organisation wants to be strengthened and promoted further. Some of the following aspects can be rewarded.

1. *Performance:* Performance needs to be rewarded, both of individuals and teams. Criteria of performance excellence and their weightages may be determined. The following criteria and weightages are suggested as an illustration:

   ❖ *Organizational level:* Profit, market share, customer satisfaction, employees satisfaction, achievement index of one thrust area to be declared every year, exceptional events like new product launch, export award, crossing a significant milestone, etc., should be celebrated.

   ❖ *Unit/Department level:* Internal customer satisfaction, innovations leading to efficiency, achievement index of one thrust area to be declared in advance, quality, culture building, team work, creativity, internal customer service, cost reduction, strategic initiatives, etc. Any of these could also become annual thrust areas or some other thrust areas could be declared by the organization or the unit/ department like export, energy saving, wastage reduction, zero defect, safety, breakthrough in chronic problems. A few Chairmen's shields may be constituted, given each year to the units/departments/being judged as the best units for the year's thrust area, and other aspects to be promoted by the organization. At RPG gives Best Region and Best Division rewards are given.

   Performance at individual level has always been emphasized. The emphasis of the new reward policy of Gujarat Gas is on rewarding "simply the best" employee. Its objective is to provide a sense of recognition and achievement motivation for the significant contribution. It gives "outperform" reward for outstanding performer of the year, i.e., performance "always exceeds expectations", RPG has 'Vacation scheme' for best employees.

2. *Speed and efficiency:* Ericsson Falcon Award is given for Speed and efficiency to promote fast, urgent work pace with speed and efficiency. The Qualifiers are – Increase in efficiency; cost savings for the company; Earnings/rewards for the company. Demonstrated Behaviours for the award are:

   ❖ Exceeds timelines consistently

   ❖ Completes projects in record time

   ❖ Always withstands pressures

   ❖ Does not wait for assignments, decides what is needed to be done

   ❖ Respond promptly to sudden/unexpected problems in own unit/department

3. *Loyalty:* When employees complete their first year with Hughes Software they are presented a watch; when they complete five year, they (and their families) are given a company paid holiday. Ernst & Young also reward people who stay in the company in considerable time.

4. *Innovation:* Gujarat Gas gives "innovation helps" reward for an idea given by an employee who has resulted in cost reduction/improved efficiency. Philips Software Centre rewards innovation Rs.5,000 for sending an idea to head office and $750 when it is filled for patent. So far more than 1,400 ideas have been filed and in the last two years 12 patents were granted. At Texas Instruments (India) Development Centre, employees feel that they really don't do peripheral work. This fact comes out quite clearly in the patent data. Over the last 16 years. TI's India centre has filed 225 patents out of India. That is more than two and a half times the next company on the list, IBM, which has 85 patents filed from India in 10 years.

At Ericsson-India Ericsson Innovator Awards are given for Innovation, Creativity and Functional Excellence. The purpose is to promote: innovation, creativity and performance excellence; initiative taking and doing an extra yard; a climate of experimentation and learning, that focus continuously on new ways to create added value for customers and shareholders. Nominations for this award should consider visible and concrete value addition in the form of increase in revenue; increase in efficiency; cost reduction; functional value addition. The following are the demonstrated behaviors for this reward:

❖   Uses opportunities to develop new and better ways of doing things.

❖   Challenges the status quo

❖   Puts generated ideas into implementation.

❖   Explores innovative and new ideas in problem solving.

❖   Reflects on past experiences to learn.

❖   Approaches problems in generally curious and open minded manner.

❖   Is able to modify and use learned concepts or methods appropriately.

❖   Makes a different, original use of the existing information.

❖   Uses intuitive approach to develop new systems and procedures to increase efficiency; Stimulates creative ideas in others.

❖   Anticipates and prepares for problems that are not obvious to others.

❖   Does not stop at the firs solution.

❖   Thinks positively even when faced with obstacles.

❖   Encourages innovation around him/her.

❖   Uses tools like brainstorming to stimulate creativity around him/her.

5. *Upholding values:* Hughes Software gives formal award for adherence to company values. Ambassador award is given for values and Business Excellence. The award is given to promote Human and business competencies which are mandatory for Ericsson employees, viz. Ericsson knowledge, customer orientation, communication, teamwork, negotiation, cultural awareness and approach to change; Ericsson values professionalism, respect and perseverance; Ericsson wanted behaviors passion to win, dedication to customer success; fast, urgent, creativity, value adding teamwork. For the award Ericsson values and behaviours should be demonstrated in the following areas: Visible market or product break-in; achieving strategic contract; successful customer partnership; great enhancements in customer satisfaction. Demonstrated behaviors are:

   ❖ Puts forth views influentially because of the deep insight in the matters.

   ❖ Handles all customer situations with confidence.

   ❖ Shares knowledge, skills and experience in a clear, concise and open manner.

   ❖ Leads teams through difficulties by soliciting ideas and eliciting their co-operation.

   ❖ Adapts to new challenges and is able to identify, accept and introduce changes in order to meet the future customer and market requirements.

   ❖ Persists in face of difficulties.

   ❖ Understands business situation and decision making process in client organization, by establishing contacts with key persons and reading the organization.

   ❖ Exerts to get ahead, is enterprising and gets the job done.

   ❖ Delivers promises with speed and a sense of urgency.

   ❖ Understands on a strategic level, the relationship between finance/technology/business areas of the company and uses it effectively in negotiating business deals.

   ❖ Understands business situation and decision making process within customers' organization, by establishing contacts with key persons and building relationships.

   ❖ Is able to take a decision even under high stress when the risks cannot be planned.

   ❖ Understands how the customer gains profit from doing business with Ericsson.

   ❖ Has knowledge of Ericsson's main competitors and their competitive strategies.

6. *Technical Solution:* Hughes Software holds employee poll for rewarding the "person with best technical solution".

7. *Learning:* Infozech Software rewards the personal achievement of the employees. For example employees who have cleared examination like; MCSD, MCSE, MCIP,

MCDBA, CISCO certification, Sun certification, they are given a cash reward in the monthly meeting.

8. *Good behaviour:* Hughes Software holds employee poll to reward "the most warm and friendly person".

9. *Sense of humor:* Hughes Software also gives reward for the best sense of humour.

10. *Teaching:* In Hughes Software, employee poll is also held for rewarding "the best teacher".

11. *Publications:* Gujarat Gas gives "the triumph" reward to an individual employee or the team who have come out with an in-house publication.

12. *Event Management:* Gujarat Gas also gives reward to persons involved in an event management without help of external agency.

13. *Social Concern:* RPG gives awards to people who have done something on social issues like riot relief or flood relief.

⌘ How to Reward? ⌘

A tricky question is how to decide who should be rewarded. In some cases the criteria may be quite objective (e.g. production, selling, etc.). However, in most cases some judgment is required. Different ways are used to reduce subjectivity in decision making. One way is to have a team decision rather than individual choices. Various methods have been used as illustrated below. Discrimination of the head of unit/department should also be given importance in rewarding employees.

For Unit/Department level rewards, survey, instruments may be prepared for assessing achievement in the selected area. Other alternative arrangements may be to have Audit Teams for each aspect, whose recommendations may be sent to the apex team for finalization of rewards.

If audit is to be used for Business/Corporate function rewards, the top management may constitute two Audit Teams. One Audit Team may cover internal customer satisfaction, strategic initiatives, and the other Audit Team may cover culture/climate, team work, and subordinate development. The Audit Teams can utilize survey data, in addition to their on-the-spot visits. Audit Teams may develop their own guidelines. The teams may core the Units/ Depts. in A, B, C categories. The top management may nominate one of the six members as Chairman of the joint teams to finalise their recommendations.

For rewarding individuals some devices have been used to make it more objective. In Hughes Software employee polls are used to pick up individuals for rewards. When the management makes decisions in rewarding employees, people may doubt that management would pick up their favourites. Employee polling is free from this kind of bias. In NIIT the HR department organizes a poll for choosing best employee. Thirty names are chosen from the poll results and these employees become members of Presidents Forum. At Net

Across one has to be nominated for the best employee by one of the department members. The information about the nominee, the criteria on the basis of which the person has been nominated, the projects he has undertaken and his accomplishments, competency, etc. are displayed on intranet and the best employee is selected after the polling. No cash rewards are connected with this.

How do Organizations Reward?

Rewards are given to recognize outstanding work of individuals, teams (units and departments including) or other connected with the organization. It is important to communicate appreciation in public. Celebrating achievement in public boosts the value of the reward. Exceptional performance by the organization, crossing a milestone or launching of a new product, etc. may be celebrated organization-wide with small gifts (the same to all employees, from the top to the lowest level). A team of 5 to 7 employees (or preferably their wives), from different levels and locations, may decide the gift to be given.

Based on the "performance" of the units/departments (all units/departments to be rated by a corporate committee as A,B,C), the units/departments may be given discretionary funds from the Reward Corpus, to be utilized to reward their employees. The recommendations made by the unit/department heads, along with justification, should be sent to the Corporate Rewards Committee. The rewards should be declared by the unit/department heads.

Individuals or team rewards may include monetary rewards, computers, family holiday plans, stock/share options, declaration in the newsletter, medals and certificates (to be given in a function by Unit/Department Head/CEO, also a person who collects four medals or so may be given some intrinsic/extrinsic reward), visit to other plants, visits abroad, etc.

Survey of customer satisfaction, internal customer satisfaction and employee satisfaction, may preferably be conducted by internal or external team (say by short placement IIM/IIT/other institute graduates). Survey forms may be developed by a Task Force, reviewed and finalised.

Empowerment

One way to reward people is to empower them, giving them autonomy with support to act in relation to their work. One good example is the public sector undertaking, BPCL, which reorganised itself and gave more freedom to people in the field. For example, territory managers in retail can award jobs up to Rs.2 crore or take action against errant dealers. In Philips Software Centre 70-80% vacancies get filled by employee referrals. Wipro Spectramind has a programme CONTACT (Cutting Out New Talent Activity) for employee referral.

Recognition

Recognition is the greatest reward. Texas Instruments, rated no.1 Great Places to Work in India, recognizes people by electing them as TI Fellows, one of the highest steps on the technical ladder. "ATI Fellow is like being a Don at Oxford. Only 0.6% of the TI population is fellows. These are the chaps who are the 'brains' – people who help TI meet its most difficult technical challenges. Becoming a fellow is difficult. Your peers and seniors evaluate your work to see if you have been innovative in your thinking right through. Staying there is even harder. You are reassessed every year. If you fall behind you can lose your fellowship as the total number cannot be more than 1% at any given time."

In NIIT there is an annual practice of naming a conference room or office or training room after the name of the most outstanding employee of the year. The naming is done ceremoniously and a car is sent to bring the family, cake is ordered, and the employees assemble in that room. At Federal Express, rated second amongst 25 great places to work in India, an employee can get one of Fed Ex's 500 aeroplanes named after his/her kid. RPG managers give certificates to their employees by on small achievements and good work that they have done.

With the belief that reward and recognition systems are some of the fundamental ways to improve motivation levels. Wipro has a unique package called Encore, which is essentially a basket of non-monetary rewards given to motivate employees and recognize excellent work performance. This basket of rewards comes at two levels – "account" level and the level of the industry or organization. For example, one account-level award is Feather-in-my-cap, which is an on-the-spot recognition of an effort that is important to a project or project team. Another award goes by the name of Dear Boss, which recognizes the positives of a good boss, including technical, managerial and leadership skills. At the organizational level, there are awards like Mastermind, which is given for the most innovative solution or idea in Wipro. The Wipro Hall of Fame recognizes superlative performances in different roles as well as superlative team performance. It stands for the highest consistent performance reward in Wipro.

Career Growth

An excellent way to reward people is to provide career growth to deserving people. In Federal Express an employee started as a receptionist, moved on to operations, and then to customer service. There each employee can tailor his/her career path. Texas Instruments has a "technical ladder", communicating to people that it does not matter even if they want to remain technical gurus all their lives. They would still be rewarded on par with people who move into management. The tool is the "technical ladder'. It is a parallel career path to the management ladder. Eli Lilly (India) career growth is promoted through cross-functional competencies. ELI recently introduced one of parent Eli Lilly's interventions – a technical competency model (TCM) – to help those employees who want to develop deep technical expertise and also want to progress in their specialized function. TCM was introduced after it was debated heavily in the cross functional teams set up to assess the pros and cons of the model.

Development

Developing people, raising their competence and qualifications is a great reward for them. Value is added to them, and their ability to carry higher responsibility increases. Several companies are increasingly investigating in employee development. Employees get more mobility and opportunities for career growth. Texas Instruments have set up Development Centre, so have Aditya Birla Group, Gyanodaya, a learning Centre. Johnson & Johnson have tied up with various business schools for MBA courses for deserving employees. Wipro Spectramind spends about Rs.30,000 per employee on training and development alone. In Jindal Iron and Steel Company shop floor workers are routinely moved and trained. The company trains them before they are given a new function. They can get Rs.10,000 allowance once in two year to pay for tuition fees. The result: productivity per worker has increased from 300 tonnes in 2000 to 575 tonnes in 2003.

At Tracmail, a BPO firm, team leaders are sent to B-schools to attend executive MBA programmes in batches. Retention rates at these levels have been very good. Employees also have opportunity to spend six months doing internal projects with various departments; if these projects are found useful, the reward is promotions to a higher level.

Celebrating and Fun

As already discussed, rewards should be celebrated. This may be in many forms. Having a party is one of celebration. In fact, more and more emphasis is being given on developing fun and joy at work place. For example, Wipro Spectramind has a budget of Rs.150-200 per employee per month to have a party either on the premises or outside or a weekend party. The company also believes in immediate rewards. Rs.25,000 to 30,000 a month are spent on on-the-spot rewards as watches, pens, caps, T-shirts, travel bags, etc. This is called Pragati initiative.

How to Link Performance with Compensation?

TABLE 9.1	Linking Performance to Compensation
Administrative Uses	**Development Uses**
Compensation	Identifying strengths
Promotion	Identifying areas for growth
Dismissal	Development planning
Downsizing	Coaching and career planning
Layoffs	

A performance appraisal system is often the link between rewards employees hope to receive and their productivity. The linkage can be thought of as follows:

Productivity → Performance appraisal → Rewards

Performance-based compensation affirms the idea that pay raises should be given for performance accomplishments rather than for seniority.

Where a performance-oriented philosophy is followed, organizations do not guarantee additional or increased compensation simply for completing another year of organizational service. Instead, pay and incentives reflect performance differences among employees. Employees who perform well receive larger compensation increase; those who do not perform satisfactorily see little or no increase in compensation. Thus, employees who perform well receive larger compensation increases; those who do not perform satisfactorily see little or no increase in compensation. Thus, employees who perform satisfactorily or better maintain or advance in relation to market compensation levels, whereas poor or marginal performers may fall behind. Also, bonuses are determined on the basis of individual, group, and/or organizational performance.

Few organizations follow totally performance-oriented compensation practices. However, in the midst of organizational restructuring occurring throughout many industries, organizations look for compensation systems that break the entitlement mode. Even in the public sector, some organizations have recognized the need to shift toward more performance-oriented re-organized compensation practices. How fast the shift occurs, given the traditions and the strength of public-sector unions, remains to be seen.

A performance orientation requires a variable pay approach in which pay goes up or down based on a measure of performance. Not everyone in the same job will be paid exactly the same, and not everyone will like the approach.

TABLE 9.2 Differences between Traditional and Total Rewards Approach	
Traditional Compensation Approach	**Total Rewards Approach**
Compensation is primarily base pay.	Variable pay is added to base.
Bonuses/perks are for executives only.	Annual/long-term incentives are provided to executives, managers, and employees.
Fixed benefits are tied to long tenure.	Flexible and portable benefits are offered.
Pay grade progression based on organizational promotions.	Knowledge/skill-based broad bands Determine pay grades.
Organization-wide standard pay plan exists.	Multiple plans consider job family, location, and business units.

Variable Pay

Pay for performance is also known as variable performance linked pay or contingent pay. Variable performance in the pay is a financially measurable reward paid to an individual based on his overall performance. This measure includes the cumulative performance of the individual, his strategic business unit and that of the organisation. Contingent pay consists of payment related to individual performance, contribution, competence or skill or to team or organisational performance.

Variable Pay is compensation linked to individual, team, and organisational performance. Traditionally also known as incentives, variable pay plans attempt to provide tangible rewards to employees for performance beyond normal expectations. The philosophical foundation of variable pay rests on several basic assumptions:

- Some jobs contribute more to organisational success than others.

- Some people perform better than others.

- Employees who perform better should receive more compensation.

- A portion of some employees' total compensation should be contingent on performance.

Contrast the assumptions with a pay system based on seniority or length of service:

- Time spent each day is the primary measure of contribution.

- Length of service with the organisation is the primary differentiating factor among people.

- Contributions to the organisation are recognized through different amounts of base pay.

- Giving rewards to some people but not others is divisive and hampers employees working together.

Variable Pay is a strategic Approach

- Take advantages of employees/Team potential/talent

- Link efforts with performance

- Link extra performance beyond "thresh hold" level performance with extra reward

⌘ Types of Variable Pay ⌘

Individual incentives are given to reward the effort and performance of individuals. Some of the most common means of providing individuals variable pay includes piece-rate systems, sales commissions, and bonuses. Others include special recognition rewards such as trips or merchandise. Two widely used individual incentives focus on employee safety and attendance. However, individual incentives can present drawbacks. One of the potential difficulties with individual incentives is that an employee may focus on what is best individually and may lock or inhibit performance of other individuals with whom the employee is competing. Competition intensifies if only the top performer or winner receives incentives, which is why team or group incentives have been developed.

When an organisation rewards an entire work group or team for its performance, cooperation among the members usually increases. However, competition among different teams for rewards can lead to decline in overall performance under certain circumstances. The most common team or group incentives are gainsharing plans, where employee teams that meet certain goals share in the gains measured against performance targets.

Often, gainsharing programs focus on quality improvement, cost reduction, and other measurable results.

Organisational incentives reward people based on the performance results of the entire organisation. This approach assumes that all employees working together can generate greater organisational results that lead to better financial performance. These programs often share some of the financial gains to the firm with employees through payments calculated as a percentage organization each employee's base pay. Also organisational incentives may be given as a lump-sum amount to all employees, or different amounts may be given to different levels of employees throughout the organisation. The most prevalent forms of organisation-wide incentives are profit-sharing plans and employee stock plans. For senior managers and executives, variable pay plans often are established to provide stock options and other forms of deferred compensation that minimize the tax liabilities of the recipients. Table 9.3 shows some of the programmes under each type of incentive or variable pay plan.

TABLE 9.3	Types of Variable Pay Plans	
Individual	**Group/Team**	**Organisation-Wide**
• Piece rate • Sales commissions • Bonuses • Special recognitions (trips, merchandise) • Safety awards • Attendance bonuses	• Gainsharing • Quality improvement • Cost reduction	• Profit sharing • Employee stock options • Executive stock options • Deferred compensation • Goal-sharing

Preconditions

1. Financial initiative linked with behavior

2. Sense of fairness

3. Goals-challenging but achievable

4. Payout formulas are simple and understandable

❊ Successes and Failures of Variable Pay Plans

Even though variable pay has grown in popularity, some attempts to implement it have succeeded and others have not. One study suggests that about 74% of companies have a variable pay plan of some sort. Of those, most feel these plans have been successful in aligning pay with performance for executives (79%), managers (73%), and exempt professionals (60%). However, only 48% felt variable pay was effective for non-exempt/administrative personnel.

Most employees prefer that performance rewards increase their base pay, rather than be given as a one-time, lump-sum payment. Further, employees prefer individual rewards to group/team or organisation incentives. Incentives do work, but they are not a panacea. The enthusiasm that many employers have for variable pay is not shared universally by workers. The success of variable pay plans depends upon the circumstances. The next section discusses several factors that affect successful variable pay plans.

⌘ Factors Affecting Successful Variable Pay Plans ⌘

Most employers adopt variable pay incentives in order to (1) link individual performance to business goals, and (2) reward superior performance. Other goals might include improving productivity or increasing employee retention. Variable pay plans can be considered successful if they meet the goals the organisational had for them when they were initiated. There are a number of different elements that can affect the success of a variable pay plan:

1. Sufficient financial resources available

2. Consistent with organisation culture

3. Clearly separated from base pay

4. Clearly communicated

5. Performance results linked to payouts

6. Current, updated plans

7. Measurable performance

8. Clear, understandable plan details

9. Results in desired behaviours

10. Linked to organisational objectives.

These factors have been categorized into three areas for discussion:

● Does the plan fit the organisation?

● Are the behaviours encouraged by the plan the one desired?

● Is the plan being administered properly?

Benefits

1. *It encourage team work:* Because evaluation and reward systems are team based, participants reap immediate incentive benefits from team orientated performance; which in turn provides measurable improvements to company performance over the medium long-term.

2. *It promotes open lines of communication:* By focusing on the sharing of information, a variable pay ensures that all employees are able to make informed decisions, which streamlines operation and reduces cost.

3. *It's all about involvement:* Employees are regularly updated about progress, expectations, feedback and changes/deviations from the moment programme design begins.

   Result: Employees feel valued for their contributions; and organisation benefits from their motivation and enthusiasm.

4. *It shows the company is committed to positive change:* Shared vision and goals replace "us and them" mentality.

5. *It aligns rewards with key business priorities:* Variable pay programme is customized to bring about improved performance.

   The more efficient reward system, the more effective reward becomes as a "Positive Reinforcer".

6. *It links compensation with profitability:* Variable pay program allows for a portion of each participant's salary to be performance based – so an organisation doesn't end up paying increasingly high salaries when it can least afford.

7. *It provides job stability:* Since variable pay links remuneration with profitability, a company facing tough times can decease the likelihood of retrenchments by reducing variable pay payouts. By doing this the threat to jobs of employees is lessened and they will be more willing to focus on their performance goals.

   Job stability creates trust, thereby increasing employee commitment to achieve those goals.

Prerequisites of a Variable Pay Plan

1. Competitive fixed/base salary

2. Transparent & simple

3. Linked to business objectives

4. Agreed targets – challenging & realistic

5. Quantum must be significant

Catalyst to Variable Pay Plan

1. *Identify Corporative Objectives:* CEO/Functional Head should constantly display their commitment to the variable pay plan and this must be perceived by employees.

2. *Ascertain Employee Readiness:* Assignment based on survey of all employees in the company will decide whether they are ready or not for the introduction of a variable pay plan.

3. *Communicate scheme details:* To ensure the smooth functioning of the scheme, it is crucial that every employee understands why variable pay has been introduced and how the scheme function.

4. *Invest in implementation:* Company should have a realistic idea as to how much time, money and effort will be needed to design and implement the scheme.

5. *Monitor & Review Scheme:* Periodic reviews help in find-tuning a Variable Pay Plan to organisation's every-changing needs.

TABLE 9.4 Fixed Pay vs. Variable Pay	
Fixed Pay	**Variable Pay**
• Day-to-day responsibilities and on-going performance • Long-term contribution • Skill /competency development and work style	• Special objectives and results • Must be re-earned each year • "Above & Beyond" expected contributions

To amplify this further

• Fixed pay determined by – Market + Inflation + Potential + Performance Rankings

• Variable Pay determined by – Results/Target achieved only

TABLE 9.5 Fixed vs. Variable Ratio			
	2001	**2002**	**2003**
Top Management	78:22	76:24	70:30
Sr. Management	82:18	79:21	75:25
Middle Management	86:14	84:16	87:13
Jr. Management	88:12	86:14	90:10
Others	94:06	94:06	95:05
Overall Average	87:13	84:16	93:17

Forms and Types of Performance Linked Reward System/Contingent Pay

There are several types of Performance Linked Reward schemes. Generally, these are designed to share with or distribute among employees as individuals, groups or collectivity, productivity gains, profit improvement, or the financial gains of the organisational performance. Such schemes fall into the following broad categories:

1. Schemes based on individual or small group performance including piece rates, traditional merit pay, and sales commissions.

2. Incentive schemes that relate pay to profit on the basis of predetermined formula.

3. Bonus schemes based on contribution to productivity and profitability according to a predetermined formula with gains sometimes distributed among the individual employees on the basis merit rating.

4. Productivity bargaining

5. Long-term incentives, Employees Stock Option Plans – ESOP

6. Competency-based pay

Main types of contingent pay are:

1. Merit pay or Individual performance related pay

2. Skill-based pay

3. Shop floor incentive and bonus schemes

4. Team rewards

5. Team/Organisation based schemes

    (a) Annual bonus

    (b) Gain-sharing

    (c) Goal-sharing

    (d) Profit-sharing

    (e) Economic value added/market value added

    (f) Share options/Stock options/EVA

6. Other cash payment

⌘ Merit Pay or Individual Performance Related Pay ⌘

A common method which has long been in existence is pay increase or bonus payment on the basis of performance rating.

The merit incentive pay scheme provides another method of recognizing and rewarding differential performance. This method could particularly be suitable for office staff. The scheme essentially involves the following steps:

(a) The determination of result-oriented merit rating procedures,

(b) The identification of job factors and their relative importance,

(c) The formulation of a scale of reward, and

(d) The communication of the basis of monetary reward.

Illustratively, job factors of salesman can be identified as (a) sales promotion, (b) realization of outstandings, and (c) goodwill calls, (d) after-sales service and, (e) investigation of complaints.

These tasks will differ in their degree of importance. This difference can be recognized by imputing numerical values to different job factors. Hypothetically, let us assign weight values of 5, 3, and 2 respectively to the above tasks. In practice, weight values can be ascertained through job analysis.

Suppose it is intended to give an incentive opportunity of 20 per cent. Correspondingly, let there be 20 performance points, each point constituting 1 per cent of basic wage. If each identified job factor has a 4-point scale, then the 20 points will be distributed as follows in table 9.6.

TABLE 9.6	Scale of Distributing Incentive Opportunity Points			
Job Factors	**Scale Values**			
	1	**2**	**3**	**4**
1. Sales tasks	0	3	6	10
2. Realization of outstandings	0	1.8	3.6	6
3. Goodwill calls, etc.	0	1.2	2.4	4

Maximum points = 20

Each degree will have to be precisely and operationally defined. Take, for example, the job factor of sales task. The four points on the scale can be defined as following table 9.7.

TABLE 9.7	Definition of a Point on the Merit Rating Scale		
1	**2**	**3**	**4**
Unsatisfactory	**Satisfactory**	**Fair**	**Good**
Sales target not achieved	Sales target achieved	3% above sales achieved	5 per cent above sales achieved

The actual merit rating score will give the percentage of basic wage or basic wage plus D.A. as incentive bonus. Given a result-oriented merit rating procedure and its objective operation in an organisation. It should not be difficult to install a merit incentive pay system. This is not to minimize the difficulties that are usually encountered in operating a merit rating system. The effectiveness of the performance appraisal system will depend on the soundness of the performance appraisal system.

Sometimes merit increments and merit awards are also given in recognition of superior performance on the part of individuals. These are poor substitutes for a system of merit incentive pay because of several shortcomings.

Under a system of merit increments, there is not prompt relationship between reward and effort. The quantum of reward at a point of time will be considered inadequate. Additional cost in the form of enhanced allowances is built for the company on permanent basis. Employees continue to benefit from their best performance even if it remains below standard in the future.

Employees getting merit awards cannot visualise a proportionate relationship between their performance and reward. The basis of determining and quantum cannot be explained to employees who are not given such awards. This may evoke jealously and friction and many thus jeopardize cooperation and goodwill.

✖ Skill-based Pay

Skill-based pay links pay to the level of schemes used in the job and sometimes the acquisition and application of additional skills by the persons carrying out the job. The term is sometimes used interchangeably with competence related pay. But skill based pay is usually concerned with the skills used by manual workers. In skill based pay, skills are more likely to be defined in terms of competition of training course, satisfactory performance in a test leading to company accreditation or attainment of national vocational qualification levels. In competency-based pay, the behaviour and attributes of an individual has to be used to perform a role effectively in addition to only the skills.

Skill-based pay can take two forms – conventional job slotting or a progression related to skills. Skill based job slotting is simply a method of locating an individual in a pay and grade structure – unskilled, semi-skilled and skilled by reference to their training, qualifications and experience. Skill based pay progression is less conventional method and links a progression to the acquisition of skills.

✖ Shop Floor Incentive and Bonus Schemes

Incentive of bonus schemes relate to the pay or part of the pay received by the employee to the number of items they produce or processes, the time they take to do a certain amount of work and/or some other aspects of their performance. They usually provide for pay to fluctuate with performance in the short term, but they can, as in major day work, provide for long-term relationship. They are often referred to as payment by result schemes. Such schemes are of following types:

1. *The main types of incentive schemes:* Individual piece work, work measure individual schemes, measure day work and group incentive schemes

2. *Alternative approaches:* High day rates, performance related pay, productivity bonus and the use of other criteria in the bonus schemes

Bonus Schemes in Different Environments

Individual Piece work: In individual or straight piece work a uniform price is paid per unit of production. Operators are therefore rewarded according to the number of pieces they produce or process, so pay is directly proportionate to results.

Most piecework schemes provide a fallback rate or minimum earning level. It is common for the minimum rate to be set at 70 to 80% of average earnings, although some companies set it as low as 30%. Companies may also provide guaranteed payments for down time due to machine failure, maintenance work or waiting for material.

The advantage to employees of piecework is that the system is easy to operate, simple to understand and can be left to run by itself. Piecework can also enable employers to estimate and control manufacturing cost effectively.

Piecework has become more inappropriate as an incentive method as new technology has changed work arrangements. In larger scale manufacturing, it has largely been replaced by work measure scheme, or some other form of incentive or bonus payment.

Work Measure Schemes: In a work measure scheme, the job or its component task is timed and the incentive payment is related to performance above the standard time allowed for the job. The amount of incentive pay received depends on the difference between the actual time taken to perform the task and the standard time allowed. If a task is done in less than the standard time, then there is a timesaving, which means that the operator's output will increase.

Incentive payments are made when performance exceeds the standard. The relationship between pay and performance usually follows either the proportional or progressive pattern. When proportional payments are made, the incentive payment increases in direct proportion to performance. In a regressive payment system (as old Halsey/Rowan schemes) the incentive payment increases less than output.

The proportionate payment method is the most suitable one but the regressive system has the advantage for employers of making mistakes in rate fixing less costly and lowering unit wage costs for output above standard performance. For obvious reasons, however, the latter approach is viewed with suspicion by trade unions and workers. It is usual and advisable to establish a sealing to the amount of incentive pay, which can be earned to avoid excessive amounts being paid out because of loose rates or some other forms of degeneration (this is sometimes called capping).

Measure Day Work: In measure day work, the pay of employees is fixed on the understanding that they will maintain a specified level of performance, but pay does not fluctuate in the short-term with their performance. The arrangement depends on work measurement to define the required level of performance and to monitor the actual level. The fundamental principles of measure day work are that there is an incentive level of performance and that the incentive payment is guaranteed in advance, thereby putting employees under an obligation to perform at the effort level required. In contrast, a conventional work measure incentive schemes allow employees discretion on their efforts level but relate their pay directly to the result they achieve. Between these two extremes there is a variety of alternatives, including banded incentive, stepping schemes, and various forms of high day rates.

Measure day work seeks to produce and effort – reward bargain in which enhanced and stable earnings are exchanged for an incentive level of performance. It's disadvantage is that the set performance target can become an easily attainable norm and may be difficult to change, even after extensive negotiation.

⌘ Team Rewards ⌘

"Teamwork is the fuel that allows common people to attain uncommon results".

A group of employees is not necessarily a "team", but either one can be the basis for variable compensation. The use of work teams in organisations has implications for compensation of the teams and their members. Interestingly, although the use of teams has increased substantially in the past few years, the question of how to equitably compensate the individuals who compose the team remains a significant challenge. As Figure 9.1 notes, organisations establish group or team variable pay plans for a number of reasons. According to several studies about 70% of large firms use work groups or teams in some way. Of those, about 36% say they use group incentives, and 10% say they use team-based pay.

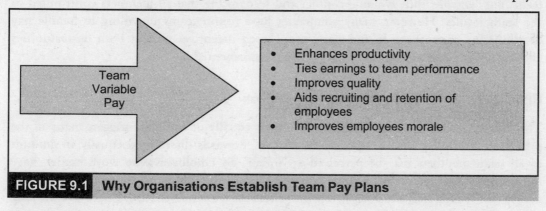

Team Variable Pay

- Enhances productivity
- Ties earnings to team performance
- Improves quality
- Aids recruiting and retention of employees
- Improves employees morale

FIGURE 9.1 Why Organisations Establish Team Pay Plans

Distributing Team Incentives

Several decisions about methods of distributing and allocating team rewards must be made. The two primary approaches for distributing team rewards are as follows:

1. *Same size reward for each team member:* In this approach, all team members receive the same payout, regardless of job levels, current pay, or seniority.

2. *Different size rewards for each team member:* Using this approach, employers vary individual rewards based upon such factors as contribution to learn results, current pay, years of experience, and skill levels of jobs performed.

Generally, more organisations use the first approach as an addition to different levels of individual pay. This method is used to reward team performance by making the team incentive equal, while still recognising that individual pay differences exist and are important to many employees. The size of the team incentive can be determined either by using a percentage of base pay for the individuals or the team as a whole, or by offering a specific dollar amount. For example, one firm pays team members individual base rates that reflect years of experience and any additional training that team members have. Additionally, the team reward is distributed to all as a flat dollar amount.

Timing of Team Incentives: How often team incentives are paid out is another important consideration. Some of the choices seen in firms with team-based incentives include payment monthly, quarterly, semiannually, or annually. The most common period used is annually. However, the shorter the time period, the more likely it is that employees will see a closer link to their efforts and the performance results that trigger the award payouts. Employers also may limit the team rewards to $1000 or less, allowing them to pay our rewards more frequently. The nature of the teamwork, measurement criteria, and organisational results must all be considered when determining the appropriate time period.

Decision Making about Team Incentive Amounts: To reinforce the team concept, some team incentive programs allow group members to make decisions about how to allocate the team rewards to individuals. For example, in one division of Motorola, teams receive a lump-sum amount, which they then decide how to divide among team members. Some teams vote, while others have a team leader decide. In other companies teams divide the team "pot" equally, thus avoiding conflict and recognising that all members contributed to the team results. However, many companies have found teams unwilling to handle pay decisions for co-workers. In summary, team based incentives present both opportunities and challenges when they are developed and implemented.

Problems with Team-based Incentives

The difference between rewarding ream members equally or equitably triggers many of the problems associated with team-based incentives. Rewards distributed equally in amount to all team members may be perceived as "unfair" by employees who work harder, have more capabilities, or perform more difficult jobs. This problem is compounded when a poorly performing individual negatively influences the team results. Also, employees working in teams have shown a relatively low level of satisfaction with rewards that are the same for all, rather than having rewards based on performance, which often may be viewed more equitably.

Generally, managers view the concept of people working in teams as beneficial. But many employees still expect to be paid based on individual performance, to a large extent. Unit this individualism is recognized and compensation programs developed that are viewed as more equitably by more "team members," caution should be used in developing and implementing team-based incentives.

Successful Team Incentives

The unique nature of the team and its members figures prominently in the success of establishing team-based rewards. The employer must consider the history of the group and its past performance. Use of incentives generally has proven to be more successful where groups have been used in the past and where those groups have performed well. However, simultaneously introducing the teamwork concept and changing to team-based incentives has not been as successful.

Another consideration for the success of team-based incentives is the size of the team. If a team becomes too large, employees may feel their individual efforts will have little or no effect on the total performance of the group and the resulting rewards. Team-based incentive plans may encourage teamwork in small groups where interdependence is high. Therefore, in those groups the use of team-based performance measures is recommended. Such plans have been used in many service-oriented industries, where a high degree of contact with customers requires teamwork. Conditions for successful team incentives are shown in Figure 9.2. If these conditions cannot be met, then either individual or organisational incentives may be more appropriate.

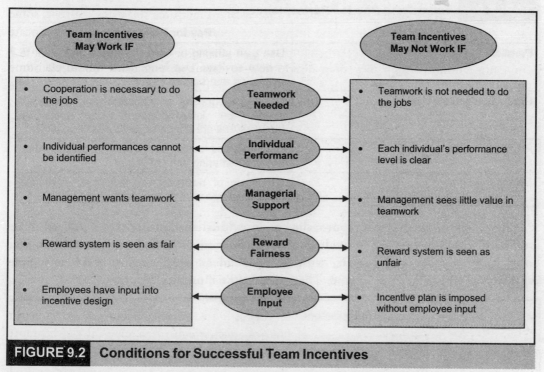

| FIGURE 9.2 | **Conditions for Successful Team Incentives** |

Teams have emerged as a widely used design approach in large organisations for a number of reasons, including the changing nature of work, they are fit with employees involvement and total quality management programmes, and the development of more and more knowledge about how to design and operate things. There are four types of team that is seen in our working – 1. Parallel teams 2. Work teams 3. Project teams 4. Management teams.

1. *Parallel teams* supplement the regular organisation structure and perform problem solving and work improvement tasks – examples, quality circles, survey feedback teams, etc.

2. *Work teams* are responsible for producing a product or providing a service and are self-contained, identifiable, work units that control the processes involved in transforming inputs into measurable outputs. They are found most frequently in manufacturing setting – examples, assembly teams, insurance claim processing teams, etc.

3. *Project teams* typically involved a diverse group of knowledge workers, such as, design engineers, process engineers, programmers and marketing manager who are brought together to conduct projects for new product development etc.

4. *Management teams* are the least frequently used and most poorly understood type of team. There are obvious advantages of a team of well-trained managers.

The fit between approaches to rewarding performance to these four teams differs because there is no one size which fits all the teams. The rewards, which are generally practiced in these different groups are given below:

TABLE 9.8	Teams and Pay for Performance
Types of Team	**Pay for Performance**
Parallel	Use gain sharing or other business unit plant to reward savings. Use recognition reward plan for teams, as appropriate.
Production and service	Use team bonuses or business unit bonuses if teams are interdependent. Use individual bonuses that are based on peer evaluations.
Project	Use bonuses based on project success. Also, use profit-sharing and stock plans
Management	Use team or business unit bonuses. Also use profit sharing and stock-based plans.

There has to be different approaches to individual reward and team reward. The individual work situation and individualists should have an individual pay-for-performance, bonus type scheme. Collectivists, with interdependent work need to have team and organisation type of reward scheme. The figure below illustrates it further.

	Independent	Work	Interdependent
Individualists	Individual bonuses		Misfit
Individuals			
Collectivists	Misfit		Team pay for performance

FIGURE 9.3 **Approaches to Team Rewards**

Traditional approaches to pay do not fit a team-based environment. They were designed to support and reward individual behaviour. As long as they remain in this mode, they are at best neutral or in most cases counterproductive to create effective teams.

Two general approaches to pay seem to potentially fit best with the teams. The first is, an emphasis on paying the individual instead of job and the second is, for performance that focuses on collective performance more than individual performance. Taken together, these two approaches can encourage individuals to learn the right skills to make teams effective and can motivate the right types of performance focus on the part of teams and organisations.

Group or Team incentive schemes provide for payment of bonus either equally or proportionately to individual within a group or team. The bonus is related to output achieved by the group in relation to define targets or to the time saved on the job – the difference between allowed time and actual time.

Group bonus schemes are in a sense individual incentive scheme writ large – they have the same advantages and disadvantages as any payment by result systems. The particular advantages of a group scheme are that it develops team working, breaks down demarcation lines and encourages the group to monitor its own performance and discipline itself in achieving targets – an essential characteristic of a high performing workgroup. In addition, job satisfaction may be enhanced by relating the team more closely to the complete operation. Group bonuses may be particularly appropriate when teams are carrying out interdependent tasks and have to operate flexibly in a just-in-time or cellular manufacturing environment.

Group or team incentive schemes are most appropriate when people have to work together and teamwork has to be encouraged. They are most effective if they are based on system of measured work, where the targets and standards are agreed by the team, which is provided with the control information, it needs to monitor its own performance. A variety of measure-day-work or a high-day-rate-system topped up with achievement bonuses related to quality, delivery to time, or cost targets may function well.

Bonus Schemes in Different Environment: Traditional incentive schemes tend to be concerned only with output and unit cost. However, significant changes have been taking place in the working environment in recent years. To maintain competitive advantage in the face of global competition, organisations have had to introduce new system of work and technology. These have led to the development of alternative approaches to pay for performance, particularly in total quality management, just in time and cellular manufacturing environment. These approaches generally take the form of bonus rather than incentive schemes.

1. *Total Quality Management:* Total quality management is a systematic way of guaranteeing that all activities within an organisation happen the way they have been planned in order to meet the defined needs of customers and clients. The emphasis is on involving everyone in the organisation, which provide for continuous improvement and for achieving sustained high level of quality performance.

    For manual workers, a quality bonus can be paid on a plant-wide basis as specific part of bonus scheme or it may be incorporated in a gain-sharing plan. One approach is to set standard of quality (zero defects) and pay a quarterly bonus of, say 10% of pay, if this standard is achieved. This bonus could be reduced on a sliding scale related to any decline from the zero defect target.

    Quality manufacturing companies can also be measured in terms of waste – the percentage of output rejected or downgraded. As the volume or proportion of waste falls, the quality bonus arises.

    Another quality measures can be delivery to time – the bonus increases on a sliding scale as the percentage of deliveries made on time increases.

2. *Just-in-Time:* The overriding feature of JIT is that material or parts are generated in the exact quantity required and just at the time they are needed. A classic JIT system consists of a series of manufacturing units, each delivering to one another in successing stages of production. The amount delivered by each unit to the next unit is exactly what the latter needs for the next product period (usually one day).

    Bonus payments in a JIT environment can be based on performance in relation to the critical success factor of JIT – like productivity, delivery, quality, flexibility, and teamwork.

3. *Cellular Manufacturing:* Cellular manufacturing involves the logical arrangement of numerically controlled equipment into groups or clusters of machine to process families of parts. By definition, processing parts in a manufacturing cell includes completing as much of the work place processing as possible within the cell before moving it to the next sequential processing, assembly or stock holding station. Cells are staffed by teams of interdependent and multi-skill workers. Cellular manufacturing system demands teamwork and flexibility within the system. Cellular manufacturing system requires multi-skilled people and is therefore possible environment for skill based pay system, although such systems are not always cost effective. It will, however, be important to ensure that a team incentive or bonus system operates in which team members are given the maximum opportunity to monitor them their own performance and take action to improve it, and are rewarded accordingly.

❈ Team/Organisation-based Schemes ❈

Annual Bonus

The twentieth century dictionary defines bonus as a premium beyond the usual interest for a loan; an extra dividend to shareholders, a policy holders share of profits; an extra payment to workmen or others. Neither the Payment of Bonus Act, 1965 nor any other industrial law defines bonus.

The concept of bonus payment to workers originated in India during the first world war in the cotton textile industry in Bombay and Ahmedabad in 1917. When the practice was discontinued in 1923, there was a general strike and the Government of Maharashtra appointed a committee headed by Sir Normal McLeod, the then Chief Justice of Bombay High Court to consider the nature and basis of payment of bonus in the cotton textile industry of Bombay. The committee observed that the cotton mills working in 1923 as compared to the situation in 1917, did not justify any payment of bonus. Thus a link between profits and bonus was established in early 1920s. During second world war the payment of bonus resumed and continued till 1945. In 1942, the bonus dispute in General Motors (India) Limited, was referred for adjudication. In this case Justice Chagla observed that it is almost universally accepted principle now that the profits are made possible by the contribution that both capital and labour make in any particular industry, and I think it is also conceded that labour has a right to share in increased profits that are made in any particular period. But the distribution of increased profits among workers is better achieved by giving of an annual bonus than by a further increase in wages. Wages must be fixed on the basis of normal conditions. The next year in the case of Standard Vacuum Mill Company the adjudicator held that, if large profits were made as a result of abnormal war conditions, it was but fair that a small fraction of such profits should be given by way of bonus without whose labour and cooperation the profits could not have been made.

In 1948 the Government of India has appointed a Committee on Profit Sharing. The Committee observed that it was not possible to devise a system in which labour share of profit could be determined on a sliding scale varying with production and favoured trying out profit sharing bonus industry-cum-loyalty basis as (a) an incentive to production, (b) a method of securing industrial peace, and, (c) a step in the participation of labour in management.

In 1950 the Labour Appellate Tribunal held, in the case of Mill Owners Association vs. Rashtriya Mill Mazdoor Sangh, that where the goal living wages has been attained, bonus, like profit share, would represent more as the cash incentive for greater efficiency and production. We cannot, therefore, accept the broad contention that a claim to bonus is not admissible where wages have (as in the case before us) been standardized at a figure lower than what is said to be the living wage. Where the industry has capacity to pay, and has been so stabilized that its capacity to pay may be counted upon continuously. It, thus, made a distinction between living wage and actual wage and held that bonus could be used to bridge the gap between the two. Five years later, Justice Bhagwati of the Supreme Court of India upheld the tribunal judgement in the case of Muir Mills Company vs. Suti Mills Mazdoor Union: It is, therefore, that the claim for bonus can be made by the employees only if as a result of the joint contribution of capital and labour the industrial concerned has earned profits. If in any particular year the working of the industrial concern has resulted in loss there is no basis or justification for a demand for bonus. Bonus is not a deferred wage. Because, if it were so, it would necessarily rank for precedence before dividends. The dividends can only be paid out of profits and unless and until profits are made no occasion, or question can also arise for distribution of any sum as bonuses among the employees. If the industrial concern has resulted in a trading loss, there would be no profits of the particular year available for distribution of dividends, much less could the employees claim the distribution of bonus during that year.

Thus, profit was considered as a precondition for bonus. Several companies including, for instance, Tata Iron and Steel Company, Indian Iron and Steel Company, Bharat Tin Plate Company and Buckingham and Carnatic Mills – have adopted voluntarily profit sharing bonuses. Notwithstanding this, there have been a series of disputes and a spate of strikes over bonus issue, with workers and their unions contending bonus to be a deferred wage. In 1961 the Government organization India constituted Bonus Commission. Based on the report of the Commission in 1964, Payment of Bonus Act was enacted in 1965 with a view to: (a) enforce statutory liability upon employers covered by the Act to pay bonus to employees in the establishments concerned, (b) define the principles of a minimum and maximum bonus and linking payment of bonus with a scheme of set-off and set-on, and, (d) to provide machinery for the enforcement of the liability for payment of bonus.

The salient features of the legislation are discussed. The legislation did not achieve the intended objective of minimising conflict on account of bonus. During the discussions before the Bonus Commission when the employers wanted a ceiling on bonus, the workers asked for a floor. With the result, the legislation provided for a minimum of bonus of 4 per cent regardless of whether a company earns profit or not. Subsequently it was raised to 8.33 per cent (section 10 of Act), which is equivalent to one month's wages. In effect, this meant 13 months wages for 12 months work, and thus bonus has actually become, at the minimum level, a deferred wage that bore no relationship whatsoever with either productivity or profitability. The ceiling remained at 20 per cent, but with a provision for bargaining production linked bonus (Section 31-A of the Act). There are instances in the public sector where sick industries had agreed to pay more than 8.33 per cent.

Gainsharing

Gainsharing is a formula based organisation or factory wide bonus plan which provides for employees to share in the financial gains made by a company as a result of its improved performance.

The formula determines the share by reference to a performance indicator such as added value or another measure of productivity. In some schemes the formula also incorporates performance measures relating to quality, customer service, delivery or cost deduction.

Gain-sharing differs from profit sharing in at least three ways. First, under gain-sharing, rewards are based on a productivity measure rather than profits. The goal is to link pay to performance outcomes that employees can control. Second, gain sharing plans usually distribute any bonus payments with greater frequency (e.g., monthly or quarterly versus annually), Third, gain sharing plans distribute payment during the current payment rather than deferring them as profit sharing plans often do.

Lawler (1971. 1990) has summarized some of the common results that have been found in research studies of gain sharing programme plans:

- Coordination, teamwork, and sharing of knowledge are enhanced at lower levels.

- Social needs are recognized via participation and reinforcing group behaviour.

- Attention is focused on cost savings, not just quantity of production.

- Acceptance of change due to technology, market and new method is greater because higher efficiency leads to bonuses.

- Attitudinal change occurs among workers, and they demand more efficient management, better planning, and good performance from their co-workers.

- Employees try to reduce overtime – to work smarter.

- Employees produce ideas as well as effort.

- When unions are present, more flexible administration of union-management relations occur.

- When unions support the plan, they are strengthened because better work situations and higher pay result.

- Unorganised locations tend to remain non-union.

There are, however, certain limitations of gain sharing plans. Perhaps the most important is differentially attracting and retaining the best performers. As gain sharing plans do not pay more for better performance, they do not necessarily motivate them to stay. Unlike profit sharing it pays bonus even when the organisation is not earning profits. Moreover, gain sharing plans do not fit in with every situation.

The concept of gainsharing is based on simple measurable improvement, for example, reduction of cost per unit. Unlike any other variable schemes, gainsharing is a group incentive scheme where a team or a group together is involved in increasing productivity, quality or customer service. Organisation has to provide a structure within which employees can work together to become responsive to customer's needs.

Gainsharing plans are based on a formula of sharing rewards in relation to measure performance. There are a number of different formulas; the traditional formulas of gain sharing are Scanlon plan, the Rucker plan, and Improshare.

The Scanlon Plan: The Scanlon formula measures employment cost as a proportion of total sales. Standard ratio, say 50%, is determined and if labour costs fall below the proportion, the savings are distributed between employees and the companies on the basis of a pre-established formula. In other words, this plan calculates gains based on standard cost reduction. It relies on employees' participation through a system of committee, to solicit, develop, evaluate and implement suggestions of work unit.

The Rucker Plan: The Rucker plan is also based on employment costs. But they are calculated as a proportion of sales less the costs of materials and supplies (i.e. value added). Allen Rucker contended that the pay proportion of value added remains a near constant share unless the organisation suffers from severe mismanagement or a drastic change of policy. On the basis of this assumption, the Rucker plan determines a constant share of whatever added value is created by the joint efforts of management and employees.

Improshare: Improshare is a proprietary plan, which is based on an established standard, which defines the expected hours required to produce and acceptable level of output. The standard is derived from work measurement. Any savings resulting from an increase in output in fewer than expected hours are shared between the organisation and employees by means of a pre-established formula.

In addition to the above, there are few other plans, which come under the purview of gain-sharing.

Value Added: Many versions of gain-sharing are based on value added as the key performance measure. Value added is calculated by deducing expenditures on material and other purchased services from the income derived from sales of product. It is in fact the wealth created by people in business.

Why organisations introduce gains-haring?

Organisations introduce gain-sharing for a number of reasons. Perhaps the most important is the feeling that it is right time to link pay to organisational performance, coupled with a belief in the desirability of communicative organisational objectives, creating team spirit, breaking down organisational barriers, increasing the flow of innovative ideas from employees, improving commitment and educating employees in business economics.

Gainsharing can be introduced as change agent in association with other structure and process initiative designed to achieve cultural change.

Increased competition: National and global or declining productivity are reasons for introducing gainsharing. It is a device for more creative pay arrangements, which stimulate both productivity and quality and keep employment cost under control.

Another reason for introducing gainsharing is that organisations have become dissolution with traditional incentives and bonus schemes.

Gain-sharing is a potentially valuable component in an organisation over all reward strategy. It has, however, to be developed and maintain as part of a integrated process of reward management and compensation management – it cannot work in isolation. It should also be kept in mind that gain-sharing is essentially a participative process. It is not, like more profit sharing schemes, simply a matter of handling out money for reasons that are beyond the control of employees. The success of gain-sharing details largely on the opportunities it presents for involvement so that employee can establish a clear link between their performance and their reward – and essential requirement for success in any pay-for-performance scheme.

Goal-sharing

Goal-sharing plans are becoming increasingly popular. Even though goal-sharing plans did not start becoming popular until recently, they many now be more common than gain-sharing plans. In some ways they are similar to gainsharing plans; indeed, sometimes they are actually called gain-sharing plans. However, they are significantly different in important ways and thus warrant a different name and separate consideration.

Like gain-sharing plans, goalsharing plans pay bonuses when performance is above a standard. They also usually cover most or all employees in a particular company or business unit. They are most frequently installed in part of a company rather than throughout. They are particularly popular when the business environment is rapidly changing and the company wants to target a particular kind of performance improvement for a limited period of time.

The key differences between goalsharing plans and gain-sharing plans are in their stability and approach to establishing measures and standards. Gain-sharing plans thrive on stability. They tend to use the same measures and the same standards year after year. They argue that this builds trust, understanding, and behavioural routines.

The logic of goal-sharing plans is quite different from gain-sharing. Goal-sharing plans seek to leverage an organisation's business strategy by measuring performance on key strategic objectives. Standards and measures are set on an annual basis and are not necessarily based on historic performance or what was measured and rewarded in past years. They are mote likely to be based on measures of what it takes to implement a strategic plan and to be successful in the current business environment. Typically, goal-sharing plans establish three, four, or more goals in areas such as quality, customer satisfaction, delivery time, cost, and sometimes profitability. They then tie specific bonus amounts to achieving one or more levels of performance on each of these measures. The plans typically last for a year; at the end of the year a different set of measures and standards may be established as part of a "new" plan, or the old plan may continue.

Goal-sharing plans are a particularly nimble reward system. They can quickly change focus as an organisation's business strategy changes, and they are usually easy to explain, so they can be used effectively by an organisation that is undergoing change and by organisations that have not had a history of employee involvement. Because of their flexibility, they can react to turbulence in the external environment and strategy changes better than gainsharing plans can.

Goal-sharing plans can and often do reward things that do not have an immediate or direct dollar payoff for an organisation. Whereas gain-sharing plans are based on measures of dollar amounts saved, goal-sharing plans simply tie measures to bonus amounts. Thus, goalsharing plans can pay bonuses for things that typically are not measured in dollars (for example, quality, customer satisfaction, and accidents). There is, of course, a risk that bonus payments will be made for performance improvements or results that do not actually affect the financial performance of the company. Examples of this are customer satisfaction and on-time delivery. It is common wisdom that they have a financial payoff, but it is often hard to quantify their impact on a company's financial performance.

The development of "Balanced Score Card" measures fits well with the idea of goal-sharing incentive plans. For a long time, accountants have neglected measures that may be important indicators of the future direction and health of organisations. Accounting measures provide a financial record of the company and are good indicators of many areas of its performance. However, they are less than perfect predictors of future performance and are not inclusive measures of present performance. Balance score card measures include such things as customer satisfaction, employees satisfaction, and quality. Goalsharing incentive plans require a type of balanced score card in order to operate effectively. The challenge which any score card approach, is to get the right measures and to weigh them appropriately so that the incentive effects are supportive of the organisation's business strategy.

Conditions for Success

For several reasons goalsharing plans run the high risk of being effective for only a short period of time. When companies misuse them by setting unrealistically high standards or changing the measures or standards indiscriminately, there is a definite risk that employees will lose confidence, not only in the plan but in management. The challenge in managing goalsharing plans is to create measures that fit the business plan and to establish goals employees see as fair, reasonable, and achievable. This must be done not just once but year after year if the goalsharing plan is to continue to drive organisational performance.

It is hard to overemphasize the difficulty of establishing and maintaining a line of sight between behaviour and rewards when organisation pay-for-performance plans are involved. It takes a significant leap of faith for employees to believe that their organisation will reward their current performance at a later date, particularly when the organisation is measuring not individual but collective performance. Anything that undermines the trust of employees and reasonableness of pay plans stands to reduce or totally eliminate a line of sight. Raising the standard, reducing bonus payouts, and unreasonably changing measures are all things that can challenge the credibility of a plan an destroy trust.

Impact of Goal-sharing

There is little systematic evidence on the success of goalsharing plans. This is because they are new and also because they often get grouped erroneously with gainsharing plans. A good guess is that in the short-term, goalsharing plans often are quite successful. It is less clear that most organisations manage them in ways that cause them to be powerful long-term drivers of strategic performance. Many organisations probably have successful goalsharing plans but over time don't do a good job of managing the goal-setting process and payouts. As a result the plans fail and are abandoned.

In the turbulent business environment that corporations face today, it is highly likely that more and more goal-sharing plans will be created. Even with their limitations they are just the kind of reward system that can help companies change by implementing new strategic focuses and processes. However, their nimbleness, agility, and ability to support change is both their greatest strength and greatest weakness. When goalsharing plan changes are not managed well, they can create mistrust and resistance to change.

Profit-sharing

Profit-sharing means paying employees a share of the net profit in addition to their wages or salary. It is payment of a dividend or a sum based on basic wage or salary, grade or seniority. It is supposed to be a stimulus for higher performance.

Profit-sharing is a plan under which an employer pays to eligible employees, as an additional to their normal remuneration, a special sum in forms of cash or shares in the company related to profits of the business. The amount shared is determined either by an established formula, which may be published, or entirely at the discretion of management. Profit-sharing schemes are generally extended to all employees of the company.

Objectives of Profit-sharing

1. To encourage employees to identify themselves more closely with the company by developing a common concern for its progress.

2. To stimulate a greater interest among employees in the affairs of the company as a whole.

3. To encourage better co-operation between management and employees.

4. To recognise that the employees have a moral right to share in the profit they have helped to produce.

There are three basic requirements for profit sharing schemes:

1. That the profit sharing reward should bear a direct relation to the effect/result

2. That the payment should follow immediately after the efforts

3. That the method of calculation should be simple and transparent.

Profit sharing is different from shareholding. Employees can become shareholders in a company by either or both of the following two ways: (a) when they offered and buy shares in the company where they work; (b) when they offered shares as a reward or incentive for better performance or seniority/loyalty or both.

Profit sharing is also different from gainsharing. Gain-sharing of the kind proposed by Joe Scanlon is called the Scanlon Plan provided for a share to the workers of the savings in input costs. This combines incentive payments with worker participation in decision-making and rewards people not necessary for working hard, but for working smart.

The main types of profit-sharing schemes are:

1. *Cash:* A proportion of profits is paid in cash direct to employees. This is the traditional and still the most popular approach.

2. *Stock:* A proportion of profits is paid in shares. This is much less popular, especially since the advent of the approved deferred share trust scheme with its considerable tax advantages.

3. *Approved profit sharing share schemes (PSSS):* The company allocates a proportion of profit to a trust fund, which acquires shares in the company on behalf of employees.

4. *Mixed schemes:* A PSSS scheme is sometimes offered in addition to a cash scheme, or the latter is made available to staff before they are eligible for PSSS shares, or as an alternative to PSSS shares.

Profit sharing, like incentives, should be in addition to regular wage, should not be considered as a substitute for it. However, economists like Weitzman consider that expected profit-sharing bonuses will substitute for the basic wage, lower wage rates and wage costs, reduce marginal cost of hiring and increase employment. Profit-sharing is considered as a useful tool in stabilizing wage costs, and yet rewarding workers when they and the company perform better. In some countries, particularly, the U.S., profit sharing schemes competed with or became complementary to pension schemes. Tax policies favoured and exempted differed payments at the time of retirement. The usual mechanism is the creation of different profit-payment trust, which invested the funds in interest carrying special bonds and released tax-free payments to workers upon retirement.

Profit sharing is supposed to contribute to productivity, worker motivation, worker participation and wage flexibility. The results may be reflected either in higher output or better financial performance through savings in input costs. When employees receive payments based on company's financial performance they become aware and concerned about factors contributing to business success and the commonality in goal with reduce mutual antagonism, if any. Thus, profit sharing is also considered to improve the general climate of employment and industrial relations.

To let employees feel and actually realize that they are getting their due share in profits requires transparency in bookkeeping practices. As of now in quite a few enterprises, both in the public and the private sectors, balance sheets are considered by their employees as excellent pieces of fiction. In some companies, there is a feeling that their managements tell one thing to their shareholders and the other the union leaders and the workers. In the absence of trust and transparency, misgivings persist.

There are also some problems with profit sharing. Profit-sharing being a group-based scheme could result in the problem of free riders. Some individual employees get reward without deserving it and a few others may feel that what they are getting as a share in the profits of the company is not in proportion to the contribution they made. Even though profit-sharing is gravy, and not a substitute to the wages or salary, some trade unions also consider that profit-sharing being a variable payment shifts risk to the employees. In the case of employee share-ownership, employees are putting not only their jobs and incomes at risk, but also their savings.

Companies Act in India provides for payment of up to 11 per cent of profits to the whole-time direction of the company. Justice Mohan Committee, which was set up to recommend pay revision for public sector executives, submitted its report in 1998 and recommended that perquisites and allowances beyond 50 per cent of pay should be linked to performance. It observed that these performances related payments should be a function of profitability at the level of a particular enterprise and emoluments at the level of the individual executive. While it is not possible to think or definitive stipulations or ceilings in these spheres, the Committee believes that some norms would be desirable. It would be appropriate to suggest that such performance related payment should not, as a norm, exceed 5 per cent of the distributable profits in an enterprise. However, there would be situations where distributable profits are not large enough for performance related payments that could suitably reward executives for turning around or significantly improving performance of an enterprise. Similarly, it would be appropriate to suggest that performance related payments should not, as a norm exceed 50 per cent of the basic pay of an individual executive. The Board should, of course, have the flexibility and discretion to go beyond this norm wherever necessary and appropriate but the justification for the relaxation should be explicitly recorded.

The major advantage associated with profit sharing plans is their impact on an organisation's culture. When profit sharing plan covers most members of the organisation, there is the potential for it to stimulate interest in the financial result of the organisation and to create a culture in which attention is focused on performance. Although profit sharing may not be terribly motivated in the sense of driving people to work harder, it may motivate them to pay attention to financial results and to try to understand the business. The effect on employees can be a better understanding of organisation and thus, more knowledge and profit focused decision-making behaviour.

Stock Options

Stock options are opportunities to buy stock at a set price immediately or sometime in future for a stated period. Stock options plan is one of the two forms of variable pay compensation package, other being profit sharing bonus.

ESOP have a long history in USA, European countries and Japan. But, it has gained currency in India after 1990-91 when Indian economy was opened up. In the year 2000, there were about 10,000 companies, which had ESOP, covering about 10,000,000 of employees. The important companies, which had introduced ESOP, are Infosys, Wipro, Godrej, GE, P&G, Global Trust Bank, etc.

ESOP are becoming popular in view of the following factors:

1. The shift from industrial to information revolution. Knowledge workers expect say and stake in the organisation in which they work.

2. Public policy in many countries favour giving employees a share in equity and profits. This is pursued in few countries through legislation and in some others; it is encouraged through voluntary persuasion.

3. In the wake of disinvestments and privatization of public enterprises, employees are offered shares with view to ease their opposition. It is apparently to give them a stake. This is also considered as an effort as redistribution of wealth.

Employer offers stock options to their employees for several reasons. Some of them are given below:

1. Attraction

2. Retention

3. Motivation

4. Financial participation by the employees in the wealth created through joint efforts

5. To garner employees commitment

6. To develop common purpose between employers and employees

7. To promote corporate performance

8. Performance based reward

9. Supplement retirement/social security benefits

10. To hedge hostile take over in future.

Stock options can be introduced not only by public traded organisations, but also by privately held firms. Stock options by foreign companies to national employees should be guided by national law and national tax policies. If the citizens are prohibited from holding foreign assets, even if foreign employer is willing to offer stock options, national law and tax policy may impose restrictions and hurdles in the way of national employees accepting such offers.

In some western countries, financial participation by employee is promoted through legislation. In UK and USA, it is encourage mainly through a variety of tax incentive for deferred profit sharing schemes and employees stock options programmes. In Belgium and Italy, it is evolved through collective bargaining. In Japan, it is highly decentralized and become a part of management of policy then public policy and legislation. In most countries, employers want profit sharing and employees stock options to be voluntary.

In India, during 1980s, a scheme was introduced by Sh. V.P. Singh, the then finance minister, whereby 5% of the new issues could be preserved for employees in the country. Over a decade later, the Securities Exchange Board of India (SEBI) issued the guidelines effective from June, 1999.

The guidelines also deal with volume funding and purchase of stocks. In the past companies offered stock options to only a handful of top ranking key managers. However, with advent of IT industries, need to attract, retain and motivate work force is making it imperative to give them both say and stake to all most all the employees. In India, mainly information technology and software organisations introduced stock options plans. But in recent years many FMCG organisations have also begun to offer stock options to their employees. The prominent companies, which have gone for stock option plans, are Castrol, CRISIL, Global Trust Bank, Godrej-GE, HCL, Infosys Technologies, Mastek, NIIT, Pentafour, Proctor and Gamble, WIPRO, Zee Network, etc. Several others are planning to introduce employee stock options.

In several public enterprises, employees were offered shares on special terms at the time of disinvestments and/or public offering. Initially trade unions in the bank and several public enterprises resisted the idea of workers owing shares because of ideological aversion to workers capitalism. However, trade union's opposition to stock options weakened because many of their own members did not want to let the opportunity go. In fact, in several cases, they asked for more shares than the government was initially willing to offer to the workers.

The salient features of the ESOP, as per SEBI guidelines are as under:

1. *Who is covered?*

    (a) Any employee except the promoter or director (holding more than 10 per cent equity)

2. *Requirements*

    (a) Setting up of *compensation committee* of the board, the majority being independent directors for administration and superintendence of ESOS

(b) *Shareholder approval* through a special resolution in the general meeting, disclosing to them such details about the ESOS as the total number of option to be granted; identification of classes of employees entitled to participate in the ESOS; requirements of vesting and periods of vesting; the appraisal process for determining the eligibility of employees to the ESOS; maximum number of options to be issued per employee and in aggregate.

(c) *Disclosure in the director's report* of all the details of the ESOS including employee-wise details.

(d) *Compliance with accounting policies*

(e) *Certificate from auditors* that the scheme has been implemented in accordance with the guidelines as also the resolution of the company in the general meeting.

3. *Non-variation of the terms of the ESOS:* The term of the ESOS cannot be varied in any manner, which may harm employee interests. However, the terms may be changed through a special resolution in a general meeting provided the ESOS has not yet been exercised by the employee.

4. *Pricing:* Companies have the freedom to determine the exercise price in conformity with the accounting policies specified. Any discount on the fair market value has to be reflected as deferred employee compensation in the accounting entries.

5. *Lock-in Period & rights of the option-holder*

(a) The company has the freedom to specify the lock-in period, with a minimum of one year between the grant of options and vesting of options.

(b) The employee will not enjoy the benefits of a shareholder, till shares are issued the exercise of the option.

(c) The amount payable by the employee, if any, at the time of grant of option, may be forfeited by the company if the option is not exercised with the exercise period or it may be refunded to the employee if the stock options are not vested due to non-fulfillment of the conditions relating to vesting of option as the ESOS.

6. *Non-transferability of option:* Options granted to an employee shall not be transferable. In the event of the death of an employee while in employment, all options granted to him or her till that date should vest in the legal heirs or nominees of the deceased employee.

Infosys introduces deferred bonus scheme for executives.

How do you retain creamy layer at the top in a highly competitive market, especially when you have put your storied ESOP on the back burner? Infosys Technologies has come up with a lucrative deferred bonus scheme for senior executives in the Associate Vice-President (AVP), Vice-President (VP) and Senior Vice-President (SVP) grade. The payouts are truly impressive ranging from $20,000 (Rs. 9.2 lakh) to $ 125,000 (Rs. 57.5 lakh) per year. Infosys expects an expenditure of about $4-4.5 million (Rs. 18.4-20.7 crore) on the scheme in the first year.

As most people in Infosys in this bracket earned Rs. 24-54 lakh last year, the bonus amount translates into an addition of 38-100% to their salaries.

The company's director and head of human resources, TV Mohandas Pai said: "The scheme will cover 160-180 people including the directors." He said : "We have introduced this scheme as an incentivising tool for senior executives and also to ensure retention." When asked if the scheme was introduced in lieu of the ESOP, he said: "This is not linked to ESOP. But after junking our ESOP, we had nothing for our employees. So, this has been introduced. It will be effective from April 2006.

There will be a variation of 25% in computation for people in India and those abroad. For example, at the SVP level, while the India-based person will get $100,000 those abroad will get $125,000, mainly to make allowances for taxes overseas.

To be eligible for the deferred bonus scheme, an employee needs to have worked with Infosys for at least a year. The first year bonus will accrue at the end of the second year. This is where the deferred and retention aspects of the scheme come in. Dispersal of the bonus is based on performance and a few other matrices.

Popular Types of Employee Ownership Stock Holding Schemes

ESOP is a type of tax-qualified employee benefit plan in which most or all of the assets are invested in the employer's stock. A stock option plan grants employees the right to buy company stock at a specified price during a specified period, once the option has vested.

An employee stock purchase plan (ESPP) is a little similar to a stock option plan. It gives employees the chance to buy stock, usually through payroll deductions over a 3-27 month "offering period". The price is usually discounted up to 15 per cent of the market price. Frequently, employees can choose to buy stock at a discount either at the beginning or the end of the ESPP offering period, which can increase the discount still further.

"Phantom equity" refers to plans such as phantom stock or stock appreciation rights (SARs) that provide employees with a payout, usually in cash, based on the increase in the company's stock value. (Employees may receive stock instead of cash, and phantom stock can include phantom dividends, etc., but the basic idea is a bonus based on the company's stock performance.)

Restricted stock involves an outright grant of stock, usually at nominal or no cost. The advantage of a restricted stock programme is the tax deferral that results from the vesting restrictions. Vesting restrictions also tend to encourage employees to focus on long-term rather than short-term objectives. Typically, an award of restricted stock will not vest until the employee has completed a specified period of service with the employer. During the restricted period, however, participants are considered the owners of the stock and will, therefore, be entitled to receive the dividends and to vote the shares during the restricted period.

The Profit sharing plan is the simplest and most flexible qualified retirement plan available to invest in employer securities. Profit-sharing plans are permitted to invest in employer securities provided that investment is authorized up to a specified percentage of the plan assets. Unlike stock bonus plans and ESOPs, however, profit –sharing plans are not required to distribute employer stock to the employees.

A stock bonus plan is a type of profit-sharing plan. Although it need not invest in employer stock, a stock bonus plan is required to distribute stock to employees whenever a distribution occurs under the plan. Alternatively, the plan may distribute cash, provided that the participant is informed and is given the right to receive stock if he chooses. Upon distribution of stock to participants, if there is no ready market for the shares, the participant must be granted the option that will require the company to purchase the shares at a fair market value purchase price.

Tax Treatment of Stock Options

While bonus and profit sharing earnings of employees are deductible expenses for companies and taxed in the hands of the employees the tax treatment of stock options is somewhat different. At present stock options are taxed as perquisite when option is granted at discounted prices. They are also taxed as a capital gain when they are converted into at discounted prices. They are also taxed as a capital gain when they are converted into cash. Stock options offered by foreign parent companies to employees of its Indian subsidiaries are also taxed under the Income Tax Act. Several companies and chambers of commerce have been pleading with the government that employee stock options be taxed as a capital gain only at the time of sale of stock options. The following are key issues in taxation of stock options:

1. In the U.K. and the U.S.A and several other industrialised countries there are a variety of legislative measures which provide tax concessions to corporates and trusts establishing employee stock options. In India, such tax concessions have not been introduced yet.

2. If stock options are given at a concessional rate how should the difference between such rate (also called acceptance price or exercise price) and the market value be treated for tax purposes?

3. Stock options are several cases part of a motivational package. It could be, in some cases in lieu of a part of salary or incentive for outstanding performance. But they are not income in the hands of the employees concerned. Therefore, the question is whether they should be taxed at the time they are granted or vested or at the time the employees actually convert those stock options into cash by disposing off their stock/ shares. In the budget for 2000-2001, the Finance Minister of India proposed to tax at the time they are offered to the employees because it is difficult to keep track of movement of shares between/among employees.

4. In April 2000 one of the companies appealed to the income tax authorities that the stock options should not be taxed upon grant because they are vested only after the lock in period is over. Therefore, there is merit, if at all, in taxing stock options after they are vested or preferably after they are encashed.

TABLE 9.9	Advantages and Disadvantages of ESOP	
Advantages		**Disadvantages**
• Funded by the market not by the organisation		• The pay-out is unpredictable
• Amounts can be sufficiently high to ensure adequate motivation		• Amounts may be insignificantly low
• Implies "ownership" in the organisation'		• Not always available as an alternative, e.g., when dilution of equity is not acceptable to the employer
• It creates a sense of employee ownership in the business		• Lock-in periods and other conditions may dilute perceived value
• Flexible in design		• Employees are subject to the vagaries of the market
• Rewards are tied to value creation		• Administrative hassles exist
• Self-funding based on economic value creation		• Lock-in periods may have a negative impact on employee returns
• It inculcates a performance-driven culture		• Performance may sometimes not lead to good pay-outs, i.e., high dependency on market conditions
• It promotes teamwork		
• It provides spectacular gains to employees, i.e., wealth creation.		• Pay-out matrix and rules and regulations are at times difficult to understand.

Though Stock plans are a relatively recent entry into the Indian corporate world, stock plans have made an impressive impact on the industry and are destined to grow. These plans can have many objectives and can be structured as simple one-off schemes or as complex ongoing ones. Linking stock plans to performance management is a widespread practice in the West. Such linkage can also serve additional objectives such as retention and commitment of the employees covered. Performance pay can be immediate or deferred and divided between cash and stock. Several organisations appear to prefer such a combination. Naturally, employees prefer cash in hand to stock in future, especially if there is no upfront bargain for them. The challenge before companies is to convince employees that there is neither such a trade-off nor any adverse implications for their long-term interests. The tax advantages for individuals are substantial. Accounting practices for stock options have an impact on the shareholders. Accounting standards may eventually dampen the accounting incentive of treating only the concession as an expense. Nonetheless, stock options will only grow in several innovative ways. There are possibilities of innovative structuring outside the SEBI guidelines and the SPV route. For instance, phantom stock or stock appreciation rights are also being used successfully in several companies. Whichever route is chosen, what is important is to link individual performance to shareholder value, and this can be achieved only through stock options.

Economic Value Added/Market Value Added

Companies are using innovative methods to raise their bottom lines and to boost up employees and investors confidence. Economic Value Added (EVA) is the latest in this direction. Economic value added measures the difference between the return on a company's capital and the cost of that capital. EVA is the surplus or deficit that remains after levying a charge against after tax operative profits for the opportunity cost of equity and debt.

The accounting concept of profit takes into consideration, interest on borrowed capital i.e. debt. The economic value added concept takes into account the economic cost i.e., not only the interest on debt but also the cost of capital invested by shareholders. EVA is calculated by a combination of three basic factors – net operating profit after taxes, capital and cost of capital. If the EVA is positive, it indicates that the company has created value for shareholders. If the EVA is negative, it signifies contrary.

Any method that anyone can employ to better the efficiency will show as an improvement in business. By cutting costs and adding to profit without adding to capital, operational efficiency can be improved. By reducing investment in assets that earn less than the cost of capital, asset management efficiency can be improved by making new investments that earn returns over and above the cost of capital, profitability can be improved. By implementing more effective financial and investor relation strategies, the cost of capital can be reduced. EVA focuses on thee and helps determine the market value of the company (MVA). EVA is linked to the market value added: EVA = Total market value less total capital employed. MVA represents how much wealth a company has created for its investors (MVA = Discounted present value of future EVA).

A sustained increase in EVA will bring an increase in the market value of a company. This is because continuous improvement in EVA brings continuous increases in shareholder wealth. EVA incorporates two basic principles of finance into management decision-making. The first is that the primary financial objective of any company should be to maximise the wealth of its shareholders. The second is that the value of a company depends on the extent to which investors expect future profits to exceed or fall short of the cost of capital. By definition, a sustained increase in EVA will bring an increase in the market value of a company. The approach has been effective in virtually all types of organisation. This is because continuous improvement in EVA brings continuous increases in shareholder wealth.

Considering the fact that EVA has its foundations in an inextricable interweaving of employee performance with company goals, is it any wonder that performance-linked pay automatically comes into the picture? EVA actually links individual performance to company profits and vice versa.

✼ TCS EVA Incentive Scheme

The EVA incentive in TCS has the following components:.

Target Bonus: Provides employees with competitive rewards for achieving expected performance

Actual EVA Improvement (deltaEVA): Year to year change in EVA

Expected EVA Improvement (EI): Performance standard consistent with TCS owners' expected return

EVA Interval: EVA Improvement (deltaEVA) above Expected Improvement (EI) that results in a 2 x Bonus declared and EVA below EI that results in a 0 x Bonus declared.

Bonus Multiple – 1.0x + (delta EVA – EI)/EVA Interval

TCS decided to link its incentive plan to EVA because it wanted to cultivate a mindset oriented to EVA and promised that it will reward those who contribute to its enhancement. If EVA is positive employees get bonus. If EVA improves, bonus increases. There are no limits to either the growth in EVA or to the bonus employees can get. EVA linked cash bonus payment being a self-funding mechanism, there are no budgetary restrictions: the more the value added, the higher the size of the bonus. If the focus is short term, it might induce some to manipulate accounts to produce results that may not be sustained over a period. In recent years, there have been many reports about the likes of ENRON and Worldcom, fudging accounts. In the EVA scheme, if the company invests one billion dollars in developing a product, the pay back is expected over, say the next five years. If the value added is not as per projections, the return on shareholders' capital will be negative. In such a situation, there is no way employees can get bonus for these five years.

TCS has three levels of management: junior, middle and senior management. The EVA is apportioned into three categories: corporate, self and individual performance. Individual managers are assessed on several performance measures on a quarterly basis. Individual managers are expected to meet their goals/targets on the balanced scorecard. In addition, they are assessed on attributes like knowledge, commitment, communication, etc. Individuals are ranked on a scale from 1 to 5. Rank 1 is awarded to those who perform below the normal TCS standards. Rank 2 is given to normal/average performers. Rank 3 is given to those who are above average and so on. Junior level managers' variable pay comes from EVA fund apportioned for individual performance. At middle management, the maximum amount of variable pay is derived from how well the unit they head performed. At the senior level, the quantum of bonus is based largely on company performance. In TCS improvement is recognized and rewarded. If a team brings down the negative EVA from 100 to 90 that team and its members will be eligible for bonus just the same way as the team which improves EVA from 100 to 110. The EVA incentive bonus scheme is linked to success in creating wealth for shareholders. Incentive bonus must be sizeable to influence employees' behaviour. The scheme does not put a ceiling on the amount of reward one can get, so long as they continue to add more value.

What are the gains for TCS? There is greater alignment between employee incentives and success in creating shareowner's wealth. There is a clear link between EVA, incentive and cell EVA targets for three years and bonus percentages. Employees are accountable for investment and asset utilization. Incentive is not paid from EVA, but increase in EVA. A level playing field is ensured for different geographic locations. Incentive bonus pool is funded from one overall measure of performance. It is simple and easy to communicate and manage. Bonus is large enough to influence employees' behaviour. Offering a bigger share in bottom line is better than a small share of top-line results. There is no need to limit bonus based on increasing sustainability and employee retention. Deferred incentive bonus in EVA bank is forfeited. All employees participate in the scheme. All these constitute gains for TCS.

TABLE 9.10	Total Compensation Components	
Wage Component	**Definition**	**Level of Risk to Employee**
Base Pay	The guaranteed portion of an employee's wage package.	As long as employment continues, this is the secure portion of wages.
Across the Board Increase	Wage increase granted to all employees, regardless of performance. Size related to some subjective assessment of employer about ability to pay. Typically an add-on to base pay in subsequent years.	Some risk to employee since at discretion of employer. But not tied to performance differences, so risk lower in that respect.
Cost of Living Increase	Same as across the board increase, except magnitude based on change in cost of living (e.g., as measured by CPI).	Same as across the board increases
Merit Pay	Wage increase granted to employee as function of some assessment of employee performance. Adds on to base pay in subsequent years.	Two types of risk faced by employees. Size of total merit pool at discretion of employer (risk element), and individual portion of pool depends on performance, which also is not totally – predictable.
Lump Sum Bonus	As with merit pay, granted for individual performance. Does not add Into base pay, but is distributed as a one time bonus.	Three types of risk faced here. Both types mentioned under merit pay, plus not added into base – requires annually "re-earning" the added pay.
Individual Incentive Plans	Sometimes this variable pay is an add-on to a fixed base pay. The incentive component ties increments in compensation directly to extra individual production (e.g., commission systems, piece rate). While measures of performance are typically subjective with merit and lump sum components, this form of variable pay differs because measures of performance are objective (e.g. sales volume).	Most risky compensation component if sole element of pay, but often combined with a base pay. No or low fixed base pay means each year employee is dependent upon number of units of performance to determine pay.
Success-sharing Plans	A generic category of pay add-on (variable pay) which is tied to some measure of group performance, not individual performance. Not added into base pay. Distinguished from risk sharing plans below because employees share in any success – performance above standard – but are not penalized for performance below standard.	All success sharing plans have risks noted in above pay components plus the risk associated with group performance measures. Now individual worker is also dependent upon the performance of other included in the group.

Contd...

Gain-sharing	It differs from profit sharing in that goal to exceed is not financial performance of organisation, but some cost index (e.g., labour cost is most common, might also include scrap costs, utility costs).	Less risk to individual than profit sharing because performance measure is more controllable.
Profit-sharing	Add-on linked to group performance (team, division, total company) elative to exceeding some financial goal.	Profit measures are influenced by factors beyond employee control (e.g., economic climate, accounting write-offs). Less control means more risk.
Risk-sharing Plans	Generic category of pay add-on (variable pay) that differs from success sharing in that employee shares not only in the successes, but is also penalized during poor performance years. Penalty is in form of lower total compensation in poor corporate performance years. Reward, though, is typically higher than for success sharing programs in high performance years.	Greater risk than success sharing plans. Typically, employees absorb a "temporary" cut in base pay. If performance targets are met, this cut is neutralized by one component of variable pay. Risk to employee is increased, though, because even base pay is no longer totally predictable.

If an employee performs well he should be paid more than a non-performer. Hence, variable pay concept. A variable pay can be worked out for an individual, a team or on the organization basis. The chapter, therefore, discusses the different variable pay schemes launched by organizations like skill based pay, gain sharing, profit sharing, employee stock option, EVA/ MVA etc.

Compensation and Appraisal of International Staff

This portion deals with the appraisal and compensation of international staff. First, the special position of international staff will be looked at. Subsequently, we shall discuss the different compensation methods used in multinational companies, such as the budget system, balance sheet system and local going-rate system. This portion sets out the criteria for appraising international staff and discusses the problems which may be encountered during the appraisal. Finally, we shall report on recent developments in this filed and draw special attention to the concept of Euro-compensation.

⌘ International Staff: A Different Compensation Perspective ⌘

The term, international staff, refers to those who hold management positions with international organizations. International staff members are not only confronted with cross-border decisions, but are also expected to cross the frontiers themselves.

Base pay still varies considerably from country-to-country. Additionally, differences in terms of performance pay or such other benefits as pensions and company cars may further increase the income gap. In the past few years, notably in Europe, attempts have been made to reduce the differences in tax and social security contributions. Although there is still a long way to go, some progress has been made. Against the backdrop of frontiers and differences which are becoming increasingly diffuse, and anticipating the globalization of what used to be domestic markets, international organizations have begun to feel the need to formulate a policy or review existing policies regarding staff who work or will be working abroad for a short or long period of time.

The manner in which organizations currently compensate their assigned staff will be described below. It would be borne in mind that the traditional expatriate of large multinationals are increasingly being replaced by a more internationally-oriented management corps. These employees must not only be internationally versatile, they also have to be fitted into a compensation policy different from the old policy aimed at individuals and consisting of one-off reimbursements for expatriate 'discomforts'. Thus, companies are increasingly seeking new forms of compensation, first to rule out the 'excrescences' of expatriation and, secondly, to be able to treat international assignments as inherent to a staff member's career, so that no special compensation is required. The final part of this chapter will set out alternative methods of compensation which may, to some extent, offset the disadvantages of the old pay systems.

One should not forget, however, that an international posting may in itself be a reward. In the first place, it can be a direct reward in that the foreign activities are an added challenge or perhaps already constitute a promotion. And secondly, it can be an indirect reward since the assignment may decisively influence an employee's future career opportunities inside the organization.

Term of the Assignment

The nature of the assignment to a large extent determines the method of compensation. An important factor is the term of the assignment.

1. *Short-term assignment:* The assignment may be for a relatively short period, such as in the case of a feasibility study. This type of assignment does not usually exceed six months. In general, assignments of up to one year are considered short-term. Family members do not generally accompany the employee on the assignment.

2. *Long-term assignment:* If the assignment is for more than one year, it will usually result in the employee and his or her family 'moving house'. Depending on the individual situation (age, family, social status and so on) and the extent to which the new local situation differs from the old one, extra efforts will have to be made to turn the assignment into a success. An assignment form the Netherlands to a developing country is likely to entail greater change than an assignment, say, to Germany. Distance is of less importance in this respect. For example, being transferred from the Netherlands to Spain may entail adjustment than being transferred to the United States.

3. *Permanent assignment:* This is when an employee signs what should, in principle, amount to a permanent employment contract with a foreign subsidiary. The assignment may conceivably fall short of the company's or the employee's expectations, so the contract is usually made for a fixed period of time. Still, the intention is for the employee to stay on.

Base pay and perquisites vary according to these categories. Generally, one can say that the longer a planned assignment abroad is, the more the principles and local environment of the host company should determine the compensation of the employee. Employees who fall into the first category are not usually called expatriates. Their assignment is of such a short duration that pay and benefits remain linked to compensation in the home country. After all, the employees must still pay the ongoing costs, such as rent or mortgage, insurances, costs for keeping the family etc. incurred in their home country. The assignment could be seen as a long business trip which 'has got out of hand'. However, the expenses incurred for food, clothing, housing and the like will often be 'liberally' reimbursed. Obviously, for longer short-term assignments, companies will allow their employees to visit their families once or twice during the term of their assignment.

Expatriates are those employees who are on long-term assignments. However, many international companies do not make a distinction between long-term and permanent assignments and thus have a number of 'permanent' expatriates on their payroll. In principle, this situation should not have any special consequences in terms of pay, because many multinationals take the view that their expatriate compensation policies are aimed at guaranteeing that the individual employee is in any case not worse off, but also not much better off, if assigned abroad. The latter is a strong understandment, which hardly reflects reality. On the contrary, there are employees who strive to become expatriates because they are so well paid. Expenses which exceed the level in the home country are almost always reimbursed, in most cases without the cheaper expenses being deducted. To be added to this are the costs of the employee and his or her family going home (by air) on leave or during a holiday. 'Additional' costs further include housing, removal, language courses and education of the children and, last but not least, measures to support the partner's position. In the next section we shall discuss in detail the compensation methods used for long-term assignments, including the local going-rate system, which should, basically, be suitable for permanent assignments.

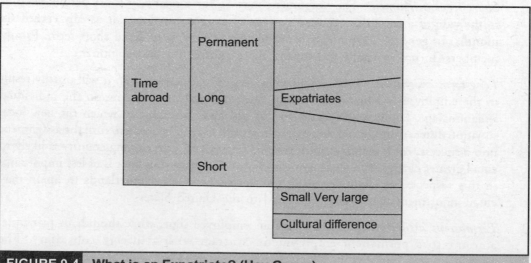

FIGURE 9.4   What is an Expatriate? (Hay Group)

We should already noted that an employee is called an expatriate in the case of a long-term assignment. It should be added, however, that an employee stands a greater chance of being considered an expatriate when assigned to a country whose culture differs significantly from that of his or her own (for example, from the Netherlands to Zambia rather than, say, France). In countries with fewer cultural differences, the assignment will have to be for a longer period if the term expatriate is to apply and any special (that is to say, more liberal) compensation to be paid. Figure illustrates this point.

⌘ Compensation of International Staff   ⌘

Objectives of Compensation

As with national compensation policies, international compensation policies are not an end in themselves, but a means to achieve certain company objectives. Robock and Simmonds (1983) argue that an effective compensation policy for international staff should strive to meet the following objectives:

1. Attract and retain employees qualified for service abroad.

2. Facilitate transfers between foreign affiliates and between home-country and foreign affiliates.

3. Establish and maintain a consistent and reasonable relationship between compensation of all of the employees of any affiliate, whether posted at home or abroad, and between affiliates.

4. Arrange reasonable compensation, in the various locations, in relation to the practices of leading competitors.

5. To this we might add:

    Be cost-effective: Of course, these objectives will often be conflicting. A generous pay package will certainly attract and retain employees, but, will not be very cost-effective. Consistent and reasonable compensation of all employees within an affiliate will often not facilitate transfers between foreign affiliates if the general level of compensation is very different between countries (see discussion of the local going-rate system below). In the next section we will discuss various methods of compensation that all attempt to meet one or more of the objectives stated above.

Methods of Compensation

There are many methods to compensate international staff. The bottom line will always be that the assigned employee must be compensated for where he or she missed out on. Economic factors play a role, but also the quality of the employee's social life. As a rule, the assignment aboard is preceded by fresh negotiations between the employer and employee, particularly where the assignment is likely to interrupt the employee's career. Almost all compensation method, however, are variations of the following three systems:

- The budget system;

- The balance sheet or home-net system;

- The local going-rate system.

The balance sheet system will be most extensively dealt with, since it is used by majority of companies.

The Budget System

This system takes in all costs incurred by the employee in both countries (the home country and host country). These costs, and the effects of the local tax system, form the basis on which the employee's income is calculated. The system is extremely expensive to keep up because of the many adjustments which need to be made, notably in high-inflation countries. This method used to be popular in the colonization era, which probably explains why nowadays it is only used by a few large, paternalistic British companies, and then especially in developing countries. An assignment form Britain to India will, for example, result in lower expenses for clothing, food and other fixed or variable private expenditure. These costs are meticulously compared and totaled. Admittedly, account is also taken of the employee's ongoing expenses in the home country. The net total is subsequently grossed up and incorporated in the (British) salary. The result is that the company completely controls the expatriate's prescribed spending pattern in an attempt to maintain the British standard of life. Problems may occur if products or services are not locally available, so the costs of importing these products are also included in the detailed calculation.

This system has been subject to criticism from expatriates. The fact that the employer determines what items will and will not be included in the budget is often seen as paternalistic. Moreover, once expatriates know what items are included in the budget, they will certainly try to get other (expensive) items on the list. They feel that they know best what they will need in the host country. Checking these items is hardly feasible without an independent company representative paying regular visits to compare local prices and needs, which would, of course, be very expensive. An added drawback is that the system may well strip up ill-feeling among host-country nationals, when 'luxury' goods such as imported cheese and whisky are considered as basic essentials for the expatriate employees.

The Balance Sheet or Home-net System

The premise underlying the balance sheet system is that the same net sum must be available in both countries. Is this context, 'net' does not mean net salary after taxes and social security contributions. It means the freely disposable income. The idea is that spending power must be identical in both countries. Consequently, allowances will have to be made for cost of living, housing and generally accepted spending patterns.

The original gross income in the home country is reduced step by step by all premiums and costs. It is essential to define beforehand what costs and premiums should be included in the comparison. So mortgage costs (or their tax consequences) or car expenses may or may not contribute to the ultimate net result, which is the freely disposable income. After that, a cost-of-living parity may be applied. Let us take as an example an assignment from the Netherlands to Denmark, which will result in a new income expressed in Danish kroner and calculated as follows.

Gross income in the Netherlands	DFL 90,000
Less pension premiums	3,200
Less social security contributions	18,800
Less income tax	22,200
Less health insurance premiums	2,500
Less housing costs	9,000
Less car expenses	12,000
Net income in the Netherlands	DFL 22,300

Subsequently, a correction may be made to maintain the spending power of the net disposable income (food, clothing, personal care, household utensils, leisure activities and so on). The spending –power parity between the Netherlands and Denmark has been set at 1.2, meaning that the same net amount buys 20 percent more in the Netherlands. At a rate of 27 Dutch cents to one Danish krone, DFL 22,300 results in DKK 99,100 (=22,300 × 1.2/0.27). The ultimate gross (Danish) income will be calculated in reverse order.

Net income in Denmark	DKK 99,100
Add car expenses	44,000
Add housing costs	28,000
Add health insurance premiums	8,500
Add income tax	142,900
Add social security contributions	2,100
Add pension premiums	12,000
Gross income in Denmark	DKK 336,600

In this example, we arrive at nearly the same income as we would have had we simply translated the gross Dutch income into Danish kroner (DFL 90,000/0.27 = DKK 333,333). This outcome can be explained the fact that although items like food, clothing and household utensils are more expensive in Denmark (the spending power of the net Danish income is lower before correction), the costs-and thus the additions-of housing, health insurance and income tax/social security, in particular, are lower in Denmark (note the different way of financing social security; in Denmark, this is done almost entirely through taxation while in the Netherlands a large portion is funded by social security contributions). Obviously, this will not always be the case.

The benefit of the balance sheet or home-net system is that the expatriate is guaranteed his home-country spending power. Moreover, it results in transparent and explainable differences between the salaries of expatriates who hold equivalent positions in different countries. A major drawback of the system is that it may, cause large salary gaps within one and the same subsidiary, particularly between parent-country nationals and host-country nationals.

The second question is – in grossing up the net income in the host country, should strictly identical items (same car and housing) be included or should the aim be to achieve a social position comparable to that in the parent country? To illustrate this dilemma, consider the example of the assignment of an American (top) manager to the Netherlands. Can he maintain his Cadillac, house and swimming pool, tennis court and four acres of land in the Netherlands, or will have to 'settle' for a Mercedes of the 500 series and a detached villa set on 1,000 square meters of land in Wassenaar, or a penthouse in the centre of Amsterdam? In view of the costs, companies will nearly always choose the second option, which does not mean to say that an assignment form the United States to the Netherlands, or even Tokyo, may not still be very problematic for the individual in question.

But it does not end there. On top of the gross income, a wide variety of allowances may be paid, such as:

- Allowances to cover the specific costs associated with a country.

- Allowances to cover personal discomfort or general hardship.

This first category may include the school fees of the employee's children, provided that the fees clearly deviate from those paid in the home country. Membership fees of social clubs are also often translated into a fixed allowance. For countries where taking on private personnel is common practice, standard sums are set. The second category concerns hardship allowances paid to compensate for a very warm or very cold climate, poor communications, language problems, food shortages, political risks, seclusion, viral epidemics, earthquakes and so on. A general allowance may also be paid to compensate for family separation. In the above example of the Danish assignment, it is highly improbable that the second category compensation for discomfort and hardship, is even so much as discussed. Even so, there are international companies which set the total sum of allowances at a fixed percentage of the salary. This parentage will, of course, vary according to country, and be revised at least once a year.

A long-term stay abroad may often only be completed successfully if the employee is allowed regularly to visit the home front. The majority of arrangements or contracts contain provisions specifying the number of paid visits that may be made (often by air). There are no general standards, but the number of visits will naturally depend not the family situation and the distance between the home country and host country, both geographically and in terms of culture. Expatriates who are joined by their families are usually granted a minimum of one visit a year. Of course, this is also a major subject of negotiation before the assignment starts.

Using the balance sheet method does not necessarily mean that the employee will hold the same income position in the host country. The Dutch income calculated above may have been reasonable or conform to market standards for similar positions in the Netherlands. In Denmark, it could be considered very low or very high. In our example, a Danish income of DKK 370,000 would have been more realistic from a market point of review. Thus, the system may generate income differences between local employees and expatriates as it fails to include market-induced compensation levels. If companies wish to take market standards into account, they should preferably use the local going-rate system.

The Local going-rate System

Under the local going-rate system, the expatriate is paid according to standards in the host country. This prevents the situation where junior staff are paid substantially higher salaries than the expatriate, who is compensated in conformity with the standards of income in his parent country. Cases in point are countries like Germany and Switzerland, where the general level of compensation is significantly higher than in other European countries. This method is considerably less popular in the reverse case. Employees would not like the prospect of being assigned to a less prosperous country under this system, as it will result in profoundly lower salaries. Thus, the local going-rate system is mostly used for assignments to countries with clearly higher compensation levels. The fact that the host country could, at the same time, have lower levels of perquisites and benefits could be a reason for an expatriate to insist on maintaining the willing to accommodate this requirements. Again, the base salary is usually increased by various allowances to compensate for extra housing costs, international schools and family visits.

Differences per Country

Basically, the way in which companies compensate their expatriates hardly differs from country to country. The balance sheet system has been the most common system so far. The organizations which render advice on what sums of compensation and extra allowances should actually be paid almost always have branch offices in many countries. They regularly adjust their compensation schedules to be able to provide an up-to-date picture. It is hardly feasible for companies to maintain such (expensive) systems themselves. In determining the actual compensation to be paid, the organizations still take as a basis the question from which country to which country the employee is transferred.

The local going-rate system is little used internationally. But with tax and social security systems increasingly converging, the system may well catch on. However, a proper comparison between countries will require the use of a job evaluation system which can be applied internationally. After all, companies need to have an insight into the usual income position of host-country nationals in equivalent jobs.

Remarkably, employees who are posted abroad on a permanent basis are often also eligible for expatriate treatment. Using a strict local going-rate system without too many allowances would seem more appropriate in those situations. In fact, international companies have begun to adjust their assignment policies by better defining this 'permanent' category and by treating them more like local employees with regard to compensation.

The belief long held by parent companies that one or more important position abroad should necessarily be occupied by staff from headquarters is on the wane, although it is still current in companies of Japanese or Anglo-Saxon origin. In other countries, assignments are increasingly looked upon form a management development angle. Business expertise very much depends on the years spent aboard. In that light, companies have begun to review their compensation policies. Clearly, the time has come to find other methods of compensation international or European managers and employees from a career point of view. We shall discuss this trend in more detail ahead with the problems surrounding the appraisal of international staff members.

Appraisal of International Staff adding an Extra Dimension to the Appraisal

A temporary or permanent transfer to a neighboring or far-off country, either with a comparable or a totally different culture, will undoubtedly contribute to the employee's experience. The experience gained by managers and specialists alike is of great value to the company. Understanding of local problems, knowledge of local methods and techniques and a better insight into the interrelation between local and central corporate interests are but a few of the many accomplishments where expertise gained can be translated into improved future performance.

In order to find out whether the newly gained experience has in fact benefited the company, a proper appraisal must be made. Besides, an appraisal is also important to the employee in material terms. A favorable appraisal will usually result in a pay rise, bonus or promotion. Properly appraising an employee is not easy; appraising expatriates adds an extra dimensions to the problem. In most cases, the final appraisal is done in the parent country, where the appraisers have little or no knowledge of local circumstance, and the context of the performance may be lost. Achieving the same results in an unknown country may well require large efforts in terms of flexibility and creativity, both of which are difficult to quantify.

In view of the geographical and communicative distance between the expatriate and the appraiser, local management are often called in to give their opinion. The are supposed to be familiar with the expatriate's performance and be able to explain the local situation and environment related factors. Their comments are, however, dictated by their local cultural background. Thus, a manager who is used to guiding and supervising a group through involvement and participation could receive a negative appraisal in a local culture where managers are expected to show strong leadership and be the ones that come up with ideas and initiatives. In such an environment, the appraisal will presumably be to the manager's disadvantage, although he may have made every possible effort and his performance would be termed excellent in the home country. The opinion of an 'ex-expatriate' would be needed to put the situation right.

Depending on the cultural gap, the first six months of an assignment be used for introduction and adjustment, before the expatriate will be able properly to fulfil his duties. Those first six months will centre on communication, that is to say, mastering the language and getting to know the culture. It is advisable to specific in advance the most important performance areas for the term of the assignment, and indicate who will appraise each area.

⌘ Appraisal Criteria   ⌘

In a number of fields, there are differences between national and international staff members working in similar positions. These differences are in many cases qualitative in nature. Thus, the criteria for appraising international staff should take in not only the differences but especially the similarities between them. After all, the international staff member must remain part of the national organization in terms of appraisal too. Table 9.11 shows the main criteria that are used. It should be noted that companies may, on the basis of these main criteria, determine whether the candidate is suitable for assignment, and subsequently, if the candidate is assigned, appraise whether he or she has performed to satisfaction. In chapter, we pointed out the importance of the link between selection and appraisal criteria. The same criteria may be applied to investigate training needs, all of which will result in a more integrated HRM policy.

Every main criterion is usually divided into a few sub-criteria. It is also decided where the emphasis will be put. A combination of criteria may be used, depending on the employee's job description. However, everyday practice shows that detailed criteria such as those listed in Table are sometimes less strictly applied and companies confine themselves to making such broad statements as: 'to close down the foreign subsidiary within one year subject to the appropriated legal restrictions'. The targets are linked to a compensation package, and it should be noted that there has been a striking shift in the types of challenge that are rewarded nowadays. We will look at this in more detail in the next section.

TABLE 9.11 Criteria for Appraisal
Qualification
• Training
• Experience
• Technical skills
• Social and language skills
Targets
• Directly derived from the company's objectives
• Directly derived from the subsidiary's objectives
• Directly derived form local objectives
• Individually dictated

Contd...

Attitude so far
• Flexibility
• Interpersonal understanding
• Ability to cope with stress
• Openness to change
Job performance
• Result areas
• Communication and decision-making
• Personal development
• Personal growth
• Individual growth targets
• Application of (newly gained) expertise

✠ Current Points of Appraisal

In any appraisal today, the following skills and qualities are considered decisive (Mitrani et al., 1992), particularly in executive staff (direction and top managers) and the more so if they have been assigned abroad.

Qualities required of Executive Staff

- *Flexibility:* The capacity to change structures and processes in order to implement changed strategies.

- *Implementing change:* The capacity to effectuate changes.

- *Interpersonal understanding:* The capacity to understand and respect others.

- *Empowerment:* To share information and promote the ideas of others, delegate responsibilities, supply feedback and undertake any such actions as are required to make employees feel more capable and motivated.

- *Team support:* The capacity to cause employees to cooperate effectively.

- *Versatility:* The capacity to adjust rapidly and perform effectively in a new environment (abroad).

All other employees are usually expected to be flexible, inquisitive, have the capacity to learn, be performance-oriented, be able to work under time pressure, be open to cooperation and be customer-oriented. All this does not mean that qualities which have not been mentioned are not important, but they are not essential to successful performance.

Developments in the Field of Euro-compensation

In the previous sections we noted that what was acceptable in the past is increasingly not so nowadays. Compensating expatriates on the basis of the best of both worlds had become not only expensive for companies, a number of employees calling themselves expatriates are on the increase, but also unacceptable in and of itself.

There are increasingly fewer situations where a hardship allowance or an overseas allowance would be in order, although hardship allowances will of course probably remain necessary, in Africa for instance. Assignment abroad and contacts with other cultures have come to be seen as inherent in the job. Inherent in the job also means that changes in work routine are not coupled with extra compensation, but are already regarded as part of the reward. According to Adler and Ghadhar these less generous, more global packages would be used mostly in multinational (global in 'our' terminology) and global (transnational in 'our' terminology) companies, while other companies would use one of the systems described above and given extra money to compensate for foreign hardships.

In this section we will first discuss some general ideas on developments in international compensation policy and then concentrate on what is called 'Euro-compensation. Despite the quite large discrepancies between base pay and perquisites in the different European countries, Euro-compensation seems a more realistic option for the short and medium term than a comprehensive worldwide compensation system. The fact that West European exchange rates have been comparatively stable for a long time (although nothing is certain since the collapse of the ERM in 1992), and the existence of a common currency (the ECU) are important facilitators for a system of Euro-compensation.

International Compensation Policy

Although the European Union's decision to eliminate the internal borders of the European labor markets may not see quick results, an internal labor market is nearing. This is particularly so for highly qualified employees who geographically speaking belongs to the more mobile group of workers. Companies in countries with lower pay levels are more and more facing competition from foreign companies in countries on the labour market. It may mean that we are on the road to Euro-compensation. Still, many obstacles are yet to be overcome. What is clear is that multinationals (especially those of European origin) are spearheading the drive for change. But so far they do not seem to be putting their ideas into practice. They probably still regard the gaps between the countries as unbridgeable, or perhaps they find the divergent legislation (tax, non-transferable pension entitlements) too much of an obstacle. It seems as if they are waiting for the fence to come down sufficiently for them to jump over. As it stands, many organizations still use the following guidelines:

1. The compensation package must reflect national custom (culture); if it is not common practice domestically to grant a bonus, no bonus is granted, no matter what home-country practice is.

2. The relative level of compensation (for example, whether a position is classified as senior or junior) must in principle be the same in all countries; absolute compensation levels may differ, however.

3. Differences in taxation and social security are not translated into different compensation levels.

TABLE 9.12	Important International Employment Conditions	
	Cash expenses	**Professional**
	Fixed annual income	Telephone allowance
	Variable income	Company car
Currently disposable	Tax-free payment	Personal expense allowance
	Loan	
	Health insurance	
	Allowance	
	Differed income	Insurance
	Pension	Supplement to sickness benefit
	Voluntary early retirement	Widow's/widower's pension

In other companies, however, compensation may already be done differently:

1. The company applies the same strategy in all countries in terms of performance-related compensation such as variable income or stock purchase plans.

2. The total compensation level of a section of the employees, or all of them, is based on the same spending-power parity.

3. The company sets minimum requirements for rules and values governing pensions, life assurance and health insurance.

The latter combination of factors reflects a more global orientation towards compensation. All employees, whether they are parent, third-or host-country nationals, are treated in the same way.

The table specifies a number of important international employment conditions. The company ay formulate a policy for each segment, subject to the applicable statutory restrictions. For each (element of a segment), regardless of whether it concerns an international or a Euro-compensation system, companies must choose any of the following three alternatives.

1. A fixed value in all countries. This means, for example, that the same net income or personal expense allowance is paid in all countries, or that the make and type of the car is the same everywhere.

2. A relative value in all countries. This means that the benefit granted depends on other values. For example, al commitments may be defined in terms of fixed income. The ultimate pension may be set at 60 percent of the last earned salary, irrespective

of what any state pension may offer. Under a supplements scheme, statutory benefits could perhaps be supplemented up to 90 percent in al countries.

3. A relative market position in all countries. This means that the organization will take a relative position in al countries. It may, for example, opt for salary position which would be labeled as market average. As regards health insurance allowances, it may choose a system which belongs to the top 25 percent of all local systems.

It is of course essential, in taking such policy decisions, that jobs are compared which are similar in terms of responsibilities. In evaluating 'job size', and thus the salary, several criteria may be used.

1. Complexity of markets.

2. Number of product/market combinations.

3. Technological level.

4. Branch of industry

5. Number of management areas to be administered.

6. Extent to which organizations are independent

7. Size of the company in terms of turnover and workforce.

On the basis of these criteria, international companies can develop a global compensation policy. Determining job size is essential to be able to compare properly between the different countries. In particular, cash and professional expenses vary greatly according to job levels. The following schedule sets out an example of a particular job size. The employment package for 'internationally' compensated staff could be as given in Table. A few components (for example, health insurance allowance) are related to the relative position in the host country; other components (for example, variable income) have the same relative value, while still others represent a fixed value.

All this does not necessarily mean that the global standard used by a company is always valid in all countries. In countries with pay levels in excess of the global corporate standard, the local pay level will take priority. If it did not, companies would lose the battle for talented managers. Consequently, the salaries paid for comparable management positions may vary considerably within one and the same group of companies. However, a massive drain of talented managers from one country to the other is unlikely. For many, the emotional and cultural obstacles are still too high.

ECU Points

Current expatriate policies are too complicated and expensive to facilitate compensation within a European context and adequately reward cross-border performance. In order to control flexibility in terms of employment conditions, the pay packages should consist of a fixed part which is not open to negotiation and a variable part to be negotiated by the employees. The variable part in particular should remain controllable. The package may take a form which could as easily be applied in the case of mergers or assignments abroad as in the case of special rewards. This type of package consists of what are called flexipoints steps will show how flexipoints are allocated.

TABLE 9.13	Example of Employment Package for 'Internationally' Compensated Staff	
	Cash	**Professional expenses**
	Annual fixed income Average income usually paid in the trade Netherlands: DFL 100,000 Denmark: DKK 395,000 Britain: £28,000	Telephone allowance Full reimbursement of all costs; tax consequences to be borne by the employee
Current disposable	Variable income 15 percent of the fixed income if targets are met	Company car Points of reference are in the same range as 'a make X-type Y'
	Health assurance allowance Average allowance usually paid in the host country	Personal expense allowance the same net allowance equivalent to DFL 1,500 in all countries
	Deferred income Pension Supplement to state pension up to a maximum of 65 percent of the last earned income; the pension age is 65	Insurance Supplement to sickness benefit supplement to state benefits up to the full fixed income during the first year of illness; supplement up to 85 percent in the second year
Commitments		Disability After the third year of illness, Benefits will be supplemented up to 65 percent of the income in all countries, regardless of state benefits Widow's/widower's pension the payment to widows/widowers amount to 65 percent of the old age pension

Step 1: Define the organization's compensation position: The position which the organization intends to hold on the pay and benefits market is clarified and defined. After that, pay and benefits components are 'translated' into total remuneration (TOTREM). In other words, the total economic value of the integral employment conditions package is defined first.

Step 2: Convert TOTREM into ECU: The TOTREM package defined in step1 must be converted into the European ECU currency. If the Netherlands is set at 1,000, at current exchange rates, the weights for Germany and the United States would be set at 1.2 and 1.8, respectively. The location weight (LW) is also important. It is an estimate of the cost of living for a given work location. For example, Paris has been set at 1.3 and Tokyo at 2.2. The third element comprises versatility and potential growth (VP). In the end, the total results in a multiplication score. The total compensation points (TCP) are standardized at 1,000 and give a unique score for each employee, for example, managers A,B and C, as follows:

Manager	LW	VP	TCP
A	1.3	1.0	1,300
B	1.0	1.0	1,000
C	1.2	1.2	1,440

Step 3: Define negotiation space: It must be determined for each organization (or division) what part of the pay package is not open to negotiation (say 500 TCP). If the organization holds a position at average level, and determines that 10 percent below that level is acceptable, then 50 TCPs will be available for further definition.

Step 4: Specify benefits package: The same operation as in step 3 is now applied to the benefits package (say 160 TCP). The choice of base pay and benefits may vary. An organization which attaches weight to a strongly caring employment package will opt for a higher TCP portion in benefits than an organization wishing to lay the emphasis on monetary rewards.

Step 5: Determine TCP-FLEX: The individual variable part must be determined, whereby TCP-FLEX is equivalent to TCP minus base pay and benefits and, if desired, plus market adjustment, variable compensation, periodic increases and so on. Employees in comparable positions may subsequently fill in their packages.

| Manager | TCP-FIXED | | TCP-FLEX | | TOTAL |
	Pay	Benefits	Cash	Benefits	TCP
A	500	160	640		1,300
B	500	160	140	200	1,000
C	500	160	340	440	1,440

Step 6: Allocation flexipoints: The actual allocation of flexipoints will, in practice, be subjected to a number of conditions. Some of them are laid down by law and may vary according to country (for example, the statutory minimum of 20 days off). Eventually, the flexipoints allocated to the employee in question will be directly linked to the spending limit of an employee's credit card. In this way, it will be easy to reward directly an exceptional performance by increasing the number of flexipoints, without having to perform a thousand-and-one calculations. At present, employees receive extra compensation if they are posted abroad for some time. It is quite conceivable that this situation will change to one where an employee receives a standard compensation for the job-related willingness to be mobile, and where he or she exactly knows, if they are assigned abroad, how many flexipoints the location weight and versatility will generate. Negotiations between the parties will no longer concern details of the employment package, but rather focus on the number of flexipoints.

Summary

In this chapter we have discussed the problems associated with the appraisal and compensation of international staff. A number of compensation systems have been reviewed. Future expatriates will, in many respects, be different 'persons' from those a decade ago. The phenomenon of expatriation will become more of a rule than an exception. An increasing number of managers and experts are eligible for expatriation. This means that the term will lose its special ring and the compensation will be less 'different' accordingly.

CHAPTER-10

Building Performing Culture
Creating Performing Organization to meet Current and Future Challenges

LEARNING OBJECTIVES

- To make students aware of the facilitating environment which motivates employees to perform

- To provide guidelines to managers to create performing condition

Introduction

Ruth Tearle has rightly said "The world has changed from horse terrain (safe and predictable) to tiger territory (turbulent and risky) and riding a nervous horse through tiger territory is "not exactly a wise choice". Market is becoming increasingly turbulent with increased competition, instability of exchanges, commodity prices and interest rates. The implication has been the need for increased flexibility and responsiveness.

Today's liberalized economic policy has opened up doors of a global market and pushed Indian industries into the global market. Globalization of market implies increase in the number of players, each one wanting to exploit opportunities available, grab and retain the target market share. This is a one rule game – "*Survival of the Fittest*".

Winds of change are blowing almost with a vengeance and organizational development and renewal have to be one of the top priority activities of the management. Organization has to build on its strengths, eradicate the weaknesses and has also to become information based, if it has to sustain the global competition.

The above situation has increased the corporate mortality rate (closure, merger, take over/acquisition). Companies die/fail young, because their policies and practices are based too heavily on the thinking and languages of economics. In other words, companies die because they focus excessively on producing goods and services and forget that the organization is a community of human beings who have to stay alive. Organization concentrating themselves on land, labour, capital and overlooking the fact that labour means real people and it is not merely a factor of production but the greatest asset of the organization.

Now a question arises: What is so special about the company which stays/sustains during turbulent times (global competition). Companies that learn and understand how to fit in the present world, value new ideas, trust their people, establish credibility, update/enlarge knowledge base, allow freedom of innovation, loosen steering and control, organize learning and shape the human community, alone can survive and grow.

Organizations which covers the path of ideas to action, believe in the aforesaid elements and follow the following algebraic formula are termed as living/learning organization/performing organization.

BOX 10.1	Organisational Attributes put as Algebraic Formula	
• Knowledge	x Skill	= Ability
• Attitude	x Situation	= Motivation
• Ability	x Motivation	= Human Performance
• Human Performance	x Resources	= Orgn. Performance

Importance of Learning/Performing Organization

Human beings and their creating capabilities are the primary source of competitive advantage, hence, organizational configuration and management choices must reflect the dynamics of creativity. Organizations cannot stay/sustain the pressure of competition unless environment ignites creativity, conserve/nurture ideas and translate the ideas into action. Ideas, initiatives and creativity comes from those who feel free, and are convinced that their jobs are worth doing. Today, organizations have to focus on decentralized communication, network culture and support freedom of expression, failing which it may be regarded as useless.

Change and learning are built right into the same fabric. What it might take for a whole organization to learn it would be the ability of all individuals to change and learn and learn to change. Unless the organization and its people change, it is not possible to cope up with turbulent time and build our future.

Today's illusions that power and authority can produce results are over.

The organization which is willing to take risks, pragmatic in nature, has definite purpose, clear direction and devoid of cookbook approach can sustain itself unpredictable/competitive environment.

Meaning enhances efficiency.

Today's illusion that power and authority alone can produce results are over. And in the present context, it is hardly conceivable to give orders without indicating the *how* and the *why* of what is being requested. In other words, meaning enhances efficiency.

"They know enough who know how to learn".—Henry Adames

In the eagerness to face the challenges of competition some of the organizations have forgotten the importance of building capabilities and focus their attention excessively on the performance. They are attracted to the management bandwagon of bookshelf and haphazardly introduce certain ideas which lead to more confusion/dilemma within the organization. Such casual approach of building competitive edge is not only disastrous, but also affects the bottom line.

To sum up, if an organization has to survive or sustain the current and future challenges of global competition, the only way is to adopt the Learning Path to Build capabilities and hence the importance of learning organization.

Creating Learning Organization

Wick & Leo define, "Learning organization is one that continually improves by rapidly creating and refining the capabilities needed for future success and is not limited to only class room training". They suggest formula for creating a learning organization and says;

Learning Org. = Leader with vision (Plan Matrix) x Information x Inventiveness x Implementation

Each or the above element is absolutely mandatory and if one element is missing, the organization will learn either the wrong things or learn at a rate less than its potential.

An organization interested in learning should not limit itself to simply training and developing individuals but learning should permeate through the procedures used through out the organization with the goal to produce the best. Such learning, when put into action, creates new competencies leading to improved performance.

Successful learning organization has –

1. Leader with clearly defined vision

2. A detailed measurable action plan

3. The rapid sharing of information

4. Inventiveness and

5. The ability to implement.

When these elements are present in any organization, it gains the capabilities to break out of the crowd of competition.

⌘ Leader with Vision ⌘

Unless the leaders are committed to learning, an organization will never achieve its potential for success. A leader is best positioned to see and articulate the performance gap between organization's current achievements vs. what is needed to achieve in future. A strong learning leader has the ability and will to close the gap despite internal skeptics and external difficulties.

"Any one who sees leadership as a means for personal gain,
doesn't have credentials to be a leader"

The leaders who have a clear and deeply held vision and consistent communication of the same enable members of the organization to appreciate what they can contribute to achieve results. In absence of clear picture which guides everyone, members either focus on the wrong things or wait to be told what to do. In either case, the company will not produce the result it is capable of. Vision also helps in focusing the efforts and ideas.

It is important for the leader/organization to have a vision but it is also important to have consistency of vision between corporate and operating units. The company should also have good ways to measure progress.

⌘ Plan/Matrix ⌘

With leader and vision in place, an organization needs the ability to develop a plan of action with detailed matrix and a system of measurement to keep the vision grounded in reality and prevent it from becoming a cosmetic exercise. The larger vision for improvement and change must be turned into specific work/action steps.

Learning organization rigorously measure their progress and hold themselves accountable, Such organization emphasize the following:

- How identified goal will be achieved?

- How progress will be measured?

- How to gauge the effectiveness of processes?

⌘ Information ⌘

A learning organization is hungry for knowledge/ information, communication with speed, honesty and openness which provide, ability to cope up with the changing business environment.

Lack of information makes an organization vulnerable to outside threats and missed opportunity inside the company. Learning organization doesn't believe that management knows it all or that their rank and file can read the minds of top management. They also do not pretend to have an accurate knowledge of what is going on outside their doors (customers, competitors and leaders in particular competencies).

Information is data endowed with relevance and purpose. The key to information based system is that every one ask "who in the organization depend, on me for information. And whom in turn do I depend on". Everyone should constantly think what kind of information we need to do our jobs effectively. The greater information flow, the less each department will be tempted to consider itself the hub of the company's activity and more "cross pollination" will occur between the job experience of different people. Managers have to come out of the illusion of power through information retention.

"Share your knowledge, intellectual selfishness is as bad as material selfishness"

Encouragement to sharing of problems and solutions with a degree of trust and ensuring that information are not tightly held by an individual or team to gain internal competitive advantage are the element of a learning organization.

Managers have to desist from sending mixed signals and double speaking. Today, some managers want to know what is going on but what they mean is to come with good news and keep the problems away. Another set of managers are in the habit of double speaking. They are heard frequently saying "if you have a problem, do not hesitate to come and talk about it", but when someone tries to consult them, they shoot back "Can't you take care of your own problems." Such double talk only 'heightens' apprehensions and feed the grapevines.

Grapevines has no place in learning organization because unchecked and unanswered grapevine blankets the work place with uncertainty and obscure the company's objective. Communication with speed and accuracy can only check the grapevine. Hence regular communications and open door policy to clarify the truth are regarded as wheels of learning organization. When the rumour mill is stopped, people feel more secure in their jobs and feel more comfortable to make decisions at the workplace as well as in their own lives.

In learning organizations, information flows freely throughout the organization to promote company-wide learning. It makes clear to the individuals that they are there in business for the good of the entire company, not for the personal gain and creates cultural norms that place high value on honesty even in the face of difficulties. Instead of covering up problems or fixing blames, such organization makes problems visible so that solutions can be found out quickly.

⌘ Innovation

Learning organizations spend little time in trying to adopt an old solution to fit new problems. They face the issue with new eyes open to fresh ideas and theories and see problem solving as real learning opportunities. Competition, customer requirement set the ground for innovation and the learning company triggers, supports and recognizes the innovativeness of individuals.

A point is made clear early and often to the members that organization is yet to reach its potential. Individuals can be good, they can be better, they can be fast, they can be faster, they can be smart, they can be smarter. There is no finish line to cross, they have to simply keep trying to better their best.

"Most innovations are based on simple ideas"

⌘ Implementation

It is a well known fact that ideas/plan without action is regarded as intention only, which doesn't yield results. Hence without action, the other elements of learning organization will remain simply a body without a soul. All learning and creativity in the world is worthless if it does not get implemented through actions.

Many companies are stuck at this juncture for one reason or the other. Some of the stumbling blocks are – risk of trying, apprehension of failure, forgetting the end purpose and being caught up in the learning process. These stumbling blocks are causes of poor abilities. Learning organization have an urgency to act and ability to execute/implement.

Implementation require perseverance, incredible tenacity and sense of responsibility to achieve goals. Learning organization never gives up.

Peter M Senge in his book *"Fifth Discipline"* has emphasized apart from other things, Personal Mastery and People's Development as important elements of learning organization.

Personal Mastery

Organizations learn only through individuals who learn. Individual, learning does not guarantee organizational learning but without it, no organization learning occurs. The most active force in any organization is "people" and people have their own will, own mind and own way of thinking.

Learning organizations focus on enlarged canvas of competence building which not only covers enhancement of knowledge, skill and attitude, but also spiritual growth of the individual and continual expansion of ability to create results in the organization as well as in their life.

Personal mastery is the expanding ability to produce result and is a lifelong discipline. They never "arrive".

Personal mastery goes beyond competence and skills though it is grounded with competence and skills. When personal mastery becomes a discipline it embodies;

- Continually clarifying what is important for the individual
- Continually learning how to see current reality more clearly

Even the best people do not consider every possibility.

Mastery does not mean more information, but expanding ability to produce results. It also does not suggest gaining dominance over people or things. It means only a special level of proficiency in every aspect of life – personal and professional.

It is a process and a lifelong discipline. People with a high level of personal mastery live in a continual learning mode. They never "arrive". They show high level of commitment, take more initiative and they have broader and deeper sense of responsibility in their work.

Development

Human beings and their creating capability are the primary sources of competitive advantage, hence organizational configuration and management choices must reflect the dynamics of creativity. The leaders of learning organization regard people as the greatest asset and as main force within the company, they commit themselves to develop their abilities for personal mastery.

In a rapidly involving world, constantly updating of knowledge is vital and it involves much more than providing occasional rehabilitation course to the employees. Some Japanese Companies spend upto 8% of their total sales on people's development.

Training breeds independence, which is the foundation of self-esteem which motivates people to create, innovate and excel. Training should be tailored to meet the organizational goals.

Group learning, through dialogue, mutual emulation and strengthening collective cohesion are some of the important factors for developments.

⌘ Prerequisites for Learning Organization ⌘

- Preparedness for change
- Manager's knowledge/grasp of fundamentals of management

- Realistic organizational structure to facilitate learning
- Clear and realistic company's goal made known to everybody
- Emphasis on result rather than process
- Leadership competent/able to
  - ❖ Set clear direction
  - ❖ Develop trust of people
  - ❖ Produce winning results

    "The spark of creating idea comes from hard work".

  - ❖ Well-defined competency development programmes and its effective implementation
  - ❖ System of information sharing communication and feed back
  - ❖ Manager's sensitivity to mobilize and motivate people.

⌘ Strategies ⌘

- Setting and communicating vision/mission statement
- Communication of norms of behaviour
- Clear-cut plan including contingency plan and its communication
- Defining structure to support
  - ❖ Learning
  - ❖ Communication
  - ❖ Innovation
  - ❖ Development
  - ❖ Motivation
  - ❖ Evaluation of training and development programmes
  - ❖ Accountability
- Setting strategic targets for learning
- Recognition of group working
- Identifying learning expeditor and inspirer for creating learning organization.

⌘ Role of HR Managers ⌘

HR managers are widely accepted as change agents within the organization and they may use this prime position to become a learning expeditor. They may play a role of inspirer to trigger creativity and learning within the organization. Their position is like that of a power boat drive who pulls a team of water skiers (Wick and Leon).

In order to assume this role, the HR managers have to come out of their cocoon of a status/ hierarchy and should be willing to work with missionary zeal. As a first step, they may make an attempt to find out whether organization qualifies as a learning organization and, if not, which are the grey area where intervention/initiative is required. They can also present the outcome of such survey to the top management for obtaining commitment.

Creating a High Performing Operating Environment: The Leadership Challenge

The leaders of any large-scale organizational change quickly learn that it's not enough to develop a new and improved set of strategies, structures and work processes. Inevitably, those formal initiatives run headlong into stiff resistance from the "informal organization"— the deeply entrenched social fabric of the enterprise.

Consequently, change leaders face two alternatives. They can leave the existing culture intact, try to work around it, and then watch helplessly as their change initiative first stalls, and then collapses, Or they can roll up their sleeves and undertake the daunting task of reshaping the organization's values, beliefs and behavior in ways that support its new business requirements.

The ultimate goal, in our view, is to create a high-performance operating environment. Simply put, that requires aligning the business strategy with the working environment – the way people do their jobs, relate to their co-workers and interact with their customers. Of course, there's nothing simple about it, and with good reason; experienced leaders often observe that when it comes to organizational change, "the soft stuff is the hard stuff."

Why is it so hard to change the operating environment? The answer goes to the very heart of successful organizational change-the ability, over time, to significantly alter the perceptions, behaviour and performance of large number of people in pursuit of clearly articulated strategic objectives. Inspired strategies, creative organization designs and streamlined processes, by themselves, will not produce lasting change in the way an enterprise conducts its business. Profound shifts in organizational performance require fundamental changes in individual behaviour.

And yet, experience shows that most organizations, faced with the threats and demands of complex change, will focus on changing their strategy, structure and work processes but avoid tackling the operating environment. That's understandable; the immediate demands of running the business, responding to customers, complying with legal requirements, and meeting financial goals – all have an undeniable immediacy.

On the other hand, issues involving people and the operating environment somehow seem less critical, and are easily shoved aside in favour of more pressing concerns. Nevertheless, there's great danger in leaving the operating environment to linger on the back burner. All too often, the existing operating environment is replete with behaviour, attitudes and beliefs that undermine the change effort and make it inherently impossible to successfully implement the newly crafted strategy, structure and processes.

Consequently, it is our view that creating a high-performance operating environment is, at once, one of the greatest opportunities and most difficult challenges facing leaders as they embark on fundamental organizational change. Toward that end, this paper explores:

- *What is it:* A description of the operating environment and a discussion of why it has such a powerful impact on performance;

- *Implications for leaders:* Principles for leading operating environment change;

- *How to change it:* A description of specific interventions; and

- *Tactical issues:* Some considerations that should influence the staging and timing of change initiatives.

⌘ What it is: Defining the Operating Environment ⌘

To many managers, the "soft side" of organizational change involves some uncomfortably imprecise concepts that are hard to measure and harder to fix. Unfortunately, their inherent murkiness had been reinforced by the use of loosely descriptive terms such as "culture" and "climate".

That's why, in recent years, we've come to refer to the social dimensions of the enterprises as the "operating environment". We do that to underscore the direct and powerful link between the way people think and behave – the way they perform their jobs, relate to their co-workers and interact with customers – and the organization's overall performance. We use it to describe the set of informal arrangements every organization develops over time along with its formal arrangements – its strategy, structure, systems, processes and explicit practices. In a sense, operating environment describe "how we run the place".

From the perspective, the operating environment is a function of the norms that emerge, the pace of the operating, and the way people work together. It describes the generally accepted "rules of engagement" that govern interpersonal interactions. It includes shared expectation about how people act and perform. It's the way people behave as they try to achieve their business objectives.

In other words, an organization's operating environment consists of the implicit patterns of behavior, activities, and attitudes shaped by a shared set of values and beliefs that characterize the way people work together. In essence, the operating environment determines:

- How people operate individually and collectively in order to successfully implement the strategy;

- What patterns of leadership behaviour are considered desirable;

- Where to focus energy and resources;

- How to think about customers, competitors and employees; and

- How people deal with each other.

Just as organizations develop strategies and operating plans, they also develop operating environments that shape the translation of those plans into tangible results and performance.

⌘ Operating Environment and High Performance ⌘

How does the operating environment affect performance? To answer that question, we'll start by looking at two fundamental characteristics of operating environments that have an impact on the way the organization functions.

Operating Environment Impacts all Parts of the Organization

At this point, we need to stand back briefly and consider the role of the operating environment as part of a larger organizational system. Our starting point is a construct known as the congruence model of organizational behaviour, an approach many organizations have found useful. The model views any organization as a system; at its heart is a transformation process whereby the enterprise, in accordance with its articulated strategy, performs work that converts input to output. This core element of the organization consists of four components – the work, or the series of tasks required to perform each function in the value chain; the people who carry out those tasks; the formal organization of structures, processes and practices that specify how work is assigned and performed; and the informal organization which includes the operating environment, including the patterns of behaviour that shape the daily interactions between people and their supervisors, employees, co-workers and customers.

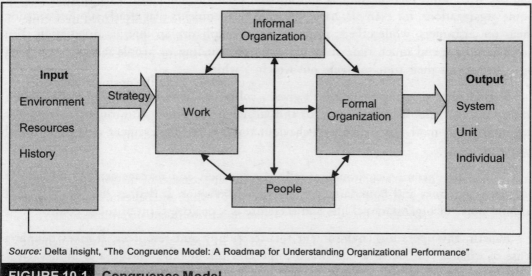

Source: Delta Insight, "The Congruence Model: A Roadmap for Understanding Organizational Performance"

FIGURE 10.1   **Congruence Model**

At any given time, each of the four components exists in some relative degree of fit, or congruence, with the other three, and with the strategy. The tighter the fit, the smaller the gap between strategic objectives and actual performance. Total congruence is the ideal goal, but in reality, in organizations, the job of managers is to constantly make decisions that will realign the fit between work, people, formal structures and the informal operating environment.

This model involves several important implications for leaders of change. The first is that major change nearly always originates in the external environment. The nature of that change will, in turn, influence the scope, intensity and sequence of changes involving the internal components. Second, the model suggests that changes in any of the internal components will have a ripple effect, altering the pattern of relationships among multiple components. Finally, it serves as a reminder that change does not occur in a vacuum; it requires that top executives demonstrate ambidextrous leadership as they simultaneously implement change while continuing to meet the ongoing demands of the business.

In this context, the operating environment is an integral part of the system that moulds performance. It shapes, and is shaped by, the other components—the strategy, work, formal organization, and people. The implication is clear – Changing the strategy or formal structures without accompanying changes in the operating environment will invariably lead to poor fit which, in turn, results in disappointing performance.

Operating Environments Directly Influence Behaviour

The congruence model provides us with a conceptual framework for thinking about the role of the operating environment. Now let's deal in more concrete terms with the ways in which the operating environment drives performance by influencing behaviour.

To begin with, the operating environment provides people with important signals that identify what kind of behaviour is appropriate, even valuable, and what is discouraged. Some organizations, for example, have operating environments that clearly support a strong focus on customers, while others, many in fact – emphasize an internal orientation. You don't have to spend much time at an organization listening to people talk and watching how they spend their time to figure out which is which.

Second, the operating environment gives a coherent identity to the workplace. This is important for establishing a sense of individual pride and commitment toward the organization. It motivates individual behaviour towards the achievement of organizational objectives.

Third, the operating environment reflects a business and management philosophy. It provides guidelines and boundaries for individual behavior. It defines the "shoulds" and "should nots" of organizational life, and therefore is a positive form of social control.

Fourth, the operating environment focuses energy and resources. It gives people a sense of what is considered a valued and important use of time, energy, and money.

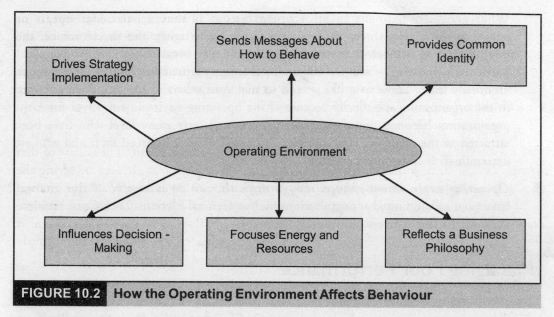

| FIGURE 10.2 | **How the Operating Environment Affects Behaviour** |

Fifth, it influences decision-making. The operating environment is a function of the underlying values and beliefs of the organizaiton's members. Values act as perceptual filters; they determine what we pay attention to and, therefore, influence how we process information and ultimately make decisions.

As a result, the operating environment is an important determinant of organizational behavior, and fundamentally affects the successful transformation of strategy into performance.

❧ Implications for Leaders ❧

Considering the essential role the operating environment plays in shaping performance, what are the implications for leaders of large-scale change? There are several implications which are given below:

1. *The single most critical factor in operating environment change is institutional leadership:* Virtually every successful CEO with whom we've worked has viewed operating environment change as a top personal priority. Each pours an immense amount of personal time and energy into articulating, communicating and reinforcing the necessary changes. Moreover, the successful CEOs quickly enlist their executive teams as advocates of change throughout the organization.

2. *Creating a high performance operating environment is a long process and requires persistence:* Operating environments are resistant to change. Once they take hold, they become self-perpetuating. That can be both a strength and a weakness. A deeply entrenched operating environment can make it difficult for the organization to adapt to changing conditions. On the other hand, a resilient operating environment can keep an organization on course, even during periods of lacklustre or incompetent leadership.

What generally happens in most organizations is that a particular operating environment develops over time because it fits the strategy and the structure, and people tend to self-select their membership in the organization. Most people – particularly managers – who feel uncomfortable in a particular operating environment, eventually leave. Those who like it tend to stay. And others of like mind are attracted to the organization specifically because of the operating environment. Over time, the organization becomes populated by employees at nearly every level who have been attracted to the operating environment, promoted by it, reinforced by it and who are determined to resist any significant changes to it.

3. *Operating environment change, though difficult, can be successful:* Major changes have been accomplished at organizations such as General Electric, Coca-Cola, Hewlett-Packard, British Airways, and Xerox Corp.

Managing Poor Performance

There is no dearth of an underperforming/poor performing employee. Such employees are a burden to an organization, which organizations of today and tomorrow can ill-afford. Therefore, improving their performance is the primary task.

Underperforming employees fail to meet their objectives, generally perform at lower standards compared to their colleagues, miss deadlines and have poor work attitude. Poor performing employees can adversely affect organizations in different ways like more complaints from customers and their failure to meet expectation can seriously affects the firm's ability to fulfill client obligation. Another potentially serious effect of having poor performers at a firm is decreased motivation for the other employees (Messmer, 2006). The Future Foundation conducted research to understand the costs associated with poor people performance. The findings revealed that American managers spend 13% of their time managing poor performers and 14% of their time correcting the poor performers' mistakes. This translates into an average of 84 days per year dealing with underperformance. So it becomes necessary to address unacceptable/poor performance as soon as it becomes apparent before the situation deteriorates or the opportunity to address the issue disappears. If the right measures are not taken at time, options are left to use the harsh measures like discipline, transfer or termination, which can prove more costly to both the organization and the individual employee. Given the cost of recruitment, it's always worth trying to help an individual to develop from poor to acceptable performance. Turning around a poor performer can recover at least a portion of what an organization has already invested in that employee, and avert the loss it would face in downtime and training a replacement.

Performance management generally tends to be seen in terms of positive process that helps employees to build on success and identification of weaknesses to aid setting development targets. The steps of performance management process including planning, mentoring, monitoring and review coaching provides the ideal framework for managing the performance generally and for dealing with poor performance when it occurs. Taking corrective action is an integral part of the ongoing performance management process, with the genuine hope and intention that most people will quickly improve and even become "high performing" again. When employees fail to function properly, a manager must assess the cause of the problem.

This chapter examines the factors responsible for poor performance, Furthers, it discusses how managers can handle poor performance. It also discusses how managers can deal with underperformer during formal performance review.

⌘ Why Poor Performance? ⌘

Job performance is the result of three elements working together: skill, effort and nature of external conditions (Peters and O'Connor, 1980). Individuals may perform badly because of lack of skill, i.e., lack of knowledge, abilities, attitude, motivation, etc. Employee may have skill and knowledge but may not perform well because of lack of motivation to perform. The third element affecting performance is the degree to which external conditions are favorable in facilitating performance. These would include external pressures, changes in requirements, system faults, inadequate resources, jobs or task allocated to people who do not have the necessary experience or attributes, inadequate induction and continuation training and poor leadership, guidance or support from the manager, team leader or colleagues. According to William Deming (1986), poor performance may not be their fault. Poor performance may be because of defective system of work, inadequate leadership or guidance, the allocation of inappropriate tasks, placement in jobs that are beyond their capabilities or insufficient training. Other reasons of poor performance of employee may be inability to manage perception or pressure, failure of priorities, conflict of personalities and styles, over-promotion and change in performance management systems or processes.

Research (Manzoni and Barsoux, 2002) indicates that poor performance at work is the result of negative behavior by managers themselves, which is then mirrored by employees. This is the 'set-up-to-fail' syndrome—whereby otherwise effective managers can inadvertently cause good employees to fail. This research shows that managers will tend to form judgments about staff performance fairly quickly. This may arise from day-to-day supervision or as a result of a single incident which leads the manager to categorize them as a 'lower performer'.

Some managers may be able to correctly diagnose the causes of performance problems of their employees, but most managers make wrong diagnosis. The typical managers often make wrong attributions about the poor performance of their employees (Knowlton and Mitchell, 1980). They often assume that poor performance stems from some characteristics of the employee when, in fact, it is frequently due to conditions that are beyond the employee's control. Further, managers often assume that poor performance is due to an employee's lack of effort, when actually the employee may not have the proper skills to do the job well. The type of attributions made by a supervisor, about the performance of employee, influences his/her attitudes and behaviour towards the subordinate. For example, a supervisor who blames an employee's poor performance on a lack of effort might be expected to take a punitive action. On the other hand, if the supervisor attributes poor performance to lack of ability or skill, the supervisor might recommend training programme or some other ways of skill building. Hence, the kind of attribution made by the boss can have serious consequences for the way subordinate is treated. The end result of this mismanagement can be quite destructive, resulting in decreased employee satisfaction and productivity. So the right diagnosis is the most crucial step to manage the poor performance. By correctly analyzing the reasons of poor/unsatisfactory performance a manager can use appropriate strategies to being employees' work up to standard.

⌘ How to Handle Poor Performance? ⌘

Different strategies are required to deal with various factors leading to poor performance to correct performance. Any time spent on trying to motivate an ill-trained employee will surely be wasted as it is inappropriate for the problem at hand, which can be better handled through skill training. A motivational strategy is appropriate in the case when employee has the skills but not the inclination. In the case of an employee who has both a poor attitude and low skill level, the major problem was probably in the selection process, and the cost of improving both skills and attitude might be so great that the employee would best be transferred or terminated. An employee with low skill levels and who has a good attitude probably requires training. In the case, when an employee has skill and motivation, the manager needs to understand the external conditions which make the employee unable to meet the right standard. The manager who reacts to a decline in performance among computer analysts by removing and bringing new or "improved" analysts in an environment in which analysts' job duties are unclear, standards of performance are missing or unclear, needed resources are unavailable, the job setting of work flow interferes with effective performance, desired performance is not rewarded, or needed information is not provided, should not expect long-term quality or productivity gains.

To manage the performance, managers must gain an understanding of the characteristics of a productive environment. People perform most effectively under the following circumstances (Bolt and Rummler, 2005):

- The task or goal is clear. They know what is expected of them.

- The resources required to do the job are readily available, including information, time, money, and the proper tools.

- The individual has the capacity, skills, and knowledge about how well he or she is doing vis-à-vis the job expectations.

- The individual is satisfied by the consequences or rewards that follow the successful performance of the job.

Performance is likely to be less than expected if any of these links are weak.

Following steps can be used to deal with poor performance (Armstrong and Baron, 2008).

Identify and agree the problem: Here manager and individual employee need to have an agreement on what the shortfall has been.

Establish the reason(s) for the poor performance: Here, the manager should not try to attach the blame. The aim should be for the manager and the employee jointly to identify the facts that have contributed to problem. Various techniques like reflections, observation of performance, listening to comments made by others about why things are occurring, reevaluating the bases of past decisions, and taking notes or keeping a work diary can help expand a manager's search for the causes of poor performance. It is necessary to differentiate the factors that are under the control of individual (skill and effort) from the factors which are outside the control of the individual (external conditions).

Decide and agree on the action required: Action may be taken by the individual, the manager, or both parties. This could include any of the actions and will depend on the reasons of poor performance. It may be to take step to improve and develop the skills, change behavior, change attitude, more support or guidance from manager, clarifying expectations, and redesign the job, etc.

Resource the action: Managers need to work as an effective leader and coach. They can define the steps that individuals may be expected to take to develop themselves. They need to provide the coaching, training, guidance, experience or facilities required to enable the agreed actions to happen.

Monitor and provide feedback: Both managers and employees monitor performance, ensure that feedback is provided or obtained and analyzed, and agree on any further actions that may be necessary.

Handling Performance Problems at Review Meetings

The manager's goal is to stop and correct poor performance and to initiate new, positive behavior. Formal performance reviews clearly provide a good opportunity to analyze and to reflect on performance problems and to agree solutions. But discussing performance problems isn't easy, and many managers prefer to avoid it at all costs, even though that isn't fair to the employee or to the supervisor.

The following steps have been suggested in Advanced Supervisory Practices, edited by John Matzer (1998) that may make a difficult task somewhat easier:

1. Managers first need to consider their own motivation. Does it stem from a desire to improve the effectiveness of the employee or from a desire to assert his/her power or control over the employee? The principal difference between constructive criticism and just plain old criticism lies in the manager's reasons for giving it.

2. A manager needs to plan how he will discuss performance problems. Without a plan, manager may lose sight of the crucial issues and can produce more anxiety for the employee and himself.

3. Managers should not guess the employee's reasons for poor performance. They need to understand the employees' perception of their performance and listen to the employee with an open mind. Problems arise when managers automatically reject any employee feedback, labelling it an excuse. Knowing how the employee views what manager see as poor performance allows a manager to propose a more productive solution.

4. Discuss the performance problem, not the employee and address the negative behaviour that needs to be changed.

5. Clarify the results of the employee's poor performance. Employees want to know how their work is linked to the overall goals of the organization, and discussing the impact of poor performance is an obvious way to demonstrate a specific relationship.

6. Offer specific examples. Do not offer them as indictments, but rather as ways of clarifying how the problem manifests itself.

7. Use discussions to understand how perceptions about performance differ. But do not inflate a rating of poor performance in order to avoid unpleasantness. After the discussions, if the manager still believes a poor rating is required, maintain his/her rating and document your reasons.

8. A manager should clarify his/her standards for the employee, and jointly develop new goals for the coming review period. This is particularly important if the employee is being placed on probation for poor performance. Expectations need to be clear as well as attainable.

9. Clarify both the employees role in changing his or her performance and any support manager will provide. Let the employee know what responsibilities he or she has for changes.

10. Set a schedule to monitor and provide feedback to the employee in connection with the new goals. Monitoring lets the employee know that change is both expected and important. Regular meetings to cite areas of improvement, as well as areas needing continued attention, are a good idea.

11. Explore with the employee whether the plan for reaching goals will work. This important step ensures that manager has not prescribed an unrealistic plan or that the employee has not agreed too quickly, just to end a difficult discussion.

12. Finally, clarify the consequences of continued poor performance. Because managers are apprehensive about their employees' reactions, they may never directly inform an employee that poor performance can result in termination. They just hope that the employee will infer this automatically, and they do not document or address the problem. But very often, employees believe that there are no consequences for poor performance beyond a series of stress-producing discussions in which the supervisor explains his or her frustrations and the employee agrees to do better.

To survive into the 21 century, organizations must offer a greater sense of meaning and purpose for their workforce. Hence, it would be pertinent to quote Indian seer, Patanjali:

"When you are inspired by some great purpose, some extraordinary project, all of your thoughts break their bonds. Your mind transcends limitations, Your consciousness expands in every direction, and you find yourself in a new, great and wonderful world. Dormant forces, faculties and talents become alive, and discover yourself to be a greater person by far than you ever dreamed yourself to be."

Evaluating Performance Management

One of the more interesting findings of our research was that only 44 per cent of organizations with performance management evaluated its effectiveness. But, as we have noted a number of times, performance management is easy to conceive but hard to deliver. To ensure that it is delivering what it was expected to deliver, it is essential to evaluate performance management, and it is quite remarkable that fewer than half the survey respondents attempted to do so.

⌘ Areas for Examination

Engelmann and Roesch (1995) have suggested that the following areas should be examined when evaluating a 'performance system':

- How well it supports the organization's objectives

- How it is linked to the organization's critical success factors

- How well it defines and establishes individual objectives

- How well it relates to job responsibilities and performance expectations

- How effectively it encourages personal development

- How easy (or difficult) it is to use

- How objective or subjective, clear or ambiguous evaluation criteria are

- Whether it addresses company policies and procedures

- Whether it is fairly and consistently administered

- How well supervisors and employees are trained to used and live under the system

- How it is linked to pay.

⌘ Diagnostic Checklist: Evaluation

To evaluate performance management, you must look for the following:

1. Performance-management processes fit the culture of the organization, the context in which it operates and the characteristics of its people and work practise.

2. There is commitment and support from top management.

3. There is shared ownership with line managers and employees generally.

4. Processes are aligned to the real work of the organization and the way in which, generally, performance is managed.

5. Performance-management processes help to integrate organizational, team and individual objectives.

6. It can be demonstrated that performance management adds value in terms of both short-term results and longer term development

7. Performance-management processes are integrated with strategic and business-planning processes.

8. Performance-management processes are integrated with other HR processes.

9. Performance-management processes can operate flexibility to meet local or special circumstances.

10. Performance-management processes are readily accepted by all concerned as natural components of good management and work practises.

11. All stakeholders within the organization are involved in the design, development and introduction of performance management. These compose top management, line managers, team leaders, team, individual employees and trade-union or employee representatives.

12. Performance-management processes are transparent and operate fairly and equitably.

13. Managers and team leaders take action to ensure that there is a shared understanding generally of the vision, strategy, goals and values of the organization.

14. Performance-management processes recognise that there is a community of interest in the organization and respect individual needs.

15. Performance-management processes are used by managers and team leaders to help people feel that they are valued by the organization.

16. Performance-management processes help to align organizational and individual goals, but this is not a matter of organizational and individual goals, but a matter of a top-down 'cascade' of objectives. Individuals and teams are given the opportunity to put forward their views on what they can achieve, and their views are listened to.

17. The focus of performance management is demonstrably on the development of people. Financial rewards are a secondary consideration if, indeed, they are associated with performance management at all.

18. There are competence frameworks in place developed specially for the organization with the full involvement of all concerned.

19. The aims and operation of performance management and how it can benefit all concerned are communicated thoroughly and effectively.

20. Training in performance-management skills is given to managers, team leaders and employees generally.

⌘ Evaluation Methods ⌘

Questionnaires following Review Meetings

Evaluation can take place by asking individuals to complete a questionnaire immediately following a review meeting. The questionnaire could ask people to rate the effectiveness of the review meetings on a points scale. They would, for example, be asked to indicate their reactions – fully agree, partly agree, partly disagree, fully disagree – to the following statements (the questions might also establish how many people actually received a formal review):

1. I was given plenty of opportunities to contribute to formulating my objectives.

2. I am quite satisfied that the objectives I agreed to, were fair.

3. I felt that the meeting to agreed objectives helped me to focus on what I would be aiming to achieve.

4. I received good feedback from my manager during the year on how well I was doing.

5. My manager was always prepared to provide guidance when I ran into any problems with my work.

6. The performance review was conducted by my manager in a friendly and helpful way.

7. My manager fully recognised my achievement during the year.

8. If any criticisms were made during the review, they were based on fact, not on opinion.

9. I was given plenty of opportunity by my managers to discuss the reasons for any problems with my work.

10. I felt that generally the comments made by my manager at the review meeting were fair.

11. The review meeting ended with a clear plan of action for the future with which I agreed.

12. I felt well motivated after the meeting.

Attitude Surveys

Attitude surveys can be conducted periodically using broadly the same questions as those referred to above. There could be an alternative to an immediate expression of opinion after a meeting.

Focus Groups

Focus groups could be used to provide more in-depth feedback on how well performance management is working. The questions for discussion could be along the lines of those set out above, but there would be an opportunity to hear extended views supported by the reasons for expressing them. Interaction between members of the group may also create useful additional insights into the effectiveness, understanding and acceptance of performance management.

PART-B

Relevant
Performance-related Concepts

1 Benchmarking

Introduction

Benchmarking – Is it driven by jealousy or envy?

Latest concern of management practitioners is "What lies beyond Benchmarking"?

Dr. Robert Camp, known as the "Father of Benchmarking", conceptualized benchmarking while working in Xerox Corporation, USA. The market share of Xerox was going down drastically as competitor products, which had flooded US markets, were sold at less than half the price of Xerox products.

Best practice benchmarking has become recognized in recent years as a valuable performance measurement, an evaluation technique which has made an important contribution in various business. It has its roots in the drive to seek enhanced competitive advantage by learning from competitive performance viewpoints. On an internal or external basis, at strategic operational and business management levels, these comparisons are based on cost, quality and delivery time, both internally and externally. Benchmarking best practices is relevant to all organizations to reach the best in class. It is limited only by imagination, creativity, innovation and resourcefulness of management and the will to succeed in improving performance.

The most critical challenge in any organization is that of strategic nature, enhancement of performance to meet the competition and more importantly the management of change to sustain the enhanced performance. Benchmarking best practice is an effective technique which can make a significant contribution in enhancing and sustaining performance. In recent years it has become recognized as a valuable performance measurement and evaluation technique, which has made important contributions in various businesses.

The profile will reflect the nature of the business, popular shorthand being or – "3 Es – Economy, Efficiency & Effectiveness". For example, service industry performances are accosted on quality, on the other hand medical professionals are assessed on their efficiency of clinical inventions. In spite of these specific changes according to the businesses, benchmarking is to know where we are now and where we want to be, and to understand and implement the transformation.

Some of the key elements of benchmarking involve understanding what competitors do and why. It is also important to know how they do it and how well they do it (in terms of products made, services provided, costs to make and service, distribution and support services, technology and how their organization works). Then the above is to be compared with what this (benchmarking) organization does. This will help to figure out what it takes to be better than the other organization in each of those areas. After getting to know all this, it is finally important to implement better policy, practice, etc.

Today, benchmarking by performance within and across the industry can not only identify the performance gap in absolute value, but can also provide a comparison of fundamental operation and management processes that provide the competitive advantage. Benchmarking can establish how much a company needs to improve to be at the highest possible level of functions and performance, and helps to ensure continuous sustaining competitive advantage at all management levels. Benchmarking rose to reach the third position as a management tool next to strategic planning and customer focus in a survey conducted by Bain & Co. in 1999.

Toyota used benchmarking to bring in the concept of "Just-in-Time" in their assembly lines conceptualized by Taiichi Ohno, after their engineers visited departmental stores in United States to study how those stores placed orders to replenish thousands of grocery goods on their shelves. A big breakthrough was achieved in the reduction of inventories for the assembly line measures in Toyota by the use of benchmarking.

Just-in-time means that, in a flow process, the right parts needed in assembly reach the assembly line at the time they are needed and in only the exact quantity needed.

Groups of companies now see benchmarking leading to the best in class achievement, which becomes a recognized standard of excellence against which similar things are compared. Benchmarking is conceived as a systematic and continuous approach to identify the best practice that enables you to become the best in class.

There are behaviours that can be encouraged and discouraged in an employee for the success of benchmarking practices. Because benchmarking involves gathering information about competitors, it can raise questions of sensitivity, fairness and integrity. Some of the practices that are to be encouraged are – asking customers about competitive equipment and prices, asking employees of well-run business about their practices, searching for information through libraries, publications, etc. the behaviors that are to be discouraged are collusion in fixing prices, talking to competitors about prices, disparaging a competitor's business to customers of others, attempting to gain confidential information about other businesses, etc.

Purpose, Process and Payoffs in Benchmarking

The purposes of best practice performance benchmarking are:

1. Development of an understanding of the fundamentals that create business success based on objective measurement of relative performance against relevant companies in areas involving official business processes.

2. Focus on continuous improvement efforts bred on ongoing analysis of essential difference between similar processes in comparable business and the underlying causes for the variants.

3. Management of overall as well as individual changes, involvement in achieving the improvement based on development action plans to measure the gaps between the companies and best in class companies with the most relevant key result variables.

The processes of best practice performance benchmarking are:

1. *Planning*

    (a) Identify the subject for benchmarking

    (b) Identify the best competitor

    (c) Determine data collection methods and collect data

2. *Analysis*

    (a) Determine the current competitive gap

    (b) Project future performance

3. *Integration*

    (a) Communicate results for analysis

    (b) Establish functional goals

4. *Action*

    (a) Develop action plans

    (b) Implement plans and monitor results

    (c) Recalibrate benchmark

The payoffs of best practice performance benchmarking are enumerated as follows.

Success of Benchmarking

The success of benchmarking lies in the organizational structure and the relationship between benchmarking and the organisation's strategic intent. Organizations have a 'mission' or raison *d'etre* to focus on customers, other stakeholders and achieving technology driven market leadership, be it product, service or solutions. Top management also lay down certain 'values' that form the culture of the organization, which become the operating principles of the organization. These values normally do not change, even after the top management moves or leaves the scene. Strategic intent, business goals, performance management and other strategies are set on the basis of the mission and values of the organization.

Benchmarking thrives in organizations where values are focused on customers, emphasis is laid on products, customer care leadership, quest for continuous improvement and innovations and fostering of knowledge management, seeking and sharing of information and networking.

Since these values are aligned with business goals and these goals are achieved through a very transparent performance management programme, benchmarking gets full commitment and support from the top management.

It is now very well-established that performance improvement can be achieved only through competency enhancement, the four foundations of this being:

1. Technology

2. Human Resources

3. Organisational Culture

4. Organisational Structure

While continuous improvements and daily management systems will result in waste elimination, cost saving, productivity improvements etc. which will lead to marginal or medium growth, introduction of 'new best practices' alone will lead the organization in achieving 'quantum jumps' in performance enhancement leading to 'radical growth' in the organization.

The choice is yours: whether you want the incremental growth for survival, or a radical growth which would sustain competition and continue to keep you on top. Anyone's guess is obviously the second choice.

Measuring an Organization's Performance

Excellent organizations manage their slack resources better than non-performing organizations. Profitability is a dubious determinant of an organization managing slack resources. The cash flow is directly proportional to the slack available in an organization at any point of time.

TABLE 1	Slack Resources

Slack Resources	
Slack Usage Measurement	**Slack Variables**
1. Sales revenue to R & D investment 2. Increase in fixed and working capital expenditure and its ratio to sales 3. Dividend pay out ratios 4. Higher the above-mentioned ratio, lesser the organisation's retention of earning to invest in future	1. Cash flow investment ratio 2. Sales vs total assets 3. R & D vs sales revenue 4. Market to book value 5. Sales per employee 6. Debt by equity ratio 7. Working capital to sales ratio; Dividend payout ratio

Profitability measures are linked to:

1. Return on sales

2. Return on total capital

3. Return on book equity

4. Net income by total assets

Productivity is another performance measure of an organisation's ability to generate slack. Employee productivity, i.e. sales revenue per employee, and capital productivity, i.e., sales revenue per total capital assets; when increased, show an increase in the slack resources of an organization. Slack variables are very important discrimination of strategic performance. Profitability and productivity need not correlate. Profitability comes from surplus contribution from external customer and productivity is the surplus which an organization receives from employees. Ability of an organisation to raise long-term resources is yet another measure of slack available to an organization. Thus, profitability, productivity and ability to raise long-term resources lead to long time availability of slack.

Current Performance Contract – Employee to Organization

Most organizations follow the performance contract entered into at the beginning of the year, with resource allocation therein. Objectives are clearly set with milestones and measuring accomplishments in absolute numbers (goals, weightages, ROI, deliverables in terms of cost, quantity and delivery cycle time, etc.)

Preset rewards (bonus, performance pay, variable pay, non-monetary benefits, etc.) are calculated and awarded on the completion of the year or period, as defined in the beginning, depending on the degree of accomplishment. If periodical reviews and feedback are done sincerely and regularly, trust and openness of the process gets enhanced and no surprises are left for the end of the year. Whether linked or de-linked, feedback and coaching take place "on the job" towards performance and competency enhancement.

An organization cannot sacrifice accountability towards the costs of flexibility, collaboration and teamwork. Performance management and measurement should focus on both converting opportunities and accomplishment of objectives.

Only what is measured will get done, if you cannot measure what you do, it is not worth doing.

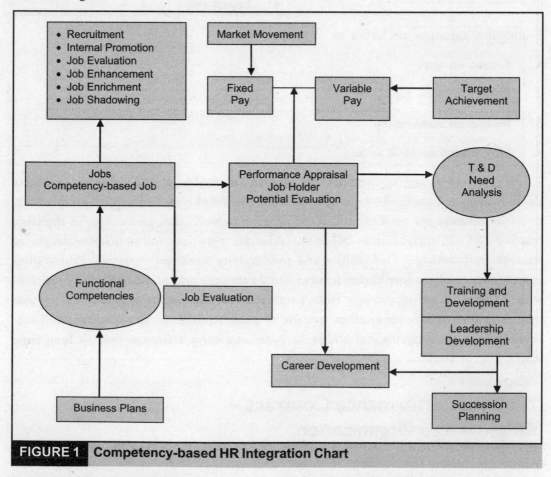

FIGURE 1 **Competency-based HR Integration Chart**

Instead of setting objectives in advance, allocation of resources, milestones to be achieved and measures of accomplishments and rewards disbursed strictly for doing what is expected, organizations are moving towards trusting their managers to claim the resources they need to seize the opportunities they come across in ever changing market conditions and dictate their strategy. This beating of the competition brings its own rewards.

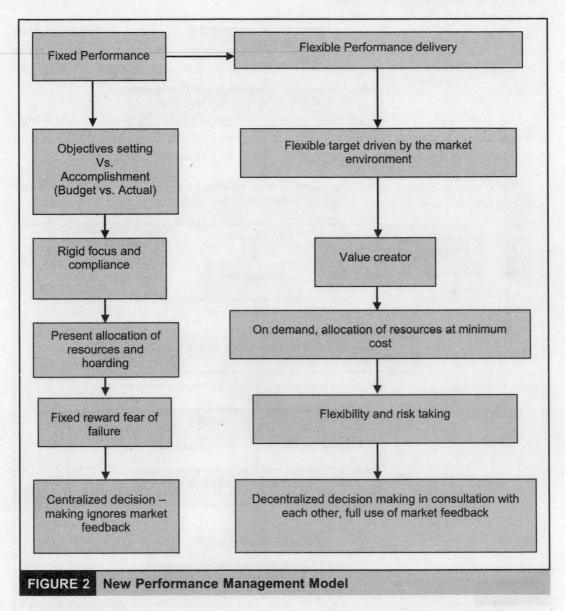

FIGURE 2   **New Performance Management Model**

The management ensures long-term adaptation of their organization to its environment through strategic management process. Strategy must be a process of innovation and discovery.

From the earlier rigid system and procedure, things have moved to flexible, continuous improving and problem-solving, innovative and collaborative team work at workplaces. Yet the strength of the old systems, that is, accountability to performance should prevail. That should be through empowerment as shown in Figure.

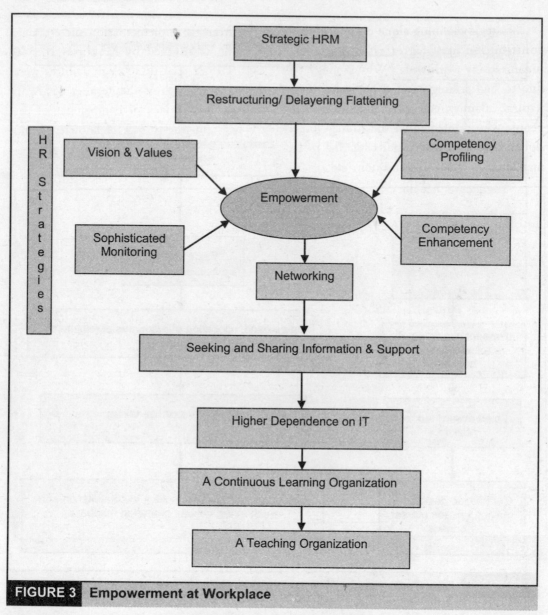

FIGURE 3 **Empowerment at Workplace**

The CEO of a very successful manufacturing and marketing organization was talking to a large number of HR professionals, "I do not ask my reportees what are the numbers they have achieved, there are people at lower levels to take care of the production and sales figures. Instead, I only ask my reportees what are the opportunities they came across and how many they converted to our business advantages. If not what is the help I could do to them to convert such opportunities for our business." Apart from ensuring the accomplishment of targets, converting opportunities to business advantages is the biggest strategic contribution that the senior management can make to the organization.

Strategic planning alone cannot work; successful strategic implementation and strategic contribution are of greatest importance. In a study conducted by Mckinsey in 340 organisations worldwide "Why strategy fails," only 17 per cent of strategic failures were due to bad strategy and 8 per cent due to other reasons such as 'September 11, War, natural calamity, etc. The remaining 75 per cent were due to lack of competency of the people who implemented the strategy precisely 40 per cent due to lack of knowledge and skills and the other 35 per cent due to lack of right attitude, i.e. willingness to change, managing feelings and emotion, etc.

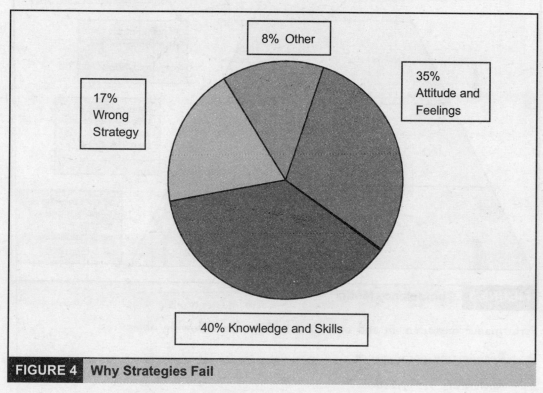

| FIGURE 4 | **Why Strategies Fail** |

"People don't resist change, they resist being changed."

– Peter Scholtes

Dr. Stephen Covey, a management guru, told a group of management experts "Any organization can hire any number of Hands' that is easy, but only those organizations who can hire 'Hearts', 'Minds' and the 'Hands', will succeed."

As health is defined by the World Health Organisation as a "state of physical, mental, emotional, spiritual and social well-being", not merely the absence of disease. Performance is only the 'tip of iceberg'. Both visible and invisible drivers, i.e. knowledge, skill, aptitude and attitude, which we call the 'competency cluster', drive performance.

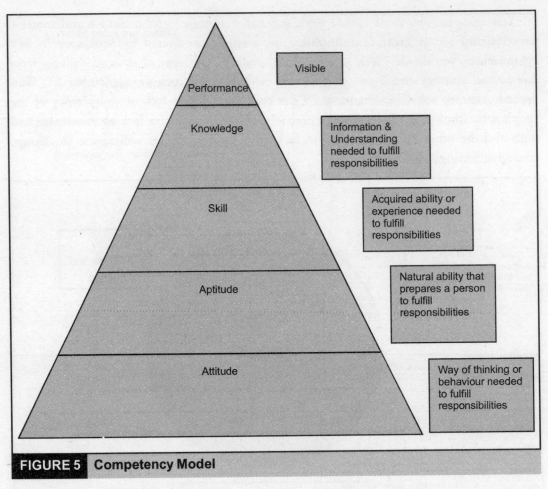

FIGURE 5 **Competency Model**

Performance measurement and management have the following objectives:

1. Recognizing performance

2. Rewarding performance

3. Identifiying and analyzing the competency gaps and initiating training and development action plans to enhance the competencies, by eliminating or bridging the competency gaps. Training and development action plans should include on-the-job training, job rotation, job enhancement, job enrichment, job shadowing, apart from classroom training, high impact training such as outbound training (OBT) programs, feedback and coaching to enhance competencies.

4. Celebrating significant accomplishments.

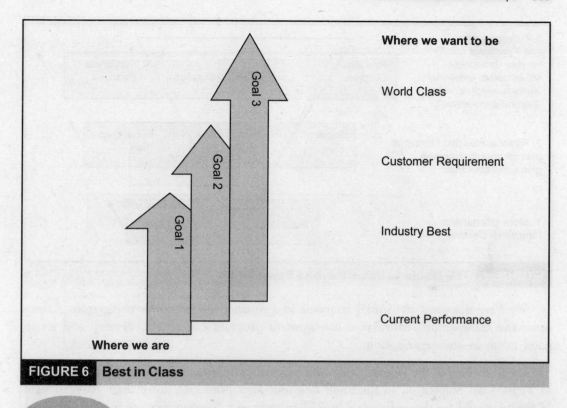

Where we want to be

World Class

Customer Requirement

Industry Best

Current Performance

Where we are

FIGURE 6 | **Best in Class**

What Lies Beyond Benchmarking?

We talked about strategy as a process of innovation and discovery. Therefore while benchmarking has taken us to the best in class, a large number of best in class organizations can not remain on the top forever. Only those organizations that move from benchmarking to "Benchmarking" will be able to remain on the top, by adapting to lateral and out-of-box thinking through innovation and creativity. According to Arthur Anderson, "The new management theory contends that benchmarking is better when oriented towards process and not product or services."

What is Process Management?

- *Basic Premise:* all problems in organizations ultimately represent failures of business processes to satisfactorily meet the requirements of customers.

- *Process Management:* Recognition that real improvement comes from factually understanding and improving their processes.

The illustration detailed below shows that we can attain 'emotional surplus' which is 'valued beyond expectation'. According to this model, rationality and functional effectiveness are directly related to emotional levels. So when both these factors rise from normal to surplus level the emotional level of the employees pertaining to commitment towards job and organization rises, creating an ownership and passion in them. (See Figure 7).

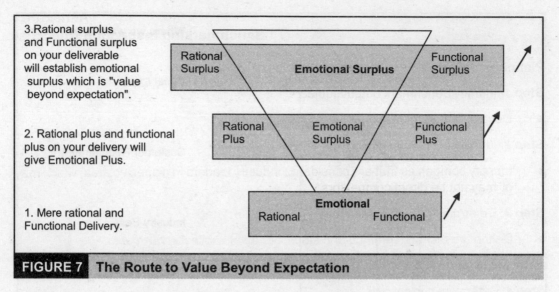

FIGURE 7 **The Route to Value Beyond Expectation**

We have discussed the initial concerns in a nutshell in the above paragraphs. A very open and transparent performance management program can attract, develop and retain good talent in any organization.

I recently read in the *Sunday Express* about a wonderful forecasting done by a philosopher in 1930. Olaf Stapledon, in his book *Last and First Man* said more than 70 years ago, "America would be the policeman in 21ˢᵗ century, the Russian Empire would disappear and Europe would become united." How could this philosopher, who was a humdrum shipping clerk, turned unionist, turned philosophy teacher, predict this strategic evaluation?

Recalling what Sun Tzu said in '*The Art of War*' a few thousand years ago, "If you know yourself and your enemy well, you can win thousands of wars." In fact, we will find a list of management strategies and techniques, including benchmarking concepts in '*The Art of War*,' which has relevance of immense relevance and application in today's business scenario.

Annexure I
Benchmarking Inspection Checklist

Planning: Steps # 1-3

Step 1: Identify Benchmark output/subject

- Develop a statement in noun/verb format.

Step 2: Identify best competitor

- Identify companies that are considered industry leaders in a specific area, which may or may not be direct competitors.

Step 3: Determine data collection methods and collect data.

- Define the research method and steps in the data collection process.

Analysis: Steps # 4 & 5

Step 4: Determine current gap

- Define benchmark performance, critical drivers of that performance, and root cause for the gaps based on the data gathered.

Step 5: Project future performance levels

- Project competitive gap based on best industry/competitive trends versus future expected internal performance.

Integration: Step # 6 & 7

Step 6: Communicate findings and gain acceptance

- Communicate results of analysis and obtain customer acceptance of analysis.

Step 7: Establish functional goals

- Revise existing functional goals to reduce competitive gaps.

Analysis: Steps # 8-10

Step 8: Develop action plans

- Prepare action plan and obtain management approval.

Step 9: Implement action plans and monitor progress

- Track results of implementation.

Step 10: Recalibrate benchmarks

- Establish criteria for recalibrating benchmarks.

Annexure II
Benchmarking—Typical Pitfalls

1. Lack of management, functional and line involvement and inspection.

2. Selecting subjects of little value; too many subjects.

3. Project scope and purpose not well-defined, insufficient resources.

4. Critical success factors, i.e., key drivers of gaps not identified or properly understood which can lead to incorrect root cause of the gap.

5. Results of analysis poorly communicated and management/customer acceptance not obtained.

6. No changes in organizational/managerial goals and objectives.

7. Expecting immediate results or analysis paralysis, excessive precision.

8. Limited benchmarking organizations and data sources.

9. Recalibration not planned or performed.

2

Six Sigma

Introduction to Bharti Airtel Limited

Bharti Airtel Limited was incorporated as Bharti Tele-Ventures Limited (BTVL) on July 7, 1995 for promoting investments in telecommunications services. As of March 31, 2006, it was India's leading private sector provider of telecommunications services with a customer base of 20.926 million customers, including 19.579 million mobile customers and 1.347 million basic telephone customers. Bharti Airtel was the first private operator to provide mobile services in all the 23 circles in India. Bharti Airtel also provides telephone services and Internet access over DSL in 15 circles. It complements its mobile, broadband and telephone services with national and international long distance services. The company also has a submarine cable landing station at Chennai, which connects the submarine cable connecting Chennai and Singapore. Bharti Airtel provides reliable end-to-end data and enterprise services to corporate customers by leveraging its nationwide fiber optic backbone, last mile connectivity in fixed-line and mobile circles, VSATs, ISP and international bandwidth access through the gateways and landing station.

The company was founded by Sunil Bharti Mittal (Chairman and Managing Director), a first generation entrepreneur, who began his career in 1976, with a small capital investment. He began with a number of trading companies. He started manufacturing and marketing the country's first push-button telephones, becoming one of the world's largest telephone producers.

Bharti began its telecom services journey in the year 1995-96 when it launched India's first mobile services under the brand Airtel in Delhi and Himachal Pradesh. By 1997-98, Bharti became the first private telecom operator to obtain a license to provide basic telephone services in the state of Madhya Pradesh. Subsequently, Bharti began providing VSAT and

Internet based solutions to their clients through the Bharti BT VSAT Ltd. and Bharti BT Internet Ltd. By the year 2000, Bharti emerged as the largest private sector telecom operator in India with the acquisition of JT mobiles (cellular services operator in Punjab, Karnataka, and Andhra Pradesh); and Skycell (mobile services operator in Chennai). In 2000, Singapore Telecommunications Ltd. (SingTel) acquired the Telecom Italia's equity stake in the company, providing Bharti the much needed technical and financial leverage.

By year 2002, Bharti had become the country's largest cellular operator through a series of acquisitions and licenses. Bharti also launched the country's first private sector national and international long distance service, aided by its submarine cable landing station — a JV with SingTel. By the end of 2006, Bharti had achieved an all-India footprint with operations in all of India's 23 telecom circles (the Indian telecom industry was structured on the basis of 23 geographic circles that were gradually liberalized by the government with the corporatization of the erstwhile monopoly of Department of Telecommunications into the Bharat Sanchar Nigam Limited —BSNL, and granting licenses for up to four mobile services operators in each circle).

The businesses at Bharti Airtel have been structured into three individual strategic business units (SBU's) — mobile services, broadband and telephone services (B&T) and enterprise services. The mobile services group provides GSM mobile services across India in 23 telecom circles, while the B&T business group provides broadband and telephone services in 94 cities. The Enterprise services group has two subunits — carriers (long distance services) and services to corporations. All these services are provided under the Airtel brand. The financial statements of the company (2005-06) are presented in Appendix 1.

Bharti Airtel Limited has created history by being ranked among the top 10 best performing companies in the world in the globally renowned *BusinessWeek* IT 100 list. Bharti Airtel, which is described by *BusinessWeek* in the report as a "highly innovative company", improves its ranking to 10 from last year's ranking of 19. Bharti Airtel is the only Indian company in the top 10 list. Bharti Airtel has ranked ahead of companies like Motorola (Rank 11), Google (Rank 13), Microsoft (Rank 37), Hewlett Packard (Rank 44) and Oracle (Rank 51).

Organization Structure

The corporate structure of Bharti Airtel Limited is depicted in Figure 1 below.

Bharti Infotel was headed by the President, and six heads of businesses (Chief Executive Officers) —four of them managing the fixed line services, one CEO long distance, and one CEO managing the enterprise business. The President's office consisted of seven major group level functions —Technical, Finance, KM and Quality, Marketing, Human Resources, Customer Relationship Marketing, and Information Technology. Each of the six business units had similar functional heads who reported to their CEOs and the group functional heads, forming a matrix organization.

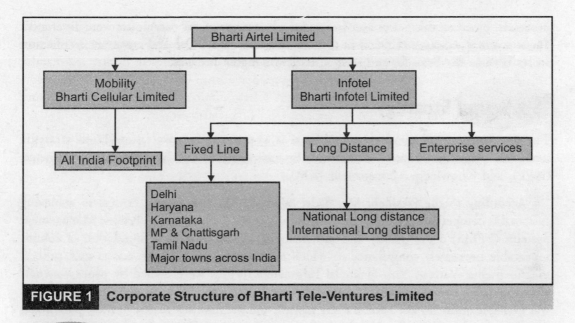

FIGURE 1 **Corporate Structure of Bharti Tele-Ventures Limited**

The Six Sigma Initiative

The speed of change in the telecommunications industry in terms of technology, regulation, and competitive actions, forced all players to focus on initiatives that will give them quick results. In an industry, where they were competing with erstwhile monopolies like BSNL and MTNL, competition cannot be sustained with only price cuts or technology. All these competitive actions were imitable, almost immediately. Therefore, the only source of competitive advantage for a telecom player was "quality of service". The service had to be "error-free" as well as "first time right". So Bharti felt a need for an initiative that will give them breakthrough results in a short period of time, rather than incremental improvements.

Bharti Infotel began implementation of Six Sigma in September 2002. There was a need in the organization to create a culture of data and measurement, rather than gut feeling and only experience. They realized that Six Sigma offered them a more analytical measure in terms of rigorous statistical tools, constant monitoring and tracking of various parameters, and explicit measurements of non-financial parameters.

✠ The "Outside-in" Approach ✠

The primary objective of implementing a quality initiative at Bharti Infotel was to improve customer satisfaction.

Other financial and non-financial benefits were by-products. Therefore, they used an "outside-in" approach. Customer data (called the Voice of the Customer or VoC) would be collected from various sources, including customer satisfaction studies, data from their call centers, their installation teams, fault repair teams, and other customer interaction points. All this VoC would be translated into internal measurable parameters under various business processes. Based on this, ratios and indices for measuring various parameters were developed. These internal measures (Critical to Quality measures or CTQs) and customer satisfaction scores became the basis for initiating specific Six Sigma projects.

Six Sigma Strategy

The Six Sigma implementation in Bharti is supported by two interrelated strategic initiatives—Business Process Management Systems (BPMS) and Non-Financial Parameters (NFP), and Knowledge Management (KM).

According to the President Mr. Badri Agarwal, "the two factors critical to achieving sustainable competitive advantage, are quality and speed." The Business Process Management Systems (BPMS) drove quality and sustenance of results through a foundation of robust, repeatable processes, compliance to which are ensured by periodic audits and process measurements. Various Non-Financial Parameters (NFPs) were owned by process-owners at various levels at the business units and the President's office. The data on these parameters was available online by the 10th of every month, and the monthly review of these parameters was done by the CEOs for their business units, functional HODs for their processes and by the President at the group level. Actions taken, and further action plans were discussed at these reviews. These meetings focused on the analysis of the exceptions—positive and negative, rather than just numbers.

The other critical factor, "speed" was achieved through their Knowledge Management (KM). Based on the philosophy that "replication of best practices takes much lesser time than the initial implementation," frequent knowledge sharing sessions were conducted, where best practice implementers shared their success stories. All the Six Sigma projects were shared as best practices (about 160 internal best practices had been shared by end July 2004) in the internal system (through emails and the intranet).

Six Sigma Project Selection

The business imperatives (called Big Y's) drove the selection of Six Sigma projects at Bharti Infotel. The big Y's were drilled down into little Y's, processes, critical to quality (CTQ) measures, and projects (as shown in an example in Figure 2 below).

The choice of projects happened through a selection from the various project proposals generated. The proposals could be generated through either of the three sources—the Customer Satisfaction (C-Sat) surveys (conducted by an external agency every six months) identify the "red areas"; the monitoring of the NFPs to identify "low performing areas"; or the set of "priority areas" identified by the top management. The CEOs and their executive committee teams then prioritized these projects, and the champion and the project leader were identified for each project. These champions and project leaders then chose their team members. The champions were identified in such a way that they were the customers of these projects, rather than the CEOs. The champions therefore, reviewed the projects' progress periodically.

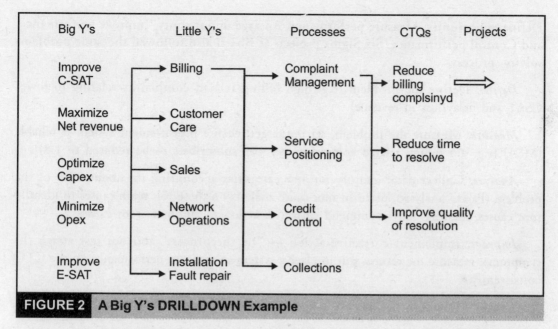

FIGURE 2   A Big Y's DRILLDOWN Example

As soon as the project team was formed, a project charter was prepared and signed (see Appendix 2 for sample project charters). These project charters defined–

- The business case

- The problem statement

- The goal statement

- The various milestones in the project

- The alignment with Big Y's

- The scope of the project

- The defect definition

- Critical to Quality (CTQ) parameters

- The various roles (sponsor, champion, master black belt, black belt, green belt, and team members)

- The projected annualized financial savings.

The project charters, thus, served as the benchmark for periodic assessment and evaluation of the projects, with the various project milestones and the annualized financial savings due to the project.

⌘ The DMAIC Methodology

The Six Sigma projects followed the "DMAIC" methodology. DMAIC is a Six Sigma problem-solving framework for improving business processes. It is an acronym for

Define opportunity, Measure performance, Analyze opportunity, Improve performance, and Control performance. Six Sigma projects at Bharti also followed the same problem-solving process.

Define: Define the problem (e.g. high billing related complaints relating to lower CSAT and delay/loss in revenue).

Measure: Measure the problem, set the target, ensure measurement system is reliable (MSA) (e.g. 4.4 billing related complaints per 100 subscribers to be reduced to 1.8).

Analyze: Collect data, identify top few categories accounting for about 80% of the problem (Pareto analysis), perform root cause analysis on these top main causes to identify root causes, identify and recommend corrective action to eliminate root causes.

Improve: Implement corrective action — "fix the process" and not just attack the symptoms, measure the results, put in place a system to measure performance on the CTQ consistently.

Control: Monitor for 2-3 months to ensure sustenance of results before closing the project.

✤ Implementing Six Sigma ✤

Six Sigma implementation began with an appreciation that the entire initiative is to achieve customer satisfaction (that was widely recognized as the only source of sustainable competitive advantage in the telecom industry) as the strategic objective.

There were both black-belt as well as green-belt projects that were undertaken at Bharti Infotel. Black belt projects involved team members who were relieved from their operational roles for at least 18 months to work on Six Sigma projects full-time. These team members reported to the master black belt or the Quality leader. Black belts were selected from employees who are already high performers in their respective functions. These black belt team members had to undergo 15 days of training before they started on a Six Sigma project.

Green belt projects, on the other hand, involved people working part-time on these projects, along with their regular operational roles. These people did their projects in their own functional areas. The green belt team members had to undergo training for 5 days, before they began a project.

The various roles in a typical Six Sigma project included the *sponsor* (typically the CEO of that business), the *champion* (the head of that particular function, for example, the CTO), the *master black belt* (the quality head in that business unit), the *project leader (Black belt or a Green belt)*, and the *project team members.*

Pilot Implementation at Two Business Units

The Long Distance business and MP & Chhattisgarh Fixed Line circle were chosen as pilots for implementation of Six Sigma in September 2002.

N. Arjun, CEO (long distance business) maintains that "the intent of our quality initiative was to bring about an attitudinal change in our people." Initially, there was some resistance among some people. Some looked on Six Sigma as just another buzzword and a fad that would go away soon. Some even said that "implementing Six Sigma was the job of the quality department and not mine." The primary challenge Arjun and his team faced was the communication of the benefits to his 500-odd people, widely spread across the country. The Six Sigma implementation required robust processes and reliable measurement systems. The silver lining was that they began documenting their processes since their inception in January 2002.

A lot of evangelization had to be done —posters were made and distributed; written and verbal messages were sent out; and a momentum had to build up. Initially, they had to coax and cajole people to take up the initial projects. About 30–35 projects were taken up in the first wave at long distance. The initial challenge was to communicate to the people that the Six Sigma projects will pay off in the short as well as the long-term.

In terms of preparation, the Long Distance business began with a "Problem Solving Methodology" (PSM) training programme for all its employees. Further a PONC (Price of Non Conformance) training was conducted. These training programmes focused on the importance of data collection and analysis in quality management. These training programs emphasized the need for rigorous data analysis and decision making based on data, rather than "gut feeling" or "experience."

Rohtash Mal (CEO, MP & Chhattisgarh Circle) believed that the primary benefits of the Six Sigma implementation had been two fold —a change in the mindset of people in recognizing and relating the rigor of analysis and thought to the business benefits; and the cultivation of the ability to step out of the box and think laterally. According to him, Six Sigma represented an evolved method of quality, and therefore involved the maximum number of people in the organization. With Six Sigma implementation, there was a lot of team work, and cross-functional respect for each others' processes had developed within the organization. Every organizational problem was shared, a common understanding was created in terms of the intent, thought process, and the core and tangential impacts of the alternatives were generated, before a solution was evolved and implemented. Everyone began seeing the full picture, rather than the specific parts.

✿ Business Benefits ✿

The major benefits for the company at the end of the first wave of projects were in the customer satisfaction scores. About 84% of the customer satisfaction scores impacted by the Six Sigma projects had shown average improvements of 80%. The direct annualized financial benefit to Bharti Infotel was about Rs.10 crores due to the implementation of first wave of Six Sigma projects within the first year.

EXHIBIT 1	Major Milestones in Six Sigma Implementation
September 21, 2002	Six Sigma implementation begins with the Leadership workshop (President, CEOs, VPs at the President's Office)
October 2002	Champions training (Long-distance and MP and Chattisgarh Fixed line circle)
Nov 02-Jan 03	Black belts training (15 days in 3 waves of 5 days each over 3 months)
March 03	Wave 1 projects closed (22 projects)
April-May 03	Green belts training at long distance and MP (5 days)
July 03	Wave 2 projects launched at the remaining units of Infotel
Aug-Sep 03	II batch of black belts training begins (6 days * 2 waves)
October 03	II batch of green belts training
May 04	Wave 2 projects end
May-June 04	Wave 1 projects audited and financial savings certified
July 04	Wave 3 projects begin

⌘ Major Shifts in Management—Impact of Six Sigma Implementation ⌘

There were three major impacts of Six Sigma implementation at Bharti.

Not only did people begin appreciating that improvements had happened, but the reasons why they happened as well. This appreciation led to an analysis of the causes of these improvements, and action towards ensuring that this improvement is sustained.

The rigour of analysis had improved significantly. People began going to the root causes of the problems, rather than just closing the issue. In terms of tools, the Six Sigma shifted people from analyzing averages to "variations," a superior indicator of defects. People began talking based on data, rather than just gut feelings or experience.

A culture of working in teams had begun as a consequence of working in these Six Sigma projects. The emphasis on customer satisfaction, process definitions, and ensuring process compliance highlighted the interdependence across various functions in the organization and the customer was owned by everyone (not just the front-end employee or sales and marketing functions). These factors, along with the fact that a larger number of associates (people working on contract) began working in Six Sigma projects led to the reinforcement of the culture of working in teams.

The shift was not just restricted to the people involved in the Six Sigma projects. As the projects matured, and the organization began replicating success stories across various business, there were far-reaching changes in the way management perceived quality as a function, the way people approached processes and problem-solving, and the way projects were selected (see Figure 3).

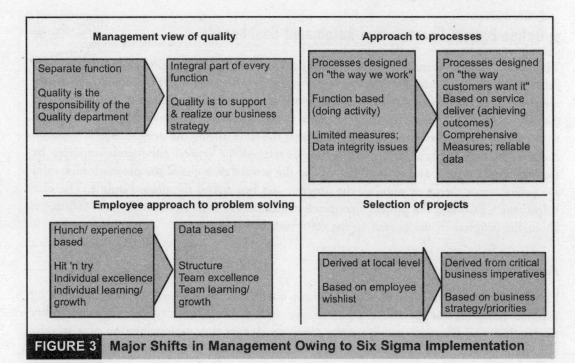

Management view of quality	Approach to processes

Separate function

Quality is the responsibility of the Quality department

→ Integral part of every function

Quality is to support & realize our business strategy

Processes designed on "the way we work"

Function based (doing activity)

Limited measures; Data integrity issues

→ Processes designed on "the way customers want it" Based on service deliver (achieving outcomes) Comprehensive Measures; reliable data

Employee approach to problem solving	Selection of projects

Hunch/ experience based

Hit 'n try Individual excellence individual learning/ growth

→ Data based

Structure Team excellence Team learning/ growth

Derived at local level

Based on employee wishlist

→ Derived from critical business imperatives

Based on business strategy/priorities

FIGURE 3 **Major Shifts in Management Owing to Six Sigma Implementation**

Institutionalizing Six Sigma

In order to ensure that Six Sigma was institutionalized in the working of Bharti Infotel, various measures were taken.

⌘ Six Sigma Guide — The Internal Strategy Document ⌘

An internal strategy document called the "Six Sigma Guide" that contained the policy guidelines for Six Sigma implementation was prepared. The document defined –

- The various Six Sigma roles

- The certification rules and processes (as Champions, Master black belts, Black belts, and Green belts)

- The weights of these roles in the individuals' performance measurements (for instance, black belts had 80% weight and green belts had 25% weight for Six Sigma projects in their performance management systems)

- The project selection guidelines, the project closure guidelines, etc.

- How to calculate the project financial savings

- How to derive project guidelines from C-SAT scores.

⌘ Online Project Charters and Automated Dashboards ⌘

The project charters were put up in the company intranet for easy access and monitoring by those concerned periodically. Monitoring of projects was done at various levels —toll gate reviews that were done by the project champions at the end of every stage of the project and the monthly CEO reviews. Standard templates and formats had been prepared and distributed to the CEOs for undertaking the reviews, so that the time during the presentation is spent on the relevant issues only. Automated dashboards tracked the critical parameters impacted by that Six Sigma project and allowed the CEOs, the project champions the project leaders, and the project team members monitor the progress and benefits of the project online. This also helped the CEOs and the project champions communicate their observations and comments about the progress of the project to the team members.

Audited Benefits

The financial benefits that the company got out of Six Sigma projects were audited by external auditors, and specific audit certificates issued. This provided very high credibility to the claims of financial savings to the company due to the implementation of a specific Six Sigma project in a particular business within the specified time frame.

Rewards and Recognition

In order to motivate people involved in the implementation of the Six Sigma projects, various awards were instituted. The Chairman's quality award at the group level, the President's quality award, and the CEO's quality award were instituted to reward best projects. Amongst all the projects completed under a CEO, the best projects were nominated for the President's award, and the best three projects from the President's award were nominated for the Chairman's award. The parameters for these awards were clearly defined, and the project teams were expected to make a presentation to the panel of judges (including external experts) in the presence of the Executive Committee (EC) members.

There were also awards for the best champions. Every CEO and every Vice President at the President's Office nominated one person each from their business/functional stream for these awards.

The Six Sigma initiative at Bharti Infotel has also been recognized outside as well. Their Six Sigma implementation had been recognized as a best practice amongst the SingTel group of companies; several leading corporates and industry associations had recognized Bharti as a benchmark for speed of implementation as well as results; and Dr. Mikel Harry, the original architect of Six Sigma at Motorola, had appreciated the process and benefits of the Six Sigma implementation. The popular and business media had also recognized their implementation and documented the initiative as a success story.

All these internal awards and external recognitions had motivated all the Six Sigma teams, by reinforcing the success story and sustaining the commitment and satisfaction of the top management.

Culture Change

The major impact of Six Sigma project on the employees was the beginning of working in teams. Various cross-functional teams began working amongst and with each other. People began appreciating the processes, and therefore could see the big picture, due to working in cross-functional teams. Significant inter-functional respect began developing. The customer came to be owned by everyone, and there was a clear focus on improvement on the critical to quality (CTQ) parameters that impact customer satisfaction. Similarly, problems were collectively owned, and a common intent was created and shared.

The Way Forward

The Six Sigma initiative at Bharti Airtel is a significant component of the company's innovation strategy including a set of strategic initiatives —Business Process Management System (BPMS) and Non-financial Parameters (NFPs), Six Sigma, and Knowledge Management. These three initiatives were designed to ensure that everyone in the organization appreciates the processes, and look at the "big picture" as they compete with entrenched erstwhile state-owned monopolies. The Six Sigma journey at Bharti Airtel is far from complete. The learning from the Six Sigma projects is disseminated across the organization through a Knowledge Management (KM) initiative to ensure replication of best practices and sustainability of the gains.

Financial Statements of Bharti Airtel Limited (2005–06)[a]

EXHIBIT	Bharti Airtel Limited Balance Sheet as at March 31, 2006		
Particular	**Schedule No.**	**As at March 31, 2006 (Rs. '000)**	**As at March 31, 2006 (Rs. '000)**
SOURCES OF FUNDS			
Shareholders' Funds			
Share Capital	1	18,938,793	18,560,889
Employee Stock Option Outstanding	505,961		–
Less: Deferred Stock Compensation	384,701	121,260	–
(Refer Note 32 on Schedule 23)			
Reserves and Surplus	2	54,395,531	34,639,403
Loan Funds			
Secured Loans	3	28,633,707	39,598,760
Unsecured Loans	4	19,329,201	10,344,149
Deferred Tax Liability		1,890,459	1,009,011
(Refer Note 12 on Schedule 22 and 31 on Schedule 23)			
Total		123,308,951	104,152,212
APPLICATION OF FUNDS			
Fixed Assets	5		
Gross Block		179,517,371	132,406,305
Less: Depreciation		49,448,600	34,756,448
Net Block		130,068,771	97,649,857
Capital Work in Progress		23,412,498	9,944,602
		153,481,269	107,594,459
Preoperative Expenditure pending allocation	6	–	–
		153,481,269	107,594,459
Investments	7	7,196,981	9,318,953
Current Assets, Loans and Advances			
Inventories	8	177,444	315,838
Sundry Debtors	9	10,761,709	7,157,443
Cash and Bank Balances	10	3,074,285	3,841,352
Other Current Assets, Loans and Advances	11	15,529,497	10,676,095
		29,542,935	21,990,728

Contd...

Less: Current Liabilities and Provisions	12		
Current Liabilities		64,655,783	42,079,834
Provisions		2,335,851	1,119,910
		66,991,634	43,199,744
Net Current Assets		37,448,699	21,209,016
Miscellaneous Expenditure			
(to the extent not written off or adjusted)	13	79,400	583,483
Profit and Loss Account		–	7,864,333
Total		123,308,951	104,152,212
Statement of Significant Accounting Policies	22		
Notes to Accounts	23		

[a]Sourced from the company annual report (2005–06) available at the company website on the Internet http://www.bhartiairtel.in/fileadmin/srijan/Results_Record/Annual-Report-2005-2006.pdf (last accessed on January 8, 2007).

EXHIBIT | **Project Charter**

Scope　　D　M　A　I　C　Step
　　　　　　　　　　　　　　　　　B

Business Case

In Scope
1)
2) Out os Scope
1)

- For a period of September - October months, Following is the outcome:-

Definition of a Defect

Goal Statement
-
-

CTQs
✧

Roles

Milestones

	SEP	OCT	NOV	DEC	JAN
Define					
Measure					
Analyze					
Improve					
Control					

Sponsor		
Champion		
CFO		
Master Black belt		
Black Belt		
Green Belt		
Team Members		

Big Y Alignment

Stakeholder	Big Y	Alignment	Annualized Financial Savings	Sigma Level	
				Z-ST	Z-LT
Business					
Customer					
Customer					

Competency Mapping/Matching

3

Introduction

Performance Management is a strategic and integrated approach for delivering sustained success to organizations by improving the performance of those who work in them and by developing the capabilities of teams and individual contributors. Development is perhaps the most important function of performance management. Performance management is concerned with outputs—the achievement of results; and with outcomes—the impact made on performance. But it is also concerned with the processes required to achieve these results and the inputs in term of capabilities (knowledge, skill and competence) expected from the teams and the individuals involved).

According to one survey, 31 percent of the organizations surveyed included some form of competency assistance in the performance management process. On the basis of the 1991 survey, Fletcher and Williams suggested that, "The interest in competencies perhaps signifies a much more explicit concern with means and not just ends", but they also remarked that if competencies are not defined on the basis of empirical research to determine which of them are associated with effective performance, then there is a danger that the competencies in themselves will lack validity and the assessments made by managers may lack reliability and validity.

Performance management is regarded as a number of inter-linked processes rather than a single system. It was, therefore, common to find performance management carefully aligned with communications strategies, competency development, job design and evaluation, payment systems and motivation practices.

What is actually a competency? Is it just functional knowledge or something more than that? Is the competency required for a technical consultant different from that of a senior manager in business? Knowledge alone does not predict job performance or success in business. Various other components are required. Generally speaking, competency is any measurable characteristic that differentiates performance in a given job or role in an organization in a given environment. It is the sun total of physical competencies, job knowledge, conceptual and strategic skills, skill in applications and emotional strength or intelligence, which is basically the capacity to act, motivate ourselves, which is basically the capacity to act, motivates ourselves, manage our emotions in ourselves and in our relationships, using this to direct and work with others, and risk-taking to achieve goals. Hence competency mapping has become an important factor in performance development and management.

⌘ Approach ⌘

In this paper, the following step-by-step approach has been taken to cover the subject of competency mapping as a performance management tool:

Performance Defined

The *Oxford English Dictionary* defines 'performance' as behaviour—the way in which organizations, teams and individuals get work done. Campbell (1990) believes that "Performance is behavior and should be distinguished from the outcomes because they can be contaminated by systems factors".

A more comprehensive view of performance is achieved if it is defined as embracing both behavior and outcomes. This is well put by Brumbrach (1988): "Performance means both behaviors and results. Behaviors emanate from the performer and transform performance from abstraction to action. Not just the instruments for results, behaviors are also outcomes in their own right—the product or mental and physical effort applied to tasks—and can be judged apart from results."

Performance could, therefore, be regarded as behaviour—the way in which organizations, teams and individuals get work done. Campbell believes that 'Performance is behavior and should be distinguished from the outcomes because they can be contaminated by systems factors.'

What is Competency?

Competencies are defined as "Skills and abilities, described in behavioral terms that are coachable, observable, measurable and critical to successful individual or organization's performance". While goals are the "What" of performance, competencies are the "How" of performance.

Companies are the knowledge, skills and personal attributes required for excellent performance in a job, role or specific business. Competency development is a carefully crafted process of research and data-gathering about firm's managers and employees as they perform their daily work, with the goal of determining the specific knowledge, skills and personal attributes required for excellent performance in these actual jobs, roles or businesses.

The competencies and the need to develop them translates into a personal development plan and the whole links into what is being tried to be achieved within the organization. Severn Trent Water has developed an interesting definition of competency as 'grouping of knowledge, skills and behaviours which may well be required in whole or in part within a variety of managerial situations'. Competency analysis is concerned with the behavioral dimensions of the roles.

Indicator of behaviours for achieving higher levels of performance can be categorized as given below:

- Personal drive

- Impact on results

- Analytical power

- Strategic thinking

- Creative thinking

- Decisiveness

- Commercial judgments

- Team management and leadership

- Interpersonal skills

- Ability to communicate

- Ability to adapt and cope with change and pressures

- Ability to plan and control projects

Performance Management

According to Lockett (1992), "The essence of performance management is the development of individuals with competence and commitment, working towards the achievement of shared meaningful objectives within an organization which supports and encourages their achievement."

Performance management is concerned with creating a culture in which organizational and individual learning and development are a continuous process. It provides means for the integration of learning and work so that everyone learns from the successes and challenges inherent in their day-to-day activities. The drive to enhance performance is making ever-greater demands on the knowledge and skills of the workforce and on people, who carry a much greater responsibility for their own performance.

Performance management for teams deserves more attention. War makes an effective team, the competencies required for teamwork and a definition of what can be regarded as a team for performance management purpose? Peer pressure in teamwork is an important factor. Performance management processes are important in tightly knit and long-standing project teams.

Some of the key competencies for team work according to Hay/McBer (Gross 1995) are:

- Interpersonal Understanding
- Influence
- Customer Service Orientation
- Adaptability
- Team Work
- Oral Communication
- Achievement Orientation
- Organizational Commitment

Performance measurement for teams will be related to the purpose of the team and its particular objectives and standards of performance.

Concept and Definition of a "Competency"

A competency is an underlying characteristic of an individual that is causally related to criterion-referenced effective and/or superior performance in a job or situation.

Underlying characteristic means the competency is a fairly deep and enduring part of a person's personality and can predict behaviour in a wide variety of situations and job tasks.

Casually related means that a competency causes or predicts behaviour and performance.

Criterion-referenced means that the competency actually predicts who does something well or poorly, as measured on a specific criterion or standard. Examples of criteria are the dollar volume of sales for salespeople or the number of clients who stay "dry" for alcohol-abuse counsellors.

The following sections in this chapter discuss each part of this definition: underlying characteristic, causally related, criterion-referenced.

Underlying Characteristics

Competencies are underlying characteristics of people and indicate "ways of behaving or thinking, generalizing across situations, and enduring for a reasonably long period of time."

Five Types of Competency Characteristics

1. *Motives:* The things a person consistently thinks about or wants that cause action. Motives "drive, direct, and select" behavior toward certain actions or goals and away from others.

Example: Achievement-motivated people consistently set challenging goals for themselves, take personal responsibility for accomplishing them, and use feedback to do better.

2. *Traits:* Physical characteristics and consistent responses to situations or information.

   Example: Reaction time and good eyesight are physical trait competencies of combat pilots.

   Emotional self-control and initiative are more complex "consistent responses to situations." Some people don't "blow up" at others and do act "above and beyond the call of duty" to solve problems under stress. These trait competencies are characteristic of successful managers.

   Motives and competencies are intrinsic operant or self-starting "master traits" that predict what people will do on their jobs long-term, without close supervision.

3. *Self-concept:* A person's attitudes, values, or self-image.

   Example: Self-confidence, a person's belief that he or she can be effective in almost any situation is part of that person's concept of self.

   A person's values are respondent or reactive motives that predict what he or she will do in the short-term and in situations where others are in charge. For example, someone who values being a leader is more likely to exhibit leadership behavior if he or she is told a task or job will be "a test of leadership ability." People who value being "in management" but do not intrinsically like or spontaneously think about influencing others at the motive level often attain management positions but then fail.

4. *Knowledge:* Information a person has in specific content areas.

   Example: A surgeon's knowledge of nerves and muscles in the human body.

   Knowledge is a complex competency. Scores on knowledge tests often fail to predict work performance because they fail to measure knowledge and skills in the ways they are actually used on the job. First, many knowledge tests measure rote memory, when what is really important is the ability to find information. Memory of specific facts is less important than knowing which facts exist that are relevant to a specific problem, and where to find them when needed. Second, knowledge tests are "respondent." They measure test takers' ability to choose which of several options is the right response, but not whether a person can act on the basis of knowledge. For example, the ability to choose which of five items is an effective argument is very different from the ability to stand up in a conflict situation and argue persuasively. Finally, knowledge best predicts what someone can do, not what he or she will do.

5. *Skill:* The ability to perform a certain physical or mental task.

   Example: A dentist's physical skill to fill a tooth without damaging the nerve; a computer programmer's ability to organize 50,000 lines of code in logical sequential order.

   Mental or cognitive skill competencies include analytic thinking (processing knowledge and data, determining cause and effect, organizing data and plans) and conceptual thinking (recognizing patterns in complex data).

The type or level of a competency has practical implications for human resource planning. As illustrated in figure, knowledge and skill competencies tend to be visible, and relatively surface, characteristics of people. Self-concept, trait and motive competencies are more hidden, "deeper," and central to personality.

Surface knowledge and skill competencies are relatively easy to develop; training is the most cost-effective way to secure these employee abilities.

Core motive and trait competencies at the base of the personality iceberg are more difficult to assess and develop; it is most cost-effective to select for these characteristics.

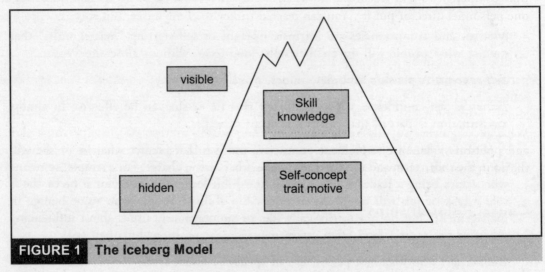

FIGURE 1 The Iceberg Model

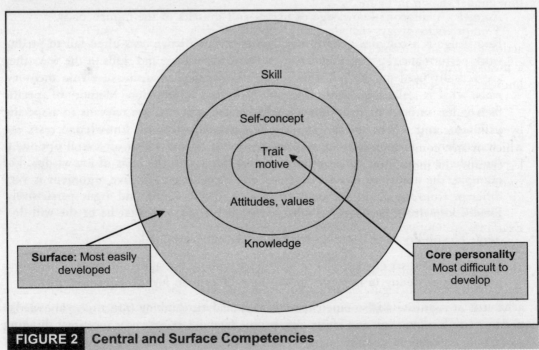

FIGURE 2 Central and Surface Competencies

Self-contempt competencies lie somewhere in between. Attitudes and values such as self-confidence (seeing one's self as a "manager" instead of a "technical/professional") can be changed by training, psychotherapy, and/or positive development experiences, albeit with more time and difficulty.

Many organizations select on the basis of surface knowledge and skill competencies ("we hire MBAs from good schools") and either assume that recruits have the underlying motive and trait competencies or that these can be instilled by good management. The converse is probably more cost-effective: organizations should select for core motive and trait competencies and teach the knowledge and skills required to do specific jobs. Or as one personnel director put it, "You can teach a turkey to climb a tree, but it is easier to hire a squirrel."

In complex jobs, competencies are relatively more important in predicting superior performance than are task-related skills, intelligence, or credentials. This is due to a "restricted range effective." In higher level technical, marketing professional and managerial jobs, almost everyone has an I.Q. of !20 or above and an advanced degree from a good university. What distinguishes superior performers in these jobs is motivation, interpersonal skills, and political skills, all of which are competencies. It follows that competency studies are the most cost-effective way to staff these positions.

Causal Relationships

Motive, trait, and self-concept competencies predict skill behaviour actions, which in turn predict job performance outcomes, as in the motive/trait – behaviour – outcome causal flow model shown in figure.

Competencies always include an intent, which is the motive or trait force that causes action toward an outcome. For example, knowledge and skill competencies invariably include a motive, trait, or self-concept competency, which provides the drive or "push" for the knowledge or skill to be used.

Behaviour without intent doesn't define a competency. An example is "management by walking around." Without knowing why a manager is walking around, you can't know which, if any, competency is being demonstrated. The manager's intent could be boredom, leg cramps, the monitoring of work to see if quality is high, or a desire "to be visible to the troops."

Action behaviours can include thought, where thinking precedes and predicts behavior. Examples are motives (e.g., thinking about doing something better), planning, or problem-solving thoughts.

Causal fowl models can be used to do "risk assessment" analyses. For example, following the causal arrows in Figure 3, an organization that does not select for, develop, or arouse achievement motivation in its employees can expect less improvement in financial outcomes, productivity, and quality, and fewer new products and services.

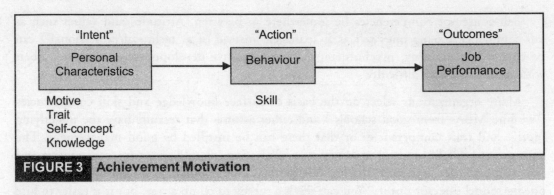

FIGURE 3 Achievement Motivation

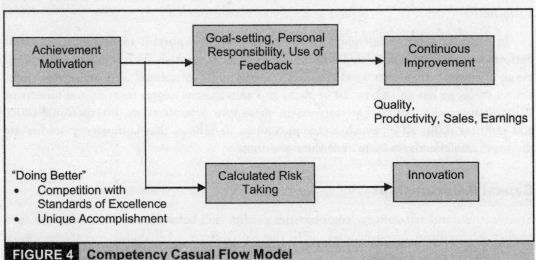

FIGURE 4 Competency Casual Flow Model

Criterion Reference is critical to our definition of competence. A characteristic is not a competency unless it predicts something meaningful in the real world. Psychologist William James said the first rule for scientists should be that "A difference which makes no difference is no difference." A characteristic or credential that makes no difference in performance is not a competency and should not be used to evaluate people.

- *Superior Performance:* This is defined statistically as one standard deviation above average performance, roughly the level achieved by the top 1 person out of 10 in a given working situation.

- *Effective Performance:* This usually really means a "minimally acceptable" level of work, the lower cutoff point below which an employee would not be considered competent to do the job.

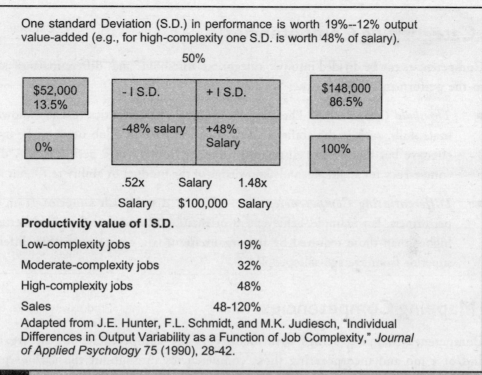

One standard Deviation (S.D.) in performance is worth 19%--12% output value-added (e.g., for high-complexity one S.D. is worth 48% of salary).

50%

| $52,000 13.5% | - I S.D. | + I S.D. | | $148,000 86.5% |
| 0% | -48% salary | +48% Salary | | 100% |

.52x   Salary   1.48x
Salary $100,000   Salary

Productivity value of I S.D.

Low-complexity jobs	19%
Moderate-complexity jobs	32%
High-complexity jobs	48%
Sales	48-120%

Adapted from J.E. Hunter, F.L. Schmidt, and M.K. Judiesch, "Individual Differences in Output Variability as a Function of Job Complexity," *Journal of Applied Psychology* 75 (1990), 28-42.

FIGURE 5 **What Superior Performance is Worth**

"One standard deviation" is used to define superior performance for two reasons. First, many research studies have documented the economic value of this level of performance to organizations. Depending on the complexity of the job, the value of one standard deviation above the mean is 19 to 48 percent of output for non-sales jobs, and 48 to 120 percent for sales. A minimum estimate of economic value of superior performance can be calculated by taking these percentages multiplied by the average salary per year for the job. In fact, this global estimate approach seriously undervalues jobs that Southeast firms found that superior salespeople (earning an average of $41,777), sold on average $6.7 million and average performers sold on average $3 million. The superior group sold 123 percent more than the average salespeople, a difference worth not 120 percent but 8,857 percent (or 89 times) the average employee salary.

These data suggest the practical economic value of a competency model that can help a firm find even one additional superior salesperson: $3.7 million—a benefit that can justify considerable investment in competency re-search.

Second, to improve performance, organizations should use the characteristics of superior performers as their "template," or "blueprint," for employee selection and development. Failure to do so is essentially to select and train to mediocrity—an organization's current average level of performance.

Categorizing Competencies

Competencies can be divided into two categories, "threshold" and "differentiating" according to the performance criterion they predict.

- *Threshold Competencies:* These are the essential characteristics (usually knowledge or basic skills, such as the ability to read) that everyone in a job needs to be minimally effective but that do not distinguish superior from average performers. A threshold competency for a salesperson is knowledge of the product or ability to fill out invoices.

- *Differentiating Competencies:* These factors distinguish superior from average performers. For example, achievement orientation expressed in a person's setting goals higher than those required by the organization, is a competency that differentiates superior from average salespeople.

Mapping Competencies

Competency Mapping beings with identifying key competencies for an organization and/or a job and incorporating those competencies throughout the various processes (i.e. job evaluation, training, recruitment) of the organization. With a competency-based job description, the second step involves mapping those competencies throughout the organization's human resources processes. The competencies of the respective job description also become factors for assessment on performance evaluation. Using competencies helps in more objective evaluations based on displayed or not displayed behaviours. Taking competency mapping one step further, the results of performance evaluation can be used to identify in what competencies individuals need additional development or training.

Building Competency Models

There are three ways in which competencies models may be developed:

1. *Behavioural Indicators:* Behavioral indicators describe the behaviours, thought patterns, abilities and traits that contribute to superior performance.

2. *Evaluative Competency Levels:* Exceptional competencies of high performers are set as standards for evaluating competency levels of employees.

3. *Competencies Describing Job Requirements:* This approach is useful for organizations having multiple competency models. Competencies required in a particular job are described. Job specific competency models help in structuring focused appraisal and compensation decisions.

Profiling Competency Framework for a Particular Role

To identify role-specific competencies required industry specific, functional and behavioural competencies, which need to be developed for enhanced performance. The approach for developing a competency framework for a particular role is as proposed below:

1. Understand strategic business context of the organizations in term of its structure and environmental variables.

2. Detail role description for positions. Defining and scaling (relative importance and mastery level) of specific behaviours for each identified competency as a measure of performance.

3. Develop competency framework taking into consideration the core values and the culture of the organizations in addition to specific functional and level requirements. This should jell with the vision and mission of the company.

4. Validate the competency framework through a workshop, which should include functional experts and top management personnel in order to define critical and desirable competencies. And also to substantiate the extent to which the competencies differentiate between high and average performers by validating the content and criteria.

The competency framework includes technical competencies, behavioural competencies and the proficiency levels required for each competency. Each competency should be detailed in terms of behavioural indicators that enable observation and assessment.

Potential Assessment Centre for Competency Mapping

The linkage between competencies and roles is achieved through a competency mapping exercise, through which the most critical, success driving behaviours for specific roles are established. Against the validated competency framework, an individual's potential is identified through an assessment centre process as outlined below:

- Design Assessment Centre

- Conduct Assessment Centre

- Map individual competencies and gaps

- Finally assess organizational capability and gaps.

A link between people and competencies is established through an effective system of measuring the proficiency of an individual on the desired competencies for the role. The link between people and roles is established through effective measuring tools that evaluate the performance of the person in the role. On-the-job performance of the individual is evaluated on the basis of a performance management system.

The Assessment Centre is a powerful tool in the hands of the management for selection and development. As a selection tool, it can be used for management promotions, fast tracks schemes, high potential list and change of functional role. As a development tool, it is helpful in succession planning, identifying training needs and career development.

Designing and conducting a potential Assessment Centre should follow basic principles in term of accuracy, fairness, reliability, legality, efficiency, multiple assessors, multiple tests and optimal stress to increase performance. It would involve two types of exercises, i.e., group exercises and individual exercises.

⌘ Group Exercises

For potential assessment, the following group exercises are conducted:

- *Assigned Role Exercises:* Used to assess negotiating skills, decision making skills, and risk taking skills;

- *Unassigned Role Exercises:* Used to assess ability to handle uncertainty, change orientation, ethical behaviour and global orientation; and

- *Team Exercises:* Used to assess ability to work in a team and solve problems efficiently.

⌘ Individual Exercises

For potential assessment, the following individual exercises are conducted:

- *In-Basket Exercises:* Used to assess ability to plan, organize, decide, manage and delegate;

- *Learning Skill Inventory/Psychometric Inventories:* Used to assess ability to learn, leverage knowledge and indicate behavioral patterns; and

- *Interpersonal Effectiveness Module:* Used to assess interpersonal effectiveness, excommunication skills, patience and interpersonal skills.

Inputs for analysis of an individual's potential and behavioural patterns are also collected through multilateral feedback (self, peer, subordinate, customer and superior assessment), behavioural event interviews, career aspiration interview, career history, etc. In order to minimize assessors' bias and ensure objectivity and uniformity, multiple trained assessors for each competencies assessment are used.

The competencies gaps can be find out by comparing the desired competency (proficiency) levels and displayed competency levels as indicated in the figure given below:

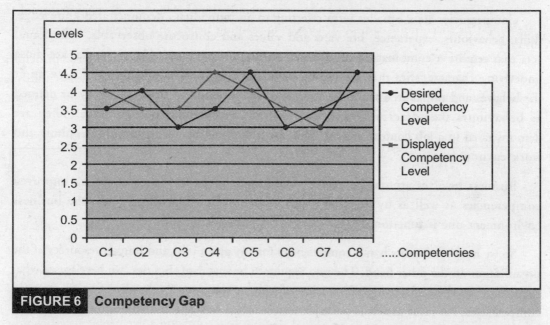

| FIGURE 6 | Competency Gap |

Based on the above exercises, feedback details for individuals on their strengths and developmental areas are prepared. Positive gaps between desired and displayed competencies indicate areas of improvement; negative gaps indicate strengths. Each gap area needs to be analyzed and prioritized into major and minor gaps. These gaps are to be addressed at the individual, departmental and organizational levels by agreeing on milestones for each individual in terms of projects, job rotations, transfer, training and job enrichment. Setting up a Development Monitoring Cell in HR would help in creating a project plan with deadlines and escalation possibilities with a feedback system for feedback from bosses and individuals. Average assessment results are used to identify strengths and gaps in an organization's capabilities.

Competency Mapping and Performance Management

Traditionally, a number of factors that gave the measure of performance were technical skills, number of years of experience, education, personality traits, IQ, etc. Organizations have been relying on scholastic achievements, standardized tests and other pedagogical measures to recruit, keep and assess their workforce. However, researchers were forced to rethink this strategy due to the fact that people fitting in these criteria were not always successful in their jobs. This issue was first publicly addressed in 1973 by a Harvard University psychologist, in his paper titled, "Testing for Competency rather than for Intelligence" wherein he observed that the most academic overachievers are not always the most successful people in their profession. According to him, job selection and performance should be based on desired, observable behaviour instead of traditional standardized tests. Although there was no empirical basis for McClelland's conclusions, the approach gained popularity and acceptance within the human resource community and continues to do so.

Competencies are a broader term referring to an individual's demonstrated knowledge, skills, behaviours, experience, life view and values and constitute observable, behavioural acts that require a combination of all these attributes to execute. Competencies are those underlying characteristics that are indicative of one's performance in terms of how he or she behaves and thinks in a work situation and over a period of time. This may be defined as behaviours that determine and demonstrate exceptional performance. They are demonstrated in a job context and, as such, are influenced by an organization's culture and work environment.

Business revolves around people. Breakthroughs in performance come via improved competencies as well as by acquiring new competencies depending upon the business environment one is functioning in.

So we have on the one hand, competencies for any given post and human resources of the organization on the other hand. The two require to be matched. Besides, we have to see what requires to be done to change the quality of human resources in the direction of required competencies. An ideal match is perhaps never reached but one can strive towards it.

Various human resource systems in an organization can be integrated with competencies as the focal point as described in Table 1.

TABLE 1	**Human Resources Systems in an Organization**	
S.No.	**HR System**	**Competencies as Focal Point**
1.	Workforce Planning	• Organization competency gap analysis
2.	Selection	• Position profiling
		• Interview questions to match positional requirement
3.	Performance management	• Competencies linked to goals
4.	Compensation	• Pay increase based on competency development
		• Recognition based on demonstrating competencies
		• Career bands based on competencies
5.	Career Development	• Competencies as road map for career development
6.	Training	• Competency assessment tools
		• Development activities linked to competencies
7.	Leadership Development	• Leadership competency profiles
8.	Succession Planning	• Planning for future leadership needs

There are four elements in the performance management process against which managers are assessed. These are:

1. *Strategic Contribution:* What managers need to do in terms of the achievement of targets;

2. *Role Performance:* What managers need to do in terms of maintaining and continually improving their core role;

3. *Common Responsibilities and Behaviors:* A measure of behavior in accordance with company values; and

4. *Competency Assessment:* What managers need to do in terms of developing their underlying skills and knowledge.

This process has been specifically designed to provide an integrated approach to managing performance by giving direction, targets and feedback and ensuring appropriate individual and team development.

Competency Model

It is the 'road map' that defines the behaviour imperative to achieve desired results. It helps employees understand how and what to deliver. It is a flexible tool and supports specific needs like employee orientation, employee development, performance management, coaching, developing career strategies, assessments and succession planning.

The initial step is to get every employee to benchmark himself. Considering that employees have different competencies, the setting up of standards should vary. When the benchmarks set are inefficient, the organization loses some of its good performers, as they believe they have accomplished the highest in the company. Similar damage is done when the standards are very high the average performers get disillusioned at the targets achieved. Benchmarks should enable the full realization of employee potential.

The main reason for the growing use of competency mapping in business lies in their strategic value as performance improvement vehicles for both organizations and individuals. Competency mapping has several performance-related benefits. These highlight the clusters of knowledge, skills and personal attributes that lead to high performance. These can be understood and learnt by all organization members through use of effective training, development, performance management and compensation systems.

Competency mapping serves as a behaviour-based standard of performance against which people and organizations can be measured over time. As such, they provide both a behavioural and conceptual vision for the kinds of performance necessary to fulfill business strategies.

Indian Oil has recently carried out this exercise for its senior executives. Based on the gap identified with respect to benchmark roles and competencies, fresh training inputs have been planned for a select group of executives. Job rotations and career successions planning would be linked to this process in due course of time.

Companies like Amoco, DuPont, Federal Express, Proctor and Gamble and Sony have been developing competency models not only to improve employee performance in the workplace, but also to improve the quality of the employees hired. Initiative has been taken by Indian companies including Indian Oil Corporation for competency mapping and they plan to integrate this with their Performance Management System.

Competency Mapping— A Tool for Optimizing the Human Capital

Competency mapping forms an excellent tool for optimizing the human capital. By identifying the key competencies for an organization or a particular position in an organization, and using it for job evaluation, recruitment, training and development, performance management, succession planning, etc. the organization effectively communicates what it actually expects from them. The competency framework serves as the bedrock for all R applications. As a result of competency mapping, all the HR processes like talent induction, management development, appraisals and training yield much better results.

Competency mapping involves identifying the competencies that will be needed by people working in an organization. The level of competency needed by employees at each level must also be specified. This depends on the type of job they do and the environment in which the organization functions. Once this is identified, the remaining process becomes easier. The next step will be to match the existing level of competencies with what is actually required, and take measures to bridge the gap.

"Can a round peg fit a square hole? So can't a wrong employee in a right organization."

The future of an organization lies with the people working there. The organization will have to find a correct person who will fulfill its expectations or will have to chisel and shape up the existing employee to fit its expectations. The more efficient they become in facing the demands of the environment, the more effective will be the organization.

⌘ Core Competencies, Behaviour Pattern and Elemental Build up ⌘

Communication Skills

This does not necessarily refer to the English-speaking skill. There are various factors leading to effective communication.

Competency	Behavioural aspects	Elements
Communication Skills	• Ability to express ones thoughts clearly • Ability to make others understand you • Ability to listen to others • Ability to write your thoughts clearly • Ability to summarize ones ideas in a precise way	• Group skill • Initiative • Empathy • Patience

Interpersonal Relationship Building Ability

This deals with how well a person is able to socialize and develop a close bond with others around him.

Competency	Behavioural aspects	Elements
Interpersonal Relationship Building Ability	• Ability to work in groups or wok as a team • Ability to initiate talks • Ability to understand other's problems • Ability to empathize with others • Courage to apologize on committing mistakes	• Group skill • Initiative • Empathy • Patience

Negotiating Ability

The need for this skill arises when two or more parties argue on a common issue and each party wants a conclusion on it prefers.

Competency	Behavioural aspects	Elements
Negotiating Ability	• Ability to reason • Ability to be ethical during the process • Ability to predict the next argument of opponents • Ability to survive till the end and not to surrender • Ability to associate various arguments and think logically	• Stress management • Risk taking • Reasoning • Responsibility taking

Critical Thinking Ability

The business environment is full of uncertainties and surprises. One must have the ability to think and act under unforeseen and critical situations.

Competency	Behavioural aspects	Elements
Critical Thinking Ability	• Ability to think logically under stress • Ability to remain confident under critical situations • Ability to take risk • Ability to take up responsibility when something goes wrong	• Stress management • Risk taking • Reasoning • Responsibility taking

Data Management Ability

The documents and files possessed by a company are of great importance. The information has to be managed effectively.

Competency	Behavioural aspects	Elements
Forecasting Ability	• Ability to receive correct data • Ability to transmit accurate data • Ability to store data in order and safely • Ability to understand how much of data is to be revealed to a person	• Data reception ability • Data transmission ability • Data storing ability

Forecasting Ability

As already said, the business environment is highly uncertain. One has to possess the ability to foresee future changes and competitions.

Competency	Behavioural aspects	Elements
Forecasting Ability	• Constant review of business environment • Updating oneself with global business happenings • Adequate logic and reasoning	• Prediction • Environment scanning • Reasoning

Creativity

It is not only the quality of the product that plays a role in the market. It is also how different our products are compared to that of our competitors, which attracts our customers. This requires creativity. This will also bring about a huge difference in the way regular day-to-day activities are carried out.

Competency	Behavioural aspect	Elements
Creativity	• Ability to think differently • A keen sense of colors • Ability to present differently • Courage to accept and present the ideas	• Accepting creativity • Practicing creativity • Encouraging creativity

Business Environment Understanding

Success is possible in business only if proper understanding and analyses of the happenings of the business environment is made.

Competency	Behavioural aspects	Elements
Business Environment Understanding	• Regular scanning of the business environment • Updating the happenings in the global business environment • Proper understanding of the happenings within the organization • Ability to relate the happenings in the outer world to the business	• Updating skill • Environmental scanning ability • Organizational understanding

Coordination/Partnership Skill

Any business cannot survive if people were to work as individuals. It requires people of one department to coordinate and work with people of other department. Also, people of the same department must be able to coordinate among themselves and also with external environment.

Competency	Behavioural aspects	Elements
Coordination/Partnership Skill	• Ability to work in teams • Knowledge about the activities of other departments • Ability to receive and transfer information	• Job skill • Information handling • Team working

Instruction Following Ability

However flat today's organizations have become, there still exists a certain amount of hierarchy. Employees must be able to receive orders from their superior and execute the instructions correctly.

Competency	Behavioural aspects	Elements
Instruction Following Ability	• Ability to listen keenly to the instructions given • Ability to accept instructions • Ability to be oriented towards the target • Ability to retain interest in the work being done. • Ability to build trust in the minds of superior about the quality of work one does	• Trust building • Target orientation • Interest retention • Instruction accepting

Knowledge Updating

Any employee must be in a position to update his/her knowledge with regard to the happenings of the outside world. This is absolutely necessary for servicing in today's business environment.

Competency	Behavioural aspects	Elements
Knowledge Updating	• Ability to scan external environment • Ability to search for information • Ability to logically relate the information obtained	• Business environment understanding • Information searching • Information relating

Presentation Skill

Employees in any organization will have to present their reports or analyses to people within the organization and also the others outside.

Competency	Behavioural aspects	Elements
Presentation Skill	• Proper body language • Ability to simplify the presentation • Ability to have a control over the audience • Ability to answer the questions asked	• Body language • simplifying the facts • Convincingly answering • Audience controlling

Analyzing/Problem Solving Ability

When faced with unexpected situations, the employee must be able to tackle it. In case any problem arises; the employee must be able to solve it.

Competency	Behavioural aspects	Elements
Analyzing/ Problem solving ability	• Ability to identify the actual problem • Ability to think under stress • Ability to reason out or think logically • Ability to give long term solutions • Ability to take up responsibility when something goes wrong	• Problem identification • Long-term solution giving • Initiative • Reasoning • Responsibility accepting

Counselling Ability

When employees have some problem, naturally their performance in the organization goes down. The problem could be in their personal life or in the organization. Whatever be the case, the employees require a good counselor who can lend their support to the employees with problems.

Competency	Behavioural Aspects	Elements
Counseling Ability	• Ability to lend a listening ear to the people with problem • Ability to listen without interrupting or advising • Ability to empathize with the other person • Ability to accept the person the way he/she is • Ability to have a proper body language	• Understanding skill • Empathy • Body language • Listening skill

Other Competencies

Apart from these competencies, there are others that are specific to the job done. The requirements of those competencies vary depending upon the time and situation. Those skills are:

- Financial forecasting ability

- Customs handling ability

- Computer knowledge

- Customer handling ability, etc.

Balanced Scorecard

Balanced Scorecard for Enhancing Performance

"The problem is that not everything that counts can be counted, and not everything that can be counted counts."

As a manager, more often than not, most of our decisions and the activities are guided by the impact they will have on the bottom line. Usually, we end up measuring an organization's performance in terms of profit made. No doubt, profitability, gross revenues, return on capital, etc. are the critical, "bottom line" kind of results that companies must deliver to survive. But if we only focus on the financial health of the organization, it may jeopardize our success in the long run because financial measures are generally "lagging indicators" of success and financial performance depends on a variety of past action and events on which we may not have immediate control. They are historical. While they tell us what has happened to the organization, they may not tell us what is currently happening or be a good.

Indicator of Future Performance

Another consequence of merely focusing on financial measures is that we lose sight of the customers who are key to our well-being. In such a scenario, we may end up taking decisions like reducing the warranty stringent to help the organization financially, but may hurt the long-term relationships with the customers, who may eventually reduce the purchases or leave altogether. Such decisions are sufficient to turn off the customers in the longer run. The world over, there are hundreds of companies which are no more talked about probably because of their obsession only with bottom line results. As they continued to do what they had been doing, very soon they realised that their competitors have displayed them from their place of imminence.

Instead of such a short-sighted, after the-fact view of an organisation's performance, a more comprehensive view is needed with an equal emphasis on outcome measures (the financial measures or lagging indicators), measures that will tell us how well the company is doing now (current indicators) and measures of how it might do in the future (leading indicators). We can't ignore the bottom line – the key indicator of what has happened (i.e., a "lagging indicator"). The *balanced scorecard* is just remedy for this kind of problem.

The origin of the balanced scorecard method can be traced back to 1990, when the research arm of KPMG sponsored a study on measuring performance in organisations. The study was motivated by a belief that existing performance measurement approaches, primarily relying on financial parameters which provide information about an organisation's past result are not well-suited for predicting future performance or for implementing and controlling the organisation's strategic plan. And it is very much relevant in the Indian context also where many big companies which were doing quite well financially at one point of time could not read the writing on the wall and as a result, they are no more talked about. By analyzing perspectives other than the financial one, managers can better translate the organisation's strategy into actionable objectives and better measure how well the strategic plan is executing. Subsequently, in 1992, Robert S Kaplan and David Norton introduced the balanced scorecard (BSC) for measuring an organisation's activities in terms of its vision and strategies which was published in the *Harvard Business Review*. It gives managers a comprehensive view of the performance of a business and have been widely adopted around the world. In fact, the *Harvard Business Review*, in its 75th Anniversary issue, cites the Balanced Scorecard as being one of the 15 most important management concepts to have been introduced via articles in the magazine.

What is Balanced Scorecard?

The Balanced Scorecard method is a strategic approach and performance management system that enables the organisations to translate its vision and strategy into implementation. The Balanced Scorecard is a conceptual framework for translating an organization's vision into a set of performance indicators distributed among four perspectives: Financial, Customer, Internal Business Processes, and Learning and Growth. Indicators are maintained to measure an organization's progress toward achieving its vision. Other indicators are maintained to measure the long-term drivers of success. Through this scorecard, an organization monitors both its current performance (finances, customer satisfaction, and business process results) and its efforts to improve processes, motivate and educate employees, and enhance information systems – its ability to learn and improve. A Balanced Scorecard enables us to measure not just how we have been doing, but also how well we are doing ("current indicators" and can expect to do in the future (leading indicators). This in turn, gives us a clear picture of reality.

The Balanced Scorecard is a way of:

● Measuring organizational, business unit's or department's success

● Balancing long-term and short-term actions

● Balancing different measures of success

❖ Financial

❖ Customer

❖ Internal Operations

❖ Human Resource System & Development (learning and growth)

Four Kinds of Measures

The scorecard seeks to measure a business from the following perspectives:

1. *Financial perspective:* Measures reflecting financial performance, for example, number of debtors, cash flow or return on investment. The financial performance of an organization is fundamental to its success. Even non-profit organisations must make the books balance. Financial figures suffer from two major drawbacks.

2. *Customer perspective:* This perspective captures the ability of the organization to provide quality goods and services, effective delivery, and overall customer satisfaction for both Internal and External customers. For example, time taken to process a phone call, results of customer surveys, number of complaints or competitive rankings.

3. *Business Process perspective:* This perspective provides data regarding the internal business results against measures that lead to financial success and satisfied customers. To meet the organizational objectives and customers expectations, organizations must identify the key business processes at which they must excel. Key processes are monitored to ensure that outcomes are satisfactory. Internal business processes are the mechanisms through which performance expectations are achieved. For example, the time spent prospecting new customers, number of units that required rework or process cost.

4. *Learning and growth perspective:* This perspective captures the ability of employees, information systems, and organizational alignment to manage the business and adapt to change. Processes will only succeed if adequately skilled and motivated employees, supplied with accurate and timely information, are driving them. In order to meet changing requirements and customer expectations, employees are being asked to take on dramatically new responsibilities that may require skills, capabilities, technologies, and organizational designs that were not available before. It measures the company's learning curve for example, number of employee suggestions or total hours spent on staff training.

Objectives, Measures, Targets and Initiatives

Within each of the balanced scorecard financial customer, internal process, and learning perspectives, the organisation must define the following:

- Strategic objectives – the strategy for achieving that perspective

- Measures – how progress for that particular objective will be measured

- Targets – the target value sought for each measure

- Initiatives – what will be done to facilitate reaching out the target.

The balanced scorecard provides an interconnected model for measuring performance and revolves around four distinct perspectives – financial, customer, internal processes, and innovation and learning. Each of these perspectives is stated in terms of the organisation's objectives, performance measures, targets, and initiatives, and all are harnessed to implement corporate vision and strategy.

The name also reflects the balance between the short and long-term objectives, between financial and non-financial measures, between lagging and leading indicators and between external and internal performance perspectives.

Under the balance scorecard system, financial measures are the outcome, but do not give a good indication of what is or will be going on in the organization. Measures of customer satisfaction, growth and retention is the current indicator of company performance, and internal operations (efficiency, speed, reducing non-value added work, minimizing quality problems) and human resource systems and development are leading indicators of company performance.

Robert S Kaplan and David P Norton, the architects of the balanced scorecard approach, recognized early that long-term improvement in overall performance was unlikely to happen through technology only and hence placed greater emphasis on organizational learning and growth. These, in turn, consist of the integrated development of employees, information, and systems capabilities.

Context and Strategy

Just as financial measures have to be put in context, so does measurement itself. Without a tie-up to a company strategy, more importantly, as the measure of company strategy, the balanced scorecard is useless. A mission, strategy and objectives must be defined. Measures of that strategy must be agreed upon to and actions need to be taken for a measurement system to be fully effective. Otherwise, it will appear as if the organisation is standing at a crossroad but unaware of which path to take.

✤ Purpose of the Balanced Scorecard ✤

Kaplan and Norton found that organisations are using the scorecard to:

- Clarify and update strategy

- Communicate strategy throughout the company

- Align unit and individual goals with strategy

- Link strategic objectives to long term targets and annual budgets

- Identify and align strategic initiatives

- Conduct periodic performance reviews to learn about and improve strategy.

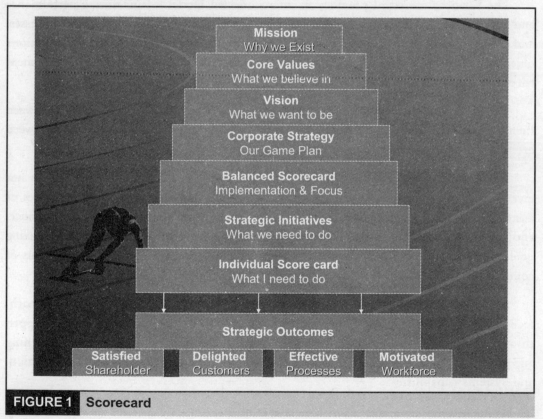

FIGURE 1 **Scorecard**

The Process of Building a Balanced Scorecard

Kaplan and Norton suggest following four step process for building a scorecard:

- Define the measurement architecture

- Specify strategic objectives

- Choose strategic measures

- Develop the implementation plan

Benefits of Balanced Scorecard

Some of the benefits include:

- Translation of strategy into measurable parameters

- Communication of the strategy to all stakeholders

- Alignment of individual goals with the organisation's strategic objectives

- Feedback of implementation results to the strategic planning process

- Preparing the organisation for the change – it provides for a front-end justification as well as a focus and integration for the continuous improvement, re-engineering and transformation process.

Avoiding Potential Roadblocks

- Lack of a well-defined strategy

- Using only lagging measures

- Use of generic metrics

- Failure at all levels

- Failure to follow through completion

How to Enhance Performance through Balanced Score Card

In such constantly shifting environments, managements must learn to continuously adapt to new strategies that can emerge from capitalizing on opportunities or countering threats. A properly constructed balanced scorecard can provide management with the ideal tool in reacting to the turbulent environment and helping the organisation to correct the course to success.

Scorecard provides managers with feedback, thus, enabling them to monitor and adjust the implementation of their strategy – even to the extent of changing the strategy itself. In today's information age, organisations operate in very turbulent environments. Planned strategy, though initiated with the best of intentions and with the best available information at the time of planning may no longer be appropriate or valid for contemporary conditions.

As companies have applied the balanced scorecard, they have begun to recognize that the scorecard represents a fundamental change in the underlying assumptions about performance measurement.

The scorecard puts strategy and vision, not control, at the centre. It establishes goals but assumes that people will adopt whatever behaviours and take whatever actions are necessary to arrive at those goals. The measures are designed to pull people toward the overall vision. Senior managers may know what the end result should be, but they cannot tell employees exactly how to achieve that result, because the conditions in which employees operate are constantly changing.

This new approach to performance measurement is consistent with the initiatives under way in many organisation: cross-functional integration, customer supplier partnerships, global scale, continuous improvement, and team rather than individual accountability. By combining the financial, customer, internal process and innovation, and organizational learning perspectives, the balanced scorecard helps managers understand, at least implicitly, many interrelationships. This understanding can help managers transcend traditional notions about functional barriers and ultimately lead to improved decision-making, problem-solving and enhanced performance. The balanced scorecard keeps organisations moving forward.

Meeting Corporate Objectives through Balance Scorecard – A Human Resource Perspective
(Three days' workshop at IMT, Ghaziabad by Prof. B.D. Singh)

Introduction

Management of business in global competitive age and navigating through turbulences has become a challenge before corporate.

The balance scorecard approach translates organization mission and strategy into a set of tangible objectives that links short term actions to long term strategies. The measures represent a balance between external measures of shareholders and customers and internal measures of critical business processes, innovations, and learning and growth. The balance scorecard approach retains traditional financial measures, but these measures tell the story of past events and story of industrial age companies. These financial measures alone are inadequate for guiding and evaluating the journey that knowledge age corporates need to create future value through investment in customer, suppliers, employees, processes, technology, innovation etc. This is must for organizational sustainability in a competitive global world.

Objectives

This innovative programme helps professionals to design and execute a way of linking HR strategy and performance by using robust performance management system, and Performance measurement system in which vital and critical factors of business will cascade down to bottom level, involving all levels.

For Whom

The programme intends to familiarize the participants with concepts and processes involved in this system. It is useful for all disciplines of management – production, project, material, finance, marketing, and HRM, specially those managers who are required to take decisions and responsible for implementing the decision.

Content

1. Emerging business trends affecting human resources management and changing paradigms of management thinking for meeting the challenges of changes.

2. Corporate strategies and balance scorecard—aligning strategies with HR architecture

3. Developing high performance system/performance appraisal system—— linking objectives/strategies with teams/individuals KPIs/KRAs.

4. Approaches and steps in implementation of balance scorecard based performance appraisal system.

5. HR as business partners – measurements and its challenges.

6. Methodology—live cases from corporate both public sectors and multinationals where balance scorecard system is in practice.

Coaching and Mentoring

Introduction

The traditional homogeneity of organizations is increasingly being replaced by encouragement of individuality, variety, innovation and difference. This, however, runs the risk of losing some of the key attractions of the traditional organization – stability and security.

Coaching and mentoring seek to bridge the gap between traditional expectations of the organization and more contemporary approaches. Several key features of coaching and mentoring, for individuals and organizations alike, make them increasingly attractive. They can encourage a culture of learning and mutual help, and combine both individual and organizational development.

Both coaching and mentoring are natural human activities, often intuitively practiced by managers. Although many managers practice them without thinking, many others have not developed these natural skills or have allowed them to stagnate or disappear.

Mentoring and coaching are distinguished from each other generally by the work-distance and time-frame of what is being discussed. Typically, managers coach those who report them, about fairly immediate work developments. A mentor is often organizationally more distant from the person they are mentoring (by seniority or by being outside the organization or department); and can work with the mentee on longer term issues of personal development and career planning.

Coaching and Mentoring in the Organization

The significance of coaching and mentoring for the modern organization lies in four key aspects:

1. The attention to the individual provided by these activities. This in itself is a shift from previous attitudes to the management of subordinates. This attention can provide a point of stability that makes people more able to respond effectively to change.

2. The individual becomes a skilful and reflective learner. This is the underlying aim of both activities. Individuals increasingly use their own experience as the key material for learning, assisted by the knowledge and wisdom of the coach or mentor.

3. The importance of the relationship. Both activities are examples of what has been described as 'developmental working relationships'. A large part of the success of the mentor or coach depends on the way they manage the relationship at a human and personal level. This ability transfers into other working areas, as not only a survival skill in the new style of organization, but as a means of sharing knowledge and expertise.

4. The effect of organizational climate, and the effect on it. Though the one-to-one relationship is clearly central in coaching and mentoring, to be fully effective it needs to be part of an organization-wide appreciation of the value of learning as a driver for relevant change. Effective coaching and value of learning as a driver for relevant change. Effective coaching and mentoring relationships can help to develop this wider process as well as deriving benefits from it.

Coaching and mentoring frequently run alongside, or are an intrinsic part of, a self-development process set in place by the organization. This process can vary with personal projects and personal development plans at one end of the continuum, and an organization-wide self-managed learning programme at the other. They are linked by an emphasis on development becoming something for which individuals have to take responsibility themselves.

One of the most important conditions for coaching and mentoring to be successful is the assumption that learning is a respectable activity, and that everyone can and should be engaged in it. The mentor and the coach challenge and support individuals in their learning, and help to provide the organizational framework in which it happens.

Success is also more likely where there is a clear, though evolving, picture of the nature of a person's job or role, and where it fits into the organization and the corporate goals. This requires a degree of clarity about job or role expectations: well-developed and thought-through criteria so success, clear regular feedback, some sense of the resources necessary to achieve the targets set, and an understanding of the work context, both internal to the organization and in the marketplace. This clarity is never easy to achieve, but a move towards it sets the scene for effective coaching and mentoring.

⌘ Coaching ⌘

Effective coaching depends not only on the skills of the coach and the receptiveness of the person being coached, but also on the conditions outlined above being present (clarity about success criteria, usable feedback, etc.) in the work setting, At the same time, when managers start to coach, if they are working effectively there is a better chance of the surrounding conditions being improved. Coaching conversations may lead to increased clarity about job expectations, for instance, and may provide regular feedback and the opportunity to think through standards and criteria for success. There is a close two-way relationship between effective coaching initiatives and a favourable learning climate, each enhancing the other.

The concept of coaching remains most easily associated with sports coaching where the purpose of the coach is to help the person they are coaching to reach their personal best. Interestingly, the nature of sports coaching is undergoing basic changes—ones which are, to some degree, mirrored in organizations. There was a time when the coach was the person who drove the athlete on, forced the pace and continually instructed. Increasingly, coaches are now moving to an approach which involves accurately targeted questioning to help the athlete become increasingly aware of 'what works'—for instance, the environment in which he or she performs best, how this feels, and what the obstacles are to achieving this repeatedly. Despite this changing emphasis, some traditional aspects of coaching remain—for example, the coach also celebrates victories and supports the athletes through bad times.

In the same way, the manager who is coaching subordinates finds a way of getting them to reflect on their performance, become aware of what they are doing and how they are doing it, so that each individual in the end learns to monitor his or her own performance. At the same time, the manager provides essential information and knowledge where there are gaps that need to be filled. While doing this, they are working to develop a climate where learning and innovation—as well as achievement—are expected and rewarded. The coaching approach challenges the manager to think about the nature of the roles of the people they may be coaching, and this is a developmental experience for the managers. Many HR functions are devolving some other their management development responsibilities to the line, and the concept of 'manager as coach' is seen as part of this trend.

⌘ Mentoring

Mentoring has something in common with coaching but, at its best, has a different emphasis. The mentor has less of a vested interest in the mentee's performance results—the mentee's results don't directly have an effect on the mentor's business performance. This makes it easier for the mentor to take a long-term view and a broader approach to the mentee in his/her working life. The mentor is free to be objective, challenging or supporting as necessary, and is able to help mentees think through their overall career development, while their immediate manager or coach may quite properly bring in the more immediate or short-term focus.

Mentors are often used to help individuals manage the process of transition: graduates entering a large organization; someone moving to increased responsibility; a person moving to a level in which they may be seen as unusual (such as women promoted to a level where there are very few women).

Many organizations now have a well-established system of mentor selection and training, induction for mentees and monitoring of the process. For example, GKN has a mentoring system for employees of high potential on a self-managed learning programmes; at supermarket chain ASDA, a senior store manager from a different area will be a mentor for people who are being prepared to be store managers; at a division of the Prudential Corporation mentoring is used for women returning to work after maternity leave; and the UK Stock Exchange has a system of external mentors to support senior management through a major change scheme.

Although widespread mentoring is a fairly recent development in Europe, it is more notably acknowledged as an essential developmental experience in Japan. Research carried out by Warwick and Stirling Universities, compared the 'factors in growing as a manager' reported in paired British and Japanese companies. The emphasis on the effect of role models and mentors was cited most frequently by the Japanese, while the British emphasized education and wider experience of life.

The process of mentoring, when mentors come from within an organization, can have an organizational impact. Senior managers come into contact with, for instance, recent recruits, and this can give the mentor a fresh view on the organization and on the new generation of thinking. At the same time, the mentor who is working at a strategic level can be in a position to convey the corporate direction to the mentee in a way that is direct and immediate. In this way, the mentoring relationship can strengthen organizational cohesion.

Challenges for Coaches and Mentors

The most challenging aspect for coaches and mentors is the change in mindset that is required. They should no longer give the impression of knowing best or insist on instructing or commanding. Instead, they should work alongside their colleagues – a position that remains rigorous and targeted but in a very different way. For people who are used to a 'telling' style, the ideas and approaches of coaching and mentoring can seem softer. In fact they are not; they are more demanding on both parties in that they require thinking, sophisticated attention, sensitivity to nuances, and a commitment to outcomes while abandoning the need to be in control of people or of situations. People surmount these difficulties more easily when they see the positive effective of working in this way, particularly in organizations which are going through changes such as restructuring, downsizing or change in corporate focus. Individuals blossom and develop, become more creative and more aware of the scope of their job and of the critical success factors. They perform better.

Skills and Activities of Coaching

There are many possible approaches to coaching. They may involve watching what a person does and giving feedback on what you notice; working on problems with someone and learning together; asking stimulating open-ended questions; taking through your own thinking processes aloud, and encouraging the other person to do the same, encouraging analysis of what really works for individuals; finding your own way of seeing the work and the learning from the other person's point of view; and using questioning as a way of helping a person understand their own thought processes.

Coaching can be thought of as two kinds of conversation – mapping-related and performance-related.

Mapping-related conversations may focus on:

- The organizational setting or culture—'what works around here?', where does this project fit into the overall strategic plan?

- Identifying problems and possible causes—'what exactly is going wrong?', 'has this happened before?'

- Establishing overall desired outcomes—'what are you trying to achieve?', 'what is the general purpose here?'

Performance-related conversations may focus on:

- What the person is doing—'what exactly did you do?', 'how are you going about this?'

- Comparisons—'is this different from what you did last time?', are other people doing the same thing?', 'can you learn from them?'

- Questions about thinking—'how are you thinking this through?', 'what evidence are you looking for?', 'what assumptions are you making?', 'do they need checking?'

- Questions about resources—'what it help to organize your resources differently?'

Managers as coaches face a number of common pitfalls in their conversations, for any of the following reasons:

- Having moved into coaching before establishing a certain amount of rapport and trust;

- Being unclear in their own minds about what they are trying to achieve by engaging in the conversation;

- Not listening properly because they are too busy deciding whether what they are saying is right or not;

- Using only those questions which demonstrate their knowledge;

- Avoiding questions to which they don't know the answer;

- Answering their own questions;

- Not picking up signals as the conversation goes along about how useful it is for the other person.

These pitfalls can be avoided by keeping in mind the purpose and desired outcome of the coaching activity.

Coaching to Improve Unsatisfactory Performance

A further and more skillful area of coaching is in the area of challenging or confronting for performance improvement. When a person is not delivering the performance required, he/she may have a variety of emotional reactions such as despair, resistance, self-justification, or even complete unawareness.

The coaching approach in this situation is to deal with these by focusing on clear expectations. Often these expectations have not been properly mapped out or clearly understood.

Gathering information and agreeing where the problem lies are essential next steps, at the same time as staying aware of the other person's reactions.

In dealing with underperformance, the following pattern, for a coach, can be useful:

- Get clear in your own mind what the situation is: what is the current performance, and what it is expected to be;

- Lay aside feelings of blame and irritation and gather information about how individuals are reacting, their awareness of the performance shortfall, and what they see as the problems.

- Get the person being coached to share in identifying the problems, adding their own perspective and ask them for possibilities to resolve them. This is a stage where it is particularly important to maintain a positive and clear relationship, focusing forward on next steps and change.

- Establish a process whereby the employee will set up a plan for informing the coach/manager of progress against clearly stated goals.

Learning to Coach

The value of coaching is that it establishes an effective and dynamic working relationship in difficult and changing situations.

In many cases, managers are encouraged to coach by 'manager as coach and developer' initiatives. These may take the form of workshops or of elements of management development programmes. As training and development responsibilities are being developed more and more to line managers, the pressure on them to work in this way increases. Lack of time or other priorities often get in the way, with the widespread feeling that in current working conditions it's quicker just to tell someone how to do things or, alternatively, to let them get on with their job, rather than taking time to coach. Because of this, there is often a certain amount of resistance to adopting a coaching style of management in the first instance; this resistance may also be in reaction to the hype that is in some cases connected with approaches to coaching.

Resistance may be overcome by starting the coaching from the top. The managers who are expected to move to a coaching style may themselves need to be coached. This experience helps them to understand the value of coaching at first hand, and to get an intuitive sense of how to do it themselves.

Skills and Activities of Mentoring

What is required of a mentor? The most favoured attributes appear to be acting as a sounding board for ideas; being a source of organizational knowledge; and helping people to see themselves more clearly. Interestingly, few potential mentors choose a role model; someone who exemplifies good practice although this is frequently the reason a mentor is chosen by a mentee.

Each variant of the mentor role requires different skills, but a core might include some familiar and well-developed techniques, to be used during a mentoring meeting:

- Listening openly without making judgments;

- Asking open-ended questions;

- Summarizing;

- Clarifying;

- Reflecting back;

- Being aware of differences between verbal and non-verbal behavior;

- Helping the mentee explore potential options and their outcomes.

Behaviours which maybe tempting but that are particularly unhelpful in a mentor include:

- Passing judgment;

- Filling in a silence too quickly;

- Asking questions when the mentee is trying to figure something out;

- Being or feeling patronizing or condescending;

- Telling the mentee what to do before he or she has started to think it through for themselves.

The main purpose of the mentoring relationship is to help mentees develop their own thinking and planning about their career and development, with someone supportive who has organizational experience and knowledge. Unhelpful behaviours such as those listed above sabotage this process.

It is noticeable, when working with potential mentors, how easy it is for them to fall into the trap of asking leading questions or of disguising statements or opinions as questions. These are habits acquired from an earlier style of management and it is easy not to be aware of them, or their inappropriateness, in the mentoring situation.

For senior managers, mentoring involves a change of behavior but an even more dramatic change of thinking. Senior managers have mainly got to where they are by being effective and decisive and by (quite appropriately) knowing what people should do and getting them to do it. Working with someone who is junior to them but whom they do not manage can initially be quite challenging. This stretch of style is one of the benefits that mentors identify as a personal gain from being involved in the mentoring process.

Learning to Mentor

Many organizations provide orientation or training for mentors, to provide a base-line or a common approach. Attending a mentoring workshop can be a welcome opportunity to engage in some personal development, to revisit the skills of listening, establishing rapport, reflecting on one's own behaviour; skills that may have become rusty in the journey to a senior position. The use fullness of mentors lies partly in their knowledge and experience; but as this becomes less relevant with changing times, mentors' key value is in their ability to help their mentees to gain knowledge and experience of their own in their current role, and to develop their ability to make effective judgments in ambiguous or uncertain or uncertain situations.

Setting up Mentoring Schemes

Key factors in a successful mentoring scheme are similar to those in any organizational initiative. That is, commitment and modeling from those with most power and influence, clear and user-friendly systems and procedures, clarity about the reasons and desired outcomes of the schemes, and widespread and appropriate communication to all stakeholders. In the case of a mentoring scheme, the stakeholders include not only mentors and mentees, but also the mentees' managers.

In some organizations, only selected people are offered a mentor in a formal scheme. Mentoring may be provided for potential high-flyers, for women, for new recruits. These choices may have an impact on those who are not offered the same provision. Communication and explanation are therefore important. Mentoring may also be seen, usually wrongly, as a 'gateway', a way through to the fast track with a powerful protector; these notions need to be contradicted if they are not the case, and the real reasons for the selection widely disseminated.

An essential element of the communication is clear briefing for al involved (mentor, mentee, mentee's manager), which may also include an element of training for mentors. Bringing mentors together at intervals supports this communication process as well as providing support for the mentors themselves.

Informal Mentoring

Many people have experience of an informal mentor; someone who took them under their wing at a crucial stage in their career. In a wide variety of organizations there are traces of this process, being, as it is, a very normal and well-respected human activity. This mentor may have been chosen in some sense by the mentee, or may have themselves chosen the mentee. One approach to promoting mentoring in the organization is to encourage this process by, for instance:

● Describing it as a valuable process;

● Encouraging new recruits to select a mentor;

● Including developmental activities such as mentoring in appraisal criteria for senior managers.

International or Cross-cultural Implications

Cross-cultural research indicates that managers in different national cultures work from different sets of assumptions and priorities. The individualist assumptions in cultures such as those of the UK or the United States, for example, contrast with the collective assumptions in Japanese or Latin American culture. Assumptions will affect the pattern of mentoring and coaching in these countries, with varying emphasis on the individual's career and personal development or the good of the organization or group. The assumptions about how status is attained (based on one's own achievements, or on the group a person was born into the their personal connections) vary between countries and cultures, and this will affect the choice of mentors, and how they are valued by mentees. Expected behaviours by mentors in different countries or cultures with a history of mentoring may also vary.

There are also implications for mentoring in multinational organizations, particularly where there are managers of different nationalities working in the same company. In the light of known cultural differences, attitudes and under standing of what mentoring is to be in the organization need careful clarification, with shared meaning being developed.

6

Pygmalion Effect

Introduction

The **Pygmalion effect**, or **Rosenthal effect**, refers to situations in which students perform better than other students simply because they are expected to do so. The Pygmalion effect requires a student to internalize the expectations of their superiors. It is a form of self-fulfilling prophecy, and in this respect, students with poor expectations internalize their negative label, and those with positive labels succeed accordingly. Within sociology, the effect is often cited with regards to education and social class.

A self-fulfilling prophecy whereby people tend to behave the way others expect them to. In a famous field experiment on the Pygmalion effect in children, carried out by the German-born US psychologist Robert Rosenthal (born 1933) and the US Schoolteacher Lenore F. Jacobson (born 1926) and published in a book titled *Pygmalion in the Classroom* (1968), the researchers applied a standard IQ test to children in an elementary school in San Francisco at the beginning of an academic year, selected 20 percent (about five children per class) at random, and told their teachers that the tests suggested that these children were potential academic 'spurters' who could be expected to show unusual intellectual gains in the year ahead. When the children were retested at end of academic year, the 'spurters' showed massive IQ gains relative to the other children, especially in the first and second grades (6-7 year old children): 20 percent of the 'spurters' gained at least 30 IQ points, and 80 percent gained at least 10 IQ points. These gains were presumably due to subtle effects of the teachers' expectations on criticized on methodological grounds. See also experimenter expectancy effect, Oedipus effect. [Named after George Bernard Shaw's play *Pygmalion* (1912), in which the linguist Professor Henry Higgins gives elocution lessons to a cockney flower-girl Eliza Dolittle and passes her off in high society as an upper-class lady—see also etymology of Pygmalionism].

By Eric Garner

"A team does as well as you and the think they can".

This idea is known as "the self-fulfilling prophecy". When you believe the team will perform well, in some strange, magical way they do. And similarly, when you believe they won't perform well, they don't.

There is enough experimental data to suggest that the self-fulfilling prophecy is true. One unusual experiment in 1911 concerned a very clever horse called Hans. This horse had the reputation for being able to add, multiply, subtract, and divide by tapping out the answer with its hooves.

The extraordinary thing was that it could do this without its trainer being present. It only needed someone to put the questions.

On investigation it was found that when the questioner knew the answer, he or she transmitted various very subtle body language clues to Hans such as the raising of an eyebrow or the dilation of the nostrils. Hans simply picked up on these clues and continued tapping until he arrived at the required answer. The questioner expected a response and Hans obliged.

In similar vein, an experiment was carried out at a British school into the performance of a new intake of pupils. At the start of the year, the pupils were each given a rating, ranging from "excellent prospect" to "unlikely to do well". These were totally arbitrary ratings and did not reflect how well the pupils had previously performed. Nevertheless, these ratings were given to the teachers. At the end of the year, the experimenters compared the pupils' performance with the ratings.

Despite their real abilities, there was an astonishingly high correlation between performance and ratings. It seems that people perform as well as we expect them to.

The self-fulfilling prophecy is also known as the Pygmalion Effect. This comes from a story by Ovid about Pygmalion, a sculptor and prince of Cyprus, who created an ivory statue of his ideal woman. The result, which he called Galatea, was so beautiful that he immediately fell in love with it. He begged the goddess Aphrodite to breath life into the statue and make her his own. Aphrodite granted Pygmalion his wish, the statue came to life and the couple married and lived happily ever after. The story was also the basis of George Bernard Shaw's play "Pygmalion", later turned into the musical "My Fair Lady". In Shaw's play, Professor Henry Higgins claims he can take a Cockney flower girl, Eliza Doolittle, and turn her into a duchess. But, as Eliza herself points out to Higgins' friend Pickering, it isn't what she learns or does that determines whether she will become a duchess, but how she's treated. "You see, really and truly, apart from the things anyone can pick up (the dressing and the proper way of speaking and so on), the difference between a lady and a flower girl is not how she behaves but how she's treated. "I shall always be a flower girl to Professor Higgins, because he always treats me as a flower girl, and always will, but I know I can be a lady to you because you always treated me as a lady, and always will."

The implication of the Pygmalion effect for leaders and managers is massive. It means that the performance of your team depends less on them than it does on you. The performance you get from people is no more or less than what you expect: which means you must always expect the best. As Goethe said, "Treat a man as he is and he will remain as he is. Treat a man as he can and should be and he will become as he can and should be".

The Pygmalion Effect

It is an interesting psychological phenomenon that people tend to fulfill the expectations that other people have of them. This phenomenon is known as the Pygmalion effect or the self-fulfilling prophecy. The idea that one person's expectations can influence the behaviour of another has been in existence for a long time. The original Pygmalion was a prince of Cyprus in Greek mythology who carved an ivory statue of the ideal woman. This statue was so perfect that he fell in love with it, and called his ideal woman Galatea. Aphrodite (the Goddess of Love) came to his rescue, and she brought the statue to life.

This interesting love story from mythological inspired the Irish playwright George Bernard Shaw to write the play Pygmalion which was the basis for the musical hit My Fair Lady. The underlying theme was that one person, by effort and belief, can change Eliza Doolittle from an ill-mannered loud flower girl into a soft-spoken sophisticated lady. In 1965, *Look* magazine in the United States contained an article titled "Sweeney's Orleans, Lousiana which at the time was headed by James W. Sweeney. According to the article Sweeney said " I am going to make a poorly educated Negro into a computer expert." Racial segregation was almost a way of life in the southern United States at the time. The poorly educated black Sweeney chose was a hospital porter named George Johnson. Johnson then worked as a janitor in the computer centre in the mornings and learned about computers in the afternoons. He was treated as a computer person and according to Sweeney he became "just about the best trainee we ever ran through the place". Johnson was eventually put in charge of the main computer room and actually trained computer operators himself. Sweeney worked hard to help Johnson make it but puts this down to a stubborn streak which he blamed on his Irish ancestry. I prefer to call it a combination of tenacity and confidence in his own ability to make a success of another person.

These examples show us that the Pygmalion effect is much more than positive thinking. It requires action in addition to thinking and beliefs. Pygmalion did not just think about his ideal woman; he helped create her. Professor Higgins also worked to help Eliza Doolittle live up to his expectations. It took many hours of hard work. James Sweeney also worked to bring about his so-called miracle. A more recent example can be seen in the popular film Trading Places. Many readers may have observed similar examples in both work and personal settings.

Mentors and Proteges

The concept of mentors and protégés also traces its origin to Greek mythology. Odysseus left for the Trojan War and put the care of his household and his son Telemachus in the hands of his friend Mentor. He believed Mentor could and would live up to his expectations. These expectations were justified as Odysseus discovered on his return. Again, the combination of expectations and action based on these expectation resulted in a self-fulfilling prophecy. While mentoring has existed in business for many years on an informal basis, only recently has it become formally entrenched in the corporate realm.

Strategic succession planning. The practice entails the assignment of a junior member of staff or a recently recruited graduate known as the protégé to a senior seasoned manager or executive known as the mentor. A mentor who knows about a subordinate's skills and talents can help that person reach his or her career goals.

Mentoring is a typical example of the Pygmalion effect in business.

The relationship of a mentor to a protégé is that of a staff capacity as opposed to a line capacity. The mentor provides advice and shares his or her experience with the protégé. The mentor must constantly act as a positive Pygmalion to make the process effective.

Positive Pygmalions

The bank's executives maintained it and took a long time for branch managers to obtain the necessary experience, knowledge and judgment to deal effectively with employee relations, customer relations and credit risks. The most effective branch managers were in their 40s and 50s with one exception, who was 27 years old, yet was in the top 10 percent of mangers in terms of effectiveness. This person had been a branch manager at 25 and did such a good job of developing his assistant that he in turn was made a branch manager at 25. The assistant had been assigned to work with two different branch managers who were very effective teachers and also positive Pygmalions. Here Livingston maintains that a young person's first manager will probably be the most influential on his or her career. If the manager sets high but achievable and challenging goals for the young person and provides the necessary support that person will most likely live up to those expectations. However, "If this manager is unwilling or unable to develop the skills the young employee needs to perform effectively, the latter will set lower personal standards than he or she is capable of achieving, that person's self-image will be impaired, and he or she will develop negative attitudes towards the job, the employer, and—in all probability—his or her career in business."

Rosenthal's "Four-factor Theory"

Rosenthal [2] offers a "four-factor theory" to explain the Pygmalion effect. These four factors include both non-verbal and verbal forms of communication. People who have been led to expect good things from their employers, clients, children, etc. appear to provide the following:

1. *Climate:* They set an accepting, encouraging social-emotional mood, or climate, for these people. These includes warmth, attention, smiling, nodding the head approvingly,

maintaining good eye contact—all position non-verbal kinds of communication, i.e. emotional support.

2.   *Feedback:* They give these people more verbal clues about their performance, more reaction, more praise, and sometimes even more criticism—all of which help to teach them what is needed for improvement.

3.   *Input:* They will literally teach more material and more difficult material to those who supposedly have more potential.

4.   *Output:* They encourage those who are chosen to ask more questions, urge them to respond more, allow more time to do a job correctly, and give them the benefit of the doubt.

Rosenthal also believes that these factors work both ways – the worker also influences the manger, the child influences the parent, the client influences the company, by his or her own verbal or non-verbal clues. This influence is known as the Galatea Effect, called after Pygmalion's ideal woman.

The important thing to remember here is to avoid having favourite subordinates. All subordinates should be given opportunities to realize their potential.

Communicating the Pygmalion effect, we can communicate our expectations in both verbal and non-verbal ways. Non-verbal messages are usually communicated unintentionally, and this makes it almost impossible for us to hide our expectations. Our tone of voice, eye contact, body posture, facial expressions, are all examples of non-verbal communication. Non-verbal messages can have negative as well as positive influence. By merely changing our tone of voice we can communicate a completely different message even though the words are the same. With verbal communication we need to be very careful with the words we use. If I give a tough task to someone and say "this is a very difficult assignment" the connotation may be interpreted as "I expect you to have problems with this one." However, if I say "This is a very difficult assignment and it means a lot to the bank. I know it's a tight deadline and you'll be pushed for time but that's why I'm giving it to you because I know you can do it. If you run into any difficulties, have any problems, or need any assistance, please let me know." The message in communication is that I have full confidence in the person's ability to complete the task successfully and also that I am available in the event of a problem. An interesting fact about communication is that people cannot communicate. For instance, when they say nothing, it is usually a sign that they are displeased. The silent treatment can communicate negative feelings even more effectively at times than a strongly worded verbal message. According to Livingston, the theory also suggests how the circle of negative self-fulfilling prophecies can be broken. This entails changing the initial definition of the situation. One must question the original assumption, arrive at a new definition of the situation and act on this belief.

Being a Positive Pygmalion

According to Walder [3] the following are the positive Pygmalion factors. These factors encourage people to live up to high expectations.

A Positive Pygmalion—

- Is easy to talk to and has time for you even when under pressure;

- Tries to see merit in your ideas even if they conflict with his/hers;

- Tries to help people to understand the company's objectives;

- Tries to give people all the information they requires;

- Displays consistent, high expectations of subordinates;

- Tries to encourage people to develop in new directions;

- Accepts your mistakes, so long as you learn from them;

- Tries to correct mistakes and figure out how they can be prevented in the future;

- Expects superior performance and gives recognition for it.

7

Job Analysis

Introduction

Gatewood and Field (1994) observed that there are probably as many different definitions of job analysis as there are writings on the topic. They suggested a definition that views job analysis as 'a purposeful, systematic process for collection information on the important work-related aspects of a job.' Others have characterized job analysis as the collection and analysis of just about any type of job-related information by almost any method for any purpose.

The Basics of Job Analysis

Organizations consists of jobs that have to be staffed. Job analysis is the procedure through which you determine the duties of these positions and the characteristics of the people to hire for the. Job analysis produces information used for writing job description (a list of what the job entails) and job specifications (what kind of people to hire for the job).

The supervisor or human resources specialist normally collects one or more of the following types of information via the job analysis:

- *Work activities:* First, he or she collects information about the job's actual work activities, such as cleaning, selling, teaching, or painting. This list may also include how, why, and when the worker performs each activity.

- *Human behaviour:* The specialist may also collect information about human behaviors like sensing, communicating, deciding, and writing. Included here would be information regarding job demands such as lifting weights or walking long distances.

- *Machines, tools, equipment, and work aids:* This category included information regarding tools used, materials processed, knowledge dealt with or applied (such as finance or law), and services rendered (such as counseling or repairing).

- *Performance standards:* The employer may also want information about the job's performance standards (in terms of quantity or quality levels for each job duty, for instance). Management will use these standards to appraise employees.

- *Job context:* Included here is information about such matters as physical working conditions, work schedule, and the organizational and social context—for instance, the number of people with whom the employee would normally interact. Information regarding incentives might also be included here.

- *Human requirements:* This includes information regarding the job's human requirements, such as job-related knowledge or skills (education, training, work experience) and required personal attributes (aptitudes, physical characteristics, personality, interests).

Use of Job Analysis Information

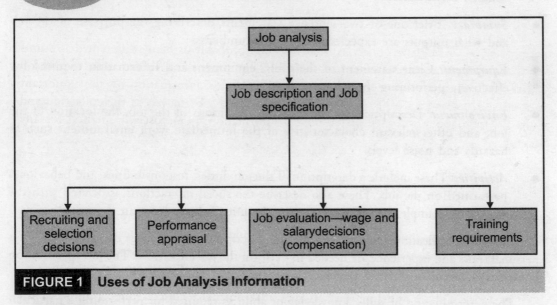

FIGURE 1   **Uses of Job Analysis Information**

Job Description and Job Specifications

How would a manager describe the openings when he advertises to hire employees? At an interview to select the best person from those who apply, what guidelines would an interviewer use? The answer, with job descriptions and job specifications.

The job description is one of the primary outcomes provided by a systematic JA. From the data gathered in JA, organizations (particularly larger ones) prepare records of what jobs are being performed in the organization (job descriptions) and the qualifications necessary to perform them (job specifications). These are used when replacement becomes necessary.

Simply stated, a job description is a written description of what the job entails. It is not necessary to overemphasise how important thorough, accurate, and current job descriptions are to an organization. Many changes occurring in recent years have increased the need for such job descriptions. These changes include:

1. The vast number of organizational restructurings that have occurred (e.g., downsizing)

2. The need to implement new and creative ways to motivate and reward employees

3. The accelerated rate at which technology is changing work environments

4. New, more stringent regulation of employment practices through legislation.

There is no standard format for job description but almost all well-written, useful descriptions will include information on (Ghorpade, 1988):

- *Job Title: Title* of the job and other identifying information such as its wage and benefits classification.

- *Summary:* Brief one-or two-sentence statements describing the purpose of the job and what outputs are expected from job incumbents.

- *Equipment:* Clear statement of the tools, equipment and information required for effectively performing the job.

- *Environment:* Descriptions of the working conditions of the job, the location of the job, and other relevant characteristics of the immediate work environment such as hazards and noise levels.

- *Activities:* These include a description of the job duties, responsibilities, and behaviours performed on the job. These also describe the social interactions associated with the work (for example, size of work group, amount of dependency in the work).

The job specification evolves from the job description. It addresses the question 'What personal traits and experience are needed to perform the job effectively? The job specification is especially useful in offering guidance for recruitment and selection.

The determination of skills, knowledge or abilities required for performing a particular job must be systematic. R. J. Harvey (1993) offers the following guidelines for arriving at the characteristics that should be included in a job specification:

1. All job tasks must be identified and rated in terms of importance (by means of job analysis techniques).

2. A panel of experts, incumbents or supervisors should specify the necessary skills for performing each of the job tasks identified.

3. The importance of each skill must be rated.

4. Any other characteristics necessary for performing the job, such as physical requirements and professional certification, should be identified.

5. Each skill that has been identified needs to be specifically linked to each job task.

Only traits and skills that are actually required to perform the job should be started in the job specification. Job specifications need to differentiate clearly between essential and nonessential skills. Essential skills are those for which alternative ways of accomplishing the job are not possible. Changing the structure or work methods of the job can accommodate nonessential skills.

A Brief History: From Specialized to Enlarged Jobs

The term, job, as we know it today is largely an outgrowth of the Industrial Revolution's emphasis on efficiency. During this time, people like economist Adam Smith and consultant Frederick Taylor wrote enthusiastically of the positive correlation between specialized jobs (doing the same small thing over and over) and efficiency. Jobs and job descriptions, until quite recently, tended to follow their prescriptions and to be fairly detailed and specific.

By the mid-1900s other writers were reacting to what they viewed as the "dehumanizing" aspects of pigeonholing workers it highly repetitive and specialized jobs. Many proposed solutions like job enlargement, job rotation, and job enrichment. **Job enlargement** means assigning workers additional same-level activities, thus increasing the number of activities they perform. Thus, the worker who previously only bolted the seat to the legs might attach the back as well. Job rotation means systematically moving workers from one job to another.

Psychologist Frederick Herzberg argued that the best way to motivate workers is to build opportunities for challenge and achievement into their jobs via job enrichment. Job enrichment means redesigning jobs in a way that increases the opportunities for the workers to experience feelings of responsibility, achievement, growth, and recognition—for instance, by letting the worker plan and control his or her own work instead of having it controlled by outsiders. Employees here, said Herzberg, would do their jobs well because they wanted to, and quality and productivity would rise. That philosophy, in one form or another, is the theoretical basis for the team-based self-managing jobs in factories like Daimler-Chryslers today.

Why Managers are "Dejobbing" their Companies

Daimler's Alabama Mercedes factory actually presents in microcosm a picture of why companies are moving to broader, simpler descriptions of jobs—**to dejobbing,** in other words, companies are grappling with challenges like rapid product and technological change, global competition, deregulation, political instability, demographic changes, and a shift to a service economy. This has increased the need for firms to be responsive, flexible, and much more competitive. In turn, the organizational methods managers use to accomplish this have helped weaken the meaning of job as a well-defined and clearly defined delineated set of responsibilities. Requiring that employees limit themselves to narrow jobs runs counter to the need to have them willingly switch from task to task as jobs and team assignments change. Here is a sampling of organizational factors that have contributed to encouraging workers not to limit themselves to narrowly defined jobs.

Competency-based Job Analysis

⌘ What are Competencies? ⌘

Competency-based job analysis basically means writing job descriptions based on competencies rather than job duties. It emphasizes what the employee must be capable of doing, rather than on a list of the duties he or she must perform. We can simply define competencies as demonstrable characteristics of the person that enable performance. Job competencies are always observable and measurable behaviors comprising part of a job.

Unfortunately, once we get beyond those simple definitions, there's some confusion over what exactly "competencies" means. Different organizations define "competencies" in somewhat different ways. Some define them more broadly, and use "competencies" synonymously with the knowledge, or abilities a person needs to do the job. Others define competencies more narrowly, in terms of measurable behaviours. Here, you would identify the job's required competencies by simply completing the phrase, "In order to perform this job competently, the employee should be able to.......

We can say formally that competency-based job analysis means describing the job in terms of the measurable, observably behavioural competencies (knowledge, skills, and/or behaviours) that an employee doing that job must exhibit to do the job well, This contrasts with the traditional way of describing the job in terms of job duties and responsibilities. Traditional job analysis focuses on "what" is accomplished—on duties and responsibilities. Competency analysis focuses more on "how" the worker meets the job's objectives or actually accomplishes the work. Traditional job analysis is thus job focused. Competency-based analysis is worker focused—specially, what must he or she be competent to do?

Three Reasons to use Competency Analysis

There are three reasons to describe jobs in terms of competencies rather than duties.

1. First, as mentioned earlier, traditional job descriptions (with their lists of specific duties) may actually backfire if a high-performance work system is your goal. The whole thrust of these systems is to encourage employees to work in a self-motivated way, by organizing the work around teams, by encouraging team members to rotate freely among jobs (each with its own skill set), by pushing more responsibility of things like day-to-day supervision down to the workers, and by organizing work around projects or processes in which jobs may blend or overlap. Employees here must be enthusiastic about learning and moving among jobs. Giving someone a job description with a list of specific duties may simply breed a "that's-not-my-job" attitude, by pigeonholing workers too narrowly.

2.   Second, describing the job in terms of the skills, knowledge, and competencies the worker needs is more strategic. For example, Canon's strategic emphasis on miniaturization and precision manufacturing means it should encourage some employees to develop their expertise in these two strategically crucial areas.

3.   Third, measurable skills, knowledge, and competencies supports the employer performance management process. As at Canon, achieving a firm's strategic goals means that employees must exhibit certain skills and competencies. Performance management means basing your employees' training appraisals, and rewards on fostering and rewarding the skills and competencies are is a prerequisite. Describing the job in terms of skills and competencies facilitates this.

Examples of Competencies

In practice, managers often write paragraph-length competencies for jobs, and organize these into two or three clusters. For example, the job's required competencies might include general competencies (such as reading, writing, and mathematical reasoning), leadership competencies (such as leadership, strategic thinking, and teaching others), and technical competencies (which focus on the specific technical competencies required for specific types of jobs and/or occupations).

Comparing Traditional Versus Competency-based Job Analysis: In practice, if you pick up almost any job description today, you'll probably find that some of the job's listed duties and responsibilities are competence-based, while most are not. For example, consider the typical duties you might find in a marketing manager's job description. Which of the duties would complete the phrase, "In order to perform this job competently, the employee should be able to:......?"

Some familiar duties and responsibilities would not easily fit these requirements. For example, "work with writers and artist and overseas copywriting, design, layout, and production of professional materials" is not particularly measurable. How could you measure the extent to which the employee "work with writers and artists" or "overseas copywriting, design, and layout?" Put another way, if you had to devise a training programme for this job's incumbent, how would you determine whether you'd adequately trained the person to work with writers and artists? In fact, what sort of training would that duty and responsibility even imply? It's not clear at all.

On the other hand, some of the job's typical duties and responsibilities are more easily expressed as competencies. For example, we could easily complete the phrase, "to perform this job competently, the employee should be able to "conduct marketing surveys on current and new-product concepts; prepare marketing activity reports; and develop and executive marketing plans and programmes."

How to write Job Competencies-based Job Descriptions: Defining the job's competencies and writing them up involves a process that is similar in most respects to traditional job analysis. In other words, the manager will interview job incumbents and their supervisors, ask open-ended questions regarding job responsibilities and activities, and perhaps identify critical incidents that pinpoint success on the job.

PART-C

Performance Appraisal Formats Practised by Corporates

1

Tata Motors

2

Tata Consultancy Services

3

SRF Limited

4

State Bank of India (Annual Appraisal Process)

5

Steel Authority of India Limited

6

Rockwell Automation

7

National Thermal Power Corporation Ltd. (A Govt. of India Enterprise)

8

Moser Baer

9

MMTC Limited: New Delhi

10

HDFC Bank

11

Example of a Performance Appraisal Form at Colt

12

The PMS Handbook – IOCL

Tata Motors

Performance Appraisal Form

Org./division/dept:		Location/based at:	
Name:	position		Ref:
Year or period covered:	Time in present position:		Length of service
Appraisal date and time:	Appraisal venue:		Appraiser:

Part A: Appraisee to complete before the interview and return to the appraiser by (date)

A1

State your understanding of your main duties and responsibilities.

A2 Discussion Points

1. Has the past year been good/bad/satisfactory or otherwise for you, and why?

2.   What do you consider to be your most important achievements of the past year?

3.   What do you like and dislike about working for this organization?

4.   What elements of your job do you find most difficult?

5.   What elements of your job interest you the most, and least?

6.   What do you consider to be your most important aims and tasks in the next year?

7.   What action could be taken to improve your performance in your current position by you, and your boss?

8.   What kind of work or job would you like to be doing in one/two/five years time?

9. What sort of training/experiences would benefit you in the next year? Not just job-skills—also your natural strengths and personal passions you'd like to develop—you and your work can benefit from these.

A3

List the objectives you set out to achieve in the past 12 months (or the period covered by this appraisal) with the measures or standards agreed-against each comment on achievement or otherwise, with reasons where appropriate. Score the performance against each objective (1-3 = poor, 4-6 = satisfactory, 7-9 = good, 10 = excellent):

Objective	**measure/stand**	**score**	**comment**

A4

Score your own capability or knowledge in the following areas in terms of your current role requirements (1-3 = poor, 4-6 = satisfactory, 7-9 = good, 10 = excellent). If appropriate, bring evidence with you to the appraisal to support your assessment. The second section can be used if working towards new role requirements.

1. Commercial judgement	Others (for current or new role):
2. Product/technical knowledge	
3. Time management	18. Corporate responsibility and ethics
4. Planning, budgeting and forecasting	
5. Reporting and administration	
6. Communication skills	
7. Delegation skills	
8. IT/equipment/machinery skills	
9. Meeting deadlines/commitments	
10. Creativity	
11. Problem-solving and decision-making	
12. Team-working and developing others	
13. Energy, determination and work-rate	
14. Steadiness under pressure	
15. Leadership and integrity	
16. Adaptability, flexibility, and mobility	
17. Personal appearance and image	

A5

> In light of your current capabilities, your performance against past objectives, and your future personal growth and/or job aspirations, what activities and tasks would like to focus on during the next year. Again, also think of development and experiences outside of job skills-related to personal aims, fulfilment, passions.

Part B

To be completed during the appraisal by the appraiser-where appropriate and safe to do so, certain items can completed by the appraiser before the appraisal, and then discussed and validated in discussion with the apprise during the appraisal.

B1

> Describe the purpose of the appraisee's job. Discuss and compare with self-appraisal entry in A1. Clarify job purpose and priorities where necessary.

B2

> **Review the complete discussion points in A2, and note the points of and action.**

B3

> List the objectives that the appraise set out to achieve in the past 12 months (or the period covered by this appraisal—typically these objectives will have been carried forward from the previous appraisal record) with the measures or standards agreed-against each comment on achieve or otherwise, with reasons where appropriate. Score the performance against each objective (1-3 = poor, 4-6 = satisfactory, 7-9=good, 10 excellent). Compare with the self-appraisal in A3. Discuss and note points of significance, particularly training and development needs and wishes, which should be noted in B6.
>
> **Objective   Measure/Standard   Self-score/App'r score   Comment**

B4

Score the apprisee's capability or knowledge in the following areas in terms of their current (and if applicable, next) role requirements (1-3 = poor, 4-6 = satisfactory, 7-9 = good 10 = excellent). If appropriate provide evidence to support your assessment. The second section can be used for other criteria or if the appraise is working towards new role requirements. **Compare scores with the self-appraisal in B4. Discuss and note agreed points training/development needs and wishes (to B6).**

1. Commercial judgement	Others (for current or new role):
2. Product/technical knowledge	
3. Time management	18. Corporate responsibility and ethics
4. Planning, budgeting and forecasting	
5. Reporting and administration	
6. Communication skills	
7. Delegation skills	
8. IT/equipment/machinery skills	
9. Meeting deadlines/commitments	
10. Creativity	
11. Problem-solving and decision-making	
12. Team-working and developing others	
13. Energy, determination and work-rate	
14. Steadiness under pressure	
15. Leadership and integrity	
16. Adaptability, flexibility, and mobility	
17. Personal appearance and image	

B5

Discuss and agree the appraisee's career direction options and wishes, and readiness for promotion, and compare with and discuss the self-appraisal entry in A5. (Some people do not wish for promotion, but everyone is capable of, and generally benefits from, personal development—development and growth should be available to all, not just people seeking promotion). **Note the agreed development aim(s).**

B6

Discuss and agree to the skills, capabilities and experience required for competence in current role, and if appropriate, for readiness to progress to the next role or roles. **Refer to actions arising from B3 and the skill-set in B4, in order to accurately identify all development areas, whether for competence at current level or readiness to progress to next job level/type). Note the agreed development areas:**

B7

> Discuss and agree to the specific objectives that will enable the **appraisee to reach competence and to m**eet **required performance in current job**, if appropriate taking account of the coming year;s plans, budgets, targets etc., and that will enable the appriasee to move **towards, or achieve the desired personal growth or experience**. These objectives must adhere to the SMARTER rules-specific, measureable, agreed, realistic, time-bound, ethical, recorded.

B8

> Discuss and agree (as far as is possible, giving budgetary, availability and authorisation considerations) the training and development support to be given to help the appraise meet the agreed objectives above.

> Refer to the guidance notes. Personal development and support must be offered to all employees, irrespective of age, gender, race, disability, etc., and not just to those seeking promotion. Development is not restricted to job skills—it includes 'whole person'. Use your imagination. Job skills training isn't restricted to courses. Think about coaching, mentoring (by and of the appraise), secondment to another role, holiday job cover, shadowing, distance-learning, e-learning, books, videos, attending meetings and workshops, workbooks, manuals and guides, researching, giving presentations; anything relevant, helpful and agreed to help the person develop. Avoid committing to training expenditure before suitable approval or availability has been confirmed. Understand development options and procedures before conducting the appraisal. Develop the whole person.

B9

> Other issues (to be covered separately outside of this appriasl-continue on a separate sheet, if necessary):

Signed and dated by appraisee: and by appraiser:

Grade/recommendation/summary as applicable:

Distribution of copies/confidentially/accessibility details:

360 Degree feedback form template. This template allows a mixture of key skills comprising one, two, three, four, an up to six elements. The number of elements per key skill/capability varies of course, so, if necessary, adjust the size of the boxes in the first column accordingly to accommodate more or less elements. See 360 Degree appraisal notes for more explanation about the purpose of each column and heading, and the feedback scoring method.

Insert your own feedback form headings and instructions: appraise name, date, feedback respondent name, position (if applicable) plus local instructions and guidelines for completion, etc.

Key skill/capability area	Skill/capability element	Question number	Feedback question	Feedback score
		1		
		2		
		3		
		4		
		5		
		6		
		7		
		8		
		9		
		10		
		11		
		12		
		13		
		14		
		15		
		16		
		17		
		18		
		19		
		20		
		21		
		22		
		23		
		24		
		25		
		26		
		27		
		28		
		29		
		30		

Optional section: Additional feedback about the appriasee—please be constructive.

The process of designing the feedback document (essentially a questionnaire) is to build it from the role's key skill areas: break these down into elements, and measure each via carefully worded questions, which the respondents answer and thereby grade the performance, i.e., give feedback in respect of the person in question.

The question as to anonymity of respondents is up to you. A grown-up organization with grown-up people should be able to cope with, and derive more benefit from, operating the process transparently but you need to decide this. Some people are happier giving feedback anonymously. And some people are not able to deal particularly well with criticism from a named person. For more information and guidance about handling and explaining this particular aspect refer—it's a powerful and helpful concept to use alongside the 360 degree feedback/appraisal process.

2 Tata Consultancy Services

New Frontiers to Performance Appraisal

In recent years, the system of performance appraisal is becoming more and more transparent wherein the employee, who is being appraised, is involved in the process. The objectives or targets are set with mutual understanding between the appraise and his immediate superior. The feedback regarding his performance is given to the apprise with areas of improvement by disclosing his strengths and weakness and the opportunities available. We will take you into details of these new frontiers to Performance Appraisal viz:

1. Management by Objectives (MBO)

2. Balanced Scorecard

3. 360 Degree Feedback

Management by Objectives

1. Management by Objectives is basically a process whereby the superior and the subordinate managers of an enterprise jointly identify its common goals, define each individual's major areas of responsibility in terms of the results expected of him and use these measures as guides for operating the unit and assessing the contribution of each of its members. Management by Objectives is primarily to change the behaviour and attitude towards getting an activity or assignment completed in a manner that it is beneficial for the organization. Management by objectives is a result-oriented process, wherein emphasis is on results and goals rather than a prescribed method. A number of companies have had significant success in broadening individual responsibility and involvement in work planning at the lowest organizational levels.

2. The concept rests on a philosophy of management that emphasises integration between external control (by managers) and self-control (by subordinates). It can apply to any manager or individual no matter what level or function, and to any organization, regardless of size.

3. Management by Objectives is a *five-sutra* process having following basic steps:

   ❖ Set Organizational Goals

   ❖ Joint Goal-setting

   ❖ Performance Reviews

   ❖ Set Check Posts

   ❖ Feedback

4. Throughout the time period what is to be accomplished by the entire organization should be compared with what is being accomplished; necessary adjustments should be made and inappropriate goals discarded. At the end of the time period, a final mutual review of objectives and performance takes place. It there are discrepancies between the two, efforts are initiated to determine what steps can be taken to overcome these problems. This sets the stage for the determination of objectives for the next period.

5. **Benefits of MBO Programme**

   (a) Helps and increases employee motivation.

   (b) Managers are more likely to compete within themselves than with other mangers.

   (c) Results in a "means-ends" chain.

   (d) Reduces role conflict and ambiguity.

   (e) Provides more objective appraisal criteria.

   (f) Forces and aids in planning.

   (g) Identifies problems better and early.

   (h) Identifies performance deficiencies.

   (i) Helps the individual manager to develop personal leadership, especially the skills of listening, planning, counselling, motivating and evaluating.

360 Degree Feedback

With the movement in the eighties to find new strengths and productivity through employee empowerment came the idea of performance appraisals from subordinates, their superiors, their peers and themselves – "360 Degree Feedback".

1. The 360 Degree Feedback process is called multisource assessment, taps the collective wisdom of those who work most closely with the employee, superiors, colleagues (peers), direct reports and possibly internal and often external customers. The collective intelligence these people provide on critical competencies or specific behaviours and skills gives the employee a clear understanding of personal strengths and areas ripe for development. Employees also view this performance information from multiple perspectives as fair, accurate, credible, and motivating. Employees are often more strongly motivated to change their work behaviours to attain the esteem of their co-workers than to win the respect of their supervisor alone.

2. As the 360 Degree Feedback process better serves the needs of employees, it serves the changing needs of their organizations too. Organizations are reducing hierarchy by removing layers of management and putting more emphasis on empowerment, teamwork, continuous learning, individual development, and self-responsibility, teamwork, continuous learning, individual development, and self-responsibility. The 360 degree Feedback Model aligns with these organizational goals to create opportunities for personal and career development and for aligning individual performance expectations with corporate values.

3. *Diagram showing the key stakeholders in a 360 Degree Feedback Process*

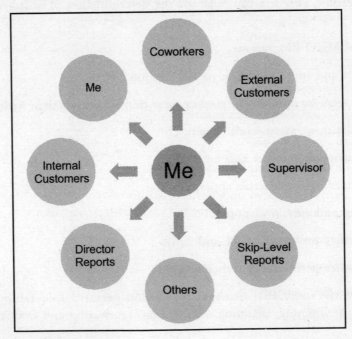

4. *Benefits to Key Stakeholders*

   The 360 Degree Feedback process offers extensive and diverse benefits to key stake holders in the organization—and the organization too:

   (a) Customers

   (b) Employees

(c)   Team members

(d)   Supervisors

(e)   Leaders and Managers

(f)   Organizations

5.   *Why are organizations adopting these systems?*

Structure and cultural factors and employee's relations have motivated organizations to begin experimenting with 360 Degree Feedback systems. For example, as organizations remove layers of management, flatten their structure, and begin using self-directed teams, the only practical option for performance feedback is for multiple sources. As organizations change their culture to align with their vision and values, 360 Degree Feedback becomes an ideal choice to communicate the new competencies required by the new values.

6.   *Structural changes*

Organizational structures have changed substantially since the mid-1980s. The 360 Degree Feedback process offers support for these structural changes, such as growth in supervisor's span of control, the increased use of technical or knowledge workers, and introduction of matrix and project management organization design, and the move to working in teams.

(a)   Increased span of control

(b)   Knowledge workers

(c)   Matrix and Project Management

(d)   Team

7.   *Change in Organizational Culture*

Revolutionary changes in organization cultures have made traditional single sources assessments illogical and impractical. Among these changes are:

(a)   Participative Leadership

(b)   Empowerment

(c)   Customer Services

(d)   Quality Focus

(e)   Reengineering

(f)   Competency-based Reward

(g)   Team-based Rewards

(h)   End of Entitlements

8. *Employee Relations*

No other information has more impact on an employee's career than information on his or her performance. Hence, the accuracy, fairness and usefulness of performance measures are critical factors to employees.

   (a) Career Development

   (b) Fair Reward Decisions

   (c) Accurate Performance Measures

   (d) Valid Performance Measures

   (e) Non-performance

   (f) Diversity Management

   (g) Legal Protection

9. *Pitfalls of 360 Degree Feedback*

   (a) 360 Degree feedback has produces some real successes; but when not done artfully, including internal preparation, it can rebound. Colleagues and subordinates are good judges of behaviour and managerial style but are not best judges of a manager's job performance. Hence, the ratings should be used with caution in decisions for pay and promotions.

   (b) In practice, peers and subordinates tend to give negative feedback about a manager due to bias or for setting scores. Such feedback may get undue importance when only selected few peers and subordinates appraise a manager.

   (c) Also, at times, the organizational culture is unable to accept the system.

10. *Options for implementation*

There are three common ways of getting 360 Degree feedback each more comprehensive and powerful in promoting change, both organizational and personal:

   (a) Using an outside consultants, minimizing any personal friction within the organization

   (b) Launching a comprehensive program in-house to get feedback on all key people, top to bottom;

   (c) Creating a comprehensive program designed to uncover not just personal flaws but systematic and organisational ones, too.

11. *The following issues need to be considered before implementation of 360 Degree feedback:*

Questions about implementing 360 degree feedback are easy to ask but not so to answer. Often times, management assumes the answers but does not openly discuss them with the result being much chaos and confusion down the road.

Among these some of these questions are:

(a) How ready is your organization to handle 360 degree feedback?

(b) Who needs to agree?

(c) Who will be involved? Which employees are to be the focus of the 360 degree?

(d) Is this voluntary or mandatory?

(e) What methods and measurements will be used?

(f) To what extent will the date be collected anonymously/or confidentially?

(g) Who what extent will the data be collected anonymously and/or confidentially?

(h) What will be done with alleged violations of laws, ethics or policies?

(i) What information will be public?

(j) What consequences will there be? What logistics and support will be necessary to make this successful?

(k) What systems changes will accompany this organizational change?

Balanced Score Card

1. Balanced Score Card (BSC) is a set of measures derived from an organization's vision and strategy. It is a concept that helps translate strategy into action. It requires an organization to balance its goals across multiple perspectives to reduce the chance that one goals will dominate others to the detriment of the organization. It leads to a realistic compromise that addresses short-term goals and longer-term staying power.

2. The balanced scorecard was developed by Robert S. Kaplan and David P. Norton in early 1990s. The article "The Balanced Scorecard Measures that Drive Performance" in the *Harvard Business Review* (year 1992) described balanced scorecard as a methodology used for measuring success and setting goals from financial and operational viewpoints. With those measures, leaders can manage their strategic vision and adjust it for change.

3. BSC links performance measures by looking at a business's strategic vision from four different perspectives: financial, customer, internal business processes, and innovation and learning. These four perspectives of the Scorecard provide a balance between desired outcomes and drives for those outcomes and between objective and subjective performance measures. BSC is prescriptive about a balanced range of measures and about how one perspective defines the drivers for the next.

⌘ Financial Perspective

The financial perspective provides a view of how the senior executives, the board of directors and the shareholders see the company. Typical metrics in this perspective might be earning per share, revenue growth and profit maximization. In the BSC, **financial measures** play a dual role: they **define the financial performance expected from the strategy and they serve as the ultimate targets for the objectives and measures of all the other scorecard perspectives.** The financial measures chosen based on the business life cycle and also the strategic theme chosen for the financial perspective. In addition to increasing returns, most organizations are concerned with the risk of these returns. Therefore, when it is strategically important, these organizations will want to incorporate explicit risk management objectives into their financial perspective.

As a conclusion, eventually all objectives and measures in the other scorecard perspective should be linked to linked to achieving one or more objectives in the financial perspective.

Customer Perspective

The customer perspective provided a view of how the customers see the company. Kaplan and Norton contend that, "to put the balanced scorecard to work, companies should articulate goals for time, quality, and performance and service and then translate these goals into specific measures." Overall, **this is a measures of how the company provides value to the customer.** Changes made to a business process output that lowers the customer's cost or allows the customer to achieve his or her objective, have value for the customer. For example, it's not enough to simply bring down the cost of an item. The delivery time and manner in which the customer is dealt during times of sales and support are important as well. It is a measures of that value that should be captured by the metrics (e.g. market share, customer satisfaction, customer loyalty, customer acquisition) representing this perspective.

Internal Business Process Perspective

The internal business process perspective provides a view of what the company must excel at to be competitive. Kaplan and Norton recommend that, "companies also attempt to identify and measures their company's core competencies, the critical technologies needed to ensure continued market leadership."

Innovation and Learning Perspective

Kaplan and Norton underscore the importance of innovation and learning in their statement that, "a company's ability to innovate, improve, and learn ties directly to the company's value." While the financial perspective deals with the projected value of the company, **the innovation and learning perspective sets measures that help the company compete in a changing business environment.** This is of principal interest to the CEO and the architects of the long-range business plan. Their focus for this innovation is in the formation of new or the improvement of existing products and processes. **This perspective looks at how effectively the organization can redesign and implement new business proves, introduce and exploit new technology and adapt to changing conditions in general.** Thus, the measures in this perspective are truly the enablers of the other three perspectives. **These measures are like the roots of a tree that will ultimately lead through the trunk of internal process to the branches of customer results and finally to the leaves of financial returns.**

With the financial, customer and internal perspectives, managers are able to identify the gaps between existing organizational resources and the ones required to be successful. The only way to close those gaps is for the organization to judicially invest in employees and information technology and to design the most appropriate organizational structure that could support their strategy. The given below diagram shows the Balance Score Card.

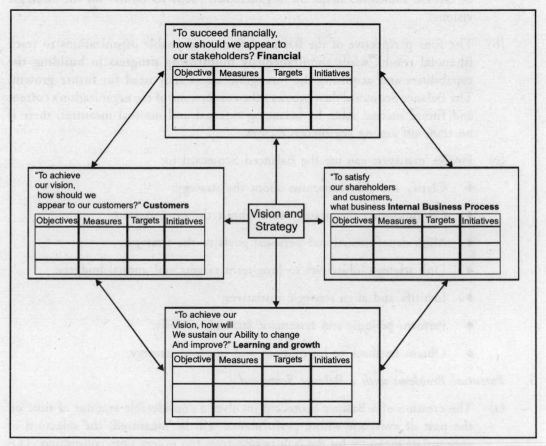

"Exhibit from "using the Balanced Scorecard as a Strategic Management System" by Robert S Kaplan and David P Norton. January-February 1996, p.76. Copyright©by the Harvard Business School Publishing Corporation; all rights reserve"

4. *The Steps of implementation are–Identifying and defining Key Performance Indicators from the multiple perspectives:*

First the multiple perspectives are to be identified, which can be as: Financial Measures, Customer Measures, Internal Process and People (Learning & Growth). After this, the main task is to identify the Key Performance Indicators (KPI) in each of these multiple perspective.

❧   Identifying Key Action Areas

❧   Implementation of Key Action Areas

❧   Monitoring Key Action Areas

5. *The advantages of the Balanced Scorecard:*

(a) First, the measures incorporated in the Balanced Scorecard are grounded in the organization's strategic objectives and competitive demands. Therefore, this set of critical indicators helps the organization focus its efforts on the strategic vision.

(b) The four perspective of the Balanced Scorecard enable organizations to track financial results while simultaneously monitoring progress in building the capabilities and acquiring the intangible assets they need for future growth. The Balance Scorecard then becomes the cornerstone of the organization's current and future success. Also, by balancing external and internal measures, there is no trade-off among key success factors.

(c) Finally, managers can use the Balanced Scorecard to:

♦   Clarify and gain consensus about the strategy;

♦   Communicate the strategy throughout the organization;

♦   Align departmental and personal goals to the strategy;

♦   Link strategic objectives to long-term targets and annual budgets;

♦   Identify and align strategic initiatives;

♦   Perform periodic and systematic strategic reviews;

♦   Obtain feedback to learn about and improve strategy.

6. *Potential Problems with a Balance Scorecard:*

(a) The creation of a Balance Scorecard involves a considerable amount of time on the part of everyone whose performance will be measured; the selection of appropriate measures for the four perspectives too is very time consuming. This is simply due to the fact that there are a large number of potential goals and targets and even more ways to measure them. People are likely to disagree about which objectives to measure and how to measure those objectives, and it will take time before consensus is achieved.

(b) The time factor involved in designing a Balanced Scorecard can be considerable since it involves a lot of people in the organization. There commitment is important not only in building the Balanced Scorecard but especially in implementing and using it. Although a Balanced Scorecard may be well-designed, lack of participation and commitment on the part of staff will make the scorecard useless.

(c) Finally, there is always a chance that too many measures will be selected. This is a problem because it is very difficult to track a large number of measures. Furthermore, some of the measures selected may be objective, such as employee turnover rates, and other measures may be subjective measures, such as employee morale or quality time spent with customers. The subjective measures, such as employee turnover rates, and other measures may be objective, such as employee morale or quality time spent with customers. The subjective measures, by definition, involve somebody's judgement and, therefore, are more prone to error. Consequently, there is a question whether subjective measures should be used and if so, how can they be made more reliable.

SRF Limited

Performance Management System Officers[7] Assessment Form (Review Period: April 2003 to March 2004)

Name				Reports to		Process		Unit	
Grade		w.e.f.		Total Experience (y/m)		Experience in SRF (y/m)		Age	
Qualifications :						Designation			
Last 2 promotions	1	Year	2	Year					

Instructions for filling up the Form

The form is divided into 2 parts as given below.

Part A

Part I   : **Performance Review:** To be filled by the Appraisee and comments by Appraiser. Appraisees/Appraisers are expected to have set goals/Control Points in the following category:

Breakthrough Management (B) / Daily Management (D)/ Growth (G) / Self Development (SD)/ Subordinate Development (SD)/Others (0). For CB, Improvement (I)/ Operational (O) should be there instead of BM or DM.

Weightage is to be given to key control points/ key goals only. Appraiser can select a few key control points/key goals out of all the control points/goals set at the beginning of the year.

Part II : **Appraisee's Voice:** Appraisee to state factors which hindered his/her performance or would improve his/her performance.

Part III : **Potential Assessment:** Appraiser to assess the competencies displayed by the Appraisee in the current role. With reference to the current role, gaps if any have to be covered through coaching/counselling and training.

Part IV : **Feedback:** Appraiser to record outcomes of feedback session in the areas of Performance Vs Goals, Strengths, Areas for Improvement, Alignment with SRF Values, Appraisee's voice related issues in part II, Any other provided by Appraisee to Appraiser during the feedback session.

Part B (Circulated Separately)

This form has to be filled up by reviewer/CEO/ Corporate Head based on the inputs from the Appraiser. The recommendation for Rewards, Promotions, CVA/HVA/KKR has to be filled up in this form. Recommendation for job rotation/re-deployment also needs to be filled in this form.

Guidelines on Rating Performance and Potential Assessment

Scale of 1 - 10 has been provided for performance as well as potential assessment. For performance score between 1- i 3 is taken as below expectations, between ^3 - ^7 is taken as meets expectation and ^7 is taken as exceeds expectations. Score of >7 can be given only if Officer has achieved more than 100% on his goals. The Appraisee has to do the self-scoring in the column provided to him/her in **Part I** and the appraiser would fill up the weightage of that control point/goal to overall goals and also fill up the score for performance. The Appraiser can add any control points/goals missed out by the Appraisee and rate the Appraisee on those control points/goals. The Appraiser should also fill up the final weighted score.

Potential assessment is being done to assess whether the person can move to the next level in the Organization. In case of potential assessment, the relative weightage of leadership, managerial and functional competencies would depend on the level of the person as given below:

Competencies	Senior Management VII to IXA	Middle Management III to VI	Junior Management I to II
	Weightage	Weightage	Weightage
Leadership	60%	40%	10%
Managerial	30%	30%	60%
Operational	10%	30%	30%

Note: The form is basically designed for measuring generic competencies (Generalists), in case an officer in Grade VI and above scores high on functional competency and low on leadership and managerial, a separate sheet may be attached if he is a specialist.

Filling of the Form

Forms may be filled either by hand or electronically.

In case the form is filled electronically, Appraisee to rename the file including his initials while forwarding the form to the Appraiser. Appraiser may also fill the form electronically and take a printout before sending it to HR Deptt...Use **Font 8** while filling the form on computer.

Time Table for Implementation

Please ensure timeliness of the process as per the responsibilities and dates given below:

Routing of the Appraisal Form

Steps	ACTIONS	Responsibility	Target Date	Actual Date	Signature*
Step 1	Kick off letter by Head HR	Corp. HR	14/03/03		
Step 2	Communication to all Leadership Team and Officers by Business HR	Business HR	17/03/03		
Step 3	Form sent to all officers	Business HR	17/03/03		
Step 4	Form submitted by Appraisee to Appraiser	Appraisee	21/3/03		
Step 5	Form filled up by Appraiser/reviewer (include Recommendation form)	Appraiser	24/03/03		
Step 6	PMS FEEDBACK TO APPRAISEE	Appraiser	25/03/03 to 1/04/03		
Step 7	Form submitted back to Business HR for compilation	Appraiser	2/04/02		
Step 8	Compilation by Business HR	Business HR	3/04/03		
Step 9	Subjected to Moderation Panel	Business HR	4/04/03, 5/04/03		
Step 10	Recommendations by Business Head	Business CEOs/ COOs	9/04/03		
Step 11	Form Given by Business HR to Corp. HR	Business HR	11/4/02		
Step 12	Compilation by Corp HR	Corp. HR	13/04/03 & 14/04/03		
Step 13	Review and Approval of recommendations by CVILL	Corp. HR	15/04/03 to 17/04/03		
Step 14	Sharing of outcome	Corp. HR	21/04/03		

Part A

Part - I : Performance Review

S. No.	Type/ Category	Description[1]	Weightage	Control Point/Goals Set[3]			Self Assessment by the Appraisee			Appraiser's Comments	Rating by Appraiser [4]
				Description	From	to	Actual	Comments	Rating[5]		

Qualitative comments; If any by the Reviewer

Breakthrough Management (B)/Daily Management (D)/Growth (G)/Self Development (SD)/Subordinate Development (SoD)/Others (O). For CB, Improvement (I)/Operational (O) should be there instead of BM or DM. $_3$ Weightage is to be given to key control points/key goals only.

Appraiser to add the goals/control points of the Appraisee not identified by Appraisee.

Scale of I - 10 has been provided for performance as well as potential assessment. Score between 1- 4 3 is taken as below expectations, between ^3 - i7 is taken as meets expectation and i7 is taken, as exceeds expectations. Score of >7 can be given only if Officer has achieved more than 100% on his goals.

Part II : Appraisee's Voice

1.	My significant contributions/ achievements and why it was significant.	
2.	My skills/knowledge/talents being utilized in my current job.	
3.	My skills/knowledge/talents not being utilized well in my current job.	
4.	Areas I would like to be trained or need coaching/guidance from Boss.	
5.	Area/s within or outside my current role that I am good at and want to improve further.	
6.	Where I want to be job rotated. By when.	
7.	Any grievances in my current job.	
8.	Factors which aided my performance.	
9.	Factors which hindered my performance	
10.	Any transfer during the year or change of Boss.	

Part III: Potential Assessment (To be filled by Appraiser)

S.No	COMPETENCY [10] (Strike out the competency not applicable. Give reason)	Score 1 to 10	Give illustration in case score is >. 7 or <. 3.
OPERATIONAL COMPETENCY			
1.	Functional expertise		
2.	Communication skills		
3.	Innovation		
4.	Problem solving & analysis		
5.	Learning orientation		
TOTAL SCORE		**Out of**	Avg. out of 10 j
MANAGERIAL COMPETENCY			
6.	Ability to work with uncertainty		
7.	Result orientation		
8.	Team playing		
9.	Emotional stability		
10.	Process orientation		
TOTAL SCORE		**Out** of |	Avg. out of 10 i
LEADERSHIP COMPETENCY			
11.	Leadership		
12.	Coaching		
13.	Networking		
14.	Environmental awareness		
15.	Entrepreneurship		
TOTAL SCORE		Out of J	**Avg. out** of 10lf

Apply weightage as per the level and work out score as given below:

Level[7]	Leadership			Managerial			Operational		
	Wt. %	Score (out of 10)	1 Weighted Score (L)[8]	Wt. %	Score (out of 10)	Weighted Score (M)	Wt. %	Score (out of 10)	[Weighted Score (O)
Total Score (L+M+O)=									

Please see Page 1 for Weightage. The product of the values in the previous two columns. Refer Annexure 2 for some self-help.

Part IV: Development Plan (to be filled in jointly by the appraiser and the appraisee)

1. *Experience Profile*

S. No.	Experience	Job Position	Nature of responsibility	Time period
a.	Outside SRF			
b.	Within SRF			

2. *PMS Data*

S. No.	Score	00-01	01-02	02-03
a.	Personal Assessment			
b.	Potential Assessment			

3. *Training Needs (for the current role)*

S.No.	Major skills and knowledge requirements (mention only 2-3)	Actions required	Time Frame
a.			
b.			
c.			

4. *Actions Required*

   Potential next career move* (Need not be an upward move and can be a lateral move also. If no move possible, mention 'None').

   a. Can he move to the next level? If yes, time period.

   b. What is the position—that he can occupy on being promoted?

   c. Do you see him today as reaching top management (CEO of a business, Corporate functional head)?

   d. In case, he has no promotion potential, how would you like to enrich his experience (additional responsibilities, lateral transfer, involvement in project/task force work).

5. *Training Needs (to move to next upward career milestone)*

S. No.	Major skills and knowledge requirements (mention only 2-3)	Actions required	Time-frame
a.			
b.			
c.			

6. *Potential successors (If no one has been identified, please mention 'None')*

S. No.	Name «	Current Designation	Unit	Readiness
a.				Within years
b.				Within years

Remarks:		
(Name of Appraiser, Signature & Date):	(Name of Reviewer, Signature & Date):	Signature of Corporate/CEO

Part V: Feedback

Checklist: Record of the feedback	
Performance Vs Goals	
Strength Areas	
Improvement areas	
Alignment with SRF Values	
Appraisee voice related issues in part II	
Any other;	
(Name of Appraisee, Signature & Date)	(Name of Appraiser, Signature & Date)

Annexure 1
Training Identification Ready Reckoner

This is not an exhaustive list. This is being provided only to enable your thinking on these lines to identify the appropriate training needs to improve performance of potential.

Knowledge related	Skills related
Commerce / Finance management related	Analytical / PSP Skills
Activity based costing	Computer skills
Basics of finance	Conceptual skills
Customs & Excise laws	Creativity and Innovation
EXIM policies	Feedback/counselling skills
Logistics & Supply, chain management	Interpersonal skills
Working capital management	Leadership skills
	Listening / Communication skills
Human Resource management related	Motivation skills
360 Degree appraisals	Negotiation skills
Factory & Labour Laws	Planning Skills
Competence mapping and assessment	Presentation skills
Compensation management	Teambuilding skills
Manpower Planning	
IT related	
MS Office (Word, Excel, PPT)	
Oracle financial	
E-commerce	**Attitude related**
Knowledge management	Assertiveness
Security systems	Achievement orientation
Messaging system	Attitude to learn
Marketing management related	Openness
Customer Relationship Management	Perseverance
Global marketing strategy	Positive / 'Can do' attitude
Sales management	Process / system orientation
	Quality orientation
Production/operations related	Respect for people / Empathy
Energy conservation in industry	Self initiative
Environmental laws	Task orientation
Industrial flow measurements	Thoroughness / Eye for details
Industrial safety management	
Maintenance management	
Others	

Contd...

Project management	**TOM / Quality related**
Strategic management	7 QC tools
Time management	Control point
	PDCA
	PSP technique
	QC circle
	Root cause analysis
	Six sigma
	TPM
	TPS

Competencies: Defined in five levels

Competency	Definition	Scale				
		1	**2**	**3**	**4**	**5**
Functional Expertise	Extent to which an individual possesses and applies job-related knowledge in the completion of work tasks and activities. Includes knowledge gained through formal and informal education or training.	Limited knowledge Has very limited understanding of body of knowledge required for the job Possesses limited formal or informal training with no experience.	Basic knowledge Has basic understanding of body of knowledge areas required for job Applies appropriate technical knowledge to some job related tasks Operates at the apprentice level, performs work under guidance.	Proficient knowledge Has proficient knowledge and abilities required for job Independently applies skills in completing job tasks Stays current on new information which applies to job Demonstrates a depth of knowledge in a specific area.	Advanced expertise Has advanced expertise in required job-related knowledge Generates novel or unique ideas in performing job related activities Considered organization-wide subject matter expert Improves systems or procedures which enhance own and others' ability to do work.	Expert Develops systems which have a major impact on organization Considered industry-wide subject matter expert Creates innovative solutions which enhance overall organizational performance Maintains in-depth knowledge of multiple functional areas.
Communication Skills	Ability to express one's thoughts and feelings with clarity and understand unspoken or partly expressed thoughts of others.	*Difficulty communicating ideas* Sends confusing and ambiguous messages Speaks disregarding others' point of view Expresses ideas which are not fully thought out.	*Appropriately communicates most ideas* Finds it difficult to drive home his point Tells more than asks. Tends to over-talk Is unsure and looks for support.	*Effectively communicates thoughts, ideas and facts* Considers audience, subject matter etc, when communicating	*Fluently communicates ideas* Is expressive and fluent Listens willingly without interrupting Presents ideas in a logical and organized manner.	*Is a dynamic speaker* Is clear, concise and unambiguous in his expression Is an active and responsive listener, respects others' view point Is confident and persuasive in his presentation.
Innovation	Ability to look at situations from multiple perspectives. Tendency or ability to do something or create something new. Creates solutions to problems using novel methods and processes.	*Lacks imagination and creativity* Cannot look at situations in different ways Does not express or indicate active imagination.	*Ideas often incomplete* Comes up with simple alternative solutions Solutions limited in scope, incomplete.	*Sees different perspective* Recognizes points for improvement and uses imagination to solve problems Able to look at situations from different perspectives.	*Creates innovative products* Experiments with new ideas, methodologies, and procedures Creates innovative products and solutions.	*Generates new insights* Generates new insights into procedures and methods Develops novel programs, processes and designs Implements ground breaking, far reaching, cutting edge plans and procedures.
Leadership		Does not create solutions	Creates simple solutions	Creates more than one solution	Identifies root cause of complex problems	Identifies relationship between complex problems

Contd...

Problem Solving & Analysis	Identification of various types of problems along with creating of solutions. Requires identification and analysis of problems, evaluation of alternatives and creation of solution	Solutions made without analyzing the problem Identifies obvious problems Doesn't create solutions/relies on others for solutions	Can identify simple solutions and create simple solutions May search 1 and collect data for reference	Identifies complex problems and creates more than one solution Performs simple analysis and evaluation to determine course of action Solutions grounded in factual information	Identifies root cause of complex problems & creates multiple solutions Uses information from more than one source for analysis and evaluation Generates alternative solutions in response to failure	Uses extensive information / research for analysis and evaluation Creates solutions which reduces chaos Evaluates alternative solutions prior to implementation
Learning Orientation	Desire and effort to acquire new knowledge and skills for work. Concern for the acquisition of new job knowledge	*Does not acquire new knowledge or skills*	*Reluctantly acquires new knowledge and skills*	*Acquires new knowledge and skills*	*Anticipates and takes initiative to learn new skills*	*Seeks knowledge from multiple sources*
		Makes no effort towards learning	Resistant to applying newly learned knowledge and skills	Acquires new knowledge and skills when necessary for job Stays current on job related information	Takes initiative, seeks opportunities to learn new skills Implements new knowledge successfully Seeks feedback concerning performance to make improvements	Creates learning environment Seeks knowledge from multiple sources Seamlessly adapts and applies new knowledge and skills in all areas of the job
Focus on suits/ Result orientation	Ability to Focus efforts on meeting a goal, mission or objective,	*Lacks it*	*Acts on opportunities to meet goals*	*Establishes and works toward ambitious and challenging job*	*Demonstrates persistence in overcoming obstacles to meet objectives.*	*Develops and implements strategies to meet objectives*
		Makes excuses and finds reasons why something cannot be done. Works individually, operates only in 'comfort zone'; needs continuous motivation	Identifies patterns or trends based on experience and current approaches. Thinks laterally to identify solutions for old problems	Exhibits high levels of energy and proactively to complete tasks and take on new ones. Is committed to perform the task to the highest possible standard	Takes calculated risks, makes cost-benefit analysis. Optimizes resource allocation and utilization. Establishes measures and criteria to monitor progress	Drives strategy through transformation Keeps track of technological, operational and financial resources needed to accomplish tasks
Team Building Team Orientation	Ability to effectively work and complete assignments in-group settings. Works cooperatively with others to achieve common goals.	*Withdrawn*	*Little involvement in group process*	*Works cooperatively with others*	*Encourages team members*	*Manage dynamics*
		Prioritizes own goals over those of the team Takes a long time to integrate into a team. Keeps information to self, tries to take personal credit for team's success.	Clarifies individual role and responsibilities Handles personal and interpersonal issues effectively. Values input from all his colleagues; shares credit for success.	Taps the strengths of individuals; is able to build and maintain team spirit. Treats others fairly and has a non-blaming attitude; builds respect for differences in opinion.	Addresses issues that are disrupting team functioning, harmony and cooperation. Acts to increase cohesion among different team roles; introduces creative team building activities.	Helps to resolve conflicts between/among team members. Drives consensus decisions in highly complex situations.

Contd...

Process improvement	Ability effectively manage continually to plan, and improve upon current processes, utilizing technological resources to the fullest extent possible, to achieve maximum utilization, efficiency and productivity	Lacks the ability Is comfortable working in already defined ways and processes. Lacks planning and does not encourage new ideas. Hesitant in trying new approach of doing things.	Open to new ideas when someone suggests the same Is open to change when presented with a new perspective, and is able to pull together ideas, issues and observations. Is prepared to 'try out' different solutions or take a different approach, when someone suggests the same.	Has innovative ideas /-thinks to identify new solutions Looks beyond the facts and thinks 'outside the box' or beyond traditional boundaries in order to suggest solutions or ways to improve.	Uses change as an opportunity Creates new concepts or modeling techniques that are not obvious to others. Adapts own thinking to meet changes or unexpected external constraints, and does things that are unique, leading - edge and new to the system.	Fosters environment Continuous improvement an of Encourages others to continually challenge the status quo. Generates and maintains a creative and change-oriented environment among or with staff and colleagues which leads to new and effective ideas that help to change the System.
Leadership	Ability to effectively manage and guide group efforts. Includes providing appropriate level of feedback concerning group progress	*Lacks the ability*	*Provides minimal instruction and feedback*	*Effectively sets goal and direction*	*Provides guidance*	*Challenges others to succeed*
		Leadership style results in counterproductive behavior among staff Plays favorites in assigning tasks Criticizes others publicly Tends to focus on failures or negative behaviors	Often sets unrealistic goals and agendas Direct reports often fail to meet goals or objectives	Provides constructive criticism Provides explanations to minimize confusion Seeks opportunities to motivate others	Provides guidance to groups, team members, or other employees Establishes mentoring relationships Uses multiple leadership styles depending on situation	Inspires others to exceed expectations Maintains organizational objectives in guiding others Creates positive morale among all employees
Coaching / Subordinate development	Overall concern for the developmental level of an individual or group. Takes steps to explain and provide guidance	No concern for the development of others Refuses or shows little interest in helping others with new tasks or procedures Belittles others mistakes	Misses opportunities to develop others Tells others how to perform tasks with little explanation Provides minimal feedback to supplement instruction Misses opportunities to reinforce good behavior in others	Concerned for the development of others Identifies need for training and coaching Provides instruction to promote others' development Offers constructive feedback about errors	Coaches others to promote knowledge Explains rationale, demonstrates appropriate behaviors Provides comprehensive feedback to supplement instruction Modifies coaching style depending on situation/ audience	Develops others using personal mentoring Creates learning environment Challenges others to seek opportunities to learn Uses assessment to identify short and long term development needs
Emotional Stability	Is aware of one's own emotions as well as that of others and acts with a sense of restraint, discipline, foresight and empathy.	Gets easily provoked and loses temper. Has an impolite and disrespectful behaviour. Is self-indulgent	Displays emotionally charged behaviour. Is insensitive to the feeling of others and at times arrogant Shows minimal concern for others.		Resists impulse to react immediately. Is somewhat sensitive to other's feelings and adjusts behaviour of self accordingly Resolves issues with mutual respect.	Stays calm and acts with restraint in all situations. Calms others in situation of stress and makes them feel comfortable Is empathetic in resolving issues.

Contd...

Ability to work in ambiguity	Ability to take initiative in unstructured situations. Ability to work in a situation without specific procedures. Ability to deliver at the end of the time line without going through routinized activities.	Can only work in a routinized setup with continuous supervision	Capable of working with or without a routinized set up but with supervision and guidance	Capable of delivering without a routinized set up but needs initial guidance to start	Capable of functioning in any project without routinized framework and supervision but quality needs to be checked on	Adapts to any environment and delivers high quality deliverables with stand-alone capabilities
		• Requires concrete framework to work with • Requires constant supervision • Contributes mostly in routine work with very little initiative on his own • Micro-goals have to be laid out for him	• Supervison is still required • Thinks on his own but cannot make concrete contributions without help from supervisor • Supervisor needs to give thrusts to him for the required initiatives • Short term goals have to laid down for him	• Capable of taking initiative on his own and making a project layout to start with • Supervisor needs to channelize his efforts to extract the desired output • Medium term goals have to be laid down for him	• When given a project, he can deliver within the given time line • Needs little or no supervision • Needs very little direction in what he is supposed to do • Quality checks need to be done periodically to bring him on track • Works with long term goals	• Contributes directly to an organizational goal • Just needs to be given the project to work on • Delivers high quality work without supervision or guidance • Works best in flexible and complex environments

State Bank of India (Annual Appraisal Process)

Introduction

Under the present system, Annual Appraisal Reports are written on all officers of the Bank. These Annual Appraisal Reports are to be compiled as on 31st March every year and the completed reports are placed in the service file of each officer.

Stated Objective of Performance Appraisal at SBI

"Performance appraisal should be used as a tool for human resources development. Reporting Authority should realise that the objective is to develop an officer so that he/she realises his/her true potential. It is not means to be a fault-finding process but a development one. The various columns in the format should be filled with due care and attention and after devoting adequate time. The Reporting Authority and the Reviewing Authority should not shy away from reporting shortcomings in performance, attitudes or overall personality of the officer reported upon".

Process of Performance Planning and Review at SBI

The Reporting Authority is expected to in the beginning of the year set quantitative/ physical/financial targets in consultation with each of the officers with respect to whom he is required to report.

In the case of those officers who have responsibility for achieving the budgeted growth of business, the settled budget for the year will be the target. As regards other officers, quantification of the responsibility in terms of identified Key Responsibility Areas (KRAs) may be done by the Appraiser in consultation with the Appraisee. Even otherwise, key responsibilities of every functionary are well known to appraisee as well as Appraiser. The targets/goals should be set at the commencement of the year.

In the case of officer taking up a new assignment in the course of reporting year he will take over the targets set for the officer whom he is replacing. However, while reporting on such officer it will be necessary to take into consideration his performance in the assignment in which he has spent maximum period. The targets should be clearly known and understood by the officer who is being reported upon.

While fixing the targets, priority should be assigned item-wise, taking into consideration the nature and the area of work and any special feature that may be specific to the nature and the area of the work of the officer to be reported upon.

Although performance appraisal is a year-end exercise, in order that it may be a tool for human resource development, the Reporting Authority and the officer report upon should meet during the course of the year at regular intervals to review the performance and to take necessary corrective step.

It is desirable that all officers submit the self-appraisal well in time so that their achievements are brought to notice of the higher authorities.

With a view to providing necessary data for writing an objective report on officers who do not have budgetary responsibility, the reporting authority and the officer concerned should evolve an action play jointly based upon KRAs, at the beginning of the year so that a criterion will be available to them at the year end to assess the performance. Where necessary mid-course review may also be done to take care of changing needs. Their appraisal will be based upon the fulfillment of the action plan and the periodical review thereof by the controller.

Only those KRAs which are circulated by Corporate Centre are valid. All KRAs/ additions or changes in KRAs have to be approved by the Organizational Planning Department at corporate centre and no KRAs should find place in the report without such approval in case of officers having budgetary responsibility, it should be ensured that the business data on the basis of which the reports are being written is shared with them. The data for all branches (division-wise data for branches with division(s), Regional Officer, Zonal Office, etc. Should be maintained by the Data Processing Centres at the Z. O/LHO and supplied to all appraisees and appraisers.

Where an officer is awarded 100 out of 100 marks by the Reporting Authority, it will be necessary to give at least three concrete work related examples/data where the officer's performance has been outstanding.

Where Reviewing Authority differs by 10% or more, the rationale should be spelt clearly.

Salient Features of the Annual Appraisal Report System

- There is only one reporting system covering all officers. The Assignment Appraisal, which was earlier complied separately, now forms part of the format.

- The format (AARF) is data-based and comprehensive (discussed later).

- The Assignment Appraisal is an annual exercise thereby obviating the need for compilation of reports years later by officials not knowing the appraise.

- The rating is by marking system. The rating system provides for a range of marks for a particular rating. For example, in AAR form III/IIIA (part A), 'Excellent' stands for a range of marks from 31 to 40 so that reporting officials could make finer distinction between degrees of excellence.

- There is provision for self-appraisal.

- The format has been devised in such a way that the reviewing authority will have to specifically record agreements/disagreements and also potentialities and accord final judgmental rating.

- The format is available in four sets making it relevant to the role and scale of officers. The following colour codes are used to distinguish the sets.

ROLE/LEVEL	CATEGORY
JMGS I to MMGS III with budgeted responsibilities	Blue
JMGS I to MMGS III with non budgeted responsibilities	Green
SMGS IV budgeted responsibilities	Black
SMGS IV and above not having budgeted responsibilities	Pink

- Separate parameters have been identified for assessing the performance with respect to qualitative aspects of the jobs of officers having budgetary responsibility and for those not having such responsibility.

  Non-budgetary responsibilities – Where no budget is given for business developments like officials at Regional officers, LHO/Corporate centre and officials at the Branches other than Branch head/Manager.

- The AARF is to be compiled on all officers as on 31st March of every year.

- The AARF on an officer will be written by his Controller as on 31st March, irrespective of the period for which the officer had worked under the said Controller.

- When there is a change in the Controller during the year, the controller as on 31st March will write the report, based on the comments recorded by the earlier Controller.

- The report will be written, based on the actual performance of the officer during the year. This period may also include when the official could have been absent (on leave, sanctioned or otherwise).

- Where an officer had been absent for the entire reporting period, the AARF will be compiled and a suitable remark mad in the report about the absence of the official. However, no marks will be awarded, since there was no performance by the official during the period. The marks will, therefore, be considered as – NIL.

Different Categories of AARF (Annual Appraisal Report Form) with their respective applicability at all levels are as below:

SMGS IV with budgeted responsibilities	Black
SMGS IV and above not having budgeted responsibilities	Pink

Different Categories of AARF (Annual Appraisal Report Form) with their respective applicability at all levels is as below:

AARF format Number	Applicability
I	All officers
II	Self Appraisals for all officers
III	For officers having budgetary and operational responsibilities
III A	For officers having no budgetary and operational responsibilities and working at administrative or branch level
IV	For JMG I, MMG II, MMG III
IV A	For SMG IV and above
V	Overall rating and summary

Objectives & Detailed Functions of these Various Formats at State Bank of India

AARF form I

The format will be completed on all officers as on the 31st March every year. This format embodies complete history of the Appraisee in terms of assignments held and other information

APPRAISAL FORMS AND PROMOTIONAL APPRAISAL FORM

Annual Appraisal Report

AS ON...................

Name_____

Date of birth _____ Age: _____ Years _____ Months_____

Provident Fund Index No _____

Present grade _____ Since_____

Educational Qualifications_____

Position regarding CAIIB/ JAIIB Position : Part I _____ Part II _____

(Date)   (Date)

Current Assignment _____ Since _____

Assignment reported upon (state period) _____

Joined the Bank on _____ as _____

Working under the reporting authority since _____

PREVIOUS ASSIGNMENTS

MINIMUM 3 ASSIGNMENTS COVERING MINIMUM PERIOD OF 5 YEARS

Position	Grade	Br./office	From	To
(a)				
(b)				
(c)				

TRAINING PROGRAMMES ATTENDED DURING THE YEAR

(Name of the Programme and the Institute)

1. _____
2. _____

✠ AARF Form II (Self-Appraisal) ✠

The form has been designed to enable the Appraisee to openly express himself to the Reporting Authority under 5 critical items on which he should have freedom to write every year before the AAR is written. It will be necessary to ensure that the forms are provided to all officers well in time to enable them to compile the report as on the 31st March every year. Though the Reporting Authority can proceed to record the report without waiting for Self Appraisal if it is not received within a month from the due date i.e. before 30th April, it will be necessary The form has been designed to enable the Appraisee to openly express himself to the Reporting Authority under 5 critical items on which he should have freedom to write every year before the AAR is written. It will be necessary to ensure that the forms are provided to all officers well in time to enable them to compile the report as on the 31st March every year. Though the Reporting Authority can proceed to record the report without waiting for Self Appraisal if it is not received within a month from the due date i.e. before 30th April, it will be necessary to ensure that sufficient opportunity is given to the Appraisee to submit the format also affords the openness which was envisaged under the KPA-based system, used earlier.

⌘ Annual Assignment Report – Form III & III A ⌘

Managerial performance needs to be evaluated on the basis of data where available and also on various qualitative dimensions of performance. The data, the qualitative dimensions and various Key Responsibility Areas (KRAs) will differ from role to role and, accordingly, the AARF will have to be filled by the Reporting Authority for each individual appraise. Where data covering business performance is concerned, the performance will have to be judged with reference to the following:

- Tenure of the appraise in that assignment
- Favourable and unfavourable aspects of environment,
- Facilitating factors or constraints in the work-environment (such as adequate or inadequate premises, availability of support of Electronic Accounting Machines etc.) and
- Budgeted goals

While the AARF III is applicable only in respect of officers having budgetary and operational responsibility such as Regional Managers, Branch Managers, Managers of Divisions, etc., the AARF III-A is applicable in respect of all other officers working in branches as well as at Administrative Officers who do not have direct budgetary responsibility.

⌘ Form III-Part A (Data-based Business Performance) ⌘

Details should be filled by adopting the following rating alternatives for expressing by the Reporting Authority his appraisal of the relevant performance of the Appraisee.

Particulars	Ratings of Performance
Average Aggregate Deposits	Excellent/Good/Above Average/Average/Unsatisfactory
Average Aggregate Advances	Excellent/Good/Above Average/Average/Unsatisfactory
Miscellaneous Business	Excellent/Good/Above Average/Average/Unsatisfactory
Total of Discount, Exchange and Commissions	Excellent/Good/Above Average/Average/Unsatisfactory
International Banking-Sales & Purchase	Excellent/Good/Above Average/Average/Unsatisfactory

The Reporting Authority should give appropriate comments. The overall performance will have to be judged on the basis of the actual performance in the light of the reasons for the variance. The rating of the performance may be done a follows:

Excellent	Goals achieved as 100% or above
Good	Between 90 % 100% achievement
Above Average	Between 70% & 90%
Average	Between 60% to 70% goal achievement
Unsatisfactory	Achievement below 60%

✤ Form III-A-Part A Key Responsibility Areas (KRAs)   ✤

A set of KRAs for various roles at Branches and Administrative Offices (given in a separate file) so that appropriate to the role of the individual appraised, the Reporting Authority is be able to evaluate the relevant aspects of qualitative performance of the appraised.

In this context, it is necessary to bear in mind that KRAs are not necessarily static. These have been broadly defined to assist qualitative appraisal by the Reporting Authority every year on the individual appraisal. It shall be the responsibility of the Reporting Authority, therefore, to critically review KRAs and maintain dialogue with the appraisee both for guiding him and monitoring his performance under laid down KRA norms. The revision of KRAs can be done for specific roles from time to time only at the all-Blank level.

The recommendations may be furnished to the Organizational Planning Department at Corporation Centre in respect of variations required in KRAs to suit the changing business environment and the changes incumbent in the responsibility dimensions.

Alignment of Business Goals and Objectives to KRAs – The Reporting Authority should bear in mind always that the Organization looks to branches as the main outlet/points of delivery of banking services and business development making "customer orientation" the principal focus of service and business strategies. The Bank ha to conduct constant review of KRAs of various roles as to make them relevant to changing situations and maintain the competitive edge.

The Reporting Authority should, therefore, have a full grasp of the Bank's commitments and the various corporate concerns so that the subordinates can be properly guided and appraised in their performance.

The Reporting Authority should also have clear perception of skill-dimensions (competencies) required for various roles in the Bank because the Reporting Authority should be able to comment meaningful on appropriateness of placements, identification of potential and skilful management of available resources.

Skill Dimensions

Banking is an area where multidimensional skills are required for effective performance.

- Basic skills,
- Advanced skills and
- Special skills

At different levels, different degrees of skills are required. In fact, it is a combination of these types of skills which makes certain managerial positions critical.

A summary of the Key skill dimensions required at different scales in SBI is as below:

Level in the organization	Skills	Job positions
JMGS	Basic Accounting Skills Basic system and procedures Basic control mechanisms Interpersonal skills Basic credit skills of SSI, Agl. And C&I Basic marketing skills Basic forex skills	Desk officer Passing officer Accountant Filed officer Manager of division BM of a small branch
MMG	Advanced Credit skills (SSI) Basic Skills of C& I Merchant banking skills Supervision and control skills Man management skills Including interpretation of service rules Planning skills Perspective building	Manager of a division(big branch) BM (medium branch) Desk Officer Manager (personal) Manager (training)
Senior management	Advanced Credit Skills Advanced IB skills Special merchant banking skills Strategic planning skills Man management skills Negotiating skills Leadership Team building Counselling Training Communication	CM large branch CM (SMECC) AGM IB AGM ops Regional manager AGM HR CM HR Faculty member

	Conceptual	
Top Executive	Strategic skills Conceptual skills Man management skills High order Team building Motivation Leadership skills Management of values Advanced credit/B/ Merchant Banking skills LRP	DGM GM CGM DGM

Technical skills get more pronounced at lower levels and conceptual skills at higher levels. As one keeps going up the hierarchy ladder, conceptualization, perspectives, macro impact, the corporate significance of decisions, etc. Get enlarged.

The managerial skills, particularly in man-management area, command, by and large, equal emphasis, although there is a perspective shift.

The configuration of technical, managerial and conceptual skills (basic+ advanced+ special skills) can be juxtaposed to each level of managerial hierarchy (grid) in the Bank on the basis of market segmentation, viz., PB segment, Development Banking segment, C&I segment, IB segment, Accounting segment

These are further refined based on special product-specific and transaction-specific divisions created at certain critical and special branches. In each market segment, depending upon the management level, the relative emphasis on skills also shifts. For example, in DBD, the skill level-whether basic/advanced or special – varies with the job position-whether Desk Officer, FO, Manager of Division (MOD), BM – and managerial level-whether JMG, MMG, SMG, TEG.

✂ Form III/III-A-Part B (Qualitative Aspects) ✂

This Form is filled by adopting the following rating alternatives for expressing by the Reporting Authority his appraisal of relevant performance of the Appraisee.

Areas of performance in this case along with the range of ratings are as follows:

1. House Keeping-always up to date to in mess

2. Customer service and complaints-excellent to not much attention is paid

3. Submission of returns-prompt and accurate to inaccurate and delayed

4. Industrial relations-harmonious and policy effective to discordant

5. Credit appraisal-comprehensive to poor

6. Quality of correspondence and promptness-high order & prompt to poor

7. Management of NPAs-effective to ineffective

8. Recovery performance-Excellent to unsatisfactory

9. Audit Rating-earlier and during incumbency

10. Follow up audit of report-quality of remarks, timely submission and rectification.

An Analysis and Review of the AARF or the Annual Appraisal
Report Format @ State Bank of India

Components of An Ideal Form	Presence of these in the SBI Forms	
	Annual Appraisal Report Format	REMARKS
Basic Employee Information	Y	AARF Form I
Accountabilities Objectives, and Standards	Y	AARF Form III & III A for budgetary targets and qualitative data; includes KRAs; written by the reporting authority; Ratings are on a 5 scale from Excellent to unsatisfactory
Competencies and Indicators	Y	Indicated in part III of the AARF, and well-defined for all levels as basic, special and advanced skill dimensions in a role; Attribute based performance assessment in part IV
Major Achievements and Contributions	Y	Usage of critical incident and supporting data by enabling employee to highlight these in the self-appraisal; Data Based business performance section in part III; Achievements of KRAs and delivery on defined skills in part III; Achievements of KRAs and delivery on defined skills in part III
Stakeholder Input	Y	Only supervisor comments and ratings
Employee Comments	Y	AARF Form II, Self Appraisal on 5 critical items
Signatures	Y	Provision made
Developmental Achievements	Y	Enables through self-appraisal and attribute based ratings in part IV
Development		

	Needs	N	
	Needs	N	No provision for recording Developmental aspects
	Goals	N	

Desirable features of an appraisal form	How Does the AARF fare on these	
	Present of these features in the AARF	REMARKS
Simplicity	Fairly simple	The language used is simple.
Relevancy	Relevant	All the sections that are given are very much relevant to adjudge an overall contribution to the job.

Contd...

Descriptive	Lacks	the form is lacking in this area. All the rating details as well as the definition of KRAs, skill dimensions and competencies have been very well and separately defined in the staff book for reference, but the personnel department must understand that the manger or the employee may not have the time to look it every time. Thus adequate descriptions may be provided in the form itself order to ensure alignment with organizational value.
Adaptability	Adequate	Since the banking operations are divided into either the branch level budgetary or non budgetary or non budgetary operations, for SBI and its associates, for its rural and urban consumers, for its various products lines, for technology advanced and educated as well as technology backward branches, the needs and behaviours of employees for success may be divers in these various facets of the bank's operations. The various components of the form however indicate towards the uniformization of services as well as a multidimensional approach to performance. Yet we feel that the form lacks adequate provisions for accounting for the various environmental factors that may have affected performance. The only mention of any constraints which may vary from place to place and across consumer segments, is there in the self appraisal report. Even if this is being discussed and recorded between the manager and the employee regularly, it is not reflected or recorded in the final form, adequately, and thus diluting the adaptability aspect significantly.
Comprehensiveness	Adequate	The form seems to meet the bank's requirement of performance standards, roles and performance culture.
Definitional Clarity	Lacks	Descriptiveness and definitional clarity in the form are missing.
Communication	Lacks	As much as description and definitional clarity is an issue in the form, this reflects on the communication aspect too.
Time Orientation	Fair	Since there is only an annual appraisal meeting to review performance, there is no continuation of performance targets set or met or reviewed form any mid term session. The form records the dates for every part and serves an administrative function of meeting the rating requirement for employees due for promotion.

Steel Authority of India Limited

Steel Authority of India Limited

EXECUTIVE PERFORMANCE APPRAISAL SYSTEM

For executives of the level

E-5 to E-7

YEAR 20..........

UNIT:

NAME:

SHRI/SMT./KUM.

DESIGNATION: PERSONAL NUMBER:

DEPARTMENT: GRADE:

DATE OF ENTRY   QUALIFICATION:

IN THE GRADE

TO BE FILLED BY THE PERSONNEL DEPARTMENT

सेल SAIL

YEAR 20................   FOR EXECUTIVES E-5 TO E-7

PART-A & B		SELF-APPRAISAL AND PERFORMANCE REVIEW & PLANNING
Name:		Personal No:
Designation:		Grade:
Department:		Section

KPAs/TASKS/ and TARGETS ASSIGNED FOR THE YEAR			
KPAs/Tasks & Targets	**Time Frame**	**April-September**	
KPA-1		Actual achievement (to be filled by Appraisee)	Comments on fulfilment (to be filled by Reporting Officer)
Tasks & Targets:			
KPA-2			
Tasks & Targets			
KPA-3:			
Tasks & Targets:			
KPA-4: .... Tasks & Targets			

KPAs/Tasks & Targets	**Time Frame**	**April-September**	
KPA-5: .... Tasks & Targets:		Actual achievement (to be filled by Appraisee)	Comments on fulfilment (to be filled by Reporting Officer)
KPA-6: .... Tasks & Targets:			
KPA-7 .... Tasks & Targets			
KPA-8: .... Tasks & Targets:			

(Please attach additional sheets, if required for filling up KPAs/Tasks and Targets.)

Signature of Appraisee   **Date:**

APRIL-SEPTEMBER

To be filled by Appraisee	**To be filled by Reporting Officer**

Special Jobs Done (Beyond Tasks & Targets)

Performance Review Discussion (strengths/Weakness/Development Needs)

Constraints Faced

Facilitating Resources

Thrust Areas for next six months

Suggestions for Improvement

	APPRAISEE	REPORTING OFFICER	
SIGNATURE			
DATE			
NAME			
DESIGNATION			
KPAs/Tasks & Targets	Time Frame	OCTOBER-MARCH	
KPA-1: .... Tasks & Targets:		Actual achievement (to be filled by Appraisee)	Comments on fulfilment (to be filled by Reporting Officer)
KPA-2: .... Tasks & Targets:			
KPA-3 .... Tasks & Targets			
KPA-4: .... Tasks & Targets:			

KPAs/Tasks & targets	Time Frame	OCTOBER-MARCH	
KPA-5: .... Tasks & Targets:		Actual Achievement (to be filled by Appraisee)	Comments on fulfilment(to be filled by Reporting Officer)
KPA-6: .... Tasks & Targets:			
KPA-7 .... Tasks & Targets			
KPA-8: .... Tasks & Targets:			

(Please attach additional sheets, if required for filling up KPAs/Tasks and Targets.)

Signature of Appraisee   Date:

OCTOBER-MARCH

Special Jobs Done (Beyond Tasks & Targets)

Performance Review Discussion
(strengths/Weakness/Development Needs)

Constraints Faced

Facilitating Resources

Thrust Areas for next six months

Suggestions for Improvement

	APPRAISEE	REPORTING OFFICER
SIGNATURE		
DATE		
NAME		
DESIGNATION		

PART-C	PERFORMANCE ASSESSMENT

FACTORS	WEIGHT	REPORTING OFFICER	REVIEWING OFFICER
		RATING FACTOR (1-5) SCORE (RATINGxWEIGHT)	RATING FACTOR (1-5) SCORE (RATING x WEIGHT)

PERFORMANCE FACTORS

	1		
Quanity of output	1	_____ _____	_____ _____
Quality of output	2	_____ _____	_____ _____
Cost control	2	_____ _____	_____ _____
Lateral coordination	1	_____ _____	_____ _____
Team spirit	1	_____ _____	_____ _____
Discipline	2	_____ _____	_____ _____
Development & quality of assessing subordinates			
Special relevant factor		_____ _____	_____ _____
....	1		

POTENTIAL FACTORS

Commitment and sense of responsibility		_____ _____	_____ _____
Planning and organization	2	_____ _____	_____ _____
Management of human resources	2	_____ _____	_____ _____
Problem analysis and decision-making	2	_____ _____	_____ _____
Communication	2	_____ _____	_____ _____
	1		
TOTAL FACTOR SCORE		_____	_____

INTEGRITY

If questionable evidence/details may be given above board_____ _____

QUESTIONABLE_____ _____

PART-C	**Comments on overall performance and potential**
	(Including comments on extereme ratings and recommendations on promotability

REPORTING OFFICER	REVIEWING OFFICER

IN CASE THE EXECUTIVE IS RECOMMENDED AS C I.E. POOR PERFORMANCE AND NON PROMOTABLE, PLEASE STATE THE REASONS FOR THE POOR PERFORMANCE AND NON-PROMOTABILITY OF THE EXECUTIVE.

REPORTING OFFICER	REVIEWING OFFICER

RECOMMENDATIONS OF REVIWING OFFICER

1. Whether the appraisee exhibits potential to grow   yes/no
2. If yes, whether the appraisee should   _____
   A) Grow in his/her own line/specialisation
       Or
   B) Be groomed for general management position
3. Any other function the appraisee should work in:
   A) Now_____
   B) In due ourse_____
4. Any other recommendation regarding
   growth of the appraisee

PART-D	DEVELOPMENT PLAN-JOB ROTATION AND JOB ENRICHMENT

REPORTING OFFICER	REVIEWING OFFICER

| | REPORTING OFFICER | SIGNATURE | |
		IN CONSULTATION	REVIWING OFFICER
SIGNATURE			
DATE			
NAME			
DESIGNATION			

COMMENTS OF HIGHER AUTHORITIES ON OVERALL PERFORMANCE AND POTENTIAL

(TO BE USED BY EXCEPTION)

HEAD OF ZONE/FUNCTION/CE/DIRECTOR	CHAIRMAN
SIGNATURE: DATE:	SIGNATURE: DATE:

PART - E	FINAL ASSESSMENT

TOTAL FACTOR SCORE	Reporting Officer	Reporting Officer	Reporting Officer	Reporting Officer
PRIMARY GRADING FINAL GRADING	O	A	B	C
	O	A	B	C

COMMENTS OF PRC IN CASE OF MODERATION IN GRADING

COMMENTS ON PROMOTABILITY

IF FINAL GRADING IS 'C', INDICATE WHETHER	PROMOTABLE	NON-PROMOTABLE

SIGNATURE OF CHAIRMAN

MEMBER OF PRC:...

NAME:..

DESIGNATION:...

If non-promotable, date of Communication to appraisee: Whether appraisee appealed for review: If yes, the final decision after Review and the reasons therof	yes/no
SIGNATURE OF REPRESENTATIVE OF PERSONNEL DEPARTMENT	

Rockwell Automation

FY 2000 Performance Review and Development Form
Note: For FY 2000 Asia Pacific has added a new competency, E-Business, to the Performance Appraisal. Individuals and their managers are to assess an individual's readiness fore-business, and what the individual's E-Business Development Plan should be to prepare them for future activities relative to e-business.

Process

1. **Employee completes:**

   Individual Performance Assessment section of the form

   -Individual Development Plan section of the form

2. Employee submits completed form to manager/leader.

3. Manager/Leader reviews employee input and then considers his/her assessment along with customer or peer feedback.

4. Manager/Leader and employee meet and discuss performance.

5. The employee or manager/leader makes revisions based on the discussion to complete the final document.

6. The employee and manager/leader sign this final document.

7. A job description must be attached if it has changed since the last review.

8. The original copy of the signed final document is sent to Human Resources.

Individual Performance Assessment

Key Business Goals/Objectives: This section includes the key prioritized individual goals/objectives established during the fiscal year. The individual goals must support overall business and department goals. List the individual's Top Five Measurable Business Goals for the upcoming Fiscal Year.

Summary of Results: Summarize individual results compared to "Key Business Goals/Objectives." Include key accomplishments, business impact and goals missed.

Competency Overview: Identify specific knowledge, skills and behaviours to describe strengths and developmental needs for employees. Use the career banding competency matrix as a guide to identify examples of required competencies.

Strengths: Areas of expertise, specific competence, skills to build upon or utilize in a broader application.

Developmental Needs: Areas with opportunity for growth, learning and areas for improvement.

⌘ Overall Assessment of Results and Competencies ⌘

Rate overall performance using the following scale:

Outstanding: Substantially and consistently exceeds established objectives and customer expectations. Exceptional performance that has significant impact on business results. Indicates performance that greatly exceeds all requirements with respect to the job.

Exceeds Expectations: Consistently meets and frequently surpasses established objectives and customer expectations. Goals achieved are well above standard performance of job requirements in terms of business impact.

Successful: Competently fulfills established objectives and customer expectations. Contributions meet and may sometimes exceed what is required with respect to the job.

Needs Improvement: Inconsistently performs against established objectives and customer expectations. Quality of results is not always acceptable and falls short of what is required with respect to the job. Development action is required to improve performance.

Unsatisfactory: Consistently does not meet established objectives and customer expectations. Results fail to meet minimum standards for a significant portion of the total job. Has not responded to developmental action. Formal performance counselling steps have or will be initiated.

New Employee: This rating should only be used for employees in new positions less than 90 days. Employees in position more than 90 days should receive a standard rating.

⌘ Individual Development Plan   ⌘

Learning and Development Assignments/Plans: Identify assignments, activities and experiences that provide knowledge, learning, skills practice during the next 12 months. Learning plans must link directly to development needs identified in the Competency Overview. Include timing by month and year. Record status or updates to learning plans throughout the year as appropriate.

Possible Next Roles: Identify future possible career enhancing opportunities or assignments. Include an estimated timing of readiness for the assignments.

Language: List any non-native language skills, check appropriate proficiency boxes

Relocation Interest: State interest in relocation within home country (Domestic) or outside of home country (International/Short Term International).

Comments: Identify location preferences or special needs/considerations

FY 2000 Performance Review and Development Form

Name_____   Position_____

Location   Department   Time in Present position: Years:_____months_____

Manager Name:_____

A-Does the employee have subordinates?	Yes____No_____
If yes, has the employee completed PM Training?	Yes____No_____
If yes, have all subordinates been appraised?	Yes____No_____
If not, when will appraisals be completed?	Date:_____

⌘ Individual Performance Assessment   ⌘

Important: If required, list upcoming year's objectives on a separate sheet.

Key Business Goals/Objectives	Summary of Results
Prior year's individual goals/objectives that support business and/or depart goals.	Summarize accomplishments and misses with specific results. Input begins with a self-assessment enhanced with feedback from your manager, peers and customers.

List of Top Five Measurable Business Goals for FY 2000

1	
2	
3	
4	
5	

Performance Management Counts! Please take the time to complete a meaningful annual appraisal. Thank you!

Possible Next Roles: Identify future possible career enhancing opportunities or assignments. Include an estimated timing of readiness for the assignments.

Language: List any non-native language skills, check appropriate proficiency boxes.

Relocation Interest: State interest in relocation within home country (Domestic) or outside of home country (International/Short-Term International).

Comments: Identify location preferences or special needs/considerations.

Rockwell Automation

FY 2000 Performance Review and Development Form

Period of Review: _____ Position: _____

Competency Overview

Note addition of E-Business Competency for FY 2000 Performance Appraisal Cycle

	Strengths	Developmental Needs
Functional Expertise Technical Skills, Professional Knowledge, Job Knowledge		
Leadership/Change Coaching/Leading Champion Change Making Decisions		
Interpersonal Communication Ethical/Integrity Teamwork		
Business Global Thinking Customer Satisfaction Company Focus		
E-Business Internet & E-commerce Awareness and Abilities Assessment of Future skill required		

⌘ Overall Assessment of Results and Competencies ⌘

Outstanding	Exceeds Expectations successful	Needs Improvement unsatisfactory	New Employee

⌘ Individual Development Plan ⌘

	Learning & Development Assignments/Plans-Upcoming Year (Projects, Formal Training, Teams, Task Forces, etc.)	Timing (MM/YYY)	Status	Date(s) of Status
FE				
LC				
I				
B				
EB				

Possible Next Roles

Responsibilities or Position	Estimated Timing

Language	Speak		Read/Write	
	Conversational	Fluent	Technical	Non-technical

	Yes	No
Domestic		
International		
Short-term International (6<months)		
Comments:		

Employee's signature _____ Date _____

Signature acknowledges discussion only.

Manager/Leader Signature _____ Date _____

7

National Thermal Power Corporation Ltd. (A Govt. of India Enterprise)

Performance and Competence for Excellence (PACE)
Form For Grades E-1 to E-5

Name			
Employee No.		Grade	
Department		Section	
Reporting Officer		Grade	
Location			

Analytical Ability	Team Player	Managerial Effectiveness	Interpersonal Skills
• Identifies problems and associated issues	• Supports and focuses efforts on the mission and goals of the team	• Regularly completes tasks in the time available 10 complete them, and get them done in order of importance	• Demonstrates sensitivity, openness, empathy and trust in work relationships
• Identifies information and data required for problem-solving	• Co-operates with other team members to offer assistance wherever needed.	• Prioritizes jobs at hand based on criticality and importance	• Respects individuals as they are
• Scans information, selecting relevant details	• Supports team work and co-operation through honest and open communication	• Draws a detailed time plan / schedule before starting an important task or project	• Exhibits tolerance for differences and disagreement based on rational and objective grounds
• Assists in problem structuring and problem-solving	• Appreciates and understands the benefits of team work.	• Follows the plan and revisits status as task proceeds	• Shows respect, courtesy and consideration for others
• Prioritizes steps to solution and evaluate criteril or optimum solution	• Places team priorities over individual needs	• Practices punctuality and shows respect and concern for other's time	• Establishes professional rapport and develops constructive work relationships with people within and outside the group and organization
• Builds alternatives and scenarios and weighs them against each other in the process of problem-solving	• Shares recognition and setbacks with the team	• Provides timely feedback to seniors to track and arrest slippages	• Honours commitments to others
• Draws logical conclusions and builds solutions	• Understands team dynamics		• Remains unbiased by background of people
• Not inherently symptomatic in identifying issues and alternatives	• Works well in cross-functional and cross-cultural teams		

Contd...

| Appreciates differences in opinion within a 'cam and works towards resolving them | | | |
| Builds consensus | | | |

Learning	Communication Skills	Decision-making	Innovation and Creativity
Demonstrates curiosity and enthusiasm to learning and sharing knowledge	Expresses opinions and views in a clear, concise and fluent manner (written as well as oral)	Provides relevant inputs and data to support and develop rationale for decision making at higher levels	Consistently challenges oneself to generate innovative ideas
Utilizes every opportunity provided by the organization i.e. formal and informal sources and garner knowledge and information.	Uses grammatically correct language to organize and communicate ideas in words.	Creates contingency plan for own area of work	Contribute to developing new products/ systems/ processes/ applications and solutions through innovative ideas and processes
Takes initiative in acquiring and mastering the skills and knowledge requirements for own position	Good listener, with openness to accepting other viewpoints	Strives for brevity and simplicity when solving complex problems	Displays willingness to experiment with new ideas
Appreciates that each one in the team has (the ability to contribute	Does not interrupt or dominate discussions	Learns from past mistakes for future decision making	Utilizes knowledge and material resources in novel and more efficient ways
Contributes to capturing knowledge to facilitate learning for others	Prepares meaningful official correspondence for delivering results	Takes routine transactions! decisions as per company systems and policies	Uses intuition and information from non - traditional sources to develop new ideas
Scans environment and laps internal and external resource for learning	Builds arguments logically and fluently to put across his viewpoints		Makes constructive suggestions and ideas* as and collaborates in TQM, Benchmarking and other such initiatives

Performance and Competence for Excellence (PACE)

Form for Grades E-1 to E-5

PACE CYCLE: From _____ to _____

Personal Data:

(to be filled by Executive)

Date of Joining of executive in Current Department at Current Location:	D	D	M	M	Y	Y
Date of Entry of Executive into the Present Grade:	D	D	M	M	Y	Y

Dates of Sign-off by Reporting Officer and Executive:

Event	Date (to be filled by Reporting Officer)
KPA setting and Competency Identification	
Mid-Year Review	
Annual Assessment	

NTP

Employee No.:

Part I: Performance Planning and Assessment

Instructions:

At the beginning of the year.

1. Reporting officer and executive to discuss KPAs by referring to the appropriate KPA directory. MoUs, functional plans, business plans etc.

2. Marks to be allocated for each KPA index and constituents

3. 3 levels of targets to be set for each KPA constituent

4. At the end of the year:

5. Scores to be awarded based on actual target achieved

Part IA

Maximum Marks	65

Dashboard of the Key Performance Areas

S. No	KPA Index	Maximum Marks	Marks Obtained (To be filled during annual assessment)
1			
2			
3			
4			
5			
6			
7			
8			
9			
10			
Total		100	

At the beginning of the year:

_____

Signature of Executive

_____

Signature of Officer

Date:

Date:

At the end of the year:

$$\frac{\text{KPA marks} + \text{Marks obtained} \times 65}{100} =$$

_____

Signature of Executive   Signature of Officer

Date: Date:

NTPC

Employee No.

Part I A- Details of KPA

S. No.	KPA Index (Marks)	Constitutions of KPA	KPA Measure	Marks of Constituents	Target Performance			Actual Target Achieved	Marks Obtained
					Stretch	Intermediate	Base	To be filled during annual assessment	
					100% marks	80% marks	60% marks		

NTPC

Employee No.

Part I A- Details of KPA

S. No.	KPA Index (Marks)	Constitutions of KPA	KPA Measure	Marks of Constituents	Target Performance			Actual Target Achieved	Marks Obtained
					Stretch	Intermediate	Base	To be filled during annual assessment	
					100% marks	80% marks	60% marks		

NTPC

Employee No.

Part I A- Details of KPA

S. No.	KPA Index (Marks)	Constitutions of KPA	KPA Measure	Marks of Constituents	Target Performance			Actual Target Achieved	Marks Obtained
					Stretch	Intermediate	Base	To be filled during annual assessment	
					100% marks	80% marks	60% marks		

NTPC

Employee No.

PART IB

Mid-Year Review

Instructions:

- Reporting officer and executive to review and discuss the progress on KPA achievements, competencies, values actualization and potential and document discussions in the space provided.

- In case of change in KPAs, Part IC to be filled up using Form IC (attached at the end of this form).

Mid-year assessment (self evaluation by executive):

Progress on KPAs:
  Achievements:

  Roadblocks/management support required:

Other achievements:

Components of reporting officer:

At Mid-Year Review:

_____   _____

Signature of Executive   Si

Date:

NTPC

Employee No. [ ] [ ] [ ] [ ] [ ]

Part II
Competency Assessment

Maximum marks for functional/technical competency	10
Maximum marks for managerial competency	10
Maximum marks fro Part II	20

PART IIA

Functional Technical Competencies

Instructions:

At the beginning of the year:

- Reporting officer and executive to agree upon at least five functional and cross-functional competencies by referring to the appropriate Functional Competency Directory.

At the end of the year:

- Assessment to be carried out using the rating scale provided carried out using the rating scale provided.

S. No.	Competencies (at least five functional and cross-functional competencies)	Ratings			
		Needs Development 1 mark	Meets Expectations 2 marks	Moderately Above Expectations 3 marks	Significantly Exceeds Expectations 4 marks
1					
2					
3					
4					
5					
6					
7					
8					
Aggregate Total Score					

Total [ ]

At the beginning of the year (upon identification of competencies):

_____   _____

Signature of Executive   Signature of Reporting Officer

Date: Date:

At the end of the year (assessment of competencies):

$$\text{Marks} = \frac{\text{Aggregate of scores of all competencies} \times 10}{(\text{no. of competencies}) \times 4} = \boxed{}$$

_____   _____

Signature of Executive   Signature of Reporting Officer

Date: Date:

NTPC

Employee No. | | | | | |

Part II B

Managerial Competencies

Instructions:

At the beginning of the year:

- Reporting officer and executive to choose 3 competencies in addition to the mandatory ones based upon direct and significant relevance to the executive's areas of responsibilities.

- Chosen optional competencies should be identified by placing a tick-mark against them.

- Remaining competencies need to be crossed out.

S.No.	Competencies	Selection	Ratings			
1	Analytical ability		Needs Development 1 mark	Meets Expectations 2 marks	Moderately Above Expectations 3 marks	Significantly Exceeds Expectations 4 marks
2	Learning					
3	Team Player					
4	Communication					
5	Managerial Effectiveness					
6	Decision-making					
7	Interpersonal Skills					
8	Innovation/Creativity					
9	Adaptability					
10	Cost Consciousness					
11	Quality Consciousness					

At the beginning of the ____ (upon identification of competencies):   Total: [   ]

_____

Signature of Executive

_____

nature of Reporting Officer
Date.

At the end of the year (assessment of competencies):

$$Marks = \frac{Aggregate\ of\ scores\ of\ all\ competencies \times 10}{6 \times 4} = \boxed{}$$

_____   _____

Signature of Executive   Signature of Reporting Officer

Date: Date:

NTPC

Employee No. | | | | | |

Part III

Core Values

Maximum Marks	5

Instructions:

At the end of the year:

- Assessment to be carried out by referring to Core Values Behavioural Guidelines provided in the PMS Policy and the Core Values Handbook using the rating scale provided.

Core Values	Ratings			
Customer Focus Has conviction that the customer is the centre of all activity; is courteous, sincere, patient and sensitive to the customers and honours commitments on time	Rarely Demonstrates value 1 mark	Sometimes demonstrates Value 2 marks	Often demonstrates value 3 marks	Always demonstrates value 4 marks
Organizational Pride Holds the company in high esteem and rejoices in belonging to it; demonstrates loyalty and commitment to the organization and has a sense of ownership and belongingness with it.				
Mutual Respect And Trust Has high regard for and faith in the fellow organizational members: believes in collaboration and openness and has good team spirit.				
Initiative And Speed Believes in taking the first step, thinking new and ahead and being swift without compromising on quality: is creative and				

Contd...

innovative and has the willingness to experiment and take risks.			
Total Quality Believes in pursuing excellence in all spheres of activity; makes continuous efforts in improving standards of performance system and processes.			
Aggregate Total Score			

Total: [   ]

At the end of the year (assessment of core values):

$$\text{Marks} = \frac{\text{Aggregate marks} \times 5}{5 \times 4} = [\qquad]$$

_____

Signature of Executive

Date:

_____

Signature of Reporting Officer

Date:

NTPC

Employee No.

Part IV

Potential Appraisal

Maximum Marks	10

Instructions:

At the end of the year:

Assessment to be carried out by referring to behavioural guidelines for potential competencies provided in the PMS policy using the rating scale provided.

S. No	Potential Competencies	Total Ratings		
1	Leadership	Needs Coaching and Development 1 mark	Somewhat Demonstrates Competency 2 marks	Always Demonstrates Competency 3 marks
2	System Orientation			
3	Resource Management and Administrative Ability			
4	Team Building			
Aggregate Total Score				

At the end of the year (assessment of potential):

$$\text{Marks} = \frac{\text{Aggregate marks} \times 10}{4 \times 3} = \boxed{}$$

_____

Signature of Executive

Date:

_____

Signature of Reporting Officer

Date:

NTPC

Employee No. | | | | | |

Part V

Special Achievement

Integrity:

☐   Nothing adverse

☐   Questionable (belief details may be mentioned below)

Instructions:

At the end of the year:

- Sections 1 and 2 to be filled by executive in consultation with reporting officer

 1. *Individual and Team Achievements and Contributions*

 Examples: Handling of emergency situations, process improvements, mentoring in-house training faculty winning awards, representing NTPC, writing the white papers, office bearer of NTPC councils/forums/committees, suggestions made etc.

Area of Achievement	Description of Contributions

 2. *Contributions (if any) for promoting Hindi*

At the end of the year:

_____

Signature of Executive

Date:

_____

Signature of Reporting Officer

Date:

3. Any remarks that the appraisee and the reporting officer would like to mak about overall performance.

Final year assessment (self-evaluation by executive)

KPA Achievement:

Roadblocks:

Other achievement apart from special achievement:

Comments of Reporting Officer

At the end of the year, the performance and other related issues discussed and feedback given.

_____

Signature of Executive

Date:

_____

Signature of Reporting Officer

Date:

NTPC

Employee No.

Part VI
Total Marks

Section A: By Reporting Officer

Part	Comments	Maximum Marks	Marks Obtained
Part I	Performance	65	
Part II (A+B)	Competencies	20	
Part III	Values	5	
Part IV	Potential	10	
	Total Marks:	100	
Signature of Reporting Officer:		Date:	

NTPC

Employee No.

Part-VII
Total Marks

Section A: By Reporting Officer

Part	Components	Maximum Marks	Marks obtained
Part I	Performance	65	
Part II (A+B)	Competencies	20	
Part III	Values	5	
Part IV	Potential	10	
	Total marks:	100	
Rational for change in marks, if any:			
Signature of Reporting Officer:		Date:	

Section B: By Reviewing Officer

Marks Awarded (after discussions with reporting officer)	Part I	Part II	Part III	Part IV	Total
Rational for change in marks, if any:					
Signature of Reporting Officer:			Date:		
Signature of Reviewing Officer:			Date:		

Section C: By Performance Management Committee

Marks Awarded	Part I	Part II	Part III	Part IV	Total
Rational for change in marks, if any:					
Signature of member of performance management Committee: Date:					

NTPC

Employee No. | | | | | |

Part I C

Mid-Year Review-Change in KPAs

Instructions:

At mid-year review:

1. This section to be used only if changes need to be made to the KPAs, weightages or targets

2. All the KPAs need to be re-filled in the table below

3. Reasons for change need to be cited at the end of the section

4. At the end of the year:

5. Annual review to be carried out with appraisal of KPAs and scores to be awarded based on actual target achieved.

S. No	KPA Index (Marks)	Constitutions of KPA	KPA Measure	Weightage of Constituents	Target Performance			Actual Target Achieved	Marks Obtained
					Stretch	Intermediate	Base	To be filled during annual assessment	
					100% marks	80% marks	60% marks		

NTPC

Employee No. | | | | | | |

S. No	KPA Index (Marks)	Constitutions of KPA	KPA Measure	Marks of Constituents	Target Performance			Actual Target achieved	Marks Obtained
					Stretch	Intermediate	Base	To be filled during annual assessment	
					100% marks	80% marks	60% marks		

Part IC Details of KPA

NTPC

Employee No. | | | | |

Revised Dashboard of the Key Performance Areas

S. No.	KPA Index	Maximum Marks	Marks Obtained (To be filled during annual assessment)
1			
2			
3			
4			
5			
6			
7			
8			
9			
10			
Total		**100**	

Reasons for Revision:

1. _____

2. _____

At Mid-Year Review:

_____

Signature of Executive

Date:

_____

Signature of Reporting Officer

Date:

At the end of the year:

$$\text{KPA marks} = \frac{\text{Marks Obtained} \times 65}{100} = \boxed{}$$

_____

Signature of Executive

Date:

_____

Signature of Reporting Officer

Date:

Part VIII
Individual Training and Development Plan

Name of employee:		Employee No:				
Designation		Department				
Grade:		Location				

Instructions: Training to be derived based on gaps identified in functions and other competencies or additional skills/ competencies required. Help of PMI and other training calendars may be taken for filling up this part of the form.

Training Area	Training Needs
Functional/ Technical (based on functional competency assessment in Part IIA)	
Managerial/Behavioural (based on managerial competency assessment in Part IIB and potential assessment in Part IV)	
Any other (specify):	

At the end of the year:

_____   _____

Signature of Executive   Signature of Reporting Officer

Date: Date:

Employee No. | | | | | |

PMS Activity Checklist

Performance Planning	Mid-Year Review	Annual Assessment
• KPAs and constituents to be identified and written in the PMS form **Source:** KPA Directory • Three levels of targets to be set • Functional/Technical competencies to be identified and written source Competency Directory • Optional Managerial Competencies to be identified and ticked in the PMS form • Sign off by the executive and reporting officer	• Performance progress to be discussed (KPAs, • Competencies, Potential and Values) • Self evaluation to be discussed and documented • Document changes in KPAs if necessary • Comments of reporting officer to be documented • Sign off by the executive and reporting	• Marks to be given for target achieved against KPAs • Summary of KPA marks to be filled in th dashboard • Competencies to be rated • Values to be rated • Potential to be rated • Summary of scores • Discuss and fill training and development plan • Sign off by the executive and reporting officer

Description of Competency Assessment Rating Scales

Level of competency	Description for assessing Functional and Managerial Competencies
Needs Development	Is able to demonstrate the competency on some occasions on the job. Displays some of the behaviours as indicated for the managerial competency. There are specific areas of development for which training interventions are required.
Meets Expectations	Is able to demonstrate the competency effectively on almost all occasions on the job with minimum supervision and training intervention. Displays all behaviours as indicated for the managerial competency. Is prepared to develop higher levels of the competency.
Moderately Above Expectations	Is able to demonstrate the competency at eh significance at a significantly higher level than that required to carry out the assigned job ob several occasions and though not an expert in the competency, has the potential to be one and can be developed with minimum training.
Significantly Exceeds Expectations	Besides demonstrating the competency effective required for the specific level is viewed as an internal expert in this competency. Peers seek his opinion across the unit/company in his domain. Uses current expertise/behavioural capability to provide coaching, guidance and transferring knowledge to subordinates and peers by conducting training programmes. Represents the organization's capability to external agencies.

Level of Competency	Description for assessing Potential Competencies
Needs Coaching and Development	Is a learner and has not yet demonstrated the behaviour/skill required for the competency as per description and requires a high degree of coaching and guidance to do so.
Somewhat Demonstrates Competency	Demonstrates some of the behaviour as of the relevant competency as per description with minimal coaching and guidance.
Always Demonstrates Competency	Repeatedly and characteristically demonstrates all behaviours of relevant competency as per description without much coaching and guidance and is a role model for others.

Observable Behaviour For Values

Customer Focus

- Is courteous to those with whom he/she deals

- Exhibits energy and enthusiasm while dealing with customers

- Communicates eagerness to serve and overcome the 'avoidance' behaviour

- Minimizes defects and errors

- Takes immediate steps to respond to customer concerns

- Demonstrates the ability to see issues from the customer's perspective

- Exudes warmth, efficiency, patience and in stills confidence while dealing with customers

- Answers calls within say 2-3 rings and responds politely

Organizational Pride

- Celebrates success and achievements of the company unreservedly

- Puts organization before self on all occasions

- Takes ownership for own actions and is willing to be held responsible for the same

- Avoids undue criticism of other functions/departments.

- Collaborates readily with others in external events/forums bringing name and fame to the organization.

Mutual Respect and Trust

- Treats others with respect and dignity

- Avoids infighting and professional jealousies

- Respects differences in perceptions, opinions and view points among co-workers

- Is always ready to help others

- Avoids stereotyping and generalizing

- Behaves in a collaborative manner with peers, subordinates and superiors, building trust and cooperation, displaying openness in communication and demonstrating team spirit.

Initiative and Speed

- Is willing to take on responsibility beyond one's call of duty

- Constantly looks for new ways of doing/handling jobs

- Develops a sense of ownership towards the task at hand and sees it to completion

- Anticipates problems and obviates or preempts them

- Cuts down costs or procedures involved in any task

- Demonstrates continuous improvement of existing approaches and adaptation to change, leading to new goals and//or approaches. Resolves problems at their source

- Is result-oriented and follows up matters to their logical end in a time-bound manner.

Total Quality

- Does things right, first time, every time

- Acknowledges and encourages quality around self

- Is organized and systematic

- Has pride in quality output

- Appreciates time and effort involved in developing quality output

- Maintains a systems approach for all tasks being performed

- Eliminates non-essential activities and concentrates on critical ones

- Ensures all individual and team responsibility is carried in pursuit of excellence

- Take part in company's programme for enhancing implementing quality systems/ excellence model.

8

Moser Baer

Goal-setting Form

Confidential

Note: The goal-setting will be instrumental in providing a clear cut understanding to the employee with respect to what the job related goals are and what parameters will determine the achievements of the same. This form will be jointly filled on a mutual agreement between the employee and their immediate Superior. A copy of the same will be provided to the employee, superiors and for personnel records. Twice a year the performance review will take inputs from the goal setting from the prescribed assessment period. At the end of each performance assessment period job related goals for the coming six months will be generated and documented accordingly.

Employee Name:		Designation:	
Date of Joining	Emp. No:	Dept.:	Head of Dept. Name:
Assessment Period-From: To:		Next Assessment Period:	
Reporting To (superior's Name): Designation/Role:		(Time Duration-Reporting) Years: Months:	

Part-I Key Goals

Goals	Activities	Measurement Parameters	Output/Results	Plan of Action

Part-II Mutual Agreement Between the Employee and His/Her Superior

Signature of Employee:_____ Dated:_____

Signature of Superior: _____ Dated: _____

(Please send back a copy of this agreement to the Human Resource Dept.)

Designation Name and Sign

Department:		
Reports To:		
Functional/ Technical Area:		
Modified By:		Modification Date:	

Position Summary: Create awareness by giving presentation on lyceum to key people in school, create a need at client end by explaining the solution benefits and advantages of lyceum, understanding the client's requirement and making a commercial, and closing the account.

Position Scope:

Reporting to:
Qualifications:
Experience (total/relevant) in years:
Technical/Functional Skills:
Supervises/Team Size:
Job incumbent would move to (next position progression)
Special Attributes: Can create and maintain good relationship with the clients.

An employee is entitled to a thoughtful appraisal. Success depends on a constructive and objective assessment, wherein constructive criticism and willingness to overcome performance barrier are top priority for both the appraiser and the appraisee. If more space is needed for any section, additional pages may be attached to this form. Please write in legible handwriting or type in the information and take a submit the same.

In the space provided, specify the goals and job-related activities, the success indicators with relation to what extent they were achieved or fulfilled. Mark the appropriate rating. Explain any change to goals that occurred during the performance assessment period. Make sure that you identify all factors that caused the success or failure of the assigned key goals.

Confidential

Pre-Appraisal Assessment/ Annual Performance Appraisal Form

Type of Assessment (Please):____ Pre-Probation____ End of Probation____ Annual Others____

Name: Shagird		Designation:	
Dept: Pre Sales	Date of Joining	(Time Duration of Reporting) Years: Months:	
Name of Reporting Superior:			
Assessment Period-Form:		Annual TC Salary Group:	
Academic Qualifications:			
How long has Employee been in the position and role?			
Total and Experience:		Relevant Skill Experience:	

TRAINING & DEVELOPMENT PROGRAMS (ATTENDED)		
Title of the Event/Program	Conducted By	Location

The Pacsoft Mission Statement
Division/Department/Group Mission Statement:

Definition Of Performance Achievement	RATING SCALE
Exceptional Performance: Unique And Exceptional Accomplishments	5
Exceeds Expectations: Clearly And Consistently Above What is Required	4
Meets Expectations: Consistently meets requirements of job in all aspects	3
Marginal Performance: Sometimes acceptable, but no consistent	2
Unsatisfactory Performance: Does not meet minimum job requirements	1

Note: Employees, under the purview of time-sheets, must attach a copy of the same, as a support document:

Confidential

Part I: (Goals specific to the employee during the Assessment Period)

Goals	Activities	Measurement Criteria	Time/Days/Date		Actions/ Results	Work not achieved. Explanation	Key Result Activity Rating	
			Initiated	Ended			Employee	TL/PL/ Mgr/H OD
Result								

Note: Employees, under the purview of time-sheets, must attach a copy of the same, as a support document,

Confidential

Part-II: Performance Categories (To be filled in by the Employee's Superior)

S. No.	Categories	standard	rating
1.	The management	Demonstrates accuracy, management of time and priorities	
2.	Work Quality	Provides accurate, through, professional work regularly	
3.	Job Knowledge—Well-informed and educated in performing to the level expected for the job		
4.	New knowledge	Seeks new knowledge, applies it to the job and shares it with others.	

Contd...

5.	Organizational and Planning	Organizes, plans, and forecast work skilfully to meet job needs	
6.	Analysis and Judgement	Analyses problems skilfully, uses skilfully, uses logic and good judgement to reach solutions	
7.	Dependability and Planning	Personality responsible, steadfast and can be called upon for difficult and pressured challenges	
8.	Communication	Communication knowledge clearly, accurately and thoroughly.	
9.	Listening skills	Listens attentively and responds thoughtfully to needs, goals and aspirations.	
10.	Interpersonal Skills	Works well with others, gets things done with people and keeps information lines open at all levels	
11.	Initiative and Drive	Employee is self directed, resourceful and strives beyond the routine	
12.	Team work	Coordinates own work with others, seeks opinions, values working relationships	
13.	Resource use	Effectively uses resources and funds available to accomplish the job	
14.	Service centered work	Regularly provides Quality Service to achieve Customer Satisfaction	
15.	Behavioural Traits	Demonstrates responsible commitment to official decorum, etiquette's and diversity	
16.	Attendance and punctuality	Regularly present and punctual	
17.	Safety and Health Observance	Regularly attentive to safety/ health regulations	
18.	Assertiveness and motivation	Follow through on assignment, modifications/develop new ideas/methods/procedures to meet changing circumstances.	
19.	Leadership/supervision	Assigns works to maximise group strengths; involves colleagues in identification and solution of work related problems; promotes teamwork and cooperation; exercises discipline and resolves conflict construct; trains, coaches and develops subordinates; delegates responsibility; motivates team in budding shared values and vision.	
(To be filled in by immediate Superior)		**OVERALL GRAND RATING**	

Note: Employees, under the purview of time-sheets, must attach a copy of the same, as a support document.

Note: Employees, under the purview of time-sheet, must attach a copy of the same, as a support document.

Part III: Performance Summary (to be filled in by immediate Superior during the Appraisal/Assessment Meeting)

Extent of accomplishments and achievements (Employee)	Areas for growth and/or improvement (Superior)	Beyond Job Related Objectives/Job Exigencies	Identify specific Actions/ Behaviours, the employees needs to either stop doing, and/or continue doing in the upcoming performance period

Note: Employees ,under the purview of time-sheets, must attach a copy of the same, as a support document.

Part IV: Development Plans

A mutual agreement is necessary between both the appraiser and appraise to identify specific work assignments and topics for training designed to increase the individual's effectiveness on the job, which will prepare the employee for future job assignments. Development plans can either take place on the job/self-study formal technical or non-technical training programmes etc. (within a specified time frame).

Identified Need/On the job requirements (mutual agreement between the Employee and Superior)	Employees Planned Action (Short- Term/long-Term)	Time frame	
		from	To
Official Training Need Identified-Company Sponsored Training (To be filled in by the Superior)	Nominated to the Training Program as stated below:		
Superior's Plan of Action and Contribution Towards Employee Development:			

Note: Employees, under the purview of time-sheets, must attach a copy of the same, as a support document.

MMTC Limited: New Delhi

PERFORMANCE APPRAISAL FORMAT

(FOR BELOW BOARD LEVEL EXECUTIVES)

NAME _____ DESIGNATION _____

FOR THE YEAR _____

Reporting and Reviewing System

1. The Appraise will be the Controlling Officer to whom the Appraisee directly reports. Similarly, Reviewing Authority will be the Controlling Officer of the Appraiser.

2. For the Finance Executives working in Regional offices or associated with various Divisions and reporting to regional Head or Division Head, their Annual Appraisal will also be reviewed by the Director (Finance) before accepted by the administrative head at the level of Director/CMD.

3. For Executives of Vigilance and Internal Audit even if working under the administrative control of Regional heads/or Zonal head their performance report will be appraised by CVO/their functional head at Corporate Officer.

4. ARs of DGMs written by the GMs or CGMs in Regions and Division at Co will be reviewed by the Zonal and Functional Directors respectively and will finally be accepted by CMD.

5. ARs of GMs working as Head or Region/Divisions at Co will be written by Zonal Incharge/CGMs and reviewed by Zonal/Functional Director respectively and accepted by CMD.

6. ARs of Zonal Incharge/CGMs at CO will be written and reviewed by Zonal/Functional Director respectively and accepted by CMD.

1	1st week of March	Blank set of KPA based format would be delivered to all Divisional/Regional Heads
2	14thth March	Forms to be given to individual officers
3	10th April	Appraisee to submit the draft performance plan to Reporting Officer.
4	21st April	Appraisee and Appraiser to have one-to-one discussion and finalize the KPA/Target and weithtage for the financial year. A copy of the Performance Plan so finalised be sent to AR Section. Performance Plan of Divisional Head/Regional Head to be put up to respective Administrative Head/Zonal Director or Director Incharge latest by 30th September.
5	By 7th of April next year	Appraisee to submit the actual achievement to be reporting officer
6	By 30th of April next year	Reporting officer to forward the ARs to the Reviewing Officer after giving the rating of Performance, Competencies, Potential and Value.
7	By 7th May next year	Countersigning authorlty I.e. reviewing and accepting authority to send to AR cell after completing the reports in all respect.

PERFORMANCE AND POTENTIAL APPRAISAL FORM

(BELOW BOARD LEVEL EXECUTIVES IN PSU's)

For the year_____

Personal data:

(To be filled in by the Appraisee/Personnel Deptt.)

NAME: EMPLOYEE NO:

DESIGNATION:

Qualification: Academic and Professional

Date of joining: date of birth:

Date of retirement:

Past position held

From	To	PSU/UNIT/Location	Position Head	Key Responsibilities

Part-I Performance

A: *Performance Plan and Mid Year Review*

Performance Areas together with measures/indicators and maximum marks to be jointly agreed upon between the Appraiser and Appraisee at the beginning of the review period and then filled in the format given below:

Performance Plan		Mid Year Review		
Key Performance Areas	Measures/Indicators	Weightage	(Actual achievement) (given by appraisee)	Review (by Appraiser)
1	2	3	4	5
1				
2				
3				
4				
5				
6				
7				
8 Staff Development				

Signature of Appraisee   Signature of the Appraiser

B: Year End Performance Review

The KPAs and measures after incorporating changes, if required, will be recast from the previous page and year-end review will be carried out.

Year end review

Key Performance Areas	Measures/Indicators	Weightage	(Actual achievement) (given by appraisce)	Review (by Appraiser)
1	2	3	4	5
1				
2				
3				
4				
5				
6				
7				
8 Staff Development				

Total Performance Marks for the year
(Prorated to total Marks of 50) $= \dfrac{\text{Total marks obtained} \times 50}{\text{total maximum marks}}$

Signature of the Appraisee   Signature of the Appraiser

- **The column 'Marks Awarded' will be filled only the Appraiser.**

Performance Review Sheet

COMMENTS ON PERFORMANCE AND REVIEW DISCUSSIONS, IF ANY, BY APPRAISER INCLUDING NEED FOR TRAINING AND DEVELOPMENT
Signature of the Appraiser

Part-II: Competencies

(This section consists of functional/technical and managerial competencies required for successful performance in the job).

S.No.	Competencies	Ratings 1-2-3-4--5
1	Business Environment Knowledge—Knowledge and understanding of economic, legal, social political trends.	
2	Profession Specific Knowledge—Knopwledge related to profession as a whole knowledge which is determined by authority and responsibility of other position, Knowledge of mission, values and standard operating procedures, policies.	
3	Making Business Decision—Use business related data to support effective and timely business decisions by systematically gathering relevant business information, identifying the strengths and weakness of a particular business line, recognising opportunities or threats and acting on them rapidly, using business facts collected in daily decision making.	
4	Vision—Develop a vision for the future of the organization by grasping the meaning of trends and inter-relationships between the organizational and its environment at the local, national and international level, identifying fundamental values and beliefs to guide the organization into the future.	
5	Systematic Thinking—Identifying connections between situations that are not obviously related using common sense, past experience and basic rules to identify key underlying issues, generating and testing hunches, which may explain complex situations or problems.	
6	Networking—To cultivate an informal network, which may help to get things done through developing contacts with people outside of the immediate work unit using network and a source of information and support.	
7	Organizing Resources—Ensure that all financial, personnel and/or other resources are in place to meet needs by identifying and acquiring the resources allocating and utilizing the resources in a timely and cost effective way, monitoring and controlling all resources required to maintain the efficiency of operation, multifunctional understanding.	

Contd...

8	Inspire People—To generate a sense of purpose for the work done by the organization through instilling enthusiasm, loyalty and commitment among team members at all levels of he organizational goals, objective, setting an example for others by behaving in ways that are consistent with espoused beliefs and values and the organization's vision and direction.	
9	Team Player—To contribute to group objectives in a team environment through co-operating and interacting well with others, contributing actively and fully to the projects working collaboratively as opposed to competitively with others, acknowledging diverse opinions, addressing relevant concerns and working towards consensual solutions that enhance the output of the team.	

Rating on competencies (Prorated to 20 marks) = $\dfrac{\text{Total of all rating} \times 20}{45}$

Signature of the Appraiser

Part-III: Values

	VALUES	**Rating 1-2-3-4-5**
1	Fairness—Decisions are made objectively free from patronage and reflect the just treatment of employees and applicants.	
2	Transparency—there is open communication about every aspect of a managerial decision, which concerns people.	
3	Trust—Trustworthiness leading to confidence, allow staff the freedom to grow and develop, relate to others on the basis of mutual respect, courage to stand by your convictions.	
4	Candour—Frank and forthright give and receive constructive criticism/suggestion openly discuss performance deficiencies and take corrective action, be consistent in words and deeds, face up to your mistakes, appreciate good performance.	
5	Collaboration—Working in tandem, be open in sharing information and in seeking suggestions/opinion be sensitive to concerns of others, honour your commitment, encourage team work across departments/functions.	
6	Involvement—Total commitment, be dedicated and committed to work, build commitment by encouraging wide participation in decision-making process to the maximum extent possible.	
7	Flexibility—Ability to participate and adapt to changing circumstances using sound judgement. Be open to accepting new ideas, be willing to learn from anyone and to do things differently, be prepared to operate and adapt to different environments.	
8	Willingness to accept challenge—Be willing to experiment, allow for freedom to fail, but learn from it too.	

Contd...

| 9 | Discipline—Adherence to accepted norms, honours the promises and adhere to agreed system, respect for others' time and space, exercise self-control. | |
| 10 | Ethical Behaviour—Demonstrate honesty and sincerity in every action, apply sound business and professional ethics, show consistency with principles, values and behaviours. | |

$$\text{Rating on Values (Prorated to 15 marks)} = \frac{\text{Total of all rating} \times 15}{50}$$

Signature of the Appraiser

Part-IV: Potential Appraisal

	Generic Attributes	**Rating 1-2-3-4-5**
1.	*Leadership Abilities:* Demonstrates ability for guiding collective decision making for succession planning, crisis management and ability to take risks.	
2.	*Team Building:* Demonstrates effectiveness in re-organizing his/her own department, manage diverse and divergent views and group processes without losing sight of objectives.	
3.	*Ability to build a strategic vision:* Demonstrates ability to mange change, focus on long-term issues, strategic thinking translate vision into goals.	
4.	*Business Sense:* Commitment to bottom line result by enhancing revenue generating by addressing interest of customers and stakeholders, Balancing need for viable Short and long-term performance, Optimizing unit/organization's contribution while supporting Corporate objectives, spotting and pursuing new business opportunities wherever possible.	
5.	*Communication Skills:* Communicate ideas and information effectively and market key points effectively through public speaking and presentation, ability to convert ideas through action plan and ensure acceptability within the organization and performance at board meetings.	

$$\text{Rating on Potential (Prorated to 15 marks)} = \frac{\text{Total of all rating} \times 15}{25}$$

Signature of the Appraiser

Appraiser's comment on Potential Suitability

The appraiser will indicate suitability of the appraise for higher position or horizontal movement in different functions/organizations and/or suitability for any specific or particular sector or further continuance.

Signature

Performance and Potential Profile/Final Marks Scored

		Total Marks	Marks Scored
Part I	Performance	50	50
Part II	Competencies		20
Part III	Values		15
Part iv	Potential		15
			100

Appraisal Grading

	Range of percentage	Grading
1.	90% and above	Outstanding
2.	80% to 90%	Very Good
3.	70% to 79%	Good
4.	60% to 69%	Above Average
5.	50% to 59%	average
6.	Below 50%	Below average

General

(i) Integrity unimpeachable   Certified   Above Board   Doubtful

(ii) State of Health

No Visible Disability_____ Indifferent Health_____ Frequently on Medical Leave_____

Suffer from a Particular Disease_____

Name of Appraiser
Date: Signature

Comments of Reviewing Officer
Date: Signature

Comments of Concerned Director
Date: Signature

Comments of Accepting Authority (CMD)	
Date:	Signature

Whether the case has been referred to the Moderation Committee   yes_____ no_____

Final overall Grade of the Officer

10

HDFC Bank

Performance Appraisal Process

1. PLAN

Job Reviewer/Job Holder meet to discuss and record

Performance Agreement

- Priority Aspects of the Role
- Key Accountabilities and Objective
- Key competencies and development indicators

Performance Management Cycle

2. MANAGE

Job Reviewer/Job Holder meet to discuss and record Actual/Desired Performance to date and any changes to the performance plan. Training/Coaching/Feedback/support continues throughout this phase.

3. ASSESS

Job Reviewer/ Job Holder meet to discuss record actual levels of and achievement and the rating

Name	Date of Joining	Grade
Job title	Date into Job	Appraisal Period
Business Unit	Reviewer	Functional Head

Frequently Asked Questions (FAQs)

1. *Who is eligible for appraisal?*

Ans. The appraisal process is applicable to full time employees who have been confirmed.

2. *What are the parameters on which the employee is assessed?*

Ans. The broad areas of assessment in Performance Management System are as follows:

Performance Appraisal Section:

❖ Key business results

❖ Competencies

Each of these areas are further broken into specific measurable parameters for the business unit. The recommended weight age for key business results and competencies is 70% & 30% respectively.

3. *How are the final appraisal determined?*

Ans. The final appraisal is determined through a combined assessment of both the key business results and competencies. We use a 4 point rating scale-Tier 1 to 4 (as defined in the corresponding page) for assessment. Post appraisal discussions of the ratings are finalised in consolation with the respective Business Head/ Group Head & then communicated to the employee. In order to ensure consistency in the application of high standard of performance rating across business groups, a prescribed pattern of rating distribution as given below is recommended for this year.

4. *How is the quantum of increments and bonus determined?*

Ans. The company has pay for performance culture where increments, bonus and incentives are linked to performance. Monetary increases/ rewards are the function of company, business unit and individual performance. Basis these key determinants and keeping the overall budget in view, the payout matrix is developed with respect to Band and Performance Ratings specifying ranges/ limits. The respective business heads then recommend on the payouts for each employee within these defined ranges. These increases are prorated for date of joining in case of lateral hires and date of confirmation in case of trainees. Whereas employees rated T1, T2, and T3 are eligible for increments, bonuses are distributed only to employees rated T1, and T2. Bonus will not be applicable to employees who are covered under separate incentive plans.

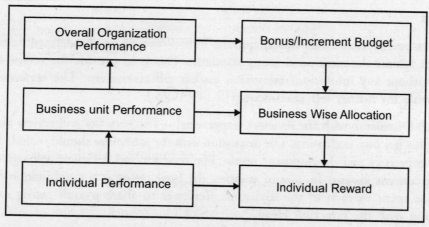

5. *What is a Performance Improvement Plan (PIP)?*

Ans. When the performance appraisal establishes that the performance levels of an individual are well below the expected standards, the reviewer in discussion with the employee puts him/her on to a time bound structured improvement program (usually 1 to 3 months) to closely track and monitor performance.

6. *Who to contact in case of any concerns or issues related to PMS?*

Ans. In case of any queries or issues, you can contact your supervisor/ skip level supervisor. Alternatively, you may also contact your respective HR.

Instructions

The PAPR form is to be jointly completed by the supervisor (REVIEWER) and the jobholder (REVIEWEE). The annual review is meant to provide a fair feedback to the jobholder about his/her performance. This form is divided into sections covering the following:

1. *Review of Business Results/Performance Targets:* This section would enable the reviewee to do self-appraisal regarding the extent of his/her achievement as against the agreed targets set at the beginning of the year (objective and measurable) which are then reviewed by the immediate superior.

2. *Competency Assessment:* To assess the review on certain personal attributes to his/her job and giving feedback on areas of strengths and improvement.

3. *Performance Review Discussion:* To discuss areas other than the business performance, but which need to be recorded for the development of the reviewee and his/her teams (if applicable).

4. *Overall Rating:* Giving an overall rating on the achievement of performance targets as well as the competency assessment. This rating is to be given by the supervisor in consultation with the Function Head/Group Head.

5. *Potential Review:* To evaluate the potential of the individual for future roles. This section to be completed only by the supervisors and signed off by the Function/ Group Head.

Process

Step 1: The review (Job Holder) will appraise himself/herself on the defined performance parameters against the mentioned rating standards. This is to provide the review a chance to state without any inhibition/reservation his/her self-assessment. The reviewee should give rationale for his/her self-assessment.

Step 2: Discussion with the reviewer (supervisor) – The reviewer will review assessment and make his/her own evaluation. The discussion with the jobholder should include feedback on the competency and development needs. The reviewer and reviewee will sign off after recording consent/dissent. In case of transfer, the final rating is a combination of rating and tenure spent in each of the divisions. Reviewer to share overall rating only after consultation with the Function Head.

Step 3: The reviewer in consultation with the Function Head shall complete the potential assessment and this form would be an input into the talent review and promotion decision after further validation using scientific assessment tools as and when required.

Step 4: The ratings will be consolidated and reviewed function-wise for all employees by their respective function heads and will be further reviewed by the Group Head for overall rating distribution of the Business Unit.

Step 5: This final approved rating shall be communicated to each employee by his/her respective supervisor.

Rating Scale

OUTSTANDING	EXCEEDS EXPECTATION	MEETS EXPECTATION	UNSATISFACTORY
Significantly exceeds targets and demonstrates high level of competence in all parameters of the job. Overall performance of the jobholder is substantially above standard with exceptional contribution. Self-driven	Exceeds targets and all essential requirements of the job. Performance of the jobholder is above standard on all major performance parameters. Requires minimal direction.	Meets targets on most key parameters of the job. Performance of the job holder is at an acceptable level and fulfils the objectives of the position. Requires regular supervision and direction. Would be acceptable performance for a person recently appointed to the job.	The results fall short of acceptable level. Performance is clearly unsatisfactory and is below minimum requirement.

Section 1: Review of Business results/Performance targets

- Each accountability should define the purpose i.e., why the job exists and should describe specific end result.

- Approximately 5-8 key accountabilities should cover all significant outputs of your job.

- Objectives should relate to an accountability and describe a specific outcome. Mark PRIMARY objectives, to which a higher weightage will be give with.

Section 1: Review of Business Result/Performance Targets

Key Accountabilities	Objectives Set for the Year	Extent of Achievement		Self Rating	Reviewer Rating
		Self Appraisal	Reviewer's Comments		

Rating for Section 1:

| ① | Outstandiang | [ ] | ② | Exceeds Expectations | [ ] |

| ③ | Meets Expectations | [ ] | ④ | Unsatisfactory | [ ] |

Section 2: Competency Assessment

Competency is a characteristic/attribute consistently applied by the individual in most situations, resulting in high performance. These are specific observable behaviours demonstrated by the individual.

1. Outstanding	• This behaviour is demonstrated with ease and with a certain level of expertise. • A real strengths of the individual.
2. Exceeds Expectation	• This behaviour is regularly demonstrated with the expected level of skill.
3. Meets Expectations	• This behaviour is sometimes demonstrated though not always to the same expected level. • The individual needs some amount of support and training to develop competencies/values appropriate to the requirement of the position.
4. Unsatisfactory	• Occasionally demonstrates this behaviour • This is an area that needs improvement.

Use the above rating scale to determine the most appropriate level for the people being reviewed. In the overall rating, this section carries 30% weightage.

Professional/Job Expertise	Self	REV
Functional/ Job knowledge: Demonstrates extensive in-depth knowledge of the functional area and continually maintains and improves this knowledge.	[ ]	[ ]
Rating for the cluster	[ ]	[ ]

	Self	REV
Banking/Finace Industry: Brings up-to-date and comprehensive knowledge of the banking industry in order to resolve work issue and managing business activities of the group.	[ ]	[ ]

Contd...

Operational Deliverables	Self	REV
Initiative: Self-dircted/Proactive/Seizes upon opportunities, improvises and streamlines processes and tasks.	[ ]	[ ]
Throughness of work and efficiency: Working towards 'zero defect' and continuous improvement of work process within the set guidelines.	[ ]	[ ]
Customer Focus: Meeting the exceptional and requirements of internal/external customers. Finds sound business solutions to satisfy customer needs. Establishes and maintains effective relationships with customers.	[ ]	[ ]
Rating for the cluster	[ ]	[ ]

	Self	REV
Meeting Deadlines/Targets: to be able to do work within specified 'Turnaround Time:	[ ]	[ ]
Business Conduct: Displays sound professional behaviour and integrity in dealing with people both within and outside the organization.	[ ]	[ ]
Adaptability/Learning ability: The ability to continuously acquire new information, different perspectives and skills. Ability to analyse problems, understand cause & effect relationship and utilities sound logic	[ ]	[ ]

Rating for Section 2:

1	Outstandiang		2	Exceeds Expectations	
3	Meets Expectations		4	Unsatisfactory	

Personal Attributes	Self	REV
Teamwork/Coordination: Easily builds rapport with others and develops a network of contacts. Deals effectively with peers, superiors and clients, Keeps all members of the team informed of issues affecting the success of the business.	[ ]	[ ]
Rating of Cluster	[ ]	[ ]

	Self	REV
Attitude: A positive attitude towards work and people. Sensitivity to service excellence.	[ ]	[ ]

Section 3: Performance Review Discussions

To be filled by reviewee and verified by supervisor.

1. Areas of strength and development should be recorded basics inputs received from Upwards Feedback/VOE/Any other as applicable.

Areas of strength	Action taken/planned	Supervisor comments
Areas of development	Action taken/planned	Supervisor comments

2. Subordinate/Team development: Outline the initiatives undertaken in the last one year and its impact (Include measurement process wherever possible)

Initiative _____   Impact _____

_____   _____

_____   _____

3. List any specific training that you would like to attend in the next one year.

Functional _____   Behavioural _____

_____   _____

4. Personal/Career Concerns if any:

_____

_____

_____

5. Mobility:

Functional Yes/No (please tick) 1. _____ 2. _____

Location Yes/No (please tick) 1. _____ 2. _____

_____   _____

Employees signature   Reviewers signature

Section 4: Overall Rating and Comments

The rating is to be given by the reviewer in consultation with the Function Head/Group Head. While assigning the overall rating, target achievement to be given 70% weightage and competency assessment 30% weightage.

| (1) | Outstandiang | ☐ | (2) | Exceeds Expectations | ☐ |
| (3) | Meets Expectations | ☐ | (4) | Unsatisfactory | ☐ |

Please specify if the reviewee is, in your assessment:

(a) In the top 5% of your Business Unit's overall outstanding performers

(b) While currently rated "3" (Meets expectations) is at the bottom end of this category and could slip to unsatisfactory if not monitored. Recommended for Performance Improvement Plan (PIP).

UNIT HEAD/BUSINESS HEAD COMMENTS:

_____

_____

_____

UNIT HEAD NAME: _____

UNIT HEAD SIGNATURE: _____

_____

HR Comments: (To be filled by HR after the appraisal is over)

_____

_____

_____

_____   _____   _____

Name   Functional Designation   Signature

Section 5: Potential Assessment

To be completed by the reviewer in consultation with his/her supervisor.

Potential refers to the inherent capability of an individual to excel at the next level and beyond. These capabilities are essential behavioural in nature and key to success in future roles.

Instructions:

- The objective of this section is to assess the individual vis-a-vis the competencies required for future roles. This does not have any impact on the rating for the year.

- This assessment would be an additional input in to promotion/career decisions—after further validating using scientific assessment tools as and when required.

- The employee is to be assessed on each competency and assigned a proficiency level as defined in the next page.

- Justification through examples/incident is to be provided by the supervisor and skip level supervisor for the level assigned to the competency.

At what highest band can you visualize the jobholder? (Please tick)

Assistant Manager ☐ Deputy Manager ☐ Manager ☐ Sr. Manager ☐

Asst. Vice President ☐ Deputy Vice President ☐ Vice President ☐

What are the areas of strengths and improvement for the employee to take on larger roles:

Areas of Strength: Areas of Improvement:

Functional_____ Functional _____

_____ _____

_____ _____

Behavioural _____ _____

_____ _____

_____ _____

Apart from your own, function/business unit do you think the reviewee is best suited for?

Job Role_____ Function _____ Business Unit _____

The individual would be ready to take on enhanced job responsibilities (not band change) in – (please tick)

(a) Less than 6 months ☐   (b) 6 months-1 year ☐

(c) 1 year-2years ☐   (d) More than 2 years ☐

Proficiency Levels:

B = *Basic:* Has an understanding of the competency and applies it successfully in a simple environment.

A = *Advanced:* Demonstrates the competency consistently in usual circumstances and applies it successfully in new and complex situations.

E = *Expert:* Is a role model for the competency. Sets benchmark for the desired competency.

Using the above scale, please assign a proficiency level for reach of the competencies outlined below. For example:

Competency	Proficiency Level	Justification (Example/Incident to support rating)	Action required for development.
Continuous Improvement: Proactively identifies areas of improvement that has an impact on key business parameters	A	Prepares a monthly analysis after studying the MIS. Has identified four projects basis the analysis and implemented them successfully.	Take up bigger challenges for improvement.

Competency	Proficiency Level	Justification (example/incident to support rating)	Action required for development
Business Acumen: • Applies Business Knowledge to take well thought out decisions keeping the big picture in mind. • Proactive identifies and evaluates opportunities.			
Personal Effectiveness: • Is able to influence others to achieve organizational objectives. • Handles multiple responsibilities effectively • Adapts to change quickly			
Communication: • Able to articulate and convincingly put across his/her point of view • Interprets and cascades relevant information • Actively gives and seeks feedback.			

Contd...

Building Relationships: • Strives to maintain inter-functional relationships • Anticipates and delivers on internal/external stakeholder expectations.			
Managing People and Performance: • Plans and monitors developed of others • Coaches others to enhance performance and creates accountability • Proactively anticipates and resolves conflict situations effectively.			
Execution Excellence: • Continuously strives for better processes and practices. • Optimizes resources and is focused on quality and results.			

Functional head/business head comments:

_____

_____

_____

Reviewer Name _____ Signature _____

Functional/Business Head Name _____ Signature _____

Org./Division/Dept:		Location/based at:	
Name:	Position		Ref:
Year or period covered:	Time in present position:		Length of service
Appraisal date and time:	Appraisal venue:		Appraiser:

Part A

Appraisee to complete before the interview and return to the appraiser by (date) ☐

A1

State your understanding of your main duties and responsibilities.

A2 Discussion Points

1. Has the past year been good/bad/satisfactory or otherwise for you, and why?

2. What do you consider to be your most important achievements of the past year?

3. What do you like and dislike about working for this organization?

4. What elements of your job do you find most difficult?

5. What elements of your job interest you the most, and least?

6. What do you consider to be your most important aims and tasks in the next year?

7. What action could be taken to improve your performance in your current position by you, and your boss?

8.   What kind of work or job would you like to be doing in one/two/five years time?

---

9.   What sort of training/experiences would benefit you in the next year? Not just job-skills—also your natural strengths and personal passions you'd like to develop—you and your work can benefit from these.

A3

List the objectives you set out to achieve in the past 12 months (or the period covered by this appraisal) with the measures or standards agreed-against each comment on achievement or otherwise, with reasons where appropriate. Score the performance against each objective (1-3 = poor, 4-6 = satisfactory, 7-9 = good, 10 = excellent):

Objective	**measure/stand**	**score**	**comment**

A4

Score your own capability or knowledge in the following areas in terms of your current role requirements (1-3 = poor, 4-6 = satisfactory, 7-9 = good, 10 = excellent). If appropriate, bring evidence with you to the appraisal to support your assessment. The second section can be used if working towards new role requirements.

1. Commercial judgement	11. Problem-solving and decision-making
2. Product/technical knowledge	12. Team-working and developing others
3. Time management	13. Energy, determination and work-rate
4. Planning, budgeting and forecasting	14. Steadiness under pressure
5. Reporting and administration	15. Leadership and integrity
6. Communication skills	16. Adaptability, flexibility, and mobility
7. Delegation skills	17. Personal appearance and image Others (for current or new role):
8. IT/equipment/machinery skills	
9. Meeting deadlines/commitments	18. Corporate responsibility and ethics.
10. Creativity	

A5

In light of your current capabilities, your performance against past objectives, and your future personal growth and/or job aspirations, what activities and tasks would like to focus on during the next year. Again, also think of development and experiences outside of job skills-related to personal aims, fulfilment, passions.

Part B

To be completed during the appraisal by the appraiser-where appropriate and safe to do so, certain items can completed by the appraiser before the appraisal, and then discussed and validated in discussion with the apprise during the appraisal.

B1

Describe the purpose of the appraisee's job. Discuss and compare with self-appraisal entry in A1. Clarify job purpose and priorities where necessary.

B2

Review the complete discussion points in A2, and note the points of and action.

B3

List the objectives that the appraise set out to achieve in the past 12 months (or the period covered by this appraisal—typically these objectives will have been carried forward from the previous appraisal record) with the measures or standards agreed-against each comment on achieve or otherwise, with reasons where appropriate. Score the performance against each objective (1-3 = poor, 4-6 = satisfactory, 7-9 = good, 10 excellent). Compare with the self-appraisal in A3. Discuss and note points of significance, particularly training and development needs and wishes, which should be noted in B6.

Objective	Measure/Standard	Self-score/App'r score	Comment

B4

> Score the apprisee's capability or knowledge in the following areas in terms of their current (and if applicable, next) role requirements (1-3 = poor, 4-6 = satisfactory, 7-9 = good 10 = excellent). If appropriate provide evidence to support your assessment. The second section can be used for other criteria or if the appraise is working towards new role requirements. **Compare scores with the self-appraisal in B4. Discuss and note agreed points training/development needs and wishes (to B6).**

1. Commercial judgement	11. Problem-solving and decision-making
2. Product/technical knowledge	12. Team-working and developing others
3. Time management	13. Energy, determination and work-rate
4. Planning, budgeting and forecasting	14. Steadiness under pressure
5. Reporting and administration	15. Leadership and integrity
6. Communication skills	16. Adaptability, flexibility, and mobility
7. Delegation skills	17. Personal appearance and image Others (for current or new role):
8. IT/equipment/machinery skills	
9. Meeting deadlines/commitments	18. Corporate responsibility and ethics
10. Creativity	

B5

> Discuss and agree the appraisee's career direction options and wishes, and readiness for promotion, and compare with and discuss the self-appraisal entry in A5. (Some people do not wish for promotion, but everyone is capable of, and generally benefits from, personal development—development and growth should be available to all, not just people seeking promotion). **Note the agreed development aim(s).**

B6

> Discuss and agree to the skills, capabilities and experience required for competence in current role, and if appropriate, for readiness to progress to the next role or roles. **Refer to actions arising from B3 and the skill-set in B4, in order to accurately identify all development areas, whether for competence at current level or readiness to progress to next job level/type). Note the agreed development areas:**

B7

> Discuss and agree to the specific objectives that will enable the **appraisee to reach competence and to meet required performance in current job**, if appropriate taking account of the coming year;s plans, budgets, targets etc., and that will enable the appraisee to move **towards, or achieve the desired personal growth or experience**. These objectives must adhere to the SMARTER rules-specific, measureable, agreed, realistic, time-bound, ethical, recorded.

B8

> Discuss and agree (as far as is possible, giving budgetary, availability and authorisation considerations) the training and development support to be given to help the appraisee meet the agreed objectives above.

> Refer to the guidance notes. Personal development and support must be offered to all employees, irrespective of age, gender, race, disability, etc., and not just to those seeking promotion. Development is not restricted to job skills—it includes 'whole person'. Use your imagination. Job skills training isn't restricted to courses. Think about coaching, mentoring (by and of the appraise), secondment to another role, holiday job cover, shadowing, distance-learning, e-learning, books, videos, attending meetings and workshops, workbooks, manuals and guides, researching, giving presentations; anything relevant, helpful and agreed to help the person develop. Avoid committing to training expenditure before suitable approval or availability has been confirmed. Understand development options and procedures before conducting the appraisal. Develop the whole person.

B9

> Other issues (to be covered separately outside of this appraisal-continue on a separate sheet, if necessary):

> Signed and dated by appraisee: and by appraiser:

Grade/recommendation/summary as applicable:

Distribution of copies/confidentially/accessibility details:

Performance Agreement (Check Sheet)

Name:	
Job Title:	Branch/Business Unit
Grade/Level:	Date into current grade:
Date into current job:	Date of joining
Period covered by report	Reviewer's Name:

- To identify objective, agree plans and timeframes, to review and record progress.

- To know where to go and to ensure that we get there.

Accountability	Objectives	Action Plans	Time Frame	Agreed Review Dates	Review and Progress
Competencies (Specify competencies as listed in appraisal form)					

Mid-year Performance Review (2008-09)

Emp. code	Job Holder Name	Job Title	Review Period (Form)	Review period (To)

(A) Overall Performance Area (Performance Score Cards/Plan or set for the individual to be used as the basis for review)	Level of Performance (Summarise/highlight through key facts and observations the performance in current role. Focus on Results and Process followed by the Job holder)
	Self Assessment Reviewer Assessment
(B) Knowledge and skills (Relates to the Functional Know-how and expertise required to perform the job)	
(C) Strengths and weakness (Refers to Behavioural Competencies that are critical to perform)	

(D) Overall Assessment (Comments) **If performance is a concern does he/she need to be put on a specific Performance Improvement plan:** **Yes/No**

Job holder
Name:

Supervisor
Name:

Business Head/Group Head
Name:

Overview:

Performance Pyramid

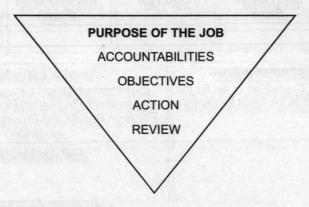

PURPOSE OF THE JOB
ACCOUNTABILITIES
OBJECTIVES
ACTION
REVIEW

Key Stages:

Planning

Managing

Assessing

Your Role...Elaborate the points

Forms: Ref. the Attachment

Performance Appraisal Form at Colt

Name	Line Manager
Country: India	Function
Length of time with COLT:	Length of time in current role:

Individual Goals

Goals are the principle deliverables specific to each role within the business during the coming year. You should ensure that your goals are linked to the Company/Function and/or Country goals. Goals for the year should be agreed by the end of January and formally reviewed on this document at mid year and at year-end.

It is important that goals are regularly reviewed and where appropriate, changed in line with the changing business needs.

Goals should be SMART: They need to be Specific; contain Measures for achievement and success; be Agreed between the individual employee and line manager; Realistic; describe how result will be achieved and focus on outcomes; and include clear Timings of when they will be achieved.

Once goals are discussed and agreed, the employee should send via-e-mail the final version to their manager. In some countries, both the employee and the manager will need to sign a copy of the agreed goals. Your local HR department will inform you if this is the case.

Goal 01-25% Order Entry

Order Entry

- To be able to perform OE tasks for at least four countries without seeking inputs from other members of the teams or manuals.

- DE,ES,PT,AT

- Success criteria

  - ❖ >95% accuracy achieved/

  - ❖ >95% of orders for the above countries entered within agreed TAT

  - ❖ Manuals fully up to date for OE for all major countries.

  - ❖ >95% order quality checked for your buddy

  - ❖ At least 45 tasks (OE+ Queries) performed per week (pro-rated)

To have established a relationship with all above countries in order to assure quality of DCS Order Entry.

1. 100% Adherence to all OE initiatives communicated during the period.

2. Able to prioritise the Xtrac work Item based on Pipeline Data and create contacts on FIFO basis.

3. Able and contain escalation at your level and let no surprises from external customers regarding OE data quality issues for above countries.

4. Regular audits of closed orders to ensure building data is transferred successfully, and report exceptions each month.

Year-end Review

97.13% orders created within TAT during Jul-Dec'07.

Quality was maintained at 100% throughout the period (Jul'-Dec'07).

All queries were handled in the best possible manner and prioritisation of work items done.

Goal 02-5% Managed Storage & Backup

New Projects (Managed Storage & Backup):-

Queue Co-ordinator and updating of Doc. and Ops Readiness

1. To learn and ensure that MS&B orders on, grid works are entered timely and accurately and monthly UBB Modification contracts generated on time.

Success Criteria:

❖ Able to support Alpha Trial(s) and all related activities related to the same, single handed and independently.

❖ 95% orders entered onto grid works within 1 Working Day.

❖ Monthly UBB billing orders are accurately created.

❖ Monthly UBB billing orders are produced 95% within agreed timelines.

❖ Responsible for at least four countries (Subject to rollout plan).

❖ >30% Contribution by each member.

Year-end Review

Acted as the SPoC and the queue manager. Facilitated the work instructions to rest of the team. Handled all escalations/queries and provided full support to the Project team as and when needed. Also helped the project team in vetting/preparation of MS&B process related documents.

Was also nominated as the Ops Champion for MS&B, which is just another feather in the cap.

MS&B Monthly UBB Billing is yet to be started so there could be no contribution from myself or any other team member in this respect.

Goal 03-15% Process PR and Associated Task

To have successfully performed all DCS Oracle Purchase Requests and associated receipting/tracking activities for all transitioned countries within agreed service levels during the period.

Success Criteria:

● >30% of the PRs prepared and queries handled (period Feb-to-Dec).

● >95% produced within 1 working day

● >95% of the PRs produced have ZERO-defects.

● >30% Purchase Request and associated receipting/query tasks performed for this period out of the total volume.

Year-end Review

All KPIs met for this objectives.

TAT was 100% for this throughout the period.

Goal 04-5% SPLA Usage Reporting

To have transitioned SPLA Usage reporting for the following countries:

- DE, ES, NL (Q3'07)
- UK, IT (Q4'07)

Success Criteria

- To have consistently submitted the SPLA Usage report per agreed process and timeliness, without failure.
- To be able to contain escalations, address all SPLA related queries and interact with SPoCs and suppliers wherever required.
- Country Procedures included in Operating Manual and are always updated.

Year-end Review

SPLA Usage report consistently submitted correctly as per the process and agreed timelines.

Operating Manuals were updated during the phases when the process was being developed. Also prepared SPLA UK manuals twice due to change in the process flow.

Trained/provided support to the Team on the complex UK SPLA as and when required.

Goal 05-20% COL T Managed Products: Service Provisioning

Be responsible to provision >30% of the total volume received.

Success Criteria

- All requests are assigned within 1 hr or Opening of Business each day.
- All assigned requests picked up within 24 hrs.
- All processes adhered within defined parameters.
- 100% of cases where CPD is assigned and adhered.
- 100% of cases where CPD is being changed for unforeseen reasons, the change is to take place before the old CPD.
- Product-wise procedures included in Operating Manual and are always updated.
- Pipeline status and 'CMS Service Delivery' mailbox is always updated.
- Master Spreadhseet(s), mail communications and documents are always saved in the required folder.
- Operational readiness and Issue Log is always updated by SPoC.

Year-end Review

All KPI's met for this objective. 30.23% orders provisioned. Apart from this provisioning was done consistently for all the available products (MBE, MES, PCB).

Conformance to CPD was 100%.

Also provided support to the team under guidance initially, especially in the case of Abridean tool.

Goal 6-15% Projects

MS&B

- Development of Charge tool,

- Enhancement on Incentra's portal

- Finalisation of Usage Charged process (Services Acceptance)

Success Criteria:

- An agreed Usage Charge Process, signed off with all stakeholders and Project Managers

- Clearly stated L4 Procedures in place.

- Clearly stated 'Out-of-scope' activities and 'Risks' associated informed to Project Team

Transition: Purchase Request

- France: To be revisited in Q4'07

Success Criteria:

KPI yet to be defined

Year-end Review

Through MS&B Project kicked off, but due to insufficient support from the third party vendor and Project Team, this is still in the pipeline and expected to be completed in Q1'08.

Its worth mentioning that initiative has been taken on my own to speak to Incentra executives and I am successful in channelizing the request to enhance gridworks portal to suit COLTs UBB requirements. Good amount of time has also been spent in consolidating the requirements, slogged during late working hours so as to attend the meetings and provide feedbacks from time to time to Incentra-U.S.A. Its my insight on charge tool that today "Thiery Motet" is able to capture the requirements and is developing the same to suit our requirements. None of these initiatives are complete, so this has to be completed in Q1'08.

Documents like MS&B Business Case and Gridwork's workflow were also presented to the Management and the Project Team respectively for their information and approvals respectively.

However, another project that has been very sincerely and judiciously taken up is Forefront License Projects in which details of the last six months licenses of (MBE Std and Bsc and Total Plus) have to be analysed and presented to the Project Manager Khurram Ijaz. This project is expected to be finished by mid-Dec'07.

As far as transition is concerned, there was not enough buy-in from the business and neither team had an opportunity to contribute to this goal.

Goals 7-10% Management Reporting and Personal Development

Management Reporting: To be able to produce the Commercial Admin Weekly Reports (includes both team and individual reports)/ Dashboards during the period.

- To ensure Order Entry/Purchase Information System database is updated on regular basis.

- Capture Issues with the help of issue logs for PRs and OE or any other BAU tasks.

- Updating timesheets accurately and on time.

Personal Development: Create and develop the skills which can be demonstrated in the following areas:

- Presentations (deliver at least 2 in each quarter)

- Project Management (lead and responsible to complete at least one small project using formalised process)

- Become subject matter experts in at least 2 areas.

Success Criteria

- To have delivered at least 6 reports without errors by agreed target dates

- Communication (convene confidential calls and able to minute the meetings in COLT format, at least one complete rounds each quarter)

- At least two presentations per quarter = Each member

Year-end Review

The reports were completed by the required time lines. And good amount of accuracy was also maintained. Presentations/workflows were also judiciously prepared.

Initiation taken that weekly meetings be cheered by individual team members rather than the team lead as this would provide an opportunity to everyone to groom themselves and get confidence in handling things in a group, this idea was also channelized and is running successfully in the team.

⌘ Goal 8-5% Process Improvement and Initiatives ⌘

To have identified and implemented at least one significant process improvement to improve overall efficiency within either PR, OE, Service Provisioning, OPT or Revenue audit (or for that matter any existing service).

Success Criteria

- Demonstrable operational/business benefits through either reducing effort or improving quality of the existing services.
- Member is responsible to revisited by end of Q3 with the line manager.

Year-end Review

Initiative was taken up to prepare the Forefront License Projects which details of the last six months licenses of (MBE Std and Bsc and Total Plus) have to be analysed.

Another initiation was made in the MS&B Ops champion group to reduce the time involved in the MS&B customer creation orders which was shared and discussed with incentra and they agreed to improve on it and the results are already being seen with improved timelines.

Wherever required training/information was provided to the rest of the team on new processes around BAU and other activities as my expertise has definitely enhanced in the two quarters.

Personal Development Plan

What training or development is needed for you to improve your performance in your current position and develop for future roles?

This may relate to knowledge, skills, attitude/behaviour or a combination of these. Once the need has been identified, consider whether it will be best met by formal training or another activity. Development that will support you with your desired career progression at COLT may also be considered here. Should any goals change during the course of the year, the development plan may need to be adapted as well.

Training or Development Needs

Activity (coaching, training course, project etc.) and time of delivery

Q3

- White Belt
- Service Provisioning: Basic (Internal Session)

Q4

- MS Access: DBMS
- eGurukul: Project Management (Basic) and other courses for developing personal skills.

⌘ **Performance Review** ⌘

The part of the document should be reviewed twice a year at mid-year and year-end. A performance review discussion between you and your manager should take place to review the goals against plan and performance.

General Review of Performance-Manager's Comments

Mid-year

Employee's Comments

Year-end

In Q3-Q4 I was able to demonstrate my skills and initiate couple of proposals on my own.

I had consciously tried to develop my skills, though Project Management is something which requires additional training and could not be picked on own.

I would like to learn more about Project Management and would like to create/find opportunities wherein my expertise could be utilised in the welfare of the organizational goals.

Also I would like to be entrusted with higher responsibilities and higher end tasks.

And I would continue making efforts to curtail all escalations/queries at my end.

Last year was filled up with new projects/activities like the Service Provisioning and Forefront Project and carrying on with the BAU activities. Services Provisioning was particularly challenging as it was technical in nature and involved lots of coordination and new tasks.

I had given my best to the term particularly in the MS&B Project area wherein my expertise is being utilised to the best for which due appreciation is also received by the management and stakeholders time and again.

Also, as a team we had won many accolades from our counterparts in the UK with reference to Service Provisioning and our PR stakeholders for being pro-active and performing with lot of enthusiasm.

Signatures (required at year-end)

Employee :   Line Manager

Date: / /   Date: / /

Review of Managerial/ Supervisory Attributes

It is to establish the employee's attributes which leads to the success of the business.

The attributes on which the overall rating of an employee is done are as follows:

1.   Taking Responsibility

2.   Job knowledge

3.   Team work

4.   Customer Focus (external)

5.   Communication Skills

6.   Reliability

7.   Attendance

8.   Punctuality

9.   Sales Orientation

10. Training Skills

The above attributes are rated on the following parameters:

Attributes	Excellent	Very Good	Good	Satisfactory	Poor
Taking Responsibility					
Job Knowledge					
Team Work					
Customer Focus (External)					
Communication Skills					
Reliability					
Attendance					
Punctuality					
Sales Orientation					
Training Skills					
Overall Rating On Attributes					

After analyzing the above section, comments are written by the HR Manager as well as the line manager for the respective employee.

12

The PMS Handbook – IOCL

PMS-Objectives, Coverage and Roles

❆ Objectives of PMS

The performance management system aims to encourage the following:

- Creation of high performance orientation at IOCL

- Stronger alignment of individual performance with organizational goals

- Higher degree of transparency, uniformity and process efficiency

- Performance ownership at the employee level

❆ Coverage of PMS

All Officers working in Grades A-I

Key Roles in PMS

Appraisee	Appraiser	Reviewer	Countersigning Officer
An individual who is assessed as part of the performance cycle	An individual who assesses the performance of one or more Appraisees that report into him/her	N individual who is responsible for reviewing the entire performance process and typically is Appraiser's Appraiser	An individual who is responsible for ensuring sanctity of process at the highest level. He will be the final authority.

Contd...

The key driver of own PMS	Helps manage performance & provides continuous feedback and counselling	Ensures objectivity, transparency & consistency	Final Authority
Facilitator/Administrator			
An individual who acts only as a facilitator and ensures adherence to timeliness and consistency in the process **Facilitates the process**			

⌘ Features of PMS ⌘

The following are system features of PMS, which have been detailed in subsequent sections of this document:

- Performance Period

- Performance Planning

- Mid-year Review

- Final Appraisal, Review & Feedback

- Cornerstones of PMS

The Features and tools of PMS have been designed to reduce subjectivity and individual biases that may impact the effectiveness of a performance management system.

Key cornerstones of Objectivity, Transparency and Consistency across IOCL have been directly addressed. While the various design features of PMS address all these cornerstones, the emphasis of each features is highlighted in the following table.

Features	Objectivity	Transparency	Consistency
Definition of Performance	✓	✓	✓
Joint Planning & Review with Appraiser	✓	✓	✓
Active role of Reviewer	✓	✓	✓
Defined & articulated Rating Scales	✓	✓	✓
Communication of Ratings upto review stage	✓	✓	✓
e-Enabled PMS	✓	✓	✓
Stretch Tool	✓	✓	✓
Definition of Competencies	✓	✓	✓

Performance Period

PMS follows an April-March annual cycle aligned to the financial year. The cycle consists of three phases, namely, Performance Planning, Mid-Year Review, and Final Performance Review. The critical calendar months and the sequence of events for three phases are represented in the following figure:

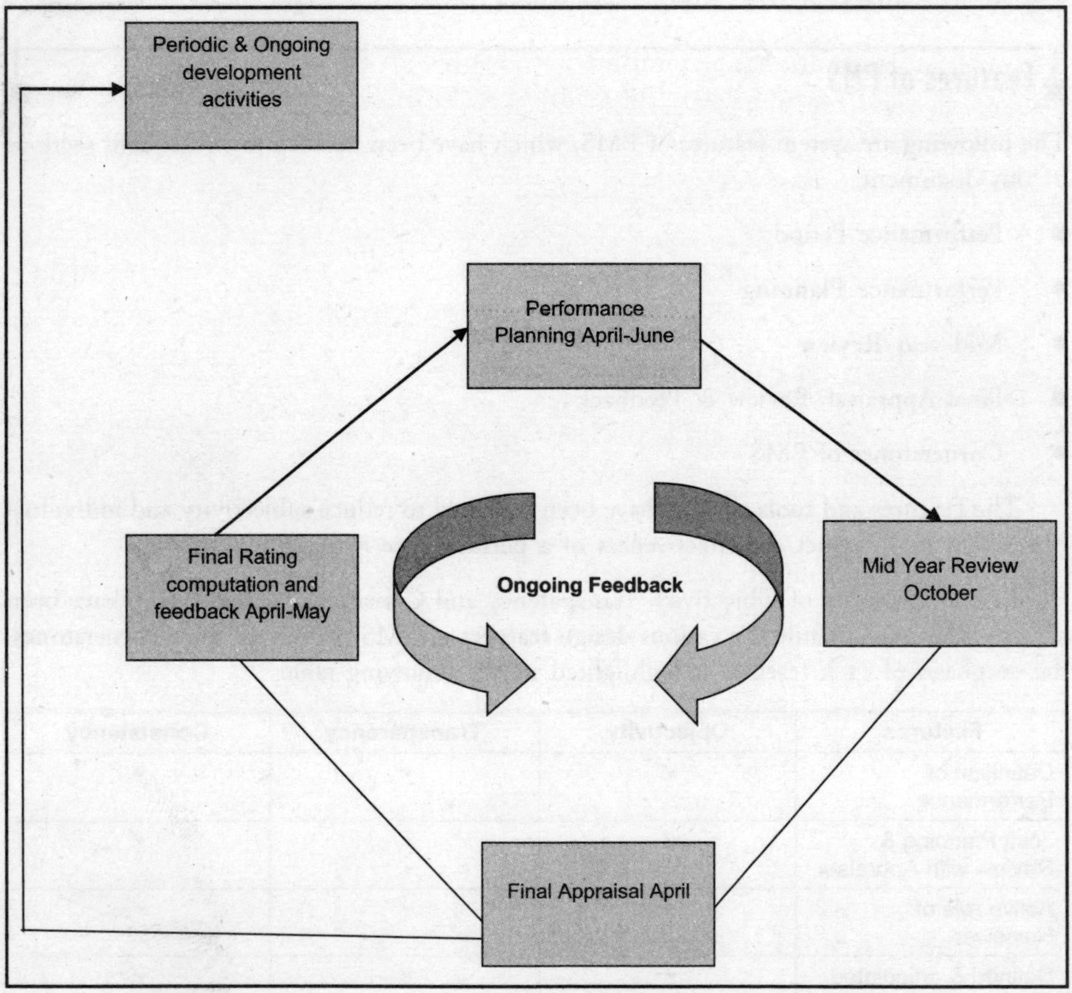

⌘ Cascading Process ⌘

Performance planning is undertaken from April to June. Once the MOU between the organization and MOP & NG is finalised, these targets are cascaded to the divisions. The division heads then cascade them down to their subordinates. This process is followed at all levels at which this is possible. At each stage of cascade, some other targets which may not necessarily be cascaded down, may also be added-these would be specific to specific roles, and may be in respect of ongoing projects and carried forward form the previous year.

This stage involves discussion between Appraisers and Appraisees to set and agree on the content of the Appraisees' performance plan parameters for the coming year. Once approval is obtained from the Reviewer, the performance plane is considered final.

⌘ Unique Roles ⌘

In order to standardize the performance planning process and measurement of performance across divisions/functions/units, each officer in the organization has been mapped to a Unique Role (UR). This also ensures strong alignment between performance plans and organizational business requirements.

These unique role profiles were created by role holders across divisions and locations, and then validated by respective functional experts.

Definition of Performance

Definition of Performance in PMS is based upon Key Result Areas (KRAs), Competencies, Values and Potential. The achievement against targets set for each of these will together constitute the Appraisee's performance.

- KRAs are identified areas of performance that support the organization's goals that are to be accomplished during the year. Each KRA is accompanied by one or more KPIs.

- Competencies are knowledge, skills and abilities described in behavioural terms that are coachable, observable, measurable, and critical to successful performance.

- Potential includes the critical attributes which do not get covered in competencies and reflect an individual's capacity to shoulder higher responsibility.

- Values are statements that express IOCL's ethical commitments and guiding principles which are timeless and will stand the test of time. Values in market forces and management practices, are the principles, an on upholding of which individuals are assessed.

The relative weight ages of these 4 sections - KPAs, Competencies, Values and Potential - has been pre-decided.

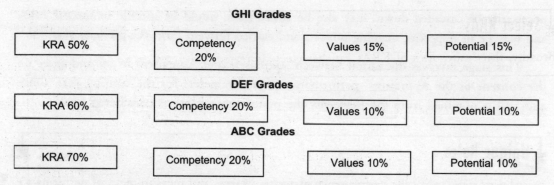

GHI Grades

| KRA 50% | Competency 20% | Values 15% | Potential 15% |

DEF Grades

| KRA 60% | Competency 20% | Values 10% | Potential 10% |

ABC Grades

| KRA 70% | Competency 20% | Values 10% | Potential 10% |

PMS allows the Appraisee to define his/her performance measures using the three categories of KRAs defined in the following section.

Additionally, to be able to focus and prioritize on the basis of importance, each KPI also has a weightage. This would be finalize between Appraiser and Appraisee during the performance planning phase.

⌘ KRA ⌘

Definition-Key Result Areas (KRAs) are "Critical outcomes towards which effort is directed to support achievement of desired business results". Each KRA in a role profile would fall in one of the following buckets:

(a) *Operational/Direct or Critical Outputs:* KRAs pertaining to functional/Operational activities, in terms of efficiency as performance in the organization.

(b) *Financial:* KRAs pertaining to direct impact on top line (revenue) or bottom line (cost) at a decision making level.

(c) *Strategy and Growth/Forward Planning:* KRAs pertaining to strategic direction setting or establishing differentiation with respect to manufacturing, selling & marketing, product & process development and delivery.

(d) *People/Team Management:* KRAs pertaining to people development, training, performance management and employee satisfaction activities for all appraisers with direct reports.

(e) *Boundary Management/Coordination and Liaison:* KRAs pertaining to liaising/ coordinating with Governmental (local, state, central), Administrative, Regulatory, Statutory bodies and vendors/customers (external & internal).

⌘ Select KRAs ⌘

Broadly, three categories of KRAs can be selected/created

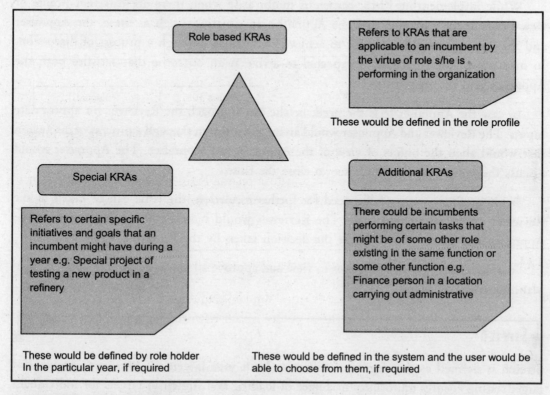

Role based KRAs

Refers to KRAs that are applicable to an incumbent by the virtue of role s/he is performing in the organization

These would be defined in the role profile

Special KRAs

Additional KRAs

Refers to certain specific initiatives and goals that an incumbent might have during a year e.g. Special project of testing a new product in a refinery

There could be incumbents performing certain tasks that might be of some other role existing in the same function or some other function e.g. Finance person in a location carrying out administrative

These would be defined by role holder In the particular year, if required

These would be defined in the system and the user would be able to choose from them, if required

⌘ Defining KPIs for KRAs ⌘

Key Performance Indicators (KPI) are specific indicators of performance to measure extent of achievement on set KRAs within a given time frame. Each KRA corresponds to specific KPIs defined to quantify or verify the extent of performance achievement in a given performance time frame.

For each KRA selected, the Appraisee should select at least one KPI. In case of Special KRAs, s/he would define a KPI.

Once the Appraisee has finalized the list of KRAs and corresponding KPIs, s/he will propose weightages and 5 levels of targets for each KPI.

S/he will also use the stretch tool to determine the stretch involved in the targets at level 3.

Note: The appraiser will finally view and accept/discuss/refer to Reviewer the performance plan.

While implementing PMS, occasions might arise when there are different points of view between the Appraiser and the Appraisee. In situations such as these, the Appraiser and the Appraisee should attempt to achieve a consensus through a process of discussion. In most cases, the Appraiser is expected to arrive at an outcome that satisfies both the Appraisee and the Appraiser.

In case the Appraiser feels the need, he/she can approach the Reviewer for appropriate inputs. The Reviewer and Appraiser would arrive at a solution through a process of discussion that would align the points of view of the Appraiser and Appraisee. The Appraiser would discuss the same with the Appraisee to close the issue.

In the unlikely event of the need for further escalation, the issue can be taken to the Reviewer on a case to case basis. The Reviewer would have a joint discussion with the Appraisee and the Appraiser where the decision taken by the Reviewer would be final.

It is mandatory for the Reviewer to view and approve all plans, before the performance-planning phase is closed.

⌘ Stretch ⌘

Stretch is defined as the degree of difficulty built into targets. A consistent process for target setting ensures uniformity in degree of loading and stretch in targets for individuals. The target setting process in PMS works on the following 5 dimensions:

- Relative to previous achievements
- Degree of dependence on uncontrollable
- Degree of complexity
- Skill Requirements
- Need for innovations

During the performance planning phase, the Appraisee proposes targets for each KPI, S/he then assesses the overall degree of stretch of each target using a four-point (high, Moderate, Low, and Nil) scale along these 5 dimensions.

Stretch needs to be calculated for the Annual target at Level 3 of performance of the target. This is the target level for MOU and Centre point of scale and also the logical definition of target based on Meets Expectations definition of scale.

The 4-point scale for each dimension is as follows:

Dimension	Nil	Low	Moderate	High
Relative to previous achievements	Nil	Standards of timeliness (deadlines), quantity, quality and costs of outcomes can be met with normal effort. Standards have been regularly met before.	Standards of timeliness (deadlines), quantity, quality and costs of outcomes require some significant effort. Standards have been met once or twice before.	Standards of timeliness(deadlines), quantity, quality and costs of outcomes require very significant sustained effort. Requires standards that have never been met before
Degree of dependence on uncontrollable	Nil	Limited support from others is necessary for success for the initiative.	Other's work or support is necessary for success, but it may be late or not complete.	Others' work or support is necessary for success, but it may take a new direction at any point
Degree of complexity	Nil	Steps, milestones and resource requirements follow a tested route.	Target requires the coordination of more resources and elements than tested route	Required steps, dependencies and time frames have not previously been planned, integrated, or executed
Skill requirement	Nil	Existing skills may be challenged, but new skills are not required.	Required skills can be developed by training with minimal disruption.	Focused and dedicated time and resources will be necessary to gain required skills.
Need for innovation	Nil	Can use standard technology and tools.	Involves some innovation in adapting existing tools or methods	Requires revolutionary innovations and technology

Stretch can reduce subjectivity but not eliminate it. Appraiser and Appraisee objectivity and process adherence are required for stretch to function adequately. Reviewer is expected to ensure balance in stretch across similar roles. The degree of Stretch varies across KPIs. But the overall stretch is the weighted average of the stretch on various KPIs. This will provide a perspective on the overall stretch of a performance plan.

⌘ Competencies ⌘

Definition---Behavioural Competencies are defined as "skills and abilities described in behavioural terms that are coachable, observable, and critical to organizational performance. Competencies form the foundation of "what" capabilities are required for the successful execution of roles and responsibilities, thereby driving functional, unit and organization performance.

The list of generic/behavioral and leadership competencies and their manifestation degrees vary. Therefore, for each role, applicable competencies from this list & the desired proficiency level for these have been identified and included in each UR. A list of detailed models for functional as well as generic competencies is available on the IOCL Intranet.

Based on the varying demands of each role, competencies and their manifestation degrees vary. Therefore, for each role, applicable competencies from this list & the desired proficiency level for each role has been identified and included in each UR. A detailed list of all competencies, generic and functional, and the proficiency levels defined for each has been provided in Appendix I.

Although the Appraisee does not have the option to select competencies defined for his role, s/he may view the competencies and proficiency levels which are applicable to his role and he is expected to demonstrate on the job.

⌘ Values ⌘

Following are the values which have been defined by the organization as essential to display for Grade A-F,

What Should I Demonstrate
1. Passion for Excellence
2. Care for all stakeholders i.e., Customers, Shareholders, Employees and Community
3. Commitment to Organization including its National obligations

How Should I Conduct Myself?
1. Honesty
2. Integrity
3. Transparency
4. Truthfulness
5. Courage of Conviction

The complete descriptions will be made available on the IOCL Intranet.

Following are the values for GHI (as prescribed by Public Enterprises Selection Board): treatment of employees and applicants.

- *Fairness:* Decisions are made objectively, free from patronage and reflect the just treatment of employees and applicants.

- *Transparency:* There is open communication about every aspect of managerial decisions which concern people.

- *Trust:* Trustworthiness leads to confidence for it

   ❖ Allow staff the freedom to grow and develop

   ❖ Relate to others on the basis of mutual respect

   ❖ Have courage to stand by your convictions.

- *Candor:* Frank and forthright
  - ❖ Give and receive constructive criticism/suggestions
  - ❖ Openly discuss performance deficiencies and take corrective action
  - ❖ Appreciate good performance
  - ❖ Be consistent in works and deeds
  - ❖ Face up to your mistakes

- *Collaboration:* Work in tandem with others, and
  - ❖ Be open in sharing information and in seeking suggestion/opinions
  - ❖ Be sensitive to the concerns of others
  - ❖ Honour your commitments
  - ❖ Encourage team work across departments/functions

- *Involvement:* Total commitment
  - ❖ Be dedicated and committed to work, build commitment by encouraging wide participation in decision making process to the maximum extent possible.

- *Flexibility:* Ability to participate and adapt to changing circumstances using sound judgment
  - ❖ Be open to accepting new ideas
  - ❖ Be willing to learn from anyone and to do things differently
  - ❖ Be prepared to operate and adapt to different environments

- Willingness to accept challenge-
  - ❖ Be willing to experiment
  - ❖ Allow for freedom to fail, but learn from it too

- *Discipline:* Adherence to accepted norms
  - ❖ Honours the promises and adhere to agreed system
  - ❖ Respect for others time and space
  - ❖ Exercise self control

- *Ethical Behaviour:* Demonstrate honestly and sincerity in every action
  - ❖ Apply sound business and professional ethics
  - ❖ Show consistency with principles, values and behaviours

The detailed set of values is available on the IOCL Intranet. The Appraisee will be able to view the set of values, applicable to his level, in the ePMS.

⌘ Potential

Following are the attributes which have been defined by the organization for Grades A-F

Grades ABC	**Grades DEF**
Adaptability to change Collaboration Cost Consciousness/Resource utilization Dependability Quality of Work/Output	Managing Change Boundary Management Entrepreneurial Leadership Enhancement of Quality and output

The complete descriptions will be made available on the IOCL Intranet.

Following are the attributes which have been defined by the organization for Grades GHL.

- *Leadership abilities:* These demonstrate ability:

  ❖ For guiding collective decision making

  ❖ For succession planning

  ❖ In Crisis management

  ❖ To take risks

- *Team building:* This demonstrates effectiveness in

  ❖ Re-organising his/her own department

  ❖ Managing diverse and divergent views and group processes without losing sight of objectives.

- *Ability to build a strategic vision:* Demonstrates ability to:

  ❖ Mange change

  ❖ Focus on long-term issues

  ❖ Strategic thinking

  ❖ Translate vision into goals

- *Business sense:* Commitment to bottomline results by:

  ❖ Enhancing revenue generation by addressing interest of customers and stakeholders

  ❖ Balancing need for viable short and long-term performance

❖ Optimizing unit/organization's contribution while supporting corporate objectives

❖ Spotting and pursuing new business opportunities wherever possible.

● *Communication skills:* Ability to:

❖ Communicate ideas and information effectively through public speaking and presentation,

❖ Convert ideas through action plan and ensure acceptability within the organization and performance at board meetings.

The Appraisee will be able to view these elements of potential which s/he is expected to demonstrate.

⌘ Editing Performance Plan ⌘

In situations, where, extraneous circumstances significantly impact performance plans, changes in the plans may be incorporated, e.g., Changes in business environment which may impact Key Results Areas, KPIs or targets of various individuals. Editing the performance plan is to be initiated by the Appraisee, the rationale for the same so to ratified by the Appraiser and the Reviewer before the change can be formalized into the system. Once approval is obtained from the Reviewer, the Appraisee is able to modify his plan and this then follows the same process as the initial performance planning module.

Performance Planning- Process steps, Roles and Responsibilities

Process step	Responsibility			
	Appraisee	Appraiser	Reviewer	Facilitator/Administrator
Initiate performance planning phase for the year				✓
Identify appropriate UR				✓
Identify Role-based KRAs	✓			
Identify additional and special KRAs	✓			
Identify overall weightage for KPIs	✓			
Propose weightage for each KPI	✓			

Contd...

Propose targets for KRAs	✔			
Validate degree of stretch	✔	✔	✔	
Achieve consensus	✔	✔	✔	
Final approval of Performance Plan			✔	
Close performance planning phase for the year				✔
Initiation of change in plan	✔			
Ratification and sign off		✔	✔	

⌘ Feedback and Counselling ⌘

The process of continuous Feedback and Counseling is an inherent and critical part of PMS.

The mid-year and final reviews are specifically focused on Feedback and Counselling and hence required the appraise and the Appraiser to have a formal feedback session.

For Feedback and Counselling to be truly effective, it should be provided and received on an ongoing basis. When used effectively, feedback & counselling are powerful means of positively impacting performance.

Feedback and Counselling helps an Appraiser in both obtaining informal and providing inputs on how an Appraisee is performing and whether or not he/she is headed in the right direction. It is also an opportunity for the Appraisee to solicit resources and help that may be required for enhancing his/her own performance.

Most people are comfortable in providing positive feedback. However, they are hesitant to initiate a conversation that involves sharing of negative or unpleasant performance-related information. Such hesitation can be overcome by considering the importance of their feedback in correcting the performance level of the Appraisee, and the consequent benefit to the appraisee's career.

Feedback is of various types:

- Positive feedback
- Corrective feedback
- Feedback focused on identifying obstacles to performance
- Feedback for the purpose of sharing information, etc.

Tips for Giving Positive Feedback	Tips for Giving Negative Feedback
Recognise good performance often	Express confidence in the Apprisee's ability to improve
Provide specific examples in your feedback messages	Focus on behaviour that can be changed, not the person
Provide timely feedback, both positive & corrective	Define the impact on you and other members
Listen to the other person's viewpoints and ideas	Offer support to help or remove obstacles
Solicit as well as provide feedback	Share your expectations for future behaviour
Catch performance problems early while they are small	Together explore options for solving the problem
Check to be sure clear communication has occurred	Describe consequences of improved/not improved performance

Remember - Giving Feedback is like Giving GIFTS

Goes both ways: Feedback should be a tow-way exchange. It is critical to listen to the Appraisee to whom you are giving feedback.

Initiated by the person who sees a need: Feedback should be initiated by the person who sees the need first. When Appraisee has requested feedback, he or she is less likely to be defensive. A climate conducive to giving and receiving feedback, and one that values honest communication, makes it easier for people to ask for feedback when it's needed.

Frequent: Feedback needs to be provided on a regular basis. If the Appraisee is surprised by the message, feedback is not frequent enough.

Timely: Generally, feedback that is given as close to the event as possible is most useful. However, timely doesn't necessarily mean that feedback must follow immediately after a triggering event, especially if there are emotions involved.

Specific: Non-specific comments leave the appraise with insufficient information about what changes or improvements he or she might need to make. Base your feedback (positive, negative, or corrective) on observed behaviour and facts, and not on inferences, assumptions, or what you've heard from others.

✠ Performance Diary ✠

The Performance Diary is a tool provided to the Appraisee to keep record of key information related to performance. The Appraisee can make entries as when required; all the entries will be stamped by the date and time entered.

Every Appraisee entry is intimated to appraiser and every Appraiser entry is intimated to Appraisee.

The Reviewer is able to view the appraisee's performance diary when he desires.

The diary is expected to ease the effort of tracking key performance events/activities. This would be used as a support document during performance reviews.

⌘ Mid-year Review

The objective of a mid-year review is to ensure that performance management is not limited to "once a year report card" but has a mid-year process for reviewing and tracking achievements. It also reduces the scope for surprises at the end of the year and ensures that the Appraisee is always aware of expectations.

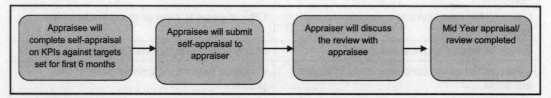

Mid-Year Review of performance for each individual is conducted during the month of October. This is initiated as a self-appraisal by the Appraisee and a review by the Appraiser. The Mid-year Review does not result in a performance score, but is a half-yearly opportunity to record comments on performance issues.

The Mid-year review is also an opportunity where under extraneous circumstances changes in performance plans may be incorporated; e.g., Changes in business environment which may impact Key Results Areas of various individuals.

Final Appraisal, Review & Feedback

⌘ Objective

Final Appraisal, Review & Feedback is an assessment phase when Appraisers assess level of achievement of KRAs, targets and routine responsibilities and demonstration of competencies for each Appraisee.

The final performance review and feedback is undertaken in the month of April-May. Ratings and feedback will be given based on what the employee has delivered vis-a-vis the set and agreed performance plan.

During the final appraisal, review and feedback phase, first the Appraisee undertakes a self-appraisal and gives a rating on all the performance parameters i.e., KRAs, Routine Responsibilities and Competencies. The Appraiser then does the assessment & rating. He/she also reviews the actions taken towards achievement of the Appraisee's development plan. The Reviewer then reviews the ratings on KRAs, Routine Responsibilities and Competencies. At any stage the Appraiser and/or Reviewer can call for a discussion with the Appraisee. The final ratings have to be a consensus between Appraisee, Appraiser & the Reviewer. In case of a dispute, the Reviewer's ratings will be treated as final and will feed into the Overall performance score of the Appraisee.

Feedback and guidance to the Appraisee should be provided on a continuous basis throughout the year. PMS provides the Appraisee and the Appraiser opportunity to input the key achievements as and when they happen through an online personal diary. This will also help capture all performance-related information and keep continuous focus on performance.

⌘ The Final Review Process

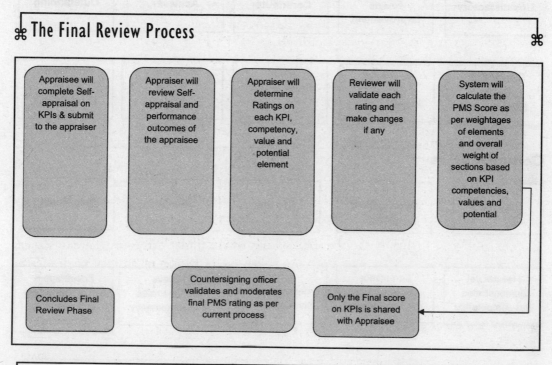

⌘ Rating Scale

All performance ratings in PMS are done on a 5-point rating scale. The scale description is different for different sections.

⌘ KPIs

KPIs have a 5-point scale with each point on the scale anchored to target metrics-reflecting degree of performance achievement against each KPI. The target metrics against the 5 levels of achievement have been proposed by the Appraisee, validated by the Appraiser and reviewed by the Reviewer during the performance-planning phase. The following is an illustration of the scale:

Level	Level	Level of Target Achievement (illustrative for Sales in INR Crores)
1	Significantly Below Expectations	120 crores
2	Moderately Below Expectations	130 crores
3	Meets Expectations	145 crores
4	Moderately Above Expectations	155 crores
5	Significantly Above Expectations	170 crores

KPIs

1 Unsatisfactory	2 Needs Improvement	3 Contributor	4 Achiever	5 Outstanding
Significantly Below Expectations	Moderately Below Expectations	Meets Expectations	Moderately Above Expectations	Significantly Above Expectations

Competencies

1 Learner	2 Development Area	3 Capable	4 Strength	5 Role Model
Has not yet demonstrated this competency	Sometimes demonstrates this competency	Often demonstrates this competency	Always demonstrates this competency	Encourage & influences others to display this competency

Values

1 Learner	2 Development area	3 Capable	4 Strength	5 Role model
Does not demonstrate these values	Sometimes demonstrates some of these values	Often demonstrates most of these values	Always demonstrates all of these values	Encourages & influences others to display these values

Potential

1 Learner	2 Development area	3 Capable	4 Strength	5 Role model
Has not yet demonstrated this attribute	Sometimes demonstrates this attribute	Often demonstrates this attribute	Always demonstrates this attribute	Encourages & influences others to display this attribute

⌘ Calculation of Stretch

As discussed in the section on performance planning, stretch is the degree of difficulty built into the target at the time of performance planning. The year end rating on each KPI will be multiplied by the stretch on it to get the performance score for each KPI.

This process will ensure that Appraisees whose targets are stretched are not disadvantaged as compared to those whose targets have lower stretch. Stretch has been considered for IOCL given the need to address issues on loading in PMS targets which may be accentuated given the planned linkage of KRA/KPI section PMS scores to Individual PIS Design.

5 Dimensions of Stretch	Degree of Stretch			
	Nil	Low	Medium	High
Relative to the previous years	0.25	0.5	0.75	1
Dependency on uncontrollable	0.25	0.5	0.75	1
Complexity	0.25	0.5	0.75	1
Skill requirements	0.25	0.5	0.75	1
Need for Innovation	0.25	0.5	0.75	1
Total Score	1.25	2.5	3.75	5
Stretch	0.25	0.5	0.75	1

The performance score is calculated based on performance on KPIs

KRA	Weight	Rating	Stretch	Individual KPI score
				(KPI weight*rating *stretch)
KPI 1	20%	3	0.85	0.51
KPI 2	30%	4	0.75	0.90
KPI 3	40%	4	0.95	1.52
KPI 4	10%	2	0.60	0.12
KPI Score				3.05

The following is an illustration of how overall performance scores can be calculated for individuals:

PMS Calculation Sheet GHI Level

KRA	Weight	Rating	Stretch	Individual KPI score
				(KPI weight*rating *stretch)
KPI 1	20%	3	0.85	0.51
KPI 2	30%	4	0.75	0.90
KPI 3	40%	4	0.95	1.52
KPI 4	10%	2	0.60	0.12
KPI Score				3.05

Competency 20%	Weight	Rating	Individual Competency Score (weight*rating)
Competency 1	33%	3	1.00
Competency 2	33%	4	1.33
Competency 3	33%	3	1.00
Competency Score			3.33

values 15%	Weight	Rating	Individual values Score (weight*rating)
Values 1	33%	3	1.33
Values 2	33%	4	1.00
Values 3	33%	3	1.33
values Score			3.67

potential 15%	Weight	Rating	Individual potential Score (weight*rating)
potential 1	33%	4	1.33
potential 2	33%	5	1.67
potential 3	33%	4	1.33
Potential Score			4.33

Over all Score	3.391

Overall Score = (KPI rating *KPI Weight + Competency rating *Competency Weight +Values rating *Values Weight +Potential rating *Potential weight)

Overall Score =(3.05*50%+3.33*20% +3.67*15% +4.33*15%) = 3.391

The Appraisee will be communicated the Performance score on KPIs upto reviewer level. This Performance score will be input into the calculation of final performance rating. However the final rating (Significantly Below Expectations/ Moderately Below Expectations/ Meets Expectations/ Moderately Above Expectations/ Significantly Above Expectations) would be arrived at not communicated to the Appraisee.

⌘ Managing Role Changes ⌘

PMS provides for handling role changes arising from transfers, promotions, change in responsibility allocation, etc. When a role change happens, the performance appraisal and review is done before transitioning to the new role, expect for incumbents who have occupied the previous role for a period of less than three months. It is to be noted that the individual undergoing a change in role needs to undertake a fresh performance planning exercise as per guidelines provided in the section on performance planning.

For the purpose of calculating overall performance rating for individuals who have undergone a change in role, a time weighted average performance rating of the roles performed by the individual is taken.

In the case of new recruits who come on board during a performance cycle, if s/he spends less than 3 months in the performance cycle, his or her performance will not be appraised and reviewed.

Performance Appraisals, Review & Feedback-Process steps, Roles and Responsibilities:

Process step	Responsibility			
	Appraisee	Appraiser	Reviewer	Facilitator/Administrator
Initiate appraisal & review phases (mid-year & final)				✔
Mid year review				
Self appraisal	✔			
Commenting on performance		✔		
Closure	✔	✔		
Final Appraisal & Review				
Self Appraisal	✔			
Year end appraisal		✔		
Year end review			✔	
Achieving consensus	✔	✔	✔	
Communication of performance score and feedback to Appraisee		✔		
Close appraisal & review (mid year & final year)				✔

Appendix I
Competency Definitions & Proficiency Levels

The following is the list of competencies that form a part of PMS:

1. Planning & Organizing
2. Strategic Orientation
3. Change Leadership
4. Championing Customer Focus
5. Performance Focus
6. Seizing Opportunities
7. Personal Effectiveness
8. Team Leadership
9. Developing Self and Others
10. Impact and Influence
11. Strategic Thinking
12. Practical Creativity
13. Openness and Learning
14. Customer Service Orientation
15. Achievement Orientation
16. Analytical Ability
17. Decision Making
18. Problem Solving
19. Negotiation Skills
20. Team Effectiveness
21. People development
22. Communication skills

Planning and Organizing

Proficiency Level 1	Proficiency Level 2
Ability to plan and organize for self	**Ability to do complex planning for self and team**
• Develops schedules to accomplish work • Develops a personal organizational system and work routine(files, to-do lists, paperwork, pending orders) that facilitates delivery of work • Prioritizes activities and issues on daily, weekly, and monthly basis and reworks plans as required	• Clearly outlines the work, deliverables, and timelines to team members, if any and helps them work out action plans • Establishes a course of action to accomplish a specific goal; plans proper allocation of time and resources. • Analyzes cost-benefit trade-off and focuses on activities that have the greatest impact • Is aware of inter-relationships among different activities and plans work assignments and allocates resources accordingly

PART-D

Live Cases

1

BHEL

Making Performance Management System a Way of Life

As a continuing process of linking HRM to market forces and stakeholder-driven policies, several new HR initiatives were put in place during the year. Having introduced Performance Management System (PMS) as a replacement of conventional Annual Confidentiality Reports (ACRs), the company become the first PSE to implement during the year, an e-enabling Performance Management System for executives called e-MAP—Moving ahead through Performance. The new Performance Management System was started by the initiative and high involvement of the top management with a drive to excel and to counter competition with domestic as well as foreign suppliers of equipment. The system, while debugging various lacunae faced in performance management systems, is aimed at boosting the productivity of employee and introducing greater transparency. It provides access to over 10,000 executives located all over the country for preparing of their performance plans and completing the appraisal on a web-enabled platform.

Five focus groups at Haridwar involving approximately 150 executives across levels, functions, locations, units and sectors were taken to test the use of MAP.

The process of e-MAP took off in 2002. The existing performance management system (ACR) was analyzed and improvement (design) measures were arrived at form the analysis. The precondition for making it user friendly and time saving is e-enablement. Simultaneously, a pilot project to develop implementation tools and processes for the new performance management system was undertaken. A combination of e-enabling and new tools and processes formed the basis to implement MAP, implementation of a communication rollout to all executives. The 2002-03 cycle process review and the report were done by Hewitt Consultants by June 2003. They also are assisting in performance planning for 2003-04.

The duration from designing MAP till rolling it out to the middle and junior level management was 14 weeks and Hewitt played an important role during this phase. BHEL played its part in rolling out the communication process and MAP to middle and junior executives. The 14-week task was divided into three phases. The first phase of two weeks duration involved designing of MAP and the communication strategy and its materials. The second mid-week phase was the change phase. The customization of e-enablement to MAP requirements was followed by pilot study in IS and power sector and then the roll-out of MAP to the pilot unit and functional templates were prepared.

The major part of this phase was spent in communicating the change and its implementation as it was important for the rese of the sub-tasks in this phase.

BHEL leadership team workshops were held and MAP was introduced for usage to BHEL middle and junior management during the third phase. It was of six weeks duration. The process was monitored till the end of its completion for the middle management and a process audit was held for the junior management.

Five hundred change agents were selected to implement the process throughout the organization. These change agents were the high job performers and key managers and executives. The communication strategy BHEL used in this task is as described hereafter.

The communication principle is to build awareness of PMS 2-0, to gain an understanding of its functioning during implementation and through feedback from users and to allay the misgivings of the system. The variables were five-fold:

1. *Events:* When are the key events taking place in the change process? And what are the key phases in these events?

2. *Audiences:* Who are the key audiences for this change? And how is this change going to affect them?

3. *Message:* What are the key messages that are required to be communicated to the audience? And what are the other appropriate messages for communication?

4. *Media:* How are the message going to be communicated? What are the key delivery vehicles? What is available? What is to be developed?

5. *Messenger:* Who are the key messengers? And what are the groups or users they are covering?

It was decided to discuss the PMS at different levels/cross-sections/units/business groups. We had the following agenda in view:

- The PMS feedback last year;

- Expectation from system;

- Culture and mindset; and

- Key concerns.

BHEL has been continuously improving upon the process/approaches for managing performance. The Performance Management System (PMS) was developed through in-house efforts, taking inputs from all concerned groups. However, in order to address certain issues, which mainly related to:

- Alignment;
- Consistency;
- Transparency; and
- Ownership;

A workshop held, with 150 participating executives across levels/functions/locations units/ business sectors.

The following inputs were collated:

1. "I was able to objectively discuss my performance with my boss."
2. "The process made us thinking about our role and contribution."
3. "We are not clear about how goals are to be set."
4. "Inadequate understanding of competencies"
5. "The process was completed only because it had to be done".
6. "We do not know what our final scores are"
7. "The system is not transparent"
8. "It is very difficult to set goals for service areas"
9. "Our superiors accumulate our targets as their targets"
10. "People have set objectives which they have already achieved or which are routine activities".
11. "We set our targets in isolation".
12. "Senior people have not devoted time to the PMS".
13. "Promotion seems to be the objective of the system".
14. "The lack of role clarity has impacted the quality of the process".
15. "Tendency to avoid stretch".

Thus, by listening to the users of the systems, the current state of the system was:

- Wide acceptance of need for PMS;
- PMS design, by and large, appropriate;

- Entire organization has attempted to implement it, with varying degrees of success; and

- Strong commitment to resolve issues and move on.

And the issues which needed to be addressed we identified as:

- *Alignment and Focus:* Executive's performance aligned to the goals of BHEL;

- *Ownership:* Executives taking responsibility and onus for their own performance;

- *Transparency:* Clear, transparent and objective process; and

- *Consistency:* Consistent application of performance principles; 'uniform loading'.

Thus, a project was taken up to make performance a "way of life" at BHEL. This was planned through:

- Redesigning;

- E-enabling; and

- Effective organization-wide implementation of the performance management system.

(M/s Hewitt Associates assistance was sought in the above area).

A comprehensive structure was put in place to prepare a road map/design the system/ design enable process and methodology to implement the same in a time-bound frame.

The system has the following features:

1. Consistency of measures through functional templates;

2. Alignment of individual goals to organizational goals;

3. Agreement between appraiser, appraisee and the reviewer;

4. Clarify and enrich the existing competencies;

5. Transpose employee to unique roles;

6. Assign competencies and proficiencies to unique roles;

7. Redesign of normalization process;

8. Effective organization-wide communication and training of new system; and

9. PMS workflow automation.

Also, the futuristic linkage of systems were discussed/ debated and included as below:

1. Direct linkage of PMS to rewards;

2. Improved measurement and target settings

3. Multi-rater feedback for a segment of the organization. E.g., senior management;

4. Better alignment of performance cycle with the performance management system;

5. E-learning-development platform;

6. Performance –potential matrix for career/succession planning;

7. Create a new competency model in line with business realities; and

8. Initiate assessment for senior managers/high performers.

The basic parameters have been bifurcated in two, as shown in Figure 1

1. Performance parameters; and

2. Capability development parameters.

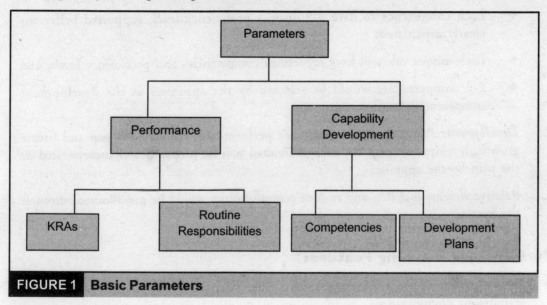

FIGURE 1   **Basic Parameters**

Performance

1. *KRAs*

    ❖   The implementation to take care of issues around the development of KRAs for service functions as well as interdependencies;

    ❖   The KRAs to recognize the efforts that create value for the organization;

    ❖   To include outcome measures as well as measures that focus on process, capability development, customer and projects; and

    ❖   Identify measures to capture relative ease of achieving performance.

2. *Routine Responsibilities*

    ❖ Appraisee to propose weightage to each appraiser to approve;

    ❖ Could be either outputs or activities depending upon roles; and

    ❖ Some roles might have very high weightage of routine responsibilities, e.g., parliamentary affairs, VIP reference, establishment, security, etc.

Capability Development

1. *Competencies*

    ❖ Consolidated from 53 to 19 competencies;

    ❖ Each competency to have 3-5 distinct proficiency level, supported behaviour clearly articulated;

    ❖ Each unique role will have predefined competencies and proficiency levels; and

    ❖ 2-3 competencies would be selected by the appraiser as the development competencies for the year.

2. *Development Plans:* Based on last year's performance, competency gap and future growth development plan for each individual will be prepared and incorporated in the plan by the appraiser.

Relative weights to KRAs and routine responsibilities would be pre-allocated through the System.

Performance Planning Features

- *Modification to the performance plan:* The change can be incorporated under extraneous circumstances.

- *Role Charge:* In the event of a transfer a time-weighted average performance rating of the roles performed by the appraisee will be taken as this performance score of the year (exception: Less than one month in the job).

Target-setting Principles Stretch/Loading

- Stretch principles: Clearly articulated six target setting principles for BHEL.

- Appraiser and appraisee establish KRAs and targets based on these target setting principles.

- Reviewer reviews the performance plan for all appraisees keeping in mind the target setting principles.

Performance Feedback and Review

- *Performance vs Effort:* Overall rating will be based on achievement of the performance parameters only. The PMS would ensure balanced KRAs, capturing capability and process building effort.

- *Frequency of feedback:* Continuous performance feedback made possible through appraisee e-PMS dairy

Competencies for Map

- 53 competencies of the present system have been consolidated into 19.

- Each competency has been defined and proficiency levels have been calibrated.

- Some to the competencies used are:

- Planning and organizing

- Initiative and drive

- Commitment to quality

- Creativity and innovation

- Interpersonal relationships

- Risk-taking

- Decision-making

- Subordinate development job knowledge

- Knowledge of business environment.

Competency and Proficiency Levels: An Example

Competency Name: 'Planning and Organizing'

Definition: It establishes systematic action plans for self and others to assure accomplishment of specific objectives.

Each competency is specified at three levels at BHEL and a corresponding behaviour description is also defined.

Level I

- Develops schedules to accomplish work

- Develops a personal system for organizing work (files, to-do lists, paperwork, pending orders) that facilities delivery of work.

- Prioritizes activities and issues on daily, weekly, and monthly basis and reworks plans as required.

Level 2

- Clearly outlines the work, deliverables, and timelines to team members and helps them prepare action plans.

- Establishes a course of action to accomplish a specific goal; plans proper allocation of time and resources.

- Analyses cost-benefit trade-off and focuses on activities that have the greatest impact.

- Is aware of interrelationships among different activities and plans work assignments and allocates resources accordingly.

Level 3

- Works with multiple teams/ projects and effectively integrates/ ensures integration of their deliverables, if required.

- Foresees potential issues that might arise and develops contingency plans to take care of the same.

- Takes cognizance of a varied number of inputs across several functions and develop long-term direction for unit/function.

These competencies are rated on a five-point scale as follows:

1. *Learner:* Has not yet demonstrated the behaviour or skill.

2. *Development area:* Sometimes demonstrates the behaviour/skill where appropriate.

3. *Capable:* Often demonstrates the behaviour/skill.

4. *Strength:* Almost always demonstrates behaviour/ skill where appropriate.

5. *Role model:* Encourages and influences others to display the skill in a job.

Unique Roles (UR) have to be created for every job under this system. Unique roles are jobs that may be held by different incumbents but essentially perform the same function. Thus, there may be certain differences in the incumbents, e.g., experience in number of years, number of people supervised by the incumbents or overall authority; but the jobs may still form one unique role if the following questions are answered:

- Do the jobs have the same primary reason of existence? Is the purpose of the jobs same?

  Required Answer: YES

- Are the roles significantly similar in duties, responsibilities and accountabilities?

  Required Answer: YES

- If you switch the incumbents of the roles in question, can they perform each other's roles with the same efficiency?

  Required Answer: YES

- Would the incumbents require a significantly different set of skills or abilities to perform each other's roles? No

  Required Answer: No.

The improvements in the new PMS (MAP) consist of

1. Design improvement;

2. Tools developed to support MAP, such as

   ❖ Unique roles and responsibilities templates;

   ❖ Measurement of stretch in targets;

   ❖ Normalization;

   ❖ E-enabling MAP,

   ❖ Users' handbook; and

3. Customizing MAP.

The Performance Cycle

It starts with:

- Unit/Business Sectors Draft Budgets (end-February)

- Office Performance Planning (March to mid-April).

- Online Performance Planning (mid-April to end-April).

- Mid-Year Review (September/October)

- Final Review and Feedback (April)

- Normalization of Scores (May)

These systems provide for ongoing feedback between appraisee and appraiser.

E-enabling

The system has been e-enabled with the objective of:

- Ease of use and implementation;

- Covers 10,000 + Executives of BHEL, via Internet;

- Consolidation of data centrally;

- Real-time analysis of data, to provide insights for business directors;

- Generalization of reports, as and when desired by users.

Competency-based Balanced Scorecard Model: An Integrative Perspective

"In the current globalization induced by abrupt changes in business environment, human resources have become the source of successful corporate strategy. This study emphasizes that human resource and HR practices are the foundation for achieving business excellence in terms of ROI, market share, employee satisfaction and customer delight. The paper explains the implementation of Balanced Scorecard by developing competencies in relation to values of the organization necessary for achieving business excellence."

Introduction

In today's dynamic world, companies are adopting newer approaches for facing competition and achieving business excellence. The new economic paradigm is characterized by speed, innovation, quality and customer satisfaction. The essence of the competitive advantage has shifted from tangible assets to intangible ones. Earlier, HR was concerned with activities such as payroll, staffing and employee welfare but rules of game have started to change completely as today organizations have to reckon with global competition and match international requirements in terms of product design, process technology, quality standards and on time delivery.

It is said today that business endeavours succeed or fail because of people involved and only by attracting the best people and making them perform their best will lead to accomplish deeds. Based on various studies (Pfeffer & Jeffrey 1994) it can be concluded that firms with more effective HR management systems consistently outperform the competition. However, evidence that HR can contribute to a firm's success doesn't mean it is now effectively contributing to success in business. It is a challenge for managers to make HR a strategic asset. This case justifies that there is a connection between human resource and business success in terms of tangible and intangible measures and establishes a framework which could assist HR professionals to make human resource a strategic asset. Based on Balanced Scorecard (Kaplan & Norton 1996) and through competency framework evident from corporate practices, the author has established a Competency-based Balanced Scorecard Model.

Balanced Score Card

Developed in the early 1990s by Kaplan and Norton (1992), the Balanced Scorecard is a management system that enables organizations to clarify their vision and strategy and translate them into action and has become a prominent strategic tool for the management.

3 EVA Incentive Scheme: The TCS Approach and Experience

TCS—An Introduction

When TCS started in 1968, it heralded the beginning of the software industry. In the 1970s it was probably the sole player in this area. Today, it is a leader in many businesses and continues to be among the leading players. TCS has a global presence with 92 branches in 29 countries. It is the largest software R&D centre in India. The revenue of TCS has doubled every two years during the past six year. It has achieved SEI-CMM Level 5 and P-CMM Level 4 and obtained the ISO 9001 certification. By 2001, TCS had a talent pool of 19,000 consultants. The annual revenue in the year was Rs. 31,420 million (USD 689).

TCS, being part of one of the largest business conglomerates – the Tata group – is known for its excellence and integrity. The Tata Group subscribes to the UN Global Compact.

What is Economic Value Added?

Economic Value Added (EVA) measures the difference between the return on a company's capital and the cost of the capital. EVA is the surplus (or deficit) that remains after levying a charge against after tax operating profits for the opportunity cost of equity and debt. The accounting concept of profit takes into consideration interest on borrowed capital, i.e., debt. The economic value added concept takes into account the economic cost of capital invested by shareholders. If the EVA is positive, it indicates that the company has created value for shareholders. If the EVA is negative, it signifies the contrary.

Any method that anyone can employ to better the efficiency will shows as an improvement in business. By cutting costs and adding to profit without adding to capital, operational efficiency can be improved. By reducing investment in assets that earn less than the cost of capital, asset management efficiency can be improved. By making new investments that earn return over and above the cost of capital, profitability can be improved. By implementing more effective financial and investor relation strategies, the cost of capital can be reduced. EVA focuses on these and helps determine the market value of the company (MVA). EVA is linked to the market value added: EVA = Total market value less total capital employed. MVA represents how much wealth a company has created for its investors (MVA = Discounted present value of future EVA).

EVA vs Earnings Growth

Increasingly, EVA is not always the same as increasing accounting profit. Rate of Return tells us how much the company's profit increases for every additional USD of capital it employs. Investment Rate is the ratio of money invested to the amount it earns as profit over the same period. For instance, look at examples A and B below:

A.   10% = 15%*66.7%

B.   10% = 5%*200%

Company A is more valuable because it needs to invest a fraction of its earnings to grow. To achieve the same level of growth in earnings as company A, B has to invest twice the amount that company A did. A can better finance growth from internally generated funds. B has to raise money. Earning a high return on capital is far more important than achieving rapid earnings growth. EVA incorporates this business maxim.

Consider the following example:

After its first year, this company wants to double sales and earnings, by doubling its capital.

Sales	100	200
Operating Costs	80	160
Profits before Tax	20	40
Tax at 40%	8	16
NOPAT	12	24
Loans	40	100
Equity	80	200
Capital	120	300
Cost of Capital	10%	10%
Capital Charge	12	30
EVA	0	-6

Note: NOPAT (-Net Operating Profit After Taxes)

The company's earnings are below the cost of capital. An additional investment of USD180 has generated only a USD12 increase in net operating profit after taxes (NOPAT). The management will earn only a 6.7% rate of return on its investments.

WHY TCS has gone in for EVA Linked Incentive?

Global competition has begun to erode profit margins. Meeting targets are not enough. To remain at the top, a company has to outperform its competitors. The company has thus to grow at a faster rate than the industry to remain viable and maintain the leadership position in the market. It has had to upscale its skills and competencies and graduate from programming and projects to developing products. The relationship between the company and its customers has to move up from short-term to long-term orientation. Unlike some other competing firms in the industry, TCS did not have stock options. TCS not being a publicity listed company, could not offer stock options to its employees. In any case, companies are slowly realizing, in hindsight, that excessive reliance on employees stock option programmes (ESOPs) is not good. Stock price movements are sometimes unrelated to company performance. Even when they are, they are not linked mainly to company performance alone, but also to industry performance and external factors at the macro level. Managers and employees are often perplexed about performance factors that drive their company's stock price. A company's stock price cannot outpace the overall stock market index indefinitely. The key challenge has been to consider other rewards, which can sustain employee motivation and improve employee retention.

TCS Compensation Plan

Individual compensation consists of two parts: Fixed Pay, which reflects experience/competency. Performance Pay which forms the variable component. Fixed pay is based on industry survey and cost of living index. Performance pay is based on EVA achieved.

The EVA incentive in TCS has the following components.

Target Bonus: Provides employees with competitive rewards for achieving expected performance.

Actual EVA Improvement (delta EVA): Year-to-year change in EVA

Expected EVA Improvement (EI): Performance standard consistent with TCS owners' expected return

EVA Interval: EVA Improvement (delta EVA) above Expected Improvement (EI) that results in a 2x Bonus declared and EVA below EI that results in 0x bonus declared.

Bonus Multiple:

$$1.0x + (delta\ EVA-EI)/EVA\ Interval$$

EVA Bank

Assume a manager has a salary of Rs. 100,000 and it is agreed that hitting EVA target should produce 25% bonus.

Salary (in '000)	Rs 100
Bonus Earned	25%
Bonus Earned (in '000)	Rs 25

Before pay-out, the bonus passes through a bank which has an Opening Balance, say of Rs. 50,000. The opening balance can come from two sources: Company Loans and Amortizes over, say next 5 years and replaces Rs. 10000 every year by employe's pay-out. The option part is contributed by the manager himself at the start of the year by way of the difference, if any, between the amount available for bonus pay out and actual bonus paid.

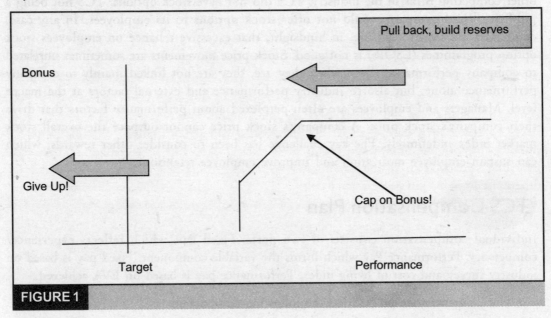

FIGURE 1

In the second year as shown below, the manager exceeds the EVA target:

TABLE 1

	Target Met (in '000s)	Great Year (in '000s)
Salary	100	100
Bonus	25%	100%
Bonus Earned, Rs	25	100
Beginning Bank Rs	50	50
Available for Pay-out	75	150
Pay-out Ratio	1/3	1/3
Bonus paid	25	50
Banked Forward	50	100

Table in the third year, suppose that EVA falls short of the target, as shown below:

TABLE 2			
	Target	**Great (in '000s)**	**Bad**
	Met	Year	Year
Salary	100	100	100
Bonus Earned	25%	100%	-50%
Bonus Earned	Rs 25	100	-50
Beginning Bank	Rs 50	50	100
Available for Pay-out	75	150	50
Pay-out ratio	1/3	1/3	1/3
Bonus Paid	25	50	16
Banked Forward	50	100	34

Employees are affected in the same way as are shareholders. Employees lose their incentive if EVA is negative. Shareholders, in a similar vein, lose or get reduced dividend. Penalty for employees and managers is shrunken bonus and depleted bank, which must first be replenished before a full normal bonus can be earned. EVA bank helps in smoothening out the bumps and grinds of business cycles. The time horizon is extended. Everyone is goaded to have one plan instead of short-term and long-term plans. The extended time horizon helps put golden hand cuffs on solid performers making it difficult for them to leave. For, EVA on investment are calculated over a period of time than in just one year.

The incentive distribution is as follows: the differences in incentive at each level are determined by cell performance and individual performance. Cell Proportion will be paid based on the cell to which an individual employee belonged during the assessment period. For getting better incentive on cell performance, what really matters is how much improvement was made over the set target (which could be positive or negative to start with). Individual performance rating is an assessment of attributes and goals met.

The performance management system in the company is designed such that it is possible to measure EVA at the lowest operational unit level. It meant cost allocation and apportionment to all the units. The revenue streams are also equally allocated and the company began to measure revenue flows, customer/project wise. The database is made comprehensive to monitor receivables, and delays in payments, if any. Earlier, first quarter results were available in the third quarter. The biggest digitization exercise launched in TCS in 2001-02 allows each project to view its EVA every month. It takes care of all direct and indirect expenses, capital costs attributable to projects and their revenues based on data at the end of each month. It takes care of all direct and indirect expenses, capital costs attributable to projects and their revenues based on data at the end of each month. This initiative links Activity-based Costing (ABC), project management and revenue systems with customer Relations Management (CRM) and supply chain management. Through computerized information system about everything concerning customers and suppliers and all activities, employees can log on to data instantly to monitor and measure the inputs and outcomes. With information available on line, the time lag is cut down drastically.

TCS decided to link its incentive plan to EVA because it wanted to cultivate a mindset oriented to EVA and promised that it will reward those who contribute to its enhancement. If EVA is positive employees get bonus. If EVA improves, bonus increases. There are no limits to either the growth in EVA or to the bonus employees can get. EVA linked cash bonus payment being a self-funding mechanism, there are no budgetary restrictions: there more the value added, the higher the size of the bonus. If the focus is short-term, it might induce some to manipulate accounts to produce results that may not be sustained over a period. In recent years, there have been many reports about the likes of Enron and WorldCom, fudging accounts. In the EVA scheme, if the company invests one billion dollars in developing a product, the pay back is expected over, say, the next five years. If the value added is not as per projections, the return on shareholders; capital will be negative. In such a situation, there is no way employees can get bonus for these five years.

TCS has three levels of management – junior, middle and senior management. The EVA is apportioned into three categories – corporate, self and individual performance. Individual managers are assessed on several performance measures on a quarterly basis. Individual managers are expected to meet their goals/targets on the balanced scorecard. In addition, they are assessed on attributes like knowledge, commitment, communication, etc. Individuals are ranked on a scale from 1 to 5. Rank 1 is awarded to those who perform below the normal TCS standards. Rank 2 is given to normal/average performers. Rank 3 is given to those who are above average and so on. Junior level managers' variable pay comes from EVA fund apportioned for individual performance. At middle management, the maximum amount of variable pay is derived from how well the unit they head performed. At the senior level, the quantum of bonus is based largely on company performance. In TCS improvement is recognized and rewarded. If a team brings down the negative EVA form 100 to 90 that team and its members will be eligible for bonus just the same way as the team which improves EVA from 100 to 110. The EVA incentive bonus scheme is linked to success in creating wealth for shareholders. Incentive bonus must be sizeable to influence employees' behaviour. The scheme does not put a ceiling on the amount of reward one can get, so long as they continue to add more value.

What are the gains for TCS? There is greater alignment between employee incentives and success in creating shareowner's wealth. There is a clear link between EVA, incentive and cell EVA targets for three years and bonus percentages. Employees are accountable for investment and asset utilization. Incentive is not paid from EVA, but increase in EVA. A level playing field is ensured for different geographic locations. Incentive bonus pool is funded from one overall measure of performance. It is simple and easy to communicate and manage. Bonus is large enough to influence employees' behaviour offering a bigger share in bottom-line is better than a small share of top-line results. There is no need to limit bonus based on increasing EVA. More EVA produces more wealth. EVA banks facilitate sustainability and employee retention. Deferred incentive bonus in EVA bank is forfeited. All employees participate in the scheme. All these constitute gains for TCS.

Excel Awards Scheme in BHEL

Objectives

The scheme aims to recognize, reward and place on record any direct or indirect outstanding and exemplary contribution by the employees towards growth profitability of the company, and also to recognize outstanding contribution to the society and all round excellence.

The scheme stipulates the following nine categories of awards each valuing upto USD 1,000 in case of an individual and USD 10,000 in the event of a group/team winning the award:

1. *An Award for All-Round Excellence:* This award has been instituted to recognize multi-disciplinary and multifaceted excellence.

2. *An Award for Excellence in Quality:* This is to recognize the outstanding achievement rating to quality of products, systems, processes, services etc.

3. *An Award for Timeliness, Speed and Response:* Instituted to recognize outstanding achievements with regard to completion of projects/assignments/tasks in record time or exemplary promptness in attending to customer complaints.

4. *An Award for Productivity:* Instituted to recognize outstanding achievement in productivity which could be in the form of significant cutting down of costs of production operations, import substitution, reduction in wastages and reworks, reduction in manpower, saving in materials, savings in fuel/power consumption etc.

5. *An Award for Technical Paper:* Instituted to promote and recognize the spirit of scientific enquiry in the field of theoretical, applied science and technology, particularly the contributions which lead to expanding the horizons of scientific knowledge.

6. *An Award for Research & Development:* Instituted to recognize the original research work of a very high standard.

7. *An award for Creativity and Innovation:* Instituted to recognize development of new products, components, processes and designs etc., leading to savings in costs, man-hours, improvement in quality, innovative solutions to problems at the shop floors, sites, customer complaints, equipment performance.

8. *An award for Customer Service:* Instituted to recognize the exemplary accolades won from the valuable customers.

9. *An award for Outstanding Contribution to Environment* of the employees towards society in general.

    While the first eight awards awarded only to the company employees, the ninth award covers spouses and dependent children of the employees.

10. *Appreciation for Good Health:* The appreciation has been kept at the unit level for employees who do not claim any medical reimbursement for self in the previous financial year and also do not avail any leave on account of sickness. The scheme was well received by a cross-section of employees across all the units. In the first year itself, about 150 employees form all units were conferred with the appreciation.

    The awards, excepting the Appreciation for Good Health are declared every year on 13th November, the day of incorporation of the Enterprise. The appreciation is declared on 7th April, World Health Day, every year.

Privileges Attached to Various Awards

1. All awards except Appreciation for Good Health carry the following privileges:

    ❖ Best nomination i.e., ranked first by the jury, in all categories will carry a cash award of USD 1,000/-, a medallion and a scroll, in case of the award is given to a group, the Chief Executive has the discretion to increase the award amount upto USD 10,000, for each award, to ensure a reasonable reward to each member of the group. The share of each team member in the reward money is specified by the jury.

    ❖ One additional training and development programme of choice at any institution within the country of maximum 15 days duration.

2. Appreciation for Good Health carries a cash prize of USD 500 and a certificate to be awarded by the Head of each unit on 7th April every year, the World Health Day.

3. To and fro journey fare for all the awardees to the capital and back to the unit is provided, with travelling expenses and hotel accommodation as per entitlement.

4. A dinner is hosted by the Chief Executive in honour of the awardees. The nominations for the nine categories of awards received from various units/divisions are evaluated

by a jury to be constituted by the Chief Executive. A glittering and large participation award presentation ceremony is held.

✄ Discussion ✄

Rewarding Excellence in BHEL

An interaction with Mr. RC Jain, Executive Director, BHEL

Q 1. How is the large amount of data required to measure the performance of an employee dealt with?

Ans. This problem is tackled in two ways:

(a) Nomination by a superior.

(b) Entry Form submitted by the employee along with a few results which could support his cause.

Q.2. How about adapting the 360 degree appraisal system?

Ans. It is not feasible, at least that is what we think.

❖ It requires a lot of maturity.

❖ There are too many groups rating the performance.

❖ Employees can not work at ease; they become too conscious.

❖ It is suitable only for knowledge-based companies.

Q.3. Are all the nominations put up before the Jury?

Ans. A summing committee consisting of a cross-functional team members from various departments shortlists the entries.

Q.4. Are the employees asked to make a presentation before the Jury?

Ans. Yes, it is a possibility.

Q.5. Is there any possibility of a person getting the award more than once?

Ans. Yes. There should not be any rotation system.

Q.6. How is the amount of cash reward estimated?

Ans. Cash reward is linked to salary, subject to certain ceilings one month's salary or Rs. 7000/- whichever is higher.

Q.7. Is there any scheme to penalize the undesirable acts done by the employees?

Ans. There is no scheme to penalize the employee on such grounds in monetary terms. One policy which could however, be followed is that the employee should not be allowed to continue working after the age of 55 years (without any compensation).

HR Balanced Scorecard and CCL

Scorecard for System Evaluation and Performance Assessment in HRM

HR Scorecard is an approach in HRM to evaluate the performance of HR function and its contribution in business operation of the company. It starts from sharing of vision to ethical operation of business and establishes HR's linkage with strategy of the company.

Renowned HR expert David Ulrich has outlined four basic roles of HR as given below:

1. *Management of Strategic Human Resources:* Aligning HR strategies and practices with the strategic need of the business.

2. *Management of the Firm's Infrastructure:* Delivering efficient HR processes such as staffing, training, appraisal, and reward systems.

3. *Management of Employee contribution:* Keeping close tabs on employee's needs and problems and seeing that these needs are met and problems are solved.

4. *Management of Transformation and Change:* HR's role in changing both the culture of the firm and the processes used within the firm.

Evolution of HR was seen into Developmental Phase

An example of HR Vision—We value the dignity and diversity of all people, excellent customer service, honesty and integrity, honouring commitment, teamwork and collaboration, open communication, simplified processes and practical solutions, innovation and risk-taking, personal accountability, job enjoyment, professional and technical expertise.

Global Economy now needs Human Resources keeping following changes:

- Expansion of economic boundaries
- Convergence to Global Economy
- Changing Contours of Business
- Digital Participation in Global Economy
- Quantitative Requirement of Human Resources
- Qualitative Matching of Manpower

Similarly, some trends in HRM have emerged which needs to be incorporated in the roadmap of HRM. Emerging Trends, as indicated below, pose challenges before organizations:

- Competition for expert workers
- Globalization
- Locus of control between organizations and individuals
- Marketability of knowledge
- Future age
- Technology explosion
- Global competitive advantage defined by ability to acquire and deploy knowledge
- Tremendous amount of information flowing within and outside organizations
- Personal computers and networking capabilities having dramatic impact of organization practices
- Presenting new challenges for HRD professionals
- Managing virtual organization

HR practices that contribute to 4Cs such as:

1. Competencies (To complete task cost-efficiently, optimal efficiency)
2. Commitment (zeal to complete the task)
3. Culture (strong culture has a lasting effect)
4. Cost-effectiveness (as competitive advantage)

Robert S Kaplan and David P Norton gave the concept of Balance Score Card (BSC), which has 4 distinct perspectives:

1. Financial
2. Customer

3.   Internal

4.   Innovation and learning

Balanced Scorecard is Prepared to Strike Balance

- between short-term and long-term objectives

- between financial and non-financial measures

- between lagging and leading indicators

- between external and internal performance perspectives

Becker, Huselid and Ulrich (Book *'HR Scorecard – Linking People, Strategy and Performance'* by Brian E. Becker, Mark A Huselid, Dave Ulrich (Foreword by David Norton of 'Balanced Scorecard' –HSS Press, 2001) extended the concept of Balanced Scorecard and gave the concept of HR Scorecard. The approach in HR Scorecard has been adopted with the following considerations:

- How to link HR's result to measures such as profitability and shareholder value

- HR's strategic role begins with designing HR architecture – the HR function, the HR system and strategic employee behaviour

- Tool to measure the effectiveness of HR

- Report card showing Performance of HR (Perception based).

There are three challenges in workforce scorecard as given below:

- View workforce in terms of contribution rather than cost

- Replace benchmarking with metrics that differentiates levels of strategic impact

- Make the line managers and HR professionals jointly responsible for getting the workforce to execute strategy

HRD scorecard reflects the extent of maturity level of HRD. It includes four dimensions of HRD that contribute to business or organizational performance:

- HRD System Maturity

- HRD Competencies in the Company

- HRD Styles, Culture and Values

- Business linkages with HRD

Steps to Implement HRM's Strategic Role and Scorecard

Organizations can follow seven steps to implement strategic role of HRM. These steps are as indicated below:

Step 1: Clearly define business strategy

Step 2: Build a business case for HR as a strategic asset

Step 3: Create a strategy map

Step 4: Identify HR deliverables within strategy

Step 5: Align HR Architecture with HR deliverables

Step 6: Design the strategic HR measurement system

Step 7: Implement management by measurement

Managers need to go by following guidelines for implementing a scorecard

1. Lead change

2. Create a shared need

3. Shape a vision

4. Mobilise commitment

5. Build enabling systems

6. Monitor and demonstrate progress

7. Make it last

HR scorecard and workforce scorecards will facilitate the management of change.

"The war for talent cannot be won in the area of recruiting but only in the area of retention" (Michael Svoboda, Head of Corporate HR Policies and Development, Deutsche Bank). Key People Challenges have been identified by some CEO in the "Best Employers in India 2004 Survey" of Hewitt Associates (I) Pvt. Ltd. These challenges need to be incorporated in the roadmap of HRM. They have identified following key challenges:

1. Attracting the right talent

2. Building a team effort

3. Building a performance culture

4. Keeping employees engaged

5. Building leadership bench strength

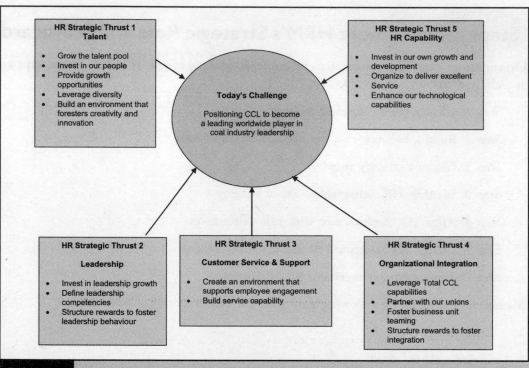

FIGURE 1 Pulling it All Together at CCL

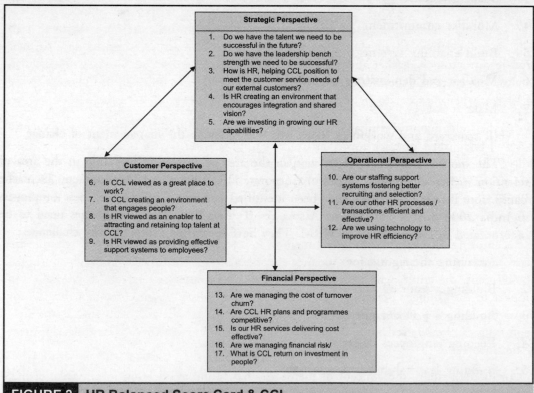

FIGURE 2 HR Balanced Score Card & CCL

Mentoring System: The NTPC Experience

"Mentoring is a brain to pick, an ear to listen, and a push in the right direction."

Mentoring: Genesis and Concept

The concept of mentoring, although centuries old, has been used as a development tool only since the 1970s. In ancient times, experienced individuals passed on wisdom to their proteges by acting as teacher and guide. In Homer's epic poem – The Odyssey, the original Mentor was entrusted the task of teaching and guiding Telemachus, son of Odysseus, King of Ithaka, when he went to fight the Trojan war.

In the Indian context, imparting *shiksha* to the *Shishya* (discipline) by the *guru* (teacher) is a well-established practice rooted in centuries-old tradition. The transfer of knowledge, skills and experience to the *Shishya* (discipline) is also very well-documented in the great epic *Mahabharat* where the story of Arjun, the powerful warrior, mastering the art of archery from his *Guru Dronacharya* gives enough testimony to learning through the *guru-shishya parampara*.

Mentoring, from the Greek work mentor, is best described as a sustained relationship between a youth and an adult for guidance and assistance to the former. Through continued involvement, the adult, who is usually an older and experienced person, offers help and support to the younger person during the growing-up phase. In this manner, the mentor shows the right way in the turbulence of life to the mentee. Viewed from this perspective, mentoring can be referred to as an initiative meant for the overall growth and development of the mentee.

In modern times, the concept of mentoring has found application in all walks of life. In academics, a mentor is often used synonymously with a faculty adviser. In families where parents are either unavailable or unable to provide responsible guidance for their children mentors can play a critical role. In business houses, mentoring is being used as a tool for social integration, assimilation and development of newly joined employees. Further, this is also being used as a powerful instrument for enhancing the performance level of employees in the corporate world.

Mentoring Initiative: Need in NTPC

Right from inception, NTPC has laid a lot of emphasis on managing and developing talent through an integrated human resource development and management system. This philosophy of integrated human resource development is reflected in the HR strategy of NTPC which focuses on building competence, commitment, culture and systems. Further, the same spirit is also expressed in the HR vision of NTPC which is to enable our people to be a family of world-class professionals making NTPC a learning organization.

The process of attracting and developing talent is a way of life at NTPC Executives in NTPC is mostly inducted through the Executive Trainee Scheme and the same talents are nurtured, developed and grown to future leadership roles through comprehensive and innovative induction, orientation and other HRD practices.

The engineering and other professional talents hired through the NTPC Executive Trainee scheme are put on a one-year training period with the right mix of classroom and on-the-job training to inculcate in them the right attitude, value systems and functional competencies. This process has helped NTPC in infusing the right attitude and skills amongst newly hired young engineers and other professionals who join NTPC fresh from colleges and other institutions. Although the overall comprehensive training module is designed to instill the required technical, behavioural, managerial skills and internalize in them the right culture and other value systems of the company, we are sensitive to the possibility of the trainees not finding their bearings in a large multi-unit organization. Being fresh from colleges and other such institutions, they sometimes need tuning and orientation to the NTPC ethos, its values and cultures. Therefore, it was decided to introduce a system to guide and counsel the young talents through a personal touch for better socialization and thus facilitate effective integration and assimilation in the organization.

As such, mentoring as a formal system/ HR initiative was introduced in NTPC in the year 1998 as an extension of the orientation practice in the workplace and township to meet the trainee's needs during and after training.

Objectives of the Mentoring System at NTPC

The mentoring system was launched in NTPC to achieve the following objectives:

- To guide and direct the new entrant during the vital and formative years in the organization;

- To clear doubts and apprehensions faced by the new entrant;
- To enable the entrant to assimilate and adapt to the organizational culture;
- To provide a companion who could be a Friend, Philosopher and Guide; and
- To act as a counselor for the new entrant.

Mentoring Model at NTPC

The mentoring system introduced in NTPC is based on the model.

Broad Features of the System

The mentoring system promotes and facilitates a relationship between the mentor and the mentee. A mentor is a fairly senior person (preferably one who had joined as an Executive Trainee himself), well versed with the working environment of the organization, having positive outlook and empathy, capacity to guide and known for his performance. A mentee as a new entrant to the organization, performance. A mentee is a new entrant to the organization, usually a fresh Executive Trainee. When the trainees join for on-the-job training, Human Resources Function catalyses the process of identification of mentor as per laid down guidelines and undertakes the role of an anchor by facilitating interaction, review meetings and social get-togethers. Further, the relationship is sustained, continued and developed through a well-defined structure in accordance with the mentoring system. Besides offering a number of opportunities for interaction and for building the relationship through socialization and guidance, the relationship is also publicly recognized through innovative practice like "Mentor's Day" which is celebrated every year on 5th September (Teacher's Day) with much fanfare and gaiety, bringing together all mentors and mentess on one platform for experience sharing and recognition. The camaraderie and team spirit is also promoted by a relaxed and playful environment created through organizing Quiz Competition, Antakshari, and indoor games and activities in which both mentors and mentees take part. The team spirit and bonding are further deepened by encouraging out-bond meets and programmes for them. To exchange progress, concerns, views, difficulties, learning from others and for networking, there is a system for formation of a Mentors Club. Although the formal mentor-mentee relationship is meant for the one-year training period, the informal relationship and dialogue usually continue beyond the training period.

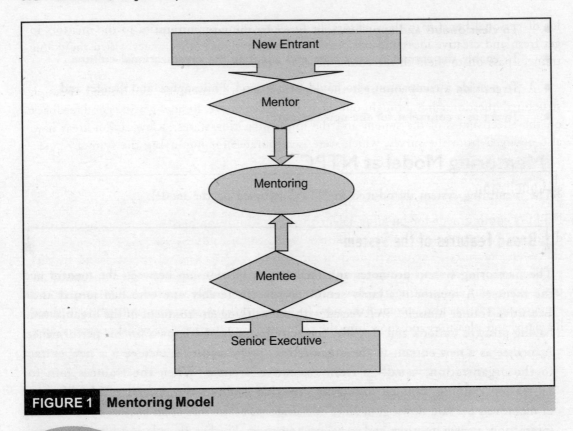

FIGURE 1 **Mentoring Model**

Unique Initiatives for Institutionalization

To hone and harness the right and positive outlook in the mentors for actualizing the initiative, organizational workshops are conducted with the help of expert facilitators. This also generates interest and enthusiasm in the system. In the initial years, this was done every year in all locations to bring about involvement, appreciation of the initiative's purpose and clarification of the concept and its value. Refresher courses are held from time to time to renew and revisit the concept and its implementation. For creating exclusive identifying and to generating good feeling, Mentors Badges are provided. Besides recognizing the service of mentors by felicitating them through "Mentor's *Samman* (honour):, a lot of other rewards and recognitions such as appreciation letters, token gifts, dinner with HODs, informal get-togethers, etc. are presented and organized to encourage and sustain the initiative.

⌘ A Reality Check ⌘

With a very focused approach, NTPC succeeded in creating and developing a pool of over 305 mentors in the organization for driving the change initiative. It was further observed that the system greatly helps the socialization process, assimilating trainees easily into the NTPC culture and systems. It has also helped in tackling work-related stress and given a lot of personal benefits to the mentors, besides providing opportunities to the mentors to get fresh and creative ideas and perspective on technical and other issues which the young trainees pass on to them in the course of their interaction.

A perception survey amongst the mentors and the mentees, conducted through structured questionnaires, brought out the results given above. Besides getting good feedback on the effectiveness of the system and the implementation status, a few action areas have also emerged from the survey, which were incorporated for improving the system.

⌘ Conclusion ⌘

NTPC's commitment for building talent through a multi-pronged strategy is paying rich dividends. Mentoring—one of the initiatives launched for guiding, directing and counselling the young recruits—has contributed in enhancing their commitment level and in this process achieved its intended purpose. Overall, this HR initiative has been successful in integrating and assimilating the new executives in the culture and value system of the organization. It has also provided the new entrant a friend, philosopher and guide to share his pains and pleasures and show him the right way in professional as well as personal life.

7

Modi Xerox Experience

Performance Management System and Performance Planning and Appraisal (PP & A)

PP&A system is consider a kind of management system which ensures that people should know what their priorities are, what should they be doing currently and what they are aiming for, how well their efforts contribute to team and company priorities, performance and individual level development needs. Carrier development, succession planning and management of motivation through rewards have been linked through the PP&A in the company.

The importance of PP&A is based on the belief that effective management of job performance is critical to the achievement of company goals. The management Endeavour through PP&A has been to gain commitment from employees, make them understand what is expected of them, provide constructive feedback, coach, counsel on individual performance and give employees the high level of empowerment and support.

Key features of PP&A have been to plan and review each person's role and required performance against objectives; to measure and improve individual performance; and, to identify and development/ training needs and actions.

Individual contribution towards common goals is through: translating company and functional objectives into individual's role, and responsibilities and objectives (RROs) having specific job holder objectives and measurements; regular performance review; counselling and coaching on individual strengths and areas for improvement; documentation of overall performance against planned objectives.

The company undertook a review of the appraisal system and found the following: a) there was no formal link between what was expected of an employee and the company goals/objectives, b) no focus on performance during the years and it was just a year-end formality, c) individual level developmental plans didn't get chalked out generally and d) linkage with increments, career and succession planning were unclear.

The Appraisal Process was accordingly changed. The system and the process of appraisal integrated the objectives of the organization with the individual. As a result, its key features were as follows:

(a) Every employee must have an agreed and signed RRO. For this, in October, the senior management committee issued a policy development blue book defining company's RROs.

(b) The HRD department released job descriptions to all department defining current accountability and updating job changes, if any.

(c) Every jobholder must receive a comprehensive and writing appraisal review by using policy deployment book and job description and also by using a previous year's appraisal.

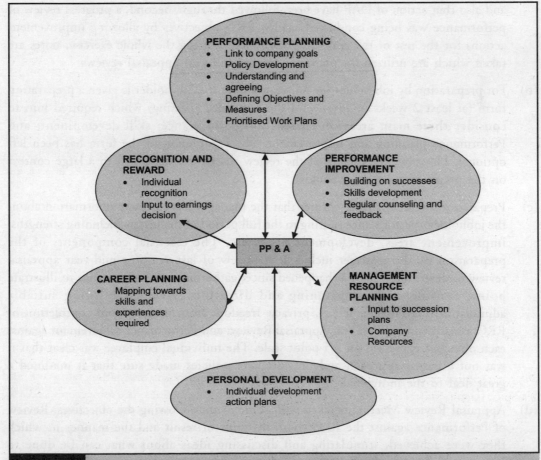

FIGURE 1 Performance Planning and Appraisal in Context

(d) Each employee will, therefore, also have a Development Action Plan (DAP) prepare from the appraisal discussion

(e) Effective use of the PP&A process is an accountability for all managers with reporting staff

(f) The content of any completed appraisal document is classified as Modi Xerox Personal Data—confidential to the job holder, the appraiser, relevant HR Manager and the next level managers. Completed forms are held in personal records.

PP&A has three elements of Appraisal Review, Performance Planning and Development Action Plan. There are four principal components of Appraisal Review: 1. A Mid-year Performance Review, 2. Preparation of Job Holder for Full-year Review, 3. Preparation by the Manager, and 4. Appraisal Review Meeting.

The Appraisal Review document becomes 'live' at the time of mid year review. Following four aspects are worth mentioning:

(a) The aim of Mid-Year Performance has been two fold. First, the manager and job holder checked the continuing appropriateness and prioritization within the RRO and also that action of DAP have been followed through. Second, a progress review of performance was being conducted against RRO objectives by allowing improvement actions for the rest of the year to be scheduled. During the whole exercise, notes are taken which are utilized for preparing for the full year appraisal reviews.

(b) For preparation by job holder for full year review, the job holder is given a preparation form (at least 2 weeks in advance of the scheduled meeting) which required him to consider three main areas of: current job performance; skill development; and Performance planning and improvement. The completion of the form has been left optional. However, the quality of the review discussion depended to a large context on the preparation of the jobholder.

(c) Preparation by the manager ensures that the manager has adequate information about the jobholder's performance relating to the full period of the review including strengths, improvement areas, development needs etc. The essential components of the preparation by the manager included: A review of last year's/or mid-year appraisal review to determine what has happened since; gathering facts and instance to illustrate point; consideration of planning and direction given; establishing suitable administrative arrangement e.g., privacy, freedom from interruption; completion of RRO assessment and Full Year Appraisal Review; and Performance achievement against each objective expressed on a 5-point scale. The individual employee was clear that it was not a casual approach and the company policies made sure that it mattered a great deal to the individuals.

(d) Appraisal Review Meeting is taken with some of the following the objectives: Review of Performance against the RRO, both in terms of result and the manner in which they were achieved; stimulating and discussing ideas about what can be done to improve performance and develop necessary skills; agreeing on personal development actions and timing for inclusion in the DAP; considering any changes in job needs or additional challenges with plans and priorities for the coming year; resolving any anxiety, uncertainty or misapprehension; and getting feedback on how effectively the job holder has been managed.

The contents of the present appraisal system were formulated also with the objective that it provides a powerful means of communication of company goals and values.

However, any new system takes time to be understood and established. Having been used to a system there was attitudinal resistance, particularly where more work was involved. The management also faced problems of understanding of DAP, coping up with the increased workload, non-acceptance (even by managers) of this system. It took a while to improve the quality of RROs.

The management, however, was committed to implementing the system and kept its eyes and ears open. When issues impending the effective implementation of the new system was identified, it: organized workshops to increase communication to line management and develop appreciation of RROs, PP&A and DAP; undertook an administrative simplification of system by re-engineering the process; and developed methodology for understanding developmental needs.

PPA and Management Resources Planning (MRP). PP&A is a process primarily concerned with current role performance improvement and skills developments. MRS is the corporate/company process to ensure the future supply and portioning of appropriately skilled people for key management roles.

MRP and PP&A are separate processes but the same time both require an assessment of key measures for management/leadership effectiveness. The PPA document requires a full year assessment against the 9 cultural dimensions and the 23 leadership attributes for managers. Whilst these are also reviewed in the MRP process, the emphasis in PP&A is on performance improvement in the current role rather than skills development for recommended future positions.

The nine cultural dimensions characterized the organizational culture of the company. It was seeking to create role model managers who served as a 'standard of excellence' worthy of imitation and operated with the following focus.

Market Connected: The management understands and is driven by the dynamics of market place. The energy is primary externally focused on customer, current and potential, our competitors, and relevant technologies and target markets.

Absolute Result-oriented: Absolute improvements strive for business results. Success is an absolute improvement in each of the priorities as measured against external benchmarks. The plan is a tool for achieving the improvements.

Action-oriented: Decisions are made and implemented in a timely and effective manner and with a peace dictated by the market. Time is recognized as a competitive advantage. Action, not activity, is encouraged and rewarded.

Line Driven: Line managers have been responsible and held accountable for running the business and achieving results. The processes are line-oriented. Line managers effectively utilize staff for their expertise.

Team-oriented: Greater good of Xerox is valued above personal, unit, or functional goals. Work has been organized to help others in Xerox to be successful. Unproductive conflict is minimized while encouraging diverse opinions and constructive debate.

Empowered People: It is ensured that decisions are made by the people who are close to the action. People are believed to be most innovative and productive when they are part of a self-managed team. They are provided with the additional information required for them to act in this manner.

Open and Honest Communication: People are encouraged to practice openness, candor and honesty. Value of diverse opinions is recognized. Open expression of differences is welcomed.

Organization Reflection and Learning: Continuous improvement is achieved through constant learning. As individuals and groups, insights are gained by reflecting on successes and failures. Attempts are made to learn from each other, competitors, and customers.

Process Re-engineering and Simplification: Productivity through constant improvement in the process is strived for.

The major leadership attributes are as follows:

Strategic Leadership

- Strategic Thinking
- Strategic Implementation
- Customer Driven Approach
- Decision-Making
- Quick Study

Organizational Leadership

- Managing Operational Performance
- Staffing for High Performance
- Developing Organizational Talent
- Empowerment
- Managing Teamwork
- Leading Innovation
- Drive for Business Result
- Use of Leadership through Quality

Managing Self and Others

- Openness of Changes
- Interpersonal Empathy and Influence
- Personal Drive
- Personal Strength and Maturity
- Personal Consistency
- Environmental and Industry Perspective
- Business/Financial Perspective
- Overall Technical Knowledge.

Performance Planning: The role of every employees has been conceived as a subset of the companies goal. It is important that each employee understood and agreed to the role. This, in essence, was an essential element of performance planning. The understanding promoted employee satisfaction and the jobholder could better relate his/her individual and team efforts to overall company goals. The company goals are the shared responsibility of all employees. RRO helped in highlighting the jobholder's objectiveness along side the company's defined goals. RRO was a process document to support the following.

(a) Individual role planning relating individual objectives to company goals; and

(b) Performance improvement enabling the jobholder and manager to agree improvement actions against various objectives and actual performance.

Role Purpose: Each jobholder in the company had and agreed RRO which was agreed, signed and dated by both the manager and job holder. The RRO was made up of a) Role of purpose which is defined as a short statement on the PP&A form and it should not be more than one or two sentences and b) Role of objectives cover things people need to do in order to fulfill their contribution to the company's common goals. These were agreed between the jobholder and the manager and must be specific to each individual role. Stress is laid to achieve a brief and easily understood statement of objectives and that these were measurable i.e. words like 'effective' and efficient' without clearly stated measures were considered insufficient.

An example of a top quality objective can be summarized as 'SMART' where:

S = Specific

M = Measurable

A = Achievable

R = Related to the job

T = Time Bound

Specific: Objectives were directly related to specific plans projects etc.

Measurable: Measurements were expected to be a balance between quantitative (objective) and qualitative (subjective).

Achievable: Objectives were expected to be achievable but at the same time, challenging. The individual was also able to control objectives.

Related to Job: Objective were relevant to the individual job role sub set of the manager's objective.

Time bound: The objectives included by 'by when' statement.

Specifically, company goals were the shared responsibility of all employees. From these goals, RROs, were derived which contained the following:

(a) *A role definition:* Why a job existed;

(b) *Objectives:* What it is the employee was expected to achieve;

(c) *Measurements:* The agreed level of performance.

Development Action Plan (DAP): The DAP intended to assist personal development and was regarded as contract between the job holder and his managers. The employee committed to completing the actions and the manager committed to provide the time and opportunity.

In essence, it was used to record all actions agreed at the review in terms of both job and personal development needs. It was completed at the full year appraisal and reviewed on a regular basis as well as at the mid-year session.

Taken together, the whole exercise of PP&A was placed a high emphasis on development of individuals in performance appraisal.

The PP&A was delinked from increments. However, it was linked to rewards, career plans and succession plans.

Process Flow Chart of Performance Planning and Appraisal showed that the process began at the beginning of 'Business Year' with issuance of set of PP&A forms by the HR Manager and included the following procedures.

(a) Through the Policy Development Blue Book, issued by Senior Management Committee, Organizational and Functional RRO's were made available. Each direct manager had then the responsibility of facilitation RRO for each jobholder within his function.

(b) To supplement the vital few from the Policy Development Blue Book, each employee was asked to look at own job description and include, those aspects of the job that are routine and which, despite not forming part of the vital few as per Policy Development, were still extremely important for the job. Where necessary, the direct manager and the HR manager concerned updated the job description to reflect current status.

(c) The direct manager when called for a meeting with the jobholder, ensured that the latter understood his role for the coming year and clear measurable objectives against which his performance was to be assessed.

(d) Mid-year review was conducted against RRP's and DAP's.

(e) A full year review was done once a year, where performance against RRO and actions against DAP were reviewed. The full year review was called the Appraisal. It was signed by both the direct and functional managers and the employee and become one of the inputs for next year's performance plan.

LTA took four years to permeate in Modi Xerox. Now it was time to take another step on quality journey to further intensify the quest for quality, Therefore, the Business Excellence Certification (BEC) programme was launched in 1992. BEC was an international Rank Xerox programme which helped assess an organization from the perspective of the external customer and enabled it to identify its strengths as also focus on actions for continuous improvement to achieve outstanding business result. In 1993, Modi Xerox was certified for 'Business Excellence' by Rank Xerox.

Modi Xerox's business goal for 'Business Excellence' by Rank Xerox was to increase the market presence at a faster rate than the competitors in the markets in which it operates. This goal was being achieved.

Modi Xerox has also started 'Market Dynamics Measurement' which too is a Xerox practice and measures the company's standing in the marketplace and how the products are performing vis-à-vis competition in different conditions. Measuring market dynamics is another way of understanding customers better.

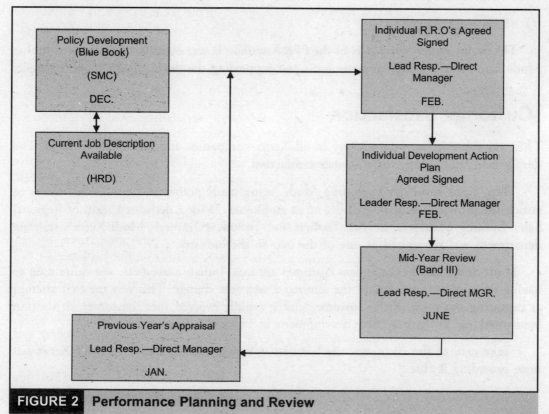

FIGURE 2 **Performance Planning and Review**

Recognition and Reward Scheme

Employee motivation and satisfaction has been a key corporate priority at Modi Xerox. Open recognition of meritorious performance motivated others even as it built people and brought a sense of accomplishment to the individual employee, team and corporation as a whole. The chairman of Modi Xerox conferred the annual awards and recognition and employee considered it very important in their service career.

For the company, there recognition and reward was a way of saying 'Thank You' to those who contributed most to business goals. It was also an excellent way to encouraging future initiative. The scheme recognized both small actions and large ideas. Small continuous improvements were as essential as major changes. Some of the awards given by the company were as follows:

(a) Achievement Award

(b) Exceptional Performance Award

(c) Honours Cult Award

(d) Quality Award

(e) Long Service Award

(f) President's Award

The award system was a part of the PP&A system. It was considered as essential tool at Modi Xerox in achieving company goals and supporting the development of their people.

Customer Satisfaction

This was the number one priority in all Xerox companies and an article of faith. The deeply held belief is that of customer satisfaction.

Thus, right from the beginning Modi Xerox made active and concerted efforts to enrich the professional quality of life of its employees. With a dedicated team of Regional Sales Training Managers, Service Trainers and Technical Trainers, Modi Xerox's training department was recognized as one of the best in the industry.

Modi Xerox also held the first customer seminar. Indian customers, not quite used to having their voice heard, found the seminar a welcome change. This was the first attempt at capturing the voice of the customer and it rapidly evolved into 'customer satisfaction benchmarking' an entirely new development in India industry.

"Take care of the customer, the business will take care of itself".—Modi Xerox has been providing it true.

Compensation

- Remuneration was linked with performance.

- The company believed in rewarding and recognizing employees who did well.

- There was a constant demand to increase salary/bonus, when production or profit increased.

- TA/DA policies have changed for better.

- In the initial stages, the number of grades amongst the workers were 17, which were subsequently reduced to 12. Amongst the managerial level, too many hierarchical levels have been reduced.

- Compensation levels in Modi Xerox have been good but now other companies have overtaken. Therefore, the flexible benefits plan. The salary which managers get today is less than half of its basic and the rest is in the form of flexible benefits, availing tax benefits. Percentage change in cash in hand is 30 percent.

After liberalization, competition has increased. The company had earlier attained number one positioning customer satisfaction which is not so now. New companies are also coming up. Company thrust on quality has increased.

The characteristics of the present work culture in Modi Xerox were being honest with integrity and high task master, practical, task oriented employees with technical knowledge and good IQ, as well as administrative ability.

Communication

Communication is a key to relationship. It was given lot of emphasis with the existence of formal forums. Every year, the Chairman talked to top executives about the performance of previous year which was then cascaded down. Similarly, a six month review was taken up. Some features of communication were the Annual Report, Open Day, Independence Day, Earth Day, departmental picnic and house journal.

More focus on communication has been put since 1990. Information sharing or any kind of communication is being done through department, family group, and was conveyed daily. Any policy change is also communicated. The union president is the leader of communication portfolio.

The following factors contributed to good communication according to the managers:

(a) House journals

(b) Adherence to annual communication plan

(c) Communication packages in Hindi

(d) Development feedback sheet both in English and Hindi provided time slots for feedback in every communication meeting.

Though, the officials felt that a lot of emphasis was given on communication, the employees felt hesitant to approach the management directly.

⌘ Conclusion ⌘

Modi Xerox experience has clearly demonstrated that people are the greatest assets. If organizations aspire to become high performing organizations they have to show through their words and deeds that they value their people. These organizations also invest in people by way of training, motivating, recognizing their contributions to organizational goals. The organization has put a good HR system including training performance management in place. Employees are also aware that there is a clear linkage between performance and reward. The organization has prepared their people to face the competition through world class quality, benchmarking in customer service and product quality.

The positive contributing factors were as following:

(a) Modi Xerox image of a professional employer

(b) Training and development of employees

(c) External and internal hiring process

The negative contributing factors were the following:

(a) Background i.e., location of the plant

(b) Compensation not equivalent to best availability in the market

(c) Infrastructure of Modi Xerox.

Strengths:

(a) Collaboration with MNC

(b) Management trained in interviewing skills

(c) Training and development process in place

(d) Business process

(e) External and internal hiring process in place

Improvement areas observed are:

(a) Compensation package

(b) Hiring process

(c) Infrastructure

Environment and Health: The Rampur unit's environment, health and safety records was matchless. The pollution free standards in the toner plant has exceeded Rank Xerox norms. It went on to win the British National Safety Council Awards for two years in a row. Recognizing its high standards of environment health and safety, the Clark University of USA selected Modi Xerox for a research project on responsible technology transfer to developing countries.

NTPC Performance Management System

Submitted to: Prof. B.D. Singh

Presented By:

Lavanya Nemali (08FN-071)

Rahul Khanna (08FN-081)

Rajesh Kumar Sahu (08FN-082)

Sharanya Shankar (08FN-099)

Sneha Gupta (08FN-106)

Amit Tiwari (08FN-110)

Introduction to Performance Management System (PMS)

⌘ Philosophy of Performance Management System ⌘

To build a culture of performance by aligning individual and organizational objectives and encouraging open communication and continuous feedback.

In government departments, promotions are given to the civil servants on the basis of seniority or merit. The most important question is how to fairly judge the merit of a candidate who is already in the service? For being fair and impartial, it is necessary to assess the performance of the individual in the organization. This is now systematically done in all the countries of the world. The assessment of an individual's performance in the organization is called Performance Appraisal. With the rise and development of modern management science, the system of performance appraisal, has gained additional significance in the study of personnel management. Since the concept of 'accountability' of the government has become more important in recent times, the need for performance appraisal of civil servants is more and more felt in all governments.

The system of performance appraisal draws upon the talent from within based on the experience gained by the employees in the organization. It compels the management to have a promotion policy based on the system of performance appraisal. It also gives justice to those employees who are efficient and capable. It serves the one short-term purpose of assessing the capabilities and usefulness of an employee to the organization and in the long-term it determines his potentials for elevation to the higher post and position.

Performance appraisal system has been defined in many ways. The simplest way to understand the meaning of performance appraisal is as follows:

"A regular and continuous evaluation of the quality, quantity and style of the performance along with the assessment of the factors influencing the performance and behaviour of an individual is called as performance appraisal."

Objectives

In government, promotions are given to the civil servants on the basis of seniority or merit. The most important question is how to fairly judge the merit of a candidate growth through optimal utilization of the human resources in the interest of the organization. The individual employee obtains feedback which enables him to develop himself to meet the objectives of the organization. Performance Appraisal is, thus, a means and not an end by itself. Performance Appraisal system is necessary not only for individual's work improvement but also for the overall improvement of the organization. It is necessary for the adoption of a fair and impartial promotion policy, which can keep the employee's morale high.

Performance Appraisal is also necessary to assess the usefulness and capabilities of a person in terms of his contribution towards the achievement of the goals of the organization. It is also needed to develop the potentials of an employee to prepare him to accept more responsibilities of the higher post, which he aspires through promotion. It helps not only in improving the viability and health of the organization but also pinpoints the shortcomings of an employee. By informing the shortcomings to the concerned persons, the superior officer can secure better utilization of services either through correction or position-change. Performance Appraisal is, thus, a very important activity of modern personnel management.

Some of the objectives for Performance Appraisal are:

- To accomplish the overall organizational vision and mission by linking individual performance to company objectives;

- To cascade company's strategic goals to individual level;

- To promote professional excellence;

- To encourage two-way communication between the executive and the reporting officer and bring about transparency in the performance assessment process;

- To evaluate the potential of the executive to assume higher responsibilities in the organization;

- To provide a source of talent for meeting the organization's growth requirements through a process of mapping the competencies and potential of executives;

- To translate future skill requirements of the organization into individual development plans;

- To identify high performers and recognize them through rewards and incentives, and

- To facilitate fulfillment of individual aspirations.

Applicability

The Performance Appraisal Process in an organization is applicable to everyone who contributes towards organization. It helps organization as well as individual both. In NTPC, the process covers the following groups:

- PMS is applicable to all executives of NTPC (E1- E9);

- Executives who join NTPC on deputation or those retaining lien while in service of NTPC are also covered by this scheme;

- Executives who join in the middle of the PMS cycle (see next section), but have served for a minimum period of three months;

- NTPC executives who are on second hand basis or are lent on service to subsidiaries and joint ventures with NTPC management.

PMS Cycle

⌘ Performance Assessment Year ⌘

Performance assessment years have been set up as follows:

For E6 and above: The performance assessment year commences from 1st April of each year and continues until 31st March of the following year;

For E1-E5: The performance assessment year commences from 1st January of each year and continues until 31st December of the same year.

⌘ PMS Process ⌘

The PMS process is broadly divided into the following stages:

- Performance Planning

- Mid-Year Review

- Annual Assessment

- Normalization

- Feedback, Coaching and Counselling

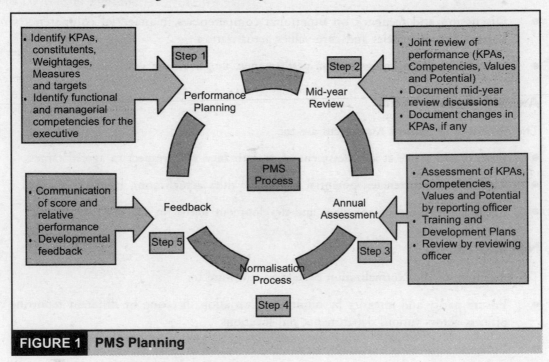

FIGURE 1   PMS Planning

Performance Planning

Performance Planning is the process of:

- Defining expectations i.e. the work to be done, the results/targets to be achieved and skills/competencies needed to achieve these objectives;

- Setting "Measures" and "Targets"

- Identifying and allocating appropriate resources (such as manpower, tools, training, budget etc.) to enable the executive to achieve the targets.

Mid-Year Review

Performance management is not an event but an ongoing process. Mid-year reviews help in the following ways:

- Reinforcing good performance in time

- Updating the status of targets i.e., progress review

- Identifying areas for "mid-course" correction

- Revisiting KPAs and goals, if necessary

- Assessing resource and skill requirements affecting the individual's performance

- Discussion and feedback on functional competencies, managerial competencies, potential competencies and core values actualization

- Providing early warnings of non-performance, i.e., avoiding year-end surprises.

Annual Assessment

The objectives of Annual Assessment are to:

- Discuss and arrive at an assessment of performance with respect to agreed targets.

- Assess the competencies, potential and core values actualization by the individual

- Agree upon improvement plans and development needs for the individual.

Normalization

The objectives of the Normalization System in PMS are to:

- Ensure parity and integrity by minimizing variation in rating by different reporting officers across various departments and locations

- Enhance objectivity and transparency in the appraisal system

- To view individual performance from the perspective of organizational achievement.

Feedback, Coaching and Counselling

In order to make PMS an open system and to enhance development orientation across the organization, feedback, coaching and counseling are essential components.

Feedback

Providing feedback on performance presents the following benefits:

- Creates transparency, making PMS more acceptable to individuals

- Reinforces good performance on time

- Enables development of coaching and mentoring relationship between reporting officer and executive

- Ensures that organizational objectives are achieved to an acceptable standard and in an acceptable form.

Providing performance feedback is a delicate matter and the reporting officer should create suitable conditions for providing performance feedback in the most effective manner.

Coaching and Counselling

Coaching is an on-the-job approach to help individuals to develop and raise their skills and levels of competence. Coaching typically consists of:

- Making executives aware of how well they are performing and their present level of knowledge and skill

- Providing guidance to individuals to enable them to complete their work satisfactorily

- Motivating individuals to learn new skills and develop themselves

- Facilitating individuals to raise their level of contribution and achievement.

Coaching and counseling together act as a feedback mechanism for the individual on his/her performance. It is often used by reviewer/reporting officer to communicate the areas for development and improvement to the executive.

PMS Linkage with Other HR Systems

Performance Management has much wider implications than purely improving individual performance in the given year. PMS provides the basis for achieving a number of fundamental aims of HR strategy for the organization as mentioned below.

Linkage with Training and Development System

PMS lays strong emphasis on continuous learning and development. The two-way communication between reporting officer and executive creates an environment of trust and self-learning.

- PMS is the basis for the organization to maintain data on an individual's skill gaps, take necessary action to meet the training needs, use it for foreign training/assignments and company sponsorship of long-term educational programmes etc.

- PMS would also provide the means to determine the collective level of competencies and strengths available within the organization as well as gaps for planning for organizational development initiatives.

- Learning and development initiatives fundamentally rest with the individual with the organization facilitating the same through creating a learning environment and providing suitable opportunities etc.

Linkage with Rewards System

- PMS is a tool for rewarding successes/achievements and contribution of individuals to motivate them to continuously strive for excellence in their respective responsibilities.

- It would provide inputs to the organization's rewards programmes.

- PMS results will be used to identify high performers for the purpose of rewards and recognition.

- Additionally, it would be used to aid counseling for improving performance and dealing with consistent non-performance.

- The detailed processes and systems are outlined in the Rewards Policy.

Linkage with Career Development System

PMS results of the executives would be used as one of the inputs in the Career Development System. It would provide inputs for assessing an individual's readiness for higher responsibility and career advancement.

The PMS Form

The PMS form is divided into seven parts as shown below:

1. *Performance Planning and Assessment*

    (a) Dashboard of Key Performance Areas (KPAs)

    (b) Details of KPA

    (c) Mid year Review

    (d) Revised KPAs (in case of change during mid-year review)

2. *Competency Assessment*

    (a) Functional/Technical Competencies

    (b) Managerial Competencies

3. *Core Values*

4. *Potential Competencies*

5. *Special Achievements*

6. *Total Marks*

7. *Individual Training and Development Plan*

Performance Planning

Performance Planning is to be done through a process of discussion between the executive and the reporting officer to arrive at the performance targets for the Key Performance Areas (KPAs).

It shall be the responsibility of the reviewing officer to ensure that KPAs identified have sufficient "stretch targets" cascaded down to achieve individual excellence.

The reporting officer shall not be below the rank of Manager (E5).

● In the beginning of the assessment year, the concerned HR department shall circulate the relevant PMS forms to the reporting officers for Performance Planning with the respective executives.

● The reporting officer will then send the PMS form to each executive reporting to him with a covering letter inviting him to participate in the performance planning process indicating time and venue and requesting the executive to complete the relevant sections of the form prior to the meeting. See Annexure for format of the invitation letter.

Identifying KPAs

1. The table entitled "Dashboard of the Key Performance Areas" is a summary of the detailed KPAs to be filled up by the executive after discussion with reporting officer in the subsequent pages of the PMS form.

2. At the beginning of the year, relevant KPAs are identified using the KPA Directory as a reference tool.

3. The KPAs should be cascaded in an open and transparent manner with each reporting officer sharing his/her KPAs and targets with all the executives reporting to him/her.

Identifying KPA Constituents and Measures

The characteristic points about the KPAs are i.e., how the KPAs are and other details about KPAs:

1. Once the KPAs are identified, their constituents, measures and targets are also identified from the KPA Directory. These are agreed upon between the reporting officer and the executive at the beginning of the assessment year.

2. The table entitled "Details of KPA" provides for detailing the constituents of the KPA index agreed upon. These are filled under the column "Constituents of KPA".

3. The measures identified for each constituent are written down in the column provided for "KPA Measures". A single constituent may have more than one measure, if necessary.

4. Total marks to be allocated to each of the KPA constituents are agreed between the reporting officer and the executive. These are filled against the relevant KPA constituent. The sum of the marks provided to the KPA constituents should be equal to the total marks allocated to the KPA Index.

5. The constituents, measures and marks provided in the KPA Directory are guidelines and may be modified by the reporting officer in consultation with the executive (the changes may be aligned as per business/functional plans, focus areas, priorities of the management, unit/department level goals etc.).

6. Each KPA constituent has three levels of targets which is to be decided jointly by the reporting officer and executive.

7. Judge the effective score.

8. At the beginning of the year, the reporting officer and the executive sign off the agreed KPA targets in the space provided in Part IA of the PMS form.

9. After the targets are agreed, the relevant column in the table is filled.

10. At this time, the reporting officer and the executive discuss in detail the identification and allocation of the various resources required by the executive (manpower, budget, tools, training etc.) to achieve the targets.

11. The columns for "Actual Targets Achieved" and "Marks Obtained" are filled at the end of Assessment Year.

Identifying Functional Competencies

The details about the functional competencies identification and its characteristics are as shown below:

1. Functional competencies are those that are required for success in a particular function or job and typically involve demonstrating technical/functional knowledge/skills/expertise.

2. In the beginning of the year, the reporting officer in consultation with the executive identifies the functional competencies applicable for the executive from the Functional Competency Directory. The Functional Competency Directory provides functional/technical and cross-functional competencies for executives at various levels and across various departments.

3. The competencies, thus, identified are written in the column provided for in the table. At least five competencies (including functional and cross-functional) must be identified.

Identifying Managerial Competencies

At each level of work, a person requires some managerial competencies which are characterized as:

1. Managerial competencies are those that are essential for the business to achieve its strategy and typically involve behavioural descriptors.

2. Six competencies are to be assessed, of which three have been identified as mandatory for that level.

3. The reporting officer and the executive need to identify three additional managerial competencies from the given set of optional competencies at the beginning of the year by placing a tick mark (") against those that the executive would be evaluated on at the year-end. These competencies are to be chosen based on the responsibilities and demands of the executive's current job. The remaining optional competencies should be crossed out (X) for clarity.

4. The chosen optional competencies should be directly and significantly related to the executive's areas of responsibilities.

5. The total managerial competencies on which the executive will be assessed would thus be six.

6. The reporting officer and executive sign off on the managerial competencies in the space provided in Part IIB of the PMS form at the beginning of the year.

⌘ Mid-Year Review ⌘

The Mid-year review consists of:

1. The concerned HR department shall resubmit the PMS forms to the reporting officers for Mid-year Review with the respective executives.

2. The reporting officer will send the PMS form to each executive reporting to him with a covering letter inviting him to participate in the mid-year review, indicating the time and venue and requesting the executive to complete the relevant sections of the form prior to the meeting.

3. The reporting officer and executive jointly review the performance in the mid-year review as per the schedule mentioned in the PMS Calendar.

Mid-Year Assessment

1. The executive completes the self-evaluation section where he/she highlights achievements to date. Further, he/she indicates roadblocks and issues faced as well as efforts made by him/her to overcome them including help/assistance obtained from the reporting officer.

2. The reporting officer records progress and performance in the space provided for "Comments of Reporting Officer". The comments should include feedback on KPA progress, functional competencies, managerial competencies, potential competencies and core values actualization.

3. Both the reporting officer and executive set aside some time to discuss the achievements and issues highlighted by the executive. The Mid-year Review is an important opportunity for the reporting officer to provide feedback on the performance to date.

4. The reporting officer and executive sign off Part IB of the PMS Form as an agreement to the amendments and comments in the Mid-year Review.

Alteration of KPAs during Mid-year Review

1. Part IC of the PMS form is to be used only if changes need to be made to the KPAs, measures, weight-ages, marks or targets. In such a case, all the KPAs need to be refilled.

2. The reasons for change need to be cited at the end of the section.

3. The KPAs may be changed under the following circumstances:

   (a) There is a significant change in the roles and responsibilities of the executives.

   (b) There are changes in the strategic business objectives of NTPC that directly impact the KPA or the specific KPA loses relevance, as in the following cases:

   ♦ Unanticipated projects

   ♦ Abandonment of projects as per corporate directives

   ♦ Situations completely beyond the control of the executive such as accidents, terrorism and other emergency situations.

4. After consultation with the Reviewing Officer regarding the need and rationale for mid-year alteration, the changes to the KPAs would be signed-off by the reporting officer and the executive in the space provided in the PMS form.

Submission of PMS forms after Mid-year Review

After completion of Mid-year Review, the completed PMS forms shall be submitted to the concerned HR by the reporting officer within the deadlines set in the calendar. Then, as per the forms submitted, each employee is then assessed among its peer group and result of the review is taken out.

⌘ Annual Assessment ⌘

The Annual Assessment process consists of:

- Re-submission of PMS forms for Annual Assessment
- Guidelines for Annual Assessment of KPAs
- Guidelines for Assessment of Functional/Technical Competencies
- Guidelines for Assessment of Managerial Competencies
- Guidelines for Assessment of Core Values
- Guidelines for Assessment of Potential/individual ability
- Summary of Scores
- Guidelines for Completing Individual Training and Development Plan

Re-submission of PMS forms for Annual Assessment

1. The concerned HR shall trigger the process of completion of Annual Assessment through resubmission of PMS forms to all reporting officers.

2. The reporting officer will send the PMS form to each executive reporting to him.

Guidelines for Annual Assessment of KPAs

1. The Annual Assessment starts with the "Details of KPA".

2. The Actual Target achieved by the executive against the KPA constituent is to be mentioned in a report.

3. Depending upon whether the target achieved is "Stretch", "Intermediate" or "Base" level, the marks are proportionately indicated in the report.

4. The marks obtained under each KPA constituent add up to the total score for a KPA Index.

Guidelines for Assessment of Functional/Technical Competencies

1. The reporting officer rates the executive on each functional/technical competency which had been identified and recorded in the form at the beginning of the year.

2. The competencies are assessed on a 4-point scale as indicated in the PMS form.

3. The aggregate marks are arrived at by adding all marks scored for the different competencies.

Guidelines for Assessment of Managerial Competencies

1. The reporting officer shall discuss each of the mandatory and the optional (as selected at the beginning of the year) managerial competencies with the executive and assign the rating on the form.

2. The competencies are to be evaluated on a 10-point scale as indicated in the PMS form by referring to the detailed behavioural descriptors for each managerial competency.

3. The aggregate marks are arrived at by adding all marks scored for the six managerial competencies.

Guidelines for Assessment of Core Values

Adoption of the company's Core Values in business dealings is an essential duty of executives at all levels.

1. All executives have a major role in the actualization of Core Values by being 'Role Models' in observing and practicing them and thereby leading by example.

2. Value actualization is assessed by observing the demonstrated behaviour of the executive in day-to-day business dealings.

3. Core Values assessment is to be done at the end of the year on a four-point scale as indicated in the PMS form.

4. At the year-end, the reporting officer shall discuss each of the value descriptions with the executive and indicate the rating on the PMS form.

5. The aggregate marks are arrived at by adding all marks scored for different core values.

Guidelines for Assessment of Potential/Individual Ability

1. Potential appraisal helps in understanding the extent to which the executive is demonstrating competencies of higher levels.

2. Evaluating these competencies will help in appreciating the preparedness/suitability of the executive for higher responsibilities along the hierarchy.

3. The prescribed potential competencies for a particular level are printed in the PMS form for the particular level.

4. The competencies are evaluated annually on a 3-point scale as indicated in the PMS form during the year-end assessment.

5. The reporting officer shall discuss each of the competencies with the executive and plot the rating on the form.

6. The aggregate marks are arrived at by adding all marks scored for different competencies.

Summary of Scores

1. At the end of the assessment year after completing each of the parts of the PMS form, the reporting officer summarizes the total of each part of PMS form.

2. The "Total Marks Obtained" is the sum of marks obtained in each section of the PMS form.

3. The PMS form duly signed by the executive and the reporting officer is then submitted to the reviewing officer for discussion, comments and approval.

4. The reviewing officer shall go through the performance of the executive in totality as finally brought out by the reporting officer.

Guidelines for Completing Individual Training and Development Plan

PMS provides the opportunity to capture the developmental needs of the executive in the Individual Development Plan. The ratings in the functional and managerial competencies provide the basis for identifying the training and development needs of the executive.

1. The development needs identified should be such that they facilitate the executive in immediate performance.

2. After receipt of completed PMS forms, the concerned HR would arrange the entire training programme.

Roles and Responsibilities

The role and responsibilities of different personnel change differently. The different roles and responsibilities identified are:

- Role of Executive
- Role of Reporting Officer
- Role of Reviewing Officer

⌘ Role of Executive ⌘

1. The executive shall attend the PMS meetings at all stages (performance planning, mid-year review and annual assessment) and be prepared to have an open and frank discussion about his/her performance.

2. The executive is required to show the necessary flexibility and adaptability to the organizational needs and display system discipline through adherence to all PMS requirements.

❖ Role of Reporting Officer

1. The reporting officer shall cascade the KPAs based on MoU targets to the executives reporting to him in a fair and achievable manner with necessary stretch for individual excellence.

2. The reporting officer should set up performance planning, mid-year review and annual assessment meetings with all the executives reporting to him within the specified periods.

3. In the event of change of KPAs, measures, targets etc., the reporting officer is required to obtain clearance from reviewing officer prior to making the change.

❖ Role of Reviewing Officer

1. The reviewing officer shall go through PMS forms for all executives under his purview and ensure that the reporting officer has been objective and unbiased in his scoring of various executives.

2. The reviewing officer shall also carry out an integrity check to ensure that the scores awarded to all the executives under his/her purview are distributed in a manner requiring minimum normalization by the Performance Management Committee.

Normalization Process

❖ Key Elements of the Normalization Process

Executives would be normalized within a cluster with a population of at least 15 executives.

1. Depending upon the level, location and the number of executives in the given level/ function, executives would be normalized either at the plant, Regional Headquarters or Corporate Centre level.

2. The composition of clusters at each grade would be notified by Corporate HR from time to time.

3. Normalization would be done by the Performance Management Committees comprising cross-functional members specifically set up for the purpose.

4. The Performance Management Committees would be the highest level of decision-making body for PMS for the respective level and cluster as the final accepting authority.

5. Constitution of the clusters and Performance Management Committees has been defined as part of the PMS policy.

⌘ Output from the Normalization Process ⌘

At the end of the process, all executives within a cluster would be categorized into the following categories:

- Top 20% of the cluster
- Middle 70% of the cluster
- Bottom 10% of the cluster

⌘ Performance Result ⌘

The performance scores finalized by the Performance Management Committee and the categorization at the end of the normalization process are final.

Normalization Steps

1. The Performance Management Committee should normalize the performance of executives within a cluster in the context of the overall performance of the unit/department.

2. KPA Targets

   ❖ Whether targets have been set at equally challenging levels across departments

   ❖ Whether "stretch targets" are truly stretch within a department's competencies

   ❖ Whether ratings have been very generous

   ❖ Whether competencies (functional/technical or managerial) have been assessed reasonably

   ❖ Whether too many executives in a department have been overrated (or underrated) on competencies (exceeds expectations)

   ❖ Whether certain executives have been overrated (or underrated) consistently on all the functional and managerial competencies.

3. After checking the integrity of the above data, the Performance Management Committee makes suitable adjustments in the scores in the relevant sections of the concerned individuals.

4. The final scores and the reasons for adjustments, (if made), are documented in the PMS form.

5. After the above steps, executives within each cluster will be categorized into the top 20% of the cluster, middle 70% of the cluster and bottom 10% of the cluster. The normalization process would be iterative until the above categorization is achieved.

6. The consolidated list of executives categorized as above for each cluster together with the final score for each employee will be signed by all members of the respective Performance Management Committee.

7. The concerned HR would facilitate the entire process of normalization in the role of a convener.

Role of HR Department

The role and responsibilities of HR department are shown below:

1. Issue PMS forms as per the PMS calendar

2. Collect forms as per schedule

3. Monitor adherence to dates

4. Highlight non-compliance/exceptions to top management

5. Send copy of Individual Training and Development Plan to concerned HRD/ EDC

6. Convene Performance Management Committee meetings

7. Consolidate feedback, final scores and relative ranking of all executives

8. Prepare "Final Score Feedback Form" for each executive and provide to respective reporting officers.

9. All the promotion decisions are taken by the HR keeping in mind the scores as provided by the PMS.

Our Learning

The key points which are major parameters for the NTPC performance appraisal process are:

1. Normalization is done for appraisal so as to bring uniformity in the process.

2. Performance appraisal split in two parts to eliminate the cumbersome process.

   (i) E1-E5 (1st April to 31st March)

   (ii) E6 above (1st January to 31st December)

3. Align company's goals with individual goals to avoid conflict of interests.

4. Encourage two-way communications between executive and reporting officer.

We noticed the following loopholes in the policies followed in NTPC:

1. Targets are set in terms of numbers which brings in objectivity and defies subjectivity.

2. The company is very rigid in its norms and adjudication criterion.

3. The company has no provision of retrenchment on the basis of performance.

4. Limited power is vested in the hands of the employees hence fast decision-making is difficult.

9 Performance-based Compensation Structure in Crompton Greaves Ltd.

Introduction

This case study deals with the introduction of a Performance-Based Compensation (PBC) package in Crompton Greaves (CG) in 1994. After a thumbnail profile of the company, the rationale for introducing PBC, its objectives, the structure, the process, and learnings are discussed.

CG is the largest multi-technology, and multi-locational electrical products manufacturing private sector company in the country. It has a sales turnover of RS.17,000 million and a workforce of 8,000 people. The company is headed by a Managing Director with four business groups and three functional areas at the corporate level.

The organization has broadly five layers of management:

1. Strategic Business Unit (SBU) and corporate functional chief-president

2. Multi-profit centre chief (in-charge of more than one profit centre)—Senior Vice President/Vice President/Sr. General Manager

3. Profit centre head – Sr. General Manager/General Manager

4. Departmental head – Dy. General Manager/Sr. Manager

5. Sub-departmental head/frontline supervisor – Manager/Asst.. Manager

Over the years, several managerial designations have come into existence within the five layers of this hierarchical structure due to operational factors such as seniority, needs of the organization and needs of individuals.

PRE-requisites for PBC Schemes

For successful implementation, monitoring and evaluation of a PBC Scheme, there are certain conditions which should be met in the organization. The organization should possess the following:

1. A corporate culture of confidence and mutual trust.

2. An image of management, being one among employees of fairness and equity

3. Clear communication throughout the organization about the mission, values, vision, objectives and goals of the organization.

4. HRM processes that are adequately positioned, including non-monetary employee development systems.

5. A professional style of management.

6. A working environment that is conducive to give employees professional and personal space for functioning.

7. Above all, scheme that is "SMART", that is:

    S : Specific

    M : Measurable

    A : Achievable

    R : Realistic

    T : Time-bound

The Raison Detre for CGs PBC for Executives

Some of the major reasons for introducing a PBC Scheme for executives in CG are as follows:

- The Government of India's decision to open up the Indian economy and markets for global competition made it imperative for the organization to make strategic interventions for gaining a competitive edge over other global players. The performance-based compensation scheme was introduced in the organizational efficiency.

- CG's compensation package was not competitive compared to other leading organizations in similar business in the country.

- The organization realised that to retain its competitive edge in the market and to achieve profitable and sustainable growth, it had to make certain HRD interventions to motivate the employees.

- CG's business of telecom, information technology (IT) products, etc., one of its strategic business, had been incurring losses for quite some time. With IT emerging as a 'sunrise industry', the organization was finding it difficult to attract and retain talented professionals.

- There was a distinct trend for rapid increase in executive remuneration in the country.

In the light of the above, CG made some critical HRD intervention. These included:

1. Restructuring and re-engineering of the organization.

2. Creation of Strategic Business Groups.

3. Redesigning the appraisal system to be compatible with the PBC Scheme.

4. Hastening the process for implementing Total Quality Management (TQM) and to bring the total population within its umbrella by 1998.

5. Introduction of a PBC package for senior executives

6. Establishing an HRD centre to further hasten competency and capacity building of employees.

The management felt that due to TQM campaign launched in the company as back as 1990, the environment in the organization was conducive for introducing a performance-based compensation scheme.

Intensive discussions were held within the hierarchy of the management. On the basis of the consultations within different levels of management, the final performance-based compensation scheme was finalized and introduced.

Of the various HRD interventions mentioned above, we will discuss only the PBC for senior executives.

Objectives of the PBC Scheme of CG

The major objectives of the scheme are:

1. To make CG's compensation package for executives comparable with that of the first three companies in similar business in the country.

2. To attract talented young professionals into the IT group without distributing the basic CG compensation structure.

3. To strengthen performance-compensation linkage in SBUs.

4. To use compensation as one of the critical motivators within the overall HRM strategy.

5. To attract and retain the best available talent in the industry.

6. To recognize, encourage and reward employees for good/exceptional performance.

7. To strengthen manufacturing and other processes and make them more predictable.

8. To prepare CG for future global competition.

Salient Features of CG's PBC Schemes

The salient features of the PBC Schemes are:

1. Measurement of performance is on the basis of four specific elements: (1) cash, (ii) profit before tax, (iii) sales and (iv) process cost.

2. Minimum and maximum compensation varies across levels.

3. The scheme takes into account the performance of the company, SBU, division and individual. Weightage is assigned to performance at difference at different levels and to different elements.

4. Less than 100% performance is also rewarded.

5. The scheme is made simple to the extent that an individual, at the end of the year, can calculate his performance and the amount permissible to him.

6. The scheme encourages teamwork as it gives details of individual performance with the division, SBU and company performance.

⌘ The 'Pride Money' Scheme ⌘

The PBC Scheme was termed as 'Pride Money' Scheme replacing the existing scheme of bonus and commission.

The 'Pride Money' scheme was conceptually different from the loosely defined concept of bonuses and commissions. Being scientific in nature and basically quantifiable, the quantum of reward to executives was on the basis of performance of the company, SBU, division and individual.

Such schemes are generally dynamic in nature and need to be periodically reviewed and redesigned, based on the changes in the external and operating environment and to keep in consonance with the organizational thrust areas.

Process of Setting Goals

Personal Goals

At the beginning of the year, the executive and the appraiser decide performance areas and set mutually agreed goals to be achieved during the year. The process has an in-built system of informal feedback to the executive by his superior. At the end of the year, the appraiser evaluates the performance on the basis of achievement of goals.

Divisional Goals

The second step in the process is setting of Divisional goals through discussions between the Divisional and Departmental heads. The divisional goals are set by the divisional head in consultation with the departmental head. As a first step in the process, the departmental head discusses departmental goals with Sectional heads.

SBU Goals

SBU goals are set by the process of discussions between the SBU Chief and the Divisional heads of the concerned SBU.

The final goals are set on the basis of discussions between the SBU Chief and the Chief Executive of the company.

Company Goals

The CEO of the company consults the SBU Chief and Corporate Heads for evolving company goals.

Performance and Evaluation Parameters

The final package under PBC scheme of each individual, depending on his position in management, is on the basis of performance of the following:

Designation	Performance of : (goals related to)
1. President	Personal, SBU and Company
2. Sr. Vice Presidnet/Vice President/Sr. General Manager	Personal, Divison and SBU
3. General Manager/Sr. GM	Personal, Division and SBU
4. Dy. GM/Sr. Manager	Personal and Division

Lessons from CG's Experience

1. There is no standardized PBC scheme which can fit all types and sizes of organizations. Business line, product range, operating environment, corporate culture, business strategy, management style and various other factors influence the shape and success of a PBC scheme in an organization.

2. The management should be clear about expectations from the scheme.

3. The review of the scheme should be an ongoing process to make it responsive to the changing needs of the organization.

4. Care should be taken to guard against "sand bagging" of goals.

5. No PBC scheme can be 100% objective. Efforts should be to reduce the subjectivity to the minimum. Efforts should also be made to reduce heartburn amongst executives of different profit centres.

6. It should be simple, measurable, achievable, realistic and time bound.

7. Finally, it is critical that a PBC scheme should fit into the overall HR strategy of the organization.

10

Performance Improvement: The IOC Experience

Introduction

In the deregulated business environment there has emerged a growing need to accelerate performance improvement to face the challenges of the free market and competition. With globalization, the oil industry in India has had to gear itself to complete effectively with the entry of private players including MNCs.

This calls for a rethinking of performance management and measurement practices and policies that are aimed at encouraging a performance-oriented culture. Among the key factors that drive performance improvement are differentiation of high performance, and recognizing and rewarding it, as also setting up a transparent communication channel.

What is Performance Management?

It is said that whatever gets measured gets done and whatever gets done is measurable. Performance measurement is a significant movement from Human Resource Development to Human Resource Management.

It is a process that measures output in terms of delivered performance in relation to expectations expressed as objectives. A forward-looking developmental approach, performance management is more a transformational rather than an appraisal process. A smart approach in goal-setting presupposes that goals are specific, measurable, achievable, relevant and time targeted.

Performance quotient is a function of emotional quotient plus intelligence quotient, which indicates that possessing intelligence or knowledge is not enough for high performance. It must be supplemented by emotional maturity.

The Oil Industry Context

The oil industry, in general and Indian Oil in particular, has been experiencing a variety of concerns in the recent past due to the opening up to the market. These concerns relate to the following:

- Extreme pressure on the bottoms line

- Commercial competitiveness

- Dismantling of the administered pricing mechanism (APM)

- Entry of big players

- Squeezed resources

- Enhanced stakeholder expectations

- Social aspect of business

In view of the above, some of the critical issues confronting the management are:

- Moving from potential to performance

- Providing an environment to excel

- Enhancing competitiveness

- Creating differentiators for performers

- Motivating people to perform

- Managing organizational and environmental turbulence

Being a leading public sector enterprise, Indian Oil has successfully faced the various challenges of the turbulent market environment and also has become a strategically of the Government of India by ensuring timely supply of petroleum products to the armed forces in wartime. Its operating performance and vast infrastructure are a clear indication of its inherent ability to face the challenge of competition and fulfill its social responsibilities. (See in Exhibit 1)

EXHIBIT 1	
About Indian Oil (2000-2001)	
Sales	**Over Rs. 1.13 lac Crore**
Employee strength	33,000
Sales record	47.8 T (53%)
Sales point	Over 21,000
LPG (liquefied petroleum gas) bottling plants	71
Aviation fuel stations	92
State offices	22
Divisional offices	47

Indian Oil owns nine of the seventeen refineries in India. It is the only Indian company in the Global Fortune 500 list. It ranks 112th in the Forbes International 500 list of largest companies outside the US and 34th among the largest 1000 Top Asian Companies of *Asia Week*.

The general assumption is that money drives performance, but that is not all. There are other factors too that drive performance. Some of these are enumerated below:

Mission (aspirations)	Very clear
	High level and inspirational
	Consistent over time
Target/Goals	Highly aggressive
	Both short and long-term & measurable
	Adjusted over time
Organization	Few layers
	Many P&L (profit and loss)
	Units ("atomized")
Performance feedback	Transparent
	Internal and external benchmarking
	Rankings made public
Consequence management	Visible and quick
	Varying severity

In the fiercely competitive market environment, Indian Oil has been working towards evolving innovative schemes to recognize and reward high performance which also can serve as a strong incentive to other employees of the organization. Towards this end, the marketing division has developed a unique scheme that recognizes the performance by various section of the marketing division. It has also evolved a highly comprehensive methodology for differentiating the high performers who deserve rewards.

Performance Management Schemes

Some of the incentive schemes implemented at Indian Oil are:

- Productivity-linked incentives bonus, region/unit-wise

- Ex-gratia (applicable for all)

- Performance-related incentives (for super perfumers)

Methodology

The steps involved in carrying out the schemes are threefold.

⌘ Step 1: Target Setting ⌘

The scheme is goal-oriented. Targets are broken down and allocated top-down across all the levels. The allocation is done by the Head Office based on annual growth projections aligned with business realities. These targets are agreed upon and owned by the business heads at various levels as benchmarks of their performance.

In accordance with the methodology, target setting is done: region-wise by the Head Office: state-wise by the regions; and location-wise by the State Offices.

⌘ Step 2: Measurement ⌘

The measurement parameters provide for the consequences of performance by assigning weightage and value to achievements, including negative marking.

⌘ Step 3: Evaluation ⌘

The final evaluation is carried out by evaluation committees at the state, regional and head office levels. The HRD department coordinates the entire process.

Towards High Performance with an Integrated Approach

To motivate teams to not only delivers performance for achieving targets but also to strive for excellence in the entire range of service, quality, safety and other related areas of performance. The Indian Oil marketing division identified the key business units and also the frontline personnel responsible for achieving critical business results. The performance parameters of the following personnel throw light on the various areas of performance taken into consideration.

1. *Best Head of State:* Performance Parameters

    ❖ Market share

    ❖ LPG enrolment

    ❖ Indane showroom computerization

    ❖ Inspections

    ❖ Growth in profitability

    ❖ Computerization, Executive information system

- ❖ Non-Directorate of Government Supply & Distribution (DGS& D) outstanding
- ❖ Revenue/capital utilization
- ❖ Stock loss control

2. *Best Head of State, Market share:* Performance Parameters

- ❖ Increase in market share MS (Motor Sprite-retail and HSD (high speed diesel), FO (Fortune oil), LSHS (Low sulphur heavy stock), bitumen/naptha/LDO (light diesel oil)/ LPG (liquefied Petroleum gas)/ special products.
- ❖ Increase in lube-fuel ratio
- ❖ Percentage of volume growth lubes
- ❖ SKO (superior kerosene oil) sales

3. *Best Divisional Manager:* Performance Parameters

- ❖ Increase in market share
- ❖ Lube/grease volume growth
- ❖ Lube-fuel ratio
- ❖ SKO allocation vs sales
- ❖ Retail outlet (RO) commissioning
- ❖ Vision 2000 upgradation (RO modernization scheme)
- ❖ Conversion from "B" site (i.e. dealer-owned, dealer-operated) to "A" site (i.e., company-owned, dealer-operated)RO
- ❖ Upgradation of state transport undertaking/railway depots
- ❖ Inspections
- ❖ Non-DGS&D and beyond, credit outstanding
- ❖ Stock loss
- ❖ Quality control index of supply points

4. *Best Depot/Terminal Manager:* Performance Parameters

- ❖ Stock loss
- ❖ Tank-truck performance
- ❖ Quality control index
- ❖ Safety maintenance and inspection (M&I) index
- ❖ Innovations

- ❖ Cost control
- ❖ Claims and Demurrages
- ❖ Disposal of scrap
- ❖ Revenue and capital budget
- ❖ Compliance with statutory provisions
- ❖ Compliance of inspection report
- ❖ Training activities

5. *Best sales Officer (Retail):* Performance Parameters

- ❖ Increase in market share
- ❖ Lube-fuel ration
- ❖ RO Commissioning
- ❖ Vision 2000 up gradation (RO modernization scheme)
- ❖ Conversion from "B" site (i.e., dealer-owned, dealer-operated) to "A" site (i.e., company-owned, dealer operated) RO
- ❖ Inspections
- ❖ Mandatory facilities at retail outlets
- ❖ Dishonour of instruments
- ❖ Irregularity at dealership
- ❖ Customers' complaints
- ❖ Pump attendants' uniform

6. *Best Sales Officer Consumer:* Performance Parameters

- ❖ Sales, volume, growth MS and HSD, FO, LDO
- ❖ Sales, volume, growth HSD (Direct)
- ❖ Sales, volume, growth FO, LDO
- ❖ New business potential tapping
- ❖ Lubes volume, growth
- ❖ Consumer pump upgradation
- ❖ Non-DGS&D collections
- ❖ Customers' complaints
- ❖ Railway Consumer Depot (RCD) inspections/meetings

7. *Best Sales Officer (Retail and Consumer):* Performance Parameters

❖ Potential customer tapping

❖ Lube-fuel Ration

❖ Lubes volume growth

❖ RO Commissioning

❖ Vision 2000 upgradation (RO modernization scheme)

❖ Sales, volume, growth MS, and HSD, FO, LDO

❖ Increase in market share MS, (retail) and HSD (retail)

❖ Sales, volume, growth HSD (Direct)

❖ Sales, volume, growth FO

❖ Servo shop

❖ Non-DDGS &D collections

❖ Inspections Retail, SKO

❖ Customers' complaints

❖ Mandatory facilities at retail outlet

❖ Night outs

For each of these awards, parameters with a significant impact on performance were involved and reward announced. (See Exhibit 2)

EXHIBIT 2	Parameters and Reward		
Unit	**Parameter**	**Reward All India**	**Others**
State Office	Overall	Singapore (3 nights)	Nepal (2 nights)
State Office	Market Share	-do-	Goa
Dividioanl Office	Overall	Nepal	-do-
Terminal	Overall	-do-	-do-
Depot	Overall	-do-	Goa
Field Officer	Retail Consumer	Nepal	

The spouse could accompany the rewardee and travel, boarding and lodging are on company account.

Officers going abroad are expected to study the practices of multinational in similar retail business.

❖ Conclusion

Indian Oil's scheme is a unique policy intervention aimed at recognition and reward of high performance by team heads and individual performers. It has gone a long way in creating a motivational climate in its marketing division, and thus, has had a highly positive impact in product sales/market share. In the post APM scenario, this scheme has been indirectly instrumental in helping IOC maintain its high sales volume and market leadership position.

The following data illustrates this point.

Year	IOC Product Sales (in mt)	Market Share (as %)
1998-99	46.05	53.1
1999-00	48.79	53.3
2000-01	47.80	52.5

Performance Management System (PMS) at Bharti Telecom

Introduction

Established in 1985, Bharti Enterprises has been a pioneering force in the telecom sector with many firsts and innovation to its credit: it was the first mobile service in Delhi, first private basic telephone service provider in India, first Indian company to provide comprehensive telecom service outside India (in Seychelles) and the first private sector service provider to launch national long distance (NLD) service in India. As on 31 July , 2002, Bharti had approximately 2,112,000 customers—nearly 1,772,000 mobile, 221,000 fixed lines and 119,000 internet customers.

Its service sectors businesses include mobile operations in circles of Andhra Pradesh, Chennai, Delhi, Gujarat, Haryana, Himachal Pradesh, Karnataka, Kerala, Kolkata, Madhya Pradesh, Maharashtra, Mumbai, Punjab, Tamil Nadu and Uttar Pradesh (West). In addition, it also has fixed line operations in the states of Madhya Pradesh, Chhattisgarh, Haryana, Delhi, Karnataka and Tamil Nadu, and nationwide broadband and long distance networks.

Bharti has recently launched NLD services, offering data transmission services for calls originating and terminating on most of India's mobile networks. The company is currently implementing a submarine cable project connecting Chennai and Singapore for providing international bandwidth. Bharti also manufactures and exports telephone terminals and cordless phones. Apart from being the largest manufacturer of telephone instruments, it is also the first telecom company to export its products to the US. Bharti provides telecom software solutions to both domestic and overseas clients. The latest addition to Bharti's business portfolio is the contact venture. Today, Bharti is the largest private sector integrated telecommunications services group in India in terms of numbers of customers.

Need of PMS

A performance orientation culture is the cornerstone of achieving excellence in any organization. Developing such a culture requires achieving clarity in understanding and managing performance within an agreed framework of planned goals, standards and required attributes and competencies. The process calls for a clear statement of the company's vision, goals and objectives and aligning statement of the company's vision, goals and objectives and aligning these with individual targets and activities. A performance management system (PMS) aimed at getting better results from teams and individuals has therefore, been introduced at Bharti.

The PMS at Bharti is based on the simple proposition that when people know and understand what is expected of them, and have participated in forming those expectations, they can and will performing those expectations, they can and will perform to meet them. This leads to the following questions:

- What do you think are the most important things you have to do?

- What do you believe you are expected to achieve in each of these areas?

- How will you or anyone else know whether or not you have achieved them?

Resolving these questions enables people to unambiguously identify their targets and plan their activities towards achieving them. It is equally essential to link recognition and rewards to such achievements to bring about and propagate a performance-oriented culture.

The PMS at Bharti encompasses the above aspects and is implemented through performance-lined incentive (PLI) scheme.

Performance-linked Incentive Scheme at Bharti

The PLI is primarily focused on individual performance, though there are schemes designed to recognize performance at the team and company levels too.

Step I: Identification of Key Result Areas (Performance Criteria)

The identification of key result areas (KRAs) is an important and systematic process. Starting with the company's goals and objectives, the KRAs are identified at all levels of management (from the top to the working levels), ensuring alignment and commonality of purpose. For instance, in production, quality, market share and profit could be some KRAs at the senior level. These are further broken down into KRAs at department and working levels. For example, production would depend upon machine utilization, and material and manpower availability, while machine utilization would depend upon power availability, preventive maintenance and availability of spares. A configuration of this type facilitates identification of appropriate KRAs at the identification of appropriate KRAs at the individual, team and company levels.

KRAs for individuals comprise of both business parameters (common for all covered by the schemes) and individual parameters. This is to ensure that while striving to achieve their individual targets, employee do not lose sight of the business goals and objectives.

Step 2: Assigning Weightage to Selected Criteria

Weightage is for each criterion is determined in proportion to its anticipated impact in terms of the company's topline, bottom line, growth strategies, etc. This enables people to prioritize their activities and expend their time and efforts accordingly. (Weightage should add up to 100 per cent.)

Step 3: Setting Targets

This is an important step and involves extensive discussions an deliberation. Care must be taken to ensure that targets are aligned to the company's budgets and strategies.

Step 4: Defining Performance Levels

Performance in these selected criteria is measured across 5 levels, level 1 being the minimum and level -5 being the maximum. The targets are normally slotted at level-3. Typically, levels-4 and 5 are set at 110 per cent and 120 percent the target respectively. Similarly, level-1 is fixed at 80 per cent and level-2 at 90 percent. However, there could be exceptions depending upon the nature and scope of the criteria. It is also possible that in some cases levels 1 and level 2 do not exist.

⌘ Performance-Payout Relationship ⌘

The payout may vary from 10 percent to 30 percent and may go upto 40 percent as well. Normally, the performance and payout are linked as follows:

Performance levels	1	2	3	4	5
Payout percent	10	13	17	23	30

As is evident, the rate of payout progressively increases at higher levels of performance. The percentages in the table are of the annual salary and normally include basic pay, house rent allowance, special allowance, conveyance allowance, LTC, medical, provident fund and superannuation.

The entire process of PLI can be illustrated with and example as below:

1. Take any job.

    Example:

    ❖ Regional Sales Manager

2. Company-wide business parameters

		Weightage
❖	Revenue	20%
❖	Profits	20%

    Individual parameters: Weightage

		Weightage
❖	Increase in market share in region (MS)	20%
❖	Increase in sales turnover (ST)	20%
❖	Increase in reliability and service level of Products (REL)	20%
	Decrease in level of outstandings(OS)	10%

3. For each responsibility, define a goal or target, for instance

    ❖ Increase market share in the region to 26 percent

    ❖ Increase sales turnover to Rs 1,500,000 lakhs

    ❖ Increase reliability and service level of products (CI index of 80 percent)

    ❖ Decrease level of outstanding to 30 days

    In the case of subjective elements, data is captured as indices.

4. Define measures of performance against targets.

    Example:

    Performance index for sales turnover will be:

❖ < RS 100 lacs	0
❖ Rs 100-120 lacs	10
❖ Rs 12-140 lacs	13
❖ Rs 140-160 lacs	17
❖ Rs 160-200 lacs	23
❖ > Rs. 200 lacs	30

The above is illustrated in the form of a PLI table.

S. No	Performance criteria	Weightage	Base year	Target	Performance levels
TABLE 1	**Individual Performance-linked Incentive Sales**				
1.	Company parameters: Revenue (20%) Profits (20%)	40%			10% ,13%, 17%, 23%, 30%
2.	Individual Parameters- -MS -ST (Rs) REL (index) -OS	20% 20% 10% 10%		26% 150 lacs 80% 30 days	220*

*Represents figure of actual achievement which corresponds to level 5. Similarly, based on the achievement, each parameter would be slotted at an appropriated level and the overall payout percentage would be determined based on the weightages.

_____

_____

Signature of Individual

Signature of Reporting officer

12

Restructuring Incentive Scheme: The Experience and Approach of National Fertilizer

Introduction

A continuous chemical industry, National Fertilizers Limited (NFL) is in the business of producing fertilizes. It basically produces urea under a trade name. Its production capacity is around 32 lakh million tonnes per year. With a market share of around 14 percent, NFL is one of the largest producers of nitrogenous fertilizers in India. NFL also manufactures and markets industrial products, namely methanol, argon, liquid nitrogen, liquid oxygen, nitric acid and carbon dioxide; sulphur is also produced as a by-product.

NFL was incorporated as a company on 23 August 1974, with two fertilizer plants, one at Bhatinda in Punjab and the other at Panipat in Haryana. Through mergers and expansion it now has one plant each at Nangal and Vijaipur as well. Its capacity has increased from 3100 mt per day to 9550 mt per day. NFL has old vintage plants at Nangal and a latest technology plant at Guna.

The capacity utilization of NFL's plants has been more than 100 percent for over the last five years. It is one of the few profit making public sector undertakings (PSUs) and has a wide marketing network spread almost all over India.

Briefly, the mission of NFL is to produce as well as market its products efficiently and economically and serve the farmer community and other customers with quality products and maintain its leading position in the fertilizer industry to the benefit of the national economy. Towards this end, the company has been striving to move its workforce to improve production capacity utilization, securing optimum manpower utilization, and reducing consumption of major process material through better operation, process control and maintenance of equipment. Therefore, various incentive schemes have been introduced from time to time. These schemes, besides focusing on the objective of the company, give an opportunity to employees to improve their earnings. After rethinking and a lot of deliberations with the help and guidance of an outside consultant, NFL has recently restricted its incentive scheme.

Incentive Schemes at NFL

There are three types of production incentive schemes in vogue in NFL.

(a)   Integrated Production Incentive Scheme

(b)   Award for achieving Monthly/Yearly Target of Production

(c)   Yearly Production Performance Award Scheme

✂ Integrated Production Incentive Scheme ✂

This scheme is base on the production capacity utilization factor, material utilization index and manpower factor.

Production Capacity Utilization Factor

The production factor takes care of better production capacity utilization. Production incentive is paid for achieving production beyond the specified base norm of production.

Matrix Utilization Index

To encourage maximum utilization of major process materials through better process control and maintenance, the material utilization index is calculated. To arrive at this index, the standard specific consumption of major input materials is compared with the actual consumption of these materials. If this index is more than the base Index, incentive is paid accordingly.

Manpower Factor

The manpower factor takes care of the optimum utilization of the available manpower by discouraging overtime and employments of casual labour. This factor is calculated for a group or department. For computation of this factor, the standard strength of the group is taken as the reference against the actual strength of the department or group coupled with the total overtime hours of the group and casual labour employed.

In order to encourage attendance and reduce absenteeism, incentive is paid to employees only for the days they are present. Overtime put in by individuals has a negating effect in computing this factor.

Depending upon the direct and indirect contribution of various groups in the production process, the whole unit is divided into two groups, namely, direct and indirect.

Groups directly involved in the production process are paid more incentive than the groups which have indirect involvement.

✤ Award for Achieving Monthly/Yearly Target of Production ✤

Introduced in 1986-87, this award is given in the form of a cash gift to all employees who achieve/exceed the base target production both on a monthly and yearly basis.

1. Rs. 401 if the month's production is equal to or above the base target first in the year.

2. Rs. 601 if the base target is achieved or exceeded the second or subsequent time during the year.

3. Rs. 601 if the base target for production is exceeded by 100 percent or above of the rated capacity even thought it may be on the first occasion during the year.

4. Rs. 801 for meeting the yearly production target of ammonia or for achieving production of 225,000 mt of ammonia for Bhatinda, Panipat and Nangal and 673,866 mt for Vijaipur Lines I & II, during the year.

✤ Yearly Production Performance Award Scheme ✤

The yearly production performance award scheme provides for an annual award of Rs 1311 to each employee on achievement of 81 percent capacity utilization in production of nitrogen. The award amount was increased or decreased at the rate of Rs 50 percent up to 95 percent in actual capacity utilization. This award is not payable if capacity utilization falls below 75 percent in a year.

The average capacity utilization of urea, the main product of the company increased from 54 percent to 73 percent after introduction of the integrated production incentive scheme in 1981 and further to 91 percent in 1986-87 when the award/gift scheme was introduced. It is, therefore, evident that the incentive schemes and reward management have been effective in improving the productivity in NFL.

✤ Other Measures Taken for Productivity Enhancement ✤

It is not possible to improve productivity by just having incentive schemes in place. It has to be a total performance improvement system. NFL has made concerted efforts in this direction. These include:

- Conducting of end-to-end survey

- Quality of cooling water upgradation

- Continuous efforts made in terms of technology upgradation and new and more reliable and energy efficient plants.

- Captive power plants installation to counter unreliable power supply system

- Emphasis on HRD activities to improve the quality of manpower

- Review of recruitment and promotion policies and introduction of necessary changes.

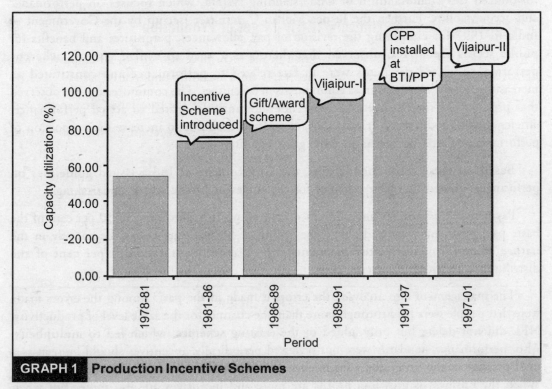

GRAPH 1 **Production Incentive Schemes**

Review of Production Incentive Schemes

With the passage of time, there was pressure on the company's resources. The government's subsidy burden on fertilizers was increasing, which resulted in the tightening of norms for fixing the retention price of urea, the main product of the company. As such, the expenditure on account of incentive schemes became too heavy for the company.

The introduction of various schemes also led to multiplicity of productivity-linked incentives in the company. In May 1999, the department of fertilizers observed that the employees were being paid through more than one channel for achieving the same objective and asked fro an integrated view to be taken of their need and relevance.

The plants were now operating at much higher capacities on a sustained basis and employees were getting incentives continuously under various schemes with comparatively less effort.

Earlier, when the incentives were payable on achievement of 70 percent rated capacity, an average capacity of 60-65 per cent was justifiable. But since the plants were not operating at much higher capacities, the break-even for incentives should be at least 95 per cent capacity utilization.

In view of globalization and the changed economic scenario, there was now a greater focus on performance and operational efficiency of public sector enterprises. The government introduced the Memorandum of Understanding system, which focuses on performance and accountability. Further, the Justice Mohan Committee, set up by the Government of India in 1997 for examining the revision of pay, allowances, perquisites and benefits for public sector executives, observed that there was a need to evolve systems, whereby performance-related payments were in fact related to performance and constituted an increasing proportion of the gross emoluments of executives. The committee further observed that productivity-linked incentives were not substantively related to actual performance, efficiency and productivity. It was, thus, considered desirable to increase the proportion of performance-related payments in their gross emoluments.

Based on these recommendations, the Government of India issued guidelines on performance-linked incentive schemes for executives in public sector undertakings.

Payments of perquisites and allowances may be up to a maximum of 50 per cent of the basic pay; payments over and above the ceiling of 50 per cent should be entirely in the nature of performance-related payments, which should not exceed 5 per cent of the distributable profited in an enterprise.

The management also analysed the errors it made in the past. Among the errors made were that people were paid through more than one channel for the same level of productivity. NFL did not delete but only added to the existing schemes, which led to multiplicity. Also, performance standards were not reviewed periodically. Incentives should be seen as a total package of the salary and adjustments must be made in the targets from time to time. When the business is growing, profits are more and incentives are also more. But when there is recession, incentives are less. People get demotivated since the take-home pay is reduced.

New Schemes

As a result of the review and study, separate schemes have been proposed for executives and non-executives. The schemes for executives are based on the overall performance and profitability of the company, while that for non-executives is based on productivity. The salient features of these schemes are given hereunder:

⌘ Incentive Scheme for Non-Executives ⌘

1. The scheme will cover all employees below the level of executives (i.e. those in the pay scale lower than E-O).

2. In order to encourage attendance and reduce absenteeism, the incentive will be paid to employees only for the days they are present.

3. The incentive payment will be related to the monthly production capacity of ammonia.

4. The incentive would be payable on achieving the base production level (i.e. 95 per cent of the installed capacity for the month).

5. At the base production index, (i.e. 95 per cent of monthly capacity utilization), the incentive will be 5 per cent of the standard wages with an increase at the rate of 1 per cent for each additional 1 per cent of monthly production capacity utilization with a ceiling of 15 percent.

6. The incentive will be paid on a monthly basis.

7. The incentive payment calculated will be expressed as a percentage of standard salary. All non-executives have been divided into four groups. The standard salary for each group will be worked out on the basis of the average of the maximum of the highest pay scale in the group and the minimum of the lowest pays scale as illustrated below:

Salary Group (Rs.)	Pay Scale (Rs.)	Standard Salary of Group
I	W-0- (3000-3480) W-1 (3500-4200)	(3000+4200)/2=3600
II	W-2 (4300-5280) W-3 (4550-5670) W-4 (4650-6000)	(4300+6000)/2=5150
III	W-5 (4650-6550) W-6 (5150-8000)	(4650+8000)=6325
IV	W-7 (5550-8910) W-8 (6100-9500) W-9 (6100-9710)	(5550+9710)=7630

8. All employees covered under this scheme will be grouped into two categories, direct and indirect. Employees in the production, maintenance and other departments who are required to work 48 hours a week will be in the direct group, while employees who have to put it in less than 48 hours per week will be in the indirect group.

9. All direct group employees will be paid 100 per cent of the payable incentive, while indirect group employees will be paid 80 per cent of the payable incentive.

⌘ Incentive Scheme for Executives ⌘

1. The schemes will cover all employees in the executive category.

2. In order to encourage attendance and reduce absenteeism, the incentive will be paid to executives only for the days they are present.

3. The total incentive earnings (TIE) of executives will be linked with the overall performance and profitability of the company as determined by the MOU.

4. The quantum of incentive will be limited to 3 per cent of the distributable profit. The profit for this purpose is the company's profit after tax.

5. The incentive amount will be determined by multiplying the MIE for the year with the incentive index corresponding to the actual MOU rating.

1. Actual MOU Rating	2. Incentive Index (%)
Excellent	100
Very Good	90
Good	80
Average	70
Poor	0

6. The incentive earning (in percentage of standard salary) for the year will be determined according to the following formula:

Incentive will be paid on a yearly basis after the accounts are finalized and the AGM of shareholders has been held.

7. The incentive payment calculated as per the scheme will be expressed as a percentage of standard salary. All executives have been divided into three groups. The standard salary for each group will be worked out on the basis of the average of the maximum of the highest pay scale in the group and the minimum of the lowest pay scale as illustrated below:

$$\frac{3 \text{ per cent of distributable profit} \times \text{Incentive index as per (5) above}}{\text{Sum total of standard salaries corresponding to MOU rating of eligible executives}}$$

Salary Group	Pay Scale(Rs)	Standard Salary of Group (Rs)
Group I	E-O (3500-6200) E-1 (4000-7150) E-2 (4800-8800)	(3500-+8800)/2 = 6150
Group II	E-3 (5400-9050) E-4 (6500-9425) E-5 (7000-9600)	(5400+9600)/2 = 7500
Group-III	E-6 (7500-9900) E-7 (8250-10050) E-8 (9500-11500)	(7500+11500)/2 = 9500

❖ The estimated average expenditure per annum on account of incentive payment for the last three years would be approximately Rs 5.6 crore (executives 3.4 crore, non-executives 2.2 crore), whereas the average payment under the existing scheme is an estimated Rs 13.5 crore (executives Rs 4.5 crore; non-executives Rs 9 crore). The estimated reduction in expenditure was Rs 8 crore.

❖ Since the earnings of the employees will fall to a considerable extent under the new incentive scheme, the scheme was implemented alongside pay revision so that reduction in earnings on account of the new scheme was compensated for by the pay revision.

Other Measures

Other measures recommended for effective implementation of the new schemes included:

1. Designing and implementation of a performance appraisal system based on KPAs and performance targets linked to MOU and strategic plan.

2. Introduction of performance management system with a customized approach.

3. Involving a consultant as a resource person and constituting a task force to design the system.

4. Involvement of hierarchy for smooth implementation.

5. Workshops for identification of KPAs and designing a performance appraisal system.

Steps Taken to Measure Individual Executive Performance

1. Role directories for selected positions based on information collected from identified companies as well as from within the organization were prepared.

2. From role descriptions, key job functions and KPAs were identified in one-to-one interaction with the role incumbents.

3. The relationships of KPA with the corporate objectives and MOU targets were examined to make them relevant and operationally functional.

4. The LPAs were prioritized, their relative importance being determined by assigning weightages to them in interaction with the role incumbent and his or her boss.

5. The job objectives were also identified on the basis of prioritized weighted KPAs with the understanding that these job objectives will change from year to year and will be determined based on one-to-one interview of the role incumbent by the reviewing officer.

6. Situational constraints that have a bearing on the achievement of performance targets were identified and taken into account in determining performance targets.

7. The competencies of each functionary were identified, but were not included for the purpose of evaluating performance. They were, however, appraised and the appraisal result used for identifying training and development needs.

8. A mid-term review was provided to identify unforeseen difficulties and to make suitable adjustments in the performance targets.

9. The rating scale as far as possible was based on performance anchors for the identified performance parameters; qualitative evaluation was used where such anchors were not easily identifiable.

10. The final appraisal was based on self-appraisal by the rate as well as a feedback meeting between the ratee and the ratee.

⌘ The Approach ⌘

The objective of the system is not to pass judgement but to improve performance by identifying impediments and evolving an action plan mutually agreed upon by the rater and ratee to reduce their impact.

Once the system gains acceptance, objectivity and transparency, the possibility of linking incentives/awards with the ratee's performance and evolving performance-linked incentive schemes will be explored.

The system data are intended to be used for linking the rewards and incentives of individual executives with their performance.

Monetary	Non-monetary
<ul><li>Financial rewards</li><li>Certificates/Mementos</li><li>Promotions</li><li>Prized postings-Perks</li><li>Member task force</li></ul>	<ul><li>Job rotation</li><li>Important assignments</li><li>Member project teams;</li><li>Participation at International/National Seminars</li></ul>

Limitations of Linking Incentive to Individual Performance

A performance-related reward system involves rewarding employees according to their performance, or the result achieved or the contribution made by them to the organization's performance as individuals or as part of a group.

The possibility of linking incentive to individual executive performance was examined but considered premature on the following:

1. There was no system of performance measurement for top executives (functional and unit heads).

2. For middle-level executives, a format based on target of performance was in place but the process and the measurement were not adequate.

3. For junior executives, the assessment was primarily on a mix of skill and supervisory quality, which was inadequate from the point of view of linking incentive payment to performance.

Looking Ahead

- Earlier, the objective was to push output and increase production. But now the industry, especially the fertilizer sector, is running at 100 percent capacity. The thrust therefore, is on exceeding 100 percent with the same resources. As such, incentives should be given over and above 100 percent capacity utilization. Cost reduction should thus, be the main aim. The objective should be to share the gains of productivity.

- The incentives must be linked to a combination of individual/team productivity, performance and profits of the organization. They cannot be totally dependent on individual productivity or totally dependent on individual productivity or totally on team productivity.

- Performance at the top level being critical, performance targets fixed and incentives should be linked with individual performance. At the lower levels, group efforts being more critical, incentives should be linked with team productivity.

- There should be separate schemes for unionized employees and executives. For the former, the incentive payments should be based on production and productivity, and for the latter, performance and profitability of the company.

- A provision must be kept to review the incentive schemes periodically, since there are ups and downs in every business.

- Unions must be involved in restructuring incentive schemes. It is much better to share the information with them and also inform them at various stages of the formulation of such schemes. It would then be quite easy to implement the incentive schemes.

- To reward individual performance of executives, some options to incentive schemes could be delegating important assignments, job rotation, participation at international and national forums, heading project groups, inclusion as a member of any task force constituted for a specific purpose, foreign assignments, timely promotions etc. However, evaluation must be objective, and for this a KPA-based performance evaluation system must be in place.

Core competencies: NFL considered it premature to include core competencies for the purpose of rating performance since competency analysis, profiling and mapping for different roles has not been undertaken. Such an exercise should consider the following questions:

- How much competency is required for each role?

- How much of it does the role incumbent possess?

- How is the gap supposed to be filled?

Role analysis and restructuring: In one-to-one interviews, it was found that some roles need to be restructured to make them more functional and operational. Deriving KPAs and defining performance objectives will be difficult unless the roles are properly defined, understood and structured.

An organizational and role analysis revealed the need for autonomy and delegation, which in turn, point to the need for organizational restructuring.

Organizational Culture: Uncertainty, falling morale and lack of succession planning can adversely affect the usefulness of KPA-based performance review system. It is, therefore, necessary to take action on all aspects and regard the performance appraisal system and KPAs as an integral part of the performance management system, culture and outlook.

Recognition and reward policy: Performance review and appraisal assume operational meaning and significance if the appraisal results are used for placement, promotion, recognition and reward, both monetary and non-monetary. A recognition and reward policy base on performance will need to be evolved both, to make the performance appraisal system meaningful and to create a performance culture.

Understanding each other's role and difficulties in achieving results is an area of concern and consideration for the organization.

It has been increasingly realized that used in isolation, performance-linked incentives have little impact on motivation for performance. Appropriate conditions in the organization, therefore have to be created for the system to be motivationally effective. These conditions include proper information dissemination, consultation, effective communication mechanisms and developing a proactive attitude and existence of a performance-oriented culture in the organization.

TATA Performance Management System

Introduction

Ensuring Development and Growth of Employees (EDGE), is what Tata Steel's Performance Management System aims at. In the past, the Performance Management System was regarded only as a tool to evaluate and reward good performance. The understanding and use of the system has today undergone a paradigm shift with emphasis on individual development and growth, in addition to performance.

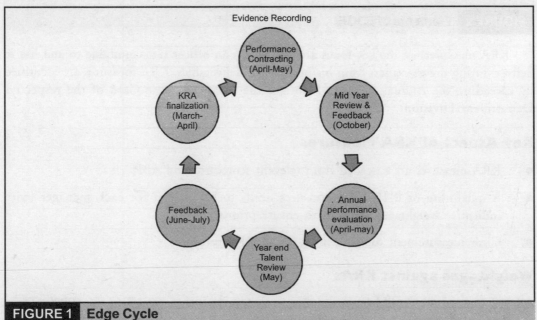

FIGURE 1 Edge Cycle

Success will depend on how we communicate the expectations, understand the needs of employees using the performance management system and address them subsequently. This alone will bring about the distinctiveness needed to achieve high performance standards throughout the organization. Once in place, it will serve as a unifying force in unleashing people's potential and providing Tata Steel the competitive EDGE.

Elements of Edge

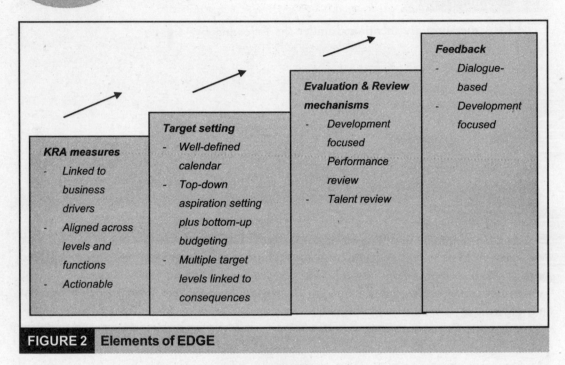

FIGURE 2 Elements of EDGE

KRA measures are the key focus areas to which an officer is accountable to and has to deliver during the year apart from his/her normal deliverables. KRA measures are identified by cascading the Annual Business Plan and the Balanced Score Card of the respective Department/Division.

Key Aspect of KRA Measures

- KRA measures are cascaded from relevant scorecards and ABP

- A maximum of 8-10 KRA measures needs to be defined for each manager (with indicative weightages attached to ensure prioritization)

- Clear measurement tools outlined for all KRA measures

Weightages against KRAs

All KRA measures should have weightages assigned to them totalling to 100%. There should not be any KRA which has less than 5% weightage.

Performance Contracting

Once the KRA measures have been identified, the next step is Performance Contracting. It is the process of arriving at targets against each KRA measure through the process of discussion between officer and superior to agree on the rating scales and qualitative grids.

Performance contracts lists down the agreed KRA measures between the superior and the subordinates.

The KRA measures are mentioned under the following five areas:

- Finance
- Customer
- Internal Business Process
- People Development
- Special Projects

Note: KRA measures are mentioned in the applicable areas only in case any of it is not applicable.

In case of dual reporting relationship, the document is also discussed with the dotted line/functional superior. There may be certain deliverables, which the functional superior may wish to include in the document. All such inputs are taken by the solid line/ current superior before finalizing the document.

Evidence Recording

Evidence recording is the process of documenting information or observations related to a subordinate's efforts/activity by superiors.

Need for Evidence Recording

- To substantiate objective and meaningful feedback to subordinates (feedback could be related to very specific dimensions of performance or very generically related to once or more competency. This way the superior is able to initiate the first activity of his subordinate's development i.e., identification of development needs).

- To aid in objective and meaningful individual case preparation for talent review (during Talent Review, the superior is not only required to present the evaluation ratings but also needs to defend these when they are challenge and discussed).

Responsibility for Evidence Recording

- Responsibility of evidence recording will rest with the immediate superior (who is closely observing the subordinate's performance.)

Process of Evidence Recording

The most common method for workplace assessment is observation of performance and making note of the person's work or demonstrated behaviour. The format for Evidence Recording provides two sheets per person: one for favourable and the other for unfavourable ones.

Mid-year Review

- The mid-year performance reviewers take place in the month of October.

- Mid-year review is done by the immediate(solid line) superiors.

- Inputs from the functional superior is also taken into account.

Mid-year review serves the following purpose:

- The objective and focus of the mid-year review is primarily feedback and

- Review of performance contracts and performance against KRAs.

- Resolve bottlenecks

- Preparation for the final end year review.

Performance evaluation is an annual exercise conducted in the month of April/May. The exercise aims at evaluating performance of an officer in the manner which

- Provides for basis of improvement in employee performance

- Provides the organization with structured record of employee performance

- Serves as one among various inputs for career development and rotation decisions

- Provides input for compensation decisions.

Apart from the above, the superior also gives his/her recommendations are made on a 5-point detailed scale on both performance and potential. The evaluator is also categorized as functional expert if he is considered to be domain expert of his/her functional area.

❖ Process of Performance Evaluation ❖

The process of annual performance evaluation starts formally during March and is captured through a structured performance evaluation form. The form has following parts:

PART-A: Self-evaluation

PART-B: Superior's evaluation

PART-C: Performance and potential categorization and classification into functional Expert

PART-D: Feedback (evaluator's comments and performance summary and Evaluatee's comments).

The process starts with the self-appraisal/evaluation. The respective filed HR managers hand over the evaluation forms to the superiors. The person evaluating performance of his direct reports (Solid-line reporting) is an evaluator. Evaluator is the current superior of the evaluate.

In case of dual reporting relationship, rating should first be done by functional superior on a separate sheet, which will be an input for final rating by the Evaluator. A blank copy of Part-B may be used for this purpose. Similar procedure is applicable for obtaining ratings from previous superior in case of transfer during the appraisal period.

Talent Review

Talent review is a mechanism, which provides a platform for a focused, fact-based and comprehensive discussion by a panel of higher level executives on performance, potential and development of group of subordinates. The whole process puts spotlight on performers and identifies high performers (listers) and under performers. For the unit, it helps in identifying talent gaps and any challenges affecting the talent pool e.g., development shortfalls, retention problems.

Talent Pools and Review Groups

Review Groups: Set of superiors who are presenting/discussing the cases of their subordinates. The review group members collectively assess individuals and assess performance and potential categories. They take key development and reward decisions for individuals and resolve all unit related issues such as high attrition, talent gaps, etc.

Talent Pools: Set of officers whose cases are being presented and discussed. The talent pools will be formed along the business lines impact level wise with adequate functional inputs.

Participants in the Talent Review Process

Presenter: Presents the case of employees reporting to him/her. Each member of the group will have responsibility of a set of cases.

Chairperson/Owner: Facilitates/co-ordinates the review group. Typically, a person to whom all review group members report.

Guest Invitee: This is optional. The chairman may call a guest invitee. They normally provide external perspective on employees e.g., functional superiors. A guest is typically the superior of the chairperson who is present toward the end of the review meeting to ensure cross calibration.

HR: It is the HR that facilitates the Talent Review discussions. They help presenters prepare the cases of individuals.

⌘ Key Features of Talent Reviews (Inputs and Outputs) ⌘

- The annual evaluations have recommendations on performance and potential of officers, which are discussed and vetted in the Talent Review.

- The final performance and potential category serve as two main inputs to that Talent Review. Each superiors who is a part of the review group is expected to go prepared with a case before discussing his/her subordinates during the talent reviews.

- The cases have details of past performance, potential, strengths, areas of improvement, evidence to support judgements and any other details which may be useful for taking decision on officer's performance and development.

- The review group decides the performance and Potential categories of the officers in review pool.

- The performance categories are finalized after debating and discussing the officer's performance and other areas of contribution by way of relative comparisons and cross calibration.

- Once performance and potential categories are decided, officers are then placed on performance-potential matrix to decide their classifications as lister, potential star, solid performance, etc. All development and rotation decisions are based on these classifications.

- Apart from performance and potential categorization, an officer is considered to be a domain expert. (Functional Experts are selected few officers who are considered to be domain experts of their functional area and their expertise is valuable for the department and the organization. Such expertise is difficult to build up).

- The output is captured in form of a report for each officer. This captures the key highlights of the Talent Review decisions and discussions on the officer.

- The Talent Review group at the end of the meeting is expected to adhere and arrive to a desired distribution/spread which are given as guidelines to all superiors during the start of annual performance evaluation exercise.

- It is at the time of Talent Review that a detailed Executive Development Action Plan is made for all listers. For others, it is made offline by respective superiors with the help of HR managers.

- It is after the Talent Review that the PDP process is also initiated.

Feedback

The feedback captures the following points:

1. The evaluator rating and the final performance and potential categorization. In Overall performance summary, key strengths, development needs and issues to be addressed next year.

2. Key decisions and discussions during talent review.

3. Once the evaluatee has received the feedback, he is required to sign the document and give his comments.

4. It is after the feedback, that the annual increment letter is handed over to the officer (evaluator).

5. The letters are handed over even in cases of disagreement/ specific issues but with a commitment that the issue will be handled and sorted out at the earliest within a months time). In such cases, the evaluatee may choose not sign the evaluation form and may sign only after being fully satisfied.

Performance Ethic Programme (PEP)

✤ Four Pillars of PEP

1. Performance Ethic Programme in Tata Steel was based on the four pillars. The total process of restructuring in TISCO brought down the levels from previous 17 to existing 5. The organization identified five major "impact levels" as IL1, IL2, IL3, IL4, & IL5.

2. These impact levels were identified by the qualitative contributions and their direct impact on the performance of organization.

3. Competency assessment is to have more transparency and authenticity. Assessment process included both for 'managerial competencies' and 'functional competencies'. Authenticity to be further strengthened by facilitating reassessment by validation, revalidation and even cross-validation of scores.

4. Jobs are to be identified and positioned according to their work content and impact levels. Matching managers against the jobs would do whole matching process. Ensure positioning the right person on the right job.

5. Strengthen the HR processes by clearly addressing the softer issues. HR uplift to be achieved by professional and upgraded HR support, target specific recruiting events and communication, individual action plans for development, consistent criteria and process for termination etc.

Success levers say that clear HRM philosophy/strategy with clear responsibilities, that are implemented with effective measures should be **Specific, Consistent, Thorough** and **Continuous**

Personal Development Plan (PDP)

The PDP outlines the developmental initiatives to be taken to improve functional and managerial competency of the individual. It addresses current needs as well as future needs using both on-the-job and formal Training methodologies.

⌘ Key Features of the PDP ⌘

- It focuses on 2-3 most important competencies to be developed during the year.

- It outlines the activity plan for the year to address those 2-3 competency needs.

- It creates alignment in the thinking between the individual and the superior and makes both their developmental responsibilities clear.

- It makes menu of Development activities available on PDP Toolkit.

- Under PDP the HR manager/line manager guides in selecting the most appropriate development option.

- It provides greater support to help people in their learning.

⌘ PDP Implementation ⌘

Process

- Discussion between superior and subordinate

- Managerial and Functional Need Identification

- Both off-the-job and on-the-job development

Responsibility

- Superior facilitated (by HR)

Compliance and Monitoring

- Regularly by superior

- Mandatory Review by HR

Timelines

*   End February

A good PDP should have operational and tactical focus and compliance.

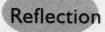

Reflection

━━━━━ ✿ **Multi Rater Feedback** ✿ ━━━━━

Overview

Reflection, as the name suggests, is exactly what this exercise of Multi Rater Feedback (MRF) is. It aims at providing a comprehensive reflection of one's own self and thereby presenting to an individual a better understanding of his/her work and behaviour styles and development areas. The feedback arrived at is objectives as the responses are given by a cross-section of people with whom he/she has interacted. It also provides a different perspective on the skills, attributes and other job relevant characteristics and thus helps to build a richer, more complete and accurate picture than could be obtained from any single source.

The Process

For each individual, the feedbacks are collected through a questionnaire. The questionnaire is sent to a fixed number of randomly selected respondents from the list of names we receive from you. These respondents are classified into the following categories – Self, Superior, Subordinates, Peers and Customers.

The Questionnaire

The questionnaire presents series of behaviours for rating and some narrative response questions.

   The questionnaire includes a few statements on each of the competencies identified for Tata Steel. In addition, feedback is also be taken on some other important behavioural attributes which are considered important at work.

   There are two open-ended questions at the end which you will also have to respond to.

Feedback (What will you as a respondent have to do?)

You will have to consider each behaviour under the various heads in the questionnaire and reflect on your observation of the person for whom you are filling the form (self if you are giving feedback for yourself) in the working environment. You need to rate each statement on a 4-point scale. Your response should not be guided by one or two incidents during your interaction with the concerned person, but should be based on a thorough analysis of the previous year's interaction and experience in an ideal scenario.

In case, you have not observed any behaviour during the course of your interaction, you can mark your response as "Not Applicable" or "Not Observed".

The Rating Scale

The rating scale is defined as follows:

"To what extent do you agree that each statement accurately describes her/his characteristic behaviour?"

Rating Scale

Not Applicable/Not Observed

Almost Never/To Limited Extent

Just Sometimes/To Moderate extent

A Lot of Times/A Great Extent

Almost Always/To a Very Great Extent

Sending the Form

Once filling up the questionnaire is completed, it is sent as suggested to HRS.

Final Report

Once all the Reflection (MRF) forms from all the respondents are received, a formal report will be sent after analysing the feedbacks.

Confidentiality and Anonymity

Needless to mention, that one need not give any personal details. Confidentiality and anonymity will be maintained all throughout the process.

Job Rotation

In TATA STEEL, job rotation is positioned to give employees developmental experiences. For officers it helps to......

1. Perform more effectively in their present position.

2. Prepare for positions of greater or different responsibility

3. Support individual professional development by offering a range of learning

❆ Guiding Principles: Job Rotation in Tata Steel ❆

The objective is of developing expertise in management and technology both.

- Reaching the top layers of the organization will require sufficient grounding and experience in both technical and management skills.

- The Tata Steel Job Rotation system will aim at balancing the needs of the organization with the strengths and interests of the individual.

The development action plans will capture rotation details for officers.

Format-1: Development Plan for Listers

Detailed career plan on the officer's movement/development with justifications, whether the person is being groomed for a particular leadership position, or is being rotated to acquire in depth knowledge in the domain area, or is being rotated to a specific group to develop his business perspective, etc.

Format-2: Development Plan for Others

For others, i.e. potential stars, solid performers, under-performers and strugglers, the decision will be taken offline by the concerned chief/head along with the respective field HR. This decisions will be consolidated in a separate format.

- The respective field HR and the heads will ensure that approximately 15% officers are rotated/transferred every year.

Rotations to out locations will be an overriding practice in all PC/CCs. All PC/CCs will recommend around 2% officers for rotations to out locations HR will consolidate and finalise the rotations to out locations.

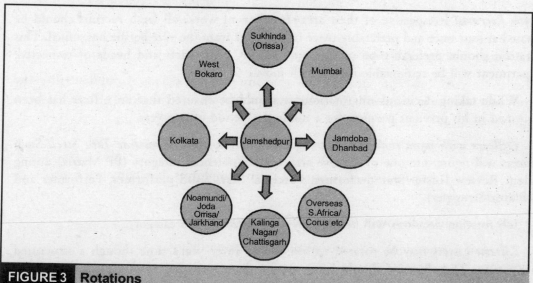

FIGURE 3 **Rotations**

Potential Category will be one of the Inputs to the Talent Review

Very High Potential (5)

Has potential and is capable of taking up responsibilities much above his current level. Has broad professional skills, aspires to higher level challenges and opportunities. Business perspectives much beyond current levels.

High Potential (4)

Capable of taking up responsibilities above his current level. Has reasonably good business perspective. Demonstrates potential to reach the next level in a year. However, progress beyond that level is difficult to predict now.

Some potential (3)

Has potential to handle expanded responsibilities at the present level. Has a business perspective appropriate for current position. Demonstrates potential to reach the next level, maybe in two to three years. However, progress beyond that level is difficult to predict now.

Yet to demonstrate (2)

At or near capacity in the present position. Progress beyond the current level is difficult to predict now. Will have to continue in the present position for some more time.

No Potential (1)

Just meets the expectations.

Job Rotation in Tata Steel is Different for Different Categories of Officers

Fresh Recruits: Irrespective of their area/ function of work, all fresh recruits should be rotated at least once and preferably twice in five years from the year he/she has joined. This rotation should preferably be in the same PC/CC. All chiefs and heads of respective department will be responsible for all such moves.

While taking decisions on rotations it should be ensured that an officer has been stationed in his pervious position for a minimum period of one year.

Officers with more than five years of experience within or outside Tata Steel: Such officers will figure into one of the five-performance/potential category (PP Matrix) during Talent Review (Lister/Star performer, Potential Star, Solid performer, Performer and C-Player/Struggler)

Job rotation decisions will accordingly flow based on the category.

Listers: Listers may be rotated within two to three year's time though a structured career plan. The objective should be to expose them to varied work situations so as to develop and keep the talent pipeline full.

- Areas to which they can be exposed will largely depend on the cluster/position they are being groomed for.

Example: Post-talent Review, if an IL3 person is identified as a lister and the group feels that he is a possible business leader and can be groomed to take up a responsible IL2 position of a business unit head, his rotation plan will accordingly be prepared.

Listers – The possible career moves of a lister can be broadly into the following areas;

- Operations
- Technology
- Maintenance
- Marketing
- Sales, Engineering
- Specialised functions (HR, F&A, Legal, IT, TOP, etc.)
- Administration and General Management

The period to be spent on such possible stations would be decided during the Talent Review as a part of the plan.

Potential Star: Such officers should be rotated in the same function once in 5 years. Such officers may also be cross-functionally exposed for 2-3 years to some task forces or assignments or areas like Business Excellence, HR Implementation, TOP, etc.

⌘ Conclusion ⌘

The HR processes practiced in Tata Steel are very robust and some of them are even benchmarks in the industry. In an organization with around 4,500 executives, the deployment of the processes in their true spirit is an issue, which needs to be addressed. If we want to achieve the desired deliverables of the processes we need to ensure that the processes are implemented uniformly and in totality across the various departments in the organization.

The study of the deployment level has brought to the fore those departments where the processes are deployed properly and pinpoints areas where the deployment needs improvement. Moreover, it also reflects the deployment across the impact levels. The project further highlights the elements within the processes that are not being strictly adhered to and are adversely affecting the deployment of the process.

The analysis of the deployment levels shows that the processes are deployed relatively better in CSI, FP and Shared Services. However, deployment needs to be more focused in Tubes and LP. However, the deployment of PMS is highest in Tubes.

Among the processes, deployment of PMS is the best followed by PDP. In PMS, mid-year review of the KRAs needs to be addressed immediately. In PDP, there has to be a regular dialogue between superior and subordinate while filling up the PDP. PDP deployment is largely affected by the deployment of training programmes. This brings to the fore the issue of on-the-job training, which is alarmingly miserable.

MRF is an extremely useful process which aims at providing a comprehensive reflection of one's own self and thereby presenting to an individual a better understanding of his/her work and behavioural styles and development areas. It needs certain improvements in terms of identification of the people from whom the feedback is to be taken.

The company needs to come up with a more comprehensive and extensive system for ensuring job rotation to provide growth avenues to the executives. Among the impact levels the processes are deployed best at IL3, followed by IL5 and IL4.

With a little improvement in monitoring mechanism and a proactive approach towards implementation of the processes, most of these issues can be taken care of.

This will reflect HR's vital role across HR processes, delivery, systems and performance improvements, thereby contributing to Business Excellence.

Bibliography

1. Arthur, J., "Effects of Human Resources Systems on Manufacturing Performance and Turnover", *Academy of Management Journal*, 1994.

2. Boyatzis, R.E., *The Competent Manager: A Model for Effective Performance*, Wiley, New York, 1982.

3. Bradford, S.B., Steve, W.J., "Goal Orientation and Ability: Interactive Effects on Self-efficiency, Performance and Knowledge", *Journal of Applied Psychology*, 2002.

4. *Business Today*, January 7-21, Managing People, 1996.

5. Delery, J.E., D.H. Doty, "Models of Theorising in Strategic Human Resources Management: Tests of Universalistic, Contingency and Configurational Performance Predictions", *Academy of Management Journal*, 1996.

6. Doz, Y., Prahalad, C., "Controlled Variety: A Challenge for Human Resources Management in the MNC", *Human Resource Management*, 1986.

7. Hunter, J., Hunter, R., "Validity and Utility of Alternative Predictors of Job Performance", *Psychological Bulletin*, 1984.

8. Klemp, G.O. Jr., Assessment of Occupational Competence, *Report to National Institute Education*, Washington DC, 1980.

9. Leopold, J. Lynette, H. And Watson T., "Strategic Human Resourcing: Principle, Perspective and Practices", *Financial Times*, Pitman Publishing, London, 1999.

10. Margaret, M. Heffeman, Patrik C.F., "An Exploration of the Relationships between the Adoption of Managerial Competencies, Organizational Characteristics, Human Resources Sophistication and Performance in Irish Organization", *Journal of European Industrial Training*, Bradford,, Vol.24.

11. Marmol, G.G., Murray, Jr., R.M., "Leading from Front", The Mckinsey Quarterly, 1995.

12. McClelland, D.C., *Assessing Human Motivation*, General Learning Press, 1971.

13. Pathak, I., *International Dimensions of Management*, Boston, Kent MA, 1994.

14. Pfeffer, J., *Competitive Advantage through People: Unleashing the Power of the Work Force*, Boston, MA: Harvard Business School Press, 1994.

15. Pfeffer, J., *The Human Equation: Building Profits by Putting People First*, Boston, MA: Harvard Business School Press, 1998.

16. Ramsay, H., Scholarios D., Harlay B., "Employee and High Performance Work Systems: Testing Insight the Black Box", *British Journal of Industrial Relations*, 2000.

17. Schneider, B., Paul J. Hanges, D. Brent Smith, Amy Nicole Salvaggio, "Which comes First: Employee Attitudes or Organizational Financial and Market Performance?", *Journal of Applied Psychology*, 2003.

18. Tovey, Laura, "A Strategic Approach to Competency Assessment", *Journal of European Industrial Training*, 1993.

19. Ulrich, D., Lake D., *Organizational Capability: Competing from the Inside/out*, New York, Wiley, 1990.

20. Wills, S., Barham, K., "Being an International Manager", *European Management Journal*, 1994.

21. Allenbagh, G.E., (1983). Coaching – A Management Tool for a More Effective Work Performance. *Management Review*, 72, 21-26.

22. Farr, J.L., & Jacobs, R. (2006). Trust Us: New Perspectives on Performance Appraisal. In W. Bennett, C.E. Lance and D.J. Woehr (Eds.), *Performance measurement: Current Perspectives and Future Challenges* (pp.321-337). Mahwah, NJ: Lawrence Erlbau.

23. Kiger,, P.J. (2002, May). How Performance Management Reversed NCCI's Fortunes. *Workforce*, 81,48-51.

24. Bacon, T.R., & Spear, K.I. (2003). *Adaptive Coaching: The Art and Practice of a Client Entered Approach to Performance Improvement*. Palo Alto, CA: Davies-Black.

25. Walther, F., & Taylor, S. (1988). An active Feedback Program can spark Performance. In A.D. Timpe (Ed.), *Performance: The Art and Science of Business Management* (pp.293-299). New York: Facts on File Publications.

26. Laumeyer, J.A., (2002). *Performance Management Systems: What to do We want to accomplish?* Alexandria, VA: Society for Human Resources Management.

27. Adapted from D.L. Kirkpatrick. *How to Improve Performance Through Appraisal and Coaching* (New York: AMACOM, 1982), 55-57.

28. Grote, D. (2002). Managing the Difficult Employee. SHRH White Paper. SHRM Online. www.shrm.org/hrresources/whitepapers-published/CMS_001865.asp.Retrieval date: March 14, 2007.

29. *Performance Management*, Michael Armstrong & Angela Baron, Published by Jaico Publishing House, 121 Mahatma Gandhi Road, Mumbai—400 001 (2006). jaicopub@vsnl.com, www.jaicobooks.com

30. *Rethinking Incentives and Reward Management* (International Management Institutes), G K Suri, C S Venkatratna , N K Gupta, Excel Books, A-45, Naraina, Phase-I, New Delhi—110028 (2003).

31. *360 Degree Feedback and Performance Management System*, Volume One, TV Rao, Raju Rao, Excel Books, A-45, Naraina, Phase-I, New Delhi–110028 (2003).

32. *Performance Management and Appraisal Systems – HR Tools for Global Competitiveness*, TV RAO, Response Books – A division of Sage Publications India Pvt Ltd, B-42, Panchsheel Enclave, New Delhi—110017 (2004).

33. *Performance Management –Concepts, Skills, and Exercises* by Robert L. Cardy, Published by Asoke K. Ghosh, Prentice-Hall of India Private Limited, M-97, Connaught Circus, New Delhi-110001, and Printed by Scanage Reprographers (Pvt) Ltd., 2-E, "Caxton House", Rani Jhansi Road, New Delhi—110055 (2004).

34. *Performance Appraisal* by Bob Havard, Published by Kogan Page India Private Limited, 2/13 Ansari Road, Daryaganj, New Delhi—110002 (2004).

35. *Performance Management—The New Realities* by Michael Armstrong & Angela Baron, published by Jaico Publishing House, 121, Mahatma Gandhi Road, Mumbai-400 023, Jaicopub@vsn.co, www.jaicobooks.com, (2004).

36. *360 Degree Feedback and Performance Management System*—Volume Two, by TV Rao, Gopal Mahapatra, Raju Rao, Nandini Chawla printed by Excel Books, A-45, Naraina, Phase-I, New Delhi—110028 (2006).

37. *Performance Appraisal and Compensation Management*—A Modern Approach by Dewakar Goel, Asoke K. Ghosh, Prentice-Hall of India Private Limited, M-97, Connaught Circus, New Delhi—110001, and Printed by Scanage Reprographers (Pvt.) Ltd., 2-E, "Caxton House", Rani Jhansi Road, New Delhi—110055 (2008).

38. *Performance Management System* by R K Sahu, published by Excel Books, A-45, Naraina, Ph-I, New Delhi—110028 (2007).

39. *Performance Management* by A.S. Kohli, T. Deb, published by Oxford University Press, YMCA Library Building, Jai Singh Road, New Delhi—110001 (2008).

40. *The 360 Degree Leader* by John C. Maxwell, Published by Dorling Kindersley (India) Pvt. Ltd., licensees of Person Education in South Asia (Registered Office: 14 Local Shopping Centre, Panchsheel Park, New Delhi—110017, India (2008).

41. *Performance Management* by Prem Chadha, published by Rajiv Beri for Macmillan India Ltd. 2/10 Ansari Road, Daryaganj, New Delhi—110002 (2003).

42. *Human Resource Management at Work: People Management and Development* by Mick Marchington and Adrian Wilkinson published by Pinnacle, 24, D.D.A. Shopping Complex Ber Sarai. New Delhi—110016., E-mail: pinnaclebooks1@gmail.com Phone-65664085 (2005).

43. *Managing Human Capital* by R P Mohanty published by Excel Books, A-45, Naraina, Ph-I, New Delhi—110028 (2006).

44. Amaratunga, D. and D. Baldry (2000), 'Moving from Performance Measurement to Performance Management', *Facilities*, Vol. 20, pp.217-23.

45. Armstrong, M. and A. Baron (2004), *Managing Performance: Performance Management in Action*, Chartered Institute of Personnel and development, London.

46. Bacal, R. (1998), *Performance Management*, McGraw Hill Publishing.

47. Banarjee, I. (2007), 'Aligning Individual Performance with Organizations: The 360 Degree Way', *Business Manager*, Vol.9, NO.8, Alwar.

48. Beer, M. and R.A. Ruh (1976), 'Employee Growth through Performance Management', *Harvard Business Review*, Vol. 54, no. 4, July-August, pp. 59-66.

49. Bidwaik, V. (2006), 'Loosing Objective of Performance Management System?' *Business Manager*, Vol.9, No. 6, Alwar.

50. Borman, W.C. (1991), 'Job Behaviour, Performance, and Effectiveness', in M.D. Dunette and L.M. Hough (eds), *Handbook of Industrial and Organizational Psychology*, Consulting Psychologist Press, CA.

51. *Compensation and Reward Management System* by B.D. Singh, published by Excel Books, A-45, Naraina, Phase-I, New Delhi-110028.

Index